Jill Ker Conway

Written *by* Herself

Volume II:

WOMEN'S MEMOIRS
FROM BRITAIN, AFRICA, ASIA, AND
THE UNITED STATES

Jill Ker Conway was born in Hillston, New South Wales, Australia, graduated from the University of Sydney in 1958, and received her Ph.D. from Harvard University in 1969. From 1964 to 1975 she taught at the University of Toronto and was vice president there before serving for ten years as president of Smith College. In 1985 she and her husband, John Conway, moved to Boston, Massachusetts where she is now a visiting scholar and professor in M.I.T.'s Program in Science, Technology, and Society.

ALSO BY Jill Ker Conway

True North

The Politics of Women's Education
(with Susan Bourque)

*Written by Herself, Volume I: Autobiographies
of American Women* (editor)

The Road from Coorain

Learning About Women
(editor with Susan C. Bourque and Joan W. Scott)

Women Reformers and American Culture

*The Female Experience
in Eighteenth- and Nineteenth-Century America*

Merchants and Merinos

Written *by* Herself

Volume II

WOMEN'S MEMOIRS FROM BRITAIN, AFRICA, ASIA, AND THE UNITED STATES

Edited and with an Introduction by
Jill Ker Conway

VINTAGE BOOKS

A DIVISION OF RANDOM HOUSE, INC.

NEW YORK

A VINTAGE ORIGINAL, SEPTEMBER 1996
FIRST EDITION

Library of Congress Cataloging-in-Publication Data

Written by herself, Volume I: autobiographies of American women: an anthology / edited and with an introduction by Jill Ker Conway.
p.   cm.
"A Vintage original"—T.P. verso.
ISBN 0-679-73633-6
Written by herself, Volume II: women's memoirs from
Britain, Africa, Asia, and the United States
ISBN 0-679-75109-2
1. American prose literature—Women authors.   2. Women—United States—Biography.   3. Autobiography—Women authors.
1. Conway, Jill K., 1934–   .
PS647.W6W75   1992
920.72'0973—dc20   92-50081
CIP

BOOK DESIGN BY ROBERT BULL DESIGN

Random House Web address: http://www.randomhouse.com/

Printed in the United States of America

10 9 8 7 6 5 4 3 2 1

CONTENTS

INTRODUCTION   VII

SECTION ONE: 1
Imperial England
"Into the blue sky with a string of camels"

Margery Perham (1895–1982)
from AFRICAN APPRENTICESHIP   2
Vera Brittain (1893?–1970)
from TESTAMENT OF YOUTH   66
Angelica Garnett (1918–   )
from DECEIVED WITH KINDNESS   117

SECTION TWO: 161
Colonial Africa
"I felt contempt for those living in safety"

Isak Dinesen (1885–1962)
from OUT OF AFRICA   162
Elspeth Huxley (1907–   )
from THE FLAME TREES OF THIKA   197
Mary Benson (1919–   )
from A FAR CRY   259
Ruth First (1925–1982)
from 117 DAYS   310
Emma Mashinini (1929–   )
from STRIKES HAVE FOLLOWED ME ALL MY LIFE   352

SECTION THREE: 389
Indian Nationalism
"Prison was a challenge"

Shudha Mazumdar (1899–   )
from MEMOIRS OF AN INDIAN WOMAN   390
Vijaya Lakshmi Pandit (1900–   )
from THE SCOPE OF HAPPINESS   438
Meena Alexander (1951–   )
from FAULT LINES   489

SECTION FOUR: 537
Postcolonial America
*"They say the loss of your mother will
cause you to sing the old songs"*

Vivian Gornick (1935–   )
from FIERCE ATTACHMENTS   538
Gloria Wade-Gayles (1938–   )
from PUSHED BACK TO STRENGTH   569
Edith T. Mirante (1953–   )
from BURMESE LOOKING GLASS   620

Editions Cited   685

INTRODUCTION

What makes someone write an autobiography? Why do we like to read them? What can the reader make of a genre that is part fiction, part narrative, rooted in events that really did occur at a unique point in time and space? Do men and women approach recounting a life history in the same way, or does the fact of being differently embodied affect the way we talk about our lives?

Up to the mid–eighteenth century the answers to most of these questions seemed self-evident to people rooted in the Western European tradition. Memoirs were the work of great men, records created for succeeding generations about important affairs of state or dramatic moments of religious conversion. These assumptions changed when Jean-Jacques Rousseau (1712–1778), one of the creators of the modern tradition of romantic individualism, changed the genre to make it the record of self-creation, an account of how one undistinguished individual forged for himself an identity and place in society. Rousseau's emotional travails along the path of asserting his will moved the focus of attention in histories of greatness from an exclusive concern with affairs of state to the mixture of public persona and private, inner creativity which Europeans came to understand through the Napoleonic hero or the artistic genius of a Beethoven.

By the mid–nineteenth century the democratic revolution, with its focus on individualism and the self-made identity, led to the appropriation of the genre by women, although the numbers of female memoirs were small in comparison to the burgeoning male production. Nineteenth-century women who set about recounting their lives had two models. They could look back to the religious reflections of women religious in medieval and early modern times (such as Dame Julian of Norwich, 1342–1423), narratives written mostly for their enclosed religious communities about their spiritual journeyings in an entirely inner relationship with God. Or they could read the accounts of women who, by reason of marriage (such as Margaret Cavendish, duchess of Newcastle, 1624–1674) or membership in a special religious confession (such as the Quaker Margaret Fell, 1614–1702), were witness to great events. These were chronicles of external events told on behalf of others who, as a result of political or religious fortunes, could not speak for themselves.

Nineteenth-century women wrote memoirs to record a special relationship to history: escaping from slavery, gaining access to education, pioneering in the wilderness, creating new professions for women, becoming famous stage performers. In so doing, they adapted the basic plot form of the romantic tradition to focus on the female journey in romanticism, a journey toward merging a female identity in her beloved—be that a male lover, a cause, or an institution. By the twentieth century, male and female narratives were also marked by differing codes about discussing sexuality and physical experience. Men might describe sexuality openly, but codes of female sexual propriety meant that women who gave birth alone on the frontier might have given birth miraculously for all the references to the female body in their stories.

Contemporary literary theorists have emphasized three problems about the genre of autobiography for women. First, since a woman has been expected to merge her identity in others and to find the meaning of life in relationships with others (husband, children, self-abnegation in the pursuit of good causes), their life histories do not fit the classic pattern of the male narrative about the self-created and bounded individual. Women often tell us about their relationships and leave the reader to interpret the silence about who they think they are.

Secondly, since women in modern social and political thought have been viewed as either failed men (as in Freudian psychoanalysis) or nonparticipants (as in the tradition of Western political thought), the cultural mirror they can hold up to themselves for purposes of self-narrative can do nothing but devalue the reality of what it is to be female. Such problems of self-imagery, however, are only crippling to the extent that the female narrator accepts that this mirror, created by the dominant male culture, offers an accurate reflection of reality.

Thirdly, theorists of language, which is, of course, gendered in a way that demeans and devalues the female, have drawn attention to the difficulty of describing the female experience while using a symbolic system which denigrates the feminine.

Because of these problems—of life plot, of cultural mirrors, and of language—women's dilemmas in storytelling are thought to be not unlike those of non-Western colonized peoples who have been taught to denigrate their native language and culture and must struggle with a hybrid sense of who they are. Postmodern cultural criticism has made language a universal cultural structure limiting human consciousness, a structure viewed in much the same way that Marxists have viewed class and race—as social and economic structures that impose an ideological straitjacket upon those lodged within them. However, we need not accept this cultural determinism about language, because its history is the history of unceasing appropriation for the user's purposes. Moreover, such a deterministic view neglects the extent to which we know and assimilate our experience through the nonverbal processes of the brain, the preconceptual thought that cognitive scientists know exists, no matter how difficult it may be to describe.

Given all these difficulties—which complicate the task of the memoirist, and especially the female practitioner of the art—why do we find its modern form so captivating? For it can be said that this genre has almost replaced the great Victorian novel as the form of fiction that the educated reader reads for pleasure, not just in Europe and its offshoots but in most modern societies.

The answer to this readers' response lies in the increasingly technical nature of most understandings of the self—be they psychoanalytic, philosophic, poetic, or historical. The general disciplines of the humanities, literary criticism, philosophical analysis, psychology, history, have developed technical languages not easily accessible to the general reader, so that a person who wants to reflect on her or his own life can do so most easily through autobiography, a form we feel is rooted enough in real events to help us define reality for ourselves. Moreover, the modern memoirist wants to communicate to a general reader in nontechnical language, an essential requirement if reader and narrator are to establish immediacy and spontaneity in sharing experience. If we try to transpose some of the great autobiographies of the past into the jargon of the modern humanities, we can easily understand the reader's problem. We have only to think of a St. Augustine trying to describe his conversion in the psychoanalytic lingo of cathexis and significant others, or of a Rousseau grappling with the concept of alterity to understand why contemporary readers rush to the biography and autobiography section of the bookstore.

Of course, reader responses are shaped by general cultural patterns. Many contemporaries, male and female, don't like reading open and unabashed female accounts of the pursuit of power or success, preferring the stereotypical self-abnegating female except for conventional film and media heroines or negative heroines of extraordinary criminality. Discussions of female sexual experience still excite comment and criticism, although such revelations are taken for granted in male narratives, so that men seem more embodied in twentieth-century literature of the self than women. However, it is clear that female sexuality if heterosexual is far more acceptable publicly than is lesbian sexuality, and that, with a very few conservative exceptions, the ultimate taboo for females remains the quest for power in one's own right, rather than the behind-the-scenes "influence" with which modern readers are comfortable.

Readers of this anthology will find a selection from the lives of twentieth-century women drawn from four continents (allowing for the inclusion of the modern United Kingdom in Europe). They show a metropolitan European culture and its colonial offshoots experiencing the great events of the twentieth century—the war of 1914–18, the Great Depression, the 1939–45 war, the postcolonial quest for authenticity—and they tell about these experiences in the female voice. Many other equally compelling selections are possible. This one is governed by the effort to see the resonance of great events in different parts of the world, the similarities and differences in experience shaped by environment and history, and by the authors' capacity to convey place, politics, passion, and inner life. They show us an imperial culture in its death throes and what that meant for the female half of a world built on subordination by race, sex, and metropolitan culture.

Readers must decide for themselves whether these women are embodied in any tangible sense, whether they are able to overcome the problems of the distorting mirror that language and history have given them, what the cost of that battle has been, and whether the cultural dilemmas of all women resemble those of their postcolonial sisters. The vigorous prose collected here represents a case study in the appropriation of language for the purposes of the feminine, supposedly the weaker grammatical category. In some instances the power of language to confuse and subdue is painfully evident, but in others we see genius miraculously transcending such limitations.

Three memoirs by Englishwomen open this anthology because they represent the root community of language from which the English-speaking world has evolved. The authors selected illustrate central themes about British imperial society and culture at the apogee of the Empire and early Commonwealth and the long, slow decline that set in after the 1914–18 war and accelerated following the cataclysm of the 1939–45 war. Margery Perham shows us the turn-of-the-century, adventurous, upper-middle-class Englishwoman of education, utterly untroubled by Freudian concerns, happy to wander the globe in search of adventure, and, supported by a community of women scholars at her Oxford women's college, free to write and speak with authority on her chosen subject, colonial government. She is a fine example of a British female type, intrepid traveler, brilliant talker, close observer of other cultures, single and happy about it.

Vera Brittain, of the same generation but from a more provincial middle-class family, exemplifies, in tragic intensity, the transformation of life for Englishwomen brought about by the 1914–18 war and the slaughter of a generation of British men. When her story begins she is a sheltered, indeed closeted, young girl, concerned with dress and her brother's school companions. By its close, she has become inured to suffering, Greek in her overpowering grief for the young men who formed her world and have died, determined with every ounce of her being to see that they have not died in vain.

Angelica Garnett bears witness to the overripe decadence of British high culture in the interwar years. The child of central figures in the Bloomsbury group, she shows us her parents' tolerance extending to silence about her own incestuous marriage; the emotional demands made on her as a child by her commanding mother, the artist Vanessa Bell, and Bell's more famous sister, Virginia Woolf; and the ease with which she slips into an affair with her future husband while his ailing wife looks on. Her early married life is an eerie prefiguring of the earth mother of the conservative 1950s, as she struggles to dance, paint, entertain ambitiously, and give birth to four children while neglecting her own identity. Her memoir chronicles the struggle, made possible by psychoanalysis, to emerge from that emotional nightmare.

Different as these profoundly British women are in background, generation, education, and political awareness, common themes cut across their life histories. For each, the death of a brother or, in Garnett's case, half brother changes the course of life. Perham's and Brittain's brothers' deaths help the sisters forge new identities and fuel their determination to become agents in their own lives. Garnett's half brother's death is the occasion for her horrified discovery of who her real father is and the beginning of a lifelong effort to come to terms with the values of Bloomsbury.

The intensity of these brother-sister relationships across so many social backgrounds makes us understand why the great English novelist Iris Murdoch, chronicler of English society after 1945,

evoked such startled response to her narrative of brother-sister in-
cest, *A Severed Head* (1961). In these three lives, the brother is a
true alter ego, whose absence leaves an emotional desert and a
young woman embattled against the demands of an older generation. Thus, the loss of successive generations of young men may be
seen as a motive force for female rebellion, political or cultural, and,
in that sense, a contributor to the rise of twentieth-century feminism.

All three women are confident that they live at the cultural center of the world. Other countries and cultures are pleasant places to
visit and to enjoy, but travel is never, for them, the journey of discovery that is a recurring theme in the lives of women from British
colonial society. Nor is political awareness so radical as to warrant
complete rejection of constituted public authority, a common theme
in the lives of women at the margin rather than the center of the old
Empire. Certainly British radical feminists were ready to embrace
civil disobedience as a political tool, but it was to force entry into
the existing political system and its spectrum of parties, not to overthrow it. And the tests of political will and physical and moral
courage faced by South African women were outside the metropolitan experience except for those few heroic Englishwomen who
worked in the Resistance in France during 1939–45. We should see
Perham, Brittain, and Garnett as each in her own way located at the
center of British society and intellectual life, typical exemplars of
the metropolitan society, excellent foils for the women shaped by
British imperial culture or its American counterpart whose narratives follow.

It is in Africa and India that the conflicts between the structures
of Empire and of racial segregation and exploitation become the
theme that overshadows all others. In these narratives differences of
class and caste are often more important than racial identities. The
coolly aristocratic assumptions of the Nehru family, rooted in their
knowledge of a great Hindu cultural heritage, enable the Nehru
women a freedom of action and authority not available to solidly
middle-class citizens of Britain's colonies of white settlement. The
Nehrus can look at the British with some disdain as well as liking
and can see some British institutions with humor derived from their
own security within a great culture.

But whatever the caste or economic background, it is the meeting of the British with the peoples of the African and Indian continents that shapes the lives of women who live on these continents
in any other than an exclusively domestic mode. In Isak Dinesen's

and Elspeth Huxley's stories of Kenya, the native people are three-dimensional and the whites less compellingly real. In South Africa, Mary Benson and Ruth First become exiles at home, defined as enemies of the state because of their identification with the black struggle against apartheid, a struggle we encounter with heartbreaking intensity in Emma Mashinini's story of resistance against crushing oppression. In India, women of education come to self-awareness through participation in the struggle for national independence or in the striving for cultural authenticity in a postcolonial world.

By contrast with the first volume of this anthology, devoted to autobiography by American women, the eleven non-American women whose memoirs appear in this volume tell us that the British and colonial societies represented did not produce the number of institutions and the scale of collective life for women so characteristic of the United States from the rise of the feminist and abolition movements in the mid–nineteenth century to the renewal of feminism in the mid–twentieth. Life in women's army services gave Mary Benson (South Africa) the experience of female sociability, but she recounts the rest of her life in terms of relationships with men. Rebellion against imperialism, racism, and bourgeois pretense took Indians or South Africans not into female-led reform organizations but into male-led left-wing political groups. There their voices were silenced by the demands of socialist realism or the party line that women's struggle for equality must be subsumed within the class or race struggle. One representative of the Indian diaspora appears in this collection, a powerful exponent of the problems of language and postcolonial expression, postmodern in her rejection of politics for the deconstruction of language and culture.

The American women memoirists in this collection represent the feminist and civil rights concerns of Americans at midcentury, and the later discovery of Southeast Asia that characterized the Vietnam generation. Just as Britain's imperial role fired Margery Perham's imagination about the African continent and its peoples, America's imperial venture in Vietnam inspired the curiosity and concern of young Americans in the postwar era, leading Edith Mirante to her career of activism in behalf of Burma's tribal people and third world women's rights.

As a group these narratives raise significant questions about women's political mobilization. What kinds of experiences politicize women? Is the process of alienation from accepted authority the same for women as for men? Do women form political bonds with the same intensity as men, and when they do, what makes a woman a leader or a follower?

Margery Perham and Vera Brittain come to political awareness because of the 1914–18 war and their battles to secure respect and collegiality as educated women. Because the young men of their generation are dead and so can never be rivals, these women's political motivations extend to all forms of subordination, though they accept unquestioningly the superiority of European culture.

Isak Dinesen and Elspeth Huxley are less certain about that superiority because their experience in Kenya shows them nobility and strength in tribal cultures that is not present in their limited white colonial society. Mary Benson, Ruth First, and Emma Mashinini make the journey to defiance of corrupt authority at different speeds, but all their journeys preclude return to life lived the old way. First is born into a political family, a dedicated fighter from youth in behalf of the new Communist world order to which her family is committed as the only credible route to racial and class justice. Benson undergoes a slow but complete progress to total commitment to the racial struggle in South Africa. We see her begin life in an island of suburban preoccupation with film stars and the mores and manners of the old British Commonwealth, and end with a dangerous double life, in which she slips out in disguise to aid and comfort a friend who has gone underground. Her politicization comes by stages—the romance she has been taught to revere by films and sentimental novels is never realized in reality, setting her free to scrutinize other cultural frauds. Her zest for adventure draws her to great causes, and her love of South Africa and its peoples leads her to decisive opposition to apartheid. Mashinini's encounter with the black labor union movement in South Africa provides her with the intellectual framework through which to resist white oppression, while her Christian faith gives her the courage for ultimate defiance.

Vijaya Lakshmi Pandit is born into one of India's principal political families, in which two generations are locked in battle with the British raj as strategists of the Congress movement for independence. Like her niece Indira Gandhi, Pandit takes her right to rule for granted, and comes into prominence when all the men in her family are imprisoned by the British. Shudha Mazumdar, product of a much less privileged caste, is also educated by the national movement, first by well-meaning British women, who urge her to abandon purdah, and then by her support of the Congress party. She too lives a double life, secretly rejoicing at the success of Indian resisters while her husband serves as a magistrate for the British. It is after his death that she assumes a more public political role and can avow her political opinions. Meena Alexander is a product of the postcolonial era, caught in the cross-currents of racial, ethnic, and gender politics, a citizen of the world in quest of authentic roots.

Gornick's Jewish tenement world is suffused with sexual politics and given a radical context by her mother's work as a Communist party organizer. Her mother's self-immolation on the altar of idealized romantic love supplies the emotional source of Gornick's passionate rejection of the bourgeois family, while her resentment at her mother's emotional demands makes her embattled in the cause of equality and mutuality of feeling between sexes and generations.

Wade-Gayles's childhood among strong black women makes achievement seem natural for a child of the civil rights movement. Her encounter, as a student in Boston, with the coolness of liberal American white culture sends her back to valuing the religious faith and human bonds that gave her strength in childhood. Marriage and maternity make her question the ideal of the self-creating individual she has embraced through her northern education. She is politicized by the civil rights movement but led back to valuing the religious culture of her childhood, once seen as apolitical but now incorporated into Wade-Gayles's definition of female strength.

Edith Mirante, like Meena Alexander, is a child of postcolonialism, unusual in living her convictions about the ethics of relationships with so-called marginal people. Unlike her essentialist American contemporaries, enmeshed in theorizing about female networks, Mirante lives with Burmese women soldiers and satirizes her tendency to crave sentimental bonds with men. Alert to the pretenses and frauds of any culture, she is nonetheless mobilized by her love of tribal peoples and her hatred of the corrupting forces of the international drug and sex trades.

Whatever the tone of these memoirs—poetic, philosophical, historical—and whatever the mood—rage, grief, triumph, despair—they prompt reflection on our own life histories, expand the viewpoints from which we can examine ourselves, and give us the chance to see how the categories by which we analyze our own lives might be changed. And with that capacity, faulty cultural mirrors, deceptive life plots, and confining language traditions assume their proper place—one element in the difficulty of understanding who we are, but only one.

—Jill Ker Conway

Imperial England

"Into the blue sky with a string of camels"

Margery Perham
(1895–1982)

Margery (Freda) Perham was born the second daughter of a British country family in which horses, shooting, books, and adventure were taken for granted. She claims that her nursery was littered with weapons, and that she and her siblings fought pitched battles over the hills surrounding the family home. She took in the color and adventure of the old British imperial world in girlhood, and, as she tells her story, her longing to see far-off places and to live a dangerous life was far more important to her than conventional dreams of romance. This longing was first gratified when she accompanied her sister to her brother-in-law's posting as a district officer in a remote part of unruly Sudan. The vision of the African continent imprinted on her mind by that journey shaped her subsequent scholarly career.

As was the case for Vera Brittain, Perham's brother was the emotional center of her girlhood, and after his death during the 1914–18 war, Perham's resolve to seek adventure was strengthened by ideals of duty and service. Coming from a family that expected higher education for its daughters, Perham graduated from St. Hugh's College, Oxford, in 1919 and endured a dreary period as an assistant lecturer in history at Sheffield University, where she was the only woman faculty member, treated with hostility and outright rudeness. From this she escaped in 1924 to a fellowship at St. Hugh's, where she pursued further African studies. The chance of her lifetime came in 1929, when she received a Rhodes Fellowship to study race relations in the United States, Australia, New Zealand, and Africa. *African Apprenticeship* is the narrative of the African part of that journey, an experience that made her a strong supporter of tribal institutions and the rights of Africa's indigenous peoples. The fellowship was continued through 1932, a period in which the groundwork was being laid for apartheid in South Africa, and contract labor began to have an impact on the traditional patterns of African rural life.

By 1932 Perham was an acknowledged expert on indigenous governmental institutions, and she continued her research through the 1930s. In 1939 she became a Reader in Colonial Administration at Oxford, and from 1945 to 1948 she directed the Institute of

Colonial Studies associated with Nuffield College, where she became a fellow in 1939.

Always a spirited defender of the rights of native peoples, she
engaged Elspeth Huxley in a series of published letters on racial
conflict in Kenya, in which Perham defended native rights and Huxley spoke on behalf of the interests of white settlers. These letters,
published as *Race and Politics in Kenya, A Correspondence* (London, Faber and Faber, 1944), helped to frame the discussion of
colonial self-government in postwar Britain, a framework Perham
elaborated brilliantly in her influential BBC Reith Lectures in 1961.
By then she was recognized as the prophet of "winds of change in
Africa" and identified as a bitter opponent of Britain's tolerance of
the system of racial oppression in South Africa. Awarded the Order
of the British Empire and many honorary doctorates, Perham remained a model for women scholars in the British world and a
model of political commitment into her ninth decade.

AFRICAN APPRENTICESHIP:
An Autobiographical Journey
in Southern Africa, 1929

The time of my life. Yes—but what sort of time? The time when
I did my best work—or what I *thought* was the best? Or the time
that was most decisive in my career? Or the time I enjoyed most?
The time of my life which was at once the most enjoyable and the
most decisive for my future was the year 1922 which I spent in the
then British Somaliland. I can make this clear only by trying to give
some picture of what I was before and after this experience. . . .

. . . Very early in my childhood I used to answer the usual
grown-ups' question of what I meant to be when I grew up with the
answer—"a big-game hunter in Africa." This, of course, was the result of my favourite reading. About Kipling's *Mowgli* and *Lives of
the Hunted*—admittedly neither in Africa and both of which should
have turned me against hunting. But *Jock of the Bushveld* and
Rider Haggard's romances—these gave me the Africa about which
I dreamed. But what hope could there be for a child, a female child
at that, and at the turn of the century, of getting to Africa, least of
all of becoming a hunter?

. . . My father was the youngest son of a large family farming in the south-west. No land was left for the last two boys so one went as a missionary to Malaya . . . while my father went into business in the north and we lived quite prosperously in Harrogate. . . . My mother came of a family of French extraction. . . .

. . . Looking back it seems to me that we had a more exciting and self-contained life than many children today. We owed little in early days to our schools. We had a nursery and nurses and as we grew older, led a busy and tumultuous life of our own. The big boys took us on immense walks over the Yorkshire moors, twenty miles was regarded as a norm. The nursery was always full of firearms and sometimes we went out to what was then a wild crag and fought campaigns among the rocks and trees with blank cartridges. . . .

. . . My great friend was my youngest brother, Edgar, three years older than myself. His enthusiasms were for music and classical studies. . . . We were inseparable except for the cruel divorce of our boarding schools from which we wrote long diary letters to each other, sometimes in verse. . . .

. . . My education was at first rather chaotic. My mother often went abroad in the winter. She did not like leaving me alone with a nurse and so sent me to boarding-school and then brought me back home on her return. So I had four or five changes before I finally went to St. Anne's, Abbots Bromley. Here, Miss Rice, the headmistress, a stately, splendidly aristocratic, devout and authoritarian woman, took firm hold of my hitherto meandering education. . . . In those days scholarships meant something, especially to girls. When I won it she persuaded me again to stay on to be head of the school and to take Responsions, the then entrance exam to Oxford. . . .

. . . Well, Miss Rice got me to Oxford—just as World War I broke out. My brother injured himself diving on our last summer holiday. So, before being able to join the army, he had his last year at Oxford taking Greats while I had my first year taking history. Then he joined up and was killed at Delville Wood. . . .

The question for me, with the war coming to an end, was "what next?" Some of the men who had taught me at Oxford persuaded me that it was my duty to fill a war-vacancy at a university ready for the flood of men which demobilization would release.

So, unwillingly, I went to Sheffield. If I am certain about the best time of my life this was just as certainly the worst. I was alone in a strange grimy city. I was not welcomed at the University. I was the first woman appointed to the academic staff. One of my first experiences was to be led out of the large warm Senior Common Room by its president, an old professor, and shown into a very small, barely furnished room next door which never had a fire. "This," he said, "is to be the Ladies' Common Room." Add to that I had my first and, I am sure, very reformative experience of poverty. My half-time salary—can you believe it?—was £100 a year. . . .

. . . Providence intervened through my sister. But how she was able to get me not only to Africa, but to what was then, perhaps, the most exciting part of the continent I could have chosen, demands quite a bit of explanation.

My sister . . . is . . . eight years older than myself. After university she was drawn by missionary ambitions to work abroad and in 1910 she took ship for East Africa. But alas! for the plans of mice and women. On the ship she got engaged and was married in Mombasa Cathedral not long after her arrival. It was through her husband, Major Henry Rayne, D.S.O., M.C., that I was now able not only to go to Africa but to go to one of the wildest, most romantic places—according to my idea—in the whole continent. . . .

. . . Henry Rayne had run away from his New Zealand home as a boy and lied about his age in order to get into the New Zealand Mounted Infantry. . . . After a full and exciting Boer War he found his way up north to the then newly annexed East African Protectorate. Here he played his full part in the rough-and-tumble of opening up that beautiful, controversial acquisition. . . .

. . . It was on the return journey from their visit to London to sell their first cotton that Rayne met my sister. Immediately after their marriage in Mombasa Cathedral he took her up to this wild country to live in bush full of lions beside a river full of crocodiles, to experience a Somali rising in which their nearest British official was murdered, and to have her first baby. . . .

. . . Marriage did not divert my brother-in-law from his adventurous career. He returned to the army in World War I and in the inter-war years commanded a joint expedition from the Sudan, Uganda and Kenya to clear raiders from Abyssinia. . . .

. . . His next employment was in the expedition of 1919–20 which at last destroyed the power of the so-called Mad Mullah who had dominated Somaliland for twenty years and, after a series of campaigns, had forced the British to retire to the coast. So 1920 saw him posted as District Commissioner of the newly regained frontier district of Hargeisa. My sister was to join him. Here, at last, was my chance! . . . To me Somaliland was the obvious, the only, the predestined place. In 1921—I forget the exact date—at twenty-four (and, as I see now, a very young and uninitiated twenty-four), my sister and I left Tilbury in a P.&O. liner.

We disembarked at Aden and my first experience of tropical heat was to have it thrown back at me like a blow from this place of solid rock. We stayed at a dingy hotel in the middle of the town—hellishly hot. I looked out from a rickety balcony on to the crowds seething below—Yemenis and Arabs of many other kinds, Somalis, Jews, Indians—also of many kinds—and Negroes—all dark, brown to black, alien, unknown, unknowable. Next day we were to cross the Gulf of Aden to Berbera to live almost alone and far inland among a population of dark people. I had an overwhelming spasm of recoil, of something more than physical fear. I referred to this in one of my Reith Lectures—a revulsion against the thought that I—how can I express it?—I, so white, so vulnerable, so sensitive, so complex, was about to commit myself to that black continent across the water; one, almost alone, among tens of thousands of strange, dark, fierce, uncomprehending people, and live away on that far frontier, utterly cutoff from my own race. . . . I suppose it was racial fear. It passed and I have never felt it again, not on the Somali frontier or later in any situation of danger or isolation in any part of Africa. Even, when alone in remote almost unadministered pagan areas in northern Nigeria, or at night alone in the African slums of Durban.

We boarded the dingy little Indian-owned cattle boat which fed foodless Aden from Somali flocks and herds. It was now on its empty run. We disembarked at Berbera, the headquarters of the Protectorate—a few white bungalows in some irrigated greenery with the native town a discreet distance up-shore. A shock awaited us. The Mad Mullah had been defeated but some of the tribes into which the Somalis were divided—there was no unity—were giving trouble. And this was down in the south along the Abyssinian frontier—my brother-in-law's district. . . .

. . . Major Rayne came up to Berbera and persuaded the Governor to let us go back. After all it was upon my brother-in-law's judgement that our safety depended. I have already mentioned his faith in Somalis as soldiers. He knew them well and had then just written a book about them and the recent final expedition in which he had taken part. It made no difference to his affection for them that Somalis had more than once tried to murder him and in one attempt killed his colleague beside him. So, backing his D.C.'s judgement, the Governor let us go. First across the burning coastal plain, then 5,000 feet up the terrifying masses of rock which led to the plateau—past Sheikh, the Governor's little hot-season retreat. On again through a sandy waste, dotted with thorn trees, rocks, ant-hills and spiky aloes. We met Somalis, very few, travelling with the mats and poles of their huts strapped on their camels. Sometimes through dim aisles of the thorn trees there would be a scurry of buck or an ugly wart-hog trundling off. And always birds, doves of many kinds and sizes. Now, for me in England, the voice of doves always recalls Africa—a harsh setting for such a gentle sound. There were other birds—why are they so numerous in semi-desert lands?—storks, vultures, hoopoes, hornbills, carrion crows and the glorious jays with feathers of a dozen iridescent blues.

At last, after threading a route of nearly two hundred miles and seeing buildings only at Sheikh, we reached Hargeisa. It is still a magic word to me. Yet there wasn't much to see—sand, thorn trees, aloes, a few stony hills, a *tug* or a dry water-course. On the other side of this *tug* from our bungalow the Camel Corps were living in tents, two Somali companies and half a dozen British officers. . . .

. . . I think the people of Africa's north-east are, by our own standards, the most beautiful in the world—slim, upright, with dry polished skins, dark hawkish eyes, fine-cut features and proud carriage. They are hard people in a hard land. I used to watch them in my brother-in-law's court litigating tenaciously for compensation after inter-tribal fights—100 camels for a man, 50 for a woman. . . .

. . . Why was I so gloriously happy in Hargeisa? There was little enough to do. We had to stay indoors during the heat of the day. But there were books to read, letters to write, and a menagerie to play with, young buck, cheetahs, two young lions and an irreconcilable little leopard. There were tennis, riding and steeple-chasing. There were the Camel Corps officers across the river-bed to be dined with in their mess tent. Or they would come across to drinks or dinner with us. There were buck and guinea-fowl to shoot for the pot. No rule against shooting sitting birds! I once shot seven with one shot—they were all bunched together and rather young. I felt like Herod. Above all there were the nights. I slept in the open on the roof. We had a breed of very large hyenas there and at night they came snooping round. They could bite off half the face of a sleeping man. Their extraordinary howl punctuated my dreams. And if the moon was up I could see them slinking around the bungalow like grey ghosts. . . .

. . . Among many memories of Hargeisa three events stand out. One was the day we found a document stuck on a tree near our house. It was a call to the Somali soldiers in the Camel Corps to cut all white throats and go with their weapons across the border into Abyssinian Somaliland and join those fighting for the deposed Muslim emperor, Lij Yasu, against the Christian contender, Haile Selassie. Obviously our throats were *not* cut: the Somali soldiers remained loyal. Lij Yasu's star sank while that of Haile Selassie rose to shine for nearly half a century and is still shining. . . .

. . . It may have been in some relation to this threat that the military authorities decided to add an Indian Company to the two Somali ones, and this led to my second thrill. . . . The newly arrived Indians needed training in Somali bush warfare. It happened that just before we arrived, many of the Mullah's soldiers had been captured and it was difficult to know what to do with them. So some of them were drafted into the Camel Corps. They were now told to take off their uniforms, put on their dervish clothes and play-act the part of the enemy. The officer in charge of them . . . said I could go with them. I am sure he must have got into trouble afterwards. But could anything have been more gloriously exciting than galloping around with this wild-looking troop, ambushing the enemy in a narrow rocky defile and later dashing madly around them like Red Indians as they formed up, and almost breaking a British square? . . .

. . . The third thrill was the best. Major Rayne had to beat the bounds of his newly reconquered district up to the Abyssinian frontier. I was allowed to go with him. . . . This meant setting off into the blue with a string of camels, ponies and mules, a handful of Somali police looking splendid in their uniforms, and a few cooks and orderlies. . . .

. . . The sun decided our routine. The cook and orderlies got up in the dark and set off with the baggage camels. We rose just as there was the first low hint of light through the trees and jogged along generally in that strange silence which the mystery of an African dawn seems to impose. . . .

. . . Night was the zenith of adventure. I slept on a camp-bed in the open with large fires on each side of me to scare potential carnivores—lions, hyenas or leopards. The police built a high *zareba* of thorn branches round our camp. They would sing themselves gutturally to sleep. Then that miracle of the tropical night of stars! If the moon was up the sand turned the colour of milk. These nights utterly fulfilled the heart's desire of my childhood for adventure in Africa. . . .

. . . The whole trek was to me, in the full sense of the word, thrilling. What especially appealed to me was that on our very blank map the word "Unexplored" was printed right across the area we were traversing. At some points there was no way of knowing for certain whether we were in British Somaliland or Abyssinia. As it was all just Somaliland and unadministered on the Abyssinian side it was only by geodetic survey that we knew where we were. As far as I knew no Europeans had ever followed our route, yet when, from time to time, we met a few Somali nomads filing through the bush with their camels they hardly turned their eyes to look at us—strangely snubbing encounters! . . .

. . . It will be obvious to anyone that the reason why this harsh corner of Africa was Heaven to me was that it provided the perfect stage in which to play the romantic role of which I had dreamed as a child. I delighted even in the costume needed then for the part I was playing—the high leather boots, the breeches—the short circular khaki skirt, the becoming double terai hat—long since discarded as an unnecessary protection; above all the rifle over the shoulder and the pistol under the pillow.

But now I was back in—of all places—Sheffield, and the lecture room, the winter slush and the clanging trams. . . .

. . . Was "the time of my life" in Somaliland to be nothing but a wonderful episode looked back to with bitter nostalgia? The rosy hues of personal adventure and self-romantization started to fade and I began to discern some of the realities which lay underneath them—the rights and needs of our African subjects—Britain's capacity to meet them—the quality of our colonial service—the ultimate goal of our imperial rule, if indeed we were aware of ultimates. . . . Suddenly . . . there was a large re-arrangement of staff and I found myself back again [at St. Hugh's] as Fellow and Tutor in Modern History. . . . You can—or you could then—lecture upon almost anything irrespective of attracting any audience. So I indulged myself with such subjects as "British Policy towards Native Races," or the "Mandates System." After a year or two of this there came another utterly unexpected intervention of fate—a letter from Philip Kerr offering me a Rhodes Trust Travelling Fellowship for a year's travel round the world looking at—I forget the definition—

native or colour questions, then an almost unknown subject of academic study.

So I set off round the world *en route* for Africa by way of America—Red Indians and Negroes—Hawaii, Fiji, Samoa, New Zealand, Australia and then at last Africa. And just as I reached East Africa I found a cable from The Rhodes Trust offering me a year's extension of my travelling Fellowship. . . .

. . . Since then I have been travelling in Africa, trying to see it at all levels from the lowest bush-station to Government House and the Colonial Office. The University invented posts for me and then Nuffield College gave me a Fellowship which allowed me to combine travel with lecturing and writing at Oxford. . . .

. . . And what about my beloved Somaliland? Alas! I never got back to study it in my new role of student. South, West and East Africa. . . . But I thought much about it and did what one writer could to project the case for the unity of all Somalis at the end of World War II. You can imagine my pleasure when I was invited to attend as the guest of the new government the independence celebrations of the united British and Italian Somalilands in the summer of 1960. So I could see again that harsh land and those handsome, high-spirited people rejoicing in their freedom and unity. . . . But nothing can change my purely personal and perhaps rather egotistical attitude to Somaliland as the place where I fulfilled so ecstatically my childhood's dream and also found a guiding purpose for my life and work—truly that year was "the time of my life." . . .

[*Perham's narrative now shifts to her arrival in South Africa from Australia in 1929.*] This morning I woke up at 5 a.m. being suddenly aware that the ship was slowing down. . . .

. . . I dressed hurriedly and went on deck. The ship was making her way across a great dull enclosed sheet of water, with docks and a town smudging the coast at one point—Durban! . . .

. . . When we had breakfasted I went up on deck. . . . Even to my ignorant eye the men were of different tribes, mostly Zulu, but—I later learned—Basuto, Pondo, Fingo as well. They looked up at us impudently, their faces nearly fell apart with their continuous laughter and every now and then they hurled themselves into a battling whirl of limbs over some small largess from the decks. The people on the boat laughed and commented:

"Look at the niggers!" "Aren't they priceless?" "Throw them a penny and see them fight for it."

I went below after a bit and sat in my cabin. I felt faint but the cause was mental rather than physical. Whether my mind had become softened with three weeks' isolation from the puzzling world, I don't know. But the sight of the Kaffirs on the docks was like a stunning blow. I seemed to feel the immensity of the problem they represented and the absurdity of my attempting to understand it. . . . I felt I dared not face this ridiculous enterprise, could hardly dare to step off the ship on to the docks, in order to begin it. . . .

. . . I made contact with one or two of the white "gaugers" in charge of the dock labour and through them I went to see the manager of one of the biggest of the firms which recruits labour from the reserves and contracts for the work on the docks. He was a hard, stringy Scot, with gimlet eyes and a mouth like a rat-trap, working in an office full of Indian clerks and Zulu foremen. Queues of natives, looking bewildered as cattle in a pen, waited their approach to the big counter behind which he sat. He could speak to them, such words as were needed, in any Bantu language and did so with a voice like a machine gun. It was impossible to tell from his tone whether he were cursing, dismissing or accepting them and equally difficult to interpret their manner as they wavered up to the counter. Some were clearly straight from the bush, others had been there before. He distinguished them, Pondos, Basutos and Zulus, down from their kraals for six or nine months, forty-five shillings a month and their keep in the compound. He explained to me:

"I have been at this for forty years and I can tell you I know my job. My firm can get all the labour it wants because we have a good reputation. They know where they are with us. We are firm but just; we give a boy his rights, no more and no less. I accept only the raw bush native. No mission boy is allowed inside this place, no so-called educated boy. Any suggestion that a boy has had the faintest connection with the I.C.U. (the native Industrial and Commercial Union which, I have since learned, is just struggling into existence) and out he goes! But the I.C.U. has been pretty well dealt with in Durban, I'm glad to say. To his shame, a white man has been mixed up with it." . . .

. . . Rather unwillingly he agreed to let me look at the compounds. But at this moment a policeman came in. He reported the death of a man who had just been killed. A rope had broken and a basket of coal had fallen on him and he had died almost at once. The policeman described the condition in which he found the body and handed over the man's belt, wallet, etc., all dripping with blood. The manager took them, excused himself from coming with me and shook hands. I withdrew mine to find it stained with the blood of No. 1102. There was nowhere to wash it off so I had to go as I was, carrying the mark. . . .

. . . The compound, though gloomy and prison-like, was not too bad. . . . I looked into everything—the kitchens where huge vats of white "mealie-meal" were cooking or cooling: the shower-baths through which they must pass on their way in from the docks: the dormitories where two rows of wooden shelves have been polished to ebony by sweat and coal dust and where groups of men were squatting, gambling, or cooking their own food in native cooking-pots. Then I went to the sick-wards, where 'flu, fever, and bronchitis had turned black men grey, and where they lay on rather dirty grids under tattered blankets. . . .

Then aboard again *en route* for Capetown [*sic*]. . . . When I did see the whole thing I was simply amazed. Nothing had prepared me for the grandeur and strangeness of the site. . . . For me it was the gateway to a continent. I knew that north and north-east of it there stretched a thousand miles of racial problems deeper and more complex than any I had yet surveyed.

The crowd is motley in Capetown streets. I saw the English in all degrees of acclimatization; brawny, tanned harsh-faced Dutch-men in big hats; Jews of all kinds, white and prosperous-looking Jews or lean, dark Jews from eastern Europe; well-dressed Malays in black or red tar-booshes; Indians; "Cape coloured" people, only a degree less respectable-looking, and very various in type and tint; and, of course, every kind of African drawn from all parts of the Union and beyond, including bare-legged women balancing pots and bundles on their heads.

. . . The sky here is famed for its almost constant and radiant blue which is given its full depth by the dry air while it has not the white glare of the tropics. . . .

I think I must just remind you of the general situation in South Africa as I arrive here in its political capital. (Pretoria is, of course, the administrative capital, Bloemfontein the judicial.) . . . General Hertzog, with the help of the Labour Party, is in power and is de-termined to swing policy in a pro-Boer and anti-African direction. Above all he plans legislation to destroy the remaining limited vot-ing rights of Africans in Cape Province, the last stronghold of those Cape liberals who, during the making of a united South Africa out of the four provinces (Transvaal, Orange Free State, Natal and the Cape) have struggled to save this last relic of racial equality.

On my last day Mrs. Cartwright took me the seventy-mile drive round the Cape Peninsula. . . . Nearly the whole of the coast is a natural rock-garden, its steep, tumbling masses of red and brown rock netted with flowers and spicy shrubs. The sands are, in real truth, almost as white as snow, and the sea is all the colours the sea can be when it is sparkling with sunlight, with cloud-shadows above and a changing floor of weed, rock and sand below. . . .

. . . I have not forgotten how in Somaliland the mountains turned opal and amethyst but here no jewel would make a simile. It is colour from the paint box, as crude and clear as colour can be. I have seen a big turret of rock catching the last shaft of the sun over the curve of the earth and its face was orange and crimson and the shadows purple. Superlatives become stale, I can only say that I stood like an idiot, struck motionless, my brain refusing to credit my eyes.

. . . The unseen Afrikaners, now the real rulers of the country; the vast dark background of the Africans—these are the forces to be understood and I do not see how it is to be done. But tomorrow I leave this lovely curtain-raiser of Capetown. I have chosen to go to the famous missionary school for Africans, Lovedale, founded in 1841, and the new University College of Fort Hare which has lately been founded alongside the school. Here at least I shall meet Africans of a kind, I hope, with whom I can talk freely.

. . . I was met at the station by the Principals of both Lovedale and Fort Hare. They had decided that I should start with the potential university, Fort Hare.

Heavens, what a day! I was up soon after seven, and we had breakfast at seven forty-five. I then went over to prayers with the Principal and sat with one of the staff. The hundred or so students filed in, including the first eight women students. I looked along the lines. The faces were of all types, a few undoubtedly, from their appearance, would support the controversial and superficial view that the African black man had smaller brain capacity than the white. . . .

The Bible lesson was very appropriate—how does it go?— "Do good to them that hurt you—pray for them that despitefully use you and persecute you." I wondered whether Christianity could and would enable these people to exercise the almost unimaginable restraint that will increasingly be demanded of them. One item in this morning's paper contains news of a raid with machine-guns and tear-gas upon natives in Durban—I must try to get there. Another, a new stringent bill against native agitation. A third item reports a strike, quite an orderly one, in which the strikers were surrounded by two or three hundred police and given five minutes in which to decide whether to go to jail or continue work.

. . . In the War, the fear of native trouble was intensified, and the establishment of the College was a sop, an amicable gesture. . . .

. . . At present the majority of students come to Fort Hare from the old-established mission schools of Lovedale and Healdtown. The students are of all tribes, mostly Fingoes and Xosas, some Zulus, Basutos and Tembus, a few coloured, and one or two Indians. Discipline presents no difficulties; they do not fight and they work only too hard.

The Principal took me round the College. In a corner in the library we found a graduate, now doing an advanced course in English literature. . . . He told me that he had not found Anglo-Saxon very difficult . . . that his favourite period was the eighteenth century and that in that period his favourite poets were Pope and Addison. . . . The vitality and humanity of the Elizabethans seemed to leave him cold, as did the romanticism and sentimentality of the nineteenth century. . . .

We talked for an hour. It was astonishing how quickly as I talked to them the impression of their ugliness faded and the intelligence and beauty of some of the faces appeared. They were soon most animated and though at first they would answer me in whispers, all at once, so that I could distinguish nothing, they soon improved, and one after another began to speak out and stand out as individuals.

. . . They questioned me eagerly about Oxford and listened with gleaming eyes to what I said of the life and the students. It was clear that dimly, far away, English student life was their ideal. It is upon *that* we shall founder with all our theories of differentiation, of adaptation to native society, etc., upon their passionate determination to accept nothing but that which will give them not only the right but the power to gain equality.

. . . Five o'clock struck, and I had to go and talk to seven selected degree course men on the verandah of the Principal's house.

. . . They began to ask me for detailed information about the exact constitutional relations between South Africa and England. It was pathetic to see in what a hopeless direction their minds were working. Soon they came into the open. They asked me terrible questions.

"What does England think of the situation out here?"

I explained that we were quite detached, that we were more liberal than South Africans but that it was easy for us to be so as our interests were not involved.

"Can England do *nothing*, then?"

"But, Miss, what do you yourself think of the way we are treated?"

Now for it! I had already asked the Principal if he objected to my talking politics in the College, and he made the very proper reply, "*Magna est veritas et praevalet.*"

I said I thought the policy was wrong: that every consideration, religious, social, economic, directed us to put all our energies into raising the black people; that so long as the reward of effort was a share in the best we had to offer, so long would they be attached to our civilization, would feel a stake in it. But then, it was easy for me, coming in from outside, to be impartial. Could they not make the effort, great though it was, to understand what the whites felt about it[?] Did they not realize, now they were educated, how great was still the gulf between their people and ours; and how the whites, one to four, feared to be swamped by a race so different from their own[?]

"Are they *afraid* of us?" It seemed a new idea. They were spellbound. I began to get a cold feeling. I had before me the first of Africa's university men, all about to take their degrees and go out, marked men and leaders of these masses, the still backward masses. I felt I had got into a position into which I must go further because I could not retreat.

"You are going out into the world highly educated, feeling and thinking almost as we do and yet you will be treated—well, you know far better than I how that will be. You will have every temptation to become embittered, to become agitators and to take short cuts. Your lives cannot be altogether happy; you have had this great privilege of education and it is going to cut you off and mark you out among your own people and among the whites. But if you do try to take short cuts the results could be disastrous. If you do all you can to make relations worse instead of better, do you know what will happen? Supposing it leads to outbreaks of violence, do you imagine for a moment you can succeed? I want you to look up and answer me. Even if there were a temporary success? England would have to back law and order in South Africa—as the whites see it. It is *your* people who would suffer, not the whites. They would crush you easily, in spite of numbers. You know that?" They all said "Yes." "A very heavy responsibility rests upon you. All your effort should go back into your people to raise them. They are not ready yet to claim and make effective use of political power. . . .

That is the gist of what I felt driven to say and from that we went on and spoke with the greatest frankness of the whole situation. I do not know if they felt the same sense of solemnity that I did because the subject was so heavy with dread. . . .

I now had to motor over three-quarters of a mile away to Lovedale, the most famous of all South African missionary institutions, a Presbyterian foundation begun in 1840. Here I again met Dr. Henderson, who took me up to the big hall, which can seat about 800 of the 1,000 pupils of all ages who fill Lovedale.

The next morning I was up early in order that I might call upon two native members of the staff before I transferred myself completely to Lovedale. First we went to see Professor Jabavu, perhaps the most famous living South African native. His father was famous, too, for the production of a South African newspaper, and both were educated at Lovedale. . . .

It was now time to leave Fort Hare and transfer myself entirely to Lovedale. Mr. Kerr took me. From the gate we went up a long avenue of trees into the untidy litter of buildings, built at many times and in many styles between 1840 and 1925, that make up Lovedale—solid stone with clock tower, modern technical block, cracked mud and tin dormitories like shabby stables and a warren of workshops. In this new country, the whole place positively smelt of tradition and was most attractive after the rather glaring newness of Fort Hare.

The Principal came out to meet us and took us in to morning tea. (Is it the Scots who have carried morning tea all over the world?) Dr. Henderson is a man of about fifty. He is reputed to be the wisest authority on the native question in Africa. . . . He shows you first the Scots lawyer, undemonstrative, silent, almost repressive. It is with surprise that you learn that he is highly strung, almost nervous. A deeply religious man, big of heart and brain, but physically not very strong. . . . The African problem has scored deep lines on his face, increasing the natural ruggedness and giving a sad expression. For he has not merely looked out upon affairs from Lovedale; he has gone out and joined in the wide struggle, writing, speaking, attending government committees, knocking on departmental doors, urged by moral indignation into activities that must be repugnant to him. . . .

. . . Lovedale operates on a very large scale, accepting contracts for big buildings and carrying through the whole work, making all the doors and window-frames in their own shops. They built part of Fort Hare and have now a contract for a big governmental agricultural school. All this work, of course, is work only for African purposes. What they perform is a proof of the capacity of the native to do the skilled work. All the work I saw, carpentry, metal work, waggon-making, counts as skilled in this country and where the colour-bar works, which is almost everywhere, the native is automatically shut out from it.

Most striking is the printing shop where I saw an African in sole charge of a type-making machine just bought from America and costing nearly £2,000. In a huge shop natives were printing and binding books in seven languages with illustrations and music, with only two white men to supervise. They are all apprentices. . . .

In the afternoon, as I had asked Dr. Henderson to interpret the country to me, he decided to take me up the hill from which a wide view of the district can be seen. . . .

This country, the Ciskei, is the area where Bantu and European first met in serious contact, and where, after a long series of wars, they were settled down side by side in uneasy neighbourhood. Land that was barely adequate for the Africans in 1875 is ludicrously inadequate for more than double the population in 1929. A people used to extensive farming, to shifting their ground in order to rest the poor land (a sanitary precaution also) are now left congested and impoverished. They are ignorant of intensive farming, even if intensive farming on such poor land could support their numbers.

The view from a spur of our hill, as interpreted by Dr. Henderson, was a most striking chart of the situation in South Africa. . . .

You must imagine one of those enormous views, clear almost to the horizon, which seem peculiar to South Africa, the country lying like a map on three sides of us, low hills hummocking round the wriggling line made by the muddy little Tynnice river. The greater part of the valley alongside the river, and the best part, was cut into European farms, with their tree-girt homesteads, squares of verdant lucerne and yellow corn. The grazing land behind, fenced into squares to allow rotation of pasture, was spotted with mimosa scrub in just the right proportation to grip the slopes and give food in the drought. Higher up the slopes, or in other depressions away from the river, was the patchwork of native cultivation, above which were the villages, the round mud huts with conical thatched roofs and the square cattle kraals made of grey-green cactus or prickly pear. Even to a novice the distribution of land was preposterous. But some of the effects were also visible. The native pasture land was denuded of scrub, the grass eaten down to the roots and this had been followed by erosion which had left great wounds in the sides of the hills. Overstocking, exhaustion, denudation, erosion—this had been the sequence, and now a yellow weed, beautiful, harmful and apparently invincible, was creeping from the pasture on to the arable and gleaming like an evil halo upon the native lands. Nature had sketched out as vivid a chart of the unjust racial situation as if a man with bold strokes of coloured crayons had tried to illustrate it.

When the sun slipped down a little the picture became even more vivid, for the outcrop of little huts, whose soft grey thatching made them almost invisible from above, were now picked out in double fashion, for the light caught one half of their circle and made it shine and threw a dark shadow behind the other. All over the hills and slopes they began to appear. . . . Emphasizing the enormous size of the native population the land was bearing. I should not say "bearing": it cannot do that. More than 60 per cent of the able-bodied men are always away in the mines and even so the people of the district are in a state of semi-starvation, strangled with debt and crowding the Lovedale hospital with evergrowing cases of malnutrition, scurvy and tuberculosis. . . .

I had some fear of a Lovedale Presbyterian Sunday. However it was all very pleasant. We had service, some 1,200 of us, in the open-air church, its aisles made of oak trees. The service was all in the native language, Xosa, except the sermon. I never saw a congregation listen to a sermon more attentively than those children. There were some very little girls in front of me who never took their eyes from the preacher, never fidgeted, although of course it was all in a foreign language, understood with difficulty. Moreover it was one of a series on the commandments and this being the eighth, the preacher was upholding the sacred rights of property, warning them against Communism. It is almost pathetic how the missionaries as pastors struggle to repress discontent with one hand while, as teachers, they give the African the fuel for this fire.

[*Perham watches a teacher training class and reflects on the problems of cultural imperialism.*] Then the little ones arrived to be practised upon and were seated on little benches round a squat table. One student gave the lesson, the others stood in a circle. It was an English lesson and the girl told these mites the story of the fox and the crane. It was really rather painful to see the teacher and the children straining after the meaning and the accent. And the white teacher reinforced the impression. She said that far too much time had to be given to English. That it would be better if it were taught as a foreign language. As it was, nearly all their lessons were in English and they were bound to talk it all the week except Sundays. It was as though the lessons in an English school were in French. The loss in education was great, the strain and the time spent enormous. In her opinion all the white teachers ought to learn Xosa. It was all the sadder, she said, as the children were so *teachable*, so eager, and docile; they could accept all that we would give.

It is a difficult problem. The pure educationalist would say, and say indignantly, that education should be adapted to their needs, that language is custom, tradition, history, expression, most of all to a primitive people whose way of life is so different from ours that their thoughts are distorted in translation. Nor is it only that they teach them so much English and teach them all their subjects in English. They are also teaching them on a syllabus set for English children. If in their reader they learnt about things familiar and interesting, or at least related to their own lives, the strain would be less, but the subjects are as remote as Mars and the moon to the kraal child. I have seen them at it. I saw Standard V struggling with *Oliver Twist*. They were at the most-quoted incident. Progress was impossible. The passage should be recalled in order to appreciate what Dickens' style means to the native child—a porringer—thin gruel—this festive composition—an almshouse. . . .

. . . But there is another set of considerations. The English language is the gateway to a new culture; they have, of course, no written literature of their own, next to no history, as we define it. And the exams are the gateway to all the professions, and even to many more lowly jobs. You cannot be a carpenter without some knowledge of maths. You cannot run any shop or small business without some knowledge of book-keeping. The South African native is in a peculiar position: he must adapt himself to white civilization and to do that he must show that he can face the same tests, hold the same ground. Not only "progress," but mere self-defence seems to demand this.

If any leaders are to hold their own with us then there must be men who have trodden the whole intellectual round and reached the goal; have taken the very best we have to offer. In higher education there can be no differentiation, no adaptation, or very little. . . .

It was time to go. We motored down to the station, and I took my leave of the two Principals, deeply impressed by their work and their spirit and by all I had seen of Scotland's gift to Africa.

To reach this, to me, all-important territory, [Transkei], I have had to go right down to the sea-coast and change trains at East London. . . .

The country we went through all day was that into which the advancing Bantu, pushed on by the Zulus from the east, were penned in by Boer and Briton from the west. . . . Lord Glenelg, one of a unique group of humanitarians, gave it back on the grounds that we were the aggressors and the natives more sinned against than sinning. Later in life Sir Harry [Smith] had to conquer it again and Sir George Grey to devise a system of government for it. And by degrees, with much trouble and many risings, it was annexed piecemeal until, in 1895, Rhodes took over the last bit, Pondoland. Meanwhile, the comparatively liberal Cape Government, imbued with British traditions, and in close touch with the mother-country, treated the land as native reserve, and built up in it, year by year, at the hands of some very good and true administrators, a system of government, which was adapted in some measure to the needs of the tribes. . . . now that there is the Union and, more to the point, motor traffic, men down from the Transvaal and Orange Free State are discovering the Transkei, and saying, "Good Heavens!" (or whatever the Afrikaans equivalent is), "Why, this is a magnificent stretch of country, about the best in the Union. And it all belongs to natives! It's monstrous." . . .

. . . In parts it is rather like the Berkshire Downs, only grander, with here and there a spine of rock sticking out as it never does in our chalk downs. In this wonderful air you can see some forty miles of these rolling grassy slopes, dotted with cattle and kraals, so that the phrase "the cattle upon a thousand hills" comes to one's mind. As the huts are mere dun-coloured mounds, not much bigger than the cattle, they do nothing to break the sense of space. And over all these huge stretches there is not a fence, nothing but the square kraals made of cactus in which the cattle are herded at night. The fences are the little herd-boys, dressed in a leather thong and a bead, who dash across country to intercept the train and run and scream and dance and sometimes roll on the ground with glee and excitement.

Yet further knowledge takes much of the pleasure out of the picture. . . . The country . . . is overburdened, with the consequent results of erosion and the growth of the yellow pest resembling rag-wort. There is now hardly grass long enough to thatch the mud huts. Much of the beautiful-seeming grass is *sawerveld*. The flocks of goats, whose funny square shapes go bobbing away from the train, are of little use except for ritual feasts. . . .

Arrival at Umtata was rather grim. No one met me and I had counted on some kind of reception, being recommended to the authorities by Dr. J. H. Oldham and the Colonial Office. So I asked for the hotel and drove there. I found the Chief Magistrate, Mr. Welsh, had booked a room there for me. He had also sent his secretary to the station. But the young man had accosted an elderly woman, saying, "Are you Miss Perm?" To which she sensibly replied, "I am, and this is my husband," and so drove off in the Chief Magistrate's car to the hotel. The secretary—looking rather foolish—told me to be ready at nine in the morning, as the Chief Magistrate would call and take me to Buntingville. . . .

Buntingville, eighteen miles away, turned out to be the head-quarters of the Wesleyan Mission to Pondoland, the last tribal area to be associated to the Transkei. The mission was celebrating the arrival of the first missionary a hundred years ago. In the solid, old-fashioned stone house we were greeted by men and women pre-served from another generation by their isolation in Africa. Furniture, clothes, even the food, spoke of a bygone age. We went to the church, stuffed to suffocation with the devout Christians of the Pondo tribe, and were wedged close to the platform. Then be-gan the speeches, the pitiless speeches of nonconformist ministers, followed by the remorseless eloquence of native orators. Yet, per-haps, if I had not felt so ill, I might have appreciated all this elo-quence for it recalled the turbulent and bloody past of this disputed region: of Zulus massacreing Pondos; of English punishing Xosas; and of later days when, as a child, Mr. Welsh himself was cut off in a beleaguered mission station. I must say, however, that the ministers who spoke did not make the best of their missionary history. Lists of achievements, mostly in figures of souls and money, were read off to mark growth and there was overmuch complacency and repetition. . . .

. . . We had now been crouched breathlessly upon narrow benches from 11 a.m. until after 2 p.m. Mrs. Welsh, the Chief Magistrate's wife, amiable mother of four daughters, saw that I was near collapse and with much fighting we got out, and I cut the centenary feast and went back to Umtata in someone's car to fall into bed. The hotel was horrible: the bed was a board with a deep hole in the middle; the servants were speechless black women who ran like hares from my desperate gesticulations. Clearly no one of importance or affluence can ever visit this centre of the most important of the native territories.

When, after a day and night of misery, I had to get up, I was handed over, body and soul, to one Mr. Barrett, the second man in the administration. He was not at first very encouraging. He was a quiet, lean, rather awkward individual, with a drawn, leathery face, and eyes too shy to meet one's own for more than a moment. . . .

He took me into his office, sat me before his spacious desk and said he was entirely at my service. It is, however, difficult, at least for me, to command, at a moment's notice, services offered so joylessly. . . . So I let him down gently with what has now become my usual demand for a place in the office where I can spend two or three days studying all the documents they think fit to put before me. The response was immediate: all this was now done. I was given a large room of my own; a huge desk was piled with records and blue-books and a clerk was told off to fetch and carry. . . .

Under these ideal conditions I sat down to read up the minutes of the rather unique Council—the Bunga—in which native chiefs and representatives sit with government officials, and which has now been working in the Transkei for about twenty-five years.

At 8.45 a.m. Mr. Barrett called for me in the Chief Magistrate's car and we set out the forty miles to the Cowley Fathers' Mission. I liked him very much and also the quiet, cold way he diagnosed the situation and interpreted the countryside. We passed ox-waggons, lashed off the road by screaming drivers, the big beasts looking half-choked and getting their six or seven pairs into clumsy tangles at the crisis. We passed many natives in Balaclava helmets and curious clothes loping along on their little, ill-treated ponies. Minute, naked piccaninnies herding cattle jumped and shrilled for glee as we passed. (Why?) Once we forded a river and startled a girl kneeling on a rock who was washing bright coloured clothes, a picture of grace and beauty. . . .

Our way led through fold upon fold of rolling grasslands, with one horizon of hills after another. One gets that sense of the land being infinite of which Rhodes used to talk when he first came out and which seems peculiar to South Africa. Alas! for the Africans it is by no means infinite.

We came to St. Cuthbert's, the mission of the Cowley Fathers. These mission institutions are much the same in form, differing mainly in the range of their activities—the elementary, the secondary school, the training for teachers, the church, the workshops, perhaps the printing press. But they differ widely in spirit. Just as Lovedale stems from Edinburgh, Aberdeen and the kirk, so St. Cuthbert's is based on Oxford and High Church. White-clad fathers with white sun helmets and silver crosses, dazzling in the African sun, on their breasts; white sisters from Wantage: and in the school the teacher, Miss Wallace, from my old college, St. Hugh's. Most characteristic of all was the weaving school, where African girls were bending over looms weaving the skirt-lengths and scarves beloved and worn by Oxford women dons (like myself) and rectors' wives. . . .

. . . No one can travel about in South Africa without realizing how old, and how great in extent, is the mission contact with the African, how late the State has come into the field of education and welfare work and still, to a large extent, limits itself to supervision and inadequate grants-in-aid. Yet, in trying to imagine a better future, it is impossible not to feel that the missionary too often gives just what is ready in his hand to give, without more careful adaptation to the needs of the native. At first sight, for instance, I was inclined to admire the weaving school. It looks so charming and equally charming pictures arise of native girls weaving away in their own homes to fulfil their own simple needs and even to sell the surplus. But, learning to distrust first impressions and getting down to hard economics, I discovered that the girls could never weave a blanket, or indeed, any other native necessity, at a price within the furthest reach of the native. His blanket, made in Germany or Japan, costs about 10s: theirs would be between £2 and £3. Well,

then, it may be said, let them make for the European market. That
is a small, capricious market, difficult to organize. . . .

. . . We drove on to the Farm School. This is one of two schools
that have been put up by the Bunga (the Transkei Council) to teach
the people agriculture. It is a very interesting experiment and both
the head of the school and his wife were intelligent people, earnestly
devoted to their work.

The strange thing about this agricultural school is that it was
thought of so late in time and need. If the native is to be taught a
subject related to his life what could be nearer to him than that of
farming which was, and within the native areas still is, his whole
life? Yet the missionaries for a hundred years have put literary and
academic training first. This they should have done if ever African
leadership is to develop but should not have left the other undone.
They have given industrial training in some missions, as at Lovedale. In both cases they fit their pupils for a profession, to go out as
wage-earners, not for the home. Too often they have merely been
giving their students keys to doors which are bolted against them
from the inside. But improved agriculture would mean improved
standards of life throughout the native lands, the raising of the
whole community. . . .

I came in unawares upon some of the students while they were
milking. They were washing hands and arms with great elabora-
tion; each beast had its udders washed; the sore ones were vase-
lined; the shed was absolutely clean. No one was in charge of their
operations. In the equally spotless dairy, with all its machinery shining as if fresh from America, a student, a little out of date, was
singing lustily "Rule, Britannia." I was told this was the favourite
song upon the farm.

We walked in the beautiful valley. The same willows I had seen
in Australasia were beside the stream but not so bright or luxuriant:
the bed of the stream was full of arum lilies and other flowers. All
round us the slopes were thick with waving grass, showing what
this soil can do when guarded and rested. Mrs. Butler and her two
charming children walked with me. She is South African, willing to
give her life and the life of her children to serve the natives—her eldest girl is to be a doctor and is pledged to native work. . . .

I was so much attracted by the Farm School and Mr. Butler had
so much to say that I knew would be valuable, that when they pressed
Mr. Barrett to leave me behind with them, I agreed. I parted from
my friend and instructor with warm thanks and mutual good wishes.

I had not so much as a comb with me but Mrs. Butler was ready to provide all, so I stayed. They had to go out at night in their car to Tsolo so now I am sitting all alone on their verandah, with the whole air vibrating with insect life and all the sky shaking with stars, so the sound and movement seem one. The sound, indeed, is beautiful enough to be the music of the spheres: when so many crickets cry all at once on different notes, the whole is blended into one harmony. And high singing notes come down from the trees where the Christmas beetles, hanging like grey-green leaves, pulsate their wings in a tremulous soprano. The frogs make the bass, a soft roar coming from the whole length of the river in the valley. In the sky I can trace the lines of Orion's belt, the throbbing group of the Seven Sisters, and a lovely constellation, shaped like a coronet of even gems, whose name I cannot learn. I do not know if there are ever wholly dark nights in South Africa: I have seen none and tonight I can trace the whole sweep of the hills, the tables and cones and sugar-loaves, not as a black outline, but in their own deep blue-violet colour.

This morning I got up early and went for a walk, trying to drink in the country so that it should not be obliterated by the many impressions that I shall be taking in. I looked at the wide rolling downs, at the mushroom-coloured huts and kraals fenced in with grey-green aloes. This is the main piece of South Africa left to the Africans, overcrowded and ill-used for all its delusive look of empti-ness and stark beauty, a country which exports not its products but its men.

Back to Umtata where my last day was hectic with work and interviews. I had a long, final talk with the Chief Magistrate, who was very frank and confirmed most of the general views I had formed about the limited scope of the Transkei Bunga, or Coun-cil. . . .

I left Umtata at night. The "poor white" who hangs about the hall, intercepting tips that should go to the natives, came down to the station with me. On the way he unbosomed himself to me. Na-tives were all swine, he said. Not one was to be trusted. I listened in silence. Argument was so obviously useless.

The train stopped at six for breakfast, and then at 9.30 a.m. threw me out upon a junction in the open veld where there was no sign of man or beast. Here I had three hours to wait. It was a desolate experience. Conscientiously I looked round to see what I might learn here. There seemed only one point of interest—the low grade of the white clerks and porters on the station: pasty, ill-developed, sullen, stupid, both Dutch and English. It made one understand the reason for the amount of ignorance and deterioration in much of the South African white stock. Those who are not concentrated in the few towns are sprinkled about this vast country, with its scanty communications, with little in the way of education or external contacts, employing people whose primitive background demands, what it can seldom get, the utmost restraint and understanding. It is not wonderful that the result in politics is what it is, especially as in the Parliament the country districts are heavily over-represented as against the towns. . . .

At last my train! . . .

All day long, running up on the line from East London to Bloemfontein, we were in rich country, rolling downs carrying immense quantities of good sheep and cattle. How different, after the native areas, were now the size and culture of the farms. The contrast was, indeed, almost shocking. After the crowded, huddling huts spotting every slope and crowning every hill, the slow train would run five or ten minutes through immense rolling grass and arable lands before the farmhouse would appear gleaming through a sudden clump of trees.

As we approached the Free State the country changed. It was no longer so grassy: we got back to the karoo again, stony flats with sheep nibbling at the dry, salt-bush clumps, or gingerly tackling the emerald foliage of the mimosa scrub, which is armed with terrible white thorns. The shapes the hills make on the skyline—mounds, cones and tables—are almost unbelievable. And here the immensity of the farms was such that I got tired of looking out of the window for that little clump of pencil-shaped poplars and the windmills that marked the farmhouses. This is the area of "dry farming." They may go for two or three years without rain but the salt bush, the mimosa and the sheep exist and all the farmers are said to be rich.

And the flowers! I realize now that it was no such strange Biblical hope that the desert should blossom like the rose. It does in truth so blossom, flowers nameless to me, their colours shimmering in the heat-haze, so that you can hardly tell flowers from what seem to be flying flowers, the millions of butterflies fluttering above them. Just as no drought seems able to stop the desert from flowering, so no poverty or hard measure can stop the African from smiling. Little gamins, reedy-limbed and pot-bellied, wave and laugh from every location and give back four-fold measure of response for any sign of greeting.

But there are other than desert flowers. Streams are choked with masses of arum lilies. Gladioli and red-hot pokers and many other flowers that are precious garden blooms to us embroider the railway embankment whilst a sort of crisp everlasting flower, bright violet, or yellow, grows profusely and patches the slope with its vividness.

From my train I saw both sunset and sunrise over the karoo. I *will* restrain myself, but indulge me for a moment—what a feast of colour and shape, what sculptured clouds flushing through all the range of colours, what weird kopjes playing with the light and what a thrilling afterglow! . . .

Poor whites again! A sight such as could not, I am told, have been seen a year or two ago. A gang on the railway wielding shovels, first five natives, then three whites, four natives and two whites. The train, to their obvious embarrassment, halted beside them. The whites hung their heads and looked away. I thought they were divided between Dutch and English. The natives went on working after one look at the train. This is a very unusual sight, I understand. Generally, when the whites are employed on the railway now—the policy of the present government—they are employed in groups by themselves, and, of course, at a much higher wage than Africans. We passed some of the places where poor whites are bred, squatters' farms, *"bijowners,"* miserable plots and houses from which the Dutch wife replenishes the earth with ignorant and landless sons.

Another night in the train, and then Bloemfontein at half-past five in the morning. One hardly appreciates a strange city when wandering about at that hour without breakfast. It is a small, squared, insignificant town. A war memorial testifies to the fact that the contingent sent from the heart of the Free State was 90 per cent British. The natives, in the hideous, cast-off and patched clothing with which they caricature their masters, were pouring out of the location to work into the city. . . .

. . . I had always hoped that on this journey I would somehow get to Basutoland. I had read the romantic history of this mountain kingdom, now surrounded by white South Africa. But to understand the drama of Basutoland's position I must insert a little history.

Early in the nineteenth century a very remarkable African, Moshesh, had gathered together the tribes broken by the bloody Zulu tyranny and had welded them together into a miniature nation backing upon these mountains. He had later been driven off his rich lowlands by the encroaching Boers but from his dramatic table-shaped stronghold of Thaba Bosiu he had called a halt to Boer invasion. Hearing that other tribes had been helped by white people called "missionaries," he sent an agent with 200 cows to buy some of these valuable beings. This man fell in with some French evangelical missionaries and so began a most useful relationship and the process of the early conversion and Western education of this rugged people.

Moshesh was a diplomat as well as a fighter. When he defeated an English force, which left forty dead Lancers on the field, he characteristically sent a message: "You have shown your power, you have chastened. Let it be enough!" What he most wanted, indeed, was British annexation to save him from the Boers and in 1868 he got his way. . . .

At the making of the South African Union in 1910 there was strong pressure from both British and Boer leaders to take over the three British-ruled native territories. Basutoland was wholly, and the others, Bechuanaland and Swaziland, mainly surrounded by South African territory. A compromise was worked out laying down the conditions under which the three territories *might* be handed over to the Union. In 1924 the first fully nationalist Afrikaner Government won the election and began to impose its repressive policies on its Africans. It also made increasingly strong demands for the three territories. . . .

. . . So here I was alighting at the little terminus of Maseru a few miles into Basutoland.

I . . . looked anxiously along the modest platform at which I had alighted. There was only one occupant, a fair, slender man, over six feet high, dressed in an immaculate whipcord suit of rather military cut. He introduced himself as the Assistant Commissioner of Maseru district (that is Assistant to his chief, the Resident Commissioner of Basutoland), and therefore in charge of me. He drove me in his car to the local hotel. It was not at all attractive but he explained that his own house was full of his family and guests.

The day was still young after my morning run in from Bloemfontein. So I asked if I could start work in the afternoon. He put me in the court, a large, simple structure, with the bare requisites of justice, a platform, a table, a dock and a witness box. It leads out of his office so that from the magisterial table where I am now sitting as I write up my diary-letter, I can call across to him for information and papers. I can already report that among all officials I have met he excels in unselfishness and courtesy. . . .

In the evening I went a long ride on one of the A.C.'s ponies which, my being very out of condition, I had a great battle to hold. A girl staying at the A.C.'s house and another official came with us and we wound up a precipitous pass on to one of the stone tables that the Basuto made impregnable. It was down this very pass that they tumbled a body of British Lancers, not one of whom escaped alive. From the top we could see inland magnificent ranges of mountains, not flat-topped but rising ever higher to jagged peaks. I felt how glorious it would be to penetrate them and leave the flat borderland far behind.

This morning the A.C. held his Court under the pine trees outside the Court House. It was rather a striking scene. A few benches for the public were filled with natives lolling in their vivid blankets and big hats. Beyond them were many more all lining up to sign on for work at the mines in South Africa. I sat beside the A.C. A guarded prisoner stood in front of us, a fine, fiery individual, whose face looked quite impassive though on close inspection the movement of his neck muscles showed him less impassive than he seemed. On one side stood a white man, a slim, rather swagger young trader who was accusing the man of theft with violence at his store twenty miles out. On a bench in front were arranged the stolen goods which had been found hidden under rocks in the mountain. A goodly selection he had made—fifteen blankets, five pairs of trousers, pants and vests in bundles, bags of tobacco, cardigans, tea, candles and soap. It was all very informal: at the adjournment for morning tea the A.C. asked the trader into his office. I began to ask about the case but stopped myself, apologizing, as the matter was still *sub judice*. But that did not seem to matter and they talked it over together. Afterwards it transpired that the big crowds of natives who had rolled up, seeing a white woman there for the first time, thought a divorce case was coming on.

This is indeed a red-letter day entry in this diary-letter. Before I arrived here the A.C. had planned a two-week trip into the mountainous interior of his district. There are no roads so it means riding with pack animals. The Resident Commissioner has now decided that I am to go with him. It is an unbelievable opportunity and a very surprising offer. The only trouble is that I am very much out of condition after all this travelling around with no exercise and I can only hope that I shall be able to stand it and not be a drag on the A.C. Those blue ranges going up and up in height look pretty formidable.

. . . Last night, the Resident Commissioner gave a big dinner-party at the Residency to give me a send-off. The whole small official world, including the Assistant Commissioner's wife, was there. We played bridge and danced. Everyone was much interested in the coming trek. To me the evening was radiant with anticipation of the adventure.

. . . We said good-bye to the car which was driven back by a Mosuto, and set out at 12:30 p.m. on the first part of the trek. I chose Stumpy to ride as one of my two horses and the one selected for the Earl of Athlone, the Governor-General, when he was up here the other day. My second mount is a grey, smaller, but more spirited. . . .

We set off at a trekking jog which reminded me of similar expeditions in Somaliland. I had been warned not to talk to the A.C. on trek, as he hated talking when riding, and had, so far, always trekked alone, making a positive rule of it. So when he made conversation I answered in monosyllables. In the end I had to explain why. But he said he would waive his rule as it was only "babbling" that he could not stand. This means, I suppose, that I shall have to try to talk intelligently but not too intelligently.

I stopped once at the sound of singing and saw a line of men all hoeing in a field, raising their hoes in time with their song and very gay about it. I got a picture of them and they roared with laughter at me. "Are you a man or a woman," they yelled, so the interpreter said.

We rode steadily uphill all afternoon, until we suddenly found ourselves on the brink of a great fall of ground, with a valley cut by a tortuous stream at the foot. It was a most precipitous descent, with no proper path, and it was almost terrifying to see right below us our pack animals finding their own way down the rocks. . . . Right underneath, wrapped in almost a circle of river, was the roof of the last trader's store on our route, shining out of a clump of trees. Here we were to spend two nights.

We dropped down, forded the river and climbed up to the store. The people who kept it were very nice and made us most welcome. The A.C. had arranged to introduce me everywhere to the natives as his sister but of course he did not attempt this with these people.

Today I had to be packed up by eight o'clock in the morning. We have the most beautiful packs and pack saddles, all solid pigskin, provided by the Government. They cost about £20 each. I have one horse and two packs for my personal belongings, another carries the tents, another the beds, three others the kitchen things. Then we have an escort of four mounted police, fourteen horses all told, and generally a guide and local headmen in their gorgeous blankets join up by the way.

We dropped down the steep kopje on which the store stands, forded a river, passed a kloof where lately some wool-stealers were trapped at midnight by the owners and stoned to death. Then away, up a high ridge, and into the heart of the mountains.

This, the first long day, has been a wonderful, but rather hard experience. I am very soft with long lack of exercise and I was not fit when I started, so I have found the strain terrific. The natives were very vague about the distance and the A.C. could not verify it from the map. Moreover, the heights are so terrific that half the time the animals are climbing like cats and for the rest go slithering down in showers of stones and dust.

We rode four hours on end in these conditions and then off-saddled for lunch. . . . The packs were off and all our goods strewed about when a storm broke. We packed up as quickly as possible and set out again in the pouring rain. The black loam turned to mud and was slippery as ice. The A.C. made me wear his huge military coat, so I kept dry while he was soaked. We went on and on for two to three hours up and down what can only be called stone precipices. . . .

. . . The rain now turned into hail. We had been trekking for about seven hours and still no sign of the valley for which we were bound. The A.C. suddenly chucked it and decided to camp then and there on a particularly bleak ledge half-way up a hill. So we rounded up the pack-horses and in the soaking, dull evening stood about while the men fumbled with the packs and at last the tents went up and, in the mysterious manner of trek life, the hill was no longer bleak for there was 4 x 12 feet of home for each of us.

I was soaked through and utterly exhausted by the strains of the ride. . . . I was thankful to get to bed and slept like a log until the rising sun, taking advantage of an angle in the mountains, poked a finger into my tent and woke me. So I got up and worked for an hour or two, having brought some books on the country in my saddle-bag.

At nine o'clock we set out, leaving our large circle of admirers to glean what they could on the camping ground. I managed to get first up the hill that had daunted us so last night, but only by dint of dismounting here and there and dragging my horse over the sudden outcrops of stone that make such dangerous angles. . . .

We were now getting really into the mountains which, from the heights that we so often mounted, could be seen rising in series, all green after the rains with a shifting blue dapple from the clouds over them. In the pit of the valley the strips of native cultivation, maize, wheat and kaffir corn, stood out from the dun rock-strewn grazing of the slopes in brilliant little green rectangles and squares.

We descended a deep gorge and waded through the biggest river we had so far forded, the Senguingave. Then, steeply up again. By pushing hard we reached our intended camping ground by two o'clock. I was not sorry as I was feeling the strain of this very rough riding.

It was bitterly cold at night, as so far it always has been. It is really extraordinary how the temperature varies. All through the middle of the day the sun is scorching like the tropics; and I can bear nothing but a silk, sleeveless shirt above my breeches. But when the sun goes in at night and there is heavy dew or frost, one must wrap up in all woollen clothes at hand. I have been thankful for the loan of six scarlet police-blankets on my bed, my rug and the A.C.'s thick military coat on top, not to speak of my battered old aluminium hot-water bottle. Even by day, if the sun goes in and you ride up over the saddle of a hill, a sudden wind cuts into you like a knife. Each night we have had to eat our dinner in a tent. . . .

We have had a long talk on native policy tonight. He is very sound and almost over-modest. Defers too much to my opinion when I am all theory and he all practice. I am not sorry to finish these notes and get to bed.

. . . We rode until two o'clock and then off-saddled on the slope of a hill. . . .

Off-saddling when you have so many animals, packs and hangers-on is an untidy business, but the A.C. is very good-tempered. He knows how to push on when need be, but he also knows how to sprawl and eat his lunch in peace. . . .

We rode on past some glorious country. As we get higher the population is getting very sparse. The way the thin rivers have cut the rocky plateaux is most intricate, cutting the mountains into zig-zag patterns. Very often our path is a shaley ledge a few inches wide on a krans (precipice), and it continually amazes me to see our free-running herd of heavily laden pack-horses filing along entirely on their own responsibility, not to speak of our two spare mounts following on like dogs.

As I had objected to the very urban and public area of the last camp, I was allowed to choose this one. I rode on ahead with our guide, Maana, and I wanted to go on and on, as I saw the country getting wilder all the time.

Finally I chose a flat space half-circled by a river and completely surrounded on one side with precipitous hill-faces, a kind of natural theatre. The river ran below a face of sheer rock on one side, and from the tent door where I am now writing, I am looking out at that face which is tufted with rock plants, salmon pink cotyledons, wild myrtles and others I cannot name, while at intervals, the yellow and golden finks, weaving their hanging nests of pale green stems, look like mobile flowers themselves.

There was no keeping out of the water. We got into our bathing dresses and rushed in, mainly in order to have a good wash. I was still feeling too bad to bathe properly and was not encouraged by a crab seizing my toe in his pincers the moment I put it in. The name of the river was Meusugave, and the meaning of that is "little black things." We had wondered what this could mean. We soon learned. When the A.C. withdrew his foot it was covered with little black wiggling worms, which adhered firmly even when he put it back in the full force of the current. Wherever the water rushes hard, there the rock is covered with these objects, all drawn taut by the water, and holding on by a little string like a spider's web. Rather a tiring way of life.

This evening the A.C. and I had another long talk, poetry, history, life in general. His books are the *Chanson de Roland* and Bertrand Russell's last book of essays; mine are a history of the Basuto and Shakespeare's Sonnets. But somehow it is hard to settle down to read. The night was so glorious, with a halfmoon and the fascinating pattern of the southern stars, that we went for a walk along the river, which here sings a particularly good song, and saw the mountain mists shifting in the moonlight up and down the valley.

It has rained all the afternoon and I now sit on the floor of my tent, while the A.C. sits in his, writing notes for me on various points in Basutoland. Tonight we shall sleep here in this glorious place and push on to the furthest limits of this mountainous district tomorrow.

A storm broke over the mountains last night and went lumbering round in circles among the hills, with tremendous echoes. Sleep was difficult with the rain blown like rifle fire on my taut tent. The forking of the lightning could be seen even through the canvas. I managed to get some sleep in spite of it and rose early to have a bathe in the stream. But the stream was now a young and lusty river, galloping over the stones and thick as coffee. It was icy cold too, and the flesh was weak. One had to risk the possibility of bright-eyed cattle-herds high up on the slopes of the mountains. There is cover from the camp for the water has cut a deep gorge, and great lines of pale reeds march along the banks. When I had finished, the A.C., who had decided against a plunge, had to go in to maintain his superiority and in the distance I heard muffled screams. It is cold and overcast now and all our retainers declare that for the moment further progress into the mountains is impossible.

. . . I shall be very sorry to leave this camp. My tent is pitched in a bed of wild mint which fills the air with a lasting fragrance as I trample on it. When we were all in train to start I had to go back again at the last minute to fix in my memory the rock-garden growing up the wall of rock that rises perpendicularly from one bank of the Mansangave river; the clumps of wild myrtle clinging to the cracks in the rock; the flowers which formed brilliant purple stars in the cushions of moss; the tall coral and yellow cotyledons on red stalks rising out of a cluster of grey-green leaves; the yellow runnuculus, called by the Basuto the "wet nose of the God." There were branches of cherry-coloured candle-flower, drooping down to rise again in vivid points. The yellow finks were busy weaving their hanging nests, which tossed in the wind and were still green with the sap in the reeds.

We climbed a plateau, 9,000 feet up, the Ditsuming, and rode along the top, the sort of place that Rhodes would have called the roof of the world. The Basuto name of the ridge is "the place where you wipe the crying eyes," and certainly the wind was like a lash and, in default of a cloak, one must drop the reins and fold arms across one's chest. But when I dared look up the view on both sides was awesome, such a wealth of hills of all sizes and shapes, with that glorious cloud-dappling on their slopes which seems a characteristic of this country and its climate.

We slithered off Ditsuming down into a deep gorge and followed all its zig-zags for an hour or more of quick riding. . . .

We have found paradise for a camp. The A.C. said it was too wet but I asserted myself for once and we stayed. We are in a small, deep valley, with a narrow stream racing quickly down it, jumping from side to side among the rocks as it goes. Beside the stream are big cushions of grass; the stems spring and curve like fountains and fall in tassels of golden seed. In front of our tents is a level damp patch. If grass is ever a carpet, this is of the finest weaving, like the oldest Persian rugs. All is to a fairy scale. The groundwork is made of tiny, brilliant spade-shaped leaves: there are mossy patches set with countless white and yellow stars, no bigger than a baby's fingernail. There is a small clover, purple-pink, yellow cups like little celandine, and here and there, close within the weaving, but unable to hide its chalk-blue petals, is a lobelia. Sometimes a tiny knoll rises out of the plain, and the little flowers have grown richly all over it. Our carpet is bordered all round by great tussocks, golden where they are alive, silver where they have faded.

It was with deep regret and many backward glances that I clambered up the stony track out of that valley. But it was difficult to indulge regret. The steep road demanded all one's care, every hill we climbed opened out new valleys and further ranges. There were other gardens, too, by the way; slopes ablaze with red-hot pokers and rocky corners choked with arum lilies.

We are here to call upon a chief, Makhaobane, a grandson of Moshesh. He is a member of the National Council and a supporter of the reforms of the Chiefs' Courts that have been suggested by the Government and utterly refused by nearly all the other chiefs. As he was much impressed by the Resident Commissioner being an M.A., the A.C. is telling him that I am something even more wonderful, though whether the A.C.'s Sesuto will run to an interpretation of Fellow and Tutor, I don't know.

We had hardly halted, unharnessed the horses and turned them loose on the veld, than the Chief appeared, his men driving a great flock of sheep and goats down to our camp. The scene, like so much of life here, was very Biblical, with the shepherds in their flowing red blankets. . . .

After breakfast . . . we went to pay our state call on the chief. . . .

The A.C. made a speech about me, the chief made a speech to me, I made a speech to the chief, and then, with the loan of the A.C.'s interpreter, I began a long cross-examination. I went on for about two hours. . . . He had been educated at Lovedale and his mind was a strange mixture of new and old, of a chief's conservatism and of a blind faith in "education." . . .

. . . We had to get over our last mountain pass, Bushman's Neck. It was not so bad going up, but the other side was steeper and longer. Rather than slither in mud we chose to go down the bed of a stream, an avalanche of stones with running water. It is the first time I had ridden down a waterfall, and I hope it will be the last. I wanted to take a picture, but these moments are too desperate for camera work and, besides, the rain was driving hard and visibility nil. My spirits were low, too, for the view before us was leading us towards Maseru, some thirty miles over the hills in front and to-morrow is the last day of our trek.

The A.C. chose to camp beside a stream not far from the first store. The rain was relentless, the ground sodden, and putting up the tents rather a discouraging piece of work. We had an hour for lunch and rest and then rode off as hard as we could go to find some Bushmen's paintings near here.

The Bushmen chose their place well. Imagine a deep-cut stream, turning abruptly between overhanging walls of rock, the rock tawny but striped with bold, black tiger markings by the action of the weather. Under the lee of this rock is a smooth panel about 100 feet long and 12 feet high. . . . The patterns were faint and at first sight I was disappointed. But, under the A.C.'s instructions, Tsaki fetched water and splashed it all over the rock, and the paintings sprang at the splash into vigorous colour and outline. Many hands have been at work at different times, figuring different animals, at different angles, and to different scales. Sometimes one is superimposed upon another: in places the rock, exposed to all weather, has flaked away. But the sum and quality of what remains is amazing. . . . Their elands and hartebeests are sketched with accuracy and care; their colours are different shades of red and ochre, with white. Their deer have always dark shaded backs and pale bellies, pale faces, too, where the model demands it. Even the lighter markings at the backs of the legs are noted. But it is the action that catches the eye. The animals stand; they graze; they run and leap. The cranes race with long necks extended; the men stoop or jump or draw arrows. They even, most wonderful, turn their heads as it were towards the artist. There is another quality too, a sense of pattern. Here and there are designs made of processions of men, advancing with the same gesture, naked, with arrows stuck in their hair, or in tall slender ranks, with long garments from head to foot. There are other marks, not to be interpreted, magical perhaps, circles and crescents.

How hard to believe, gazing at this art of a vanished race, that the contents of their life were so limited, their evolution arrested so low in our scale of measurement, these men with eyes to see, hands to execute, skill to find pigment that withstands the long attacks of time and weather. The A.C. chose the outline of a partridge, a bold, rapid sketch in dark red, as his favourite; better than Thorburn, he said. I chose an eland and two young, all stooping their long necks to graze. Also a whiskered lion, evidently at bay, and beautifully maned.

The damp on the wall dried, the colour faded, and we found our horses, crossed the stream, left the paintings panelling that lonely gorge and went on at a gallop through a driving rain.

Dinner over, and the horses all penned in a kraal, for they may not run free here, the men all went off to the big neighbouring village. We made ourselves as warm and dry as possible and discussed the native problem in its economic aspect, the League of Nations, the Boer War, and finished up with Shakespeare's Sonnets. I am now very tired, and have a long last day in front of me tomorrow. Alas and alas, for the end of the trek.

The A.C. brought me coffee at six, and we looked at the day with a night of rain just dripping into a dull morning. . . .

We left the packs and rode on hard with Kaswell. We had much to do and, in this more populous part, many chiefs to visit. . . .

It was now getting terribly hot. Our clothes dried on us as we rode on as hard as we could until the mountain Thaba Basiu came into sight. This is the most famous mountain in the country. It is a completely flat table, rising at a sharp slope and then crowned by a

sheer wall of rock. It is absolutely impregnable except for three
places which can be, and once were, barricaded and defended. . . .

At the foot of the mountain was a large village where an important chief lived. We sent the interpreter ahead to announce our
visit and slackened pace. By the time we reached the village the men
were all out staring and the women, in their bright dresses, twittering. The rocky hillside looked, in the distance, like a garden full of
purple, orange and crimson flowers.

"Eh, Morena," they yelled, deep in their throats, and then were
at a loss how to address me. Then a woman decided I was one of
her sex and in her excitement rolled back laughing on the ground.
Yet it is difficult to believe that they had never seen a woman
dressed in boots and breeches. . . .

[The chief] looked me up and down and asked who I was. The
A.C. made his usual speech about me, which I knew by heart, even
in Sesuto. I struck in.

"Greetings, Khoabane. I am happy to see what good rain you
have had."

The Basuto is nothing if not blunt. He looked at me pityingly
and said they had had a drought until yesterday. The A.C. chipped
in with the story of our wanderings. Their eyes grew wide, and the
chief looked in horror at us, clicking his tongue in depreciation and
looking from one to the other of us as if we were mad. He made us
repeat the names of the furthest places we had reached.

"Well, well, tch-tch, such journeys are not for me. I should be
killed. I cannot go out at all. I cannot sit so long as that on a horse."

"Do you good to get some exercise," said the A.C., English
fashion.

"Take off some of your fat and make a new man of you."

Secret smiles from the retinue at this.

"And now, Khoabane," I said, "we mean to climb the mountain to find the grave of your father Moshesh and pay our respects
to his memory."

. . . He promised to provide an escort. He doubted if horses
could ride up (it must indeed be bad going if a Mosuto says this) but
he would send a guide ahead to choose a path.

"God be with you and bring you safely home (you poor fools),"
he said the last with his eyes.

"God be with you Khoabane, and give you good rains and
large crops and healthy beasts."

We mounted and rode away from the village, all the crowd staring at us until we were out of sight.

Now began our last steep ascent away from the kraal, piled mountain high with manure, which the women were working into little cakes for the fire, and then upwards painfully, between the showers of boulders which had fallen down one of the three possible ascents. We were not surprised to learn from our guide that not even the Zulus had chosen to storm on this side. Riding soon became impossible, so we dismounted and left our horses to climb after us alone as best they could. From running free with the pack they had become very clever at mountaineering.

At the top was a large, flat space, with ruined remains of old villages. . . . We rode around among goats and aloes and came to an untidy muddle of stone mounds. This was the royal cemetery of Basutoland. The graves might have been placed there yesterday, so fresh do the yellow rocks keep under the sun and rain. . . .

Now we must descend. . . . The old man led my horse, stopping every now and then to push the big stones out of his way. On the level at last and now a long canter towards the store where we were to have lunch and make our re-entry into civilization. I was as sorry to see the kind, white face of our hostess as I had been glad to wave good-bye to the last storekeeper we had seen some two weeks ago.

The car sent for us had not been able to reach the store as the river was in flood, but half-way through lunch a note arrived to say that a car was waiting on the other side. The trader offered to drive us the four miles to the river. It was difficult to refuse but I explained that I could not miss one mile of the last ride. And though we had been riding hard for four hours I was now so gloriously fit that I felt fresh as paint.

We rode rather sadly to the river. It was turgid and running fast. On the other side the car—a new saloon—was glittering with metal and navy panels and seemed to belong to another world. We plunged in, the muddy water racing past us above the knee and emerged the other side, to dismount, greet the A.C.'s two young sons—very nice-looking boys, too—and a woman, a guest at the A.C.'s house. We said good-bye to the horses and the police for they must jog along the fifteen miles behind us to Maseru.

Hotel dinner alone, a stuffy evening's work, and a stuffy, hot bed. The descent from the mountains to the plain, from a tent to a stuffy hotel, was sudden and adaptation difficult.

———————

A letter from the Chief Native Commissioner in Pretoria, scolding me for not being in Zululand and telling me to get there as quickly as possible. . . . Clearly, in apportioning my time in South Africa, I have been here too long. I think I had better go to Johannesburg. The mines and the miners can't shut down even for Christmas.

A long day's work at the office, 8:45 a.m.–5 p.m., with a quick lunch in the middle. The A.C. pushed aside all his arrears of work, and turned himself into my secretary, looking up facts and having stuff typed for me. . . .

In the evening the A.C. took me to see Fort Hare's cricket team play Maseru. It was all very sober and correct, and it seemed to me, having played the game at school and college, very good cricket. I was glad to see the Fort Hare people and they were much surprised when I met them on the field. One or two of my especial friends were there. The A.C. is extremely good with all the natives and always attends their functions. He was much intrigued by the way the students talked to me. "It makes me feel I ought to ask them round to dinner." But that, even in Basutoland, would be too much of a novelty.

I have had another long day's work up to 5 p.m. Then we visited the leper settlement. We went in pouring rain, and splashed about in muddy yards, with the lepers all huddled in wet blankets or lying in their rooms.

There were about five hundred people in the settlement, in all stages of the disease, from those whose extremities were dropping away from them, or who had the repulsive nodular type, to comely young people who showed no visible signs of rottenness and yet who were doomed in spite of their youth. . . .

The A.C. was evidently a popular visitor. He talked to them all very cheerily. And reproved me for my silence. 'Have you forgotten your Sesuto?' I realized that I was not even greeting the lepers: I was looking at them as at things—cases—not people, absorbed in my own horror, rather than giving real sympathy. I tried my best after this and the attempts to respond through those dulled eyes and perished faces showed that humanity was still alight in them. . . .

This is my last day in Basutoland. I worked the usual hours, which included taking down full notes of a long interview between the A.C. and the chief Jaccottet, heir to Koabane, the chief of Thaba

Basiu, who is going to hold a Pitso (a general meeting of the people) to advocate the new reforms of native government which were turned down by the National Council. It was fascinating, though I hardly knew how to stop myself from intervening.

After dinner the A.C. and his wife called and we all went to the Fort Hare concert. Though we arrived a little late, there was no sign of anyone. No preparations seemed to have been made. The A.C.'s wife argued that it was bad for prestige to wait for them like that so she went home. But the A.C. and the rest of us decided to wait.

. . . Vinikulu, the captain, conducted: they had no piano, they stood all huddled together, with a dim lamp throwing a transverse light on their shining, dark faces. Absolutely motionless, seemingly mesmerized by the conductor—"Svengali," whispered the A.C.— they sang. It was marvellous. They sang, in parts, the most ambitious songs, English and African, and some Negro spirituals. I do not think that any European cricket team, chosen for cricket and not for voices, could have touched them. . . . It was not only the richness and variety of the voices and the perfect tune and time into which they had trained themselves but also the restraint and feeling with which they sang. "Stealing Away to Jesus" and "One More River" were most poignant. You feel that when they sing they are speaking your language more than when they talk; a universal language of art and emotion which they speak as well or better than ourselves. Better, certainly. . . .

Having packed at night, I was free to put in a long last morning at the office. . . .

At two o'clock the A.C. called to motor me the eighteen miles to Marseilles in the Free State, there to pick up the train to Bloemfontein.

The contrast as you cross the Basuto border struck me forcibly. No more mushroom clusters of huts, no more wavering little strips of agriculture. Instead, vast level areas of grazing, with tall, rich grass and with great fat, square Friesians browsing; fences, which stand for efficiency, if not for the very life of the veld. And not a human habitation to be seen, except once or twice, wreathed in poplars and gums, the solid farm of the prosperous Boer owner. This is the land they took from the Basuto.

The train crawled up at last. I need not say that it was hard to say good-bye to the A.C. who had been such a good trek-comrade as well as an expert informant upon Basutoland. As soon as I boarded the train I went on to the swaying platform between the two carriages of which the train was composed. I was determined to see the last of the territory. In spite of a scattered hill or two cropping up alongside the railway there was no difficulty in seeing Basutoland. Right along the eastern horizon stood its magnificent wall of mountains growing more blue with each decline of the sun's light. Some of them I could still pick out as old friends—the two like a woman's breasts; the one like a devil's head, above all Machachne, the mighty one. Only a few days ago I had been among them, right up on their shoulders, sleeping between their knees, bathing in their cold streams. Because I knew that I should almost certainly never see them again I was forced to watch them as long as the light and the distance allowed. . . .

As I went back to my empty carriage in this almost empty little train I was possessed of a fierce hope that this little mountain-state, embedded in the Union of South Africa, should be saved from the threatened grip of the Afrikaner Government which is pressing for its incorporation. The Basuto are not angels but in spite of their dependence upon the Union's labour market, they have a spirit of freedom long crushed out of many of the tribes within South Africa. I can only hope that the issue will not be settled before I get home and that I may be able to throw what small influence I can wield on behalf of the Basuto.[1]

. . . A wretched night in the train and I woke in the Transvaal—good veld and big farms and the famous Reef in the distance. It wasn't much fun, after leaving Basutoland, to arrive in Johannesburg at six-thirty in the morning and find I had booked at a vile hotel.

1. I was able to join in the controversy after my return to England and I wrote articles upon it for *The Times*. I clashed with a formidable antagonist, Mr. Lionel Curtis. He wrote three articles in *The Times* during May 1935 urging acceptance of the South African demand. I therefore wrote a further article for *The Times* published on 16 May to controvert his views and remind the public of the history of Basutoland and of the other two Protectorates, Bechuanaland and Swaziland. Mr. Curtis proposed that our articles should be published in a single book and generously allowed me to have both the first and the last words in the ensuing publication, *The Protectorates of South Africa* (Oxford University Press, 1935). As what I have written applies equally to the Bechuanaland Protectorate, which was also demanded by the South African Government, I have repeated this information at the end of the chapter on Bechuanaland (p. 210).

I hate this city. I know this is a hasty and stupid attitude, very improper in a student of affairs in the subcontinent. . . . and to be mastered as soon as possible. But, to begin with, it is hideous. Right along the Reef are piled the entrails of the earth, higher than anything to be seen round English mines and of various sickly colours, ochre, grey, but mostly a pale sulphur. I had been led to expect something rather showy and glittering in the town itself but here, too, I was disappointed. . . .

This morning I renewed a very interesting and valuable contact. This was with Margaret Hodgson, a South African woman whom I had known at Oxford when we went together with our weekly essays to Grant Robertson at All Souls College. She is now on the staff of the University here as a history lecturer. She holds very liberal views upon native affairs and it was both exciting and instructive to meet her again in her own setting. . . . It was an immense encouragement to meet an able young South African academic with such a vigorous and well-informed liberalism.

She confirmed views about South Africa that have been gradually forming in my mind; of the low standard of intelligence among many of the scattered and agricultural Dutch; of the decline of the British tradition; of the near impossibility of influencing Dutch opinion. She fights the temptation, which I have found in so many people here who have sensibility, to get out of the country.

In the afternoon Margaret and I went a long trek down to the Western Native Township and Sophiatown. The former is a new municipal location, very neat and well spaced, but dreary beyond description, hundreds of tiny, mud-coloured, two-roomed hutments— I cannot call them cottages. Even they cannot be leased at an economic rent with native wages what they are so the municipality subsidizes them and the employer keeps down the wages.

We went into a great barn-like hall, built as a speculation by a Jewish contractor. We were the only Europeans in the audience at what was advertised as a monster meeting for agitation on various points. . . .

Presently another European arrived, a youngish man, looking rather harassed behind his high-powered glasses. This was the famous (or, in most South African eyes, infamous) Mr. Ballinger, who has recently come out from England with British trade union support to try and develop the nascent trade unionism among the natives and to save their own Industrial and Commercial Union which is threatened not only by the Boer authorities but also by inexperience and by tribal fissures.[2]

The meeting was billed for 2:30 p.m. but at 2:45 a message came from the chief speaker, Professor Jabavu, that, knowing his people and their unpunctuality, he always waited until the meeting had fully gathered and had sent for him. This was rather annoying but then I don't suppose that he expected any Europeans to attend. We were handed a printed programme of speakers the length of which appalled me. But even this was not complete for it omitted to mention two lectures by Mr. Ballinger, one on wages and one on the pass laws. The programme showed the extraordinary mixed grill that is served to an African urban audience and the extent of their appetite. Hymns are mixed with an agitation which is full of dangers for them.

Professor Jabavu gave a speech that rather disgusted me. It was of the real Mark Antony technique, one designed to raise the maximum amount of racial-feeling with the minimum amount of indiscretion on his own part. He is the leading African intellectual, at least in reputation; a Professor at Fort Hare, where I had met him. The natives, who worship academic qualifications, seem to regard him almost as a god. . . .

Then Ballinger, with two interpreters, into Xosa and Sesuto, took over. "Do you know that your labour is worth twice what you are being paid for it? The average wage is £3 5s a month. You must ask for a minimum of £7. There is nothing peculiar about your situation. The same thing happened to us in Britain. Our people were forced off the land and into the towns and paid inadequate wages, until they united to secure better conditions. Your greatest enemy is your own disunity."

---

2. I must insert a note here about the subsequent history of Margaret Hodgson and Mr. W. Ballinger. In 1936, after a long struggle, the Afrikaner Government succeeded in abolishing the Cape native franchise, which they hated less for its political effectiveness than for the principle of racial equality upon which it was based. A new measure allowed for the election by Africans of three white members of Parliament for the Cape. Margaret Hodgson was one of these. She married Mr. Ballinger, who himself became a representative of the Africans in the Senate. In 1960 all representation of the Africans in both houses was abolished by an Afrikaner Government determined to rid white rule of any element of African participation, however indirect. The story of [Margaret Hodgson Ballinger's] able and devoted political life in relation to the whole grim record of Afrikaner imposition of political and social *apartheid* is told in her book *From Union to Apartheid* (Capetown, 1969).

More hymns, more speeches, votes of thanks, interruptions, ever increasing heat and smell, and below us all those rows of sweating black faces from every part of South Africa, cut off from their tribes and lands; herded in dreary locations and compounds; hedged round by restrictive laws and customs; all advance checked by a colour-bar; educational facilities practically nil—a bewildered, amiable people, just learning to resent their exploitation. It takes more than one meeting to make a revolution but meetings will increase yearly and some day the amiable, bewildered African giant may learn his own strength and use it.

We came out through the dreary municipal location, mile upon mile of tiny uniform brick huts, a model location, I am told. And though the natives pay rates they get neither light nor water in their huts. (This is still true of most locations though not of all.) They cannot pay an economic rent for their huts so they pay less and thus the big employers are subsidized out of the rates. Transport to and from town is admittedly dear and inadequate. But the locations are a model beside the real slums where entrepreneurs buy small plots of land, run up shelters of tin and charge 25s a month for them. . . .

At night I had dinner with Margaret Hodgson and Mr. Ballinger, and was able to find out a great deal about the I.C.U. (the new black Trade Union).[3] . . .

Today (24 December) I went to lunch with Professor Macmillan, the historian protagonist of the native races of South Africa, the apologist for the old "sentimental" missionary and the academic hammer of the Dutch. A red-headed Scot, South African born, he dragged himself up from the MSS of his third book—on the present "native" problem—and we began without ceremony on that subject.

He is bitter. How a man can bear to live in this country, feeling as he does, with his working hours filled with the grim history of

3. Upon this, as upon other matters, I was, of course, doing all I could in the time allowed, to collect literature and take notes of interviews. In this diary, written for my family and a few friends, I could not deal fully with such a subject as trade unionism. However, as this matter was so important to me, not only in Johannesburg but also later in Durban, it may be useful to mention here a book describing events in this context by a man who was active at this time on more extreme lines than those followed by Mr. Ballinger. This was Edward Roux's retrospective book, *Time Longer than Rope* (London, 1948).

native policy and his leisure with its present injustices, I do not know. In a long, and to me, deeply interesting talk, we came to the following conclusions.

The Dutch were originally emigrants of mainly low class. As a result of their long isolation from Europe and the more complete isolation of the veld far in the interior away from government, they have developed a kind of permanent inaccessibility to ideas and are all but invulnerable to outside opinion. The majority of them are, at a certain low level, born politicians and quite unscrupulous. They have not and they will not alter their attitude to the native as being the eternal inferior. Deprived of the system of slavery, they are elaborating a system of legalized serfdom to meet their needs.

I cannot help thinking, myself, that the British are guilty of a betrayal of the native, a moral, in some cases, almost a legal, guilt. In the first half of the nineteenth century we sponsored the native, recognizing his potential equality and, in the Cape, granting him the franchise and at least theoretical equality before the law. Our support of the native was one reason for Britain's conflict with the Boer, with all the resulting disturbance of the middle and late nineteenth century. With the growth of imperialism, with Disraeli, and then Chamberlain, a change came over our hostility towards the Boers; the native began to fade out of the foreground. After the Boer War, the Liberals came in, full of ardent generosity towards the defeated Dutch enemy; all the more so as some of them had doubts about the justifiability of the Boer War. So, in a series of handshakes, progressively warmer, the breach was apparently healed and the Union achieved. But as it is difficult, if not impossible, for us to be liberal towards Boer and native at the same time, the native now tended to get left. . . .

I suppose that few in Britain foresaw that the Dutch might rise again and swamp the British, using, instead of the rifles of 1900, the political weapons of the majority which we had put into their hands.

Now it has happened. Well may the bewildered, frightened native rub his eyes. "But," he says—some have said this to me—"I don't understand." These people were your enemies and our enemies. We accepted your rule, in some cases we voluntarily handed ourselves over to you, in order to get your protection against them. You taught us an unbounded confidence in your strength and justice. You fought them again in the Boer War and we showed you our loyalty and prayed for your victory. And now—here are the Dutch ruling us. . . ."

The most disquieting fact as regards native policy is the position of the British. Even if some may have feared that the Dutch might be beyond assimilation, surely none feared that many of the British would be influenced by the Dutch. But the South African Party now has little or no policy: it is divided between the old stalwarts of the Cape and those, especially from Natal, who would vote with the Dutch on the native question. British liberal traditions have worn thin; fear is catching and the poor white, who is sometimes British and who has a vote, is the greatest enemy of the native. . . .

I went down at midday to Ektuleni, the House of the Peacemakers, where Miss Maude works, the daughter of the Bishop of Kensington. . . .

Miss Maude, the head of this mission, is well known and beloved in her district. She took me out afterwards and the passage of her car was hailed by one long scream of greeting from waving children. She drove me into the Western Native Township which I had passed before and where little two-roomed brick houses are built in endless rows. . . . No trained investigator can understand how these people live on their wages. I have seen dozens of specimen family budgets drawn up, all showing, even on the most modest estimate of expenses, that the expense must largely exceed the income. The impossible is made possible by nearly all the women doing washing or charring or brewing illicit native beer but also by the unquestioning way in which they all help each other. It must be remembered that native wages are low, based on the idea that the standards are primitive, and yet the urban native is on almost the same footing as the white who earns seven or eight times the wage— that is, he must pay almost as much for transport (perhaps more where he is pushed miles outside the town), also for food, and, indeed, for all that he buys in shops. He and his family must wear European clothes. Yet his wages are kept down artificially. This is partly because the colour-bar prevents a natural advancement and partly because of the system of buying cheap labour on contract to the Union. . . .

Now the mines, though they abstract dangerous percentages of men out of some of the African reserves, are short of black labour.

They are crying out for at least 20,000 more. This does not, as in normal conditions it would, lead them to offer more wages. Instead they ask that the law forbidding them to recruit north of latitude 22 degrees be repealed. It was because the health of the natives from the further north suffered in the mines that the ban was laid. Now the mines declare they can meet the health danger with better knowledge and equipment. Perhaps the growing value of the African will lead to his being less wastefully used and financial competition will do what humanity has failed to achieve. But we shall not deserve nor get any thanks from the African.

After the mines with their compounds came the city with its slums. . . .

. . . Here the owners have run up rows of tiny tin hovels, about 8 x 5 feet, and let them for 25s a month. "No worse than the slums in England," says the South African in defence. I have seen the worst slums of Sheffield and some other towns and I found these in Johannesburg bad beyond all comparison, beyond imagination. . . .

When I got back we motored out to the Country Club. . . . This is one of the prizes for which men strive, with a car good enough to hold its own in the car-park, with beautiful frocks for wife and daughter so that they can sit in confidence upon the flowery terrace to drink their cocktails. And the whole elegant superstructure is built on black labour; men and women from those seething yards work in white houses and hotels and even take the washing back home. . . .

Dined with Professor Macmillan and he told me how the Government sent him to make a report on a certain native area and when he told them that the area was overcrowded, exhausted and neglected, they simply suppressed the report. He is now going to publish it in his new book. He, too, is very despondent. We worked out with maps and figures the proportion of land held by the natives, the vast majority of the population. It worked out, I think, at about one-thirteenth. Though some of the reserves are fairly good, the proportion is balanced by including a stretch of Namaqualand, which is largely barren. . . .

The refusal to regard the native as an integral part of the township for which he works is all part of the bluff about segregation. Regard him as temporary and you can neglect his interests as a ratepayer, deny him light and water and deny him also any political power, municipal or national. You can neglect him if he is ill or starving. And you can also go on talking about the native develop-ing "along his own lines." I should like to ask these Dutchmen what *is* his line in the Johannesburg slums. Having got him there, broken or weakened his contact with his own tribal area, the white man af-fects not to see him. I saw the advertisement of a little watering place near East London—whose location I visited—saying—"Come to bright, clean X. All white area. No native locations." I wonder how long that will last and whether the workers live underground.

Government House is big, pure white, owing something to do-mestic Dutch architecture but with a classical touch to give it more grandeur. I was the only visitor, though there was a large house-party there, mostly familiar English titled names. All was done in state. We waited until the double doors were thrown open and H.E. (Earl of Athlone), Princess Alice and her daughter, Lady May Cam-bridge, came in. I really forget exactly who Princess Alice is, being bad at royalties, but she seems to have a slight resemblance to Queen Victoria and the Prince of Wales, though she is pretty and well dressed. I was very shabby, being just as I was from my jour-ney, but I have (almost) got over worrying about that sort of thing. I had to sit next to H.E. at lunch. He is a tall man, with a little turned-up white moustache and rather a varnished expression. I had, of course, had talks with him in Capetown.

. . . H.E. went off on to the chiefs and said very hard things about them. I ventured to protest and even to offer my own inter-pretation for it will be too silly if, after indulging them all these years, the Government suddenly allow themselves to get exasper-ated and that is what I think I see coming. . . .

. . . H.E. was also very down on the educated native, and criti-cized Lovedale and Fort Hare. I realized that the views of both the Governor-General and the Princess were very conventional but I soon saw it would be silly to attempt an argument. . . .

I walked away from Government House through rows of mod-ern, pillared houses, whose rock-gardens were formed by the out-cropping stone of what were bare kopjes not long ago; along roads hewn out of purple and orange rock, under avenues of young jacarandas, soon to burst into the purple blossoms for which Preto-ria is famous. . . .

Communications in Pretoria are appalling and taxis extortion-ate. Trams go once in half an hour and the distances are immense for the town is spread widely in its trough between the hills. The result was that I walked four miles in the afternoon heat in my best tight shoes before reaching the Union Department for Native Affairs.

I did not know whether to laugh or to cry when I saw it. It is absurd. Everyone admits the native to be *the* problem in South Africa, everyone who thinks; he is four and a half to one in numbers. But his affairs for the whole Union are housed in a makeshift office, a small, dark, dilapidated private house. The land-bank, a few doors away, is two or three times the size, and brand new. . . .

Next day . . . I went down to the local Native Affairs Office for Pretoria and district and called on Mr. Hook, Native Commissioner. He allowed me to do what I wanted, which was just to watch him at work and see what sort of contact of white and black he has to handle. In one corner of his enclosure, lying patiently on the ground, were the raw natives from the country, trying to get into the towns. They were to be examined by the doctor and turned back or sent to hospital if diseased. If admitted, they go to the municipal compound, have their clothes sterilized and are bathed. There they get a six-day permit to look for work, and start on their rounds—on foot, because they are not allowed on the trams and no special trams are run for them. This must make for great hardship, as distances are great and the location far out, especially for natives who have to be in early for work. It is just these small inconveniences that mount up to such a sum in the life of the native and which, in his unrepresented state, he has no hope of redressing. His treatment on the railways is very bad, and, as far as I can see, much of his life in towns is spent hanging round Pass Offices or in jail as a result of contravening the Pass and Liquor Laws, both very elaborate and hard to keep.

I have come down to Capetown to attend as much as I can of a course at the University on Bantu studies for administrators. It is, of course, as much to meet these men as to attend the instruction that I have come. The result is that I have been kept so busy all day with lectures, talks and in-between discussions, plus work at night. . . .

I had better confess . . . that I have succumbed to a temptation which, when I set out, I had resolved to resist, but to which I succumbed in New Zealand over the Samoan crisis. I have been playing politics. I had no sooner got to Capetown than I was followed by a very urgent letter from the A.C. in Basutoland to the intent that the High Commissioner, Lord Athlone, was proposing to coerce the Basuto chiefs into accepting a limitation of their jurisdiction and this in defiance of the Resident Commissioner's promise to the chiefs. . . . I felt certain that the new policy was wrong and arose from accumulated exasperation with the conservatism of the chiefs, and perhaps the dishonesty of some of them. . . . I even questioned, presumptuously perhaps, whether these officials living in the Union really understood the situation in Basutoland and the part played by the chieftainship, imperfect though it is, in holding the endangered little state together. That the paramount chief is at present a woman does not help the situation. . . . I . . . have decided to meet all the people most directly concerned with the issue and to put to them my views on the territory, favouring gradual reform but bringing out how deeply pledged we are to the system of indirect rule, how much the abuses of the chiefs are exaggerated and the general contentment of the people in contrast with the South African natives. . . .

I was fortunate enough to sit next to the Imperial Secretary at table when the Athlones, now back in Capetown, invited me to dinner. I found, however that he could beat me at talking and as soon as I raised the subject in an abstract, tentative kind of way he engaged me so hard that—most improperly—I never even knew who was sitting on my other side. But I managed to get across enough of my views to excite his interest and after dinner he took me into a corner and we went at it until midnight when the Earl and the Princess brought the party to an end. . . .

. . . There was nearly a scene with the party at the luncheon table when I confessed to my friendship with Ballinger who, they asserted, was in Russian pay! Wherever I go I make a point of defending this brave man who I find is regarded as a sort of monster, a renegade to his country and his colour. In this connection I have managed to persuade the conference which—on and off!—I am attending at the University to invite Ballinger to an after-dinner discussion. This, though composed mainly of officials, produced a most interesting exchange during which all hostility towards him faded away and many of the participants confessed to me afterwards that a man like Ballinger was a boon to the country. His honesty, moderation and good temper impressed them all and especially his unique knowledge of the urban native.

I met Ballinger again for a talk. We sat for two hours on a seat in some public gardens, it being difficult to find a *locus* for such a meeting. We were watched all the time by no less than three detectives. The same day they had stolen his bag, full of papers, from the railway cloakroom. I assumed that my meetings with him were all reported to Major Herbst, Afrikaner head of the Native Affairs Department. Ballinger told me something of his privations and the times when he hardly had enough to eat. He has indeed had a grim time between the natives and the authorities, a lonely time, too, which only a man of his exceptional courage and resolution could have endured.

. . . This day, 28 January, is my last day in Capetown. . . .

I had plenty of Dutchmen [this] morning but of another generation. It will hardly be credited that there exists in the Union only one set of fully accurate maps showing native areas and the meagre fragments now being released for native purchase. These maps are owned by the Native Affairs Department and are battered with much transit between Pretoria and Capetown and much thumbing by official Committees on Native Affairs. They are large, amateurish and inaccurate. I got permission to photograph them. Where, in what light, and with what exposure and focus were questions that soon collected the entire staff of the entire Native Administration Department out of their offices. (Men love to give technical advice to stupid women.) . . . In the end we got the largest map out into the yard. A native boy, one Julius, climbed out of an upper window and, leaning perilously down, held the top; the Under-Secretary lay flat on his back in the yard and held it from below to prevent the wind blowing it: all the others yelled advice in Dutch and Dutch-English from windows and doorways. As the maps went up there were appropriate comments. The Orange Free State, which forbids natives to hold land, was nearly all white.

"Now Julius, hold up the Free State. Ah! this is the prize map. Don't smile, Julius, or it will be taken as evidence on the photograph that native opinion is satisfied with the allocation of land in the Free State.". . .

. . . Then I went to the Law Courts where Sir James Rose-Innes had arranged to have me taken round the various courts. . . .

. . . Speaking generally . . . the native gets a better deal in the law courts than elsewhere. . . . But . . . the native commits, inevitably, a large number of technical offences which, if his skin were not black, would be civil and not criminal, or would not be offences at all. These are mostly offences under the Pass, and Masters and Servants, Acts, and I believe that seven-tenths of the natives in gaol at any one time are there for these technical faults. . . .

The native, except perhaps in the High Court, certainly does not get equal justice with the white man. He is punished much more heavily for the same offences and in any case in which a white woman is concerned, anything may happen. This is especially true of the magistrates' courts. When it comes to murder, as in parts of America, the jury system becomes a danger. The murderer of the white man gets the rope every time; the murderer of the black man is unlucky if he gets a few years. The white jury does not trust the judge and so is more likely to acquit completely a white man. . . .

My time in South Africa will soon be running out. . . . I must take a look, however brief, at the great and tragic Zulu people. . . .

. . . I have come from Capetown to Maritzburg, the capital of Natal. It has taken two days and three nights to get here from Capetown and once again I had to endure crawling round the north of beloved Basutoland and looking again at the marvellous panorama of those so well-remembered mountains and passing the junction for Maseru.

The Zulu kraal is circular, with cattle in a stockade in the middle. Round each kraal you see the veld patched with the miserable, untidy bits of cultivation which is all this tribe seems capable of. . . .

It was icy cold and not even a glorious sunset over an immense basin among the mountains, with every range swimming in violet light, could make me sorry to see little Nongowa sitting on top of a high hill and to find a great log fire in the tiny hotel. . . .

We drove out early this morning. . . . We reached the Court House. . . . Inside, the official, a little cross and thirsty, sits at his littered, dusty desk, and wrestles with forms and registers and licenses when he should be away out in his district, sitting under a tree and listening to the old men talking themselves out and so forging links of sympathy between black men and white rulers.

This man was born in Germany and is approaching retiring age, an unkempt, insignificant man to look at but from whom a few faint sparks of humour and interest could be struck. All his work had been with the Zulus. I gently suggested criticisms of stagnation and neglect against the administration. He smiled wearily. "The Zulu has only one answer," he said, when you suggest reforms to him. "Who complains?" His favourite proverb is to be translated "Tomorrow is also a day." Progress and reform! "Why? Why?" he asks. "And have we any answer? For what future can Africans strive in this country?"

. . . Fear of the Zulu sank deep into the mind alike of both British Natalian and Boer, so great was the military power and aggressiveness of the Zulu kingdom against black and white alike. But Dinizulu's annual meeting is at present a tame affair. The representatives pay £5 for the privilege of coming. This goes into the Zulu National Fund and such is their faith in their chief that no one has ever asked what becomes of it. . . .

They all loathe the Dutch like poison. In the nineties, when there was a division within the reigning family, Botha and some other young men offered to help one section against the other in return for some land. The Zulu story is that when the final claim was made it turned out to be for an immense tract of Zululand and now the Zulus gaze at this great wedge, some of the best land in their country, as bitterly as do the Basuto at the abundant flats of the Orange Free State. . . .

Our next point of call was the Alobane coal-mine under a hill on the summit of which the Zulus inflicted a nasty little defeat upon us. . . .

. . . My object now was to examine a remote colliery, for Ballinger had told me that here the conditions were appalling, or so he heard for he had not been able to get there. It seems strange to see the gear of a coal-mine, so much connected in my past with the gloom of crowded black industry in and around Sheffield, held up aloft against the African sky on the slope of a lonely kopje. Whether there is something in the nature of coal that invites sordid conditions I don't know, but here, almost unimaginably in its rural setting, I came upon one of the foulest slums.

. . . These were tiny shacks, all but windowless and divided into two, a whole family in each single room. The huts were in a state of disrepair and their interiors, which were bare of all but dirty litter, showed signs of utmost poverty. Piles of ashes and rubbish lay outside the doors. But worst of all was the stench. A few, tiny, filthy runnels crept between the houses, and from the smell of these, half-blocked by rubbish, I assumed that they were the chief means of sanitation. . . .

We went on to the single men's compound where they had about a thousand, a mixture of all tribes. There were heavy wire entanglements round the place. Why? Here, too, were foul, evil-smelling, broken-down huts, sixteen men to one smallish room, and a system, or lack of systems, of sanitation that made it unbearable to breathe in the compound. The men came in just as they were from the mine, brown bodies black with sweat and grime and lay down at once on the dark floor to rest. The African is so naturally cheerful that the dullness and silence of these men was startling. We questioned one who had been in the place for many years. He came from Nyasaland. He did not know whether he would ever get back home because he could not eat the food and had to spend his wages buying his own. There were other long-term men who said vaguely that they had wives at home.

It was quite clear that no attempt had been made to give these people any education. There was an entire lack of imagination. . . .

The boy who took us round told us that there were quite a lot of desertions but that the men were generally caught and brought back. It must be remembered that to break a contract of work, as also to strike, is in South Africa, for Africans, a penal offence, so that the man can be fined or sent to jail. If fined, he must work longer than his contract in order to pay it. You may ask why he goes to such a bad mine since labour is legally voluntary. The answer is that in his ignorance and simplicity he may know no better: or he may be the prey of unscrupulous white labour-recruiters who get a large bonus for each man secured and who have under them native assistants who get 10s a head per recruit. The possibilities opened up by this can be imagined.

So came to an end this rather grim, disturbing tour through the country of a famous warrior tribe whose warlike traditions and resistance had only made their defeat more bitter and their subjection more complete. . . .

A long and exciting day today, 1 February. A stifling night made sleep difficult so I got up early and worked and dashed up the town to buy a dress and get money from the bank.

Back at 9:30 to find Durban's Superintendent of Native Locations and his car waiting for me. He took me first—very honestly—to see one of the bad parts, a long row of single-room hovels, with mixed Indian and native families bulging out of the dark doorways.

Then we went to see the compounds, where he can hold 3,000 natives and is always needing space for double that number. . . .

We then went down to the headquarters of the native trade
union, the Industrial and Commercial Union. It is in a very low part
of the town reached through crowded slums of mixed races. We
found it hard to discover as the last I.C.U. premises were wrecked
by the whites in the recent serious anti-native riots, when there were
deaths on both sides. The Natal I.C.U. is the most militant of all
and, under its Zulu leader, Champion, has broken away from the
main stem which Ballinger advises. But just because it is violent it
attracts more support and has a large income. The I.C.U. premises,
which are masked behind a warehouse door, are enormous, an old
sweet factory, dark and inclined to rot, but with several huge
rooms.

We found Champion in an office blocked off from an upper
room in the factory. We went through crowds of natives to get
there. It was an act of great courage on the part of Mr. X, my guide,
and an official, to bring me here. I am afraid, if it should get out, he
will be in for trouble, for of course, to white Durban, there is only
one opinion about Champion and that is that he should be put up
against a wall and shot.

Champion . . . said there would be a huge gathering on Saturday night of natives of every sort and kind. Had I the courage to
come? To the native population of Durban it would be a great event
that a white woman, and one from England, should come down to
their gathering. I did not know what to say. I was attracted and
frightened. And I could feel the horror of the official at my side. I
hedged and said I would let him know and I saw he feared this was
a refusal. Outside we saw rows of clients waiting for Champion. He
escorted us through the great, mouldering, dark, barrack-like place
and into the sordid street.

. . . In the evening I trammed around Durban, having another
look at it and calling on people. I was thinking all the time, however, of the night, and being torn between fear and attraction. I have
no doubt that Champion, from a white man's point of view, is an
unprincipled and dangerous man. Having brooded on ways and
means and not liking the idea of going down into those parts with
an Indian taxi-driver I decided to get hold of a reliable white driver
who would take me and fetch me away. So I rang up Champion,
who said he was already making preparations, counting on my
coming, and that he would see to my being fetched and taken back.

That cut out my plan for possible retreats. So I fell back on another. I left for the hotel-keeper a note giving the name and whereabouts of the place to which I was going and saying that if I were not back in the hotel by 11 p.m. then arrangements would have gone wrong and I must be fetched. . . .

It was a stifling night, loaded with wet heat, and all the hotel people were sitting out along the *stoep*. A woman who heard I was interested in natives came up and sat beside me, and proceeded to blackguard them and, by inference, me, in the most outrageous manner. She was a handsome, white-haired woman, in a beautiful evening dress, and loaded with jewels. I really felt quite sick as I listened to the usual flow of words—spoiled—lazy—animals—keep them down. She knew nothing—nothing. She boasted a life-time in the country, and knew not the first fact of the situation. And the unprovoked vindictiveness with which she attacked me for daring to study the question! "You wait until you have been ten years in the country before *you* advance an opinion." I don't know whether I was a bit tired and therefore nervy, but I could not stand it. Argument was useless, and I did not want a scene on the *stoep*, especially as Champion would shortly arrive and run the gauntlet. So I got up and said it was useless to answer her, so wide apart were we in outlook. Then I went to another seat. Presently a smart new Buick swung up to the doorway with some natives in it and Champion came out. Fortunately no one recognized him and I hurried into the car before people had time to realize what was happening.

. . . When at last we drew up at the I.C.U. there was a dense crowd of natives round the door and along the pavements. Champion shouted and swung his arms to make a lane and they parted, staring in silence. The building, a large disused factory, was like a hive of bees, every part of it packed. There must have been several thousands of natives there and the heat and smell were overwhelming. Champion took me to an upper room where several hundred natives were already sitting on benches and many more standing and squatting all round. He sat me at a table in front of them and got up to make a speech. For my benefit he spoke in English and had it interpreted. He said that already they all knew about me as he had addressed them earlier about my visit. He paid various compliments to me and my country and the idea that I should "tell England" of their wrongs roused, alas!, a cheer.

. . . The audience . . . comprised every type, young bucks in short-cut double-breasted waistcoats and Oxford trousers (these *very* popular with the Bantu) through all possible grades and shades of shirts and collars to the collarless and the coatless, to men with hair plaited in porcupine spikes and women in nothing much but brass wire and beads. They sat or stood, shining with sweat, staring at me with their big black-brown eyes and absolutely dumb. Then the choir, probably from some secessionist church, and looking highly respectable, appeared and at Champion's order, since they were to sing to *me* and not to the audience, stood right on top of me and sang an anthem about the captivity of Sion. Champion, evidently deeply moved, or acting, rose to say that for Sion he read Africa and asked when God would turn *her* captivity.

The whole audience now stood up and, singing in harmony, roared out the Bantu national anthem, "Africa." It was most inspiring, the word itself kept recurring in different tones, mournful or defiant. I must try to get the words.

It was now my turn to speak. I got up, fully aware how careful I must be in what I said. I was greeted with stimulating applause and Champion came forward to interpret. The pause, for interpreting, checks the flow, but enables you to keep them waiting for the point in a way that with practice, I imagine, could be made very effective. This was my speech as far as I can remember.

"Tell your people not to be afraid that I am going to make a long speech. I only want to tell them why I am here. I should not dare make a speech. Africans are so much better at speech-making than white people." ("I don't agree with that," said Champion.) "I had the privilege of hearing Dr. Aggrey speak and he was the best orator, white or black, I ever heard. But I have also heard old chiefs up in the Transkei and in the Basutoland mountains make speeches I could never hope to equal.

"Why am I here tonight? It is not because I agree with Mr. Champion. I don't agree with him, with much of what he is doing, and much of what he has said. But I have come because I want to learn. I want to see all sides of this problem of South Africa and it is a great pleasure for me to be able to spend an evening here among you, in your own place, and see how you enjoy yourselves." Then I told them something of my travels and of my hope, when I returned to England, of lecturing and perhaps writing on what I had learned. I finished up by telling them about Fort Hare and warning them about the difficulties of education, and the danger of thinking it was a cheap or easy thing to gain but that, in the long run, it was the only salvation.

But the big event was preparing below. Soon a muffled noise I had been hearing began to grow and grow, and Champion came and asked me if I were prepared to see what they had got up for me. "It is the real thing, you know," he explained, half apologetic. I went down and found the huge hall that is the entire ground-floor of the factory filled literally to suffocation. They must have run into hundreds, though it was difficult to see them all in the big, half-lit space. They were all men, and all naked but for a thong round the loins and metal armlets and anklets and on their heads a few trimmings of metal and fur such as suited each man's fancy.

The great bulk of them were squatting at the back in ranks, each armed with a heavy stick, with which he struck the floor as he shouted his song. There was hardly room between my chair and these men for the first dance team to come in, especially as they must dash in at a gallop, and whirl their sticks round their heads. "Don't be frightened," said Champion. "However near they come to you, they won't hit you." But I remembered this from Somaliland and how men, frenzied with the dance and apparently quite unseeing, will, with quite reliable accuracy, miss you with their spears by a few inches.

. . . The dance was really splendid. One after another the teams, each about two or three hundred strong, replaced each other. They got more worked up as the night wore on. It was impressive, almost beyond bearing, to have a row of a hundred or more naked brown men, leaping and yelling within a few inches of you, their faces drawn into terrific grimaces, their eyes glassy with excitement, their mouths wide open to shout and scream and their whole bodies contorted with movements that demanded their whole strength to perform. I thought the rickety old floor would give way under the crash of their feet, especially as each crash was accompanied with the pounding of hundreds of sticks, and a simultaneous shout so that the rhythm was deafening. One team did a dance founded on the British Tommy, and evolved, I suppose, by a native labour corps in France. It was a priceless burlesque. They marched in ranks, formed fours, saluted, bringing their hands down with a resounding smack on their bare thighs, carrying their sticks like rifles, whistling famous half-remembered tunes of the war, and trying to imitate the stiff march of the white man, so unlike their own gazelle-walk.

But their own war-dance was the best of all. There were about three hundred dancers, all wearing white fur rings round knees, ankles and wrists, and carrying sticks festooned with white feathers.

The joints of their arms were bound with gold and silver wire; some wore baldrics of leopard or catskin or embroidery of white and scarlet beads. The Zulu physique can be magnificent; many were slim and tall and some looked more Hamitic than Negro. Certainly this dance showed the Zulu off in all his glory.

The impressiveness became almost overwhelming. I was surrounded by these flashing brown bodies with muscles running up and down skins glossy with sweat. Yet it was beautiful, this living frieze of dark bronze bodies. Now they advanced, singing with sticks levelled at me like spears. Champion shouted the translation in my ear:

> Who has taken our country from us?
> Who has taken it?
> Come out! Let us fight!
> The land was ours. Now it is taken.
> We have no more freedom left in it.
> Come out and fight!
> The land is ours, now it is taken.
> Fight! Fight!
> Shame on the man who is burned in his hut!
> Come out and fight.

I was relieved when, with one great final roar, the dancers all fell flat on the floor, their bodies nearly dovetailed into each other and the sticks laid out in a long straight line. Champion said that the dancers were mostly men who had lately come in from the kraals, the majority of them working as house-boys. I could see another line of young men in the red-bordered calico of domestic service filing in, each carrying a little bundle containing the precious trappings of tribalism.

As I looked it suddenly struck me that these splendid young men could be the grandsons of the Zulu warriors who inflicted such a terrible defeat upon British regular troops at the battle of Isandhlawana in 1879, killing with assegai and rifle 800 regular British soldiers and as many native levies. Did they ever recall those days of their great military power as they stooped to menial tasks under their white masters or were nagged in the kitchen by white housewives? How those Durban matrons would have stared to see how their docile house-boys spent their Saturday night!

I had lost all sense of time. I looked at my watch. It was well after eleven! It was a terrible moment—I had far more to fear than

Cinderella. I remembered my note on the manager's desk which told him where I had gone. Suppose they sent police to fetch me out of here—if police dared to come. "Take me to a telephone," I shouted in Champion's ear. He read my face: he asked no questions. We rushed up to his office. I found the number but in the continuing din from below I could neither hear or be heard. Champion guessed the danger: in a few minutes I was in the car with him being raced through the docks and slums—now mercifully empty—until I jumped out of the car and ran into the hotel. I rushed to the manager's room. There on his desk lay my note—unopened! Clearly he was having a night out! I felt faint with the realization of what might have been. My only defence was that I had not realized the extent of recent disorders, of how police and unofficial white men had lately used their revolvers on Zulu strikers with loss of life on both sides, nor had I any idea of the kind of entertainment Champion had prepared for me.

. . . I . . . left Durban, feeling a little battered after my night out with the Zulus and deeply shocked by the disgraceful housing and starvation wages of the African workers. So on via Johannesburg and to the train that runs far north to Bulawayo. A long night in the train as we skirted along the eastern edge of Bechuanaland. I was up early to alight at Palapye, the junction for Serowe, headquarters of the largest tribe in the Protectorate [of Bechuanaland], the Bamangwato.

I think I must pause here in order to explain why I was so anxious to . . . call in at Serowe in the Bechuanaland Protectorate, one of the three native territories retained under direct British rule. . . .

I was . . . eager to meet the best educated chief in Southern Africa and to learn how he was facing the threat from Hertzog's South Africa to take over his country along with the other two High Commission territories. . . . The powerful British South Africa Company had long held concessions for mineral rights in Tshekedi's country and now it appeared that there might be gold not far from Serowe and the Company wanted to assert their rights. Tshekedi knows only too well what a young Johannesburg would mean to his people, no less than their demoralization and ultimately their annexation, and he is fighting tooth and nail to beat off the concessionaires. His strong will plus his education make him no mean antagonist. But the odds against him are huge.

. . . As an experience, flat, dry, Bechuanaland could offer nothing comparable with Basutoland's mountains. . . .

I had a lot to learn at Serowe. I first visited the native school. This, in striking contrast with the Zulu school I had recently visited, has been built and is entirely run by the people themselves without any help or supervision from the white man. As far as buildings, equipment and cleanliness are concerned, I have seen very little to touch it in South Africa. . . .

I went on to visit the royal Kgotla. This is an open space at the foot of the central kopje. The chief holds his court under the trees in front of a half-circular palisade. The people bring their little carved stools and sit about in the shade of some large trees. . . .

. . . I am immensely impressed by [the chief] and feel drawn to him. He has character as well as intelligence. It is impossible not to admire his strength of will. But he can be pleasant, too, when he likes, and he was open and friendly to me. But he would not admit that, following his father's example, he was about to journey to England to lay his case before the Secretary of State. But then the District Commissioner had told me that I had no business to know that as it was a secret.

The chief's attitude is this: "Give my people a chance to develop a little further before you push this industrialism upon us. The gold will keep. In fifty or a hundred years we shall be ready at least to co-operate in its mining and the whole thing will injure us far less than it will today. But if I am to develop my people I must have more funds. Give me back some of the taxation to spend upon education and agriculture. Try me, and I won't fail in the trust." But will Sir Ernest Oppenheimer wait? Not he!

I think that the time I spent talking to Tshekedi in his house was, in political interest, the high-water mark of my visit to South Africa. It was not that he was the most fully "westernized" African that I had met during these months, if I must use an unsatisfactory term. I had met a number of men with whom I could talk "on the level" in Johannesburg. But the combination of this young man's intelligence, sensitivity, good looks (by our standards) and the fragile cause of independence for which he was fighting against such odds, all made a strong appeal to one's mind and heart. I looked round at his considerable library. He has a good collection of *Africana,* including the blue-books and official reports which he needs so much if he is to understand the complex dangers which threaten the status of his country. I could hardly realize that, outside, his house was encircled by a vast mass of little huts representing no great population in numbers and yet the largest purely "native" town in all southern and eastern Africa. Beyond that stretches a vast dry region, the pasturelands of his tribe and the home of the remaining Bushmen and of wild animals. It did not seem much of a base from which to fight South Africa. Yet he can still laugh. "Look," he said, "what happens to the gold that is dug up out of the earth on the Reef at so much cost in human toil and dislocation. Most of it goes off at once into deep vaults under the earth in America, Britain or elsewhere. Why not get expert geologists to estimate roughly how much gold lies under my people's land, make a nominal distribution between the Company and my State and leave it there until we are sufficiently advanced to carry out its excavation ourselves."

Note Added in 1973 by the Author

The visit to Serowe was the last incident of my South African travels. But it did not, of course, mean the end of my interest in the subcontinent. With regard to the three High Commission territories, I found on my return to England, late in 1930, that the controversy about their transfer to the South African Government was still dragging on. Hertzog's Government continued to press its claims and British ministers, supported by such public opinion as there was on the issue, continued to use evasive tactics. Public opinion was suddenly concentrated upon Bechuanaland by the action of Tshekedi in 1933 in sentencing a white youth to flogging for assaulting a native woman. Tshekedi, as acting-chief, had shown a very strong and independent spirit. This was regarded by the British authorities as the last straw. At the time of the incident it happened that a naval officer was acting High Commissioner in South Africa for Britain. He sent a naval party up to Serowe, complete with guns which were dragged with difficulty across the soft sand. Tshekedi was temporarily deposed. The incident roused very wide interest which in Britain was favourable to Tshekedi because of the dignity of his bearing through the incident.

Meanwhile the issue with South Africa over the future of the Protectorates dragged on. I did what I could, working in a junior capacity in a movement led by Lord Lugard and also by Lord Selborne, who had played a major part in the achievement of South African unity and in the definition of the status of the Protectorates.

I wrote articles for *The Times* in 1933 and 1934[4] and found myself crossing swords in its pages with a distinguished opponent, Mr. Lionel Curtis, one of Lord Milner's famous "Kindergarten" which had played such an important part in constructing the Union. Mr. Curtis wrote a series of articles in *The Times* in favour of transfer on the grounds that the Afrikaners would respond to a policy of trust. I continued the argument in person, Mr. Curtis being a Fellow of All Souls. In the end we decided to put our opposing views together in one book in which he generously allowed me to have the last words.[5]

I met Tshekedi and Seretse in England and had the pleasure of entertaining Tshekedi as a guest staying in my house. . . . His nephew, Seretse, aided by his English wife, is now the successful Prime Minister of the independent state of Botswana, formerly Bechuanaland which, with mingled poverty and promise, shows what Africans can do even under the shadow of a powerful neighbour which denies both the human rights and the potentialities of their race.

Conclusion, Written in 1973

It was while I was in Southern Rhodesia that an idea which had been slowly gathering shape in my mind developed into a definite purpose. This was to devote myself entirely to the study of the government of "native" races, especially in the African regions administered by Britain. The Principal of my college, Miss Gwyer, kept the many letters I wrote to her while on my tour and this year she handed them back to me. I find in one written from Salisbury on 24 February 1930, this first avowal of my new ambition:

I had a long letter from H. A. L. Fisher today, four big sheets, defending Smuts against me. He says that Rhodes House is to go ahead as a centre of African studies but, of course, does not suggest that there is any place in it for me. I do not enlarge here upon my plans and hopes because you will know without my saying it that I want to go on with what I am only now beginning. A book on native administration, for me at any rate, would be a colossal enterprise and I

---

4. 28 September 1933 and 6 July 1934. Reprinted in the book of my collected papers *The Colonial Sequence* (1967).
5. M. Perham and L. Curtis, *The Protectorates of South Africa* (Oxford University Press, 1935).

should need to give all my time and strength to it if it is to be of any use. It is for you to tell me my duty to the College as at present I am, perhaps, a little overwhelmed by my duty to this work, this cause, if you like. The situation in Africa is among the most complex the world has ever had to face and some political machinery has got to be invented that will enable the twentieth-century European to live with "primitive" man without the latter swamping the former or the former exploiting the latter. So far our present machinery offers little help. There should be as many people as possible thinking, studying and writing on these problems. If I can go on with this work and have some status in the University and some connection with the College, so much the better. If not, I think I ought, as soon as the College can spare me, to leave and try to manage on my own resources. I know that it would be better for me to have some status, with a recognized obligation to get the work done in a certain time. Not that I fear I should ever slack but I might go on and on and be submerged by the size of the subject.

I don't think I write of myself in any egotistical spirit. I have seen something of the world now and I know how small in it are even the great ones. I can, however, see myself as one upon whom money has been spent and opportunities given that make it possible for me to offer some small contribution. But life is short and the flesh is weak and it seems a waste that I should not be free to make that contribution. But *you* see all round the subject—the College, Africa, me personally and officially, and your judgement I trust. I don't want you to rate too highly what I could do. It will be, and it must be, very little. But I have said enough. I am not holding you to ransom. I shall, if necessary, be ready to take up my work in October, in the right spirit.

The sequel to this letter was in the form of two cables which reached me soon after I had begun to work in East Africa. One was from Philip Kerr to say that the Rhodes Trust were offering to extend the Travelling Fellowship for a further year. The other was from my College to say that if I accepted I must resign my Fellowship. I at once sent off two cables in the sense of "Accept" and "Resign" and then proceeded to rearrange my plans for East Africa upon a more thorough basis.

Vera Brittain
(1893?–1970)

Vera (Mary) Brittain, daughter of a prosperous but provincial British middle-class family, faced a battle to escape from suffocating domesticity in which her principal ally was her younger brother, Edward, a gifted musician and composer. With Edward's help she extracted reluctant permission from her family to study at Somerville College, Oxford, although she remained only one year before the extent of the European catastrophe unfolding in 1914–18 propelled her into war work to serve alongside her brother, her fiancé, and the group of friends she came to know from their boarding school and respective regiments.

Testament of Youth is her passionate account of the experience of serving as a nurse while her fiancé, her brother, and all his friends were killed in battle. Although Brittain was later to become a committed feminist, in *Testament of Youth* the heroes are all male, and Brittain's fiancé, Roland Leighton, is transformed into a combination of Greek hero, holy saint, and redemptive victim. By contrast Brittain describes many demon matrons and punishing female figures, and her bitter rebellion against her mother's expectation that her daughter will come home to care for her in her seeming inability to live without servants is presented in counterpoint with her brother's death in the closing months of the war. The power of her narrative comes from her compulsion to tell every detail of her life and those of her brother, her fiancé, and her friends in the months and years leading up to their deaths. Just as survivors of the Holocaust can make its horror palpable only by piling detail on detail, Brittain makes us experience a doomed generation going willingly to slaughter because she remembers every detail—what she wore, what she ate, what the train station looked like when she parted from her fiancé for the last time, what the hotel was like where she waited for Leighton to come on leave and where instead she received the news of his death. No other account has been so influential in conveying to later generations the slaughter that took place between 1914 and 1918. Brittain's focus on the horror of the death of an entire generation gives the book its strength. She makes no mention of war aims, European politics, battle strategy. We simply live with her dread, as one by one everyone she loves dies.

It was Brittain's return to Somerville, and her first, unantici-
pated encounter with women as intellectual peers, and indeed superiors, that combined with her wartime experiences to make her the
feminist, pacifist novelist, essayist, and poet known to British and
American readers in the 1940s and '50s.

Her *Poems of the War and After* (1934) conveys the same tone
of elegy for a doomed generation as her memoir of the war years,
although critics rightly pointed out that her talent for prose far ex-
ceeded her achievement as a poet. *Honorable Estate* (1936) is a fictional examination of the constraints imposed on women by marriage,
an institution she now knew more about through her happy marriage to an American academic. This fictional exploration of marriage marked Brittain's own deeper involvement in feminism and
her effort to ground her feminism in systematic study of the institutions that confined women. Throughout the 1940s she courageously wrote against the grain of popular sentiment, exploring the
concept of honor and its expression outside military institutions,
the psychological cost of war, and the reality of the psychological
damage done to men in battle, something later generations would
call posttraumatic stress syndrome. In 1957 her second memoir,
Testament of Experience, appeared, although its depiction of happiness in middle life did not excite the popular response that *Testament of Youth* received. More compelling was Brittain's *Chronicle
of Youth,* drawn from her war diaries and published in 1981, when
readers of the nuclear age were again ready to consider the futility
of war.

TESTAMENT OF YOUTH:
An Autobiographical Study
of the Years 1900–1925

For nearly a decade I have wanted, with a growing sense of urgency, to write something which would show what the whole
War and post-war period—roughly, from the years leading up to
1914 until about 1925—has meant to the men and women of my
generation, the generation of those boys and girls who grew up just
before the War broke out. I wanted to give too, if I could, an impression of the changes which that period brought about in the
minds and lives of very different groups of individuals belonging to

the large section of middle-class society from which my own family comes.

The way to set about it at first appeared obvious; it meant drawing a picture of middle-class England—its interests, its morals, its social ideals, its politics—as it was from the time of my earliest conscious memory, and then telling some kind of personal story against this changing background. . . .

When the Great War broke out, it came to me not as a superlative tragedy, but as an interruption of the most exasperating kind to my personal plans.

To explain the reason for this egotistical view of history's greatest disaster, it is necessary to go back a little—to go back, though only for a moment, as far as the decadent 'nineties, in which I opened my eyes upon the none-too-promising day. . . .

I must have been about eighteen months old when my family moved to Macclesfield, which was a reasonable though none too convenient railway journey from the Potteries. Here, in the small garden and field belonging to our house, and in the smooth, pretty Cheshire lanes with their kindly hedges and benign wild flowers, I and my brother Edward, less than two years my junior, passed through a childhood which was, to all appearances, as serene and uneventful as any childhood could be. . . .

Edward . . . I remember . . . at the age of seven, as a rather solemn, brown-eyed little boy, with beautiful arched eyebrows. . . . Even in childhood we seldom quarrelled, and by the time that we both went away to boarding-school he had already become the dearest companion of those brief years of unshadowed adolescence permitted to our condemned generation. . . .

When, a few years before the War, I first went to St. Monica's, the young school had not yet reached the high educational standards of its later days, and though my budding ambition to go to college—which developed as soon as I discovered that such places as women's colleges existed, and learnt what they stood for—met with real sympathy from both Principals and staff, it received no practical preparation for the necessary examinations, which were not then taken as a matter of normal routine. No doubt my father's persistent determination throughout my schooldays that I should be turned into an entirely ornamental young lady deterred both my aunt and Miss Heath Jones from the efforts that they would otherwise have made on my behalf. . . .

My classroom contemporaries regarded my ambitions, not un-naturally, with no particular interest or sympathy. Many of them were fashionable young women to whom universities represented a quite unnecessary prolongation of useless and distasteful studies, and they looked upon my efforts to reach the top of a form, and my naïve anxiety to remain there, as satisfactorily exonerating them from the troublesome endeavour to win that position for themselves. . . .

I had . . . in my last term at school, misguidedly pleaded for a few months in Paris or Brussels. . . .

Baulked of the minor alleviation, I returned again and again to the major attack; the desire for a more eventful existence and a less restricted horizon had become an obsession, and it never occurred to me to count on marriage as a possible road to freedom. . . .

Each fresh refusal to spend another penny on my education (though the cost of my music lessons, and of the expensive new pi-ano which was ungrudgingly bought for me to practise on, would have paid for nearly a year at Oxford) plunged me into further depths of gloom. . . .

Even at eighteen, a mentally voracious young woman cannot live entirely upon scenery. . . . The holidays were more bearable, for Edward's return from Uppingham always brought with it a fresh outburst of music, which lent, if only vicariously, some object to life. I was never more than a second-rate pianist, for my hands were too small to stretch an octave easily, but Edward—already a skilled and passionate violinist—depended upon me to accompany him in the complicated sonatas and concertos that he brought home from school. . . .

By the time that Edward reached nineteen, he had acquired a charming, easy-going manner (another inheritance, perhaps, from our musical grandfather) which won him a good deal of popularity and was particularly effective in interviews with senior officers and War Office officials; but beneath the agreeable surface I and others who knew him well continually came up against something adamant and rigid through which we could not penetrate—"like a vein of flint in a soft rock," as I described it in my diary in 1914. Mentally, I suppose, he was intelligent rather than intellectual; his taste in lit-erature was limited to plays, short stories and a few poems most of which had some practical significance, and though he won a good many prizes as a small schoolboy, he continually missed them as he grew older. At Uppingham he was invariably second or third in his form; his school reports, apart from those of his music-masters, were never brilliant and never unsatisfactory.

His one absorbing passion was music, to which he added the persistent determination that our unlucky grandfather had so conspicuously lacked. At seventeen he had already begun to compose songs and concertos; as soon as a sheet of music paper was in his hand he became a different creature, irritable, alert, absorbed. On instruments other than the violin—the organ, the piano, the viola— he became a tolerable performer after a very few lessons. How gifted he really was as a violinist, how promising as a composer, I cannot now tell. . . .

In spite of his limited qualities of scholarship and his fitful interest in all non-musical subjects, the idea of refusing Edward a university education never so much as crossed my father's mind. I loved him too dearly even while he was still at school to be jealous of him personally, particularly as he was always my gallant supporter, but I should have been far more patient and docile than I ever showed any symptom of becoming if I had not resented his privileged position as a boy. The most flattering of my school reports had never, I knew, been regarded more seriously than my inconvenient thirst for knowledge and opportunities; in our family, to adapt a famous present-day phrase, what mattered was not the quality of the work, but the sex of the worker.

The constant and to me enraging evidences of this difference of attitude towards Edward and myself violently reinforced the feminist tendencies which I had first acquired at school, and which were being indirectly but surely developed by the clamorous drama of the suffragette movement far away in London. . . .

Early in 1913, when my hopes of ever escaping from provincial young-ladyhood were almost abandoned, came the first unexpected intimations of eventual release.

One spring evening a Staffordshire acquaintance—an old family lawyer—came to spend the night at our house. . . . he began at dinner to talk about Oxford, and I learnt that his elder son, who had won a scholarship there, had only just gone down after taking a brilliant degree. . . .

My father, not to be outdone in parental self-congratulation, thereupon not only mentioned his determination to send Edward to Oxford, but threw in my own continual requests to go to college to make up the balance. To his surprise, our visitor took this expression of feminine ambition entirely as a matter of course. . . .

There is an unduly optimistic proverb which declares that God tempers the wind to the shorn lamb. My subsequent history was hardly to justify such naïve faith in the Deity, but on this first occasion Providence at least let me down gently by giving me a year at college before pitchforking me, a willing victim, into the crudities of Army service. . . .

Overwhelmed though I was by the exciting relief of the news, amazement rather than jubilation remained my prevailing emotion. The gate to liberty was not yet completely open, for the Oxford Senior, to me far more formidable, still barred my way into Somerville. But before I resumed my work for that intimidating final test which awaited me in the summer, something occurred that was destined—at any rate for the next few years—to affect me far more deeply than success in examinations. . . .

Late one night the previous holidays, my mother, noticing the light still burning in Edward's room, had gone up to see if anything was the matter. . . . He was setting to music, he told her, a poem called "L'Envoi," which the captain of his House had written for last summer's school magazine. . . .

In April 1914, Edward invited the author of the poem to Buxton to stay with us for part of the Easter holidays. He looked forward to his friend's coming with definite pleasure but also with a little trepidation, for Roland, besides being captain of their House, was considerably Edward's senior, and had an enormous school reputation for brilliance and unapproachableness. . . .

Although my interest threatened effervescence, I managed to be out of the house when Roland arrived. Coming in purposely late for dinner, I greeted with a lofty assumption of indifference the unknown young man who rose hastily from his chair as I opened the door. But I had not been with him for ten minutes before I realised that in maturity and sophistication he was infinitely the superior of both Edward and myself. . . .

Tentatively I broached the subject of Uppingham, and found my mother perfectly willing to take me with her to Edward's last Speech Day; no doubt she welcomed anything that would deflect my attention—to say nothing of my conversation—from the imminent Oxford Senior. The fact that this ordeal would follow immediately after the Speech Day lost, for the moment, its importance, and I settled down to work and to wait with as much patience as juvenile adulthood could muster. . . .

Absorbed in Unseen Translations and the Binomial Theorem, eagerly looking forward to seeing Roland once more at Uppingham, and mitigating the interval by a heartless retrospective flirtation with my would-be suitor of the previous summer, I entirely failed to notice in the daily papers of June 29th an account of the assassination, on the previous morning, of a European potentate whose name was unknown to me, in a Balkan town of which I had never heard. . . .

When . . . I saw Roland—who like Edward was in the Officers' Training Corps—wearing his colour-sergeant's uniform at the corps review on the Middle Field next morning, I did not feel inclined to tease him any more. On his mother's side he had military ancestors, and took the O.T.C. very seriously. He and Edward and their mutual friend Victor, the third member of the devoted trio whom Roland's mother had christened "the Three Musketeers," were going into camp together near Aldershot for a fortnight after the end of the term. . . .

. . . I do not believe that any of the gaily clad visitors who watched the corps carrying out its manoeuvres and afterwards marching so impressively into the Chapel for the Speech Day service, in the least realised how close at hand was the fate for which it had prepared itself, or how many of those deep and strangely thrilling boys' voices were to be silent in death before another Speech Day. Looking back upon those three radiant days of July 1914, it seems to me that an ominous stillness, an atmosphere of brooding expectation, must surely have hung about the sunlit flower gardens and the shining green fields. . . .

As Roland had no relatives there of his own . . . he sat with me after luncheon at the school concert. This function gave Edward, who had as usual been second or third in every subject, the opportunity to atone for his lack of prizes by playing a violin solo, Dvořák's "Ballade.". . .

The afternoon was so hot, and our desire for conversation so great, that Roland and I were relieved when the concert ended, and we could lose ourselves in the crowd at the Headmaster's garden-party. I remember to-day how perfectly my dress—a frilled pink ninon with a tiny pattern, worn beneath a rose-trimmed lace hat—seemed to have been made for our chosen corner of the garden, where roses with velvet petals softly shading from orange through pink to crimson foamed exuberantly over the lattice-work of an old wooden trellis. But even if I had forgotten, I should still have Roland's verses,

"In the Rose-Garden," to renew the fading colours of a far-away dream.

I have written so much of Uppingham Speech Day because it was the one perfect summer idyll that I ever experienced, as well as my last care-free entertainment before the Flood. The lovely legacy of a vanished world, it is etched with minute precision on the tablets of my memory. Never again, for me and for my generation, was there to be any festival the joy of which no cloud would darken and no remembrance invalidate.

To my last week of mathematics and Latin I returned apprehensively enough—the more so since Oxford had begun, dimly and for the first time, to represent something more than the object of unmitigated ambition. I even permitted myself, at the close of a long day's work, to visualise a pair of dark, intent eyes examining with me the Joshua Reynolds windows in New College Chapel, and to picture a scholar's gown swinging up St. Giles's on its way to Somerville.

On July 20th, exactly a fortnight before the world as I had known it crashed into chaos, I went to Leek to take my Oxford Senior. . . .

War had already broken out, and the map of Europe was undergoing daily transformation, when I learnt, in the last week of August, that my papers had reached the "required standard." . . . no sooner had I, for the moment completely forgetting the state of Europe, begun proudly to announce this final triumph, when my father—though he soon relented—gave way to an outburst of fury. It was useless for me, he thundered, to think of going to Oxford now this War was on; in a few months' time we should probably all find ourselves in the Workhouse!

. . . The controversy ended, none too satisfactorily, with Edward remarking, placidly but firmly, that if I could not be sent to Oxford he wouldn't go either.

For the time being I simmered wrathfully in anger and hopeless resentment. By means of what then appeared to have been a very long struggle, I had made for myself a way of escape from my hated provincial prison—and now the hardly-won road to freedom was to be closed for me by a Serbian bomb hurled from the other end of Europe at an Austrian archduke.

It is not, perhaps, so very surprising that the War at first seemed to me an infuriating personal interruption rather than a world-wide catastrophe.

. . . Roland . . . wrote that his application for a commission had been refused on account of imperfect eyesight—a defect which his youthful vanity had hitherto concealed from me. . . . The possibility that he would be at Oxford with me after all came once more into the foreground.

"Come what may," he told me in sudden enthusiasm after hearing that I was safely through my Oxford Senior, "I *will* go now. And I look forward to facing a hedge of chaperons and Principals with perfect equanimity if I may be allowed to see something of you on the other side."

In the early autumn, Edward . . . had at last been given reluctant permission by my father to apply to the Senior O.T.C. at Oxford for training as an officer.

And it was . . . then that Roland wrote that he had, after all, some chance of a commission in a Norfolk regiment.

So I went up to Oxford, and tried to forget the War. . . .

In the intervals snatched from . . . Greek and religion, I saw something of Edward. . . .

Towards the end of November he was gazetted to the 11th Sherwood Foresters, and the next day he left Oxford for Sandgate. With his tall figure, his long beautiful hands, and the dark arched eyebrows which almost met above his half-sad, half-amused eyes, he looked so handsome in his new second-lieutenant's uniform that the fear which I had felt when he returned from Aldershot on the eve of the War suddenly clutched me again. Reluctantly I said good-bye to him in the Woodstock Road at the entrance to Little Clarendon Street, almost opposite the place where the Oxford War Memorial was to be erected ten years afterwards "In memory of those who fought and those who fell."

I often thought of him in camp as the November rain deluged the city and churned the Oxfordshire roads into mud, and once again the War crept forward a little from its retreat in the back of my mind. One student in my Year had a brother who was actually at the front; I contemplated her with awe and discomfort, and carefully avoided her for the rest of the term.

[Brittain makes an expedition to London to see Roland Leighton during a leave.]

. . . His [Roland's] uniform and little moustache had changed him from a boy into a man, and one so large and powerful that even in the splendour of the rose-trimmed hat and a new squirrel coat

given me by my father, I felt like a midget beside him. Months of intimate correspondence had bound us together, and yet between us
was this physical barrier of the too conscious, too sensitive flesh. It
was getting dark and all the streets were dim, for the first German
air raid had occurred just before Christmas, and the period of
Darkest London had begun. In the sky the searchlight, a faint, detached glimmer, quivered at the edges of the clouds, or slowly
crawled, a luminous pencil, across the deep indigo spaces between.
Roland, who had worked one himself, was immensely amused at
my naïve absorption, and for the first time tentatively took my arm
to guide me across the darkening streets. . . .

In spite of the War, the next day was heaven.

At the Florence Restaurant, still aunt-chaperoned, I lunched
with Roland and was quite unable—and indeed did not try very
hard—to shake him off at my dressmaker's or my milliner's, or even
in the underclothing department at D.H. Evans. I hardly knew what
I was buying; the garments and the furniture which had interested
me so intensely had somehow lost their fascination. . . .

At Charing Cross, with half an hour to wait for the last train to
Purley, we walked together up and down the platform. It was New
Year's Eve, a bright night with infinities of stars and a cold, brilliant
moon; the station was crowded with soldiers and their friends who
had gathered there to greet the New Year. What would it bring, that
menacing 1915?

Neither Roland nor I was able to continue the ardent conversation that had been so easy in the theatre. After two unforgettable
days which seemed to relegate the whole of our previous experience
into a dim and entirely insignificant past, we had to leave one another just as everything was beginning, and we did not know—as in
those days no one for whom France loomed in the distance ever
could know—when or even whether we should meet again. Just before the train was due to leave I got into the carriage, but it did not
actually go for another ten minutes, and we gazed at one another
submerged in complete, melancholy silence.

. . . The previous night I had become ecstatically conscious that
I loved him; on that New Year's Eve I realised that he, too, loved
me, and the knowledge that had been an unutterable joy so long as
any part of the evening remained became an anguish that no words
could describe as soon as we had to say good-bye. . . .

At the beginning of 1915 I was more deeply and ardently in
love than I have ever been or am ever likely to be, yet at that time

Roland and I had hardly been alone together, and never at all without the constant possibility of observation and interruption. In Buxton our occasional walks had always been taken either through the town in full view of my family's inquisitive acquaintances, or as one half of a quartette whose other members kept us continually in sight. At Uppingham every conversation that we had was exposed to inspection and facetious remark by schoolmasters or relatives. In London we could only meet under the benevolent but embarrassingly interested eyes of an aunt. Consequently, by the middle of that January, our desire to see one another alone had passed beyond the bounds of toleration.

In my closely supervised life, a secret visit to London was impossible even *en route* for Oxford; I knew that I should be seen off by a train which had been discussed for days and, as usual, have my ticket taken for me. But Leicester was a conceivable *rendez-vous,* for I had been that way before, even though from Buxton the obvious route was *viâ* Birmingham. So for my family's benefit, I invented some objectionable students, likely to travel by Birmingham, whom I wanted to avoid. Roland, in similar mood, wrote that if he could not get leave he would come without it.

When the morning arrived, my mother decided that I seemed what she called "nervy," and insisted upon accompanying me to Miller's Dale, the junction at which travellers from Buxton change to the main line. I began in despair to wonder whether she would elect to come with me all the way to Oxford, but I finally escaped without her suspecting that I had any intention other than that of catching the first available train from Leicester. The usual telegram was demanded, but I protested that at Oxford station there was always such a rush for a cab that I couldn't possibly find time to telegraph until after tea.

At Leicester, Roland, who had started from Peterborough soon after dawn, was waiting for me with another sheaf of pale pink roses. He looked tired, and said he had had a cold; actually, it was incipient influenza and he ought to have been in bed, but I did not discover this till afterwards.

To be alone with one another after so much observation was quite overwhelming, and for a time conversation in the Grand Hotel lounge moved somewhat spasmodically. But constraint disappeared when he told me with obvious pride that he had asked his own colonel for permission to interview the colonel of the 5th Norfolks, who were stationed some distance away and were shortly going to the front, with a view to getting a transfer.

"Next time I see the C.O.," he announced, "I shall tell him the colonel of the 5th was away. I shall say I spent the whole day looking for him—so after lunch I'm coming with you to Oxford."

I tried to subdue my leaping joy by a protest about his cold, but as we both knew this to be insincere it was quite ineffective. I only stipulated that when we arrived he must lose me at the station; "chap. rules," even more Victorian than the social code of Buxton, made it inexpedient for a woman student to be seen in Oxford with a young man who was not her brother.

So we found an empty first-class carriage and travelled together from Leicester to Oxford. It was a queer journey, the memory of its profound unsatisfactoriness remains with me still. I had not realised before that to be alone together would bring, all too quickly, the knowledge that being alone together was not enough. It was an intolerable realisation, for I knew too that death might so easily overtake us before there could be anything more. I was dependent, he had only his pay, and we were both so distressingly young.

. . . When the grey towers slid into view, unsuitably accompanied by the gas-works and the cemetery, I put out my hand to say good-bye. With sudden vehemence he pressed it against his lips, and kept it there until the train stopped. I could not speak any more, but at the station I looked back at him walking forlornly down the platform; as a final irony I had allowed him to send off the telegram saying that I had arrived safely. Later he told me that he had followed me in a hansom to Somerville and had walked up and down outside the circumspect red walls until it was time for his train to leave. He did not say how he had retraced the tedious journey to Peterborough, but he admitted that the prolonged travelling had cost him three days in bed. "'Do I still think it was all worth while?' Can you ask?"

[Brittain became ill and left Oxford early, before the end of term]
. . . I was thankful . . . to be carried off home, three days before the official date for going down. . . .

I . . . opened a letter from Roland which had been forwarded from Somerville. Ten minutes after reading it I was dressed and staggering dizzily but frantically about the room, for it told me that he had successfully manoeuvred a transfer to the 7th Worcestershire

Regiment and was off to the front in ten days' time. Assuming that I was going down from Oxford at the official end of term, he had asked me to meet him in London, where he was staying for his final leave, to say good-bye.

My parents returned the next day to find me still feverish and excited. As it would have been "incorrect" for me to go alone to London, and as I was, in any case, still hardly fit to do so, they agreed that Roland, who had telephoned that he could manage it, should come to Buxton for the night. My father, however, did inquire from my mother with well-assumed indignation "why on earth Vera was making all this fuss of that youth without a farthing to his name?"

"Sometimes," I told him, "I've wished I'd never met you—that you hadn't come to take away my impersonal attitude towards the War and make it a cause of suffering to me as it is to thousands of others. But if I could choose not to have met you, I wouldn't do it— even though my future had always to be darkened by the shadow of death."

After tea we walked steeply uphill along the wide road which leads over lonely, undulating moors through Whaley Bridge to Manchester, twenty miles away. . . .

It was a mournfully appropriate setting for a discussion on death and the alternative between annihilation and an unknown hereafter. We could not honestly admit that we thought we should survive, though we would have given anything in the world to believe in a life to come, but he promised me that if he died in France he would try to come back and tell me that the grave was not the end of our love. As we walked down the hill towards Buxton the snow ceased and the evening light began faintly to shine in the sky, but somehow it only showed us the more clearly how grey and sorrowful the world had become.

Time, so desperately brief, so immeasurably precious, suddenly seemed to be racing. . . . We were left to ourselves in the dim, lamplit drawing-room.

. . . We sat on the sofa till midnight, talking very quietly. The stillness, heavy-laden with the dull oppression of the snowy night, became so electric with emotion that we were frightened of one another, and dared not let even our fingers touch for fear that the love between us should render what we both believed to be decent behaviour suddenly unendurable.

I was still incredibly ignorant. I had read, by then, too much to have failed to acquire a vague and substantially correct idea of the

meaning of marriage, but I did not yet understand the precise nature of the act of union. My ignorance, however, was incapable of
disturbing my romantic adoration, for I knew now for certain that
whatever marriage might involve in addition to my idea of it, I
could not find it other than desirable. . . .

The next day I saw him off, although he had said that he would
rather I didn't come.

In the early morning we walked to the station beneath a dazzling sun, but the platform from which his train went out was dark
and very cold. In the railway carriage we sat hand in hand until the
whistle blew. We never kissed and never said a word. I got down
from the carriage still clasping his hand, and held it until the gathering speed of the train made me let go. He leaned through the window looking at me with sad, heavy eyes, and I watched the train
wind out of the station and swing round the curve until there was
nothing left but the snowy distance, and the sun shining harshly on
the bright, empty rails.

The determination to work hard and to plan out the days so
that each moment would be occupied became singularly hard to
fulfil, for I could not open a book without finding some subject that
I had discussed with Roland or seeing words which reminded me of
his characteristic phrases. . . .

How fortunate we were who still had hope, I did not then realise; I could not know how soon the time would come when we
should have no more hope, and yet be unable to die. Roland's letters—the sensitive letters of the newly baptised young soldier, so
soon to be hardened by the protective iron of remorseless indifference to horror and pain—made the struggle to concentrate no easier, for they drove me to a feverish searching into fundamental
questions to which no immediate answers were forthcoming.

The fight around Hill 60 which was gradually developing, as-
sisted by the unfamiliar horror of gas attacks, into the Second Battle of Ypres, did nothing to restore my faith in the benevolent
intentions of Providence. With that Easter vacation began the wearing anxiety of waiting for letters which for me was to last, with only
brief intervals, for more than three years, and which, I think, made
all non-combatants feel more distracted than anything else in the
War. Even when the letters came they were four days old, and the
writer since sending them had had time to die over and over again.
My diary, with its long-drawn-out record of days upon days of

miserable speculation, still gives a melancholy impression of that
nerve-racking suspense.

To this constant anxiety for Roland's life was added, as the end
of the fighting moved ever further into an incalculable future, a new
fear that the War would come between us—as indeed, with time,
the War always did, putting a barrier of indescribable experience
between men and the women whom they loved, thrusting horror
deeper and deeper inward, linking the dread of spiritual death to
the apprehension of physical disaster. Quite early I realised this possibility of a permanent impediment to understanding. "Sometimes," I wrote, "I have feared that even if he gets through, what he
has experienced out there may change his ideas and tastes utterly."

. . . To become a nurse was now my intention. It was not, perhaps, an obvious choice for a Somerville exhibitioner, but I was
then in no mood for the routine Civil Service posts which represented the only type of "intellectual" war-work offered to uncertifi-
cated young women. I never even dreamed of patiently putting in
the two remaining years of self-qualification before taking part in
the War. . . . I longed intensely for hard physical labour which
would give me discomfort to endure and weariness to put mental
speculation to sleep.

On Sunday morning, June 27th, 1915, I began my nursing at
the Devonshire Hospital. The same date, exactly ten years afterwards, was to be, for me, equally memorable. Between the one day
and the other lies the rest of this book.

From our house above the town I ran eagerly downhill to my
first morning's work, not knowing, fortunately for myself, that my
servitude would last for nearly four years. The hospital had originally been used as a riding-school, but a certain Duke of Devonshire, with exemplary concern for the welfare of the sick but none
whatever for the feet of the nursing staff, had caused it to be converted to its present charitable purpose. . . .

In the early days of the War the majority of soldier-patients belonged to a first-rate physical type which neither wounds nor sickness, unless mortal, could permanently impair, and from the constant
handling of their lean, muscular bodies, I came to understand the
essential cleanliness, the innate nobility, of sexual love on its physical side. Although there was much to shock in Army hospital service, much to terrify, much, even, to disgust, this day-by-day contact
with male anatomy was never part of the shame. Since it was al-

ways Roland whom I was nursing by proxy, my attitude towards him imperceptibly changed; it became less romantic and more realistic, and thus a new depth was added to my love.

In spite of periodic encounters with the Sister, my new life brought me tranquillity to exactly the extent that it diverted my mind from the letter that had not come or the telegram that might be coming. . . .

When a fortnight passed in which no letter came from Roland at all, I was glad to have attached myself so securely to the hospital.

"If it were not for the nursing I do not know how I could bear this," I confessed. "I feel as if I couldn't go on much longer without news of some sort, and yet it is no good feeling like that because one *has* to go on, come what may. . . ."

A day or two afterwards, Edward arrived home for a long leave which seemed likely to be his last; it was now possible, he told us with his usual serene aloofness, that the 11th Sherwood Foresters might be ordered to the Persian Gulf. . . .

Together Edward and I looked at *The Times* History of the War, picked out a newspaper paragraph stating that the total estimate of European war casualties was already five million dead and seven million wounded, and studied with care the first official account of Neuve Chapelle.

"It is quite impossible to understand," I commented afterwards, "how we can be such strong individualists, so insistent on the rights and claims of every human soul, and yet at the same time countenance (and if we are English, even take quite calmly) this wholesale murder, which if it were applied to animals or birds or indeed anything except men would fill us with a sickness and repulsion greater than we could endure."

On the last evening of his leave, we celebrated the first anniversary of the War by a long walk between the dark moorlands up the Manchester Road. Again, as in the garden at Micklem Hall, Edward expressed the haunting premonition that he himself would not survive to see the coming of peace. It wasn't, he said, as though he were a full-fledged and well-known composer; he couldn't see that his life at present was of much use to anyone, including himself. Everything, it seemed, after he had gone the next day, was being taken from me—my future, my work, my lover, and now my brother. Life was melancholy indeed. . . .

[Brittain's narrative now moves to Roland Leighton's second leave.]

Eventually we decided to tell Roland's mother that we were engaged "for three years or the duration of the War," but to say nothing to my family until Roland's leave was over. Exhausted and excited as I was, I felt unable to face either conventional congratulations or the raising of equally conventional obstacles. My father, I was convinced, would want to spend precious moments in asking Roland how he proposed to "keep" me—an inquiry which I thought both irrelevant and insulting. I was already determined that, whether married or not, I would support myself, preferably by writing, and never become a financial burden to my husband. I believed even then that personal freedom and dignity in marriage were incompatible with economic dependence; I also laboured under the happy delusion that literature was a profession in which self-support was rapidly attainable.

My parents, who not unnaturally expected some explanation for the series of journeys upon which Roland and I proposed to embark together, were obviously puzzled by our silence and by the casual brusquerie with which we treated both them and one another. When, a few days later, I did tell them that we considered ourselves engaged, they received the news with calmness if not with enthusiasm, and protested only about our failure to mention the fact. . . .

. . . To the disappointment of his mother, who thought a ring the only true symbol of union between a man and a woman . . . we both reacted violently against the idea of an engagement ring. Roland saying that he "detested the obvious," and I fiercely determined to exhibit no "token of possession." I could not endure the thought of displaying a conventional jewel in order to indicate to other men that I was "appropriated" and to suggest to other women that I had won a long-sought prize after a successful hunt; it seemed too typical of the old inequality.

Throughout the remaining hours the shadow of the approaching end of day—and perhaps of so much more—lay heavily upon us. I made Roland go to Dunlop's and choose himself a pipe, and he bought me an extravagant bouquet of deep red roses, but despite these lover-like transactions we felt jarred and irritated by the knowledge that the little time left to us had to be spent in the noise and tantalising publicity of shops and streets. At Savory & Moore's he restocked his medical case with morphia; I was glad, later, to remember that he had bought a good supply.

After tea—for both of us a sullen, subdued meal, at which we had joined his mother and an old novelist friend—I had to go to St.

Pancras to catch my train back to Buxton. I felt sadder and more listless than ever; so much that I had meant to say to him was still unsaid, and yet it seemed of no use to say anything more. He told me at last, very bitterly, that he didn't want to go back to the front; he had come to loathe its uncongenial monotony, and this glimpse of England and "real life" had made him hate it more than before.

At St. Pancras there was no empty carriage in which we could talk for the few moments left to us, so we had perforce to walk up and down the noisy platform, saying nothing of importance, and ferociously detesting the cheerful, chattering group round my carriage door.

But when, suddenly, the shriek of the whistle cut sharply through the tumult of sound, our resolution not to kiss on a crowded platform vanished with our consciousness of the crowd's exasperating presence. Too angry and miserable to be shy any more, we clung together and kissed in forlorn desperation.

"I shan't look out of the window and wave to you," I told him, and he replied incoherently: "No—don't; I can't!"

To my amazement, taut and tearless as I was, I saw him hastily mop his eyes with his handkerchief, and in that moment, when it was too late to respond or to show that I understood, I realised how much more he cared for me than I had supposed or he had ever shown. I felt, too, so bitterly sorry for him because he had to fight against his tears while I had no wish to cry at all, and the intolerable longing to comfort him when there was no more time in which to do it made me furious with the frantic pain of impotent desire.

And then, all at once, the whistle sounded again and the train started. As the noisy group moved away from the door he sprang on to the footboard, clung to my hand and, drawing my face down to his, kissed my lips in a sudden vehemence of despair. And I kissed his, and just managed to whisper "Good-bye!" The next moment he was walking rapidly down the platform, with his head bent and his face very pale. Although I had said that I would not, I stood by the door as the train left the station and watched him moving through the crowd. But he never turned again.

"I could have done so well without love—before it came—I with my ambitions and life work . . ." I wrote in my diary. "I shall never again now be able to work towards worldly triumphs with the same disinterested concentration. It was so pleasant when I had only myself to care for most instead of someone else. My peace of mind is gone for ever—it will never completely return again."

———

As September wore on and the Battle of Loos came nearer, an anxious stillness seemed to settle upon the country, making everyone taut and breathless. The Press and personal letters from France were alike full of anticipation and suspense. Roland wrote vaguely but significantly of movements of troops, of great changes impending, and seemed more obsessed with the idea of death than ever before. One letter, describing how he had superintended the reconstruction of some old trenches, was grim with a disgust and bitterness that I had never known him put into words:

> The dug-outs have been nearly all blown in, the wire entanglements are a wreck, and in among the chaos of twisted iron and splintered timber and shapeless earth are the fleshless, blackened bones of simple men who poured out their red, sweet wine of youth unknowing, for nothing more tangible than Honour or their Country's Glory . . . but look at a little pile of sodden grey rags that cover half a skull and a shin-bone and what might have been Its ribs, or at this skeleton lying on its side, resting half crouching as it fell, perfect but that it is headless, and with the tattered clothing still draped round it. . . . Who is there who has known and seen who can say that Victory is worth the death of even one of these?

On Sunday, September 26th, came a brief note from Roland, written three days earlier:

> I have heard nothing definite yet, but they say that all posts will be stopped very soon. *Hinc illæ lacrimæ.* "Till life and all.". . .

All that autumn Edward expected to be sent to France to join one of the numerous battalions of Sherwood Foresters already out there; in consequence his "last leaves" were legion, and on one occasion he invited for the night his now beloved friend from the regiment, a young subaltern whom we all knew as Geoffrey. When that reticent idealist with visions of a clerical career in a slum parish first entered our house, he was so shy that his few remarks were almost inaudible. . . .

. . . Perhaps his most surprising quality was his beauty, which I cannot remember having seen equalled in any young man. Over six feet tall and proportionately broad, he had strongly marked, rather large features, deeply set grey-blue eyes with black lashes, and very thick, wavy brown hair. . . .

The very term in which I had gone up to Somerville and Edward had spent his few weeks in Oxford, Geoffrey had been due there at University College. . . . The three of us read, rather sadly, in *The Times* of October 15th, the customary account of the opening of the Michaelmas Term at Oxford, and speculated whether we should ever again see as students the grey walls clothed in their scarlet robes of autumn creeper. Would Roland, I wondered, read the article in France, and share both the poignancy of our regret and the bitter obstinacy of our determination to go on repudiating the life of scholarship that we had once chosen with such ardent enthusiasm?

On the following day, as if to justify my decision to remain away from college, my orders came from Devonshire House, telling me to report at the 1st London General Hospital, Camberwell, on Monday, October 18th. . . .

. . . Twenty-four hours later, in the midst of the rapid clearing-up and packing to which I was to grow so tediously accustomed during the next three years, I walked up and down the familiar roads, bidding a hurried good-bye to all the places made dear to me, even in Buxton, by association with Roland. It might be a long time, I thought, before I saw them again, and I was not mistaken, for I have never revisited the town since that Sunday afternoon. The leaves were falling fast, and a misty twilight quenched the autumn tints into greyness. Now that the moment of departure had come, I felt melancholy and a little afraid.

. . . My first experience of convoys—the "Fall In" followed by long, slowly moving lines of ambulances and the sudden crowding of the surgical wards with cruelly wounded men—came as a relief because it deprived me of the opportunity for thought.

"I had no time to wonder whether I was going to do things right or not," I noted; "they simply *had* to be done right."

But afterwards the baffling contrast between the ideal of service and its practical expression—a contrast that grew less as our ideals diminished with the years while our burden of remorseless activities increased—drove me to write a puzzled letter to Roland.

"It is always so strange that when you are working you never think of all the inspiring thoughts that made you take up the work in the first instance. Before I was in hospital at all I thought that because I suffered myself I should feel it a grand thing to relieve the sufferings of other people. But now, when I am actually doing something which I know relieves someone's pain, it is nothing but a matter of business. . . ."

Now that the time of waiting for [Roland] was measurable, going on night-duty early in December seemed a new and exciting experience. . . .

It was disconcerting a day or two later to be sent for, together
with several V.A.D.s who had joined the hospital at the same time,
and be told by the Matron that we were all due (as V.A.D.s were invariably "due" whenever the season was unpropitious and none of
the Sisters wanted to go away) for a week's leave of our six-monthly
fortnight. . . . When the others went out I stood my ground and
asked if I could speak to her alone. My cheeks turned scarlet and
my hands, which suddenly seemed to have become four times their
normal size, stole irresistibly towards the starched pockets of my
clean apron as I explained the circumstances of Roland's leave and
begged to have mine a little later.

"You see," I stammered, "he's been at the front nearly nine
months, and I've only seen him once all that time. . . ."

I fully expected, in common V.A.D. parlance, to be "jumped on,"
but to my astonishment the Matron gave me a sweet smile—and
wasn't it, too, most amazingly, just a tiny bit amused?—and answered
benevolently: "Certainly, nurse; I'll postpone your leave.". . .

On my next half-day I occupied an entranced hour or two in
taking a tram to Victoria. . . . At Gorringe's in Buckingham Palace
Road—already the scene of many large and satisfying off-duty
teas—I spent all that was left of two months' pay, and the whole of
the supplementary pocket-money sent to me at intervals by my forgiving father, upon a stimulating selection of brave new garments.
After a comprehensive examination of half the contents of two or
three departments, my choice fell, colourfully rather than judi-
ciously, upon a neatly cut navy coat and skirt, a pastel-blue blouse
in soft crêpe-de-Chine, an unusually becoming fawn felt hat
trimmed with crimson berries, and a black taffeta dinner dress with
scarlet and mauve velvet flowers tucked into the waist. With this I
decided that I could still wear the black moiré rose-trimmed hat
purchased the previous winter in Manchester.

. . . When the final information did come, hurriedly written in
pencil on a thin slip of paper torn from [Roland's] Field Service
note-book, it brought the enchanted day still nearer than I had
dared to hope.

"Shall be home on leave from 24th Dec.–31st. Land Christmas
Day. R."

As Christmas Eve slipped into Christmas Day, I finished tying up the paper bags, and with the Sister filled the men's stockings by the exiguous light of an electric torch. Already I could count, perhaps even on my fingers, the hours that must pass before I should see him. In spite of its tremulous eagerness of anticipation, the night again seemed short; some of the convalescent men wanted to go to early services, and that meant beginning temperatures and pulses at 3 a.m. As I took them I listened to the rain pounding on the tin roof, and wondered whether, since his leave ran from Christmas Eve, he was already on the sea in that wild, stormy darkness. When the men awoke and reached for their stockings, my whole being glowed with exultant benevolence; I delighted in their pleasure over their childish home-made presents because my own mounting joy made me feel in harmony with all creation.

At eight o'clock, as the passages were lengthy and many of the men were lame, I went along to help them to the communion service in the chapel of the college. It was two or three years since I had been to such a service, but it seemed appropriate that I should be there, for I felt, wrought up as I was to a high pitch of nervous emotion, that I ought to thank whatever God might exist for the supreme gift of Roland and the love that had arisen so swiftly between us. The music of the organ was so sweet, the sight of the wounded men who knelt and stood with such difficulty so moving, the conflict of joy and gratitude, pity and sorrow in my mind so poignant, that tears sprang to my eyes, dimming the chapel walls and the words that encircled them: "I am the Resurrection and the Life: he that believeth in Me, though he were dead, yet shall he live: and whosoever liveth and believeth in Me shall never die."

Directly after breakfast, sent on my way by exuberant good wishes from Betty and Marjorie and many of the others, I went down to Brighton. All day I waited there for a telephone message or a telegram, sitting drowsily in the lounge of the Grand Hotel, or walking up and down the promenade, watching the grey sea tossing rough with white surf-crested waves, and wondering still what kind of crossing he had had or was having.

When, by ten o'clock at night, no news had come, I concluded that the complications of telegraph and telephone on a combined Sunday and Christmas Day had made communication impossible. So, unable to fight sleep any longer after a night and a day of wakefulness, I went to bed a little disappointed, but still unperturbed. Roland's family, at their Keymer cottage, kept an even longer vigil; they sat up till nearly midnight over their Christmas dinner in the hope that he would join them, and, in their dramatic, impulsive fashion, they drank a toast to the Dead.

The next morning I had just finished dressing, and was putting on the final touches to the pastel-blue crêpe-de-Chine blouse, when the expected message came to say that I was wanted on the telephone. Believing that I was at last to hear the voice for which I had waited for twenty-four hours, I dashed joyously into the corridor. But the message was not from Roland but from Clare; it was not to say that he had arrived home that morning, but to tell me that he had died of wounds at a Casualty Clearing Station on December 23rd.

That was all. There was no more to learn. Not even a military purpose seemed to have been served by his death. . . .

Later, night after night at Camberwell, watching the clouds drift slowly across the stars, I dwelt upon these facts until it seemed as though my mind would never contain the anguish that they brought me. . . .

All the same, gazing fixedly out of the ward window at a tall church spire blackly silhouetted against banks of cloud pierced by a shaft of brilliant moonshine, I would whisper like a maniac to the sombre, indifferent night: "Oh, my love!—so proud, so confident, so contemptuous of humiliation, you who were meant to lead a forlorn hope, to fall in a great fight—just to be shot like a rat in the dark! Why did you go so boldly, so heedlessly, into No Man's Land when you knew that your leave was so near? Dearest, why did you, why did you?"

. . . The growing certainty that he had left no message for us to remember seemed so cruel, so baffling. To-day, after one or two experiences of shattering pain, I understand the degree to which both agony and its alleviations shut out the claims of memory and thought, but at that time, in spite of six months in hospital, I did not allow for the compelling self-absorption of extreme suffering or the stupefied optimism induced by anaesthetics, and it seemed as though he had gone down to the grave consciously indifferent to all of us who loved him so much. . . .

When my leave came . . . to an end, it was Edward who took me back to Camberwell. . . .

Even death was evidently better than paralysis, I reflected miserably, vainly endeavouring to defeat thought by working my way with resentful conscientiousness through the pile of correspondence that had descended upon me. At the beginning of 1916 the amount and variety of letters of sympathy were still overwhelming, for reiteration had not yet wearied the pens of the sympathisers, but out of them all only two really counted. One of these came from my English tutor, to whom also the War had brought a measure of personal sorrow. Her brief, grave note, suggesting as consolation the living beauty of the life that was gone, assumed a degree of contemplative detachment of which I was then quite incapable. . . . Yet it was to the other letter, so great a contrast in its shy abruptness, that I turned still oftener.

"I'm so very, very sorry," Geoffrey had written from the bleak perils of the Salient, vainly striving for words that would express his acute sensitiveness to another's pain. There were times, he said, when letters were but empty things, and he could not write.

At the beginning of February my night-duty ended, and with tears falling into my trunk I packed up to move from my quiet hut to Denmark Hill. . . .

It was just at this moment that Edward wrote to say that his orders to go to the front had come at last and he was leaving London for France on February 10th. The date was memorable for other reasons, since it brought conscription into operation in England for the first time in history. . . . My mother and I saw him off from Charing Cross on one of those grey, unutterably dismal afternoons in which a London February seems to specialise. . . .

A week later a letter came to say that he was already in the trenches.

"It is quite easy for me now," he wrote, "to understand how Roland was killed; it was quite ordinary but just unlucky. . . . I do not hold life cheap at all and it is hard to be sufficiently brave, yet I have hardly ever felt really afraid. One has to keep up appearances at all costs even if one does."

A day or two afterwards, looking anxiously as usual at the casualty list in *The Times,* I noticed with cold dismay that Geoffrey's name was among the wounded. Almost immediately my mother, who had heard from his family, wrote to tell me that he was now a patient at Fishmongers' Hall, in the City; he had escaped with shell-shock and a slight face wound from a heavy bombardment in front of Ypres, which had caused many casualties among the 10th Sherwood Foresters.

On my next afternoon off duty I went to Fishmongers' Hall, and found him, in a green dressing-gown, huddled over a gas-fire with a rug across his knees. Though the little wound on his left cheek was almost healed, he still shuddered from the deathly cold that comes after shell-shock; his face was grey with a queer, unearthly pallor, from which his haunted eyes glowed like twin points of blue flame in their sunken sockets. Ill and nightmare-ridden as he looked, I was impressed once again by his compelling, devotional beauty.

At first our conversation was slow and constrained, but as he grew accustomed to me, and I did not mention Roland, he began to talk, as though throwing off a burden of memory with painful relief. He was not, he told me, a successful officer as he knew Edward to be; in the trenches he always felt afraid. . . .

Roland's death, Edward's departure and Geoffrey's readiness to take up once more a life which he knew must break him physically or mentally in a very short time, all increased my certainty that, however long the War might last, I could not return to Somerville while those whom I loved best had sacrificed, and were sacrificing, everything that they cared for in the world. I even began to face, bitterly and reluctantly, the possibility that I might never return at all. The Germans were now hammering remorselessly at Verdun, and pessimists had already begun to discuss the chances of a ten-year war. "The first seven years will be the worst!" was now an accepted slogan amongst the men, and even the spirit of the *Punch* cartoons, once so blithely full of exhortations to stand up "For King and Country," had changed to a grim and dogged "Carry On!"

So on a half-day in March, I went up to Oxford to discuss the uncertain future with the Principal of Somerville. . . .

. . . I saw the Principal, of whom I had strangely ceased to be in awe. She was so much less terrifying than most hospital Matrons, so I told her finally that I should not return to college until after the War.

Back at Camberwell, I found a notice pinned to the board in the dining-hall asking for volunteers for foreign service. Now that Roland was irretrievably gone and my decision about Oxford had finally been made, there seemed to be no reason for withholding my name. It was the logical conclusion, I thought, of service in England, though quite a number of V.A.D.s refused to sign because their parents wouldn't like it, or they were too inexperienced, or had had pneumonia when they were five years old.

Their calm readiness to admit their fears amazed me. Not being composed in even the smallest measure of the stuff of which hero-

ines are made, I was terrified of going abroad—so much publicity
was now given to the German submarine campaign that the possibility of being torpedoed was a nightmare to me—but I was even
more afraid of acknowledging my cowardice to myself, let alone to
others. . . .

So I put down my name on the active service list, and never
permitted my conscious self to hear the dastardly prayer of my unconscious that when my orders came they might be for anywhere
but a hospital ship or the Mediterranean.

At the end of June, the hospital received orders to clear out all
convalescents and prepare for a great rush of wounded. We knew
that already a tremendous bombardment had begun, for we could
feel the vibration of the guns at Camberwell, and the family in
Keymer heard them continuously. The sickening, restless apprehension of those days reminded me of the week before Loos, but now
there was no riverside bank beside which to dream, no time to spare
for the somnolent misery of suspense. Hour after hour, as the convalescents departed, we added to the long rows of waiting beds, so
sinister in their white, expectant emptiness.

On June 30th, a tiny pencilled note came from Edward. "The
papers," it announced tersely, "are getting rather more interesting,
but I have only time to say adieu."

Obviously the moment that I had dreaded for a month was imminent, and I had no choice but to face it. How much longer was
there, I wondered, to wait in this agony of fear? Had I time to get
one last message through to Edward before the attack began? I decided to try; and sent off a letter that night.

. . . Was Edward still in the world—or not? At the hostel, after
supper, I wrote to my mother; I did not know how much Edward
had told her, but if he was dead it seemed better that she should
share my knowledge and be forewarned. It surprises me still that I
was able to write so calmly, so unemotionally. The whole of my
generation seems always to have worn, for the benefit of its parents,
a personality not quite its own, and I often wonder if, in days to
come, my own son and daughter will assume for me the same alien
disguise.

"The news in the paper, which we got at 4.0 this afternoon, is
quite self-evident," ran my letter, "so I needn't say much about it.
London was wildly excited and the papers selling madly. Of course
you remember that Edward is at Albert and it is all round there that

the papers say the fighting is fiercest—Montaubon, Fricourt, Mametz. I have been expecting this for days, as when he was here he told me that the great offensive was to begin there and of the part his own regiment was to play in the attack."

For the next three days I lived and worked in hourly dread of a telegram. Had it not been for the sympathy of Geoffrey and Victor, and the knowledge that they too were watching and waiting in similar anxiety, this new suspense would have been overwhelming. Geoffrey wrote from Brocton Camp, in Staffordshire, where he was once more temporarily attached to the 13th Sherwood Foresters, to tell me that nine officers were going to the front from his battalion next day; he would have been going himself were he not on a course which lasted five more weeks. He'd been thinking about us all more than usual, he said, and only hoped that Edward would be as well looked after as himself "out there." For many things, he concluded, he yearned to be there once more, and yet he knew that when the summons came again he would dread it—"or, to use a balder word, funk it"—which was, he seemed to think, an awful confession to make, "as it's absolutely the only thing now."

On Sunday, the day after the battle, Victor came up from Purfleet to see me, for he too had had a note from Edward similar to mine. "The remark 'One can only hope they will follow' now applies. I am so busy that I have only time for material things. And so I must bid you a long, long adieu."

Throughout the brief hour of my off-duty time we walked up and down St. James's Park, staring with unseeing eyes at the ducks fluttering over what was left of the lake—which was being drained to make room for Army huts—while Victor vainly tried to convince me how excellent were Edward's chances of survival, since he was the kind of person who always kept his head in a crisis.

Next day we were told that the first rush of wounded was on its way to Camberwell.

At the usual "break" for 9:30 biscuits and apron-changing next morning I had only a few moments' respite, as the "Fall In" had already sounded for the first expected ambulances. But on my way to the dining-hall I went—as I had gone at every available opportunity during the past three days—to the V.A.D. sitting-room to take another fearful glance at the letter-rack, and there, high above the other letters, I saw a crushed, pencil-scrawled envelope addressed in Edward's handwriting. In a panic of relief—for at least he couldn't be dead—I pulled it down, but even then I could hardly open it, for the paper was so thin and my fingers shook so.

The little note was dated July 1st, and the written words were faint and uneven.

"DEAR VERA," it said, "I was wounded in the action this morning in left arm and right thigh not seriously. Hope to come to England. Don't worry. EDWARD."

For a moment the empty room spun round; then I remembered the waiting ambulances and the Sisters' injunction to "hurry back." In the effort of pulling myself together I recalled, too, that I could save my father and mother, whose letters arrived in Macclesfield a day later than mine, another twenty-four hours of cruel anxiety. Regardless of the indignant glances of Sisters who knew that V.A.D.s were allowed to run only in cases of hæmorrhage or fire, I dashed like a young hare down the stone corridor to the telephone and asked my uncle at the National Provincial Bank to wire to the family.

After breakfast [the next day] I went to my own ward as usual, and was in the midst of preparing dressing-trays—with which, regardless of floors and lockers, the day now began—when I heard a voice agitatedly calling: "Brittain! Brittain! Come *here!*"

I turned, and saw to my great astonishment the elder of the two V.A.D.s from J standing in the doorway. She was panting so much from hurry that she could hardly speak, but managed just to gasp out: "I say—*Do* you know your brother's in J ward?"

By pure good luck I managed to avoid the complete wreckage of my dressing-bowls, and gasped in my turn: "*What!* Edward in J?"

"Honestly, he is," she answered jerkily; "I've just been washing him. Sorry I can't stop—only got permission to come over and tell you!" And she rushed back across the road.

I was excitedly explaining the situation to my Charge-Sister, when Matron—the stony-eyed and somewhat alarming successor to the first Matron, who had left the hospital a few weeks earlier for work in another field—rang up to say that Second-Lieutenant E. H. Brittain had come in with the convoy that morning and was asking for his sister. I could see him, she added, as soon as I could be "spared from the ward." Overwhelmed with work though we were, the Sister told me that I might go and need not return at once, so, half-dazed with surging emotions, I raced over to the College.

. . . I stood in the doorway of J and looked for Edward in vain. Then, half way down the ward, a blue pyjama-clad arm began to wave, and the next moment I was beside his bed.

For a minute or two we gazed at each other in tremulous silence. One of his sleeves, I saw, was empty and the arm beneath it stiff and bandaged, but I noticed with relief, as I looked with an instinctively professional eye for the familiar green stain, that the outer bandage was spotless. With his one available hand he was endeavouring to negotiate a breakfast tray; I helped him to eat a poached egg, and the commonplace action restored to both of us the habit of self-control.

Even then, neither of us could say much. He seemed—to my surprise, for I remember Geoffrey's haggard depression after a much smaller wound—gayer and happier than he had been all through his leave. The relief of having the great dread faced and creditably over was uppermost in his mind just then; it was only later, as he gradually remembered all he had been through on July 1st, that Victor and Geoffrey and I realised that the Battle of the Somme had profoundly changed him and added ten years to his age.

That afternoon and for several successive days, I was allowed to have tea with him in his ward. Except for a brief good-night it was my only chance of seeing him, for I was on duty without a break for nearly a fortnight. Even the end-of-day ten minutes were difficult to wrest from the J Charge-Sister, a cynical old curmudgeon who could not be persuaded that I really wanted to talk to Edward, and not to flirt with the twenty other officers whose beds surrounded his in the crowded ward. . . .

The first gaiety of relief was by now slowly evaporating. He still remained tranquil and controlled, but his left arm was stiff and the fingers immovable; the bullet had badly damaged the central nerve, and he secretly worried about its possible effect upon his violin playing. I learnt the details of July 1st only by degrees. . . .

Edward's award was officially announced in *The Times* of October 21st, 1916, under the heading of "REWARDS FOR GALLANTRY: SHORT STORIES OF BRAVE DEEDS":

"Temp. Sec.-Lt. EDWARD HAROLD BRITTAIN, Notts and Derby R.— For conspicuous gallantry and leadership during an attack. He was severely wounded, but continued to lead his men with great bravery and coolness until a second wound disabled him.

But when I read this notice, I was far away from both Edward and England.

With the coming of summer weather and increased activity on the various fronts, small groups of Sisters and V.A.D.s had begun to leave Camberwell for foreign service, chiefly in France. . . .

At the beginning of September I was due for leave . . . and I left Euston for Macclesfield, where my parents were still living, with a sense of profound relief.

On Macclesfield station my father met me with the news that a telegram awaited me at the house. Hurrying there in a taxi, I opened and read it; it announced that I was ordered on foreign service, and recalled me to Camberwell at once.

. . . It was almost midnight when I tramped wearily through the silent slums between Camberwell New Road and our flat, but Betty was lying awake in bed, waiting for my return. When she heard me at the door she called through the window that both of us were ordered east, probably to Malta.

I was still at Imtarfa when I received my first letters from England.

My worst fears now were for Geoffrey in France; he had grown into a very dear friend whose intelligent understanding never failed the most exacting demands, and my admiration for his determined endurance of a life that he detested was only enhanced by his shy self-depreciation and his frequent asseverations of cowardice. . . .

"Promise me faithfully this one thing," I urged Edward in reply to his first letter from home; "if anything important happens to either you, Geoffrey or Victor, will you cable to me at once? . . .

"I never thought," I added, "that there was Tah's [Victor's] to look for too"—for Edward's letter had contained the surprising news that Victor had gone unexpectedly to the front by transferring from the Royal Sussex Regiment into the King's Royal Rifle Corps. "On the Monday after you left," he wrote, "a wild telegram from Tah announced that he was going to France. I met him in town, helped him with all his shopping (and you can image he needed some help)—it was an awful business as he didn't like most things and knew nothing about anything; occasionally he would suddenly take a violent dislike to a most necessary article of clothing and refuse to have it until I had wasted about 1/2 an hour conjuring up an imaginary situation in which he couldn't possibly do without the thing in question."...

By the middle of March the sunny afternoons had become as hot and sleepy as an English July. In Gargar Ravine, a deep valley where the greenest grass in Malta was strewn with grey boulders of incalculable age, scarlet anemones and a dozen varieties of vetch— yellow and mauve and cerise and orange and purple—sprang up beneath the old stumpy trees, with their dry, hollow trunks and dark, smooth leaves....

Now that Edward, who had been ordered to take two successive officers' courses, was safely in England for a few more months, I should have been drugged into comfortable peace by the calm, drowsy weather and the lovely, serene flowers, had not my letters from France continually sounded a note of apprehension, a warning yet again of approaching calamity. Geoffrey wrote ruefully that leave was remote, and a course for which he had hoped to be sent to the Base had been cancelled, while Victor deplored his lack of a consoling religious philosophy, and regretfully described himself as "an awful atheist." He only wished, he confessed, that he were not, for in the New Army soldiers were made, not born, and with the knowledge of a coming ordeal in the near future, a man required something more to fall back upon than self-manufactured ideals....

The next night, just after I had gone on duty and was making the usual tour of the wards, an orderly brought me a cablegram. Standing between the beds of two patients, I opened it and read the words:

"Victor dangerously wounded; serious."

"I hope it isn't bad news, Sister?" exclaimed one of the men, who must have gathered from my face that it certainly was.

"A great friend of mine's been dangerously wounded in France," I replied, surprised to find that I could speak quite quietly. "He's been dangerously wounded—and it doesn't say how!"

It didn't say how. Now that I knew so much about wounds, that vagueness seemed the telegram's worst infliction. After the Somme I had seen men without faces, without eyes, without limbs, men almost disembowelled, men with hideous truncated stumps of bodies, and few certainties could have been less endurable than my gruesome speculations. Long afterwards I learnt that the cable had been sent by my father, who, with the kindest possible intentions, had believed that he was letting me down gently by suppressing the exact truth.

I had to wait four days before a reply came from Edward, to whom I had cabled because I knew that I could trust him to spare me nothing.

"Eyesight probably gone. May live."

So that's it, I thought. He's blind. His eyes are gone. I wonder if his face is gone too? No, not that; if it had been, Edward would have told me.

Poor dear "Three Musketeers," [Brittain wrote her mother] it doesn't seem fair that Roland should be dead and Victor blind, to say nothing of Edward's bad arm. What a good thing we had no knowledge of what was in store for them in the future to spoil that last Speech Day.

I learnt from the next two mails that Victor had been wounded on April 9th at Arras, first in the arm—which he had disregarded—and then in the head, while leading his platoon to attack the inexorable redoubt known as "The Harp." At Rouen a hospital Matron had summoned his father, thinking that he could only last a few days. But unexpectedly he had rallied, and was sent home to the optical ward in the 2nd London General Hospital, Chelsea, where the care of the best eye specialists in England or France represented his only chance of sight.

The reports from France had been so conflicting that Edward, who sent me these details from Stafford, had vetoed all cables until nine days after the battle.

Immediately after the battle, the Colonel of the 9th K.R.R.C. had written to tell Victor's father that he had recommended him for the Military Cross; "he did exceedingly well that day and . . . I have no doubt he will get it."

The M.C. was in fact awarded to Victor a few weeks later, but this tribute did little more than intensify the stricken confusion into which his family had been plunged since the telegram from Rouen. After living in Sussex for many years, peacefully indifferent to foreign affairs, and politics, and all the other sources from which irrelevant calamity can descend upon the unprepared heads of inoffensive citizens, they found it almost as difficult to credit Victor with a supreme act of military courage as to grasp the overwhelming fact of his blindness.

To Edward also the prospect of Victor's Military Cross brought no consolation; he had worn the purple and white ribbon himself for nearly a year, and knew that the attractions of being a hero were apt to lose their staying power when they were expected to compensate for severe physical damage.

"Victor got a bullet right through the head behind the eyes," he wrote miserably on April 22nd to Geoffrey, who was waiting for dawn in the trenches on the Scarpe. "I'm afraid the sight has gone entirely; the left eye had to be removed in France and a specialist here thinks there is no hope for the right eye; the optic nerve is severed. It is a tragedy which leaves one stupefied and he had such beautiful eyes."

But Geoffrey, the only person who could have comforted him, never read the letter, for on April 23rd he was killed in action at Monchy-le-Preux.

I had just got into bed on May Morning and was drifting into sleep, when the cable came from Edward to say that Geoffrey was dead.

When I had read it I got up and went down to the shore in my dressing-gown and pyjamas. All day I sat on the rocks by the sea with the cable in my hand. I hardly noticed how the beautiful morning, golden and calm as an August in Devon, turned slowly into gorgeous afternoon, but I remembered afterwards that the rocks were covered with tiny cobalt-blue irises, about the size of an English wood violet.

For hours I remained in that state of suspended physical animation when neither heat nor cold, hunger nor thirst, fatigue nor pain, appear to have any power over the body, but the mind seems exceptionally logical and clear. My emotions, however, in so far as they existed, were not logical at all, for they led me to a conviction that Geoffrey's presence was somewhere with me on the rocks. I even felt that if I turned my head quickly I might see him behind me, standing there with his deep-set grey-blue eyes, his finely chiselled lips and the thick light-brown hair that waved a little over his high, candid forehead.

I had to wait for nearly a month before I received permission "to proceed to the United Kingdom" by the overland route. . . .

In the interval I received news from Edward of both Victor's progress and Geoffrey's end. "Tah," he told me, "is perfectly sensible in every way and I don't think there is the very least doubt that he will live. He said that the last few days had been rather bitter. He hasn't given up hope himself about his sight and occasionally says, 'If I get better.' "

On April 30th, when Edward wrote from Brocton Camp, he had heard only that morning of Geoffrey's death, and did not yet know that he had been killed by a sniper while endeavouring to get into touch with the battalion on his left some hours after the attack on the Scarpe began. Shot through the chest, he died speechless, gazing intently at his orderly. The place where he lay was carefully marked, but when the action was over his body had disappeared and was never afterwards found.

"I have been afraid for him for so long," ran Edward's small, precise handwriting—an incongruous medium for such abysmal grief, "and yet now that he has gone it is so very hard—that prince among men with so fine an appreciation of all that was worth appreciating. . . . Always a splendid friend with a splendid heart and a man who won't be forgotten by you or me however long or short a time we may live. Dear child, there is no more to say; we have lost almost all there was to lose and what have we gained? Truly as you say has patriotism worn very very threadbare. . . . This is an unlucky place—I was here when Roland died of wounds, when Tah was blinded and when Geoffrey was killed."

The 2nd London General Hospital opened out of a short street in the Chelsea half of the monotonous and dreary buildings which run almost continuously from the public house appropriately known as World's End to Fulham and Hammersmith. Two schools formed part of the building, and their joint play-grounds made a large open space which held quite comfortably the collection of huts and tents that sprang up wherever a few hundred mangled heroes were gathered together. It was not nearly so big as the 1st London General, and had several wards exclusively devoted to head wounds and eye cases.

I found Victor in bed in the garden, his pale fingers lethargically exploring a big book of Braille. His head was still copiously bandaged, and one brown eye, impotently open, stared glassily into fathomless blackness. If I had not been looking for him I should not have known him; his face seemed to have emptied and diminished until what was visible of it was almost devoid of expression. "Hallo, Tah!" I said, as casually as I could, self-consciously anxious to keep the shock of his appearance out of my voice.

He did not answer, but stiffened all over like a dog suddenly hearing its master's call in the distance; the drooping lethargy disappeared, and his mouth curved into the old listening look of half-cynical intelligence. "Do you know who it is, Tah?" I asked him, putting my hand on his.

"Tah!" he repeated, hesitating, expectant—and then all at once, with a ring of unmistakable joy in his voice, "Why—it's Vera!"

———————

I did not see Edward until he appeared on June 1st for a week-end leave. When he did come he was an unfamiliar, frightening Edward, who never smiled nor spoke except about trivial things, who seemed to have nothing to say to me and indeed hardly appeared to notice my return. More than his first weeks in the trenches, more even than the Battle of the Somme, the death of Geoffrey and the blinding of Victor had changed him. Silent, uncommunicative, thrust in upon himself, he sat all day at the piano, improvising plaintive melodies, and playing Elgar's "Lament for the Fallen."

Only a week later—the day after a strange early morning shock like an earthquake had shaken southern England with its sinister intimation of the terrific mine-explosion at Messines Ridge—my mother and I went to Chelsea to find the usually cheerful, encouraging Matron with a face grown suddenly grave and personal. There was an unexpected change, she said, in Victor that morning. He had told his nurse that during the night something had "clicked" in his head, like a miniature explosion; since then he had gradually grown vaguer and stranger, and had begun to wander a little. . . . She thought that perhaps it would be wise to send for his people.

. . . Left alone with him for a few moments while the others went to see the Matron and the doctor, I looked down at his quiet, passive paleness with a sense of heavy finality. So much human wreckage had passed through my hands, but this . . . well, this was different.

"Tah—dear Tah!" I whispered, in sudden pitying anguish, and I took his fingers in mine and caressed and kissed them as though he had been a child. Suddenly strong, he gripped my hand, pressed it against his mouth and kissed it convulsively in return. His fingers, I noticed, were damp, and his lips very cold.

That night Victor's relatives stayed with us in Kensington; the doctor had advised them not to risk returning to Sussex. Next day, just before breakfast, his father was summoned to the public telephone on the ground floor of the flats; my parents had not yet had a private telephone installed. The message was from the hospital, to say that Victor had died in the early hours of the morning. . . .

Victor's body had already been taken to the mortuary chapel; although the June sunshine outside shone brilliant and cheerful, the tiny place was ice-cold, and grey as a tomb. Indifferently, but with the mechanical decorum of habit, the orderly lifted the sheet from the motionless figure, so familiar, but in its silent unfamiliarity so terrible an indictment of the inept humanity which condemned its own noblest types to such a fate. I had seen death so often . . . and yet I felt that I had never seen it before, for I appeared to be looking at the petrified defencelessness of a child, to whose carven features suffering and experience had once lent the strange illusion of adulthood. With an overwhelming impulse to soften that alien rigidity, I laid my fragrant tribute of roses on the bier, and went quickly away.

Back at home, the aunt, kind, controlled, too sensitive to the sorrows of others to remember her own, turned to me with an affectionate warmth of intimacy which had not been possible before and would never, we both knew, be possible again.

"My dear, I understand what you meant to do for Victor. I know you'd have married him. I do wish you could have. . . ."

"Yes," I said, "I wish I could have," but I did not tell her that the husband of my imagination was always Roland, and could never now be Victor. The psychological combats and defeats of the past two years, I thought, no longer mattered to anyone but myself, for death had made them all unsubstantial, as if they had never been. But though speech could be stifled, thought was less easy to tame; I could not cease from dwelling upon the superfluous torture of Victor's long agony, the cruel waste of his brave efforts at vital readjustment.

As for myself, I felt that I had been malevolently frustrated in the one serious attempt I had ever made to serve a fellow-creature. . . .

When Edward went back to France in the last week of June 1917, I did not go back with him to Victoria, for I had come superstitiously to believe that a railway station farewell was fatal to the prospect of meeting again.

Instead, I waved to him from the window as his taxi rounded the corner of the square, and then helped my mother to wrap up his violin and put it away once more. In the dining-room hung his portrait by Graham Glen; painted while his wound was still painful, the face above the Military Cross ribbon looked pale and sad and retrospective, as it had been for many months after the Somme.

On the wet afternoon of August 3rd, feeling rather sick after a rough crossing and a hasty second inoculation against typhoid done

only the day before, I sat in the stuffy *salon* of the Hôtel du Louvre
at Boulogne, writing out endless "particulars."

The rest of the draft were similarly engaged; most of them were
new to foreign service, and I had felt all the veteran's superiority towards their awkwardness over their life-belts, and their light, nervous conversation about submarines. It had seemed a little strange
starting off without Betty, but familiarity with the routine was a
very fair compensation for solitude.

When the forms were filled in, a Sister from Headquarters ordered me to go to No. 24 General Hospital at Étaples; I was told to
"proceed" the next day, and to spend the night in Boulogne. So I
wired to Edward that I had arrived in France, and shared a room
for the night with S., a talkative, red-haired V.A.D. some years
older than myself. By the time that Edward replied to my telegram
the 11th Battalion had moved up to the Salient, to take part in the
series of offensives round Ypres which began on July 31st and continued, futile and expensive, till the middle of November.

Our train next day did not leave until the afternoon, so I spent
the morning in the English Church at Boulogne commemorating
the Third Anniversary of the War. The Chaplain-General to the
Forces, once Bishop of Pretoria, preached to the packed congregation of officers and nurses a sermon to which I only half listened,
but I paid more attention to the prayers and the collects:

"Remember not, Lord, our offences, nor the offences of our
forefathers; neither take Thou vengeance of our sins; spare us, good
Lord, spare Thy people, whom Thou hast redeemed with Thy most
precious blood, and be not angry with us for ever."

A phrase from my Pass Mods. days at Oxford slipped into my
mind; I had quoted it not long ago to Edward in a letter from
Malta:

"The gods are not angry for ever. . . ."

It came, I thought, from the *Iliad* and those quiet evenings
spent with my Classical tutor in reading of the battles for sorrowful
Troy. How like we were to the fighters of those old wars, trusting to
the irresponsible caprices of an importuned God to deliver us from
blunders and barbarisms for which we only were responsible, and
from which we alone could deliver ourselves and our rocking civilisation!

. . . I saw the congregation as a sombre rainbow, navy-blue and
khaki, scarlet and grey, and by the time that the "Last Post"—with
its final questioning note which now always seemed to me to ex-

press the soul's ceaseless inquiry of the Unseen regarding its ultimate destiny—had sounded over us as we stood in honour of the
dead who could neither protest nor complain, I was as ready for
sacrifices and hardships as I had ever been in the early idealistic
days. This sense of renewed resolution went with me as I stepped
from the shadowed quiet of the church into the wet, noisy streets of
Boulogne. The dead might lie beneath their crosses on a hundred
wind-swept hillsides, but for us the difficult business of continuing
the War must go on in spite of their departure; the sirens would still
sound as the ships brought their drafts to the harbour, and the wind
would flap the pennons on the tall mast-heads.

   . . . It has often been said by pacifists . . . that war creates more
criminals than heroes; that, far from developing noble qualities in
those who take part in it, it brings out only the worst. If this were
altogether true, the pacifist's aim would be, I think, much nearer of
attainment than it is. Looking back upon the psychological processes
of us who were very young sixteen years ago, it seems to me that his
task—our task—is infinitely complicated by the fact that war, while
it lasts, does produce heroism to a far greater extent than it bru-
talises.

   To-day, when I go on holiday along this railway line, I have to
look carefully for the place in which I once lived so intensely. . . .

   Between rows and rows of long wooden huts splashed with the
scarlet and yellow of nasturtiums, we found the white placard: No.
24 GENERAL HOSPITAL. The camp, which I had noticed from the train
only a few weeks before, seemed quite familiar. . . . Although I had
been such a short time in England, with its diminishing rations, it
was quite strange to see unlimited butter and sugar again.

   "Here," I wrote to my mother, exactly two years after the Battle of Loos, and in language not so different from that used by
Roland to describe the preparations for the first of those large-scale
massacres which appeared to be the only method of escape from
trench warfare conceivable to the brilliant imagination of the
Higher Command, "there has been the usual restless atmosphere of
a great push. . . . I hope I shall hear something of Edward soon; I
seemed to be thinking of him and listening to the bugles going
through the whole of last night."

   It was during this offensive that he came to be known as "the immaculate man of the trenches." In addition to his daily shave, he
wrote most considerately whenever he could to let me know that
he was still "quite alright." "In the second half of September," he

finally summed up the position on October 2nd, "we only had 3½ days out of the line, which is heavy work for the Salient when straffing."

This was war in real earnest, yet to my tense anxiety he did seem to bear the proverbial charmed life. So long as he remained, even though the others were dead, hope remained, and there was something to live for; without him—well, I didn't know, and blankly refused to think. . . .

At the end of October came the Italian collapse at Caporetto. As von Bülow pursued his demoralised opponents to the River Piave, and one by one captured the heights between the Piave and the Brenta which protected the Venetian plain, there was much speculation in France over the fate of Venice. For the moment I took little interest in these discussions, never dreaming that the route of an Italian Army in a remote mountain village could concern me for the rest of my life, nor that a time would come when I should not be able to look at a map of the Italian front without a tightening of the throat.

But on November 3rd, when the Flanders offensive was subsiding dismally into the mud and Edward was daily expected home on leave, a brief, mysterious note came from him, written in the vaguely remembered Latin of the Sixth Form at Uppingham.

Calling desperately upon the elusive shades of Pass Mods., I managed to gather from this letter that Edward's battalion had been ordered to join the British and French Divisions being sent from France . . . to reinforce the Italian Army. . . .

Although I was glad that Edward had left the Salient, I couldn't help being disappointed that he was going so far away after I had manoeuvred myself, as I had hoped, permanently near him for the duration of our wartime lives.

"Half the point of being in France seems to be gone," I told my family, "and I didn't realise until I heard he was going how much I had . . . looked forward to seeing him walk up this road one day to see me. But I want you to try and not worry about him more because he is there.". . .

Except for the weather it didn't seem much like Christmas, with no Roland or Victor or Geoffrey to buy presents for, and Edward so far away that the chance of anything reaching him within a week of the proper time was discouragingly remote. Wartime

Christmases anyhow had long lost their novelty, but Mary and I got up early all the same and made shopping expeditions to the village, walking back in pitch darkness through the frozen mud laden with fruit and sweets and gaudy decorations. Christmas Day itself was less unhappy than I had expected, for after a tea-party with the men in my ward, I spent the evening warmly and sleepily at a concert given by the convalescents from the two next-door huts, of which Hope Milroy was now in charge by day.

On January 12th, a hard, bitter morning, a telegram suddenly arrived from Edward: "Just got leave. Can you get it too?" I went at once to the humane Scottish "Red-cape" who had succeeded the Matron of the autumn; I had been in France for nearly six months, and she told me that she would put in for my leave immediately. In a day or two my orders came through, and I packed up and started for England.

As I was too late for that afternoon's boat I had to spend the night in Boulogne, where I scarcely slept for a burning head and a dull ache all over my body. Next morning a very rough and pro-longed crossing made me feel so ill that I hardly knew how to bear it, and as the freezing train from Folkestone did nothing to aid my recovery, I reached Kensington in a state of collapse very different from the triumphant return from Malta. Edward, who had arrived from Italy four days earlier, had gone to Victoria to meet me, but in the crowd and the dark confusion we had somehow missed each other.

Fortified by a large dose of aspirin from Edward's medical case, I went to bed at once, but woke next morning with a temperature of 103 degrees, and for several days had such high fever that the London doctor thought I should be obliged to overstay my leave. The particular "bug" that had assailed me was difficult to locate, but was obviously a form of "P.U.O." or trench fever not dissimilar from the Malta disease in 1916. Perhaps, indeed, that old enemy was reasserting itself, stimulated by overwork or by my fatigued failure to dry my bedclothes sufficiently one recent morning when I had come off duty to find them saturated by a snowstorm which had blown open my hut window during the night.

After a week of feverish misery I was thankful to find myself be-ginning to feel better. The aches and pains had been bad enough, but worst of all was the conscience-stricken sense that I had spoiled Edward's leave and overburdened my mother. Her health was cer-tainly none too good; with one indifferent maid she had felt her powers taxed to their limit by the care of the flat, and must have been driven nearly frantic by the simultaneous appearance of a sick daughter who needed quite careful nursing, and a vigorous son who continually demanded her society at concerts or urged her to accompany him in a newly acquired selection of violin sonatas.

As soon as my temperature went down it seemed like a pleasant dream to have Edward once more beside me, telling me stories of the journey to Italy, and describing the grey rocks and dark pine forests of the Asiago Plateau. But by the time that I was able to go out, rather shakily holding his arm, only three days of his leave were left; and all that we could manage to achieve alone were two theatres and a few hours of Bach and Beethoven.

Our short time together, so long anticipated and so much discussed in letters, had been completely upset by my absurd illness, and on January 25th, almost before we had talked of anything, he was obliged to go back. I had missed so much of his society that I broke my resolution to avoid stations and saw him into the return leave-train for Italy at Waterloo; I compromised with superstition by leaving the platform before the train went out. At the flower-stall on the station he brought me a large bunch of the year's first Parma violets, and though we did not mention it, we both thought of a verse in the song "Sweet Early Violets," which he had bought for his gramophone in Italy and played over to me at home:

> Farewell! Farewell!
> Tho' I may never see your face again,
> Since now we say "good-bye!"
> Love still will live, altho' it live in vain,
> Tho' these, tho' these, my gift, will die!

How handsome he is now, I thought, but so grave and mature; it's obviously an ageing business to become a company commander at twenty-one. Dear Edward, shall we ever be young again, you and I? It doesn't seem much like it; the best years are gone already, and we've lost too much to stop being old, automatically, when the War stops—if it ever does.

Remembering the eager feminism of my pre-war girlhood, and the effervescent fierceness with which I was to wage post-war literary battles in the cause of women, it seems incredible to me now that I should have gone back to hospital completely unaware that, only a few days before my leave began, the Representation of the

People Bill, which gave votes to women over thirty, had been passed by the House of Lords. I had been equally ignorant of its passage through the Commons the previous June, when my thoughts were occupied with Victor's death and the daylight air-raid, but my indifference to the fact that, on February 6th, 1918, woman suffrage became a part of English law only reflected the changed attitude of the war-absorbed Pankhursts themselves. With an incongruous irony seldom equalled in the history of revolutions, the spectacular pageant of the woman's movement, vital and colourful with adventure, with initiative, with sacrificial emotion, crept to its quiet, unadvertised triumph in the deepest night of wartime depression.

However long I may be destined to survive my friends who went down in the Flood, I shall never forget the crushing tension of those extreme days. Nothing had ever quite equalled them before—not the Somme, not Arras, not Passchendaele—for into our minds had crept for the first time the secret, incredible fear that we might lose the War. Each convoy of men that we took in—to be dispatched, a few hours later, to England after a hasty wash and change of dressing, or to the cemetery after a laying-out too hurried to be reverent—gave way to a discouragement that none of us had met with in a great battle before.

"There's only a handful of us, Sister, and there seem to be thousands of them!" was the perpetual cry whether the patient came from Bapaume or Peronne or St. Quentin, where the enemy hordes, released from the Eastern Front, were trying to smash the Allied resistance before the rescuing Americans arrived in force. Day after day, while civilian refugees fled panic-stricken into Étaples from threatened villages further up the line, and the wounded, often unattended, came down in anything that would carry them—returning lorries, A.S.C. ambulances and even cattle-trucks—some fresh enemy conquest was first incredulously whispered and then published tentatively abroad. . . .

"I won't talk about your push as you will have too much to do with it already," considerately wrote Edward on Easter Sunday, when the offensive was ten days old, "but I am glad we have recaptured Albert if only for memory's sake; if the Hun cannot break our line, and I don't think he can, I should think that the end of the War is fairly near. We are in the line with snow all about us—a great change as it is very cold but we are just getting used to it. There have been wonderful sights to see—huge peaks covered with tall pine trees—marvellous roads with hairpin bends and everything

solid rock where the snow lies until June. . . . Early this morning we
had a most extraordinary communion service about 300 yards behind the front line behind a knoll—a most original performance."

. . . Within the next few weeks a good night's rest proved impossible for most of us. The liability to be called up for late convoys
had already induced a habit of light, restless dozing, and the knowledge that the raiders meant business and might return at any moment
after sunset did not help us to settle down quietly and confidently
during the hours of darkness. Whenever a particularly tiring day
had battered our exhausted nerves into indifference, the lights went
out as the result of alarming reports from Abbeville or Camiers and
revived our apprehensions. Rumour declared that we were all to be
issued with steel helmets, and further spasmodic efforts were made
to provide us with trenches in case of emergency.

Three weeks of such days and nights, lived without respite or
off-duty time under the permanent fear of defeat and flight, reduced
the staffs of the Étaples hospitals to the negative conviction that
nothing mattered except to end the strain. England, panic-stricken,
was frantically raising the military age to fifty and agreeing to the
appointment of Foch as Commander-in-Chief, but to us with our
blistered feet, our swollen hands, our wakeful, reddened eyes, victory and defeat began—as indeed they were afterwards to prove—
to seem very much the same thing. . . .

Only a day or two afterwards I was leaving quarters to go back
to my ward, when I had to wait to let a large contingent of troops
march past me along the main road that ran through our camp.
They were swinging rapidly towards Camiers, and though the sight
of soldiers marching was now too familiar to arouse curiosity, an
unusual quality of bold vigour in their swift stride caused me to
stare at them with puzzled interest.

They looked larger than ordinary men; their tall, straight figures were in vivid contrast to the under-sized armies of pale recruits
to which we had grown accustomed. At first I thought their spruce,
clean uniforms were those of officers, yet obviously they could not
be officers, for there were too many of them; they seemed, as it
were, Tommies in heaven. Had yet another regiment been conjured
out of our depleted Dominions? I wondered, watching them move
with such rhythm, such dignity, such serene consciousness of self-
respect. But I knew the colonial troops so well, and these were dif-

ferent; they were assured where the Australians were aggressive, self-possessed where the New Zealanders were turbulent.

Then I heard an excited exclamation from a group of Sisters behind me.

"Look! Look! Here are the Americans!"

I pressed forward with the others to watch the United States physically entering the War, so god-like, so magnificent, so splendidly unimpaired in comparison with the tired, nerve-racked men of the British Army. So these were our deliverers at last, marching up the road to Camiers in the spring sunshine! There seemed to be hundreds of them, and in the fearless swagger of their proud strength they looked a formidable bulwark against the peril looming from Amiens.

Somehow the necessity of packing up in a hurry, the ignominious flight to the coast so long imagined, seemed to move further away. An uncontrollable emotion seized me—as such emotions often seized us in those days of insufficient sleep; my eyeballs pricked, my throat ached, and a mist swam over the confident Americans going to the front. The coming of relief made me realise all at once how long and how intolerable had been the tension, and with the knowledge that we were not, after all, defeated, I found myself beginning to cry.

Just when the Retreat had reduced the strip of coast between the line and the sea to its narrowest dimensions, the summons came that I had subconsciously dreaded ever since my uncomfortable leave.

Early in April a letter arrived from my father to say that my mother had "crocked up" and had been obliged, owing to the inefficiency of the domestic help then available, to go into a nursing-home. What exactly was wrong remained unspecified, though phrases referred to "toxic heart" and "complete general breakdown." My father had temporarily closed the flat and moved into an hotel, but he did not, he told me, wish to remain there. "As your mother and I can no longer manage without you," he concluded, "it is now your duty to leave France immediately and return to Kensington."

I read these words with real dismay, for my father's interpretation of my duty was not, I knew only too well, in the least likely to agree with that of the Army, which had always been singularly unmoved by the worries of relatives. What was I to do? I wondered desperately. There was my family, confidently demanding my presence, and here was the offensive, which made every pair of experienced hands worth ten pairs under normal conditions. I remembered how the hastily imported V.A.D.s had gone sick at the 1st London during the rush after the Somme; a great push was no time in which to teach a tyro her job. How much of my mother's breakdown was physical and how much psychological—the cumulative result of pessimism at home? It did not then occur to me that my father's sense of emergency was probably heightened by a subconscious determination to get me back to London before the Germans reached the Channel ports, as everyone in England felt certain they would. I only knew that no one in France would believe a domestic difficulty to be so insoluble; if I were dead, or a male, it would have to be settled without me. I should merely be thought to have "wind-up," to be using my mother's health as an excuse to escape the advancing enemy or the threatening air-raids.

Half-frantic with the misery of conflicting obligations, I envied Edward his complete powerlessness to leave the Army whatever happened at home. To-day, remembering the violent clash between family and profession, between "duty" and ambition, between conscience and achievement, which has always harassed the women now in their thirties and forties, I find myself still hoping that if the efforts of various interested parties succeed in destroying the fragile international structure built up since the Armistice, and war breaks out on a scale comparable to that of 1914, the organisers of the machine will not hesitate to conscript all women under fifty for service at home or abroad. In the long run, an irrevocable allegiance in a time of emergency makes decision easier for the older as well as for the younger generation. What exhausts women in wartime is not the strenuous and unfamiliar tasks that fall upon them, nor even the hourly dread of death for husbands or lovers or brothers or sons; it is the incessant conflict between personal and national claims which wears out their energy and breaks their spirit.

. . . The next day I went to the Matron's office and interviewed the successor to the friendly Scottish Matron who had sent me on leave, and whose health had obliged her to leave Étaples and return to the calmer conditions of home service. The new Matron was old and charitable, but she naturally did not welcome my problem with enthusiasm. The application for long leave which I had hoped to put in would have, she said, no chance at all while this push was on;

the only possibility was to break my contract, which I might be allowed to do if I made conditions at home sound serious enough.

"I'm giving you this advice against my will," she added. "I'm already short of staff and I can't hope to replace you."

So, with a sinking heart, I asked for leave to break my contract owing to "special circumstances," and returned to my ward feeling a cowardly deserter. . . .

I was glad that my orders did not come through until almost the end of April, when the offensive against the British had slackened, and we knew for certain that we had not yet lost the War.

Early one morning I bade a forlorn farewell to my friends and went down alone in an ambulance to the station.

As the train passed through Hardelot, I noticed that the woods on either side of the line were vivid with a golden-green latticework of delicate leaves. For a whole month in which off-duty time had been impossible, I had ceased to be aware of the visible world of the French countryside; my eyes had seen nothing but the wards and the dying, the dirt and dried blood, the obscene wounds of mangled men and the lotions and lint with which I had dressed them. Looking, now, at the pregnant buds, the green veil flung over the trees and the spilt cream of primroses in the bright, wet grass, I realised with a pang of astonishment that the spring had come.

As soon, therefore, as I had re-established my father in the flat, I brought my mother back from the costly ground-floor dreariness of Mayfair to her own high bedroom, where she could at least look upon the wooded park with its vivid, blossoming trees, which alone of all creation seemed unaffected by the grey, life-draining economy of 1918. Throughout the hot, dusty months of that comfortless summer, I proceeded to "run" the flat with a series of ever-changing, inefficient maids, varied by servantless intervals in which I played the part of nurse, cook and maid-of-all-work.

. . . It was not until late in the summer, while my mother was away in the country, that I happened by chance upon a black-haired, beetle-browed girl whose quick-tempered abruptness concealed an honest disposition and a real capacity for hard work. After I had engaged her, comparative peace descended upon our household for over a year.

I can look back more readily, I think, upon the War's tragedies—which at least had dignity—than upon those miserable weeks that followed my return from France. From a world in which life or death, victory or defeat, national survival or national extinction, had been the sole issues, I returned to a society where no one discussed anything but the price of butter and the incompetence of the latest "temporary"—matters which, in the eyes of Kensington and of various acquaintances who dropped in to tea, seemingly far outweighed in importance the operations at Zeebrugge. . . .

Keyed up as I had been by the month-long strain of daily rushing to and fro in attendance on the dying, and nightly waiting for the death which hovered darkly in the sky overhead, I found it excruciating to maintain even an appearance of interest and sympathy. Probably I did not succeed, for the triviality of everything drove me to despair. The old feeling of frustration that I had known in Buxton came back a thousand times intensified; while disasters smashed up the world around me I seemed to be marooned in a kind of death-in-life, with the three years' experience that now made me of some use to the Army all thrown away.

Temporarily reassured about [Edward's] safety, I went on grieving for the friendly, exhausting, peril-threatened existence that I had left behind at Étaples. To my last day I shall not forget the aching bitterness, the conscience-stricken resentment, with which during that hot, weary June, when every day brought gloomier news from France, I read Press paragraphs stating that more and more V.A.D.s were wanted, or passed the challenging posters in the Trafalgar Square, proclaiming that my King and Country needed me to join the W.A.A.C., or the W.R.N.S., or the W.R.A.F.

And it was just then, a few days before midsummer, that the Austrians, instigated by their German masters, decided to attack the Allies on the Asiago Plateau.

On Sunday morning, June 16th, I opened the *Observer,* which appeared to be chiefly concerned with the new offensive—for the moment at a standstill—in the Noyon-Mont-Didier sector of the Western Front, and instantly saw at the head of a column the paragraph for which I had looked so long and so fearfully:

ITALIAN FRONT ABLAZE
GUN DUELS FROM MOUNTAIN TO SEA
BAD OPENING OF AN OFFENSIVE

The following Italian official *communiqué* was issued yesterday:
From dawn this morning the fire of the enemy's artillery, strongly
countered by our own, was intensified from the Lagerina Valley to

the sea. On the Asiago Plateau, to the east of the Brenta and on the middle Piave, the artillery struggle has assumed and maintains a character of extreme violence.

"I'm afraid," I thought, feeling suddenly cold in spite of the warm June sunlight that streamed through the dining-room window. True, the *communiqué* didn't specifically mention the British, but then there was always a polite pretence on the part of the Press that the Italians were defending the heights above Vicenza entirely on their own. The loss of a "few small positions," however quickly recaptured, meant—as it always did in dispatches—that the defenders were taken by surprise and the enemy offensive had temporarily succeeded. Could I hope that Edward had missed it through being still in hospital? I hardly thought so; he had said as long ago as June 3rd that he expected to be "back again in a few days."

However, there was nothing to do in the midst of one's family but practise that concealment of fear which the long years of war had instilled, thrusting it inward until one's subconscious became a regular prison-house of apprehensions and inhibitions which were later to take their revenge. . . .

A day or two later, more details were published of the fighting in Italy, and I learnt that the Sherwood Foresters had been involved in the "show" on the Plateau. After that I made no pretence at doing anything but wander restlessly round Kensington or up and down the flat, and, though my father retired glumly to bed every evening at nine o'clock, I gave up writing the semi-fictitious record which I had begun of my life in France. Somehow I couldn't bring myself even to wrap up the *Spectator* and *Saturday Review* that I sent every week to Italy, and they remained in my bedroom, silent yet eloquent witnesses to the dread which my father and I, determinedly conversing on commonplace topics, each refused to put into words.

By the following Saturday we had still heard nothing of Edward. The interval usually allowed for news of casualties after a battle was seldom so long as this, and I began, with an artificial sense of lightness unaccompanied by real conviction, to think that there was perhaps, after all, no news to come. I had just announced to my father, as we sat over tea in the dining-room, that I really must do up Edward's papers and take them to the post office before it closed for the week-end, when there came the sudden loud clattering at the front-door knocker that always meant a telegram.

For a moment I thought that my legs would not carry me, but they behaved quite normally as I got up and went to the door. I knew what was in the telegram—I had known for a week—but because the persistent hopefulness of the human heart refuses to allow intuitive certainty to persuade the reason of that which it knows, I opened and read it in a tearing anguish of suspense.

REGRET TO INFORM YOU CAPTAIN E. H. BRITTAIN M.C. KILLED IN ACTION ITALY JUNE 15TH.

"No answer," I told the boy mechanically, and handed the telegram to my father, who had followed me into the hall. As we went back into the dining-room I saw, as though I had never seen them before, the bowl of blue delphiniums on the table; their intense colour, vivid, ethereal, seemed too radiant for earthly flowers.

Long after the family had gone to bed and the world had grown silent, I crept into the dining-room to be alone with Edward's portrait. Carefully closing the door, I turned on the light and looked at the pale, pictured face, so dignified, so steadfast, so tragically mature. He had been through so much—far, far more than those beloved friends who had died at an earlier stage of the interminable War, leaving him alone to mourn their loss. Fate might have allowed him the little, sorry compensation of survival, the chance to make his lovely music in honour of their memory. It seemed indeed the last irony that he should have been killed by the countrymen of Fritz Kreisler, the violinist whom of all others he had most greatly admired.

And suddenly, as I remembered all the dear afternoons and evenings when I had followed him on the piano as he played his violin, the sad, searching eyes of the portrait were more than I could bear, and falling on my knees before it I began to cry "Edward! Oh, Edward!" in dazed repetition, as though my persistent crying and calling would somehow bring him back.

When the sound of victorious guns burst over London at 11 a.m. on November 11th, 1918, the men and women who looked incredulously into each other's faces did not cry jubilantly: "We've won the War!" They only said: "The War is over."

[After her brother's death Brittain insisted on returning to nursing.] From Millbank I heard the maroons crash with terrifying clearness, and, like a sleeper who is determined to go on dreaming after being told to wake up, I went on automatically washing the dressing bowls in the annex outside my hut. Deeply buried beneath my consciousness there stirred the vague memory of a letter that I had written to Roland in those legendary days when I was still at Oxford, and could spend my Sundays thinking of him while the organ echoed grandly through New College Chapel. It had been a warm May evening, when all the city was sweet with the scent of wallflowers and lilac, and I had walked back to Micklem Hall after hearing an Occasional Oratorio by Handel, which described the mustering of troops for battle, the lament for the fallen and the triumphant return of the victors.

And as I dried the bowls I thought: "It's come too late for me. Somehow I knew, even at Oxford, that it would. Why couldn't it have ended rationally, as it might have ended, in 1916, instead of all that trumpet-blowing against a negotiated peace, and the ferocious talk of secure civilians about marching to Berlin? It's come five months too late—or is it three years? It might have ended last June, and let Edward, at least, be saved! Only five months—it's such a little time, when Roland died nearly three years ago."

Late that evening, when supper was over, a group of elated V.A.D.s who were anxious to walk through Westminster and Whitehall to Buckingham Palace prevailed upon me to join them. Outside the Admiralty a crazy group of convalescent Tommies were collecting specimens of different uniforms and bundling their wearers into flag-strewn taxis; with a shout they seized two of my companions and disappeared into the clamorous crowd, waving flags and shaking rattles. Wherever we went a burst of enthusiastic cheering greeted our Red Cross uniform, and complete strangers adorned with wound stripes rushed up and shook me warmly by the hand. After the long, long blackness, it seemed like a fairy-tale to see the street lamps shining through the chill November gloom.

I detached myself from the others and walked slowly up Whitehall, with my heart sinking in a sudden cold dismay. Already this was a different world from the one that I had known during four life-long years, a world in which people would be light-hearted and forgetful, in which themselves and their careers and their amusements would blot out political ideals and great national issues. And in that brightly lit, alien world I should have no part. All those with whom I had really been intimate were gone; not one remained to share with me the heights and the depths of my memories. As the years went by and youth departed and remembrance grew dim, a

deeper and ever deeper darkness would cover the young men who
were once my contemporaries.

For the first time I realised, with all that full realisation meant,
how completely everything that had hitherto made up my life had
vanished with Edward and Roland, with Victor and Geoffrey. The
War was over; a new age was beginning; but the dead were dead
and would never return.

Angelica Garnett
(1918–   )

Angelica Garnett is the daughter of British artist Vanessa Bell (sister of the more celebrated Virginia Woolf) and Bell's artist-lover, Duncan Grant. A child of the worldly, sophisticated, and obsessively intellectual Bloomsbury circle, Garnett did not know until young girlhood that Vanessa Bell's legal husband, the art critic Clive Bell, was not her father. Nor did she learn until well after her marriage to David (Bunny) Garnett in 1942 that he was a spurned lover of her mother and an actual lover of Duncan Grant, her biological father.

Garnett was raised in the permissive world of Bloomsbury, where extramarital affairs were normal, homosexuality accepted, and intellectual or artistic creativity worshiped. Her memoir is an account of a quest for psychological stability and the emotional distance to come to terms with her extraordinary family circle. By showing us Bloomsbury through the eyes of a child, Garnett conveys the uneasy confusions of a world of multiple liaisons and no formal taboos. The child who sits in John Maynard Keynes's ornate bathtub in his London apartment and is showered with many-colored bath salts by the great economic sage gives us a new perspective on Bloomsbury, and a sense of its potentially suffocating but also emotionally distant relationship to children.

Not surprisingly, Garnett viewed her courtship by and marriage to Bunny Garnett—something opposed by Vanessa Bell and Duncan Grant, although their real reason was never given—as a game pursued by an older generation, in which she was an unsuspecting pawn. Lengthy psychoanalysis after the breakup of her marriage and the seven-year effort to compose this memoir gave her the freedom to pursue her own career as writer, painter, and sculptor, now successfully exhibited in Milan and London.

DECEIVED WITH KINDNESS:
A Bloomsbury Childhood

In 1975 I was living on the north side of London in Islington, a prey to loneliness and regret, following a love affair with someone much younger than myself. My lover had gone abroad, leaving me without news of any kind, and I spent many months of doubt and anxiety before compelling myself to admit that he would never return. My children had by that time left home, and my husband, David Garnett (called Bunny by myself and our friends), from whom I had separated several years earlier, lived in France. Now I found myself alone in one of those tall London houses, with nine empty rooms, not so much unhappy as disoriented.

What else had I ever been, however, in spite of a longing to prove the contrary? I had friends, of course, but I did not feel particularly close to any of them. Either they were friends of my youth with whom the links had become attenuated by time and a change of interests, or they were those of an older generation who were friends of mine mainly because they had known and loved my parents. With them I always felt secure, but also ill at ease, sensing that there was some profound inadequacy in me to which, in their kindness, they did not allude. Our relations were inhibited either because we could not achieve a sufficient intimacy together, or because I imagined that I had nothing to offer our friendship. . . .

Preoccupied with myself as I was, I began to be aware of the profound and disturbing emotions I felt for my mother, Vanessa Bell, and my father, Duncan Grant. I was beginning to question their behaviour towards me.

In 1961, when she was eighty-one and I was forty-two, my mother died. Her image and personality had always obsessed me: on the one hand I felt compelled to imitate her, while on the other I resented her dominance. With Duncan I had had a different relationship: light and easy, affectionate and undemanding. . . . But recently I had become aware of currents beneath the surface, of unsatisfied desires and longings which, partly because I did not know what they meant and partly because Duncan himself seemed so unaware, had become deeply repressed. . . .

Writing my diary proved helpful, for it provided a means of increasing my insight. Then another lifeline was held out to me by a young American called Frank Hallman, who wrote asking for permission to publish an article by my aunt, Virginia Woolf, and subsequently a memoir by Vanessa. At first we carried on a lively correspondence, and later in the summer he arrived in England. . . . We liked each other immediately, a feeling which on my side was all the warmer because I hoped that here at last was that particular kind of intimacy for which I longed. I did not fall in love, but something in his manner affected me like an elixir. . . . It was a reflection of what he felt for my mother, for whom he had conceived an enormous admiration. . . . Unlike most people, he had responded more strongly to Vanessa [as a painter] than to Duncan. It was Frank who dropped into my mind the idea that Duncan was not necessarily as attractive to everyone as he appeared to me. . . .

Since Vanessa's death, Duncan had lived on in the country at Charleston. I often went down to see him, making the two-and-a-half-hour journey by car, assuming, much in the way small children do, that I should always be welcome. Undemonstrative though he was, Duncan never made me feel otherwise, and in that place and in his presence I had the sensation, a false one as it turned out, of being a whole and integrated person. . . . Every day I saw Duncan slowly ageing in front of his easel, dedicated to his painting and responding happily to a host of faithful admirers, while I, rigid with suppressed love and a misery in which there was more than a tinge of jealousy, suffered from his obvious lack of interest in my life.

He was by now very old and, unable to live alone, was looked after devotedly by the poet Paul Roche, a friend of long standing, who filled the house with his grown-up children and their companions. . . . Provided he could continue to paint, which he was at the time doing very well, he preferred to remain detached, apparently unconcerned with what went on around him, although an occasional spark of life showed he was not as oblivious as he seemed. . . .

. . . I was worried about the future of Charleston, full as it was of paintings, decorations and objects of every kind—a testimony to the life we had lived there—and I wanted to find a way of preserving it. It had been obvious for some time that the work should be undertaken as soon as possible, but my reluctance to disturb Duncan had made it difficult to know how to begin.

. . . My correspondence with Frank Hallman continued and, in the course of his other visits to London and one to Sussex, our friendship deepened. But in the summer of 1976 the telephone rang, and a voice on the other end of the line told me that Frank, on the previous day, had dropped dead of an aneurism. . . . A year later I sold my house in Islington and went to live at Charleston, from where Duncan had again departed to Aldermaston, as it turned out for the last time. I thought I could keep it going until his return in the spring, but living there again was a psychological experiment which held greater risks than I had imagined.

I loved the place and all that was in it, but there was a sense of compulsion about my return, as though this time I were going back to the cave of the enchantress, the role in which I saw Vanessa. Surrounded by the subtle and glowing colours which splashed and streaked every surface, transforming walls, mantel-pieces, doors and furniture, all familiar to me from childhood, I was too close to see things dispassionately, and yet I could not tear myself away. . . .

Obscurely, I felt it necessary to come to terms with them in a place where I had spent a large part of my childhood and which I had always thought of as my home. At the same time the force of personality of both my parents, together with their philosophy or attitude to life, constituted a threat which until then I had never properly considered. . . .

Immediately after Duncan's death I began to suffer from a continuous headache. At first negligible, after a time it felt as though, when I bent my head, a set of billiard balls clashed together in the middle of my forehead. Activities such as gardening became impossible. Examinations revealed nothing and pills were useless; finally a violent pain seized the back of my neck and more or less prostrated me. As I lay in Vanessa's bedroom I had the sensation of being sucked into a vortex from which, as in a nightmare, it was imperative but impossible to escape.

Weeks went by during which no one was able to suggest what was wrong, weeks when I felt less and less capable of normal emotion. There was a moment when I thought of the pond as a solution. . . . I decided to move into a nursing home in London, where I was told I was suffering from a depression: a psychiatrist gave me jade green pills to swallow. I shall never forget the moment when, lying in bed in the evening, I felt an unmistakable trickle of vitality wriggle down my spine. I simply lay there, allowing this miracle to take possession of me, like an urn being filled with water.

It was a long time before I felt completely normal, but I could at least lead the life of an ordinary human being, and I returned to

Charleston to an exceptionally beautiful spring, when the Japanese cherry that I had put in the year before flowered with the palest pink almond-scented blossom. . . .

When [Vanessa] was alive, I had seen her . . . as a monolithic figure who stood in my way, barring my development as a human being. Unable to wrench myself away from her for whom I had such feelings, I burdened her instead of myself with the responsibility for my life. The result was that when she died I felt almost nothing save the oppressive shadow of her presence and the faint hope that I might one day be free of it.

Why had I not revolted while there was still time, thus discovering my own self-respect and the ability to love Vanessa while she was still alive? . . . Now that she was no longer there it was impossible to say, but the idea that it might be possible to hold a dialogue with the dead began to form in my mind. . . .

. . . As I read Vanessa's early letters to her sister and to her husband Clive, I was astonished by a vitality that I had not known was there; it was like uncovering a spring of silver water. An earlier identity glowed tantalisingly through these pages and through other people's memories and allusions, calling to life the mother I had always wanted, and with whom so many had fallen in love. Such a woman had invented the vibrant colours and shapes that surrounded me. . . .

. . . It is only now, and still with hesitation, that I feel I can portray her from a greater distance and affirm my separation from a personality I have spent so much time thinking about. I hope to be excused a skeleton of biographical facts without which, to my mind, her behaviour would lack meaning.

Although she eventually formed part of a society that was to have lasting influence, it was a small group within which Vanessa exerted her power, a group very susceptible to personal ascendancy. Some of its members, notably Virginia Woolf and Maynard Keynes, gained world recognition, but there was some element in Vanessa which refused to compete, restricting her energies to a more personal arena, where she reigned supreme.

She reminded me of a mountain covered with snow: at its summit the sun shone with warmth and splendour, and there was a sweetness and gaiety in the air. Further down the clouds gathered, plunging the lower, more arid slopes into darkness. At the centre of the mountain ran a deep river, glimpsed only at intervals, when it

surged through a rift in the hillside with unexpected and disconcerting power. . . .

Vanessa was not only Virginia Woolf's sister, she was also the
eldest of the Stephen family by her father Leslie's second marriage
[to Julia Duckworth]. . . .

The gap in age was considerable, however, whereas that between Vanessa and her full brothers and sister was as close as possible, as was their intimacy. Next to Vanessa came her adored
brother Thoby, also of great importance in her emotional development; then Virginia who through the accident of sex was thrown together with Vanessa, for a time becoming a psychological burden of
considerable proportions; and lastly Adrian who as an unwanted
child was spoiled, over-protected and inhibited. According to Virginia, Vanessa felt her responsibilities towards them keenly: thrust
into a maternal role by nurses and Julia alike, she had no choice but
to respond, tempted by rewards of love and affection, and proud no
doubt of being thought capable and worthy. . . .

After the death of Julia, and her stepsister Stella shortly afterwards, Vanessa's sense of maternal responsibility, already forced
into precocious maturity, became a vulnerable point in her make-
up. Left exposed as the one who was expected to take charge of the
large and—by our standards—formal household, she was obliged
to account for every penny, week by week, to her persistent and
guilt-ridden father. . . .

. . . In a family that was highly articulate and self-conscious,
Vanessa held herself a little apart, perhaps because she was the eldest.
Her reactions were slower and more instinctive than Virginia's—
possibly more so than Thoby's—and she often preferred to main-
tain a mute independence which impressed the more volatile
Virginia with a sense of strength and responsibility. . . .

In spite of her superiority of years and experience it was from
her sister that Vanessa often felt the need to protect herself. While
still a child Virginia, possessed of precocious insight, christened
Vanessa "the saint," knowing that such a nickname would embarrass Vanessa by its suggestion of disingenuous self-righteousness. . . .

Vanessa was fifteen when her mother died, after some weeks of
illness—she was forty-nine. She looked far older, worn out not only
by a life of service to others but also, one is tempted to think looking at the later photographs, from an indefinable inner anguish.
When two years later, after a few months of marriage, Stella died,
the family was doubly bereft, while the display of extreme emotion

indulged in by Leslie brought his children together in a common dislike of hypocrisy. . . .

Virginia's feelings for Vanessa were two-fold: love, admiration and understanding played their part but were inextricably mixed with jealousy and envy, stimulated by Vanessa's cool detachment and evident if unconscious superiority. . . .

With Thoby at Cambridge Vanessa came to know a number of his friends, among them Clive Bell. Vivacious, amusing and somewhat of a libertine, Clive came from a family of *nouveaux riches* whose extreme conventionality had driven him to escape first to university and then to Paris. . . . He fell in love while she was still living at Hyde Park Gate, but though his feelings were at first unreciprocated he persevered and, after her removal to Bloomsbury, continued to see a great deal of her.

In 1906 Vanessa, Virginia, Thoby, Clive and other friends went for a holiday to Greece, and on their return Thoby fell ill with an infection that was not immediately diagnosed. . . . Thoby, considered by all his friends as a brilliant and promising young man, died at twenty-six—almost the same age as Stella. Two days later Vanessa accepted Clive's proposal of marriage. . . .

Initially their union was a great success. She was twenty-eight and had waited a long time for sexual experience. Now that it had come, she was transfigured; she was bowled over not only by sex itself but by the intimacy it conferred on their relationship. All her tender, delicate and most endearing qualities came to the surface; he teased, joked and laughed, enjoying the half-private, half-public parade of their feelings for each other. In addition, she soon found she was pregnant: in 1908 her elder son Julian was born.

It was during this supremely happy and fulfilled period that Virginia took it into her head to flirt with Clive, an act which paralleled in its incestuous nature that of Vanessa falling in love with Jack Hills. But its character was entirely different. Vanessa's feelings had, one may imagine, been prompted by despair at losing her sister and a desire to identify with her through the loved one by means of sexual attraction, whereas Virginia's feelings for Clive were barely sexual, and owed much of their vivacity to a common delight in the processes of the intellect. Both he and she were carried away by a youthful effervescence which ignited a whole train of intellectual fireworks in a style that was not in Vanessa's nature. Clive's manner, though flattering and suggestive, carried with it none of the undertones of feeling which would have frightened Virginia, but was exactly calculated to promote a flirtation which, as they must both have been aware, was outrageous in its apparent disregard of Vanessa's existence. . . .

With the birth of her sons Julian in 1908, and Quentin in 1910, Vanessa's second passion in life, maternity, was fulfilled. At Asheham, the house in Sussex taken by Virginia and shared with Vanessa, she effortlessly organised a life where friends, children and animals lived together in acceptable though primitive conditions. Surrounded by other painters, and visited by a shifting population of guests, among whom were Roger Fry and Duncan Grant, she enjoyed working in their company while controlling their existence with gentle laissez-faire. Her sense of humour, her flair for improvisation and her sympathy for other people's emotional difficulties, together with her unquestionable capacity to get what she wanted, gave her a special place among that group of friends who were later to be called Bloomsbury. . . . Most of these friends were young men, many of them, though not by any means all, homosexual. Vanessa, though a sympathetic friend and listener, did not take their love affairs very seriously: sexual emancipation, though a source of some trouble and a good deal of amusement, was hardly as important as friendship. . . .

. . . After Quentin's birth in August 1910, the relationship between Clive and Vanessa seems to have deteriorated. He had never ceased to have extra-marital relations and when Quentin's refusal to put on weight was causing Vanessa considerable anxiety, Clive offered her little support. It was then that Roger Fry, whom she had known for some time, showed a sympathetic understanding which, coming from a man, was new to her. Their friendship, already stimulated by a common excitement about the latest developments in art and his inauguration of the first Post-Impressionist Show in November of the same year, grew steadily more intimate. In 1911, together with Clive, they went to Turkey, where Vanessa became seriously ill. While Clive absented himself as much as possible from the sick-room, Roger revealed himself an expert, if unconventional nurse. On Vanessa's recovery and their return to London, it was evident, at least to themselves, that they were very much in love. . . .

. . . Vanessa was a prey to intermittent but crippling bouts of lethargy lasting over a couple of years, suggesting that she suffered from a severe depression, different in effect but not perhaps unrelated to Virginia's instability. Whatever their cause, these periods of forced inactivity and withdrawal certainly coloured her attitude to her love affair, which had begun with her as the victim and Roger as the knight errant, rescuing her from the dangers of inertia and despair; later, when she discovered that his very vitality exhausted her and that he demanded an attention she could not give, he became a prey to self-pity while she felt a growing indifference. . . .

. . . In the end Roger understood that perseverance was useless, and gave up his place in her affections to another artist and friend of both, Duncan Grant. The spirit in which Roger watched the development of this new relationship, though not without moments of jealousy, was remarkable for its generosity. . . .

Duncan Grant was a cousin of the Stracheys, whom Vanessa had known well all her life. His world was therefore much closer to hers than either Clive's or Roger's, although, like that of the Stracheys, it had a strong Anglo-Indian flavour. Duncan's father had spent his professional life in India, and Duncan lived with his parents there and in Burma until he was seven. His parents staying on, he then lived with the Stracheys, and went to various schools in England. . . . Like Vanessa, Duncan decided early in life that all he wanted to do was to paint, an ambition encouraged by his grandmother, Lady Strachey. He went to Paris for a year, from where he returned to enter the London art scene. He was a homosexual with bisexual leanings, though at what age he realised this is not clear—perhaps he had always known it. On the surface he seemed singularly candid and uncomplicated, with an unselfconscious charm that had an almost hypnotic effect on those who knew him. . . .

He was a sympathetic companion, beautiful rather than handsome and extraordinarily sensitive to the prevailing atmosphere. . . . With Duncan [Vanessa] knew that the slightest allusion to aesthetics or the process of painting would be understood and appreciated, while at the same time she need not be over-serious. . . .

. . . Had it been possible to lead a normal social life, their relationship might not have continued. But it was wartime and Duncan, as a conscientious objector, was forced to live in the country and work on the land. . . . First at Wissett in Suffolk and then at Charleston, they succeeded in creating a life that seemed like an idyll snatched from the horror that surrounded them, and Vanessa found herself a role which exactly suited her, that of mother-housekeeper and presiding genius as well as artist. Lack of food, comfort and intelligent servants was not enough to destroy their optimism, to which the existence of two lively boys added its own special quality. . . .

Both in the house at Suffolk and afterwards at Charleston, Vanessa found she had to share Duncan with David Garnett, who, younger even than Duncan, had allowed himself to be seduced. Duncan was very much in love, and Vanessa saw that if she was to keep Duncan in her life she would have to accept not only David but many others. One might imagine that such a situation would be difficult if not painful for all three—and perhaps it was. But Vanessa knew exactly what she wanted. She persuaded Duncan to give her a child, prepared to take the responsibility on herself provided he remained close to her. For her he was a genius, his offspring destined to be exceptional.

I was born on December 25th, 1918, a date which to Vanessa seemed auspicious, and which, later, she taught me to associate with the unusual, as though the accident of being born on Christmas Day was a virtue of my own. . . .

Presumably it was with his approval that Vanessa and Clive decided to ignore the fact that Duncan was my father. It was arranged between them that Duncan, on my arrival in this world, was to telegraph Clive's parents, Mr. and Mrs. Bell, in Clive's name. They, innocent and conventional, would never suspect, it was supposed, that I was not their grandchild. Clive was anxious to avoid the inexplicable which was not so much that his wife had been unfaithful to him—and he to her—but that this made little difference to the amity of their relations. . . .

It was characteristic, however, of Clive's urbanity and Vanessa's tact; if it was unnecessary to say anything, why say it? . . .

When, many years later, [Vanessa] came to tell me of my parentage, she offered Duncan's youth as an excuse for his behaviour, the only sign as far as I remember that she was aware of anything wrong. He was at that time thirty-three or thirty-four. She thought of him as, above all, an artist; to see him as a father seemed unreal, and perhaps unnecessary, since she herself felt equal to being both father and mother. Duncan's own feelings are unknown to me. . . .

As far as intimate friends were concerned, my birth was an open secret. . . . Owing to my likeness to Duncan, even my grandmother Ethel must soon have had her suspicions. I was the only person successfully kept in the dark.

Charleston, the house where I was born, was a large, compact Sussex farmhouse, standing by itself just under Firle Beacon, the highest point in the range of downs that extends from the River Cuck in the east to the Ouse in the west. At the foot of the Beacon was a cornfield, and between this field and the house lay the farm buildings, dominated by a magnificent flint barn and granary, underneath which stood the hay-wagons and tumbrils, at the time still in use. . . .

With the arrival of peace, however, the *ménage à trois* was to split up; though Duncan and Bunny were both there when I was born, they were longing to get back to a semblance of normal life in London after the rigours and isolation of the war, and Bunny, whose tastes had been only temporarily homosexual, was already attracted by the idea of other and quite different love affairs. It was only Vanessa who was immobilised—worried by a domestic crisis and almost certainly by the fear that Duncan might finally desert her, in spite of the fact that he was now the father of her child.

In addition, almost immediately after my birth I fell ill, an illness reluctantly admitted by the local doctor. . . . I began to thrive on Gray's Powders and cow's milk. My two brothers, Julian and Quentin, ten and eight years older than myself, showed their feelings at my arrival in the world by running amok in the schoolroom, and were sent to stay with Virginia, while Vanessa lay in bed in a house without running water, electricity or telephone. True, the war was over, but food and coal were still scarce, and in addition to her anxiety on my account, Vanessa had difficulty in finding servants. . . .

My first conscious memory is not of Charleston but of France, always to me a second home, and of being carried, probably by Vanessa, up a flight of dark stairs, to find at the top a small, voluble lady in black, who gave me violet *bons-bons*. We were in Paris and she was almost certainly Angela Lavelli, a friend of Roger Fry, who occasionally offered her services to Vanessa as chaperone for her children. Whether the horns of the taxis honking in the rain, typical of the voices of Paris, belong to the same occasion I don't know; and whether being put to sleep in the luggage-rack is real or only hearsay I am not sure. I seem to have felt the string of the rack, like a hammock swaying to the rhythm of the train; and when I was given soda water to drink for the first time, astonished by its autonomous activity. . . .

It is at Charleston that I am next aware of myself. In photographs

of the time I am grave, round-eyed and healthy, held by a smiling
Nellie [the nanny] or a Madonna-like Vanessa, whose long straight
fingers are too apt to find their way into every crevice of my body.
It was then, at the age of five, that I first became aware of my own
identity, and with it of an exaggerated sweetness in Vanessa which
troubled me. Alongside the everyday brown-bread-and-butter of
my life in the nursery ran my relationship with her, conducted in
the very different atmosphere of drawing-room and studio. My
earliest sensations were of her propitiatory attitude, as though I
held a weapon in my small, fat hands. Anxious not to provoke, she
continually soothed and lulled me into acceptance. Cries, screams
or the sight of tears upset her; if she could buy peace she was satisfied. I longed for her to want me to be strong and independent,
whereas apparently all she desired was to suffocate me with ca-
resses. . . .

More than half our time was spent in London, where Vanessa
was now sharing No. 46 Gordon Square with Maynard Keynes. It
was a large, tall house with high rooms looking onto the square. On
the first floor, French windows opened onto a balcony with a black
iron railing that ran across the width of the house and was repeated
all along the row. Vanessa lived in the upper part, where the rooms
were much smaller and the ceilings sloped as in a country cottage.
Here, in her attic sitting-room, I was handed over to her every day
after tea, to play in front of the gas fire, its intricate cones of blue
and white changing to red and yellow, the little bowl of dusty water placed on the hearth like an offering in front of a shrine. I sat on
the chequered coconut matting, rough and uneasy to my bottom,
sheltered from the heat by Nessa's knees, while her hands would
take from the mantel-piece, and bring down to my level, the dried
oranges and lemons she used for darning socks. I gazed at them in
wonder, and threw them into the shadows. Nellie's sudden appearance at the door provoked screams of anger, and she would carry
me away, scarlet and protesting, leaving behind an anguished Vanessa.
    At bedtime I was sometimes allowed, as a privilege, to have my
bath in Maynard's bathroom, more splendid than ours. It was a
luxury chiefly because of its larger size, but there were glass jars full
of sponges and bath salts, and I well remember Maynard, in his elegant city suit, standing over me and showering me with these as I
sat in the water. . . .

Another London scene of that time is of Duncan standing stark naked in the back bedroom. Coming in by chance, I was amazed at the sight of him; what on earth was this strange appendage hanging between his legs? Seized by embarrassment but devoured by curiosity, I turned my back on him, bent down and, putting my head between my own legs, continued my rapt examination of his anatomy, prompted by the feeling that if I was upside down no one would spot the focus of my attention. Carried away by a smiling Vanessa, I burst into tears.

Another, quite different, occasion is also connected with Duncan. The large L-shaped room on the first floor is full of people. There are many children among the grown-ups, and in the warmth everyone is moving about and talking. There is the Christmas tree, decorated and lit with candles, and the long heavy curtains are drawn close. Standing by the sofa, I am suddenly accosted by a rather small Father Christmas. Whether he gives me anything or says anything to me I can't remember, but I am enchanted by his presence. I turn away to call attention to him, and when I turn back he has disappeared! Dismayed and disappointed, I look for him everywhere, particularly behind the curtains where it is suddenly dark, cold and frightening. Vanessa, to whom I appeal, only smiles and shakes her head; for some reason I am convinced it was Duncan—and feel horribly defrauded. . . .

One of the rare but regular events was tea with Leonard [Woolf] and Virginia. Virginia I knew would treat me as a special person—almost as Vanessa did. Leonard, however, was another matter, and was the only member of the family who could successfully refuse me something I wanted, whose very tone spelt the finality of real authority, against which there was no appeal. . . .

With the Hogarth Press in the basement and the solicitors on the ground floor I found myself in a rigorous world of machinery and accounts, very different from our own. Occasionally I collected Virginia from her writing-room in the basement, where she sat by a tiny gas fire surrounded by a wall of books done up in brown paper parcels as though to shelter her from a bombardment. I felt the austerity of their lives compared with ours—which was much fuller of wine and laughter, and of the ribaldry supplied by Julian and Quentin. Virginia and Leonard's work allowed them only just time for a frugal meal; preoccupied with thoughts of the *New Statesman* or the House of Commons, Leonard encouraged no elbows on the table, cigars or liqueurs—he was off, like a secretary-bird, to more gripping occupations. . . .

A year or two earlier than this Nellie went and Louie came. I accepted the change with a good grace, especially as from the first Louie possessed a moral ascendancy over me that attracted me enormously—to Vanessa this was a miracle. . . . Small and dark, she had a face like a squashed red apple with pips for eyes, and her short hair was tied up on one side by a floppy black ribbon. . . . Unafraid of my tantrums, she exercised an authority based partly on affection, and partly on values inherited from generations of country people. Quite rightly, Vanessa trusted Louie and was relieved to be able to leave me in her hands; I was completely happy. Her great virtue was that she was rough and solid, and with her I learnt to a certain extent to think of things outside myself. But she was also repressed and limited, her mind like a Stilton cheese, riddled with airless little tunnels that ended in dust. . . .

At Christmas, we spent two or three days with Clive's family at Seend in Wiltshire. For me, stimulated by the celebration of both Christmas and my birthday, the visit was one of excitement and pleasure, while for Vanessa it was an annually recurring period of boredom and misery. Her dislike must have grown with time, as she felt less and less justification in being there, constantly reminded by my presence that this was neither her place, nor mine. Ignorant of both facts I was unaffected by them, but Vanessa could remember her early years there as the eldest daughter-in-law, when her visits had been unbearably long. . . . I took it all at its face value, sniffing the Victorian smells with pleasure—the leather bindings of the *Illustrated London News*, the chrysanthemums in the jardinière, the smell of the spotless earth-closet and the polish on the oak floorboards. All these, added to the formality of our existence there, the presence too of the impeccable servants (some of whom were my friends), the hierarchy of the household, meant much to me: they created a yearly dip into romance, calling to mind the books I was fond of, such as *Little Lord Fauntleroy* and *The Secret Garden*. . . .

The house was a kind of petrified zoo. In the library a lamp stood on a tripod of hooves, once those of a deer, and on the writing-table, furnished with the thickest of inlaid writing-papers, was an ink-well made from another, larger hoof, perhaps that of the moose in the hall, king of all these relics. In the dining-room, pepper and salt were shaken out of a pair of silver owls, not of course stuffed and for that very reason more attractive. Every feather on their backs was etched with care, and they stood proud and steady on their metal feet. Most of the pictures were of animals—hounds, horses, dogs, including a large, unctuous chow, one of the dynasty which reigned over the life of Grandmamma. . . . Fond though the Bells were of animals, I doubt if they understood them more than most people. They looked to them for support, needing their loving if mute approbation. . . .

In 1927, while in the south of France with his mother and her sister Daisy McNeil, Duncan became ill with an infection diagnosed first as pneumonia, then as typhoid, in those days a much more common and frightening illness than now. Vanessa's anxiety was increased by the fact that she was not on the spot, and had little trust in Mrs. Grant's common sense. As soon as she could, she went to Cassis, a small fishing town between Marseilles and Toulon, accompanied by Grace and myself. She rented the Villa Corsica, almost opposite the Villa Mimosa, the much older house where the Grants lived. . . .

. . . Peter Teed . . . lived in the Château de Fontcreuse, a miniature château a couple of miles up the valley from Cassis. He owned the ruined shell of La Bergère, a small cottage previously inhabited by farmworkers, to which was attached a story about a miser and a shepherdess, of whom Vanessa painted a picture over the chimney-breast in the dining-room. She paid for the rebuilding of the house, consisting of five or six rooms, and in return was granted possession for ten years, which came to an end at the beginning of the war. The whole family used it, going there at different times of the year. Clive and Quentin enjoyed it in the hot summer months when the town was full of visitors and social life was amusing and, I gather, quite demanding. Vanessa, Duncan and myself went there in the comparative coolness of spring, when our translation from the dark English winter to the crystal clarity of the Mediterranean was a miracle. . . .

Installed eventually in La Bergère, Vanessa and Duncan were both completely happy, able at last to combine the pleasures of French life with the comfort of being in their own house. Our existence was always quietly domestic, and Vanessa's responsibilities scarcely diminished, but the fact that everything was French made it automatically delightful. Vanessa was an ardent Francophile and

believed that the French were vastly superior to the English in all
departments of practical life: better mechanics, electricians, dress-
makers, cooks, better at inventing domestic gadgets, at making
easels, stretchers, canvases and paints. So sensible to have paperback books, to dress their children in black pinafores and allow
them to stay up late, to have invented the siesta and go to market
every day returning with such delicious bread, to have invented
champagne, *Petit Larousse* and mayonnaise. . . .

If in the Cassis countryside there was no grass and no streams
or ponds, there was the pervasive fragrance of woodsmoke, the
sudden whiff of rosemary and thyme and the delicious smell of
resin. When the wind blew strongly the pines swayed and moaned
with self-flagellating pleasure, imitating the sound of the sea, as
though they who were rooted to the spot were overcome with longing to see the furthest corners of the world. The little road which
ran past the Villa Corsica climbed towards the Couronne de Charlemagne which dominated the town. Beneath it lay the Baie de la
Reine, a lonely half-circle bitten out of the pine-waving cliff, car-
peted with black straps of seaweed which stuck to one's wet skin
and got into the picnic basket. It was like fodder for horses, and we
sank up to our ankles in its dry, carbonised straw. Grey boulders
clustered at either end of the bay; if one clambered among them one
might find shells, dried sea-horses, coloured pebbles or desiccated
starfish. . . .

Vanessa sent me to boarding school when I was ten—or rather,
I went at my own request, after the idea was put into my head by
Louie, who wanted to leave us in order to get married.

. . . Vanessa . . . finally chose Langford Grove, near Malden in
Essex, which was run by an Irishwoman of character and charm,
called Mrs. Curtis, or Curty for short.

Vanessa had long ago made up her mind that schools—and education in general—were a waste of time. The best education was
assuredly self-acquired, and this was gained after one had left
school. I do not know what she expected to occur while one was
there, but she set little store by discipline, and hardly more by
processes of the intellect. Herself uninterested in knowledge, or in
the historical approach to any subject, she could hardly believe that
anyone close to her might feel differently. When, as in the case of
both Julian and Quentin, it became obvious that they did, she smilingly declined to involve herself, on the grounds of her fundamen-

tal incapacity. "You're so clever, darling, but I'm afraid I can't follow you," was in effect what she said, and though she never raised a finger to stop anyone doing what they wanted, such an attitude was in itself unhelpful.

She assumed that I would feel the same as she did, and by a gentle persuasion and reluctance to inculcate in me any spirit of objectivity, had made it impossible for me to do otherwise. Convinced that I was going to be an artist, she decided that I needed no more education than she had had herself. Seeing also that I had showed promise of being good-looking, she thought that I would "get along all right" without training of the mind: such indeed was her attitude of laissez-faire that one sometimes had the impression that she despised the intellect—or perhaps she only denied my right to develop mine, since she certainly admired the erudition of many of her friends, including her sister. . . .

Sending her children to school was therefore more of a practical measure—it would have been very difficult for her, with her professional life to take into account, to do otherwise. The best schools could do was to provide companionship, but she also thought that boys differed from girls: boys needed something tougher and more demanding than she could provide at home. Even so, schools were thought of as a necessary evil, their hardships were to be palliated whenever possible—Quentin, for instance, spent a term of his school life in France. Although I was younger when I started my formal education than either of my brothers, this was simply because I asked for it. I had "got it into my head" that I wanted to go, and her overriding principle was permissiveness.

Though my desire was only an instinct, it was surely a healthy one. I was aware of the cloying atmosphere that surrounded me, contributing to the disquieting "difference" I felt between myself and my friends. I did not realise that going to school would not dispel it, given that Vanessa's presence was to pursue me, undermining the whole purpose of the experience. I wanted to find firm ground but couldn't: I was prevented at every turn either by Vanessa or Curty singling me out for special treatment. It was as though some secret agent had hold of me, and, struggle as I might, my feet would never hit the earth. . . .

Thus on the level where I really needed help, school did nothing for me, and one could say that Vanessa's prejudice was justified. But she herself was on the side of the devil, since she persuaded Mrs. Curtis to let me drop any subject I found difficult. Latin, arithmetic

and allied subjects, games and some other disciplines were succes-
sively crossed off my timetable until, in addition to music and the
arts, I learnt only history, French and English. . . . If the school had
been more intransigent Vanessa would have disliked it—as it was,
the school itself aided and abetted her in sabotaging its purpose.
She could not believe that I wanted to learn anything—or that, if I
did, such a wish was worth supporting. . . .

Langford . . . was indeed an extraordinary school where one
was dragged out of bed late at night to take part in a play by W. B.
Yeats; where often, instead of going to church, one was prized out
of the brown crocodile of waiting girls to go on a picnic with Curty
or to spend the day with her son Dunstan on his yacht. On these occasions we were treated as grown-up only to find ourselves on the
following day back in the puerile, competitive atmosphere of a lot
of small girls thrown together, out of touch with the outside
world. . . .

To others our narcissism must have been painfully evident,
while to ourselves it seemed as though we were exhibiting the
purest spirit of objective detachment—in either case it was hardly
an atmosphere which welcomed outsiders, and the very fact that we
thought of them as such was a betrayal of our attitude. . . . I was
probably the worst offender, copycatting my elders without their
wit, always able to raise a laugh by such means, until one day
Bunny, my future husband, said, "You must stop being so disdain-
ful of those who are unlike yourself." It was one of those rare occasions when criticism really sinks in, and I *did* stop, as though
provided with a pair of brakes. . . .

School was becoming a bore: allowed by Vanessa to evade the
exam for which everyone else was working as the crowning effort
of their scholastic career, I was simultaneously deprived of this goal
and alienated by yet one more difference from my own generation.
At the same time I was permitted a certain amount of freedom. I
went from Langford to London once a week to join Vanessa and
Duncan in the National Gallery on Copying Day, when the public
were discouraged from entering by being asked for sixpence. I felt
self-conscious standing before Piero's "Baptism," painstakingly
copying the two angels behind the tree. The rare people who did
come would sometimes ask me my age—I was fifteen—and one day
I found myself pictured in a magazine, looking tall, thin and austere,
dressed in clothes more suitable for a woman of thirty, a reflection
of Vanessa. (Oddly—or perhaps logically—it was this photograph

which, in later days, Bunny kept pinned to the wall of his study.) It was, however, an immense pleasure to be in the cool, calm spaces of the Gallery, surrounded by pictures with which I soon began to be familiar, occasionally strolling round to look at other artists, some of them sitting on high stools, reproducing a famous masterpiece with infinite care.

Back at Langford, both music and the theatre became alluring passions. Louie had been the first to fire my enthusiasm for music, and had taught me the rudiments of the piano. Later I was sent to have lessons with Mrs. Smyth, a plump little lady in black satin and a noted teacher of children. I learned to play with fluency, although I never heard a professional soloist until after I went to school. . . .

It must have been about now that Curty tried to separate Beetle [a fellow student] and myself. Our relationship had become suspicious and she did all she could to prize us apart. It was a mistaken insight, as, far from being in love, we were slowly disengaging ourselves from a friendship we recognised as exhausted. All Curty did was to revive a dying flame, and encourage us, from natural perversity, to persist a little longer. Thus, though Beetle was supposed to spend her prep-time in the library where I was not allowed, all I had to do was to invent some excuse for wanting a book, and the sight of me would be enough for her to follow me through another door into the shrubbery, where we would hold long, intimate conversations. It was on one of these occasions that she suggested, on a note of moral superiority, that I was illegitimate, the daughter of Duncan. I was indignant, suspecting from her tone of voice that to be illegitimate meant to be ostracised, but while protesting that I was Clive's daughter, a flash of clairvoyance told me that she was right. There was, however, no more to be said, and I soon forgot about it.

Meanwhile life at Charleston continued, bathed it seemed in the glow of a perpetual summer. The household fell into two halves: on the one hand the painters, on the other the writers. If we lived happily together it was largely because, like birds or animals, we each had our own territory, duly respected by the others. . . .

But a divide of some kind, vague and unadmitted, stood between Vanessa and all of us. In our case it had nothing to do with class, and as she so evidently adored us, nothing to do with love and affection—and yet it had the effect of a seeming lack of sympathy and feeling, a black hole of impalpable depth. She herself was aware of it and would have given anything to cross it, but it affected all of us—those who, like myself, she could not bear to relinquish, and those like Clive, whose hold had slackened in an attempt to remain in touch, for whom she could no longer summon more than a stale affection. . . .

. . . She and Duncan would retire down the long passage to the studio, which was half work-room and half sitting-room, redolent of oil and turpentine. Easels and paintboxes stood about, brushes, sometimes festooned with cobwebs, emerged from jugs or jam jars, palettes and tubes of paint lay on stools or tables, while there was often a bunch of red-hot pokers and dahlias arranged in front of a piece of drapery. The gun-powder-coloured walls were hung with canvases of many shapes and sizes, and some of Duncan's favourite objects, such as a jointed—or rather disjointed—Sicilian wooden horse, a silver table-watch once given by her admirers to Lydia Lopokova, a fan and perhaps a child's drawing, could be seen balanced on the mantel-piece or pinned to a spare piece of wall.

On either side of the large stove were two chairs where they sat, Vanessa smoking the first of her self-imposed allowance of cigarettes, Duncan one of an endless chain always hanging from his lips. Plans for the present and the future were discussed at this time of day, as though life could not be lived until it had been decided exactly how to do it. . . .

If Duncan was elusive, egotistical and selfish in his love affairs, he submitted to Vanessa in every other area. She accepted this as a mother accepts the faults of a son; her compensations lay partly in the intense pleasure she took in Duncan's personality, partly in the reassurance she got from working with him. . . . It gave her courage to find that her ideas were understood almost before she had made them visible, and that, where painting was concerned, she could often be of help to him. . . .

The studio was the citadel of the house, the sanctuary in which I spent the most treasured hours of my life. It was here, basking in the atmosphere of hard work and concentration, that I felt the most important things would happen; I was a dragonfly that hovers, disappears and returns, a law unto itself. As in a hot-house, I was both protected and stimulated, without a shadow of responsibility. I can imagine nothing better than sitting on the studio floor engrossed in some manual occupation while those patient elders concentrated in their own dreamlike fashion on their art. I absorbed much in that atmosphere that I afterwards valued, aware that it was a privilege to have been there, but it was a little like giving a child strong alcohol. . . .

At week-ends visitors filled the house: Clive's friends, Lytton Strachey, Francis Birrell and Raymond Mortimer. . . .

There was however one man about whom I had no reservations, and that was Roger Fry. Equally welcome to both painters and writers, his arrival at Charleston was always an occasion for joy and sometimes amusement, as when, startled by the view of Bunny's aeroplane landing in an adjacent field just as he was driving up the lane, he immediately backed into the gatepost. For the Bloomsbury generation cars were an innovation, and while they welcomed them in theory, they never became accustomed to them in practice, and the machinery appeared to take control of them rather than the other way round. Intent on mastering it, however, Roger treated his car like some continuous scientific experiment, improvising various cures for its unpredictable behaviour with string, elastic bands or anything else that came to hand. . . .

To me he was a grandfather with paternal and avuncular overtones, whom I had no qualms in asking to perform miracles. Thus he would teach me to tie knots designed never to come undone, make for me paper birds that flew, stick things together for me without the faintest sign of impatience, his deep voice purring gently, a forgotten smile hovering over his features. . . .

I did not know then that Roger and Vanessa had been lovers, although I could not be unaware of the special consideration with which he treated her, the intimacy mixed with deference, and his way of listening to what she said, almost as though he still hoped for a message that had gone astray. . . .

It was to Roger that I owe my first taste of asparagus; he brought bundles of it down to Charleston, having obtained it cheaply from some unusual source. I had made up my mind to dislike it simply because everybody was so concerned I should do otherwise, but when it appeared on the table, limp rods of jade and ivory, I allowed him to persuade me to try it—and then, naturally, could not have enough. He nearly always brought something with him—on one occasion a paper kite in the shape of an eagle, on another a matchbox decorated by himself with a small piece of jewellery inside. I remember his sensuous feeling for objects, and the passionate quality of his interest in the subject of the moment, blind to all else. . . .

It was on a summer's afternoon in 1934 that Clive, coming out to find me on the gravel in front of the house, told me that Roger had died. He told me no details, only hugged me so tight that I could scarcely breathe and certainly could not ask questions: my one desire was to get away from his suffocating grip, which seemed actually responsible for this dreadful news, and held no comfort. It was the first death I had experienced, and the unreality of it left me disorientated. . . .

Vanessa was at Monk's House, with Leonard and Virginia, and when the news came she fainted. I don't remember her return to Charleston, but the following day, on going near her bedroom, I heard her howling in anguish. The door was closed, and it was beyond me to open it—indeed I dared not, almost fearing that the creature who made those noises could not be my mother. I fled from the house, and walked far over the fields before I could persuade myself to return.

One day, while looking for a pen or pencil on Vanessa's desk, I came across a letter describing how Roger had slipped on the polished floor, to lie there for a long time until he was found, and how in hospital he had died of pneumonia, unconscious of what was happening—and I felt the healing comfort of reality, the certainty that no one was trying to shield me from the truth—I was free to make of it what I could. . . .

Our intimacy with the Woolves, as we called them, was close in spite of the fact that the atmosphere we breathed was very different. . . .

Neither Virginia nor Leonard pretended to be other than they were; there was no facile morality or talking down to children—on the contrary Virginia was less remote than Vanessa and insisted on a reciprocity that filled the air with tension, which if sometimes alarming, was also stimulating. . . .

It was at teatime that I remember Virginia's arrival at Charleston, pacing through the house, followed by Leonard and Pinka, the spaniel, whose feathered pads would slap on the bare boards beside her master's more measured footfall. Virginia, seeing myself and Vanessa sitting by the fire or under the apple tree in the garden, would crouch beside us, somehow finding a small chair or low stool to sit on. Then she would demand her rights, a kiss in the nape of the neck or on the eyelid, or a whole flutter of kisses from the inner wrist to the elbow, christened the Ladies' Mile after the stretch of sand in Rotten Row, Hyde Park, where Vanessa in the past had ridden on a horse given her by George Duckworth. . . .

. . . My objection to being kissed was that it tickled, but I was only there to be played off against Vanessa's mute, almost embarrassed dislike of the whole demonstration. After a long hesitation during which she wished that some miracle would cause Virginia to desist, she gave her one kiss solely in order to buy her off. . . .

Leonard, like a vigilant and observant mastiff, remained unmoved by this behaviour. He was made of different material from the rest of us, something which, unlike obsidian, couldn't splinter, and inevitably suggested the rock of ages. . . .

For my birthday one year he gave me a splendid Victorian copy of *Pilgrim's Progress,* filled with pictures of Christians marching onwards in stiffly engraved wooden drapery. For some reason this book meant a great deal to me, and my eyes met those of Leonard across the festive tea-table in a moment of intense understanding I seldom experienced. For once I felt limpid and transparent, purged by emotion of all the dross of puerile secrecy and prevarication that usually submerged me. I had unwittingly come into contact with the passion in Leonard's character, which was both convinced and inflexible, contrasting with Vanessa's tendency to compound and procrastinate in favour of those she loved, and Duncan's ability to laugh away and ignore things he didn't like. . . .

As I grew older and she grew richer, Virginia made herself responsible for my dress allowance, which was £15 a quarter, quite enough for clothes and minor pleasures. Although the money was hers, Virginia had often forgotten to bring it with her and had to ask Leonard to pay me by cheque. It was a little like extracting water from a stone. Although Leonard did not protest, he went through a process of finding and putting on his spectacles, which made him look like a hanging judge, plunging his hand into some inner pocket to draw out his cheque book, then his pen, from which he unscrewed the cap with some difficulty, and finally writing out and signing the cheque with a trembling hand in complete silence—all of which seemed a test of my endurance. In the end he handed it over with a half-smile, like the flash of a needle under water. . . .

With hindsight I can see, though she never said so, that Virginia was disappointed in me: she wished I was more intelligent, more disciplined, and probably agreed with Leonard about my education. She would have liked me to have had more enterprise and

independence, to have been less predictable. Longing none the less
to seduce me, she succumbed to the more conventional ploy of trying
to improve my appearance, doing things which did not come naturally to her such as taking me to my first hairdresser, giving me jewels and feminine knick-knacks. But she also gave me her copy of
Mme. du Deffand's letters, presented to her many years before by
Lytton, and encouraged me to talk to the Rodmell Women's Institute on the theatre, helping me with my script. She tried to probe
and loosen my ideas, and, when she forgot to be brilliant and amusing, showed a capacity for intimacy which I found illuminating. At
such moments her critical faculties and insight were used intuitively,
and never made one feel inferior. I felt too that there was in her a
toughness and courage to which she clung through thick and thin,
of which one was aware under all the jokes and laughter.

Anxious to go to Italy before the heat became too severe,
Vanessa took me away from Langford after Christmas 1935, without entering me for the school certificate; I was barely sixteen. We
travelled to Rome in the unaccustomed grandeur of Vita Nicolson's
chauffeur-driven car, accompanied by Quentin. After a few days at
the Hassler Hotel, just off the Piazza di Spagna, we found a studio
in the Via Margutta, traditionally the artists' quarter. . . .

On the whole . . . we escaped confrontation with the régime,
and continued unalarmed in a hermetic but enjoyable existence.
Vanessa and Quentin painted every day in the Forum or in the
Medici Gardens under the ilex trees, while I wandered in the sun or
sat on a tomb learning the part of Juliet, for it had now been decided that I should go on the stage, and I immersed myself not only
in Shakespeare but in Bram Stoker's life of Henry Irving and any
other books I could find in the English Library. Every morning,
evading with some difficulty the lecherous old men on the bus, I
went to have lessons in Italian with Signorina Boschetti, who seemed
to have had as a student every English girl who had ever been to
Rome. There I pored over Italian verbs and the most famous of
Dante's sonnets, unable to concentrate, my thoughts drawn inex-
orably to their own secret but well-worn paths.

Duncan arrived at last, and took another studio in our building, from the roof of which we could see far out over Rome. He
continued to work on his decorations for the liner, the *Queen Mary*,
for which he used me as a model, while in the evenings we sat in the
marble interior of the café Greco drinking grappa, teasing him

about various relationships with virginal spinsters supposed to be in love with him, while half-hypnotised by our reflections in the sombre perspective of the café's mirrors. Afterwards we strolled home in the warm evening air past the theatrical decor of façade and fountain.

Finally we decided to hire a car and tour south to Naples, Pompeii and Paestum. We included the cascades of the Villa d'Este as well as those of Caserta, and stopped at every village market in the hope, often realised, of buying pottery or seductive if tattered pieces of silk and brocade. The weather became oppressively hot, and every evening, after a day spent in the back of a closed car, I suffered from an excruciating headache. Fearing Vanessa's solicitude, I tried to hide my pain, and by the time we had seen the sights and eaten the inevitable stodgy spaghetti, my one desire was to collapse on my bed. We seldom if ever stayed in a good hotel, indeed probably there were none. Our lavatory was usually a stinking hole in the ground, and hot water was difficult to procure. . . .

On our return to Rome Vanessa found a letter from Julian waiting for her; he had accepted a teaching job at the University of Wuhan, near Hankow, and was leaving for China in a month. Though not completely unexpected, this news was a shock to Vanessa who had probably not dreamt that China—four to five weeks away by boat, to her a country unknown and almost unreal—would be Julian's objective. She at once packed our things and set off for England, amazed and perhaps disappointed to find that I was in a state of excitement, not at the thought of saying goodbye to Julian, but at going down to Langford for the last two days of term. The temptation of flaunting my newly found independence was too great to be resisted.

In London I found Julian in a state of euphoria, shopping for topees and tropical suits, deciding on which gun and which books to take, as though he were going to be away for a lifetime. . . .

For Julian it was a supreme effort to gain his freedom, without if possible hurting his mother. He could not doubt, however, that he did cause her pain, but although this gave him a certain anguish, it could not quench his curiosity and enthusiasm. His love for Vanessa remained paramount: no other woman would come near her. She and he were more like lovers than mother and son. . . .

. . . I learnt much from the warmth of his embraces, which resembled those of a lover and were exactly what I needed. I had seen little if any physical contact between my parents, no sharing of a bed or kisses snatched at odd moments, and I was deprived of sensuality; as a consequence I was, in spite of a hidden preoccupation with sex, deeply repressed. Both Duncan and Vanessa and Leonard and Virginia were, as couples, asexual if not virginal, and unable to initiate me, and there was something about Clive's well-meant overtures that repelled me. Julian's tenderness was therefore all the more important and all the harder to lose, especially at a time when I was on the threshold of my own sexual advances.

I was lively, flirtatious and I think affectionate, with, like Virginia and Vanessa, an intense longing to be loved. I was not entirely stupid, but I was uninquisitive, timid and blinded by the egotism which, I think I may truthfully say, I had always been encouraged to manifest: I was insensitive to the needs and feelings of other people. My unbalanced flights towards independence were mere emotional flashes in the pan, unsupported by thought or reflection. Some strength of purpose I must have had, but even now I am unable to say what it was. . . .

. . . Weighed against those of other people, my feelings, even to myself, seemed to count for nothing. I had to nurse them in private to convince myself of their validity, and was unaware that this was the worst mistake I could have made. I lacked the ability to remain true to myself through thick and thin, in spite of the fact that I often appeared to other people as obstinate and intolerant—but this was a mere smokescreen, like the ink of the cuttle-fish. I was in reality a ready victim, and once I had been knocked down was unable to regain my balance. I was easily demoralised, and my need for affection led me to practise self-deception and subterfuge in order to get it. . . .

Though I was indifferent to such things, I could not remain . . . insensitive to the menace of the international situation. . . .

. . . Never again would we know those calm country silences, when all noises were either animal or human, when the sound of a tree falling two miles away defined the distance between it and ourselves, or the twittering of a lark in the sky measured the spaces of blue air above; even the mechanical hum of the threshing machine called forth a sympathetic echo from the empty, sunbaked fields. Now these sounds were rapidly becoming drowned by the noise of car, lorry and aeroplane, never, in the foreseeable future, to be silenced. Lying in the grass listening to phrases about bayonets and fifth columnists, Hitler and Fascists, I froze, like a mouse, in my place, hoping that these terrifying images would pass me by.

The next year was in many ways an exciting one. For the first time in my life I found myself living away from home, in a foreign and highly sympathetic environment. . . . I went to Paris to live with some friends of the Bussys with whom, as one is apt to do in those years of one's life, I fell deeply in love—a love affair of friendship that has lasted to this day.

François Walter, handsome and bearded, was a civil servant and at the same time a left-wing agitator for peace, editing a paper called *Vigilance*. At the threat of a *coup d'état* by the *Action Française*, François learnt to shoot with a pistol, lending our lives a quality which in England would have been termed overdramatic but in France seemed merely realistic. Zoum, his wife, came from a family of Belgian artists, and she herself looked like a figure from a picture by Georges de La Tour, dignified, ample and superb. She too was a painter; her easels and canvases were to me a familiar adjunct of life, although her paintings were quite unlike any I had seen before. Deeply in love, she would become desperately anxious if François were late for supper, and hang out of the window on the sixth floor, hoping to hear the sound of his taxi. When he eventually returned, he was bitterly reproached and then passionately embraced before being given a delicious meal. Immediately afterwards François would plunge into editing his paper, pacing up and down the apartment until far into the night, sustained on minute cups of black coffee.

To me such scenes were a revelation of the possibilities in human relationships hitherto suspected only through literature.

On my return to London in the spring of 1936 I went almost immediately to the London Theatre Studio as a pupil of Michel Saint-Denis, whom I had last seen as Noé in the Compagnie des Quinze. . . . As a student I was lost in love and admiration for him, seeing in him a Zeus-like father figure for whose good opinion I craved. . . .

. . . When, for example, I played the part of one of the heroines in a comedy by Dryden, Michel told me that for five minutes I had succeeded in acting—"You *can* act!" This was a red-letter day, its greatest merit being that, not having put it to the test, I can still dream that it might have been true. Michel was always particularly kind and charming to me, but his treatment of me as someone "special" added to my sense of unreality: I felt like a paper doll trying to enter an alien world. . . .

In spite, or perhaps because of, the growing threat of war—as though the light while it narrowed also grew brighter—life in London was very pleasant. Vanessa, Duncan and I lived at No. 8 Fitzroy Street, now destroyed but then one of those mid-nineteenth-century houses with large rooms and heavy cornices . . . while the upper regions were allocated to various tenants. I had a room at the top which, though it looked on to the street, was reasonably quiet. . . .

It was at this time that my adoration of Duncan was at its peak. If, at the age of six or seven, I had chosen him as my "husband" in preference to Clive, it was probably because I felt instinctively that he was my father; but it was also because he was younger, more approachable and more gentle. He was never didactic, he never bullied, and seldom offered advice unless it was asked. Many people, afraid of seeming insensitive, exaggerate their emotional reactions. Duncan never did so; neither did he appear to repress his feelings, but remained intimately in touch with his instincts. Considerate and good-mannered, there was a sense of proportion in all he did. . . .

Eventually, after about a year and a half, Julian came home, resigning from his post at Wuhan University partly as the result of an amorous indiscretion, partly because he could no longer ignore the Civil War in Spain. He had grown thinner and was changed, and so was I. . . .

Appropriately enough, I was dancing at the London Theatre Studio in a dramatic ballet on the theme of Goya's *"Desastros della Guerra."* It was my most successful part and one I very much enjoyed. In June that year we gave a fortnight's showing to friends and public. One evening after the performance had started Duncan suddenly appeared in the narrow alleyway outside the theatre: Julian had been killed, would I come home immediately? Trembling, I climbed the ladder leading to the lighting platform from where Michel watched all our shows. Seeing something serious was wrong, he immediately came down with me and, hearing what had happened, put his arm round me. Of course, if someone else could take my part, I could go home.

Before long we were at Charleston again, and Vanessa lay on a daybed in the studio looking down the empty garden path, occasionally weeping, more often exhausted. It was decided to publish a book made up of Julian's letters from China and other writings with contributions from such friends as Maynard and Bunny. . . .

I remember that summer as endless, hot and tiring. One day when Vanessa was better she took me into the drawing-room at Charleston and told me that Duncan, not Clive, was my real father. She hugged me close and spoke about love: underneath her sweetness of manner lay an embarrassment and lack of ease of which I was acutely aware, and which washed over my head like the waves of the sea. It is hard to say what prompted her to tell me just at that moment—how much was due to a plan conceived long ago, and how much because of her actual state of emotion. It is very likely that she felt, however obscurely, that she owed this gesture to Julian's memory. Not only would the knowledge she was about to impart help me to mature, but he would approve of the honesty of her gesture. . . . Anxious about how I was going to take it, she said it need change nothing, since it was the intimacy of the present, not the facts of the past, that was important: my love for Quentin, for example, need not be affected by the fact that I now knew he was my half-brother. I remember the curious little shock this assertion gave me and I recognised the fact that I did indeed love him, though never before had I thought of saying so, which may indicate what an undemonstrative family we were. Although Julian had written to her that I was even more emotional than he was himself, I was not an outgoing child. If Vanessa expected me to show surprise at her information, she must have been disappointed: I hardly batted an eyelid, though when she left me to myself I was filled with euphoria. It was a fact which I had obscurely known for a long while. Whatever explosion there may have been occurred far below the surface: at the time I simply felt that a missing piece had been slotted into place.

Still, I did not talk to Duncan: perhaps I was afraid he would deflate my exultation. I preferred to gloat alone, unable to overcome my feeling that, with such a father, I had been marked for a special destiny. I was the little girl, red rose in hand, who falls in love with the prince, the hideous and charming beast. It never occurred to me that I was fantasising a Duncan that could never be. Nor did I realise, in my desperate need of a father figure, the true nature of my sacrifice. I should have spoken to Duncan. As it was, Vanessa said no more, he said nothing, and I remained closeted in dreams.

My relation to Duncan never got beyond this: I adored him, but the will to be his daughter was all on my side, and was received with no more than a bland serenity. It was an asexual barrier of simplicity and kindness which baffled me. I could not see round it, but—I cannot now help wondering—was there anything further to see? Assuredly there was, but it was too nebulous, private and self-centred to respond to the demands of a daughter. As a result our relationship, though in many ways delightful, was a mere simulacrum. . . . My dream of the perfect father—unrealised—possessed me, and has done so for the rest of my life. My marriage was but a continuation of it, and almost engulfed me.

Although Vanessa comforted herself with the pretence that I had two fathers, in reality—emotional reality, that is—I had none. It was impossible to associate Duncan with any idea of paternity— and he never tried to assume such a role. Clive acted better, but carried no conviction, for he knew the truth. How different it would have been if we had all acknowledged it. . . . Vanessa never reflected that perhaps he too was inhibited by her prevarication, just as she never realised that, by denying me my real father, she was treating me even before my birth as an object, and not as a human being. No wonder she always felt guilt and I resentment, even though I did not understand the true reason for it. . . .

As a result I was emotionally incapacitated—though it would be a great mistake to think that, had she told me before that my father was Duncan, my life would have been easier. My difficulties might indeed have been much the same, since his character would have remained constant. It was knowing the truth, instead of being deceived by those who had not fully considered the consequences of their lie, that would have changed everything.

But curiously enough, when the moment came, being told the truth made the world seem less and not more real. No one seemed capable of talking openly and naturally on the subject: Vanessa was in a state of apprehension and exaltation, and Duncan made no effort to introduce a more frank relationship. They gave the impression of children who, having done something irresponsible, hope to escape censure by becoming invisible.

Vanessa imagined that she herself could shoulder the entire situation, but although this was meant well, it was a gesture compounded of arrogance as well as generosity, and showed blindness, if not indifference, to reality. It would be easy to say she failed to recognise the importance of the relationship between father and daughter, but I do not think this was so—she evidently hoped that the one between myself and Clive would be fruitful—but she may not have understood that a daughter longs to be possessed by her father, and this Clive was in no position to do.

He did, however, show a greater sense of responsibility towards me than Duncan—although my general insecurity prevented me responding to it wholeheartedly. I suffered from reservations which I attributed to his inherent coldness, or to certain innuendoes and implications to sexual subjects, which I found embarrassing. Within certain limits, however, we got on very well, although as I look back on our relationship I regret that, at the time, I did not do his intentions justice.

Clive had welcomed my arrival in the world with generosity, and had continued to show a warm interest in my existence, even on rare occasions taking Vanessa's place when she wanted to go away—something Duncan never did. Of course, Nellie or Louie was always there, but as a point of reference, Clive was reliable, calm and good-humoured. When, as a very small child with mumps, appositely and without tears, I said, "Oh dear, I've fallen out of bed," he was delighted at my natural philosophy, and repeated the story at intervals for the next twenty years—a reiteration which irritated and blinded me to the affection that lay behind it. I remember too an occasion when I was rude to him. I was still small, but old enough to know what not to say, yet my tongue, like a lizard's, seemed to act on its own, and I came out with something now lost in the limbo of the unconscious—some remark met on his side with a blank surprise, a disbelief which showed that he was wounded, although I never heard any more about it.

On another occasion, having reached the age when Seend no longer seemed the magical place it once had been, I asked Vanessa whether I need go there for Christmas. She referred me to Clive, and with some trepidation I went to see him in his study at No. 50 Gordon Square, where he sat in his cane-backed chair puffing his pipe. Although innocent of all desire to cause pain, I have little doubt that my manner was tactless: young as I was, I did not realise that he was and always would be fond of a place and people that I, with youthful inconsistency, had just rejected. Clive looked at me over his spectacles in silence, and I knew that his feelings were hurt.

Diplomatically, however, he promised that, if I went to Seend this year I need not go the next. For me it was a milestone because, even if he did not realise it, it was the first time I had talked to him as an adult, capable of doing something from choice rather than because I was told to.

. . . Clive enjoyed showing me off. He was also, however, sensitive to my predicament, and knowing that Duncan was incapable of showing an interest in my sexual education, gave me *Daphnis and Chloe* to read—pastoral and poetic and perfectly adapted to my stage of development. As my French improved he gave me *Manon Lescaut,* followed by the rather curious choice of *Les Liaisons Dangereuses,* which, as I might have known, was a Bloomsbury favourite. It was thanks to Clive that I became an enthusiastic admirer of Mérimée, enjoying *Carmen, Colomba, La Vénus d'Ille,* and some of the *Lettres à une Inconnue.*

Between Clive and Duncan there was not the faintest shadow of jealousy—indeed it seems absurd to mention such a thing—and although this was no doubt largely because Duncan was a homosexual and that there was therefore no masculine rivalry, they also had a deep affection and understanding for each other. Clive, while he teased Duncan mercilessly for giving himself the airs of a colonel or major of some long-forgotten regiment, or for his almost uncritical catholicity of taste in art, or for any of his other idiosyncrasies, never patronised him, was always generous and never inconsiderate. It would have been only too easy for him to treat Duncan as an escaped lunatic or an *enfant terrible,* but this he never did. His respect for Duncan's personality was always evident, even if never directly spoken of. On his side, Duncan understood Clive and appreciated his sophistication, his erudition and the scope of his reading, which would often form the topic of their conversation. . . .

My relations with my husband David Garnett had begun flirtatiously in 1936 or '37, when I was still at the London Theatre Studio, and had gathered in intensity until, in 1938, it had become a courtship—though not a love affair—about which I had very ambivalent feelings. I had known him all my life and had been to stay at Hilton Hall, his house in Huntingdonshire, where I met his wife, Ray, a sister of Frances Partridge, and her two small sons, Richard and William. Ray was quiet and still, very gentle; sitting before the open fireplace she asked me friendly questions, but as she always remained in the country I never got to know her well.

Bunny began to take me out to restaurants and theatres, for picnics in the country or to see his mother in her woodland cottage. He told me long stories to which I listened with hungry avidity: through them I caught glimpses of a vigorous mentality as well as of a life full, it seemed, of adventure—a life I longed to have experienced myself. In a continuous saga he exposed his own personality—or that part of it which he felt would create the best impression. I could hardly have been more gullible, whereas he, though appearing guileless, was certainly not without skill. He talked about his past—so very much longer than my own—and presented me with a youthful Corydon, unsophisticated, rash, adventurous and innocent, who attracted such people as D. H. Lawrence, Edward Thomas, H. G. Wells, and other writers whom, through him, I came to love. When he told me about his attempt to rescue the Indian political leader Savarkar from prison, I immediately saw him as another Rudolph Rassendyll, albeit without the aristocratic overtones. His visit to Russia as a boy of twelve, when he learnt the language by spending long days with the shepherds on the steppe, and his association with the revolutionary emigrés such as Prince Kropotkin and Sergei Stepniak, were incidents which seemed to connect me by a direct line with the world of the Russian novelists that I was just beginning to know. The fact that, when young, Bunny never had a penny in his pocket, went everywhere on foot or on bicycle and was an only child, gave him the aura of the fool in the fairy story who always wins the princess in the end, either by fair means or foul.

He never disguised the fact that he had had many love affairs, though he left out those which might have touched me more nearly. As a child of Bloomsbury I took all this for granted, just as I felt it perfectly natural for him to make love to me while at home he had a wife and children. As it was he who took the initiative, I felt it was more his affair than mine—no other attitude occurred to me. I was already in the grip of a personality a hundred times more powerful than my own, in which I put far too much trust for the good of either of us. The accounts of his amorous exploits caused me no pangs of jealousy; his experience with the novelist Dorothy Edwards and his love affair with the artist's model Betty May—the tiger woman—were, for me, sealed in a past that was long over, packed away like a trunk in the attic. But as he opened it to take out a piece of crumpled brocade, with his slow speech, his evident strength of feeling and natural warmth, he had an unerring sense of the dramatic. He sat broad-shouldered in the lamplight, on his face a lop-sided smile; his blue eyes looking straight at and through me, deprived me of the ability to see that, under an urbane and charming exterior, Bunny was a bulldozer.

However intimately connected with Vanessa and Duncan, Bunny came from an entirely different background (although no doubt his grandfather, Richard Garnett, Keeper of Printed Books at the British Museum, knew Leslie Stephen). Bunny's parents, however, had no thought of being stars in the literary firmament, but belonged to its very core. They were less creative than professional, his mother a translator, his father a publisher's reader, both remarkable and highly intelligent people. They were hard working, frugal, blind to visual pleasures and indifferent to luxury. . . .

One day early in our relationship Bunny invited Duncan and myself for the week-end to Hilton. As we drew up outside in his car, he turned round in his seat and surprised me with a long, sexy kiss, which Duncan in the back can hardly have avoided noticing. Bunny, although he had talked to me much of his years at Charleston in 1916–18, had been less than explicit about his love affair with Duncan—he was indeed never completely open about it. Neither had he told me that when I was born he had boasted that one day he would marry me. His kiss, though primarily addressed to me, was an unmistakeable warning to Duncan of his intentions, which it was a pity that Duncan ignored: Bunny, however, knew instinctively that he would. The place chosen was also significant, being within sight of the window from which Ray, at that moment, might be watching for our arrival.

She was already ill and Bunny was even then worried about her health. She had been operated on for cancer, and during the year 1938–39 her slow deterioration was always at the back and often in the front of his mind. His imaginative understanding of physical pain increased his distress, as did his guilt at the failure of their marriage, and the recognition that Ray had been, to a large extent, the victim of his own egotism. His appeal for sympathy as a repentant husband added to his attraction: he offered me a role in a tragic adult situation in which I had no responsibility. Ray was hardly real to me, and, although she was an object of genuine sympathy, I could not fail to realise that my youth and vitality were, in contrast, a strong attraction for Bunny.

The progress of our love affair was slow compared with Bunny's usual style with women; but he remained patient and tactful. There were many outings in London, some week-ends at Charleston, usually with the family, although on one occasion when we very much hoped to be alone, Vanessa and Duncan turned up at the last minute with the obvious intention of supervising us. Eventually I gave way to Bunny's insistence and lost my virginity, appropriately enough, in H. G. Wells's spare bedroom.

But however strong the physical attraction, I refused to say I loved him; I felt obscurely that real love was a different matter, and my heart was full of doubts which refused to disappear, although I could not put them into words. . . . The grown-ups, as I still thought of them, were lined up behind me waiting expectantly to see what I would do; and, at the time, I failed to recognise that Bunny belonged to their generation, not to mine. That was why, I later realised, no one of my own age had stood a chance beside him.

. . . Although it was natural for him to want me to share his own enthusiasms, his behaviour was addressed as much to Duncan and Vanessa as to myself. It was very much as though he was saying to them, "Stop me if you can!"

These moments of mixed happiness and anguish took place against a background of the Civil War in Spain and the growing certainty of a European war. In anticipation of this, Bunny had entered the Air Ministry, spending half the week in Fitzroy Street, where he had rented a room opposite my own, and the other half at Hilton. In the autumn I started going to the Euston Road School as an art student, but the following term was almost entirely taken up by an illness which, foolishly concealed, proved to be painful though not dangerous. As none of our bed-sitting rooms was suitable for an invalid, Bunny put me in a nursing home—a rather dramatic development which brought Vanessa to London in a state of intense anxiety. It would have been more tactful to put me to bed in her studio and call the family doctor, but Bunny realised how little I relished being nursed by Vanessa. . . .

In September war was declared: we listened to Chamberlain on the radio in the garden at Charleston, which was glowing with the reds and oranges of the dying summer. The unreality of the occasion was in itself frightening, and yet there we all were—except for Julian—untouched and uncommitted, and seemed likely to remain so. As the suspension of hostilities continued throughout the autumn, so our sense of reality declined in direct ratio to the mounting tension: each day we expected and almost wanted something to happen, but were relieved when it did not.

In the early spring Ray died, and Bunny took a farmhouse in the Weald, about five miles from Charleston. It must have been about this time, one day at Rodmell, that Virginia took me aside and asked me whether I was going to marry Bunny, implying that it would distress Vanessa very much if I did. At the time I had little thought of the future, a future threatened with the unknown caprices of war and social upheaval, and I said in good faith that I had no intention of it.

Meanwhile from our farmhouse we watched the Battle of Britain, seeing the Messerschmitts and Spitfires spiralling to earth as the smoke from their fuselage streamed upwards. In the air the planes were like toys, and it was hard to believe that the airmen manipulating them held our fate in their hands, so abstract seemed their performance from below. . . .

It was here at Claverham that I last saw Virginia, who with Leonard—and in spite of petrol rationing—came over to tea. With more than her usual insistence she clung to her "rights," to which I reacted with more than my usual impatience. Perhaps I sensed a greater intensity than ever under her endearments, and for some reason could not respond with as much warmth as she would have liked—but then when could one ever have done so?

Three days later I went down to the village to telephone to Charleston, and Clive told me she had disappeared, and was believed drowned. When, on returning to the house, I called out to Bunny, he put out his arms to embrace me with a warm bearlike gesture that in a crisis I learnt to expect from him.

At Charleston I found a fragile but not overwhelmed Vanessa: it must have been an event she had expected for most of her life, and now that it had happened it had lost its power to shatter. Virginia's death merely confirmed the general pessimism and sense of futility which surrounded us. On Duncan's arrival from London she broke the news to him, and we all three clung together in the kitchen, in a shared moment of despair, feeling that the world we knew, and the civilisation Virginia had loved, was rapidly disintegrating. Leonard, white from exhaustion, though as always objective and dispassionate, sat in the drawing-room and told us how they had found her body in the river, the river that Julian had loved, and where I could remember a dolphin that had once tempted Virginia down to the bank to stand beside us, watching its strange and lovely antics.

Bunny, who on Ray's death had been given compassionate leave from the Air Ministry, was now transferred to a secret propaganda department at Bush House. For the time being we lived in a service flat in Clifford's Inn. It was a new block, built between the wars, and predictably depressing. . . .

It was in these hideous and claustrophobic surroundings that Bunny began to talk of marriage, a proposition which at first I firmly resisted. Now that I was living with him in London, Vanessa and Duncan's presence impinged on us far less than it had the year before, since they had become more or less settled at Charleston. Vanessa, who had always been in favour of a love affair, thought that marriage would be a fatal mistake. She foresaw responsibilities that she thought me unprepared for, as well as the sacrifice of my freedom to paint. She thought that Bunny at forty-eight was too old and that my feelings for him were unlikely to last; she was also afraid that I would suffer from his being something of a libertine.

She told me none of these things, however, emitting a vague feeling of worry and distress, the effect of which was to exasperate me. Her fears were not only for me but for Duncan, who had shown himself to be upset and jealous. Had the situation been less fraught with unavowed emotion, much of it impossible for me to understand, I might have felt free to enjoy my love affair without committing myself; but the feelings it provoked floated just beneath the surface, incomprehensible and menacing. Vanessa hovered in an anguish that I now find so easy to understand, holding long tête-à-tête conversations with Bunny. Her one desire was to protect both myself and Duncan, as it appeared, from life itself, when what I most needed was liberty and freedom. I should of course have asked questions; but I had been told the "truth" so often that I thought I must know it.

To many people it must have been obvious that my feeling for Bunny was not that of a wife, or wife-to-be; Maynard, for instance, appealed to him not to go on with the marriage. Bunny, however, had the bit between his teeth and not even Maynard's eloquence and authority could stop him. He was always immensely attracted by youth, drawing from it a strength which enabled him to remain young himself for an amazingly long time. . . .

. . . Perhaps it was natural that no one told me the one fact that seems to make sense of Bunny's behaviour: that he had proposed bed to Vanessa and had been rejected. Even though I now know this, I still find it hard to believe he was in love, since nothing he ever said pointed to more than a natural affection for her. But his affection coexisted with an unacknowledged resentment, and its only outlet lay in abducting her daughter.

When Bunny said at the cradle-side that he meant to marry me, no one took him seriously, it was so evidently an extravaganza disguised as a compliment, and neither Duncan nor Vanessa was in the habit of analysing other people's behaviour. But Bunny meant it literally, and did not forget it, and, knowing his nature, I find it impossible to believe that it was unconnected with jealousy, and perhaps with a desire to assimilate one who had been a part of both Duncan and Vanessa. Bunny longed to be loved, and to take possession of the loved one. . . . It seems clear enough now that when he carried me off to live as his wife and be a stepmother to his sons, his purpose was, at least in part, to inflict pain on Vanessa.

He knew also that he was driving a wedge between Vanessa and myself, one that in fact remained for ever. It was in this situation that Vanessa showed an almost saintly generosity, not only proving Virginia's early dictum true, but putting into practice the virtues of tolerance and forbearance so dear to Bloomsbury. . . . Once more in the drawing-room at Charleston there was a scene between Vanessa and myself. She may have tried to tell me what her feelings really were, but became hysterical—an unnerving experience, which I could not face the risk of repeating. It is only now that I wonder what it was she was trying to tell me. My inadequacy as comforter, and my lack of the most rudimentary understanding, haunt me to this day.

. . . I . . . had . . . [never] really allowed myself to realise how close Bunny and Duncan's relationship was from 1915 to 1918. I paid lip-service to the broad-mindedness of my parents, but I was shocked, not morally but physically, by the idea of homosexuality—a natural result perhaps of Duncan's lack of response to me—and I was unable to bring myself to think about it. Neither did I understand how incestuous my relationship with Bunny was. . . . The story of our marriage could be summed up as the struggle on his side to maintain the unlooked-for realisation of a private dream, about which in spite of an almost wilful blindness, he must have had deep misgivings; and on mine the slow emancipation from a nightmare, which was none the less painful because I thought of it as almost entirely my own fault. Years later he would never admit that there was anything out of the ordinary in his love for the daughter of an old friend and her lover, with whom he had been so intimate. . . .

. . . Bunny, . . . had I not married him, . . . would have been a perfect friend, one in whom I could have safely confided and who would always have given me good advice. When I eventually left him, although he was deeply hurt and never really recovered, he could not wish me ill: whatever he failed to understand he courageously tried to put up with.

We did not invite Vanessa and Duncan to the wedding, an omission which Quentin tried to repair. But we did not listen to his arguments, and I now see that it would have been impossible for Bunny to tolerate their presence at a ceremony which so flagrantly symbolised his victory. They were deeply wounded, and never afterwards alluded to what they probably considered as a piece of boorish stupidity.

The wedding took place at the substitute for the Guildhall, which had been bombed. We invited Frances and Ralph Partridge as our witnesses, together with my stepson William, who had just left school. I had on a too-short pink cotton dress and a straw hat more suitable for a woman of forty, into which I had pinned a rose. Standing in the small dreary room where the ceremony was held, I was for a moment almost overcome by panic: supposing, when the clerk asked for my consent, I said, "No"? What a marvellous way out, what a simple solution! But I said, "Yes," and the deed was done. I drowned my sense of guilt in champagne at the Ivy, Clive's favourite restaurant, where we had lunch. Then we caught the night train to Northumberland, where Bunny had just bought a small property.

As for myself, I seemed unwittingly to have plunged into a stagnant pool where nothing ever changed. My effort towards liberation from Vanessa had ended in a feeling of guilt and its concomitant paralysis. Although she was now over a hundred miles away, Vanessa was omnipresent: I still had not understood that some kind of confrontation was necessary—running away would solve nothing. With the birth of my children I undertook too many responsibilities, in an effort to disguise the fact that I was both lost and unhappy. Vanessa had always said, "All I want is for you to be happy, darling,"—and now that I was not so, it seemed that the least I could do was pretend. . . .

It was in 1944, when I was pregnant with my second daughter, that Vanessa discovered a lump in her breast, which she mentioned to me in a letter, telling me at the same time that she expected to be operated on almost immediately. I was in Yorkshire with Bunny when I received a telegram from Duncan to say that the operation had been successfully performed. No one called it a mastectomy or said it was cancer: the severity of the ordeal was submerged under a veil of stoicism and mystery. Vanessa must have suffered enormously from an experience for which in those days there was no psychological preparation and no support to be found from sharing it with others. For someone of her temperament this would in any case have been difficult, and she retired to the wartime austerity of Charleston rather as a wounded animal creeps into its lair, where Quentin's gentleness and Duncan's optimism may have done something to allay her natural anxiety. It was Vanessa's misfortune that at that time cancerous illnesses were regarded almost as though they were family scandals, to be brushed under the carpet; no one quite realised what she had been through, least of all myself. With the passing of time, however, she regained her strength, and salvation came to her through my children—she completely surrendered herself to their spontaneous affection.

By 1947 I had four daughters, the youngest twins. The years of their childhood gave me infinite pleasure—more than I can put into words. I felt and was very close to them, and at least one of them has told me that as a mother I was vivacious and full of gaiety. I certainly did not spend all my time moping about the failure of my marriage since, for one thing, I could not bear to admit that it was a failure. I was young and energetic, I loved country life. . . .

. . . One of the reasons for my lack of emotional growth was the amount of hard work which I put into running my household. We lived in the same house in Huntingdonshire that Bunny and Ray had occupied when Duncan and I visited them before the war. Ray had left traces of her own personality on this charming seventeenth-century house, and the effect was so sensitive and fragile that I was afraid to touch it. It was only very gradually that, as walls and furnishings needed to be repainted or replaced, I felt free to impose my own more robust taste. We had little money and no luxuries, the house was unbelievably cold and draughty, our methods of heating antiquated, our supplies of hot water inadequate. For the first seven years of their lives the children were, it seemed, always ill, especially in winter.

It is true I had help, but as I refused to give up music and painting I was in a constant state of fatigue, and went to bed each night almost giddy with exhaustion. As I have said, a lot of this was unnecessary—a way of escaping thought and reflection. But it happens to many young mothers; once the extraordinary and irreplaceable experience of maternity has receded, one's horizon becomes limited to that of the children and one is temporarily incapable of further development. Even if there had been time to make new contacts I would have found it impossible to profit from them, and holidays offered only physical relaxation, not spiritual renewal.

Although Bunny was helpful and sympathetic, my dulled sensibilities only made our relationship less equal. In addition, there was social life. The house was often full of visitors: we had many friends in Cambridge as well as in the village, and, seeing my life through their eyes, I built up an image of myself as the perfect young mother-housewife-hostess, and spent much of my energy living up to it. The only drawback—and it was a very serious one, symptomatic of what lay underneath—was my growing misunderstanding with Bunny, and his shattering rages, which, disconcertingly and tragically, often included the children.

In early days I was swept off my feet by Bunny's concern for me: never had I experienced anything of the kind, except for certain brief moments with Julian. Either I was blind to his excess or, having been deprived of displays of feeling, I hungered for them. When we were man and wife, however, I gradually became repelled by his emotionalism, which always seemed just off the mark. I became afraid it would distort my own emotions, and took to keeping them more and more to myself. I began to imitate Vanessa's habit of reserving her most precious feelings to herself, and appeared far colder and more critical than I really was; and this to Bunny was anathema.

During my entire marriage my relation to Duncan and Vanessa remained far too close. . . . Incestuously bound up with each other, we found each other's company more familiar, less exacting and, by the same token, less stimulating than anyone else's. For me there seemed to *be* no one else; domesticity put me out of bounds on the one hand, and on the other my close association with my parents hedged me round with invisible barriers.

In spite of my inability to keep away from them, my relation with Vanessa had not changed, and was as negative as ever. When I visited Charleston, I would sit with her by the studio stove, unable to utter a word. Neither of us knew what was wrong: we were submerged by inertia and depression. I do not know what prevented me from taking the initiative, why I did not think of asking questions, of opening up the past—and with this way blocked, there was no other. . . .

According to Paul Roche, in 1918, the year of my birth, Duncan had told Vanessa that he felt incapable of having further sexual relations with her. Thus her victory, if it was one, in keeping Duncan for herself was at best pyrrhic, gained at a cost she failed to assess. She seems to have accepted it as a necessary sacrifice for the privilege of living with this immensely attractive yet incomplete human being, to whom she was so passionately attached, and there must have been a strong element of masochism in her love for him, which induced her to accept a situation which did permanent harm to her self-respect. . . .

I remember [a] . . . holiday on the Yonne at a small inn, the patron of which had been an active member of the resistance. . . .

The last of these holidays was as late as 1960, when Vanessa and Duncan rented the Bussys' house, La Souco, in Roquebrune near Menton. This time they were not in a hotel but in a home from home, accompanied by Grace to do the cooking. . . .

On their return to England, Duncan and Vanessa continued every fortnight to spend two or three nights in London at Percy Street, where they now had Saxon Sydney-Turner's old rooms. . . .

In the winter of 1960 she became seriously ill in Percy Street with pneumonia. The flat was inconveniently placed at the top of the house and suddenly seemed poorly equipped and squalid. When the worst was over and Vanessa was a little stronger, she was driven down to Charleston. Clearing up after her departure, I was shocked by the dirty sheets, the dust on furniture and floors, the filth in the kitchen. It brought home to me Vanessa's age and her growing incapacity, disguised so far by her determined independence: later I realised that this was a happy state of affairs rather than otherwise, since it implied that she had remained in command very nearly until the end.

In the spring of 1961 Clive was ill in the London Clinic. Late one afternoon he telephoned me at Hilton: Vanessa had again developed pneumonia and was not expected to live through the night. I took the first train from Huntingdon, crossed London in a taxi and just caught the train to Lewes. Although it had been obvious for some time that Vanessa was failing, the thought that she might die was unbelievable, terrible and at the same time inadmissibly exhilarating. Like the disappearance of some familiar monument, her absence would reveal a new perspective in which I might be able to find freedom. It was thus that my thoughts ran, or rather burst to the surface like bubbles from a stagnant pool, as I sat in the train.

Taking a taxi from the station, I arrived at Charleston to find Duncan and Quentin in a state of shock, though perfectly calm. Duncan, in whose eyes there were tears, took me to Vanessa's ground-floor bedroom, which looked onto the garden: she had died only an hour before. She was lying on her bed, white but austerely beautiful. Duncan suggested that I should do a drawing of her—but of this I was quite incapable. He did one himself, which I still have.

I was puzzled by the fact that I had not even known that Vanessa was unwell. Why had not Duncan, instead of Clive, telephoned me? The more I thought of it the more stunned and the more excluded I felt, especially when I realised that her illness had lasted for about ten days. . . .

Vanessa was buried in Firle churchyard. . . . There is now a stone there giving her dates: 1879–1961. Oddly enough, it was difficult to believe she was eighty-one, in spite of the fact that she had always seemed such an elderly mother. . . .

Short as it is, this book has taken me seven years to write. To a professional author this must seem ridiculous, but to me it represents nothing so much as an emergence from the dark into the light.

. . . I owe my eventual emancipation from Bunny's domination to a chance contact with the works of Karen Horney, a Freudian psychologist. Something in me responded to her writing, and I was conscious that I had found one of the keys to freedom, although, still suffering from timidity, my progress was erratic and ill-informed. Later, I was galvanised by one of my daughters, who not only had her own problems but a very clear idea of what she wanted. Her crisis had a deep emotional impact and brought me to life—it also taught me much; but I have learnt precious lessons from all my children.

At about the same time that I made up my mind to leave Bunny, I, like Vanessa, had to have a mastectomy. It was a devastating experience, and I knew then what she must have suffered. If I mention it now, it is only to say that I am convinced it was a result more of my unhealthy state of mind than of my body. Luckily for me, it seems to have been in the nature of a warning, which even then I was beginning to heed.

It is generally believed that to understand all is to forgive all, but apart from the fact that it is impossible to understand everything, to talk of forgiveness smacks too much of superiority. Understanding is enough—if one can achieve it—but there is no doubt it comes and goes. There are moments when I feel hard done by, and others when I recognise that Vanessa meant me no harm. It was a sin of omission; and although those are the sins that have the worst effect, they are the ones which must—there is no way of avoiding the word—be forgiven. Writing this book has in itself made me try to understand, and I can say now, with untold relief, that I am now more able to see Vanessa through other people's eyes.

I now see my childhood as a precarious paradise, slung like a cradle over a cloud, but none the less full of delight. And yet it seems to me that one's maturity should be a better time than one's childhood, however wonderful that may have been. Mine has only just begun. Although retarded by some thirty years or more, it is still worth having, but in the effort to gain it I may have painted Vanessa in darker colours than she merited, having no doubt distorted her for my own purposes. In the nature of things, however, an autobiography cannot pretend to be objective. I have tried to describe my own ghosts, and, in doing so, to exorcise them.

Colonial Africa

"I felt contempt for those living in safety"

Isak Dinesen

(1885–1962)

Isak Dinesen (Karen Christentze Dinesen, Baroness Blixen) was born in Rungstedt, Denmark, to an aristocratic family and educated at Oxford and the Royal Academy of Copenhagen, followed by private study of painting in Paris and Rome. Troubled by her father's suicide and uncertain about the path she should follow in life, Dinesen, when thwarted in her attraction for one of her second cousins, Hans Blixen, married his twin brother, Baron Bror Blixen-Finecke, in 1914. Bror Blixen was a hunter of African big game who took Dinesen to Kenya, where, with money invested by her family, the couple established a coffee plantation, in the mountains in what is now the outskirts of Nairobi.

Since Blixen was unfaithful and infected his wife with syphilis, their unhappy marriage ended in divorce in 1921, but not before Dinesen had fallen in love with Kenya and coffee growing. So she remained alone on the plantation until it failed completely as an economic venture in 1931. During this decade her passionate relationship with the British big-game hunter Denys Finch-Hatton formed one pole of her emotional life, along with her love for Africa and African peoples.

After 1931 Dinesen became a highly successful and much admired writer in Denmark, publishing her acclaimed volume of suspense and the supernatural *Seven Gothic Tales* in 1934. Her longing for a heroic dimension to life, her love of adventure and of the exotic suffuse the elegant prose of her memoir *Out of Africa* (1937), which won instant recognition as a classic. Dinesen's training as a painter gave her a capacity to evoke the African landscape unrivaled in letters in any European language, and her way with words, whether in English or Danish, etches the images on the reader's mind.

Further volumes of Gothic stories followed until her *Last Tales* (1957). By that time she had been twice nominated for the Nobel Prize and held a unique position in English and European literary circles. Her will provided that her literary estate should support the establishment of a bird sanctuary on the family's Danish estate, Rungstedtland, and her love of nature and of the heroic was recaptured in the 1985 film version of *Out of Africa*.

OUT OF AFRICA

I had a farm in Africa, at the foot of the Ngong Hills. The Equator runs across these highlands, a hundred miles to the North, and the farm lay at an altitude of over six thousand feet. In the daytime you felt that you had got high up, near to the sun, but the early mornings and evenings were limpid and restful, and the nights were cold.

The geographical position, and the height of the land combined to create a landscape that had not its like in all the world. There was no fat on it and no luxuriance anywhere; it was Africa distilled up through six thousand feet, like the strong and refined essence of a continent. The colours were dry and burnt, like the colours in pottery. The trees had a light delicate foliage, the structure of which was different from that of the trees in Europe. . . . Upon the grass of the great plains the crooked bare old thorn-trees were scattered, and the grass was spiced like thyme and bog-myrtle; in some places the scent was so strong, that it smarted in the nostrils. All the flowers that you found on the plains, or upon the creepers and liana in the native forest, were diminutive like flowers of the downs,—only just in the beginning of the long rains a number of big, massive heavy-scented lilies sprang out on the plains. . . .

Looking back on a sojourn in the African highlands, you are struck by your feeling of having lived for a time up in the air. . . . In the middle of the day the air was alive over the land, like a flame burning; it scintillated, waved and shone like running water, mirrored and doubled all objects, and created great Fata Morgana. Up in this high air you breathed easily, drawing in a vital assurance and lightness of heart. . . .

The Mountain of Ngong stretches in a long ridge from North to South, and is crowned with four noble peaks like immovable darker blue waves against the sky. It rises eight thousand feet above the Sea, and to the East two thousand feet above the surrounding country; but to the West the drop is deeper and more precipitous,— the hills fall vertically down towards the Great Rift Valley.

The hills from the farm changed their character many times in the course of the day, and sometimes looked quite close, and at other times very far away. In the evening, when it was getting dark, it would first look, as you gazed at them, as if in the sky a thin silver line was drawn all along the silhouette of the dark mountain;

then, as night fell, the four peaks seemed to be flattened and
smoothened out, as if the mountain was stretching and spreading itself.

From the Ngong Hills you have a unique view, you see to the
South the vast plains of the great game-country that stretches all the
way to Kilimanjaro; to the East and North the park-like country of
the foot-hills with the forest behind them, and the undulating land
of the Kikuyu-Reserve, which extends to Mount Kenya a hundred
miles away,—a mosaic of little square maize-fields, banana-groves
and grass-land, with here and there the blue smoke from a native
village, a small cluster of peaked mole-casts. . . .

In my day, the Buffalo, the Eland and the Rhino lived in the
Ngong Hills,—the very old Natives remembered a time when there
were Elephants there. . . .

Up on the very ridge of the hills and on the four peaks themselves it was easy to walk; the grass was short as on a lawn, with the
grey stone in places breaking through the sward. Along the ridge,
up and down the peaks, like a gentle switchback, there ran a narrow game-path. One morning, at the time that I was camped in the
hills, I came up here and walked along the path, and I found on it
fresh tracks and dung of a herd of Eland. The big peaceful animals
must have been up on the ridge at sunrise, walking in a long row,
and you cannot imagine that they had come for any other reason
than just to look, deep down on both sides, at the land below.

We grew coffee on my farm. The land was in itself a little too
high for coffee, and it was hard work to keep it going; we were
never rich on the farm. But a coffee-plantation is a thing that gets
hold of you and does not let you go, and there is always something
to do on it: you are generally just a little behind with your work.

Coffee-growing is a long job. It does not all come out as you
imagine, when, yourself young and hopeful, in the streaming rain,
you carry the boxes of your shining young coffee-plants from the
nurseries, and, with the whole number of farm-hands in the field,
watch the plants set in the regular rows of holes in the wet ground
where they are to grow, and then have them thickly shaded against
the sun, with branches broken from the bush, since obscurity is the
privilege of young things. . . .

. . . When the plantation flowered in the beginning of the rains,
it was a radiant sight, like a cloud of chalk, in the mist and the drizzling rain, over six hundred acres of land. The coffee-blossom has a
delicate slightly bitter scent, like the black-thorn blossom. . . .

I had six thousand acres of land, and had thus got much spare land besides the coffee-plantation. Part of the farm was native forest, and about one thousand acres were squatters' land, what they called their *shambas*. The squatters are Natives, who with their families hold a few acres on a white man's farm, and in return have to work for him a certain number of days in the year. My squatters, I think, saw the relationship in a different light, for many of them were born on the farm, and their fathers before them, and they very likely regarded me as a sort of superior squatter on their estates. . . .

Nairobi was our town, twelve miles away, down on a flat bit of land amongst hills. Here were the Government House and the big central offices; from here the country was ruled.

The Masai, the nomadic, cattle-owning nation, were neighbours of the farm and lived on the other side of the river; from time to time some of them would come to my house to complain about a lion that was taking their cows, and to ask me to go out and shoot it for them, and I did so if I could. Sometimes, on Saturday, I also walked out on the Orungi plains to shoot a Zebra or two as meat for my farm-labourers, with a long tail of optimistic young Kikuyu after me. I shot birds on the farm, spurfowl and guineafowl, that are very good to eat. But for many years I was not out on any shooting expedition.

. . . From my first weeks in Africa, I had felt a great affection for the Natives. It was a strong feeling that embraced all ages and both sexes. The discovery of the dark races was to me a magnificent enlargement of all my world. If a person with an inborn sympathy for animals had grown up in a milieu where there were no animals, and had come into contact with animals late in life; or if a person with an instinctive taste for woods and forest had entered a forest for the first time at the age of twenty; or if some one with an ear for music had happened to hear music for the first time when he was already grown up; their cases might have been similar to mine. . . .

It was not easy to get to know the Natives. They were quick of hearing, and evanescent; if you frightened them they could withdraw into a world of their own, in a second, like the wild animals which at an abrupt movement from you are gone,—simply are not there. Until you knew a Native well, it was almost impossible to get a straight answer from him. . . .

We could not know, and could not imagine, what the dangers were that they feared from our hands. I myself think that they were afraid of us more in the manner in which you are afraid of a sudden terrific noise, than as you are afraid of suffering and death. And yet it was difficult to tell, for the Natives were great at the art of mimicry. In the shambas you would sometimes in the early morning come upon a spurfowl which would run in front of your horse as if her wing was broken, and she was terrified of being caught by the dogs. But her wing was not broken, and she was not afraid of the dogs,—she could whir up before them the moment she chose,—only she had got her brood of young chickens somewhere near by, and she was drawing our attention away from them. Like the spurfowl, the Natives might be mimicking a fear of us because of some other deeper dread the nature of which we could not guess. . . .

On our Safaris, and on the farm, my acquaintance with the Natives developed into a settled and personal relationship. We were good friends. I reconciled myself to the fact that while I should never quite know or understand them, they knew me through and through, and were conscious of the decisions that I was going to take, before I was certain about them myself. For some time I had a small farm up at Gil-Gil, where I lived in a tent, and I travelled by the railway to and fro between Gil-Gil and Ngong. At Gil-Gil, I might make up my mind very suddenly, when it began to rain, to go back to my house. But when I came to Kikuyu, which was our station on the railway line, and from where it was ten miles to the farm, one of my people would be there with a mule for me to ride home on. When I asked them how they had known that I was coming down, they looked away, and seemed uneasy, as if frightened or bored. . . .

Kamante was a small Kikuyu boy, the son of one of my squatters. . . .

I came upon him for the first time one day when I was riding across the plain of the farm, and he was herding his people's goats there. He was the most pitiful object that you could set eyes on. His head was big and his body terribly small and thin, the elbows and knees stood out like knots on a stick and both his legs were covered with deep running sores from the thigh to the heel. Here on the plain he looked extraordinarily small, so that it struck you as a strange thing that so much suffering could be condensed into a single point. When I stopped and spoke to him, he did not answer, and hardly appeared to see me. In his flat, angular, harassed, and infinitely patient face, the eyes were without glance, dim like the eyes of a dead person. . . .

Kamante to my surprise turned up at my house the morning after our first meeting. He stood there, a little away from the three or four other sick people present, erect, with his half-dead face, as if after all he had some feeling of attachment to life, and had now made up his mind to try this last chance of holding on to it.

He showed himself with time to be an excellent patient. He came when he was ordered to come, without fault, and he could keep account of time when he was told to come back every third or fourth day, which is an unusual thing with the Natives. He bore the hard treatment of his sores with a stoicism that I have not known the like of. In all these respects I might have held him up as a model to the others, but I did not do so, for at the same time he caused me much uneasiness of mind.

. . . They had a very good hospital at the Mission, and at the time when I was there, it was in charge of a philanthropic, clever head-doctor, Dr. Arthur. They saved the life of many of the people from the farm.

At the Scotch Mission they kept Kamante for three months. During that time I saw him once. I came riding past the Mission on my way to the Kikuyu railway station, and the road here for a while runs along the hospital grounds. I caught sight of Kamante in the grounds, he was standing by himself at a little distance from the groups of other convalescents. By this time he was already so much better that he could run. When he saw me he came up to the fence and ran with me as long as it was following the road. He trotted along, on his side of the fence, like a foal in a paddock when you pass it on horseback, and kept his eyes on my pony, but he did not say a word. . . .

Kamante came back to my house on the morning of Easter Sunday, and handed me a letter from the hospital people who declared that he was much better and that they thought him cured for good. . . .

. . . As slowly, slowly, he unwound the bandages from his knee to his heel there appeared, underneath them, a pair of whole smooth legs, only slightly marked by grey scars.

When Kamante had thoroughly, and in his calm grand manner, enjoyed my astonishment and pleasure, he again renewed the impression by stating that he was now a Christian. "I am like you," he said. He added that he thought that I might give him a Rupee because Christ had risen on this same day.

He went away to call on his own people. His mother was a

widow, and lived a long way away on the farm. From what I heard from her later I believe that he did upon this day make a digression from his habit and unloaded his heart to her of the impressions of strange people and ways that he had received at the hospital. But after his visit to his mother's hut, he came back to my house as if he took it for granted that now he belonged there. He was then in my service from this time till the time that I left the country,—for about twelve years.

Kamante began his life in my house as a dog-toto, later he became a medical assistant to me. There I found out what good hands he had, although you would not have thought so from the look of them, and I sent him into the kitchen to be a cook's boy, a marmiton, under my old cook Esa, who was murdered. After Esa's death he succeeded to him, and he was now my Chef all the time that he was with me.

Natives have usually very little feeling for animals, but Kamante differed from type here, as in other things, he was an authoritative dog-boy, and he identified himself with the dogs, and would come and communicate to me what they wished, or missed, or generally thought of things. He kept the dogs free of fleas, which are a pest in Africa, and many times in the middle of the night, he and I, called by the howls of the dogs, have, by the light of a hurricane-lamp, picked off them, one by one, the murderous big ants, the *Siafu*, which march alone and eat up everything on their way.

. . . He was a thoughtful, inventive doctor's assistant. After he had left this office, he would at times appear from the kitchen to interfere in a case of sickness, and give me very sound advice.

But as a Chef he was a different thing, and precluded classification. Nature had here taken a leap and cut away from the order of precedence of faculties and talents, the thing now became mystic and inexplicable, as ever where you are dealing with genius. In the kitchen, in the culinary world, Kamante had all the attributes of genius, even to that doom of genius,—the individual's powerlessness in the face of his own powers. If Kamante had been born in Europe, and had fallen into the hands of a clever teacher, he might have become famous, and would have cut a droll figure in history. And out here in Africa he made himself a name, his attitude to his art was that of a master.

Kamante, in all cooking matters, had a surprising manual adroitness. The great tricks and tours-de-force of the kitchen were child's play to his dark crooked hands; they knew on their own everything about omelettes, vol-au-vents, sauces, and mayonnaises. He had a special gift for making things light, as in the legend the infant Christ forms birds out of clay and tells them to fly. He scorned all complicated tools, as if impatient of too much independence in them, and when I gave him a machine for beating eggs he set it aside to rust, and beat whites of egg with a weeding knife that I had had to weed the lawn with, and his whites of eggs towered up like light clouds. . . .

He had a great memory for recipes. He could not read, and he knew no English so that cookery-books were of no use to him, but he must have held all that he was ever taught stored up in his ungraceful head, according to some systematization of his own, which I should never know. He had named the dishes after some event which had taken place on the day they had been shown to him, and he spoke of the sauce of the lightning that struck the tree, and of the sauce of the grey horse that died. . . .

Kamante showed his good will towards me, outside of the kitchen as well. He wanted to help me, in accordance with his own ideas of the advantages and dangers in life.

One night, after midnight, he suddenly walked into my bedroom with a hurricane-lamp in his hand, silent, as if on duty. It must have been only a short time after he first came into my house, for he was very small; he stood by my bedside like a dark bat that had strayed into the room, with very big spreading ears, or like a small African Will-o'-the-wisp, with his lamp in his hand. He spoke to me very solemnly, "Msabu," he said, "I think you had better get up." I sat up in bed bewildered; I thought that if anything serious had happened, it would have been Farah who would have come to fetch me, but when I told Kamante to go away again, he did not move. "Msabu," he said again, "I think that you had better get up. I think that God is coming." When I heard this, I did get up, and asked him why he thought so. He gravely led me into the dining-room which looked West, towards the hills. From the door-windows I now saw a strange phenomenon. There was a big grass-fire going on, out in the hills, and the grass was burning all the way from the hill-top to the plain; when seen from the house it was a nearly vertical line. It did indeed look as if some gigantic figure was moving and coming towards us. I stood for some time and looked at it, with Kamante watching by my side, then I began to explain the thing to him. I meant to quiet him, for I thought that he had been terribly frightened. But the explanation did not seem to make much impression on him one way or the other; he clearly took his mission to have been fulfilled when he had called me. "Well yes," he said, "it may be so. But I thought that you had better get up in case it was God coming."

To the East of my farm lay the Ngong Forest Reserve, which then was nearly all Virgin Forest. To my mind, it was a sad thing when the old forest was cut down, and Eucalyptus and Grevillea planted in its place; it might have made a unique pleasure-ground and park for Nairobi.

An African Native Forest is a mysterious region. You ride into the depths of an old tapestry, in places faded and in others darkened with age, but marvellously rich in green shades. You cannot see the sky at all in there, but the sunlight plays in many strange ways, falling through the foliage. The grey fungus, like long drooping beards, on the trees, and the creepers hanging down everywhere, give a secretive, recondite air to the native forest. I used to ride here with Farah on Sundays, when there was nothing to do on the farm, up and down the slopes, and across the little winding forest-streams. The air in the forest was cool like water, and filled with the scent of plants, and in the beginning of the long rains when the creepers flowered, you rode through sphere after sphere of fragrance. One kind of African Daphne of the woods, which flowers with a small cream-coloured sticky blossom, had an overwhelming sweet perfume, like lilac, and wild lily of the valley. . . .

Lulu was a young antelope of the bushbuck tribe, which is perhaps the prettiest of all the African antelopes. They are a little bigger than the fallow-deer; they live in the woods, or in the bush, and are shy and fugitive, so that they are not seen as often as the antelopes of the plains. But the Ngong Hills, and the surrounding country, were good places for bushbuck, and if you had your camp in the hills, and were out hunting in the early morning, or at sunset, you would see them come out of the bush into the glades, and as the rays of the sun fell upon them their coats shone red as copper. The male has a pair of delicately turned horns.

Lulu became a member of my household in this way:

I drove one morning from the farm to Nairobi. My mill on the farm had burnt down a short time before, and I had had to drive into town many times to get the insurance settled and paid out; in this early morning I had my head filled with figures and estimates. As I came driving along the Ngong Road a little group of Kikuyu children shouted to me from the roadside, and I saw that they were holding a very small bushbuck up for me to see. I knew that they would have found the fawn in the bush, and that now they wanted to sell it to me, but I was late for an appointment in Nairobi, and I had no thought for this sort of thing, so I drove on.

When I was coming back in the evening and was driving past the same place, there was again a great shout from the side of the road and the small party was still there, a little tired and disappointed, for they may have tried to sell the fawn to other people passing by in the course of the day, but keen now to get the deal through before the sun was down, and they held up the fawn high to tempt me. But I had had a long day in town, and some adversity about the insurance, so that I did not care to stop or talk, and I just drove on past them. I did not even think of them when I was back in my house, and dined and went to bed.

The moment that I had fallen asleep I was woken up again by a great feeling of terror. The picture of the boys and the small buck, which had now collected and taken shape, stood out before me, clearly, as if it had been painted, and I sat up in bed as appalled as if someone had been trying to choke me. What, I thought, would become of the fawn in the hands of the captors who had stood with it in the heat of the long day, and had held it up by its joined legs? It was surely too young to eat on its own. I myself had driven past it twice on the same day, like the priest and the Levite in one, and had given no thought to it, and now, at this moment, where was it? I got up in a real panic and woke up all my houseboys. I told them that the fawn must be found and brought me in the morning, or they would all of them get their dismissal from my service. They were immediately up to the idea. Two of my boys had been in the car with me the same day, and had not shown the slightest interest in the children or the fawn; now they came forward, and gave the others a long list of details of the place and the hour and of the family of the boys. It was a moonlight night; my people all took off and spread in the landscape in a lively discussion of the situation; I heard them expatiating on the fact that they were all to be dismissed in case the bushbuck were not found.

Early next morning when Farah brought me in my tea, Juma came in with him and carried the fawn in his arms. It was a female, and we named her Lulu, which I was told was the Swaheli word for a pearl.

Lulu by that time was only as big as a cat, with large quiet purple eyes. She had such delicate legs that you feared they would not bear being folded up and unfolded again, as she lay down and rose up. Her ears were smooth as silk and exceedingly expressive. Her nose was as black as a truffle. Her diminutive hoofs gave her all the air of a young Chinese lady of the old school, with laced feet. It was a rare experience to hold such a perfect thing in your hands.

Lulu soon adapted herself to the house and its inhabitants and behaved as if she were at home. During the first weeks the polished floors in the rooms were a problem in her life, and when she got outside the carpets her legs went away from her to all four sides; it looked catastrophic but she did not let it worry her much and in the end she learnt to walk on the bare floors with a sound like a succession of little angry finger-taps. She was extraordinarily neat in all her habits. She was headstrong already as a child, but when I stopped her from doing the things she wanted to do, she behaved as if she said: Anything rather than a scene.

Kamante brought her up on a sucking-bottle, and he also shut her up at night, for we had to be careful of her as the leopards were up round the house after nightfall. So she held to him and followed him about. From time to time when he did not do what she wanted, she gave his thin legs a hard butt with her young head, and she was so pretty that you could not help, when you looked upon the two together, seeing them as a new paradoxical illustration to the tale of the Beauty and the Beast. On the strength of this great beauty and gracefulness, Lulu obtained for herself a commanding position in the house, and was treated with respect by all.

. . . My dogs understood Lulu's power and position in the house. The arrogance of the great hunters was like water with her. She pushed them away from the milk-bowl and from their favourite places in front of the fire. I had tied a small bell on a rein round Lulu's neck, and there came a time when the dogs, when they heard the jingle of it approaching through the rooms, would get up resignedly from their warm beds by the fireplace, and go and lie down in some other part of the room. Still nobody could be of a gentler demeanour than Lulu was when she came and lay down, in the manner of a perfect lady who demurely gathers her skirts about her and will be in no one's way. She drank the milk with a polite, pernickety mien, as if she had been pressed by an overkind hostess. She insisted on being scratched behind the ears, in a pretty forbearing way, like a young wife who pertly permits her husband a caress.

When Lulu grew up and stood in the flower of her young love-liness she was a slim delicately rounded doe, from her nose to her toes unbelievably beautiful. She looked like a minutely painted illustration to Heine's song of the wise and gentle gazelles by the flow of the river Ganges.

One evening Lulu did not come home and we looked out for her in vain for a week. This was a hard blow to us all. A clear note had gone out of the house and it seemed no better than other houses. I thought of the leopards by the river and one evening I talked about them to Kamante.

As usual he waited some time before he answered, to digest my lack of insight. It was not till a few days later that he approached me upon the matter. "You believe that Lulu is dead, Msabu," he said.

I did not like to say so straight out, but I told him I was wondering why she did not come back.

"Lulu," said Kamante, "is not dead. But she is married."

This was pleasant, surprising, news, and I asked him how he knew of it.

"Oh yes," he said, "she is married. She lives in the forest with her *bwana*"—her husband, or master. "But she has not forgotten the people; most mornings she is coming back to the house. I lay out crushed maize to her at the back of the kitchen, then just before the sun comes up, she walks round there from the woods and eats it. Her husband is with her, but he is afraid of the people because he has never known them. He stands below the big white tree by the other side of the lawn. But up to the houses he dare not come."

I told Kamante to come and fetch me when he next saw Lulu. A few days later before sunrise he came and called me out.

It was a lovely morning. The last stars withdrew while we were waiting, the sky was clear and serene but the world in which we walked was sombre still, and profoundly silent. The grass was wet; down by the trees where the ground sloped it gleamed with the dew like dim silver. The air of the morning was cold, it had that twinge in it which in Northern countries means that the frost is not far away. However often you make the experience,—I thought,—it is still impossible to believe, in this coolness and shade, that the heat of the sun and the glare of the sky, in a few hours' time, will be hard to bear. The grey mist lay upon the hills, strangely taking shape from them; it would be bitterly cold on the Buffalo if they were about there now, grazing on the hillside, as in a cloud.

The great vault over our heads was gradually filled with clarity like a glass with wine. Suddenly, gently, the summits of the hill caught the first sunlight and blushed. And slowly, as the earth leaned towards the sun, the grassy slopes at the foot of the mountain turned a delicate gold, and the Masai woods lower down. And now the tops of the tall trees in the forest, on our side of the river, blushed like copper. . . .

A bird began to sing, and then I heard, a little way off in the forest, the tinkling of a bell. Yes, it was a joy, Lulu was back, and about in her old places! It came nearer, I could follow her movements by its rhythm; she was walking, stopping, walking on again. A turning round one of the boys' huts brought her upon us. It suddenly became an unusual and amusing thing to see a bushbuck so close to the house. She stood immovable now, she seemed to be prepared for the sight of Kamante, but not for that of me. But she did not make off, she looked at me without fear and without any remembrance of our skirmishes of the past or of her own ingratitude in running away without warning.

Lulu of the woods was a superior, independent being, a change of heart had come upon her, she was in possession. . . .

Kamante touched my arm with one finger and then pointed it towards the woods. As I followed the direction, I saw, under a tall Cape-chestnut-tree, a male bushbuck, a small tawny silhouette at the outskirts of the forest, with a fine pair of horns, immovable like a tree-stem. Kamante observed him for some time, and then laughed.

"Look here now," he said, "Lulu has explained to her husband that there is nothing up by the houses to be afraid of, but all the same he dares not come. Every morning he thinks that to-day he will come all the way, but, when he sees the house and the people, he gets a cold stone in the stomach,"—this is a common thing in the native world, and often gets in the way of the work on the farm,—"and then he stops by the tree."

For a long time Lulu came to the house in the early mornings. Her clear bell announced that the sun was up on the hills, I used to lie in bed, and wait for it. Sometimes she stayed away for a week or two, and we missed her and began to talk of the people who went to shoot in the hills. But then again my houseboys announced: "Lulu is here," as if it had been the married daughter of the house on a visit. . . .

One day, as I came back from Nairobi, Kamante was keeping watch for me outside the kitchen door, and stepped forward, much excited, to tell me that Lulu had been to the farm the same day and had had her Toto,—her baby—with her. Some days after, I myself had the honour to meet her amongst the boys' huts, much on the alert and not to be trifled with, with a very small fawn at her heels, as delicately tardive in his movements as Lulu herself had been when we first knew her. This was just after the long rains, and, during those summer months, Lulu was to be found near the houses, in the afternoon, as well as at daybreak. She would even be round there at midday, keeping in the shadow of the huts.

Lulu's fawn was not afraid of the dogs, and would let them sniff him all over, but he could not get used to the Natives or to me, and if we ever tried to get hold of him, the mother and the child were off.

It . . . seemed to me that the free union between my house and the antelope was a rare, honourable thing. Lulu came in from the wild world to show that we were on good terms with it, and she made my house one with the African landscape, so that nobody could tell where the one stopped and the other began. Lulu knew the place of the Giant Forest-Hog's lair and had seen the Rhino copulate. In Africa there is a cuckoo which sings in the middle of the hot days in the midst of the forest, like the sonorous heartbeat of the world, I had never had the luck to see her, neither had anyone that I knew, for nobody could tell me how she looked. But Lulu had perhaps walked on a narrow green deerpath just under the branch on which the cuckoo was sitting. . . .

The league between Lulu and her family and my house lasted for many years. The bushbucks were often in the neighbourhood of the house, they came out of the woods and went back again as if my grounds were a province of the wild country. They came mostly just before sunset, and first moved in amongst the trees like delicate dark silhouettes on the dark green, but when they stepped out to graze on the lawn in the light of the afternoon sun their coats shone like copper. One of them was Lulu, for she came up near to the house, and walked about sedately, pricking her ears when a car arrived, or when we opened a window; and the dogs would know her. She became darker in colour with age. Once I came driving up in front of my house with a friend and found three bushbucks on the terrace there, round the salt that was laid out for my cows.

The years in which Lulu and her people came round to my house were the happiest of my life in Africa. For that reason, I came to look upon my acquaintance with the forest antelopes as upon a great boon, and a token of friendship from Africa. . . .

———

We had many visitors to the farm. In Pioneer countries hospitality is a necessity of life not to the travellers alone but to the settlers. . . .

When Denys Finch-Hatton came back after one of his long expeditions, he was starved for talk, and found me on the farm starved for talk, so that we sat over the dinner-table into the small hours of the morning, talking of all the things we could think of, and mastering them all, and laughing at them. White people, who for a long time live alone with Natives, get into the habit of saying what they mean, because they have no reason or opportunity for dissimulation, and when they meet again their conversation keeps the native tone. . . .

When one of Denys Finch-Hatton's long Safaris was drawing to its end, it happened that I would find, on a morning, a young Masai standing upon one long slim leg outside my house. "Bedâr is on his way back," he announced. "He will be here in two or three days."

In the afternoon, a Squatter Toto from the outskirts of the farm sat and waited on the lawn, to tell me, when I came out: "There is a flight of guineafowl down by the bend of the river. If you want to shoot them for Bedâr when he comes I will come out with you at sunset to show you where to find them."

To the great wanderers amongst my friends, the farm owed its charm, I believe, to the fact that it was stationary and remained the same whenever they came to it. They had been over vast countries and had raised and broken their tents in many places, now they were pleased to round my drive that was steadfast as the orbit of a star. They liked to be met by familiar faces, and I had the same servants all the time that I was in Africa. I had been on the farm longing to get away, and they came back to it longing for books and linen sheets and the cool atmosphere in a big shuttered room; by their campfires they had been meditating upon the joys of farm life, and as they arrived they asked me eagerly: "Have you taught your cook to make an *omelette à la chasseur*?—and have the gramophone records from 'Petrouchka' arrived by the last mail?" They came and stayed in the house also when I was away, and Denys had the use of it, when I was on a visit in Europe. "My Sylvan Retreat," Berkeley Cole called it.

As far as Berkeley Cole and Denys Finch-Hatton were concerned, my house was a communist establishment. Everything in it was theirs, and they took a pride in it, and brought home the things they felt to be lacking. They kept the house up to a high standard in wine and tobacco, and got books and gramophone records out from Europe for me. Berkeley arrived with his car loaded up with turkeys, eggs, and oranges, from his own farm on Mount Kenya. They both had the ambition to make me a judge of wine, as they were, and spent much time and thought in the task. They took the greatest pleasure in my Danish table glass and china, and used to build up on the dinner table a tall shining pyramid of all my glass, the one piece on the top of the other; they enjoyed the sight of it.

Berkeley, when he stayed on the farm, had a bottle of champagne out in the forest every morning at eleven o'clock. Once, as he was taking leave of me, and thanking me for his time on the farm, he added that there had been one shadow in the picture, for we had been given coarse and vulgar glasses for our wine under the trees. "I know, Berkeley," I said, "but I have so few of my good glasses left, and the boys will break them when they have to carry them such a long way." He looked at me gravely, my hand in his. "But my dear," he said, "it has been so sad." So afterwards he had my best glasses brought out in the wood.

It was a curious thing about Berkeley and Denys,—who were so deeply regretted by their friends in England when they emigrated, and so much beloved and admired in the Colony,—that they should be all the same, outcasts. It was not a society that had thrown them out, and not any place in the whole world either, but time had done it, they did not belong to their century. No other nation than the English could have produced them, but they were examples of atavism, and theirs was an earlier England, a world which no longer existed. In the present epoch they had no home, but had got to wander here and there, and in the course of time they also came to the farm. . . .

The particular, instinctive attachment which all Natives of Africa felt towards Berkeley and Denys, and towards a few other people of their kind, made me reflect that perhaps the white men of the past, indeed of any past, would have been in better understanding and sympathy with the coloured races than we, of our Industrial Age, shall ever be. When the first steam engine was constructed, the roads of the races of the world parted, and we have never found one another since.

Denys Finch-Hatton had no other home in Africa than the farm, he lived in my house between his Safaris, and kept his books and his gramophone there. When he came back to the farm, it gave out what was in it; it spoke,—as the coffee-plantations speak, when with the first showers of the rainy season they flower, dripping wet, a cloud of chalk. When I was expecting Denys back, and heard his car coming up the drive, I heard, at the same time, the things of the farm all telling what they really were. He was happy on the farm; he came there only when he wanted to come, and it knew, in him, a quality of which the world besides was not aware, a humility. He never did but what he wanted to do, neither was guile found in his mouth.

Denys had a trait of character which to me was very precious, he liked to hear a story told. For I have always thought that I might have cut a figure at the time of the plague of Florence. Fashions have changed, and the art of listening to a narrative has been lost in Europe. The Natives of Africa, who cannot read, have still got it; if you begin to them: "There was a man who walked out on the plain, and there he met another man," you have them all with you, their minds running on the unknown track of the men on the plain. But white people, even if they feel that they ought to, cannot listen to a recital. If they do not become fidgety, and remember things that should be done at once, they fall asleep. The same people will ask you for something to read, and may then sit all through an evening absorbed in any kind of print handed them, they will even then read a speech. They have been accustomed to take in their impressions by the eye.

Denys, who lived much by the ear, preferred hearing a tale told, to reading it; when he came to the farm he would ask: "Have you got a story?" I had been making up many while he had been away. In the evenings he made himself comfortable, spreading cushions like a couch in front of the fire, and with me sitting on the floor, cross-legged like Scheherazade herself, he would listen, clear-eyed, to a long tale, from when it began until it ended. He kept better account of it than I did myself, and at the dramatic appearance of one of the characters, would stop me to say: "That man died in the beginning of the story, but never mind."

Denys taught me Latin, and to read the Bible, and the Greek poets. He himself knew great parts of the Old Testament by heart, and carried the Bible with him on all his journeys, which gained him the high esteem of the Mohammedans.

He also gave me my gramophone. It was a delight to my heart, it brought a new life to the farm, it became the voice of the farm.—

"The soul within a glade the nightingale is."—Sometimes Denys would arrive unexpectedly at the house, while I was out in the coffee-field or the maize-field, bringing new records with him; he would set the gramophone going, and as I came riding back at sunset, the melody streaming towards me in the clear cool air of the evening would announce his presence to me, as if he had been laughing at me, as he often did. The Natives liked the gramophone, and used to stand round the house to listen to it; some of my houseboys picked out a favourite tune and asked me for it, when I was alone with them in the house. It was a curious thing that Kamante should stick, in his preference, with much devotion to the Adagio of Beethoven's Piano Concerto in G-Major; the first time that he asked me for it he had some difficulty in describing it, so as to make clear to me which tune it was that he wanted.

Denys and I, however, did not agree in our tastes. For I wanted the old composers, and Denys, as if courteously making up to the age for his lack of harmony with it, was as modern as possible in his taste of all arts. He liked to hear the most advanced music. "I would like Beethoven all right," he said, "if he were not vulgar."

Denys and I, whenever we were together, had great luck with lions. Sometimes he came back from a shooting Safari of two or three months vexed that he had been unable to get a good lion for the people from Europe whom he had taken out. In the meantime the Masai had been to my house and had asked me to come out and shoot a certain lion or lioness which was killing off their cattle, and Farah and I had been out, camping in their manyatta, sitting up over a kill, or walking out in the early morning, without as much as finding the track of a lion. But when Denys and I went for a ride, the lions of the plains would be about, as in attendance, we would come upon them then there at a meal, or see them crossing the dry river-beds.

On a New Year's morning, before sunrise, Denys and I found ourselves on the new Narok Road, driving along as fast as we could go on a rough road.

Denys, the day before, had lent a heavy rifle to a friend of his who was going South with a shooting party, and late in the night he remembered that he had neglected to explain to him a certain trick in the rifle, by which the hair-trigger might be put out of action. He was worried about it and afraid that the hunter would come to some sort of harm by his ignorance. We could then think of no better remedy than that we should start as early as possible, take the new road, and try to overtake the shooting party at Narok. It was sixty miles, through some rough country; the Safari was travelling by the old road and would be going slowly as it had heavy loaded lorries with it. Our only trouble was that we did not know if the new road would have been brought through all the way to Narok.

The early morning air of the African highlands is of such a tangible coldness and freshness that time after time the same fancy there comes back to you: you are not on earth but in dark deep waters, going ahead along the bottom of the sea. It is not even certain that you are moving at all, the flows of chilliness against your face may be the deep-sea currents, and your car, like some sluggish electric fish, may be sitting steadily upon the bottom of the sea, staring in front of her with the glaring eyes of her lamps, and letting the submarine life pass by her. The stars are so large because they are no real stars but reflections, shimmering upon the surface of the water. Alongside your path on the sea-bottom, live things, darker than their surroundings, keep on appearing, jumping up and sweeping into the long grass, as crabs and beach-fleas will make their way into the sand. The light gets clearer, and, about sunrise, the sea-bottom lifts itself towards the surface, a new created island. Whirls of smells drift quickly past you, fresh rank smells of the olive-bushes, the brine scent of burnt grass, a sudden quelling smell of decay.

Kanuthia, Denys's boy, who sat in the back of the box-body car, gently touched my shoulder and pointed to the right. To the side of the road, twelve or fifteen yards away from it, was a dark bulk, a Manatee taking a rest on the sands, and on the top of it something was stirring in the dark water. It was, I saw later, a big dead Giraffe bull, that had been shot two or three days before. You are not allowed to shoot the Giraffe, and Denys and I later had to defend ourselves against the charge of having killed this one, but we could prove that it had been dead some time when we came upon it, though it was never found by whom or why it had been killed. Upon the huge carcass of the Giraffe, a lioness had been feeding, and now raised her head and shoulder above it to watch the passing car.

Denys stopped the car, and Kanuthia lifted the rifle, that he carried, off his shoulder. Denys asked me in a low voice: "Shall I shoot her?"—For he very courteously looked on the Ngong Hills as my private hunting-ground.—We were going across the land of the same Masai who had been to my house to bewail the loss of their cattle; if this was the animal which had killed one after the other of their cows and calves, the time had come to put an end to her. I nod-ded.

He jumped from the car and slid back a few steps, at the same moment the lioness dived down behind the body of the Giraffe, he ran round the Giraffe to get within shot of her, and fired. I did not see her fall; when I got out and up to her she was lying dead in a big black pool.

There was no time to skin her, we must drive on if we were to cut off the Safari at Narok. We gazed round and took note of the place, the smell of the dead Giraffe was so strong that we could not very well pass it unknowingly.

But when we had driven a further two miles there was no more road. The tools of the road-labourers lay here; on the other side of them was the wide stony land, just grey in the dawn, all unbroken by any touch of man. We looked at the tools and at the country, we would have to leave Denys's friend to take his chance with the rifle. Afterwards, when he came back, he told us that he had never had an opportunity to use it. So we turned back, and as we turned we got our faces to the Eastern sky, reddening over the plains and the hills. We drove towards it and talked all the time of the lioness.

The Giraffe came within view, and by this time we could see him clearly and distinguish,—where the light fell on to his side,—the darker square spots on his skin. And as we came near to him we saw that there was a lion standing on him. In approaching we were a little lower than the carcass; the lion stood straight up over it, dark, and behind him the sky was now all aflame. *Lion Passant Or.* A bit of his mane was lifted by the wind. I rose up in the car, so strong was the impression that he made, and Denys at that said: "You shoot this time." I was never keen to shoot with his rifle, which was too long and heavy for me, and gave me a bad shock; still here the shot was a declaration of love, should the rifle not then be of the biggest caliber? As I shot it seemed to me that the lion jumped straight up in the air, and came down with his legs gathered under him. I stood, panting, in the grass, aglow with the plenipo-tence that a shot gives you, because you take effect at a distance. I walked round the carcass of the Giraffe. There it was,—the fifth act of a classic tragedy. They were all dead now. The Giraffe was look-ing terribly big, austere, with his four stiff legs and long stiff neck, his belly torn open by the lions. The lioness, lying on her back, had a great haughty snarl on her face, she was the *femme fatale* of the tragedy. The lion was lying not far from her, and how was it that he had learned nothing by her fate? His head was laid on his two front paws, his mighty mane covered him as a royal mantle, he too was resting in a big pool, and by now the morning air was so light that it showed scarlet.

Denys and Kanuthia pulled up their sleeves and while the sun rose they skinned the lions. When they took a rest we had a bottle of claret, and raisins and almonds, from the car; I had brought them with us to eat on the road, because it was New Year's Day. We sat on the short grass and ate and drank. The dead lions, close by, looked magnificent in their nakedness, there was not a particle of superfluous fat on them, each muscle was a bold controlled curve, they needed no cloak, they were, all through, what they ought to be.

As we sat there, a shadow hastened over the grass and over my feet, and looking up I could distinguish, high in the light-blue sky, the circling of the vultures. My heart was as light as if I had been flying it, up there, on a string, as you fly a kite. . . .

To Denys Finch-Hatton I owe what was, I think, the greatest, the most transporting pleasure of my life on the farm: I flew with him over Africa. There, where there are few or no roads and where you can land on the plains, flying becomes a thing of real and vital importance in your life, it opens up a world. Denys had brought out his Moth machine; it could land on my plain on the farm only a few minutes from the house, and we were up nearly every day.

You have tremendous views as you get up above the African highlands, surprising combinations and changes of light and colouring, the rainbow on the green sunlit land, the gigantic upright clouds and big wild black storms, all swing round you in a race and a dance. The lashing hard showers of rain whiten the air askance. The language is short of words for the experiences of flying, and will have to invent new words with time. When you have flown over the Rift Valley and the volcanoes of Suswa and Longonot, you have travelled far and have been to the lands on the other side of the moon. You may at other times fly low enough to see the animals on the plains and to feel towards them as God did when he had just created them, and before he commissioned Adam to give them names.

But it is not the visions but the activity which makes you happy, and the joy and glory of the flyer is the flight itself. It is a sad hardship and slavery to people who live in towns, that in all their movements they know of one dimension only; they walk along the line as if they were led on a string. The transition from the line to the plane into the two dimensions, when you wander across a field or through a wood, is a splendid liberation to the slaves, like the French Revolution. But in the air you are taken into the full freedom of the three dimensions; after long ages of exile and dreams the homesick heart throws itself into the arms of space. The laws of gravitation and time,

> . . . in life's green grove,
> Sport like tame beasts, none knew how
> gentle they could be!

Every time that I have gone up in an aeroplane and looking down have realised that I was free of the ground, I have had the consciousness of a great new discovery. "I see:" I have thought, "This was the idea. And now I understand everything."

One day Denys and I flew to Lake Natron, ninety miles South-East of the farm, and more than four thousand feet lower, two thousand feet above sea level. Lake Natron is the place from where they take soda. The bottom of the lake and the shores are like some sort of whitish concrete, with a strong, sour and salt smell.

The sky was blue, but as we flew from the plains in over the stony and bare lower country, all colour seemed to be scorched out of it. The whole landscape below us looked like delicately marked tortoise-shell. Suddenly, in the midst of it was the lake. The white bottom, shining through the water, gives it, when seen from the air, a striking, an unbelievable azure-colour, so clear that for a moment you shut your eyes at it; the expanse of water lies in the bleak tawny land like a big bright aquamarine. We had been flying high, now we went down, and as we sank our own shade, dark-blue, floated under us upon the light-blue lake. Here live thousands of Flamingoes, although I do not know how they exist in the brackish water,— surely there are no fish here. At our approach they spread out in large circles and fans, like the rays of a setting sun, like an artful Chinese pattern on silk or porcelain, forming itself and changing, as we looked at it.

We landed on the white shore, that was white-hot as an oven, and lunched there, taking shelter against the sun under the wing of the aeroplane. If you stretched out your hand from the shade, the sun was so hot that it hurt you. Our bottles of beer when they first arrived with us, straight out of the ether, were pleasantly cold, but before we had finished them, in a quarter of an hour, they became as hot as a cup of tea.

When Denys and I had not time for long journeys we went out
for a short flight over the Ngong Hills, generally about sunset.
These hills, which are amongst the most beautiful in the world, are
perhaps at their loveliest seen from the air, when the ridges, bare
towards the four peaks, mount, and run side by side with the aeroplane, or suddenly sink down and flatten out into a small lawn.

Here in the hills there were Buffaloes. I had even, in my very
young days,—when I could not live till I had killed a specimen of
each kind of African game,—shot a bull out here. Later on, when I
was not so keen to shoot as to watch the wild animals, I had been
out to see them again. I had camped in the hills by a spring half way
to the top, bringing my servants, tents, and provisions with me, and
Farah and I had been up in the dark, ice cold mornings to creep and
crawl through bush and long grass, in the hope of catching a
glimpse of the herd; but twice I had had to go back without success.
That the herd lived there, neighbours of mine to the west, was still
a value in the life on the farm, but they were serious-minded, self-
sufficient neighbours, the old nobility of the hills, now somehow reduced; they did not receive much.

But one afternoon as I was having tea with some friends of
mine from up-country, outside the house, Denys came flying from
Nairobi and went over our heads out Westwards; a little while after
he turned and came back and landed on the farm. Lady Delamere
and I drove down to the plain to fetch him up, but he would not get
out of his aeroplane.

"The Buffalo are out feeding in the hills," he said, "come out
and have a look at them."

"I cannot come," I said, "I have got a tea-party up at the
house."

"But we will go and see them and be back in a quarter of an
hour," said he.

This sounded to me like the propositions which people make to
you in a dream. Lady Delamere would not fly, so I went up with
him. We flew in the sun, but the hillside lay in a transparent brown
shade, which soon we got into. It did not take us long to spy the
Buffalo from the air. Upon one of the long rounded green ridges
which run, like folds of a cloth gathered together at each peak,
down the side of the Ngong mountain, a herd of twenty-seven Buffalo were grazing. First we saw them a long way below us, like mice
moving gently on a floor, but we dived down, circling over and
along their ridge; a hundred and fifty feet above them and well

within shooting distance; we counted them as they peacefully blended and separated. There was one very old big black bull in the herd, one or two younger bulls, and a number of calves. The open stretch of sward upon which they walked was closed in by bush; had a stranger approached on the ground they would have heard or scented him at once, but they were not prepared for advance from the air. We had to keep moving above them all the time. They heard the noise of our machine and stopped grazing, but they did not seem to have it in them to look up. In the end they realized that something very strange was about; the old bull first walked out in front of the herd, raising his hundred-weight horns, braving the un-seen enemy, his four feet planted on the ground,—suddenly he be-gan to trot down the ridge and after a moment he broke into a canter. The whole clan now followed him, stampeding headlong down, and as they switched and plunged into the bush, dust and loose stones rose in their wake. In the thicket they stopped and kept close together, it looked as if a small glade in the hill had been paved with dark grey stones. Here they believed themselves to be covered to the view, and so they were to anything moving along the ground, but they could not hide themselves from the eyes of the bird of the air. We flew up and away. It was like having been taken into the heart of the Ngong Hills by a secret unknown road.

When I came back to my tea-party, the teapot on the stone table was still so hot that I burned my fingers on it. The Prophet had the same experience when he upset a jug of water, and the Archangel Gabriel took him, and flew with him through the seven heavens, and when he returned, the water had not yet run out of the jug.

My farm was a little too high up for growing coffee. It hap-pened in the cold months that we would get frost on the lower land and in the morning the shoots of the coffee-trees, and the young coffee-berries on them, would be all brown and withered. The wind blew in from the plains, and even in good years we never got the same yield of coffee to the acre as the people in the lower districts of Thika and Kiambu, on four thousand feet.

We were short of rain, as well, in the Ngong country, and three times we had a year of real drought, which brought us very low down. In a year in which we had fifty inches of rain, we picked eighty tons of coffee, and in a year of fifty-five inches, nearly ninety tons; but there were two bad years in which we had only twenty-five and twenty inches of rain, and picked only sixteen and fifteen tons of coffee, and those years were disastrous to the farm.

At the same time coffee-prices fell: where we had got a hundred pounds a ton we now got sixty or seventy. Times grew hard on the farm. We could not pay our debts, and we had no money for the running of the plantation. My people at home, who had shares in the farm, wrote out to me and told me that I would have to sell.

I thought out many devices for the salvation of the farm. One year I tried to grow flax on our spare land. Flax-growing is a lovely job, but it needs much skill and experience. I had a Belgian refugee to give me advice on it, and when he asked me how much land I meant to plant, and I told him three hundred acres, he immediately exclaimed: "*Ça Madame, c'est impossible.*" I might grow five acres or even ten with success he said, but no more. But ten acres would take us nowhere, and I put in a hundred and fifty acres. A sky-blue flowering flax-field is a marvellously pretty sight,—like a piece of Heaven on earth and there can be no more gratifying kind of goods to be turning out than the flax fibre, tough and glossy, and slightly greasy to the touch. You follow it in your thoughts as it is sent away, and imagine it made into sheets and nightgowns. But the Kikuyu could not, in the turn of a hand and without constant supervision, be taught to be accurate enough in the pulling and retting and scutching of it; and so my flax-growing was no success.

Our real trouble was that we were short of capital, for it had all been spent in the old days before I took over the running of the farm. We could not carry through any radical improvements, but had to live from hand to mouth,—and this, in the last years, became our normal mode of living on the farm.

If I had had the capital, I thought, I would have given up coffee, have cut down the coffee-trees, and have planted forest-trees on my land. Trees grow up so quickly in Africa, in ten years' time you walk comfortably under tall blue gum trees, and wattle trees, which you have yourself, in the rain, carried in boxes from the nurseries, twelve trees in a box. I would have had then, I reflected, a good market for both timber and firewood in Nairobi. It is a noble occupation to plant trees, you think of it many years after with content. There had been big stretches of native forest on the farm in the old days, but it had been sold to the Indians for cutting down, before I took over the farm; it was a sad thing. I myself in the hard years had had to cut down the wood on my land round the factory for the steam-engine, and this forest, with the tall stems and the live green shadows in it had haunted me, I have not felt more sorry for anything I have done in my life, than for cutting it down. From time to time, when I could afford it, I planted up bits of land with Eucalyptus trees, but it did not come to much. It would be, in this way, fifty years before I had got the many hundred acres planted up, and had changed the farm into a singing wood, scientifically run, with a saw-mill by the river. The Squatters of the farm, though, whose ideas of time were different from those of the white people, kept on looking forward hopefully to the time when everybody would have abundance of firewood,—such as the people had had in the old days,—from the forest that I was now soon going to plant.

It is a heavy burden to carry a farm on you. My Natives, and my white people even, left me to dread and worry on their behalf, and it sometimes seemed to me that the farm-oxen and the coffee-trees themselves, were doing the same. It appeared to be agreed upon, then, by the speaking creatures and the dumb, that it was my fault that the rains were late and the nights so cold. And in the evening it did not seem right that I should sit down quietly to read; I was driven out of my house by the fear of losing it. Farah knew of all my sorrows, and he did not approve of my walks at night. He talked about the leopards that had been seen close to the house when the sun was down; and he used to stand on the Verandah, a white-robed figure just visible in the dark, until I came in again. But I was too sad to get any idea of leopards into my mind, I knew that I did no good whatever by going round on the roads of the farm in the night, and still I went, like a ghost that is just said to walk, without any definition as to why or where to.

Two years before I left Africa I was in Europe on a visit. I travelled back in the coffee-picking season, so that I could not get news of the harvest before I came to Mombasa. All the time on the boat I was weighing the problem in my mind: When I was well and life was looking friendly, I reckoned that we would have got seventy-five tons, but when I was unwell or nervous I thought: We are bound to get sixty tons in any case.

Farah came to meet me in Mombasa, and I dared not ask him about the coffee-crop straight away; for some time we talked of other news of the farm. But in the evening as I was going to bed, I could not put it off any longer and I asked him how many tons of coffee they had picked on the farm in all. The Somalis are generally pleased to announce a disaster. But here Farah was not happy, he was extremely grave himself, standing up by the door, and he half closed his eyes and laid back his head, swallowing his sorrow, when he said: "Forty tons, Memsahib." At that I knew that we could not carry on. All colour and life faded out of the world round me, the bleak and stifling Mombasa hotel-room, with the cemented floor, old iron bedstead, and worn mosquito-net, took on a tremendous significance as the symbol of the world, without any single ornament or article of embellishment of human life in it. I did not say anything more to Farah, and he did not speak again, but went away, the last friendly object in the world.

Still the human mind has great powers of self-renewal, and in the middle of the night I thought, with Old Knudsen, that forty tons was something, but that pessimism,—pessimism was a fatal vice. And in any case I was going home now, I would be turning up the drive once more. My people were there, and my friends would come out to visit me. In ten hours I was to see, from the railway, to the South-West, the blue silhouette against the sky of the Ngong Hills.

When I had no more money, and could not make things pay, I had to sell the farm. A big Company in Nairobi bought it. They thought that the place was too high up for coffee, and they were not going in for farming. But they meant to take up all the coffee-trees, to divide up the land and lay out roads, and in time, when Nairobi should be growing out to the West, they meant to sell the land for building-plots. That was towards the end of the year.

Even as it was then, I do not think that I should have found it in me to give up the farm if it had not been for one thing. The coffee-crop that was still unripe upon the trees belonged to the old owners of the farm, or to the Bank which was holding a first mortgage in it. This coffee would not be picked, handled in the factory, and sent off, till May or later. For such a period I was to remain on the farm, in charge of it, and things were to go on, unaltered to the view. And during this time, I thought, something would happen to change it all back, since the world, after all, was not a regular or calculable place.

In this way began for me a strange era in my existence on the farm. The truth, that was underlying everything, was that it was no longer mine, but such as it was, this truth could be ignored by the people incapable of realizing it, and it made no difference to things from day to day. It was then, from hour to hour, a lesson in the art of living in the moment, or, it might be said, in eternity, wherein the actual happenings of the moment make but little difference.

In this way I was the last person to realize that I was going. When I look back upon my last months in Africa, it seems to me that the lifeless things were aware of my departure a long time before I was so myself. The hills, the forests, plains and rivers, the wind, all knew that we were to part. When I first began to make terms with fate, and the negotiations about the sale of the farm were taken up, the attitude of the landscape towards me changed. Till then I had been part of it, and the drought had been to me like a fever, and the flowering of the plain like a new frock. Now the country disengaged itself from me, and stood back a little, in order that I should see it clearly and as a whole.

The Natives of the farm, in the stark realism of their souls, were conscious of the situation and of my state of mind, as fully as if I had been lecturing to them upon it, or had written it down for them in a book. All the same, they looked to me for help and support, and did not, in a single case, attempt to arrange their future for themselves. They tried their very best to make me stay on, and for this purpose invented many schemes which they confided to me. At the time when the sale of the farm was through, they came and sat round my house from the early morning till night, not so much in order to talk with me as just to follow all my movements. There is a paradoxical moment in the relation between the leader and the followers: that they should see every weakness and failing in him so clearly, and be capable of judging him with such unbiased accuracy, and yet should still inevitably turn to him, as if in life there were, physically, no way round him. A flock of sheep may be feeling the same towards the herd-boy, they will have infinitely better knowledge of the country and the weather than he, and still will be walking after him, if needs be, straight into the abyss. The Kikuyu took the situation better than I did, on account of their superior inside knowledge of God and the Devil, but they sat round my house and waited for my orders; very likely all the time between themselves expatiating freely upon my ignorance and my unique incapacity.

You would have thought that their constant presence by my house, when I knew that I could not help them, and when their fate weighed heavily on my mind, would have been hard to bear. But it was not so. We felt, I believe, up to the very last, a strange comfort and relief in each other's company. The understanding between us lay deeper than all reason. I thought in these months much of Napoleon on the retreat from Moscow. It is generally thought that he went through agonies in seeing his grand army suffering and dying round him, but it is also possible that he would have dropped down dead on the spot if he had not had them. In the night, I counted the hours till the time when the Kikuyus should turn up again by the house.

Denys Finch-Hatton had come in from one of his Safaris, and he had stayed for a little while on the farm, but when I began to break up my house and to pack, and he could stay there no longer, he went away and lived in Hugh Martin's house in Nairobi. . . .

But most of the time when we were together, we talked and acted as if the future did not exist; it had never been his way to worry about it, for it was as if he knew that he could draw upon forces unknown to us if he wanted to. He fell in naturally with my scheme of leaving things to themselves, and other people to think and say what they liked. When he was there, it seemed to be a normal thing, and in accordance with our own taste, that we should sit upon packing-cases within an empty house. He quoted a poem to me:

> You must turn your mournful ditty
> To a merry measure,
> I will never come for pity,
> I will come for pleasure.

During those weeks, we used to go up for short flights out over the Ngong Hills or down over the Game Reserve. . . .

Denys sometimes talked of making Takaunga his home in Africa, and of starting his Safaris from there. . . .

In the month of May of the year when I left Africa, Denys went down to Takaunga for a week. He was planning to build a larger house and to plant Mango trees on his land. He went away in his aeroplane and was intending to make his way home round by Voi, to see if there were any Elephants there for his Safaris. The Natives had been talking much of a herd of Elephants which had come on to the land round Voi from the West, and in particular of one big bull, twice the size of any other Elephant, that was wandering in the bush there, all by himself.

Denys, who held himself to be an exceptionally rational person, was subject to a special kind of moods and forebodings, and under their influence at times he became silent for days or for a week, though he did not know of it himself and was surprised when I asked him what was the matter with him. The last days before he started on this journey to the coast, he was in this manner absent-minded, as if sunk in contemplation, but when I spoke of it he laughed at me.

I asked him to let me come with him, for I thought what a lovely thing it would be to see the Sea. First he said yes, and then he changed his mind and said no. He could not take me; the journey round Voi, he told me, was going to be very rough, he might have to land, and to sleep, in the bush, so that it would be necessary for him to take a Native boy with him. I reminded him that he had said that he had taken out the aeroplane to fly me over Africa. Yes, he said, so he had; and if there were Elephants at Voi, he would fly me down there to have a look at them, when he knew the landing-places and camping-grounds. This is the only time that I have asked Denys to take me with him on his aeroplane that he would not do it.

He went off on Friday the eighth: "Look out for me on Thursday," he said when he went, "I shall be back in time to have luncheon with you."

When he had started in his car for the aerodrome in Nairobi, and had turned down the drive, he came back to look for a volume of poems that he had given to me, and that he now wanted with him on his journey. He stood with one foot on the running-board of the car, and a finger in the book, reading out to me a poem that we had been discussing.

"Here are your grey geese," he said:

> I saw grey geese flying over the flatlands
> Wild geese vibrant in the high air—
> Unswerving from horizon to horizon
> With their soul stiffened out in their throats—
> And the grey whiteness of them ribboning the enormous skies
> And the spokes of the sun over the crumpled hills.

Then he drove away for good, waving his arm to me.

While Denys was down in Mombasa, in landing he broke a propeller. He wired back to Nairobi to get the spare parts that he wanted, and the East Africa Airway Company sent a boy to Mombasa with them. When the aeroplane was fixed, and Denys was again going up in it, he told the Airway's boy to come up with him. But the boy would not come. This boy was used to flying, and had been up with many people, and with Denys himself, before now, and Denys was a fine pilot and had a great name with the Natives in this capacity as in all others. But this time the boy would not go up with him.

A long time after, when he met Farah in Nairobi and they were talking things over, he said to Farah: "Not for a hundred rupees would I, then, have gone up with Bwana Bedâr." The shadow of destiny, which Denys himself had felt the last days at Ngong, was seen more strongly now, by the Native.

So Denys took Kamau with him to Voi, his own boy. Poor Kamau was terrified of flying. He had told me, at the farm, that when he got up and away from the ground, he fixed his eyes at his feet and kept them there till he got down to the earth again, so frightened did he feel if ever he cast a glance over the side of the aeroplane, and saw the landscape from its great height.

I looked out for Denys on Thursday, and reckoned that he would fly from Voi at sunrise and be two hours on the way to Ngong. But when he did not come, and I found that I had got things to do in Nairobi, I drove in to town.

Whenever I was ill in Africa, or much worried, I suffered from a special kind of compulsive idea. It seemed to me then that all my surroundings were in danger or distress, and that in the midst of this disaster I myself was somehow on the wrong side, and therefore was regarded with distrust and fear by everybody.

On this Thursday in Nairobi the nightmare unexpectedly stole upon me, and grew so strong that I wondered if I were beginning to go mad. There was, somehow, a deep sadness over the town, and over the people I met, and in the midst of it everybody was turning away from me. There was nobody who would stop and talk to me; my friends, when they saw me, got into their cars and drove off. Even old Mr. Duncan, the Scotch grocer, from whom I had bought groceries for many years, and with whom I had danced at a big ball at Government House, when I came in looked at me with a kind of fright and left his shop. I began to feel as lonely in Nairobi as on a desert island.

I had left Farah on the farm to receive Denys, so that I had nobody to talk with. The Kikuyus are no good in such a case, for their ideas of reality, and their reality itself, are different from ours. But I was to lunch with Lady McMillan at Chiromo, and I thought that there I should find white people to talk to, and get back my balance of mind.

I drove up to the lovely old Nairobi house of Chiromo, at the end of the long bamboo avenue, and found a luncheon-party there. But it was the same thing at Chiromo as in the streets of Nairobi. Everybody seemed mortally sad, and as I came in the talk stopped. I sat beside my old friend Mr. Bulpett, and he looked down and said only a few words. I tried to throw off the shadow that was by now lying heavily upon me, and to talk to him of his mountain-climbings in Mexico, but he seemed to remember nothing about them.

I thought: These people are no good to me, I will go back to the farm. Denys will be there by now. We will talk and behave sensibly, and I shall be sane again and know and understand everything.

But when we had finished luncheon, Lady McMillan asked me to come with her into her small sitting-room, and there told me that there had been an accident at Voi. Denys had capsized with his machine, and had been killed in the fall.

It was then as I had thought: at the sound of Denys's name even, truth was revealed, and I knew and understood everything.

Later on, the District Commissioner at Voi wrote to me and gave me the particulars of the accident. Denys had been staying with him over the night, and had left from the aerodrome in the morning, with his boy in the aeroplane with him, for my farm. After he had left he turned and came back quickly, flying low, at two hundred feet. Suddenly the aeroplane swayed, got into a spin, and came down like a bird swooping. As it hit the ground it caught fire, the people who ran to it were stopped by the heat. When they got branches and earth, and had thrown them on the fire, and had got it out, they found that the aeroplane had been all smashed up, and the two people in it had been killed in the fall.

For many years after this day the Colony felt Denys's death as a loss which could not be recovered. Something fine then came out in the average colonist's attitude towards him, a reverence for values outside their understanding. When they spoke of him it was most often as an athlete; they would discuss his exploits as a cricketer and a golfer, and of these things I had never heard myself, so that it was only now that I learned of his great fame in all games. Then when the people had been paying tribute to him as a sportsman, they would add that, of course, he had been very brilliant. What they really remembered in him was his absolute lack of self-consciousness, or self-interest, an unconditional truthfulness which outside of him I have only met in idiots. In a colony, these qualities are not generally held up for imitation, but after a man's death they may be, perhaps, more truly admired than in other places.

The Natives had known Denys better than the white people; to them his death was a bereavement.

When, ☙ Nairobi, I was told of Denys's death I tried to get down to Voi. The Airway Company was sending down Tom Black to report on the accident, and I drove to the aerodrome to ask him to take me with him, but as I got into the aerodrome, his aeroplane lifted and sailed off, towards Voi.

It might still be possible to get through by car, but the long rains were on, and I had to find out what the roads were like. While I sat and waited for the report on the roads, I remembered how Denys had told me that he wished to be buried in the Ngong Hills. It was a strange thing that I had not recollected it before, but it had been so far from my thoughts that they should mean to bury him at all. Now it was as if a picture had been shown to me.

There was a place in the hills, on the first ridge in the Game Reserve, that I myself at the time when I thought that I was to live and die in Africa, had pointed out to Denys as my future burial-place. In the evening, while we sat and looked at the hills, from my house, he remarked that then he would like to be buried there himself as well. Since then, sometimes when we drove out in the hills, Denys had said: "Let us drive as far as our graves." Once when we were camped in the hills to look for Buffalo, we had in the afternoon walked over to the slope to have a closer look at it. There was an infinitely great view from there; in the light of the sunset we saw both Mount Kenya and Kilimanjaro. Denys had been eating an orange, lying in the grass, and had said that he would like to stay there. My own burial-place was a little higher up. From both places we could see my house in the forest far away to the East. We were going back there the next day, for ever, I thought, in spite of the widespread theory that All must die.

Denys had watched and followed all the ways of the African Highlands, and better than any other white man, he had known their soil and seasons, the vegetation and the wild animals, the winds and smells. He had observed the changes of weather in them, their people, clouds, the stars at night. Here in the hills, I had seen him only a short time ago, standing bare-headed in the afternoon sun, gazing out over the land, and lifting his field-glasses to find out everything about it. He had taken in the country, and in his eyes and his mind it had been changed, marked by his own individuality, and made part of him. Now Africa received him, and would change him, and make him one with herself.

I often drove out to Denys's grave. In a bee-line, it was not more than five miles from my house, but round by the road it was fifteen. The grave was a thousand feet higher up than my house, the air was different here, as clear as a glass of water; light sweet winds lifted your hair when you took off your hat; over the peaks of the hills, the clouds came wandering from the East, drew their live shadow over the wide undulating land, and were dissolved and disappeared over the Rift Valley.

I bought at the dhuka a yard of the white cloth which the Natives call *Americani,* and Farah and I raised three tall poles in the ground behind the grave, and nailed the cloth on to them, then from my house I could distinguish the exact spot of the grave, like a little white point in the green hill.

Later on, Denys's brother, Lord Winchilsea, had an obelisk set on his grave, with an inscription out of "The Ancient Mariner," which was a poem that Denys had much admired. I myself had never heard it until Denys quoted it to me,—the first time was, I remember, as we were going to Bilea's wedding. I have not seen the obelisk; it was put up after I had left Africa.

In England there is also a monument to Denys. His old schoolfellows, in memory of him, built a stone bridge over a small stream between two fields at Eton. On one of the balustrades is inscribed his name, and the dates of his stay at Eton, and on the other the words: "Famous in these fields and by his many friends much beloved."

Between the river in the mellow English landscape and the African mountain ridge, ran the path of his life; it is an optical illusion that it seemed to wind and swerve,—the surroundings swerved. The bow-string was released on the bridge at Eton, the arrow described its orbit, and hit the obelisk in the Ngong Hills.

After I had left Africa, Gustav Mohr wrote to me of a strange thing that had happened by Denys's grave, the like of which I have never heard. "The Masai," he wrote, "have reported to the District Commissioner at Ngong, that many times, at sunrise and sunset, they have seen lions on Finch-Hatton's grave in the Hills. A lion and a lioness have come there, and stood, or lain, on the grave for a long time. Some of the Indians who have passed the place in their lorries on the way to Kajado have also seen them. After you went away, the ground round the grave was levelled out, into a sort of big terrace,

I suppose that the level place makes a good site for the lions, from there they can have a view over the plain, and the cattle and game on it."

It was fit and decorous that the lions should come to Denys's grave and make him an African monument. "And renowned be thy grave." Lord Nelson himself, I have reflected, in Trafalgar Square, has his lions made only out of stone.

Elspeth Huxley

(1907–   )

Elspeth Huxley (Josceline Grant) was born in London, the daughter of Major Josceline and Lillian (Grosvenor) Grant, and raised in Kenya, where her parents established a coffee plantation outside Nairobi when Huxley was five. Educated at Reading University, where she received a diploma in agriculture in 1927, and at Cornell University, where she studied agricultural science in 1927–28, Huxley retained a strong interest in agriculture all her life, although her principal career was as a writer.

At twenty-four she married Gervas Huxley, a British tea commissioner whose work took the couple to wherever tea was produced in the old British Empire. Huxley began writing detective stories with exotic colonial settings to while away the time on the long voyages to far-flung points of empire, completing twelve in the couple's peak years of travel from 1937 to 1965. These travels were balanced by love of the farm in Wiltshire the couple purchased in 1939.

Huxley experienced the same enchantment with Africa so vividly recounted by Isak Dinesen, though her child's eyes gave her a splendid narrative vantage point from which to comment on both black and white societies. Her greatest talent, the ability to comment with insight and irony on the small but telling details of social life, gives depth to her detective fiction and led critics to compare her autobiographical writing with the prose of the Mitfords or Jane Austen.

Always concerned with African affairs, Huxley became a broadcaster in England during the 1950s, speaking regularly on Africa. She served on the Monckton Commission on the Future of Central Africa and was awarded the C.B.E. (Commander of the British Empire) in 1960 for her extensive writing and commentary on African history and politics.

In 1948 she published *The Sorcerer's Apprentice: A Journey Through East Africa,* describing the postwar changes in her childhood world. In 1954 and 1955 works on West Africa and on Lord Delamere's role in building the colony of Kenya followed. Three volumes of autobiography chronicled her relationship with the African continent: *The Flame Trees of Thika: Memories of an African*

Childhood (1959), *The Mottled Lizard* (1959), and *Love Among the Daughters: Memories of the Twenties in England and America* (1968). Besides these volumes Huxley exchanged a series of letters with **Margery Perham** on the respective rights and obligations of white settlers and native peoples in Kenya, in which Huxley argued the claims of the white settlers. *On the Edge of the Rift: Memories of Kenya* (1962) completed Huxley's story of her life in Kenya. *Race and Politics in Kenya: A Correspondence* (1944) launched Huxley on her postwar travels in Africa and brought her to public attention as a commentator on Britain's postcolonial role.

A truly cosmopolitan traveler and an industrious writer, Huxley published one unsuccessful novel, *Red Strangers,* in 1939 and a number of murder mysteries. Critics are agreed that *The Flame Trees of Thika* is a classic of its type, conveying a child's love for the colorful world of British colonial society in Kenya, yet allowing the political undercurrents of the era to figure in the narrator's growing love for her African home.

THE FLAME TREES OF THIKA:
Memories of an African Childhood

We set off in an open cart drawn by four whip-scarred little oxen and piled high with equipment and provisions. No medieval knight could have been more closely armoured than were Tilly and I, against the rays of the sun. A mushroom-brimmed hat, built of two thicknesses of heavy felt and lined with red flannel, protected her creamy complexion, a long-sleeved white blouse clasped her by the neck, and a heavy skirt of khaki drill fell to her booted ankles.

I sat beside my mother, only a little less fortified in a pith helmet and a starched cotton dress. The oxen looked very thin and small for such a task but moved off with resignation, if not with speed, from the Norfolk hotel. Everything was dusty; one's feet descended with little plops into a soft, warm, red carpet, a red plume followed every wagon down the street, the dust had filmed over each brittle eucalyptus leaf and stained the seats and backs of rickshaws waiting under the trees.

We were going to Thika, a name on a map where two rivers joined. Thika in those days—the year was 1913—was a favourite camp for big-game hunters and beyond it there was only bush and plain. If you went on long enough you would come to mountains and forests no one had mapped and tribes whose languages no one could understand. We were not going as far as that, only two days' journey in the ox-cart to a bit of El Dorado my father had been fortunate enough to buy in the bar of the Norfolk hotel from a man wearing an Old Etonian tie. . . .

Robin, my father, did not come with us in the cart. He was there already, locating the land and, Tilly hoped, building a house to receive us. A simple grass hut could be built in a couple of days, but this needed organization, and Tilly was not counting on its being there.

"I only hope that if he builds one, he will do so on the right farm," she said.

Farm was of course the wrong word. My father had picked out on a map five hundred acres of blank space with a wriggling line, presumed to be a river, on each side. . . .

Robin bought the five hundred acres between the wriggling lines at Thika. He paid four pounds an acre, a fabulous price in those days. As this was much more than he could afford, he also bought a share in the syndicate in Uganda which . . . was certain to make a great deal of money in a very short while and which would therefore enable him to finance the coffee enterprise at Thika. . . .

Robin got a map from the Land Office with a lot of lines ruled on it, from which the position of our holding could be deduced. Nothing had been properly surveyed. The boundary between the land earmarked for settlement and land reserved for the Kikuyu was about a mile away. . . .

It became very hot in our ox-cart, or on it rather, as we had no covering. Tilly hoisted a parasol with black and white stripes which helped a little, but it had not been made for tropic suns. I was fortunate; being only six or seven, I wore no stays or stockings, but Tilly was tightly laced in, her waist was wasp-like, her skirt voluminous, and the whole ensemble might have been designed to prevent the circulation of air. In a very short while the dust and sweat combined to make us both look like Red Indians, with strange white rings around our eyes.

Once out of the town the oxen flagged, and no wonder, and the driver shouted less. He fell into a kind of shuffle beside the beasts, who were coated now with flies. We had to keep flapping flies off our own faces. . . . We were immersed in a thick red fog which made us choke and smart and settled over everything. The stunted thorn-trees and shrubs beside the road were coated with it and we travelled always with its sharp, dry, peculiar smell tickling our nostrils.

One cannot describe a smell because there are no words to do so in the English language, apart from those that place it in a very general category, like sweet or pungent. So I cannot characterize this, nor compare it with any other, but it was the smell of travel in those days, in fact the smell of Africa—dry, peppery, yet rich and deep, with an undertone of native body smeared with fat and red ochre and giving out a ripe, partly rancid odour which nauseated some Europeans when they first encountered it but which I, for one, grew to enjoy. . . .

"We might see a lion," Tilly said, "if we keep a sharp lookout." Lions were often observed to stroll about in broad daylight among their potential dinners, who displayed no alarm. But we did not see any lions; Tilly said they were asleep in the patches of reed and papyrus we passed from time to time. She longed to stop the cart and get out to look for them, as people sometimes stopped the train from Mombasa if they saw a fine specimen. We jolted on, getting hotter and hotter, and more and more irritable and sore. At last we reached Ruiru, about half-way. We were to stop there for the night. . . .

Before the sun was really hot next morning the little weather-beaten oxen with their humps and sagging dewlaps were inspanned and we set off again down the wagon track. . . .

We had with us in the cart a cook-cum-houseboy called Juma.

Juma was a Swahili from the Coast, or said he was: Swahilis were fashionable, and quite a lot of people who were nothing of the sort appointed themselves as members of this race, with its Arab affinities. He also claimed to be a Muslim, though it was hard to say in what this consisted. We never saw him at his prayers and doubted if he knew the direction of Mecca. His only strict observance was his refusal to eat meat unless the throat of the animal providing it had been cut. . . .

"These oxen," Juma grumbled, "they are as old as great-grandmothers, their legs are like broken sticks, this driver is the son of a hyena and lacks the brains of a frog. When the new moon has come we shall still be travelling in this worthless cart."

"No more words," Tilly said snappily. Juma had a patronizing air that she resented, and she doubted if he was showing enough respect. . . . Indeed respect was the only protection available to Europeans who lived singly, or in scattered families, among thousands of Africans accustomed to constant warfare and armed with spears and poisoned arrows, but had themselves no barricades, and went about unarmed. This respect preserved them like an invisible coat of mail, or a form of magic, and seldom failed; but it had to be very carefully guarded. The least rent or puncture might, if not immediately checked and repaired, split the whole garment asunder and expose its wearer in all his human vulnerability. . . . So Tilly was a little sensitive about respect, and Juma was silenced.

We came at last to a stone bridge over the Chania river, newly built, and considered to be a great achievement of the P.W.D.'s. Just below it, the river plunged over a waterfall into a pool with slimy rocks and thick-trunked trees all round it, and a little farther on it joined the Thika. This meeting-place of rivers was a famous hunting-ground; not long before, Winston Churchill had slain a lion there, and many others came to camp and shoot. The game, like the soil's fertility, seemed inexhaustible; no one could imagine the disappearance of either.

A hotel had been started just below the falls. It consisted of a low-roofed, thatched grass hut whose veranda posts were painted blue and gave the place its name; of three or four whitewashed rondavels to sleep in, and a row of stables. . . .

Robin rode down on a mule to meet us at the Blue Posts.

"Is the house built?" Tilly asked hopefully.

"Not exactly," Robin answered. "I've picked out a splendid site, only there doesn't seem to be any labour to build it with.". . .

"Well, we've got tents," Tilly said. I think she was glad, really; already she had fallen in love with camp life and was in no hurry to become civilized again.

"There are said to be some chiefs in the reserve," Robin added. "I shall go and see them. The bush is much heavier than Stilbeck led me to believe. I shall have to do a lot of clearing before I can plough any land."

All the clearing had to be done by hand, by young men with pangas. They started off in blankets but soon laid these aside and glistened in the sun like red fish, jingling with charms and ornaments. They did not work hard, and rested often, and their wages were very low. Generally speaking they could earn the price of a goat in thirty days. This was about four rupees. The goat would be added to a flock being slowly assembled to pay for a bride.

"I can only find one river," Robin added. "The other seems to be just a sort of gully with no water in it. And there are several *vleis* which won't be much use. . . .

. . . "There's a lot of red oat grass, which everyone says means high fertility. The stream that *is* there has a nice fall and we shall be able to put in a ram. Later on perhaps a little turbine might be possible. . . . There's building stone by the riverbank. And lots of duiker and guinea-fowl; we oughtn't to go hungry, anyway."

It all sounded wonderful, except the ticks. I had already found a lot crawling up my legs and had learnt to pluck them off and squash them in my fingers. They were red and active, and itched like mad when they dug into the skin. They left an itchy little bump and, if you scratched it, you soon developed a sore.

There were also jiggas. These burrowed under your toenails, laid their eggs, and created a swollen, red, tormenting place on your toe. To extract it, you had to wait until the jigga was ripe. Juma was an expert at this. He would seize a needle which you first held in a match-flame, grip your toe with thumb and forefinger, and plunge the needle in with such skill and dispatch that in a few moments he had cleared a pathway to the jigga and extracted on the end of his weapon the neatest little white bag, about as large as an onion seed, containing the eggs. . . .

We had reached, now, the end of the road. . . . and we had to make our way through roadless country to our piece of land. This lay uphill, towards the Kikuyu reserve.

"I don't know how the cart will get there," Robin mused. "For one thing, there are no bridges."

"Then we must get some built," Tilly replied. She never dwelt for long on difficulties. . . .

Robin borrowed a mule for each of us from Major Breeches and we set out early next morning, before the heat of the day. A steepish hill immediately confronted us. Dry, wiry-stalked brown grass—hay, as it were, on the hoof—reached up to the mules' shoulders and wrapped itself round my legs and knees. There were trees, but this was not forest; each tree grew on its own. Most of these were erythrinas, about the size of apple-trees, with rough bark and twisted boughs—rather tortured-looking, not calm and dignified like cedars; they bore their brilliant red flowers on bare branches, and only when these were over turned their attention to leaves. Tapering ant-hills like spires, or the ruins of castles, thrust themselves above the grass and bush; they were hard as sandstone, and the same colour. These were the craft of termites and underneath each one, if you dug, and if it was still in use, you would find a big, fat, slug-like white queen, large as a sausage, manufacturing egg after egg for years on end.

It soon grew very hot. The erythrinas were in bloom, and glowed like torches: Tilly called them sealing-wax trees. Small doves with self-important breasts cooed from the branches. The country undulated like the waves of the sea.

We followed a native path that corkscrewed about like a demented snake. There was not a straight stretch in it, and one could not see why, it did not seem to be avoiding anything, or even linking up dwellings. Its convolutions must have made the journey three times as long. Our attempts at short cuts were unsuccessful. . . .

. . . It seemed a very long five miles, and the heat stifled us like a heavy blanket. Cicadas kept up a shrill, continuous chorus that quivered like the heat in the air, and the heads of the grasses. It seemed that everything was quivering—air, heat, grass, even the mules twitching their hides to dislodge flies who paid no attention; the strident insect falsetto seemed like the voice of air itself, chattering through all eternity to earth and grass. The light was blinding and everything was on a high note, intensified, concentrated: heat, light, sound, all blended into a substance as hard and bright and indestructible as quicksilver.

I had never before seen heat, as you can see smoke or rain. But there it was, jigging and quavering above brown grasses and spiky thorn-trees and flaring erythrinas. . . .

. . . We crossed a treeless *vlei* whose grass was short and wiry and where a duiker leapt away from under the mules' feet. Robin pulled up and said, "Here we are." We did not seem to be anywhere. Everything was, just the same, biscuit-brown, quivering with heat and grasshoppers. There was not even an erythrina tree.

"You mean this is the farm?" Tilly asked. Her voice suggested that her feelings were much the same as mine. Even Robin did not sound very confident when he replied that it was.

None of us quite knew what to say, so Robin began to praise our surroundings in a rather hearty voice he always used when bolstering-up was needed. . . .

. . . He himself had already furnished the site with a large mansion equipped with running water and electric light, with a garden, an avenue of flame trees, with several hundred acres of fruiting coffee trees.

"This is where I thought we'd put the house," he added, leading the way up a slight rise to command a prospect of more brown grass, dark-green spiky bush, and scattered trees. "There's a good view towards Mount Kenya, and we can ram the water to a reservoir on top of the hill and feed it down by gravity to the house and factory. . . ."

. . . Robin talked on; the whole place was thriving and making several thousand pounds a year before Tilly had managed to dismount and sit down on an old eroded ant-heap to wipe her face, coated with sweat and red dust as all our faces were, and start to pull ticks off her ankles.

"And in the meantime," she said, "it would be nice to have a grass hut to sleep in, or even a few square yards cleared to pitch the tent."

"Oh, that won't take long. But just for the next night or two, perhaps we'd better put up at the Blue Posts."

Robin had never ploughed anything in his life before. He had been in other parts of Africa, but had spent his time prospecting, and going into partnership with men who knew infallible ways to make money quickly without having any capital. By a series of extraordinary mischances, something invariably went wrong, and it was always Robin's little bit of cash that vanished, together with the partner. Unfortunately his father, dying young, had left him some money, so instead of learning how to make it in the ordinary humdrum manner, . . . he had vanished to seek a new fortune in the colonies, as they then were, and I had attached myself to Tilly, instead of a nanny, at the home of relatives. . . .

. . . All the good reports he had heard about the country seemed to him more than justified. Letters . . . fired Tilly, also, with a longing for this land of splendour and promise that offered sunshine, sport, and adventure, with the prospect of independence and the rebuilding of lost fortunes; and here we now were, again united, and the owners of a ninety-nine-year lease of five hundred acres of land. . . .

With hard work and patience, the vision could become real: a house could arise, coffee bushes put down their roots and bloom and fruit, shady trees grow up around a tidy lawn; there was order waiting to be created out of wilderness, a home out of bush, a future from a blank and savage history, a fortune from raw materials that were, as they then existed, of no conceivable value at all.

All this would take, perhaps, longer than Tilly and Robin had at first counted on, it would need more money than they had, it would be a harder struggle than they had anticipated; but they were young, hopeful, and healthy, and what others had done before them could be done again. Their spirits had rallied by the time they got back to the Blue Posts, and although we were sore, hot, exhausted, and bitten, although no cool grass hut awaited us, no span of oxen ready for the plough, by the time I was sent off to bed they had already harvested their first crop, bought a motor-car, built a stone house, and booked their passages for a holiday trip home, when they would stand their relations expensive meals and take a grouse-moor in Scotland for the rest of the summer. . . .

. . . Everything was unpacked and made into loads for porters to carry on their heads. Robin was to make a camp, enrol some labour, and start to clear land, and we would follow in a few days when tents were pitched and everything in order.

Robin rode off on a mule at the head of a peculiar cavalcade. Bedding, tents, chairs, tables, and boxes of stores made loads that were conventional if uncomfortable; as well as these, we seemed to have a lot of oddments, like a side-saddle, a grindstone, an accordion, the Speckled Sussex pullets, an amateur taxidermist's outfit, a pile of enamel basins, a light plough with yokes and chains, rolls of barbed wire, and a dressmaker's dummy which a friend of Tilly's had given her, assuring her it was indispensable for a woman in the wilder parts of Africa. . . .

. . . They sang, however, and marched off in fine style, though they were only what Major Breeches called a scratch lot, and did not get far before various loads fell off, or got tangled in trees, and several of the carriers grew disheartened, dumped their burdens, and fled. But the distance was only five miles, so the safari did not have to be highly organized. . . .

The gramophone had been suggested to Robin as a convenient way of breaking the ice with the natives. It enticed them, as a light attracts insects; once, as it were, captured, the advantages of signing on for work could be explained, and some would feel bold enough to try the experiment. So Robin took the gramophone and, when we were installed in tents, hopefully played "The Bluebells of Scotland" and "The Lost Chord" over and over again. As the records were scratched and the gramophone an old one, extraordinary sounds emerged from its trumpet to be lost very quickly in the surrounding bush and long grass. Its only effect was to deflect Juma from his labours; he listened entranced; and one of the mules was found gazing pensively down the trumpet. . . .

. . . After I was sent to bed, I lay awake and watched people moving about by lantern-light and the flickering of the camp fire, a small speck of warmth and comfort amid a great encircling continent where cities, friends, and civilized ways were not to be found, not for thousands and thousands of miles across plain and bush and forest.

At such times, when all the furtive noises of the night beyond that speck of firelight crept unasked like maggots into your ears, you could feel very isolated and lonely. At such times, I think, Robin and Tilly, although they did not say so, wondered why they had come, and what they were doing, and whether they had set their hands to a hopeless task. For until you actually saw it and travelled across it on foot or on horseback or in a wagon, you could not possibly grasp the enormous vastness of Africa. It seemed to go on for ever and ever; beyond each range of hills lay another far horizon; always it was the same, pale-brown grass and bush and thorn-trees, rocky mountains, dark valleys, sunlit plain; there was no break and no order, no road and no town, no places even. . . .

And here they were, on all sides only blankness, committed to the task of somehow shaving off a patch of bush in the middle of nowhere and ploughing it up and getting little plants put in, and a house built in the wilderness: surely a daunting task for two people not at all well equipped to tackle it. Like rusty hinges, frogs croaked from surrounding *vleis*, the air was pierced by the ceaseless cry of cicadas: how many between here and the Indian Ocean? . . .

. . . The young men arrived about a week later. Robin remarked ruefully that he appeared to have summoned up a sort of Zulu *impi* rather than a labour force. They were painted as for war, or perhaps a dance, with chalk and red ochre and feathers tucked into their freshly decorated hair, and they arrived in a column stamping and chanting and waving spears. At the first sight of them Tilly and Robin were somewhat alarmed, but it soon became apparent that this was all in fun, so to speak, and to show that they were ready for anything. With them were some of the elders and, at a safe distance, a party of shy and giggling young women heavily greased and ochred and covered with beads.

When they had calmed down and communication had been established, each man who wished to work was given a small square of cardboard ruled into thirty squares and called his ticket. One square was crossed off for each day on which he worked. When he completed the ticket, which might take him several months, he was paid. When it came to accepting tickets, only a small proportion of the *impi* proved to be stayers; the rest had come to see what was going to happen, and to join in the fun.

The young men's first task was to build themselves sleeping quarters, which they did in an amazingly short time merely by felling trees, driving branches into the ground, and tying together bundles of long, dry grass to make walls. But they would not thatch the huts themselves, as this was against their custom.

Everything except the thatch was prepared on the first day. On the second, the house was assembled. The young men had erected the walls and the skeleton of the roof by midday. Then a file of young ladies arrived, each one bearing on her back a bundle of reeds cut from a river-bed and previously dried in the sun. These maidens, clad in short leather aprons, clambered up to the skeleton roof and tied the thatch in place with twine made from forest creepers. It was very well organized and, in two days, the huts were done. The Kikuyu had a strict rule that every building must be completed between sunrise and sunset; if a hut were to be left unroofed overnight, evil spirits would move in and nothing, apparently, could be done to dislodge them. This was a most fortunate belief, from a European point of view.

After they had completed their own houses, Robin put them on to building one for us. It was to have a single living-room flanked by two bedrooms, all in a straight row like a stable—not, perhaps, inspired architecturally, but this was to be a temporary arrangement, until a proper stone residence went up. . . .

To build a rectangular house naturally took longer. Its roof was a major difficulty: the structure of rafters, purlins, and a ridge-beam was a total novelty and Robin's explanations got nowhere, although when he clambered up—we had no ladder—and, with the aid of many willing but unpractised hands, secured the main poles in position, much interest was shown. We started off with nails, but after the first day all the long ones vanished; we had no safe or store to lock things in and these handy little lengths of iron, just right for turning into ornaments, proved irresistible to the Kikuyu. Robin cursed and swore and made up his mind to ride to Nairobi on a mule to get a fresh supply, but Njombo considered this quite unnecessary.

"Those things," he said (the Swahili word for things came in for heavy use), "they are useful, but it is wrong to put iron in houses. Iron is for weapons and for ornament. Let us build the house according to our custom and keep the iron for bigger things."

"The house will fall down without nails," Robin said.

"Why should it fall down? Our houses do not. And if it does, you can build another."

So Robin agreed to let them try, and they bound the poles together with twine in their customary fashion. The house was standing when we left the farm fifteen years later and never caused us any trouble, and the roof withstood many storms and gales. . . .

After the grass walls had been tied in position, the house was lined with reed matting. The floor was made of earth rammed into a hard red clay which could be swept as if it had been tiled, and it was soon covered, at least partially, with skins of leopards, reedbuck, Grant's gazelle, and brown-haired sheep. Its only disadvantage was the shelter it offered to jiggas, and at some later stage, though not for several years, we put down a layer of cement. This was the only material that did not come from the farm, or from the bush round about.

The house was airy, comfortable, cool, and most companionable, for a great many creatures soon joined us in the roof and walls. The nicest were the lizards, who would stay for hours spread-eagled on a wall quite motionless, clinging to the surface with small scaly hands, like a very old woman's, whose claws looked like long finger-nails. They would cock their heads a little on one side and then scuttle off suddenly in a tremendous hurry, or vanish into the thatch.

This thatch was always full of sounds, little rustling, secretive noises from unseen fellow-residents meaning no harm—except for white ants, those termites who will destroy anything with their tiny but ferocious jaws, and betray themselves by little tunnels, like long blisters, marking their passage across walls and beams. A constant war was waged against termites and it must have been largely successful, as our house did not get eaten away. The whole house took about a fortnight to build and its cost, which no one ever worked out, could not have been above £10. Our light came first from safari lanterns, but later we acquired a pressure lamp that had to be pumped up at frequent intervals, emitted a faintly sinister hissing like a snake, made the room too hot, and leaked paraffin. . . .

Most of our furniture was made out of the packing-cases that

had sheltered our few salvaged possessions, such as a French bureau with ornate, curly legs, used by Tilly as a writing-desk and
adorned always by two tall, embossed silver flower-vases. She also
had a delicate little work-table where she kept her embroidery, and
a fat-bellied commode used as a medicine-chest, full of queer brews
of turpentine, ether, linseed oil, camphor, and other strong-smelling
liquids, together with calomel, castor-oil, iodine, and that sovereign
remedy for almost everything, Epsom salts. No more unsuitable
tenants could possibly have been found for the commode. . . .

It was fortunate that . . . when both Tilly and Robin were exhausted and on edge, Randall Swift arrived to see how things were
going. He had to push his bicycle most of the way from Thika, and
he was always anxious to get back quickly to Punda Milia, but I
think the inexperience and general unpreparedness of Robin and
Tilly worried him, and . . . he made it his business to see if he could
help. . . .
. . . Randall said cheerfully, "You need a headman here who
knows a bit about these Kikuyu fellows. I think I can find a man for
you, and I'll send him along.". . .

The prospect of a party, even if it consisted only of one guest
with nothing beyond a clean pair of socks in his saddle-bag, always
gave Tilly's eye a sparkle and her laugh a new contagious gaiety. . . .
By now Tilly's attempts to preserve an appearance of leisured
elegance, never perhaps very determined, had gone by the board.
She was by nature a participator, and had a dozen enterprises under
way. While Juma took care of the domestic chores, she was abroad
in the sunshine laying out a garden, supervising the planting of coffee seedlings, marking out a citrus plantation, paying labour in a
corner of the store that served as an office, rendering first-aid, and
in many other ways filling her day with occupations that made her
hot, dirty, and tired. Now she had a chance for once to dress up like
a lady, and she took it. She wore grey, a kind and gentle background
for her corn-gold hair and milky skin and wild-rose complexion,
and her emerald ear-rings shone with the radiance of a sunlit beech-
leaf in spring. . . .

Randall was entranced, as indeed he might have been, for she
was a handsome woman in the fullness of youth and she had besides that flame of animation without which all beauty is petrified.

I think he fell in love with her a little that night and never lost his admiration afterwards. . . .

Randall kept his word about a headman, and in due course Sammy arrived. He was a tall, beak-nosed individual with fine, almost Asiatic features and thin bones; instead of the usual blanket he wore a shirt and shorts and a pair of leather sandals. He brought a chit from Randall which said: "You will find this boy reliable and clever, so long as you keep him off the drink. He is half a Masai, so despises the Kikuyu, but the other half is Kikuyu so he understands them. If you give him grazing for his cattle, he will think you a king."

I became friends with Sammy. To the Kikuyu he was stern and often arrogant, but to us he was always polite and dignified. . . .

Sammy took more note of things. He showed me nests of the small golden weavers that built in swamps; neatly-woven purses, lined with seed-heads, depending from bent-topped reeds and giving them a look of pipes with long, thin, curved stems; he followed the yellow-throated francolin whose clutch of speckled eggs, laid under a grass-tuft, was as hidden as the weavers' nests were plain.

Also he introduced about half a dozen of his little native cattle to graze on our land.

"This is a bad place for cows," he said, "so I shall bring only a few, enough to keep me from hunger."

"Where are the rest?"

"My father herds them for me with his own."

It was his father who was the Masai. "My father's cattle are as many as the gazelle on the plain. When he moves them, it is like droves of zebra who seek water in the dry season. My father's cattle are fat as lice. These Kikuyu cattle, they are thin as grasshoppers.". . .

. . . Robin and Tilly spoke to Sammy as they would speak to a fellow European. In return, Sammy gave them his complete loyalty. African society was feudal then, and Europeans who were used to the system fitted in without any trouble. . . .

About twice a week we sent a syce down to the post at Thika on a mule. Not much, as a rule, came back, except on those exciting occasions when an English mail-boat had arrived. But one day Robin received a letter from Roger Stilbeck that ran:

"Some people you will like have just bought a block of Thika land. His name is Hereward Palmer, you may have heard of him.

He was in the 9th. She was a Pinckney, and is a dear. They are new to the game and I told them I was sure you'd give them a helping hand. She will be a friend for Tilly. I expect you have seen that good coffee land is now fetching up to £10 an acre. You got yours cheap. When are you coming in for the races? Look us up when you do. There is talk of starting a country club and I dare say I could put you up for it if anything comes of the idea.". . .

Hereward Palmer was a Captain. Although no one could have disliked the Army more than Robin had when he was in it, now that he was not, it had acquired in his mind a certain enchantment. At times he thought of himself as a great soldier *manqué,* and after prolonged struggles with reluctant oxen, broken implements, weather that refused to do what was expected of it, and Kikuyu who had very little idea of what they were expected to be doing at all, he yearned for the prospect of communication with more orderly minds. . . .

Although it is so long ago, and afterwards she changed so much, I can still remember Lettice Palmer as I saw her then for the first time: friendly, eager, and above all handsome in a stylish, natural, and entirely unselfconscious manner. Her skin was the finest I have ever seen, as fresh and translucent as the petal of a columbine. Her eyes were amber-brown and her hair an unusual colour, like a dark sherry; she had the spring and cleanliness of health about her, and a trick of tilting her head back and arching her nostrils, almost wrinkling them, when attentive or amused. . . .

[Captain Palmer] was a good-looking man: fair, with hair brushed straight back off a high forehead, a long bony face, strong features, and a vigorous moustache. He could have been nothing on earth but an English officer and the observant might have placed him in the cavalry, perhaps from his heron-like legs and his walk. . . .

After they had settled into their grass huts—larger and better ones than ours—the Palmers rode over on their superior ponies to lunch, and in the afternoon Robin showed Captain Palmer his development. There was not much to see, but what there was had been won hardly. The clearing of the bush was slow and difficult, especially the digging out of tree stumps. When you came to do it, there were more trees than you thought, and their roots were remarkably tough and prolific. The Kikuyu had never wielded picks before and used them rather as if they had been toothpicks, prodding gently round the stump as if afraid of touching a nerve. Eventually, when all the roots were freed, the ox-boys lashed a chain to the stump and their team, with luck, hauled it away. But the chain often snapped or slipped, and the oxen were apt to pull in several directions at once; and the more the Kikuyu shouted and flapped, the more confused and stubborn the oxen became.

However, at last the stumps had been drawn from a level piece of ground near our camp, and the land had been ploughed and worked down to a seed-bed that would have appalled an English farmer, but that was adequate for coffee, which was planted as seedlings ten or twelve inches high. In the dry weather before the long rains, a hot and dusty period, Robin had spent many sweaty and frustrating hours holding one end of a chain composed of thin steel rods, each three feet long. A Kikuyu warrior held the other end, and Sammy went down the chain putting a stick into the ground at each joint, to mark the site of a future seedling. This was complicated by the spacing of the seedlings in triangles, and the forest of sticks which soon arose sometimes grew confused, and had to be uprooted to enable everyone to start again.

Eventually, however, the Kikuyu dug holes for the seedlings. This task was supposed to be finished before the rains, but of course was not, and then came a crisis when the seedlings Robin had bought arrived before the ground was ready for them. In future years the plantation would be supplied from a nursery beside the river, under Tilly's care, where coffee berries were planted in long mounds, like asparagus beds, and thatched with banana fronds to prevent the sun from drying out the moist riverine soil. . . .

In theory, Tilly disapproved, at least in Africa, of everything that Lettice was or represented, but in practice she could not help being entertained by Lettice and enjoying her company.

"This country frightens me," Lettice [said]. "I don't mean the insects and the *idea* of snakes (I haven't actually seen one), or even the lions and rhinos—why people should be so much more nervous about wild animals, who nearly always run away except when provoked, than about other human beings, who are so much more dangerous and vindictive, I've never been able to understand. No, it isn't that which alarms me. It's a sort of quiet, smiling, destructive ferocity. Doesn't it strike you as strange that nothing people have created here has survived? Not even a few traces? No ruins of cities or temples—no ancient over-grown roads—no legends of past empires—no statues hidden in the ground—no tombs or burial mounds? No sign that generations of people have lived here, lived and died. Do you realize that quite soon *we* shall be the past? And what will there be to show that we have ever existed? We shall be swallowed up like everything else into a dreadful, sunny limbo.". . .

And so the Palmers, by and large, were a success. Lettice even paid some attention to me. I had at this time a hospital for sick animals, which included a lame hen, a baby duiker, and a pigeon with a broken leg. This I had bandaged with tape and set in splints made of two matches, and to everyone's surprise the bird had not yet died. (A hospital for sick animals has a quick turnover, since very few wild creatures that are both injured and in captivity will survive.) Lettice helped me to rearrange the pigeon's splints and to feed the duiker from a bottle; I do not think it was sick, it was merely small and deprived of its mother.

"I once knew a woman," Lettice said, "who wore a live snake instead of a necklace at dinner parties; she said it kept her neck cool. That sounds a very tall story, but it's true."

"There's a python in the river," I suggested hopefully.

"It would be more a question of the python wearing the woman, I'm afraid. . . . Which is your favourite animal, among all that you have seen since you arrived?"

Even Lettice, I thought sadly—even Lettice who fascinated me like some brilliant-plumaged flashing bird, or like a clown on a magic bicycle—even she did not avoid that distressing adult habit of asking enormous questions to which there could be no sensible reply. Cornered, however—I did not want to disappoint her—I fell back on my chameleons. . . .

After they had left Robin said . . . "I hope he's got as much money as he seems to have. One can never be sure."

"There's something queer about them," Tilly said. "At least, about their being here."

"He's a pompous sort of cuss, but there's nothing very queer about that."

"Why did they come? They're not the type," Tilly insisted. "My guess is they ran off together and have to live abroad; anyway, I bet there's a scandal mixed up in it somewhere.". . .

. . . A few days later a *toto* arrived with a wicker basket and a chit for Tilly. Inside the basket, on a bed of leaves, sat two green chameleons, a present to me from Lettice. "I hope they are a he and a she, but no one seems able to tell," she wrote. "At any rate they appear to be friends." Tilly and Robin thought of various fancy names for them but in the end we called them George and Mary, because

Robin thought their crests looked like crowns, and they had the dignified, deliberate movements proper to royalty.

If I put them on a tartan rug, Robin told me, they would explode. I believed him, and refused to try the experiment. Their repertoire of colour was not very wide, but they could change from green-all-over to a patchy greenish-brown with touches of yellow (suitable for bark) in about twenty minutes. It was fascinating to watch the lightning dart of their long, forked tongues—as long as their whole bodies—which would nick a fly off a leaf too swiftly for the eye to follow. They were just like miniature dragons. When they had gulped a fly whole, their expression of complacent self-satisfaction seemed to intensify and they sat completely motionless. Robin said they looked like aldermen at a city banquet who had eaten themselves into a stupor. But their expression was not stupefied: it was watchful, calm, and impassive.

We built a large cage of wire netting around a shrub, where they could lead a natural life. To begin with I caught flies for them, but they ignored my offerings. They were independent creatures, and waved their legs as if they were cycling when I picked them up, wriggling desperately; yet they were not frightened of me and never tried to run away. . . .

I was sitting one day designing a cloistered court with statues when Lettice Palmer walked in, smelling faintly of heliotrope and looking, as she always did, fresh and elegant, although she had ridden over in the heat of the day.

"Now come, I've a surprise waiting for you outside."

A syce stood on the lawn, or what was destined to become a lawn, holding two ponies, her own alert South African and one I had not seen before: a small, white dumpy animal with short legs, a short neck, and a suspicious expression.

"You've got your wish," she said. "Make the most of it, because when you're older that will very seldom happen to you, and when it does, you will often find you wished wrong."

As I did not understand her meaning, I did not reply.

"Well, have you been struck dumb?"

This was even more embarrassing, and I was still tongue-tied.

"This pony is a present for you," Lettice patiently explained. "That's what you wanted, isn't it? Or have you changed your mind, and would prefer a party frock or a talking doll?"

I shook my head, now much too overcome for speech, and

gazed at the pony, which gradually changed before my eyes. From a stumpy, rough-coated Somali it became a splendid milk-white charger, fleet of foot and proud of eye, and yet not too proud to acknowledge me as its friend and master. It looked at me, I perceived at once, with a meaning withheld from other people, a look of recognition and mutual conspiracy.

An ability to match my thanks to the gift was quite beyond me; I muttered a few disjointed words and patted the pony. His nostrils were soft and springy, like woodland moss, and his breath sweet. He cocked an ear as if to say that he accepted my advances, and understood that he had come to stay.

"You'll have to find a name for him," Lettice said. "Something very fine and grand like Charlemagne or Galahad. He came from a place called Moyale."

That was the name that stuck to him, Moyale. I thought of several others but Njombo paid them no attention. Moyale did not mean anything, but he could pronounce it.

Tilly and Robin were nearly as surprised and overcome as I was. Tilly grew pink with embarrassment and was almost grumpy, she did not like receiving presents on a scale much too lavish to reciprocate, yet of course Moyale could not be returned.

"Ian Crawfurd got him for me," Lettice said. This was a name I had not heard before, but one that was to crop up often in my elders' conversation.

"It came down with a batch from the Abyssinian frontier," she added. "They drove the ponies through the desert where only camels live as a rule, but there had been rain. One night they were attacked by raiders and had a pitched battle, and another time lions broke in and stampeded the ponies, and they lost three or four."

More than ever did Moyale become an object of romance and enchantment. Caparisoned in gold and crimson, with a silver bridle and a flowing mane, he had carried princes on the tented battlefield, and galloped through the night to bring news of victory to maidens with hibiscus flowers in their dark hair, imprisoned in a moated fortress.

"I hope that he is salted," Tilly said.

"You aren't going to eat him, surely?" Lettice inquired. But this was a term, Tilly explained, to indicate that a pony had recovered from horse-sickness and was thenceforth immune.

Njombo, who was used to mules, professed himself delighted

with Moyale. "What a pony!" he cried. "He will gallop like a zebra, he is strong and healthy and yet not fierce; now you have a
pony fit for King George."

We found a brush, and groomed him every day. His hide had
many scars and gashes, and a brand on the flank. To me these scars
were relics of spear-thrusts and sabre-strokes delivered in
battle. . . .

For a prince's charger full of battle-scars, he was surprisingly
placid. I think he had a lazy nature which he was at long last able
to indulge. He would amble peacefully along with one ear cocked
forward and the other off-duty, as it were, in a resting position, but
life had imposed a wary sense upon him, and sometimes I could feel
a current of alertness running through his body. Once he shied violently and threw me off sideways into a prickly bush, but waited
politely for me to remount. His main fault was a hard mouth, an inevitable result of the long, brutal bits used by Somali and Boran
horsemen. . . .

Soon after this Ian Crawfurd arrived, to stay with the Palmers,
who asked Tilly and Robin over for the evening. I had to go too, as
I could not be left, and they arranged for me to sleep there, rather
than ride back late at night. I was given a tent, much to my satisfaction, for there was nothing I liked better than tents. . . .

. . . Ian Crawfurd was a young man who left a wake of laughter as he skimmed along. Hereward Palmer was the best-looking
man I knew, but Ian Crawfurd was much more attractive. He was
even fairer—his hair looked almost silver in the lamplight—and his
face drew your eyes because its expression was always changing,
like cloud-shadows on mountains, and because the bones were so
beautifully formed. They seemed to have been very carefully
moulded out of some malleable material like plasticine, whereas
Hereward's were rigid, as if cast in iron. The hollows of his cheeks
and temples were soft and delicate, like curves in Chinese porcelain. . . . His eyes, blue-grey in colour, were candid and clear.

Ian Crawfurd was a friendly person who found life entertaining
and agreeable, as indeed it could be for the young, healthy, and adventurous. He had arrived on horseback attended by a tall, thin,
proud Somali who wore a shawl of bright tomato-red wound
loosely round his head, and who appeared to disdain all that he
saw. . . .

When I awoke, a blade of sunlight had thrust under the flap of
my tent, and outside the doves gurgled like cool water tumbling

from a narrow-necked jar. Also came the three notes in a falling cadence, half a whistle, half a call, of a nondescript but vociferous bird the Kikuyu called the "thrower of firewood"—why, goodness knows. I got up to pay my morning visit to Moyale and found Ian Crawfurd at the stable preparing for an early ride. His hair shone like kingcups in the morning light. He wore a leather strap, for some reason, on his right wrist, and looked as slender-waisted as a whippet in his shirt and breeches.

"I'm glad you liked the pony," he said. "I picked him out from a batch of twenty or so; I thought he was the nicest, if not perhaps the most beautiful."

"Did he belong to a prince?"

Ian Crawfurd looked thoughtful, and replied that, in a sense, he had. "He belonged to a Ras, and a Ras is a kind of prince, if frequently a villain also: I daresay the two go together more often than not. The Ras didn't want him to leave Abyssinia, even though he accepted a red cloak and a Winchester rifle and gave me his word; so he had to be smuggled out, with his nineteen companions."

"Let's ride up the ridge," Ian Crawford said. "and you shall tell me who lives where, and what sort of animals you'd turn them into if you had been apprenticed to a witch who knew how."

Everyone (he went on to explain) had some affinity with a bird or beast or reptile—and not always the one that you would think. Doves, for instance, were unpleasant characters who squabbled, scolded, and were greedy and cross, whereas eagles were very shy, and cobras liked nothing better than to curl up in someone's bed and go peacefully to sleep in the warmth, and only spat when they were terrified.

I thought Mrs. Nimmo might become an ostrich because she had a large behind which waggled when she hurried, and he assigned to Captain Palmer the giraffe because he was long and thin and had large feet and a thick hide. . . .

When I mentioned Lettice Palmer, he laughed and shook his head.

"We must leave her out of it," he said.

"But why?"

He pointed with his whip at the sun, which was climbing quickly above the tawny ridge towards some fluffy clouds as light as meringues. "Suppose the sun entered the sign of Virgo, the tide turned, and an eagle perched upon the Sphinx all at the same moment, it might really happen; and we should look fools if we got back to breakfast and found our hostess had become a wallaby."

I felt disappointed in Ian; like nearly all grown-ups, he had started something sensible and let it tail off into stupidity. But when I looked at him it was impossible to be annoyed, he was so gay and spirited, and smiled with such goodwill. . . .

"Perhaps she'd be a sort of bird," I suggested, determined to persist with the game. "With lovely feathers. A kind sort, of course."

"I'm not sure there are any," said Ian, who did not seem to have a high opinion of birds. "Rather, I think, 'the milk-white hind, immortal and unchanged,' if that isn't blasphemous.". . .

. . . The guinea-fowl were regarded as a pest by the Kikuyu because they came into the shambas and scratched up seed, and boys hunted them with sticks and hit them down from trees at night when they had gone to roost. The Kikuyu therefore welcomed the idea of a shoot, and so did we, because we grew tired of eating tough native sheep or oxen with very little flavour, or small skinny fowls, and looked forward to a meal of plump, succulent birds. So off we set one morning on mules and ponies with a picnic luncheon packed in saddle-bags: the Palmers with Ian Crawfurd, Alec Wilson, and our three selves.

At first we rode through the khaki grass, the scattered erythrinas and fig-trees, the clumps of dark-green aromatic bush that we were used to, seeing very little sign of life beyond a flock of glossy-coated goats with their attendant, a small naked boy. But quite soon we entered the reserve and, although no boundary was marked, the nature of the country quickly changed. Circles of round huts appeared, each fenced with split poles, and the hillsides were patch-worked with small, irregular plots of cultivation. Each young maize plant showed up against the rich red of the turned earth like a halma peg on a chocolate-coloured board. . . .

After a steep climb up a slippery hillside we paused to rest our mounts and gaze about us at the chequered ridges, the forest darkening the scene ahead, the thatch of huts poking like mushrooms through bush and floppy-leaved banana-trees which partially concealed them. The Kikuyu liked privacy; each homestead was bush- or forest-sheltered, each had its own twisting path that could be guarded by spells. The country was greener here than on our farms, and more fertile; the rainfall, you could see, was higher, the air more crisp, and the bush full of wild flowers, bright flowering creepers, and big flowering shrubs, especially one, a kind of cassia, that bore spikes of golden florets as vivid and as bold as gorse.

"We have seen nothing but women and children," Lettice remarked. "Surely there must be men about somewhere."

"Lying under trees asleep, or swilling beer," Hereward announced, "while their wives do all the work. Lazy scoundrels."

"Lucky dogs," Robin said wistfully.

Hereward's moustache bristled. "Young dogs should be made to work, if they won't do it voluntarily. No discipline, that's what's the trouble. This Government."

"I suppose we were all like that once," Lettice interrupted hastily, "going about in woad and making human sacrifices, until the Romans came. It seems odd to think that we were civilised by Italians.". . .

Kupanya was waiting for us under a large fig-tree outside his fenced enclosure, which had almost the dimensions of a village, because he had so many wives and children.

"Do people become chiefs because they are rich, or rich because they are chiefs?" Lettice inquired.

"The two advance side by side," Ian answered.

Kupanya had dressed up in a cloak of grey monkey-skin and wore a kind of shako made of some other fur, together with a great many ornaments and charms. This was a compliment to us; normally he wore a blanket like everyone else, and merely carried a staff with a brass knob on it to indicate his chiefly status. . . .

He gave us native beer, which Hereward spat out with a grimace, and Ian sipped with interest, remarking that it tasted of sour yeast. Alec said that it would give you a bad headache if you drank more than a mouthful. . . .

The guinea-fowl could not be shot until the sun was more than half-way down the sky and so we found a shady tree some way from Kupanya's village for the picnic. In our circle of cool shade, as if under a rustling green parasol, we inhabited a different world from the sun-soaked Kikuyu ridges that stretched to meet a far, enormous sky, blue as a wild delphinium and decorated with vigorous clouds that threw shadows as large as islands on to the hillsides and valleys. It was as if we sat in a small, darkened auditorium gazing out at a stage which took in most of the world. . . .

. . . We lay under the tree in silence, watching the sky wink at us through gently-moving leaves and hearing the rustle of heavy-seeded grasses, the far tinkle of goat-bells, the never-ceasing chirrup-ing of crickets that seemed to concentrate the essence of heat and brightness into sound. . . .

Ian lay on his back creating for himself, it almost seemed, with his bright hair, a little tarn of sunlight. It had become a fashion among the younger men (set I think by the Cole brothers, Berkeley and Galbraith) to wear round their shoulders one of the light, fine woollen shawls affected by the Somalis, and Ian had one, on which he was reclining, that exactly matched the sky. Lettice was propped on one elbow, scratching patterns in the soil with a twig. On Tilly's dressing-table stood a little pin-tray made of mother-of-pearl whose cool, smooth, iridescent lustre, haunted by the ghosts of colour, was the nearest match that I had seen to Lettice's complexion.

Ian was watching her with a look of concentration, almost of puzzlement. She raised her eyes and they gazed at one another in si-lence. Not long ago, Robin had blasted some rock out of the quarry. After he had lit the fuse, we had waited several hundred yards away for the bang. Now I had the same sort of feeling, as if we all waited for something big and dramatic; but of course there was nothing like that to come in this peaceful, drowsy afternoon lull under a tree.

An ant carrying a speck of food hurried across the dusty plain under Lettice's eye. With a twig, she gently pushed it aside to change its direction, but each time it turned back to resume the course on which it was set.

"Such a little thing," she remarked. "And yet its resolution is stronger than mine. I shall tire of this battle of wills before the ant."

"You are playing the part of fortune, who is rightly called a woman," Ian said.

"The part is too big for me." Lettice threw aside her twig. "Let the ant carry his prize to his family."

I rode with Lettice along the winding paths while shadows be-gan to advance up the red and green hillsides, turning the interven-ing valleys into pools of darkness. The round thatched huts on the ridges glowed like fresh honey and, on the hillsides, a feathery grass with pink and silver seed-heads bent before the breeze in a manner that, for no reason, always made me feel sad. The beaters made a great deal of noise walking through the shambas below us, waving sticks. Guinea-fowl are great runners; the difficulty is always to get them off their feet. We heard a number of bangs and a good deal of shouting. Small buck were also about, and this worried me, for any duiker in the district might well be a relation of Twinkle's, or might leave an orphan behind it, if it were killed, who might never be found, and die in the bush.

"Why don't they shoot goats, instead of duikers?" I wondered. "There are far more."

"For one thing, the goats belong to people," Lettice explained. "And for another, they would not provide sport for the guns."

I inquired why.

"Because they stand still, and don't run away."

Obviously this was sensible of the goats, and I felt a new respect for them. It was the same, I noticed later, with birds; if a guinea-fowl sat in a tree Hereward would not shoot it, but waited until someone made it fly away. This increased the likelihood that he would merely wound the bird, but once when I remarked as much he grew angry, and said that I did not know the meaning of the word sport. . . .

At the last stream to cross before reaching home, Ian was waiting for us, sitting on a boulder with his blue Somali shawl flung over his shoulder. When he mounted his pony his movements had the same sort of grace as those of an antelope, lithe and economical. Hereward stumped about like an intruder, but Ian moved as if, like the antelopes and the Kikuyu, he had grown from the soil.

"I have shot enough guinea-fowl," he said. "The others have gone to beat the last lot of shambas. Hereward is happy, he is teaching Tilly, and thinks that she is hanging on his words."

"You mustn't be unkind about Hereward," Lettice objected.

"Perhaps not; but he is such a fine specimen, he ought to be stuffed."

We had to ride in single file in order to keep to the narrow paths, but when we reached a stretch of open grazing, Ian again drew up beside Lettice.

"You will be going away soon," she said, looking ahead of her, and not at him.

"Yes: we have planned another Abyssinian safari. But I hope it will be my last."

"Have you made a fortune, and mean to retire?" Lettice asked lightly.

"Neither: but after a while I think the pursuit of freedom only turns one into a slave."

They rode in silence and I followed behind them, not at all interested in the conversation, and anxious to get back to Twinkle. Yet I could feel again a tension in the air that made their words memorable.

"There was a scandal when I ran away with Hereward," Lettice said. "You know that I was married before."

"I am afraid all that makes no difference," Ian said, rubbing the backs of his pony's ears with his whip. "But of course it is very interesting."

"Well, it is the plot of many hackneyed plays and novels. I was married at eighteen to a man much older than myself. I believe there was a rumour that my father lost me at cards, but I should doubt if that was the case. It's true this man was pushed down my throat, so to speak, by my parents, but I think that I imagined myself in love."

"There's an Eastern flavour to this story," Ian commented. He had tied the blue shawl round his waist, and rode close to her side. "Ahmed would think that it was all a great fuss about nothing. The only point of interest for him would be the sum your father lost at cards."

"Perhaps his is a better point of view, but I was not acquainted with it at eighteen. And I was most unhappy, which was inconsiderate of me, since the arrangement suited everyone else so well. Hereward was sympathetic, handsome, and kind. He was also impulsive, and we eloped. Of course he had to send in his papers, and it was some time before I realized quite what that meant to him. Hereward is a born soldier. So now here we are. He gave up a lot for me and I hope that he will find this life a compensation. I think he will: I think he is discovering a new purpose. So now you understand, Ian, why you must keep your freedom, or find someone else to surrender it to."

Ian was silent for so long I thought he had forgotten where he was, and when he did remember he spoke so quietly I could scarcely hear.

"You have warned me off, but I am not the type to go in search of tigers in Bengal, or the highest peaks of the Himalayas. Nor to feel my heart bleed for Hereward. We are both young, and time is on my side."

"It is when one is young that time is too precious to waste."

Ian pulled up his pony and laid a hand on the reins of hers. "Look at that sunset: time can never be wasted when there are such sights to look at, and such things to enjoy."

The sunset was, indeed, spectacular. The whole western sky was aflame with the crimson of the heart of a rose. Deep-violet clouds were stained and streaked with red, and arcs of lime-green and saffron-yellow swept across the heavens. It was all on such a scale that the whole world might have been burning.

"Wonderful, but extravagant," Lettice said. "There is no restraint in it."

"Yes it is the sort of sky that angry Valkyries might ride across," Ian agreed.

"There is more beauty in a butterfly's wing or a seashell than in that sunset; but it has a barbaric splendour in it, and an element of terror.". . .

. . . An atmosphere that was not exactly sullen, but was not cheerful either, prevailed on the farm. Robin complained that people skimped their work even more than usual and no longer sang when they cleared bush or weeded. Several of the regular and, up till now, reliable Kikuyu disappeared. Sammy said vaguely that they were ill, or had sick relations. It was curious how pervasive such an atmosphere could be. The air was bright and sunny, rain came when it was needed, flowers bloomed, work progressed, and yet there was something oppressive and uneasy. Hereward said that it was all imagination and we needed a change. Fortunately, one was in sight; Ian Crawfurd had written to suggest that, when his latest journey in the north was over, he should take the Palmers, Tilly, and Robin on a game-shooting safari.

"Get away from all this pettifogging detail for a bit," Hereward approved. "Good for Lettice, especially. Stop her moping."

"Is Lettice moping?" Tilly asked. "I hadn't noticed it."

"Difficult country for women," Hereward said vaguely. "The vertical rays of the sun." He had taken to riding over quite often to ask Tilly's advice. Perhaps he found her cheerfulness and energy inspiriting. Tilly never moped, and disregarded the vertical rays of the sun.

Njombo . . . too, shared the general malaise. Now that we had three ponies, his job was an important one, for they needed more attention than mules. He had a real talent for looking after them, and was intelligent, so he was one of the few individuals, apart from Sammy and Juma, whom we looked upon as a prop and stay.

It was therefore very disappointing when one day he disappeared without a word to anyone. When Robin made inquiries, he was told: "Perhaps Njombo is sick," but no one seemed to know, and Sammy simply shrugged his shoulders and said that Njombo was as foolish as a chicken, and that others could be found to do his work just as well.

This was untrue, and Sammy knew it. Although desertion, as it was called, among the labour was quite common, and could be dealt with through the District Commissioner, farmers did not as a rule pay much attention unless it was on a big scale, or connected with theft or some other crime. But on this occasion Robin was annoyed. Njombo had a position of trust, and had gone off without even leaving a message. Robin sent an urgent summons into the reserve, but nothing happened, so he rode up in a temper to see Kupanya. The chief received Robin with his usual bland courtesy and presented him with a chicken, which ruffled Robin further still, because he had forgotten to bring anything to give Kupanya in return.

"I will send for this man," Kupanya said, when he had heard the complaint, "but it may be that he is sick."

"If he is sick then he should have treatment," Robin replied.

"There are doctors for white men and doctors for black men. It may be that he has come to consult a black man's doctor."

"Then he is a fool," Robin retorted, unable through the limitations of the language to denounce superstition and quackery, as he would have wished. "Tell him to come back at once or I will bring a case against him before the D.C."

Njombo did return about a week later, and received in silence the dressing-down from Robin which he no doubt expected, and did not assimilate. He had lost weight, and looked a sick man. His return only seemed to accelerate matters. Quite suddenly he shrank, his bones stuck out, his cheeks grew hollow and his skin dry, as if something had literally been drained out of him. Robin said he looked as if he had been attacked by vampires, and Tilly dosed him in vain with Epsom salts, cough mixture, cooking port, and quinine. . . .

Tilly put him in her sick-bay and ordered Juma to feed him on beef tea. He had no will or life of his own, and refused the beef tea, and no member of his family came to nurse him. It was sad to see him, who had been so bold and smiling, reduced to this pitiable condition, like a blighted plant whose roots have rotted; and to be helpless to apply a remedy.

"I don't see how it can be poison," Tilly said, "because he eats nothing; the sickness must be in his mind. We must convince him that the spell, or curse, or whatever it is, is all imagination, and hasn't really any power to hurt him."

"That is rather difficult," Robin pointed out, "when it so obviously has."

"Only because he thinks so. It's a question of faith." . . .

On our return we found Alec waiting, and consulted him. He got on well with the Kikuyu and, probably because he was a bachelor and had no one else to talk to, generally knew more than our other neighbours of what was going on. . . .

"There is only one man who can save Njombo," Alec said, "and that is Sammy; it was he who put on the spell, because he thinks it was Njombo's magic that [caused the injury of] his son; and he must take it off again."

"You make it sound like a mackintosh," Robin protested. "Sammy simply ignores what I say."

"Well, we must look for his Achilles heel. And that is easy, with a Masai."

"You mean his cattle."

"Of course. If you round them up and tell him that you'll cut their throats unless Njombo recovers, or hand them over to Njombo's father, I think your Sammy will very soon come to heel."

Robin tried this, but it was not a success. His trouble was that he was never really convinced of his own authority. A little worm gnawed away at the back of his mind: what shall I do if they refuse? How shall I make them obey me? To squash the worm, he assumed a very stern demeanour and spoke abruptly, like a sergeant on parade. This was most unlike his ordinary manner, which was dreamy and benign. . . .

He summoned Sammy to his office in a corner of the store, smacked the table with his palm, and said:

"Sammy, you are the headman and you have had a quarrel with Njombo which is very wicked. You are behaving not like a man who can read, but like a savage. Do you not understand that these Kikuyu customs are bad and old-fashioned? If Njombo dies, you will be a murderer."

"I do not understand what you are saying," Sammy stubbornly replied.

"You will understand very quickly when I seize your cattle and shoot every one of them myself. Every one. I shall do this, Sammy. If by tomorrow evening you have not undone this thing, if Njombo does not begin to recover, that is what will happen. Every one of your beasts will die."

Sammy glowered like a black mountain and his eyes rebelled, but he said nothing. While he was enraged, Robin's threat did not convince him.

"Very well: finish Njombo's illness or your cattle die," Robin barked. "Go at once and arrange it. At once. That is all."

Robin knew that, if he had the chance, Sammy would spirit his cattle away to a friend in the reserve, so he had them driven into the thorn-protected *boma* where our own oxen spent the night.

"What shall I do if Sammy *doesn't* de-witch Njombo?" Robin wondered. "I can't really kill sixteen head of cattle, and have the D.C. after me. I suppose all this is highly illegal.". . .

As the day developed, everyone realized that nothing was being done to de-witch Njombo and that our bluff had failed. Robin got out his rifle and left it about in obvious places as a hint.

"A lot of dead cattle won't save Njombo," Tilly remarked. "I think that one of us ought to see Kupanya. Njombo is his relation, and surely he must have some authority."

"Sammy married his daughter," Robin pointed out. "That was what started all this trouble, I suppose."

"If Njombo dies, we can report the case and make things awkward for him with the Government. At any rate we can try."

Robin did not like to leave the farm with so much tension in the air, so Hereward offered to escort Tilly, and I was allowed to go with them. . . .

Hereward explained our mission in his barking voice and poor Swahili, as if giving orders on parade. The chief listened with a heavy afternoon face and briefly answered:

"Njombo—I do not know this man."

"Do not give me lies! He is one of your own relations."

"If he has left my land to work for Europeans he is not mine, but theirs."

"Whether he is yours or ours does not matter," Tilly said. "Listen carefully. Someone is trying to kill Njombo with medicine. If this does not stop at once, today, or at any rate by tomorrow morning, we shall tell the D.C. that you have allowed it. And then the D.C. will send askaris to arrest you. He will put you in jail and fine you hundreds of goats, and take away the staff of the chief. And he will give that staff to another. That is the plain truth. And here is our warning. If the magic has not been taken off Njombo by noon tomorrow, the D.C. will know about it before the sun sets."

Kupanya stood for a while in silence with his eyes on the ground, and a look as heavy as the thunderstorms we could feel mounting up just beyond the horizon. The air was motionless, the flies clung, and when a goat picked its way across the compound, the little puffs of red dust that its feet created hung there and drifted back on to the ground as slowly as thistle-down.

"I do not understand these words," Kupanya said at last. "All this has nothing to do with me. If the D.C. wishes to come, I am ready for him."

"The D.C. will not come," Tilly retorted. "He will send askaris to take you away with bracelets on your wrists. Have you not heard that the Governor has said there must be no more bad magic? So now you must put a stop to this affair. You have till noon tomorrow; and if Njombo dies first, the D.C. will know that you have murdered him."

With this parting shot, Tilly sprang on to her mount and we rode off without waiting for protests or denials. . . .

It was extraordinary how quickly a huge black cloud had appeared from nowhere and filled the sky. The air grew blacker and more sinister and the ridges crouched beneath a lurid, leaden light as if waiting for the crack of doom when the earth would spew up its dead. A cold wind shook the trees like a vicious cavalcade of ghostly horsemen riding the air, and then a fork of lightning lit the whole scene with an unreal whiteness, as if a crack in the surface of reality had for an instant revealed an underworld full of hidden devils and advancing doom. Trees bent before the onslaught and perhaps dug their roots into the ground.

The crash that followed brought our ponies to a halt, quivering all over. We slid off them and held tightly to their bridles. The whole air was electrified, explosive, and black. Huge raindrops came down as cold as ice and with a personal malignance. It felt as if they wanted to tear the clothes off our bodies; the drops splashed over our feet and the next flash of lightning blinded us, and for several moments everything was invisible and yet full of painful light.

"The bananas," Hereward shouted, and started to run with his pony plunging beside him. We were near a stream between two ridges, and banana-trees with their arching fronds grew beside it, dropping over the water. The storm burst fully as we reached the banana clump. The air was filled with fury, as if a wild, colossal monster was setting on the earth with tooth and claw to tear it to shreds. The banana fronds were quite unable to offer shelter, they were whipped about like shreds of rag. We huddled together with the quivering ponies and in a few moments were drenched to the skin. It was terrifying, yet there was something splendid and invigorating about the raging wall of icy water assailing us. . . . It was hard not to believe, as the Kikuyu did, that God himself was in a fury and was raging through the storm, and that the lightning was the flashing of his sword as he lunged at the devils who had offended him.

The storm rolled down the valley, leaving us cold and soaking wet, but exhilarated and thankful. . . .

"That was a near thing," Hereward said in a stiff voice. "I don't want to see lightning as close as that again. Are you all right, Tilly?"

"You can see I am," Tilly replied crossly, thereby showing that she, too, had been badly frightened.

"I'd never have forgiven myself if anything had happened to you."

"It would hardly have been your fault, Hereward. And it would have happened to us all."

"Well, there are many worse ends. I sometimes think it would be the best way out for me."

"What nonsense!" Tilly cried, trying to tighten one of [her horse's] girths. "Why should you wish to get out of anything? You have everything you want."

"I am glad I have given that impression." Hereward sounded anything but glad, in fact rather offended, yet determined to forgive the offender. "I think most men would include his wife's affection among the things he wants."

"Are you trying to say that Lettice . . ."

"I may be a fool of a soldier, but I'm not blind as a bat."

"Oh, come off it, Hereward. . . . I wish you'd help me with this girth."

Hereward, his moustache at the bristle, responded with agility, slipping a hand over Tilly's as he reached for the wet leather and obliging her to wriggle it free.

"'Nuff said, my dear. I think we understand each other. You're a very plucky woman, you know."

"I'm a very wet one. And I want my tea."

It was not a pleasant ride back. The cold and slippery saddle rubbed my bottom, everything clung to the skin, and poor Moyale slid and slithered up and down slopes now traversed by miniature red rivers. . . .

The storm had deluged the farm, and lightning had blasted a fig-tree half-way up the river slope. Robin said that he had felt the flash strike the earth, and it was like the entry of the demon king in a very expensive pantomime.

Apart from the rain, the night was very silent, but once I awoke to hear the bone-chilling howl of a hyena, close to the house. Hyenas were said to be cowards, but in their midnight howlings there was something intimate, knowing, and sly, as if they were saying: it will be your turn one day, your flesh will rot as other people's, you too will join the great legion of the faceless and dissolved. The hyenas were no doubt waiting for Njombo, and perhaps while I lay in bed their jaws were pulling at his limbs, so that there would be no more Njombo, nothing to show that he had lived, laughed, and existed, and everything that was a man had ended in a few moments of satisfaction for these heavy-shouldered shadows of the night.

I was awakened, as always, by the high, metallic ring of iron on iron (a bar struck by a rod) that was our daily summons to work. In such a soft and golden morning, alert with the praise of birds, night fears were silly; the *siafu* had gone, the doves were cooing, Twinkle sparkled like a queen, her fur dew-beaded, and picked fastidiously at shrubs that shot miniature cascades of cold water over her black, quivering nose. The Kikuyu greeted us and each other with smiles, one could not imagine the existence of terror and pain. Yet Njombo lay as before in the dark hut—alive still, Tilly reported, but only just; his limbs were so light and fragile it was a wonder there was any blood in them. She had propped him up and tried to make him drink but he seemed too weak to swallow.

"It's today or never," she said. She told the syce who had replaced him to saddle a mule and be ready to start at noon with a note for the D.C., hoping that news of this would convince Kupanya's spies that we meant business.

"What will happen," Robin asked, "if Sammy and Kupanya pay no attention?"

"Then we must put Njombo into the mule-buggy and take him to Fort Hall, dead or alive. That will force a case, anyway, and get someone into trouble, even if it doesn't save his life."

The strangest part of it all was that none of Njombo's relations had turned up to look after him. A Kikuyu is normally embedded in his family like ore in the rock, or a tooth in the jaw: organically a part of it, unable to conduct a separate existence. . . .

Alec Wilson came over next day full of gossip. It was Kupanya, he said, who had saved Njombo, and Kupanya had intervened only because the storm, coming immediately after our visit, had convinced him that God was angry, and did not wish Njombo to die. "Kupanya didn't give two hoots for the D.C.," Alec said, "but he was a bit reluctant to take on the Almighty."

"It's always a good thing to have friends in high quarters," Tilly remarked.

The chief had sent for a wizard, who had broken the spell, and so cheated Sammy of his revenge. Sammy was furious, for he believed that Njombo, out of jealousy and spite, had killed his young wife by witchcraft and caused the detonator to injure his son. There was no doubt at all that if Kupanya had not changed his mind, Njombo would have run down like an unwound watch, and died.

"I should never have believed it," Tilly said, "unless I'd seen it with my own eyes." . . .

It was remarkable how quickly Njombo recovered, considering that he had been, as Tilly said, as near a goner as made no difference, and looked as bony as a barbel when he first emerged from the hut. He never spoke of his experience to any of us, and we never questioned him, but I always looked upon him as a man who had been raised from the dead. . . .

One day Hereward rode over to ask for Robin's help. The piano had arrived at the station in a crate, and required the united efforts of both farms to convey it to its destination.

"We shall need two span of oxen," Hereward said. "I think we shall have to cut some trees down first to widen the road."

The actual operation took on a military character, with men stationed at strategic points to direct the drivers, others held in reserve at steep places to add manpower to ox-power, and various people warned to keep the track clear on the morning of the move. The worst danger-point was a river crossing with a steep bank on either side. The stream had been roughly bridged with logs, but these were submerged in rainy periods and sometimes washed away, and the banks put a severe strain on our teams. Wagons

sometimes ran backwards and Hereward was afraid the grand piano might end up on its back in the stream. . . .

We all rode down to Thika to see the crate loaded into a
wagon. A gang of lifters had been assembled, a much larger group
of onlookers had assembled itself, the Indian station-master bustled
round, and Hereward, looking as usual perfectly turned-out in
jodhpurs, barked brisk orders that no one obeyed and deployed
forces who merely ignored his plan of attack.

"I wonder what the boys think is inside," Tilly observed. "A
house, perhaps; it's almost as big as one of theirs."

When Njombo, who had by now recovered, and accompanied
us on a mule, did in fact inquire, the limitations of our Swahili
forced her to reply:

"It is a thing with which you make a noise."

Njombo, startled out of his calm, let out a long exclamation
and remarked: "It must be a very big noise indeed."

"Not big, but good. You make it with your hands."

"But who will be able to?"

"Memsabu *Mrefu.*" Hereward's official native name was
mrefu, meaning tall; but he had another meaning praying mantis,
never used to Europeans, I suppose because they might have considered it an insult to be compared with an insect that could be
crushed even by a child.

"How can memsabu's hands use such a thing?" Njombo asked
skeptically. "It would be a giant's affair."

Tilly gave up trying to explain the piano and stood in the shade
of the station-master's tin office to watch Hereward and Robin
marshalling their wagon and teams into a suitable position. The piano was eventually loaded upside down, and this made Hereward
angry, but he was powerless to reverse it. Lashed to the wagon, it
swayed off along the rutted track, a far cry from the concert halls
and drawing-rooms for which its makers had doubtless intended it.

"Stupid notion, really," Hereward commented. "Lettice would
have it, but what use is a piano out here?"

"I suppose Lettice will enjoy playing it."

"Oh, well, if it makes her any happier, I shall feel it's been well
worth while. You're her best friend out here, Tilly, so I can say this
to you. I'm worried about Lettice. I sometimes doubt if this is the
right life for her. She gets queer notions into her head." . . .

Hereward gave a sharp bark like a jackal.

". . . Now she wants to go off on this safari of Crawfurd's. Stupid idea—for her, I mean. All right for a fine, strong woman like you."

Tilly looked displeased at the compliment. "It might be good for Lettice. And they say Ian Crawfurd is a splendid shot and knows the country inside out."

"A young puppy, if you ask me. But of course I don't expect my opinions to carry any weight."

We had reached the river, and a crisis was developing upon the farther bank. Egged on by a tremendous shouting, cracking of whips, and general furore, the oxen had taken a run at the steep part of the bank and would have crested the rise had not the crate unfortunately caught on the branches of a tree. The oxen heaved in vain, the wagon started to slide backwards, dragging the little beasts after it, and Robin, who was riding by the team, bellowed, "Stone, stone, stone," at the top of his voice. Everyone took up the cry; it echoed round the hillside like a battle-cry while the sliding wagon gathered pace, the frantic oxen scrabbled with their little hoofs, and several people tried to hang on to the spokes. A couple of Kikuyu at length rushed up with boulders to put under the wheels, a simple expedient which arrested the runaway in the nick of time. The crate, dislodged by the tree, was now hanging dangerously over to one side, and a few more yards would have seen it topple over and smash itself against the rocks.

A considerable audience had by now sprung out of an apparently deserted countryside to proffer advice, while the drivers and their mates re-told the more dramatic parts of the episode with a great many gestures and pieces of mime, so that one could see again the oxen heaving, the wagon creeping forward, the impact of the tree, the wagon slipping, the oxen giving way, the threatened disaster, the yawning abyss, the heroic struggle of the driver to arrest the wagon, and finally the brilliant last-minute triumph of the two men with boulders who flung themselves into a position of danger and saved the day. . . .

"Silly idiots," Robin said. "They forgot the wheel-chocks. And I told them about three times."

"What can you expect?" Hereward agreed. "I suppose God gave them brains, but they'll do anything to avoid using 'em."

One could see, then, that the drivers had not been very bright; but what a story they would have to tell when they got home!

The wagon reached the Palmers' without further adventures,

and a week or two later we were asked for a piano-warming. By now they had moved into their stone bungalow, which seemed to everyone the height of luxury; it had three spare rooms, teak floors, bow windows, a bathroom, and gables in the Dutch style, with curlicues. Lettice had hoped for a tiled roof, but this was too expensive even for Hereward, and they had fallen back on the usual corrugated iron, painted green.

"You've done your hair in a new way," Tilly remarked. Lettice wore it piled on top of her head in soft, gleaming swathes and she had a fillet of small bronze leaves somehow woven into it.

"I thought I had better dress up like a concert pianist, even if I can't play like one," Lettice explained. ". . . I thought we might all sing choruses. Ian has come back, did you know? And wants us all to go off soon with him on the safari.'

It was good news about Ian, and I went off hopefully to find him. I had been reading about Prester John, so Abyssinia had become a place of riches and mystery, where princes wore crowns that flashed with rubies, and dwelt in castles set on the cloud-enfolded crests of lowering mountains.

Ian said he had met a prince, but without a crown, though he did have jewels set in the handle of his sword, which he used to cut off chunks of raw meat at a banquet; and a cup-bearer, a boy of twelve or so, had poured the wine from a golden goblet, and knelt on one knee before his prince, after the taster had taken the first sip. And although Ian had seen no castles, he had visited a monastery on top of a hill so steep that no pony could clamber up, inhabited by holy men with long beards, and by five princes, relations of the Emperor, whose eyes had been burnt out in their youth, so that they could never lay claim to the throne nor lead armed revolts against the Lion of Judah.

Hereward was moved to exclaim: "Revolting cruelty! What barbaric devils they are."

"Yes, they are barbarous," Ian agreed, "but they did it to preserve unity and avoid civil wars."

"I see no need to make excuses for them."

"Their point, I suppose, is that it's better to blind four or five young men than to plunge the country into dynastic struggles later on, at the cost of thousands of lives."

"I don't believe they thought of that at all," Hereward said. "You'll be defending next their habit of mutilating prisoners, like the wretched Italians taken at the battle of Adowa." . . .

"[That is] quite enough," Lettice observed. "I can see that I must deputize for Orpheus, without any of his genius. You must please be charitable to me, if not to the Abyssinians or to Ian's morals."

Our ears had grown accustomed to rhythm and dissonance, to cadence and chant, but not to melody. Although Lettice may not have been a player of the first quality, the skill of her hands, darting like butterflies above the keys, in summoning from the instrument a torrent of harmony seemed to be a kind of miracle. A hissing lamp threw a circle of light over her gleaming chestnut hair with the bronze leaves in it, over her pale skin and her dancing hands, and over the piano's shining surface, still and deep as a lake among mountains; this was a moment of magic revealing to us all, for a few moments, a hidden world of grace and wonder beyond the one of which our eyes told us, a world that no words could delineate, as insubstantial as a cloud, as iridescent as a dragon-fly, and as innocent as the heart of a rose.

When she had finished her piece there was a silence no one cared to break, it seemed to have a tangible existence of its own. Lettice herself dissolved it by arranging some music and starting to sing. Probably her voice was not the equal of her playing, but it was true and gentle, and she sang lively little songs in French. Ian jumped up and stood beside her, looking over her shoulder, as natural and easy as one of the Somali horsemen whose lives he often shared. I suppose the music had tautened our perceptions and made me see them, together in the lamplight, as something other than they were, more handsome and accomplished, more of the spirit and less of flesh and blood, more of the ideal and less of the matter-of-fact—or had woven for reality a richer garment than it usually wears.

At any rate, they looked very fine, and full of laughter as they sang together songs as light as bubbles, and as gay. Ian's voice was clear and simple and made me think of sherry poured into a crystal glass the Palmers had—the look of it, not the taste, which I did not know. I cannot remember any of the songs that evening except one in which we all joined, the French-Canadian jingle *Alouette;* and afterwards, whenever I heard this little tune, it reminded me of that evening, and Lettice at the piano with Ian by her, the others joining in with more enthusiasm than accuracy, the sense of gaiety and friendship, and the room with a spicy scent peculiar to everything that Lettice owned.

Robin decided that he was too busy to go on the safari Ian Crawfurd had arranged, and Tilly said she would not go without him; but he urged her so earnestly to seize the chance, and Hereward implored her so convincingly to keep Lettice company, that she gave way, and the bustle of a coming departure stirred the life of the farm. Ian was collecting porters, equipment, and stores in Nairobi, but Tilly wanted to contribute, and for some days there was a great roasting of chickens, a boiling of marmalade, and a concocting of lotions according to a most valuable formula, handed down by a member of the family who had lived in India, which infallibly healed bites, alleviated sunburn, and prevented the festering of sores.

Ian marched the safari out from Nairobi and camped at Thika, and Tilly and the Palmers rode down to meet him there accompanied by Robin and myself, who were to breakfast with them at the Blue Posts and see them leave for their long journey.

As we descended the last bit of hill above the Blue Posts, we saw the safari passing just below. The porters were marching smartly with their morning strength and chanting a vigorous song. Their loads were of all shapes and sizes: long tent-poles which, though jointed, poked out such a distance fore and aft that to manoeuvre them through bush must have presented appalling difficulty; a tin bath full of lanterns; folding-chairs and tables; rolls of bedding; chop-boxes of food; everything you could think of. It was a miniature army on the march, guarded by three or four askaris looking fierce and superior with nothing to carry but their rifles and water-bottles. The porters wore all sorts of nondescript clothing— tattered shorts, vests consisting mostly of holes, football stockings, discarded greatcoats, red blankets. . . .

As the porters swung by with their bobbing loads, their song of challenge rose among the rocks, a dusty halo hung about the backs of the rear-guard askaris, two men left behind with slipping loads half-walked, half-ran after them, and the column wound out of sight along the wagon-road that dipped to cross the river by a log bridge. They were gone, marching to far romantic places beyond the last farm, the ultimate shamba, where the wild game of Africa had their wide plains and secret reeded water-holes all to themselves, and when you camped among the thorns beside a dry sand-river, and dug for moisture in the hot sand, it might be that you were treading where no man, white or black, had ever set his foot before. It was a moment to lift the heart, but also to fill the mind with anguish because the others were going, and I was left behind, and would never see these far imagination-torturing places, or taste the solitudes where nature keeps her pure and intricate balance free from the crass destructiveness of man.

At the Blue Posts we ate a large breakfast, and sat on the veranda while Hereward busied himself checking girths and bridles, and once more examining the armoury, helped with an air of lofty disdain by Ahmed, clad now in a khaki suit but with a green shawl loosely wrapped round a proud, small head held on a slender neck as erect as a tulip—a little like the gerenuks and giraffe soon to be his companions. Ahmed was headed for his own land, his own people, and there was a suggestion of eagerness and tension in his bearing.

"I would entrust my life to him a dozen times over," Ian said, "but if an unarmed, harmless youth annoyed him, he'd be as likely to stick a knife into him as to hold my stirrup when I mount, and think no more of it either." And he told us more of Ahmed's people: of the constant fights between the tribes, the deeds of bravery, the feats of endurance in this desert world so different from our own and existing side by side with ours, absorbed in its own life and struggles, and quite oblivious of us and of all our complications and intentions.

"They wear white robes, and gaily coloured skirts, and turbans as bright as jewels," Ian said, "and shawls thrown over their shoulders, and swords at their belts, and they can ride any pony born, and walk for three days across the lava rock without water or the camels' milk they live on, which makes them lean and strong and gives a healthy bloom to their skins. . . . They worship Allah, and think no man fit to take a wife who hasn't killed an enemy; but they respect cunning, and if they can outwit you and take you unarmed, so much the better. They do not fear death as we do; it will come to all, and cannot be avoided, like storm or famine, so must be taken as it comes."

The time came for their departure; I cried, and so did Tilly, when she said good-bye; and we watched them mount their mules and jog away along the dusty road, and turn to wave at the corner, and disappear round a bend of the road.

I was delivered like a parcel to Mrs. Nimmo, together with instructions that I was to weave a receptacle for dead-heads (Tilly had

taken up basket-work from a book), memorize the Kings of England and the *Lady of Shalott,* learn the multiplication tables
(which had somehow got overlooked) and the life-cycle of the liver-
fluke, and draw the signs of the Zodiac. I was to have an examination when they returned and if I was successful I would get another
saddle for Moyale (his was almost in pieces), whereas if I failed I
should have to go to bed early for a week.

Twinkle was the main reason why I did not want to go to Mrs.
Nimmo's. Not only did I hate parting from her, but I was afraid that
she would meet with some disaster. At night she was safe in her hut,
but by day she wandered sometimes to the river and had been seen
to drink from the pool beside our coffee nursery, just below the waterfall, where the python lived. In some ways he was a harmless reptile—he did not emerge from the pool to threaten people working
in the nursery—but if anything was rash enough to venture into the
water, or to stand on its edge, he satisfied his hunger.

Robin had resolved to kill the python, but it was cunning and
elusive; after swallowing its prey it disappeared, perhaps into a cave
behind the waterfall, and he had never been able to get a shot at it.
I had seen it once or twice—a glistening black and speckled coil on
a black rock, its body thick as a man's thigh, like a wicked elemen-
tal shape spewed up from the ocean's caverns. I was haunted by the
fear of Twinkle being sucked, still breathing, down the great black
tunnel of its body, to be digested alive.

When I expressed these fears to Njombo he said, perhaps half
mockingly:

"Why do you not get a charm to protect her from the python?"

I asked him where one could be got.

"From the *mundu-mugo;* he has charms for everything, and
certainly one against a snake."

Mundu-mugos were the good witch doctors, the anti-sorcerers,
and it seemed that several lived close at hand, either on our farm or
on those of our neighbors.

"Would it be expensive?" I inquired.

"No, because you are a child. If you gave him one rupee . . ."

"But I haven't got a rupee."

Njombo laughed to reassure me. "Perhaps he will do it just to
help you. I will see."

The *mundu-mugo* turned out to be a thin, light-coloured man
with a narrow nose and sharp eyes who worked for Alec Wilson
and belonged, in some complicated manner, to Kupanya's family.

Mrs. Nimmo allowed me to ride over to tea with Robin several times a week, provided I was escorted by Njombo, who was by this time accepted as a trustworthy chaperon. So we left early, and Njombo took me to the *mundu-mugo*'s dwelling, which lay across a log bridge just above the waterfall, and we sat down in the shade of a tree. Njombo had told me to bring a few hairs from Twinkle's coat; I had snipped them off and carried them in a match-box, and I also brought a pencil for a present, and a packet of needles.

The *mundu-mugo* carried with him on his business two or three long gourds with stoppers made of cows' tails, and some smaller gourds, the size of snuff-bottles, containing all sorts of powders and medicines, hanging by fine chains from his neck. He scooped a little depression in the earth and laid in it a banana leaf, like a dish, and poured some brown liquid into it from an old whisky bottle. It was a great relief to me that we did not have to sacrifice a goat and use the undigested contents of its stomach, the basis of so many Kikuyu potions and magics. After he had added various powders from his gourds, Twinkle's hairs, one or two feathers, and some ground chalk, and stirred it all into a paste, he built round it a little *boma* of twigs from a particular shrub, and uttered a number of incantations, at the same time smearing paste on his neck, wrists, and ankles. Then he wrapped the remaining paste neatly in a leaf and presented it to me with the air of a marshal proffering the crown on a velvet cushion.

"You are to rub this on the head and legs of the animal," he told me, "and put a little on his tongue, and then he will be able to go to the river and the snake will leave him alone."

I thanked the *mundu-mugo* warmly but he refused both my presents. "It is not because he does not like them," Njombo explained, "but he does not want to take anything, he will help you because he is your friend."

I carried the folded leaf carefully home in my pocket, where it exuded a very peculiar odour, and managed to smear some of the paste on Twinkle's head, but she evidently liked the smell no better than I did and bounded away whenever I advanced towards her. With Njombo and two helpers clinging on to her, I managed to rub it on her legs, but her tongue seemed impossible, and she struggled so frantically that we let her go.

Resorting to guile, we fetched some rock-salt from the store and put it down in front of her. Like all antelopes, Twinkle relished salt, and soon she sniffed her way up to it and rasped her tongue along its glistening surface. I picked it up and proffered it in my hand. At first she shook her head with an impatient gesture, flicked her ears, minced away, and had a little frolic round, kicking up her heels; then she cautiously returned, sniffed gently at the rock-salt with her blue-black nose, and gave it an exploratory lick. Reassured, she licked more vigorously while I scratched her neck behind the ears and, having lulled her, basely held out a piece of salt with a little of the paste on it. She took one sniff and then recoiled, wrinkled her nose, and bounded off with her neck stretched out before her.

"She did not eat it," I said.

"If the medicine touched her tongue, that was sufficient. This it did: why else should she run away?"

I was not really satisfied; she might have been put off merely by the smell. However, Njombo was confident and he knew more than I did about charms and spells, so I hoped that Twinkle was now fully protected against the python. All the same, I thought, it would be better for the python to be shot. But Njombo said:

"It would be very bad to shoot the python. Then we should not get any rain."

"What has the python to do with rain?"

"Have you not seen the big snake of many colours that lies across the sky when the rain falls? That is the snake who lives in the waterfall. If you look down into the waterfall you can see him there sometimes. His colours are many, like the flowers your mother grows."

"But the python is black," I objected.

"When he goes into the waterfall he puts on his bright clothes. They are so bright that they shine up into the sky. If you kill the snake there will be no colours and no rain."

Robin, I recalled, had said that he would give the python's skin to Tilly, and she could have shoes and bags made from it. I was glad that I would be able to warn him, as we needed rain for the young coffee, and if Tilly wore shoes made from such a magical creature she might disappear.

The news I had so long half-dreaded now came down like a flood. Twinkle was gone. She had vanished the day before. That night her *boma* had been left open, but she had not returned. Because I had sometimes imagined this disaster, it was not any easier to bear.

"Twinkle will be safe, did you not get a charm to protect her?" Njombo said. "Perhaps she has gone to find a bwana of her own."

Every night I prayed that Twinkle might be preserved. I had faith in the charm, if only I could have been certain that it had been properly applied. With charms, everything had to be done exactly right, and when they failed, it was because some detail of their application had been faulty.

Njombo came to me a few days later and said:

"I have news for you. There is a buck up there"—he pointed with his chin—"that perhaps is Twinkle. Will you go to see?"

Mrs. Nimmo did not allow rides into the reserves with Njombo, but I pleaded with Robin, and so, with some reluctance, he agreed to come too. We followed the twisting path up the ridge that led to Kupanya's, but when we had gone about half-way we diverged, and halted by a homestead whose occupants Njombo engaged for some time in conversation. At length an elderly man in a blanket led us through some shambas and up a hill to a large boulder, and, with a monkey's agility, clambered to the top. We followed. Evening shadows had already darkened the bottom of the valley but the boulder had the warmth of day stored in it, the warmth of life, as if it were the living flesh of the earth.

Our elder pointed across the river and spoke in Kikuyu, and Njombo translated. "He says that two buck come every evening to the river there."

"But why does he say that one of them is Twinkle?"

"The owners of the shambas have set traps, and these duikers walk round them. A man threw a spear, he was as close to it as that tree, and the spear turned aside."

This was just as I had feared: the enmity and wit of the Kikuyu were turned against Twinkle, no charm could be strong enough.

"They will kill her," I said miserably.

"This man says that the medicine is powerful."

We waited for perhaps half an hour while shadows crept like a stain up the hillside, killing the gold and chestnut and copper in which the tree-trunks and the shambas had been bathed, and drawing the parrot-green from the young maize and bean-growth as one might draw wine from a flask, leaving it dull and empty. Yet the umbered purple of the shadows gave the valley its own beauty. . . . At last the old man pointed across the stream and said softly: "Look."

In the pool of shade, two darker shapes were moving across a flat stretch of grass. They went jerkily, stopping often to look and listen, and now and then to crop a blade of grass, or the leaf of a shrub, as fastidiously as a queen plucking a flower for her lover. One of them wore two sharp points on his brow. Was the other Twinkle? How could I tell? Yet at that distance, in the dark shade, I felt that I recognized her, and the grace of her movements, and the proud lift of her head. As I watched her, she stood still, sniffed the air, and, I could have sworn, looked straight at me, as if to say: I see you, I know you, but although I shall remember you I cannot come back, for I have returned to the freedom which is my heritage.

"I must go and call her," I said.

"She will run away," Njombo warned. "She belongs now to her bwana, not to the house any more."

Nevertheless I set off down the hill and when I plunged into a plantation of bananas near the river I could see them standing stock-still on the farther bank. The bananas blotted out the view, and then the stream had to be crossed by stepping-stones. At last I emerged on the other side, climbed a steep place, and stood at the foot of the slope where the duikers had browsed. The hillside lay silent and lifeless, the duikers had vanished; sunlight was withdrawing from the crest of the ridge and guinea-fowl were crying in the shambas.

I called to Twinkle, but my voice sounded alien and futile, a sound that belonged to nothing, that intruded on the valley's ancient secrecy—water whispering to stones, a soft hissing of banana fronds, goat-bells from a distance, a guinea-fowl's chatter, a francolin's call. I knew then it was no good trying to follow Twinkle, that the cord of trust had snapped for ever.

We rode back silently through the darkening landscape, Moyale jiggling, even prancing sometimes, in his anxiety to be back in his stable with his evening meal. I did not mention Twinkle again, and nor did Robin, but next time he went to Nairobi he brought me a new paintbox and a book about Buffalo Bill.

From the veranda of our grass hut we looked over the Kikuyu ridges to Mount Kenya, which could be seen only in the early mornings, and in the evenings, at certain times of the year. Unless you knew it was a mountain you would have thought it a persistent cloud, the shape of a breast, with the twin peaks, Mbatian and Nelion, blending at this distance into the semblance of a nipple. In colour it was a bluish-purple, like a grape, save for a white cap of ice and snow from which arose cold, clear little streams bringing life to the Kikuyu uplands that formed the shoulders of this great mountain, below the moorland and forest surrounding its peak.

The snow and glaciers were also the dwelling-place of God, according to Njombo, and if you wished to pray to God, you looked across towards the peaks and hoped that he would hear you; though this was only possible if you had offered a sacrifice. "Would you expect a chief, or any man of importance, to hear you unless you first gave him a present?" Njombo explained. "How then can God hear without a present?" No one had ever seen God, Njombo added; he dwelt by himself without a wife, or father and mother, but he had given land and sheep and goats to the first Kikuyu, and he watched over them so long as they obeyed his laws.

The twin peaks of Kenya, Nelion (the lesser) and Mbatian, were called after two great Masai *laibons,* or priests, the real rulers of the tribe. As to Nelion, no one seemed to know much about him, but when Sammy was a boy he had seen Mbatian, who had prophesied the great outbreak of smallpox twenty years earlier that had ravaged the Masai and Kikuyu tribes, and had foreseen also the coming of the white man in the head of a snake. He had told his people not to fight them, and that is why the Masai did not drive away the Europeans when they brought their snake, which was the railway, from the sea, and put an end to the greatness of the Masai people who had held the highland with sword and spear and the prowess of their warriors.

Every morning the mountain floated in the sky as if sketched in lightly with a pencil, and I thought of Tilly and the safari, for it was somewhere beyond those peaks, to an unimaginable far country, that they had travelled. They would see the face of the mountain that was always turned away from us, and I wondered whether from that unknown angle they might catch a glimpse of something shining in the snow, a bit of God perhaps—a bead on his cloak, or the tip of his spear.

I thought also of Ian when I looked at the mountain, for I had heard him say that he was going to climb it, and drink a bottle of Tokay on the topmost peak on the feast of Stephen. . . .

I did not doubt that what he set out to do, Ian would achieve. Yet when an exploit was behind him, he seemed to take no further interest in it. Before he came to Africa, I had heard Lettice say, he had done many remarkable things; in the Rocky Mountains he had killed a ferocious bear by stabbing it, and won some great cowboy contest in Canada, for which the prize had been a pair of silver spurs. Once Lettice had asked him what, in his heart of hearts, he wanted most to do. After some thought, Ian had lit one of the small cheroots he smoked, no larger than short pencils, and replied that his true ambition was to be a lock-keeper on the Thames.

"There life would flow past you in an orderly manner, and you would stand among your snapdragons and phloxes and watch it go by," he had told her, "instead of going forth to seek it in the raw places, and perhaps being swept like a twig out to sea."

"That is an ambition it should be possible to satisfy," Lettice had said, "by the pulling of strings." Ian had replied that lock-keepers' posts were reserved for retired master mariners, so that to get one you must first serve thirty or forty years at sea.

At this time of year Mount Kenya seemed to move closer to us, the base became more purple, the outlines darker, the crest more white. By eight o'clock the peak had always disappeared behind a cloudy muffler. The cumulus clouds that drifted all day long across a sun-filled sky reminded me of huge swirls of whipped cream, but these clouds were heavier and denser, like bands of curd, and the colour of rosemary flowers. All this meant the approach of the rains, and the planting of many more coffee seedlings. In the shamba, big holes had been dug, at intervals of nine feet, to receive them. In Sammy's absence, the organization of the labour was in some confusion; the office work, Tilly's province, had been left largely to Kamau, and confusion was doubtless a mild word to describe the state it was in. In order to keep the household up to scratch—or so he hoped—Robin announced every morning that Tilly would be back next day, and the house was in a state of constant readiness, at least in theory; in fact, the Kikuyu had their own secret antennae to pick up the vibrations of coming events, and did no more than say: "Yes, bwana, we will get ready," and continue in their own ways undisturbed.

The long rains, which in those days were expected on 25 March exactly, arrived punctually at two o'clock in the afternoon. A deluge of enormous chilly drops beat with a noise of thunder on Mrs. Nimmo's iron roof, turned our surroundings into a mess like melted chocolate, poured in rivers down every slope, and swept through the unglazed windows of the rondavels on to sacks laid on the mud floor to absorb it. I could not ride over that day to the farm, but next morning was cold and drizzly, Mrs. Nimmo was busy supervising the repair of leaking roofs, and I was allowed to go.

Rain had stirred the people on the farm as it stirred the *siafu*, they too were scurrying about in a black stream, although not of course in such numbers. They carried on their heads boxes of bright-leaved young coffee trees, dumped them in the shamba and hurried back to the nurseries for more. The shamba-boys placed each seedling carefully in a hole and packed in the chocolate mud, which they pressed down with their naked feet. Most of them had discarded their blankets, and their bare satin skins glistened with moisture and made them look like seals. No African could perform any action of this kind for long without setting it to rhythm; some of them punched down the earth with a swaying motion, intoning a chant whose beat ended with a grunt as they threw their weight on to the foot whose toes were feeling round the infant tree to bed it in, as a mother might tuck in her child. . . .

There was an art in planting young coffee, because if the little tap-root was not put in absolutely straight, if it had the least kink in it, the tree would die; so Robin hurried to and fro among the planters trying to ensure that every root was true. All the Kikuyu on the farm had been pressed into service, even Kamau, who had for the moment forgotten the cabalistic insignia of his art, the pens and digits and ruled papers, and was levering treelets gently from boxes with his fingers with a look of great concentration on his scraggy face. Njombo was there also, in the capacity of a self-appointed overseer, shouting encouragement and enjoying himself very much indeed.

"Now the rains have come and we will make a coffee shamba like a forest," he cried. "As big as a forest, with trees taller than the olive or the cedar, and their fruit will fill many, many wagons and our bwana will be richer than King George."

Robin would not let me plant any trees, I suppose because he did not trust me with the tap-roots; however, I was allowed to help scoop moist earth round the seedlings, and press it in with my fingers, which had all the delight of making mud pies with the added pleasure of utility; for children are bored with pointless things and, when they play, attempt by pretence to add the dimension of reality to their actions. Now there was no need to pretend, the mud pies had a purpose and so the making of them was delightful, at least until I grew tired.

"Memsabu will be back tomorrow," Njombo said. "The safari is not far away."

If this was so, it was time I came home; so when the planting was over, I asked Robin if I could stay, instead of riding back to Mrs. Nimmo's.

"Not until your mother returns."

"Njombo says she will be back tomorrow."

"Then Njombo knows a great deal more than I do," Robin replied. "I have heard nothing about it, and you must stay where you are.'"

[The next day proved that] Njombo had been right, although Robin could not imagine how, for he had only heard himself the night before when a syce sent to Thika to collect the mail had brought a telegram dispatched from Fort Hall. This said that Tilly was getting a lift by car for the last stage of the safari, and would be at the Blue Posts by lunch-time. So Robin and I rode down, leading Lucifer, and there she was, sitting on the veranda in her divided riding-skirt, her tight waist, and a clean blouse for the occasion, a little thinner than when she went away, but with her bright hair shining over its wide frame, and her skin still rosy in spite of the deserts she had tramped over and the heat she had endured.

"Thank goodness you're safe," Robin said, beaming with pleasure, after they had embraced. "I have missed you. . . . I'm planting out the coffee and everyone is hard at it, and the office work has got chaotic and Sammy is away."

"It's lovely to see you," Tilly responded. "And you look well. . . . Do you know I shot a lion: not a very large one, but definitely a lion: the skin is coming on with the safari, so we shan't need another rug in the living-room."

"I've got the still in working order, except for one or two small details, and I think we shall be able to start on the geraniums in a week or two if this rain keeps on."

"In a way I didn't want to shoot it, but it sloped off into a *donga,* and when I saw something tawny moving in the grass I let fly and hit it in the leg."

"We've had a bit of bad luck with the oxen, one broke its leg, and another died of colic, probably a poisonous plant, I should say; and the boys broke the axle of the water-cart, but I've made a start on installing the ram."

Clearly it was more blessed, or at any rate more enjoyable, to give news than to receive it, and they continued in this independent vein for some time. Then Robin suddenly asked:

"But what has happened to Lettice and Hereward?"

"They've stayed behind at Nyeri—Hereward's had an accident, and must go down to Nairobi as soon as he can be moved."

When Robin asked what sort of accident, Tilly said a buffalo had charged him; and gave me her glass, telling me to get it refilled. We had lunch at the Blue Posts and rode back afterwards in the heat of the afternoon, which Tilly said was cool compared with the banks of the Guaso Nyiro river. They had shot many animals, it seemed; in fact it had been a successful safari except that a mysterious cloud had fallen over it towards the end.

"And Ian?" Robin inquired. "I suppose he is hardly sitting at Hereward's bedside, giving him ice-packs and enemas?"

"Ian is involved in a *shauri* about Ahmed."

"Ahmed! He's in trouble, I suppose."

"No, it's Ian who's in trouble, up to a point. Ahmed went back to his tribe in Somaliland, or wherever he comes from."

"Ian will miss him."

Tilly agreed, and added: "You must never breathe a word about all this."

Everyone was delighted to see Tilly. Andrew had returned, limping, to his duties, and we now had a Masai houseboy as well. These haughty, long-shanked young men had shaved their pigtails when they donned the *kanzu* of office, and looked noble and heraldic in their green sashes, like figures from Egyptian friezes. Tilly said she never grew entirely used to seeing them in the house, it was as if one were to come across a couple of panthers in the boudoir. She had dosed them heavily when they had arrived for several kinds of parasite, and dressed several kinds of sore. They trod softly and were delicate in their movements, and seldom broke things, as the heavier-handed Kikuyu were apt to do, and they dusted with the care of a woman; there was, indeed, something strangely effeminate about the warriors of this aggressive, battle-hungry tribe. They greeted Tilly with an upraised arm, as if a chieftain had resumed his kingdom, but with reserve; the Kikuyu were more demonstrative, and full of questions about the lands she had travelled in, the lions she had shot, and the people she had encountered.

"You see, we have looked after bwana very well," they said, giving themselves a share in all this goodwill. "We have seen that he has not gone hungry and that his cattle and horses have not fallen sick, and that his shamba has thrived; and the *toto* also, we have looked after her."

It must have been about a week later that Lettice, heralded an hour or two before by a note in her large sloping hand on royal blue paper, came over to see us. Most people did not notice me when they arrived, but Lettice always did; she kissed me and said:

"You see, I was right: you have grown older since we've been away, and learnt many new things. But I am distressed to hear that you have had a great sorrow. It is just as sad for you to lose Twinkle, as it is for older people to lose their brothers and sisters or sons, and perhaps one's first great sorrow is the worst of the lot. But Twinkle may be happier, even if you are not; and Ian is bringing you a new pet, not perhaps so lively as Twinkle, but with a charm of his own. He wears a handsome black and yellow armour, and comes from the dry country in the north and can only speak Somali, so you must keep him warm and teach him English. He is called Mohammed, and eats grass."

Mohammed was a tortoise, and Ian would escort him to Thika in a few days.

Tilly imported from England twelve more Speckled Sussex pullets and a cockerel to make a new start. We rode down to meet them at the station on a cool, wet day with low clouds, and an inclination to drizzle: we had weather like that sometimes in July and August, but it did not last.

We met several neighbours at the station and they all discussed the same topic, bad news from Europe, and the probability of war. Austria and Serbia were fighting, Belgrade was in flames, the Bank of England had closed its doors. All this came as a complete surprise to Tilly and Robin. People said the Army was mobilizing and that, if England went to war with Germany, we should at once invade German East Africa, and everyone would volunteer.

"I had better go to Nairobi and see what's happening," Robin said. Tilly replied:

"Let's get these pullets settled in first, for goodness' sake. I don't want to lose them all a second time."

Both my parents were rather silent on the ride home. There was a lot to think about. What would happen to the farm? To Tilly and me? To the crops and plans?

"It won't last long long, that's certain," Robin remarked. "No country could afford it, for one thing."

Robin belonged to some kind of reserve force, having been in the Yeomanry, and began to fuss about getting back to his regiment.

Next day he had a cable saying: "European war inevitable." So he packed his bag and rode off the following day to the station to catch a train to Nairobi. Tilly felt restless, worried, and out of things. No one thought of lessons, she busied herself with looking after the new chickens and organizing the labour force.

"It's no good leaving me alone with your still," she had said to Robin. "You will have to come back and show me how to work it."

"It's very easy," Robin had assured her. "There are just one or two little parts it needs. I can get them in Nairobi and bring them back when I come."

"What will Hereward do, I wonder?"

"Of course, he'll be recalled to his regiment, and I suppose go home by the next boat."

"I'm glad someone will be pleased about the war," Tilly had said.

Narrowly avoiding Bowker's Horse, Robin got himself a job to do with Intelligence. He was delighted with it, and even more delighted to delve into a tin trunk in the store and extract his kilt and its accoutrements. Whether it was needed for Intelligence I do not know, but he took it off to Nairobi, and that was the last we saw of him for some time. It was decided that Tilly was not to stay by herself on the farm, but was to take part in Nairobi in the starting of a military hospital. Alec Wilson offered to look after the farm; later on, he also took over the Palmers', and led a more strenuous life than many people did who had joined the Army. There remained my own future to be settled. Ian Crawfurd had an elder-brother, Humphrey, with a farm upcountry, and a wife. Tilly had met them both and liked them; and when Mrs. Crawfurd wrote to offer me a sanctuary she accepted gratefully, and threw in the Speckled Sussex pullets for good measure. I was not allowed to take George and Mary, the chameleons, nor Mohammed the tortoise, but Njombo promised to look after them as faithfully as if I had been there. To part with Moyale was the worst of all. It was a bitter moment when he ate his last lick of sugar from my hand, nuzzling me with his soft muzzle, and cocking one ear forward and one back. Moyale would look next day for his sugar, his carrots, his patting, his exercise, and I should not be there. Would Njombo keep his promises? Or would some *shauri* claim his interest and Moyale grow neglected and forlorn?

"We are not going for ever," Tilly said. "I expect we shall be back before Christmas, and meanwhile I shall come out at week-ends to see that things are all right."

"But I don't want to go!"

"Well, you must blame the Kaiser, he is the one. . . . Don't forget to clean your teeth, and try not to scratch your head so often, and when you ride for heaven's sake keep your toes straight and your heels down, and your elbows in, and don't look so much like a performing monkey."

At the end of the track, I told myself, would be Mr. Crawfurd, and he would be just like Ian only rather larger, because he was the elder of the two. But Humphrey Crawfurd was another surprise. He was not like Ian at all, in fact I did not believe that they were brothers. Humphrey was certainly much larger, but dark instead of fair, with a heavy moustache and big thick hands; indeed he was heavy all over, bulky, silent, he did not sparkle at all. . . .

In the Crawfurds' sitting-room there was a photograph of Ian, looking young and handsome in a kilt. I hoped that he would come to see his brother, but Mrs. Crawfurd said that he had gone to a district called the Trans Nzoia, wild and uninhabited, to take up land the Government had given out, and start a farm of his own.

"But of course he won't stay there when he hears about the war," she added. "He will go straight down to Nairobi to join up. But I don't know how the news will reach him, there are no posts, and he said he wasn't coming back until he'd built a house and planted a crop, what sort of crop I can't imagine, and it's really quite unlike Ian to stay in one place and be a farmer, he will probably go off into the blue as soon as he gets wind of a herd of elephants. Do you think he will ever make a farmer, Humphrey?"

"No."

"Although, of course it may be a sign that he's wanting to settle down, and perhaps for the usual reasons; it is high time that he was married, although I can't imagine him as a domesticated husband with a little woman fetching him his slippers. . . ."

"No."

Soon after the buffaloes were shot I rode with Dirk [an employee of the Crawfurds] to Londiani, which was then railhead for the Uasin Gishu plateau and all the country beyond—the Trans Nzoia, the far and fabulous Mount Elgon, and great valleys and escarpments only visited by hunters, and by very few of them.

The Crawfurds had not wanted me to go with Dirk, whose object was to get some cartridges, but Kate Crawfurd was unwell, Mr. Crawfurd was busy, and I insistent, and so they gave way. Dirk had not wanted me either, but he had little choice; I mounted the pony the Crawfurds had lent me, a white one called Snowball, and set out at his side. On the whole he was a good-natured young man, and used to children. He had grey eyes and a skin that, although sunburned, was so fine-grained as to look almost transparent. Years later, I saw a pumpkin hollowed out for Hallowe'en with a lighted candle inside. The pumpkin's flesh shone with a deep golden glow that suddenly reminded me of Dirk's complexion as I had noticed it on this long ride.

Dirk had come to the country, as a boy, seven years earlier, with a party of Boers conducted from the Transvaal by a patriarch called Mr. van Rensburg, a modern Joshua leading his people to the Promised Land on the last of all the treks of the Afrikaner people. . . .

By the time Dirk had finished telling me this, and much else besides, we had reached Londiani, or at least seen the roofs, which shone like a pool of water in a fold of the downs. The corrugated iron threw back the sunlight and we seemed to be arriving at a city of splendour and glory, like the ancient capitals of Lanka that were copper-domed.

Londiani shrank, however, on our approach, as if it had drunk from the bottle Alice found at the bottom of the rabbit-hole; it shrank, withered, and turned into a single rutted street with a few *dukas,* some sheds beside the railway, a *dak* bungalow, and a D.C.'s office with a flag-pole.

"Is that all there is?" I asked.

Dirk laughed. "What are you expecting?"

Whatever it had been, Londiani did not possess it. I was by then tired, sore, and hungry, despite a sandwich and some roasted mealies Dirk had shared with me as we rode along.

"Now what shall I do with you?" Dirk wondered. Had I been a pony, he would have turned me out to graze.

"I'm hungry."

"We had better go to the D.C."

"Will he have some breakfast?"

"Certain to."

District Commissioners were accustomed to deal with any situation that might arise, and I do not remember that this one showed any great surprise at being handed over a stray child. He passed me on to his wife, who gave me a feast. On farms, the bread was made with yeast brewed from bananas or potatoes and imported dried hops, and was nearly always sour, and hard as old boots, so that one of the luxuries farmers most enjoyed when they visited a town, even a little one like Londiani, was baker's bread. Mrs. Pascoe's toast was pliant and delicious, and she even had apples and sausages, the rarest of treats. Nothing in the world tastes better than a crisp and spicy sausage, steaming from the pan, after a long ride on a sunny morning.

Mrs. Pascoe was a kind-hearted woman with a well-developed sense of duty; these two attributes had made her into a dumping-ground for other people's pets, and a soft option of the locals, who caught birds and animals in the forest to bring to her for the six-pence she would generally pay to rescue them from their misery, and so the house was full of small beasts like bush-babies and mongooses, and larger ones occupied pens outside.

Mr. Pascoe soon appeared looking rather harassed, and no wonder; the war had upset everything, and this was mail-train day, so his office was full of citizens with *shauris* needing immediate attention. No one expected to be kept waiting, and everyone felt that his turn ought to come first.

"What are we going to do with this child?" Mr. Pascoe demanded. "We can't keep her here, like those infernal mongooses."

"I'm going back with Dirk," I said.

"That young Dutchman? What makes you think he's going back to the Crawfurds?"

"He came to get some cartridges."

"Cartridges my foot. He's probably on the way to the plateau by now, or else to Nairobi to join the party."

"But he's got Mr. Crawfurd's pony."

Mr. Pascoe only laughed. "*That* won't bother him."

"I don't think we've any right to jump to conclusions," Mrs. Pascoe said. "He is probably quite an honest young man."

"Not if he's a Dutchman," Mr. Pascoe said ferociously. "They're in my office all day long. Permits to move cattle that turn out to be pinched from the Nandi—cases against each other that turn out to be faked—beacons moved about in the night—slippery as eels, the whole blessed lot of them. Now, what are we going to do about this brat?"

"I can go home by myself," I said.

"You certainly can't. Perhaps there'll be someone on the train who can take you to Molo, and then the Crawfurds can collect you there. As if I hadn't enough to do without playing nursemaid to a stray female brat!"

He was not really a savage man, just a little gruff and disconcerted; and in the end he called for Snowball, who had also breakfasted, and allowed me to ride with him to the *dak* bungalow to
find out if anyone had seen Dirk.

The bungalow, a railway rest house, was full of bearded, dust-
stained Dutchmen who fell silent as Mr. Pascoe approached; when
he spoke they greeted him politely but with a wary, almost shifty
look, behaving a little like wildebeeste that smell a lion about; they
do not panic and gallop off, but tend rather to huddle together, stop
grazing, and stand ready for action, although uncertain what to do.
Mr. Pascoe addressed a man who looked exactly like a leathery,
bearded Boer, but spoke with the accents of Scotland.

"You're wearing your boots today, Sandy."

"Aye, my feet are looking after them. It's necessary, in a thiev-
ing crowd like this."

Sandy was one of the few transport-riders who was not a Boer.
He was said to keep his boots in a knapsack and to walk barefoot
beside his oxen in order to save the leather, and to have travelled
back to Scotland on a third-class railway ticket from Londiani to
Nakuru. Another story was that he once rode on muleback for
three days into the Kavirondo country to retrieve a stolen pair of
socks; but others said this was untrue, because he had never owned
any socks.

When Mr. Pascoe inquired about Dirk, Sandy said:

"Och, he'll have gone after his brother, up to Sixty-Four. The
brother came through by the last mail, to fetch his gun before he
went for a soldier."

"You mean he took the pony?" Mr. Pascoe said.

Sandy looked astonished. "You don't think there's a Dutchman
living who'd pay for transport when he could get his legs across a
nag?"

In spite of Sandy's certainty and Mr. Pascoe's smile, I felt sure
that Dirk would return the pony. Although Mr. Crawfurd would no
doubt regard his present action as a theft, to a Dutchman or to an
African it would appear merely as a rather long borrow.

Mr. Pascoe had decided that I was to stay the night and accompany the Montagus to Nakuru next day, where the Crawfurds
would meet me. He had sent a syce to Molo on Snowball with a
note to this effect. I knew that Mrs. Crawfurd would be worried
and Mr. Crawfurd angry, and wanted to ride back on Snowball my-

self, but Mr. Pascoe would not allow it, and there was nothing to be done. However, when we boarded the train it appeared that we were to travel in the guard's van, and this redeemed the disappointment.

Even the Uganda Mail, which ran three times a week, was not a very fast train, and our goods made no pretences. Several steepish gradients so much exhausted our little locomotive that it paused a long time to regain strength, while its boilers cooled and the logs that it devoured were re-stacked. Once or twice it failed altogether at the first attempt, retreated, and took a longer run, while some of the passengers got out and walked, as if to help it. At every station it drank prodigious quantities of water while the crew, and various attendants who had attached themselves to it, got off to bargain with vendors of bananas, cooked maize, chickens, eggs, gruel, oranges, and the many other comestibles on offer at every halt. In fact our train made something of a triumphal progress, with long pauses to allow the people to admire at close quarters a creature so strange and inexplicable, that brought to remote places a flavour of adventure, a whiff of the mystery of unknown lands.

We arrived in Nakuru latish in the evening, and made our way to the hotel. I was sent to bed in a cubby-hole too noisy to permit easy sleep. The kitchen quarters were nearby, in the public rooms people stumped about on bare boards, and in the bar a sing-song developed, interrupted by shouts and laughter, and once by the smashing of glass. The hotel belonged to Lord Delamere and sometimes, when he felt the need of a rough-house, he would drive into Nakuru in a buggy and start to break up his own property.

Sometime in the night, a commotion arose. The station was very close, and I awoke to hear an engine panting and grinding, bells clanging, whistles blowing, shouts and cries. Had the Germans captured Nakuru, were we all to be lined up and shot? As I did not wish to be shot in my pyjamas, I dressed and went out to investigate.

A train was in, the platform was alive with khaki men, like giant ants whose nest has been disturbed. But Germans would be grim, orderly, and helmeted; these men wore slouch hats or no hats at all, and even in the hard, shadowy light looked young and gay.

"It's the Mounted Rifles on their way back from Kisumu, they've won a great victory."

I looked round to see the thin and smiling face of Ian Crawfurd.

"I hear you are staying with Kate and Humphrey; you must give them my love, and say that I shall write, and that I hope they are very well."

"All right. . . . Thank you very much for Mohammed," I said. "But I had to leave him at home."

"Yes, he would not at all enjoy Molo; you would have had to make a coat for him from a blanket, with a hole to push his head through."

"I didn't want to leave him at Thika, but . . ."

Above all I wanted to hold Ian's attention, not to lose him, and to find some thread to lead me on to all the questions I longed to burst out with. But it was no use, they jammed my tongue. The moment passed, Ian turned away. . . .

He took my hand for a moment to say good-bye.

"Did Ahmed come back?" I managed to eject one of the questions, even if it was a minor one, out on the perimeter.

"Funny you should mention that. He did, and he's joined a troop of Somali scouts and has a pony and a rifle, and glorious dreams of war and loot. So he's all right. Give my love to Tilly when you see her, and to everyone else. . . ."

He stood for a moment as still as a fish-eagle above a swirling muddy stream, looking down at me, his hat in one hand and the other resting lightly on his belt. I thought he looked thinner even than before, older perhaps. The name in both our minds lay unspoken between us like a barrier, and yet uniting us, for this fleeting instant, like fish caught in the same net. So strong was this impression that I thought I heard through the chatter a clear musical voice and sensed among the stale platform odours, and the lingering reminder of bread, the sunny scent of heliotrope.

Ian hesitated; perhaps he, too, did not want to put to flight the ghosts of happiness whose presence there beside us turned all the khaki men of flesh and blood into puffs of vapour. Then he slipped from one wrist a little bracelet he wore—such things were then in fashion—of plaited hair pulled from a lion's tail.

"He had courage: some people eat the heart, but I doubt if that's necessary."

I took it without finding anything to say, but I knew in my own heart that it was not for me. He smiled at us, waved a hand, and vanished into the throng and bustle of the train, which was now preparing for departure.

A couple of days later I, too, found myself in the train and bound in the same direction, although not for the war. The Crawfurds, who came down from Molo together, had decided not to keep me any longer. Humphrey said he was tired of my disappearing act, and that Kate had other things to think about; and they had heard from Tilly, who had done all she could for the time being at the hospital, and was returning to Thika, that she would like me back again.

Tilly was at Nairobi station.

Robin was still away somewhere on the railway, or perhaps on the German border, no one knew; the next day we took the train to Thika and once more rode out to the farm.

Several of the flame trees, now taller than I was, flanking the future drive, had burst into flower. The young coffee trees were looking healthy and had a few green berries on them, their first. I was thankful to discover Moyale in excellent health, too plump if anything.

Here on the farm the war, except for Robin's absence, might not have existed at all.

A chit came one day from Lettice: she had returned, and invited Tilly over for the night. I went too, because there was no one to be left with, and for the same reason a syce carried over a woven-reed basket containing a pair of carrier pigeons Tilly had bought from a man who kept a *duka* in the farthest depths of the Masai reserve, and used a pigeon post to Nairobi. Tilly anticipated a need for carrier pigeons when our troops were pursuing Germans beyond Tabora and hoped, by breeding them, to make a small contribution to the war.

Lettice we found pale and tired; her eyes looked huge and dark, a peaty brown. She kept patting her hair and making other nervous gestures, and she had taken up smoking. The smell of heliotrope was still there, but almost overlaid by Turkish tobacco.

"Hereward expects to get a passage any time now, and I shall follow by the next ship I can get on to."

They fell silent, with an unspoken question lying heavily between them. Lettice had taken up her tapestry work, but she was only fiddling with it. She sat on a low stool of plaited thongs before the open fireplace, her head, with its chestnut hair loosely gathered up, bent over the neglected work, and Tilly was on the deep velvet sofa, frowning a little over her thoughts, which might have been of

Lettice and her troubles, or of the pigeons and theirs, or of Robin, or of some new notion that was coming to birth.

Lettice was able to say:

"I saw Ian in Nairobi."

"Yes. . . . May I try one of your cigarettes?" I had never seen Tilly smoke before. She puffed experimentally, blowing out the smoke in little jets.

"You know he took up some land at the back of beyond, near a mountain. He said it had caves full of bats, and wonderful butterflies. His nearest neighbour brought a house out from England in bits, carried for the last hundred miles or so by porters, and kept a cheetah chained to his veranda."

"Ian is chasing Germans on the border, if they're not chasing him, and Hereward's heart is absolutely set on becoming a hero. . . . Oh, Tilly, what am I to do?"

Lettice had jumped to her feet and was prowling round the room, changing the position of an arum lily in a vase, patting out a cushion, winding up a little leather-coated clock on her writing table.

We rode back next morning with the pigeons, and a few days later Robin came home on leave, bringing me a present of a pair of German field-glasses, and a lot of news about the war, which was not going very well. However, the Mounted Rifles were patrolling the border and hoped to meet the Germans in a fair fight at any moment, and of course to win a victory. So far the enemy had avoided open battle in a typically Teutonic way; the bush was exceedingly thick, and more trouble had been caused by rhinos than by Germans; hyenas were so bold that, at night, the men made pillows of their saddles, and even then sometimes the leather was chewed. Malaria was the worst enemy. A secret force was said to be coming by sea from India to land on the German flank, and that would turn the balance, Robin believed.

"After that I shall be able to get home without any trouble, except that all the ships are full. There's a rumour that my battalion has gone to France already. It's maddening to be stuck out here."

I cannot remember how long it was after Robin's leave that Alec Wilson appeared, looking for Tilly.

I found Tilly on the veranda, with Alec, having a late cup of tea. They both looked gloomy, and Tilly's eyes were red.

"Run along now and play with something," she said.

"With what?"

"Oh, never mind. Why don't you sit down and read a book?"

I went inside and looked at an atlas lying on the table, but I could hear them talking on the veranda.

I knew that someone was dead. People often died, animals and people; I had seen a dead body once, lying in the grass by the side of the road; a cloud of flies had risen from it, the ponies had shied, I had been hustled past it, and past the stench of putrefaction. It did not make any great impression. But none of that could be connected with Lettice, or with anyone I knew.

When I sat over my supper, and the lamps had been brought in, I asked Tilly if anything was wrong with Lettice.

"Nothing, so far as I know."

"Are you going to see her tomorrow?"

"Probably."

"Can I come too?"

"No, you have been neglecting your lessons; you must learn some French verbs."

"We should have lost Mohammed, if it hadn't been for the string; do you know, he dug himself a hole under the Cape gooseberries. Will Ian come back soon?"

"Ian—well, if you must know, he has been killed. Now don't ask any more questions, and I'll read to you for twenty minutes before you go to bed."

This was a great treat—we were reading *Robbery Under Arms* at the time—and so I did not think any more then about Ian, but when I was in bed I remembered how I had seen him on the station platform, and how his hair had shone in the lamplight like a golden sovereign, and the bracelet he had given me made from a lion's tail. I had it wrapped in tissue paper and tucked safely into my scrapbook, too valuable to wear. It was hard to imagine a dead Ian, lying limply in the grass with blood on his face and flies buzzing over him, so hard in fact that I gave it up and thought of him as I had seen him when we had found the whydah birds dancing, and when he had lain under the fig-tree talking to Lettice, and when they had sung together after the piano had arrived. I had not seen Ian many times, but each time had been like a special treat, even though nothing unusual had happened; when he had been there it had seemed as if the sun had been shining, and I thought that he would never altogether disappear from my mind.

The life of the farm continued as usual on the surface, but underneath there was a feeling of suspense and uncertainty. Our time at Thika was running out and everyone knew it, even though no word had been said.

Tilly was waiting for news of Robin, of the war, of our departure; and when news did come, it was never good.

I put away the bracelet, and for a long time valued it. When I was away from Africa I would sometimes take it out and look at it, and think of the tawny lion crouching among wiry grasses and grey boulders, and the heat and aromatic smell, and dust and dryness, and the flat-topped acacias with their tightly clustering yellow sweet-smelling flowers, and the big clouds with their crowded sail throwing patterns on the furrowed hills, and the doves cooing, and the whistling thorns.

To be torn up by the roots is a sad fate for any growing thing, and I did not want to leave Thika for the unknown.

I took Moyale for a farewell ride in the reserve.

It was, as I remember, a cloudy day, with a sky of storms, low and threatening. Yet the sun threw long, triumphant shafts down the ridges to make huts and trees and goats look hard and solid, as if carved from wood, like objects in a toy farmyard. The green of the new grass was so intense and fierce that every hillside seemed afire with an emerald flame, rising to meet a sky of glutinous indigo. Moyale's progress was dignified; nothing would hurry him.

"Kiss each of the four walls of the living-room," Tilly said, "and you will come back for sure." I did so, and fingered Kupanya's bead necklace with the men, women, and children in it, and felt better. This was only an interlude, like going to Molo, and everything would still be here to greet us when we returned after the war.

Mary Benson

(1919–)

Mary Benson was born in Pretoria to Cyril and Lucy Stubbs Benson, members of a prosperous professional family. She lived the conventional childhood of an affluent white family, the home of her youth in sight of the Pretoria jail, where so many fighters against apartheid were to endure torture and solitary confinement.

Benson left home in 1941 to serve as an officer in the South African Women's Army. Her service opened a much larger world to her through work in Cairo, North Africa, and Europe. A passionate affair with an already married British officer helped to further dislodge her from her comfortable family life and set her looking for adventure in the film world in Hollywood and the United Kingdom, where she became secretary to the British movie producer David Lean.

By the late 1940s Benson was emotionally involved with and politically committed to Michael Scott, one of the Anglican clerics who first took up the cause of black South Africans and set about publicizing the evils of apartheid. With him Benson became in 1950 a cofounder of the Africa Bureau, a volunteer news and information service about South Africa and a center of lobbying to influence British opinion on South African affairs. Here she met Tshekedi Khama and the young Nelson Mandela, both figures about whom she later wrote biographies.

Encouraged by the South African novelist Alan Paton, whose best-selling novel *Cry the Beloved Country* introduced English-speaking readers to the evils of racial oppression in South Africa, Benson became an increasingly articulate speaker and writer on South African affairs, finally returning to her native land in 1958. By now a recognized and outspoken critic of the apartheid regime, Benson gave testimony before the United Nations on the effects of oppression on black South Africans in 1963 and also to the U.S. Congressional Committee on South Africa in 1966. Her descriptions of the poverty of shantytowns like Sharpeville and Soweto, and of the increasing surveillance of opponents of the government by the South African police, led to her banning, or house arrest, in 1966. Shortly thereafter she left the country, a political exile. Back in England she wrote plays and novels describing the evils of the

South African regime; *Nelson Mandela and the Rivonia Trial* (1972) and *Robben Island* (1976) were among the most successful.

One of the most moving passages of Benson's memoir describes her bittersweet friendship with the increasingly desperate and hunted Afrikaner lawyer Bram Fischer, one of the few members of the legal profession of Boer descent who insisted on fighting for the maintenance of due process in the trials of opponents of the government. Fischer, a respected member of the bar, eventually felt obliged to denounce the proceedings in the trial of Nelson Mandela and the other members of the African National Congress tried for treason in 1964. In her mid-forties, Benson suddenly became a new kind of lawbreaker, putting on disguise to meet Fischer, giving emotional support to a man doomed to capture and heavy reprisals. After Fischer's death from cancer while serving a life sentence in the same Pretoria prison around which she had played as a child, Benson set out for England, bereft, like every South African exile, at the moment of farewell to the natural beauty of South Africa and the cause to which she had given half her life.

Benson's adventure-packed life and free spirit infuse her story with zest for life, although she has been plagued since young womanhood by arthritis and has frequently lived in severe pain. Her tone is totally free from self-pity, although even she is able to admit the horror of being a banned person, to whom others can speak only at their peril.

A FAR CRY:
The Making of a South African

Our small brick house in the hospital grounds stood next door to the jail. Nanny—Mrs. Eliza Miles, a Cockney from London, England, starch-aproned, snug-corseted, smelling of Sunlight soap and Reckitt's Blue—took Poppy and me for walks, through the front gate to the sound of loud Zulu gossip from Sam the cook and the "garden-boy," and up Potgieter Street, past the red-brick turreted wall with its small barred windows from which black faces peered down. Then on we went, past the warders' houses, where black convicts hosed and mowed neat lawns, watched by a white warder who slouched over his rifle, to Magazine Road, where the Boers had stored gunpowder—might it blow up?—and across to the shade of gum trees lining the dusty track leading to the old Boer fort. Around us was the veld, with aloes and suikerbos and, mocking from a branch, a Pietmyvrou.

The prison was part of our everyday landscape. Warders' sons stole peaches from our orchard, a warder's daughter gave me piano lessons, we waited outside its formidable doors for trams into town. Long afterwards I learned that its bleak iron-barred interior contained the gallows, where many hundreds of black men and women, and occasionally whites, were hanged. We were surrounded by symbols of a system that was to become infamous, a system which I was to spend much of my life opposing and of which I was at that time totally oblivious. That small colonial prison has grown to be a vast conglomeration and, at its heart, political prisoners, black and white, are held.

Photo after photo in the family album recording those early years has the same background: the high walls, the small barred windows of the prison and, in the foreground, our smiling faces.

I was determined to escape from a life centred on the Country Club. From the age of fifteen I had been making plans. Half-way up the koppie stood a big rock. There I sat dreaming of a future alive with possibilities. I might fly around the globe like Amelia Earhart, or play tennis at Wimbledon, or be the first girl to explore the South Pole. Above all, I dreamt about Hollywood, about how I would become a movie star.

During 1940 I got a much-coveted secretarial job on the staff of the British High Commissioner. One of its attractions was travelling between the Transvaal and the Cape, as the diplomatic corps accompanied the Government on its annual journeys from the administrative to the parliamentary capital. The war against Hitler's Germany and Mussolini's Italy had broken out and, remote though we were, the girls on the staff felt tremendously patriotic. I longed to get away from South Africa, to take part in this great adventure. The chance came in August 1941. Women were wanted to relieve men from desk jobs in Middle East headquarters and, together with two friends, I volunteered. Joining the South African Women's Auxiliary Army Service as privates, we were known as WAASIES.

I returned to South Africa's midsummer heat in December 1945. The old life in Pretoria was ended, not simply because my family now lived in Johannesburg but because friends had been killed in action in the Western Desert, over the Mediterranean, in Italy. I did not yet know about the other role white South Africans had played in the war: the activities of pro-Nazi Afrikaner extremists, among them a man who would one day be Prime Minister, J. B. Vorster.

Once again I was determined to leave. As soon as I'd earned the fare, I sailed for England.

"There is a lovely road that runs from Ixopo into the hills. These hills are grass-covered and rolling, and they are beyond any singing of it."

I read those words one momentous day in 1948. They still strike at my heart. Exile gives them added poignancy. Through its revelation of South Africa, the landscape, the people—the black people—*Cry, the Beloved Country* crashed open the mould in which my white consciousness had been formed. This complex and marvellous country was *my* country. The place I had found boring and kept running away from was my heritage.

The little I knew of the author came from the dust cover: born in 1903, he was married with two sons and for twelve years had been Principal of a reformatory for delinquent African boys.

So from thousands of miles apart, Paton and I wrote to each other, imagined presences, he from his house at Diepkloof Reformatory in the Transvaal, I from an attic in Kensington. Of course, I was flattered and excited by his letters and I wanted to know all about his life. Originally a teacher, he had gone on to run a reformatory, and he described how, on arrival there, he'd found "a prison . . . well equipped with gates and barbed wire and bars and locks and sentry bars. Punishment was the great weapon. It was a hard and unlovely place; it contained about 600 native boys, among them some of the hardest and unhappiest of human beings."

Shortly before the Christmas of 1949, . . . I was spellbound by a profile in the London *Observer* which told the dramatic story of an Anglican priest in South Africa. In Johannesburg he'd lived among Africans in the dangerous squalor of a shantytown called Tobruk and been arrested for trespass; in Durban he'd joined Indian passive resisters and with them gone to jail; in the Transvaal, after exposing near-slavery conditions on farms, he'd been threatened with lynching by angry farmers.

Of course, this was the man Alan Paton had spoken of whose name had meant nothing to me at the time, Michael Scott. Something else Paton said was borne out by the article. Increasingly, as Scott's reputation for fearless championship of the Africans spread, his name became associated with trouble, and white South Africans regarded him as a dangerous crank, a misinformed fanatic. Those who knew him best spoke of his diffidence and reserve, yet where principles of justice and humanity were involved, he was totally uncompromising. Aged forty-two, despite ill-health he was in appearance "still youthful, with a strikingly handsome face," as the article expressed it, "which had something about it of the saint and something of the rebel."

He was virtually penniless; tribesmen and a handful of Indian friends had collected money for him to fly to the United Nations in New York. There he represented the tribes of South-West Africa, who were protesting against the South African government's attempt to incorporate this mandated territory. With no organization to back him he had made a spectacular breakthrough and had testified on their behalf. He had also appealed for the policy of apartheid to be referred to the Security Council as "a threat to peace and racial harmony."

[Benson became Michael Scott's assistant.] Towards the end of 1951 I flew home to be with my father, who was very ill with pernicious anaemia. That year the UN session was in Paris. It was hard to leave Michael, fragile as ever, to cope virtually alone, but at least the daily papers kept me in touch. South-West Africa has front-page news. Very early each morning, the moment I heard the *Rand Daily Mail* land with a smack on the verandah of our small house in Pretoria, I hurried to read it. After Michael's years of lobbying for the tribal leaders to put their own case, the UN finally cabled an invitation to the chiefs to appeal before the Assembly in Paris. The South African government was called upon to "facilitate" their "prompt travel"—whereupon its delegate promptly walked out of the UN Committee. And even in this well-known liberal newspaper Michael Scott was referred to as "a hostile foreigner." Britain was among the minority to vote against the invitation—because "correct procedure" had not been followed.

[Scott requested Benson's help for the South-West African chiefs.] Now, facing a reality I had never before experienced, I wondered what it would be like actually confronting the South African authorities in Africa.

A seat was available on next morning's flight to Windhoek, due to a fortuitous cancellation.

I was surprised and enchanted by my mother's sensitive anticipation of events. She had returned from town one morning looking flushed and pleased; she had emptied her savings account to lend me £100. Now, wearing her familiar blue dressing-gown, she ironed my dresses and helped me pack.

At the airport I climbed into a car advertising the Continental, which proved to be a big, brash and expensive hotel. I hoped to be anonymous there.

Next morning the wife of an Anglican priest drove me along the main *strasse* of the picturesque Germanic town to the mission school on the outskirts of Windhoek. One of the teachers was sent for, a tall, bright young African who ran to shake my hand. "You have come from Father Michael!" He was Berthold Himumuine. He acted as the Chief's interpreter and would arrange a meeting that afternoon at St. George's Cathedral.

In the hall attached to the tiny cathedral, Berthold waited with three other men. One was tall and grave and very old. He was dressed in a worn grey suit and Homburg hat and the aristocratic distinction of his features was already familiar to me from Scott's film: Chief Hosea Kutako. The embodiment of his people's history. As a young man, he had wanted to become a minister of religion; instead, he had found himself chosen to lead back across the desert the refugees who had survived the German massacre. From them, the present tribe was descended; under him the Herero people had been re-created.

We discussed the question of permits to go to the UN. Chief Hosea, with the Chief of the Namas, had indeed written to the Administrator some weeks before and, although ill, he had then journeyed from his home in Gobabis to await the reply in Windhoek.

Next day, the Chief Native Commissioner, Mr. Neser, a brisk, bespectacled man, received me courteously. When I asked why the Secretary for the Interior had told me that no application to go to the UN had been received from the chiefs, when in fact they had applied, he corrected me. No application for *passports* had been received. He added that the "natives" going to the UN would do far more harm than good and they would be "spoiled."

Just as my association with Michael aroused misgivings or hostility in the old familiar South Africa, in my "new" world it meant spontaneous trust. So it was that Walter Sisulu, Secretary-General of the African National Congress, warmly welcomed me. He was a calm, homely man, wearing heavy-rimmed spectacles. The office in Johannesburg's business section was small, rather dark and dilapidated, reflecting a paucity of funds. . . .

He whole-heartedly supported Scott's work; indeed, he suggested that Michael should represent the ANC in London. Their confidence in him would be greatly appreciated, I said, but Michael thought it important and urgent for them to have their own, African, representatives there—to which I added the advice that to have any influence with Western governments, they should not seem too left-wing. Sisulu explained that there was no question of being able to send their own people abroad at this time. The ANC was wholly preoccupied in organizing a campaign to defy apartheid laws. It was to be non-violent and would be launched in three months' time. He wanted me to meet leaders of the Indian Congress involved in that organizing.

The conference, when it took place in Johannesburg's City Hall, was packed with Africans as well as Indians.

From where I sat at the back, I could see only one other European—a dark-haired, striking young woman, clearly Jewish and a journalist. This was Ruth First, who, when I met her much later, would become a valued friend.

No whites had protested at Scott being prohibited from returning to the country but now the Indian Congress did so, and passed a resolution acclaiming his "magnificent untiring and heroic labours" in putting before the UN the case of the African people in South-West Africa, as well as the "oppression and injustice perpetrated by Malan's government."

At 5:45 I left for a party in my other world. At 6:00 police raided the conference, arresting ten people.

But much of the work was taken up with British colonial policies. Travelling between Britain and Africa, we aided the people of Nyasaland and Northern Rhodesia in their opposition to Federation in Central Africa. We lobbied for urgent political, economic and educational reforms in the colonies and in the three High Commission Territories: Basutoland, the Bechuanaland Protectorate and

Swaziland—Britain's "shop window" in southern Africa, as we euphemistically called them. Our small staff seemed always to be battling against actions which showed lamentable disregard for the wishes of the African people. The "man on the spot" on whom the British government relied was invariably a local white official or settler. We attempted to educate the British people in the facts of life in Africa through meetings and through our publications.

Meanwhile, I had been finding it increasingly painful to type. Rheumatoid arthritis was diagnosed but each drug prescribed gave only temporary relief.

"Michael Scott is of no fixed abode." The South African government had once made the point in attempted derogation, and as he moved from the Friends' Centre to a series of small hotels and bedsitters, I too became increasingly aware of this handicap. Since he wanted my companionship, a nomadic round of restaurants, cafés and cinemas was the background to our times together. Loving him as I did, I grew rebellious at this lack of privacy. There was one solution that could bring an end to the enervating routine: that we should marry.

And marriage became the theme of obsessive nagging on my part, but Michael simply continued to reiterate that there could be nothing personal in his life. But what could be more "personal" than the confidences we shared? And clearly he *did* care. The very word "personal" drove me to a frenzy of frustration which left him drained and bewildered, while I felt sickened at dragging this good man down into a banal desire for marriage, for sex—a word never uttered between us. "Can't you see," asked David Astor, who was close to both of us, "that for Michael marriage is an impossibility?" I could not and would not see. David believed that renunciation of self and therefore of the "personal" had in part contributed to Michael's greatness and specialness. My own belief was that my love could liberate him from his inhibitions and help him to be yet more effective in his work.

We worked together for seven years and that is what mattered; all we shared, all I learned from him, enriched and influenced the rest of my life.

[Benson became the guide of many African leaders visiting London.] Thickset, with a bull-like quality to his powerful, fine head, he plunged through a swarm of photographers and journalists and strode towards the official from the Commonwealth Office who had come to welcome him at Victoria Station. His fierce energy belied his forty-six years.

That was my introduction to Tshekedi Khama on his arrival in London early in 1951. He was the first African I came to know; working for him gave me a great leap forward in experience—both human and political—and seven years later it was through him that I became a writer.

Tshekedi had been Regent of the Bangwato in Bechuanaland while his nephew, Seretse, was being educated and prepared for chieftainship. The young man's sudden marriage to an English girl, Ruth Williams, provoked widening controversy. Tshekedi bitterly disapproved of this flouting of tribal tradition, while the South African and Rhodesian governments—horrified by the idea of a mixed marriage just across their borders—put pressure on Britain's Labour government, which exiled Seretse from the Protectorate. Soon after, Tshekedi was also exiled, not from the entire Protectorate but from his tribal area. Actions which predictably turned controversy into chaos among the Bangwato.

In coming to Britain to negotiate or, if necessary, campaign for his return home, Tshekedi naturally sought assistance from two old friends. One was Scott, the other was Margery Perham, Oxford academic and a distinguished authority on Africa, who had first encountered a furious young Tshekedi in the High Commissioner's office in Cape Town in 1930—after a quarrel with a senior official, he had nearly knocked her over as he rushed down the stairs. Now there were intense consultations with her at David Astor's country house near Oxford before Tshekedi and Scott moved to London.

Early every morning they set out from our makeshift office in the Friends' Centre—the short, heavy-shouldered African and the Englishman, very tall and thin and pale, both carrying bulky briefcases, striding through Tavistock Square as they headed for Whitehall or Westminster or Fleet Street. They were a great team, discussing and arguing by the hour: Tshekedi the strategist and Scott the lobbyist. Though mulishly obstinate, Tshekedi valued intelligent advice. Putting his case to the Secretary of State for Commonwealth Relations, he used arguments as a general deploys troups. Meanwhile, he flooded the Ministry with long and complex memoranda. When eventually negotiations broke down he rallied his forces for a brilliant campaign.

As his secretary, I found those five months enormously exciting.

I succumbed to his magnetism and was stimulated by a curious combination of tension and a sense of his unassailable authority. His laughter was infectious, starting deep down, breaking out, then rippling on in shoulder-heaving titters; not only an expression of amusement but of irony, as a disguise for anger. Taking dictation or typing until my fingers swelled ominously and I drooped with exhaustion, I also had first-hand experience of his slave-driving propensity.

It took another year's struggle and a change of government in Britain before Tshekedi achieved his objective. His return to Bangwato territory did not endanger the peace of the tribe. Not for the first time he'd proved the "man on the spot" wrong—the white official, whose advice was religiously followed by the British government in preference to that of the equally "on the spot" black inhabitants. In Bechuanaland he was able to add pressure for the return of his nephew. Their cases were an object lesson in the failure of political parties to fulfil enlightened electoral promises once they have acquired power, and they were yet one more example of British subservience to the South African government.

As Regent, Tshekedi continued to face almost insurmountable obstacles: huge distances, prolonged droughts, outbreaks of foot-and-mouth disease and poverty—the Protectorate was known as the Cinderella of the British Empire. Meanwhile, he was repeatedly distracted by the South African government's threat to incorporate the Protectorate and the other two High Commission Territories, Basutoland and Swaziland. For three decades he played a unique and historic role in organizing effective opposition, exposing the injustice of South Africa's system, its colour bar and degrading pass laws. . . . He personally organized protests against South Africa's threatened incorporation of South-West Africa, protests not just from fellow-chiefs in Bechuanaland but from black intellectuals who were leaders of the African National Congress in South Africa.

Visiting Serowe, the Bangwato capital, meeting councillors and teachers and members of the royal family, I learned more about Tshekedi's manifold activities and came to see him as a high-powered engine relentlessly driving the old-fashioned vehicle of the tribe through an arid wilderness towards a productive, more prosperous and enlightened future.

Within months of that visit, I had to go into hospital in Pretoria. Afterwards, while convalescing in Cape Town, I was asked to write a biography of Tshekedi Khama. With a small publisher's advance, supplemented by an annual grant generously provided by David Astor, I began.

Under a tropical sun the Natal coast was just as I remembered from my youth: the smell of damp earth in the belt of jungle, where chattering monkeys cavorted and lizards darted back and forth across the path leading to white sands and the dazzling expanse of the Indian Ocean. But instead of breaking into a trot at the first sight of the sea, I limped creakily and, far from plunging into the surf, cautiously lowered myself into a pool carved in the rocks. Lazy days on the beach, which at seventeen had seemed bliss and were precisely what the doctor had ordered, at thirty-seven bored me. Yet as I breathed, gazed, listened and touched, senses long atrophied were reanimated in moments of pure happiness. And at night, when the Milky Way filled the sky, I discerned that familiar modest constellation, the Southern Cross. I had come home.

After sailing from Southampton early in January 1957, the ship had made its customary brief stop at each port in turn. In Cape Town I caught haunting glimpses of the mountains and vineyards, all too brief between intense encounters with dissident politicians, academics and writers.

I met Alex Hepple for coffee. A Member of Parliament and leader of the Labour Party, he spoke excitedly about the Treason Trial, which had recently opened in Johannesburg. The 156 men and women who had been arrested had shown tremendous spirit and, in a remarkable show of unity, liberal and left-wing whites had come together with the African National Congress and the Indian Congress to rally support for their defence. Rich and poor alike had provided bail and the Bishop of Johannesburg, Ambrose Reeves, chaired the Defence Fund committee. Leading the defendants, the ANC's president, Chief Lutuli, exuded confidence and calm. The trial, Alex emphasized, would be *the* issue for a long time to come.

I went on to a boarding house to visit Aunt Annie—very old, but spirited as ever.

Aunt Annie was staying with her son, Tiny, and his loyal wife. They well knew [the] suffering [caused by alcoholism]. During the First World War, as a sixteen-year-old, Tiny had joined the Royal Flying Corps. It was the time of his life. When everything afterwards proved a disappointment, he found relief in alcohol. Recently he'd got a humble job in the Bantu Administration Department—he thought himself fortunate to have such security and would have

been hurt and insulted by my perception of him as a petty bureau-
crat juggling with lives under the Group Areas Act. His section organized the "endorsing out"—a euphemism for forced removal—of
"Bantu" from the Western Cape to remote reserves in the Transkei
and Ciskei. Since those poverty-stricken areas offered few jobs, the
displaced persons in despair returned to the city, risking imprisonment, to reconstruct demolished shacks. "Reserves," "black spots,"
"locations"—white South Africans were adept at coining words
which expunged humanity and turned families into ciphers which
could be scattered at the stroke of a pen.

Small, vain, vulnerable, with red-gold wavy hair artistically
brushed back, Cousin Tiny dutifully carried out Pretoria's departmental instructions by day. In the evening, returning to the boarding house, he settled down at the piano in the lounge and lost
himself in the music of Chopin and Debussy. His playing was a part
of childhood in the house by the koppie: Poulenc's *Mouvement Per-
pétuel* never fails to evoke sun-filled mornings with Cousin Tiny at
the upright piano in our living-room, smilingly obeying my command to play it once more.

At the next port of call, the industrial centre of Port Elizabeth,
in a sunlit house Christopher Gell was propped up in bed, his emaciated body just visible above the sheets, his whole being concentrated in a thin amused face and sparkling bespectacled eyes. He
wrote regular articles which powerfully challenged the state and
ironically analysed each new apartheid law. And he carried on a
running battle with those white liberals who urged blacks to compromise or saw reds under the beds of black leaders. Of course, his
telephone was tapped. Norah warned that he must return to the
lung within forty-five minutes. Since he could only breathe by using
neck muscles and had to speak from his throat, he wasted no time
on the frills of social exchange. He was an honorary member of the
African National Congress and expressed the firm belief that an integrated state was possible. Unfortunately, he added, most whites
were incapable of realizing that Africans didn't have to be literate to
understand about politics, incapable of understanding that whereas
they themselves had everything laid on from the start, blacks had
"one long problem from birth to death."

I was not yet sure what I wanted to do. The Treason Trial kept
cropping up, even in the unlikely surroundings of the small railway
station at Glencoe, where I waited for a train to Pretoria to visit my
father. The Afrikaner who ran the refreshment room raised the sub-

ject while I was having a remarkably good meal. We'd talked about his family, then about the "native problem" and he'd expressed the view that if people were educated, it was only natural they should want political rights. That led on to his confiding that at first he'd thought the trial a serious matter of treason, but before long he'd come to the conclusion that the arrests were a political move by the government, and he was unhappy that people like himself, in the Civil Service, were afraid to speak their minds. Before leaving I tipped the black waiter—an extraordinary event to judge from his excessive gratitude and his boss's explanation that "the madam" was not an Afrikaner but from England.

As the train journeyed north towards the Transvaal, I wondered how many other lonely Afrikaners in small dorps harboured his heretical views. And I wondered whether he would have been so forthcoming had he realized that I was not English but South African.

"The Treason Trial's Defence Fund urgently needs a secretary," wrote Ambrose Reeves. "Can you start at once?" Knowing of my physical problems, he assured me that typing assistance would be provided; the pay would be £35 a month and I could stay with him and his family until I'd found a permanent place. The appeal was irresistible. Within days I had settled into his lively household and the busy Defence Fund office at the Labour Party's headquarters.

During my first lunch-hour, somewhat nervous at the prospect of encountering 156 "traitors," even though I already knew several of them, I set off by tram for the Drill Hall. A colonial, iron-roofed barn of a hall, it had been crudely converted into a court for the preliminary hearings. High Treason? The atmosphere was startlingly informal. Even the armed police seemed phlegmatic and at the back of the hall defendants were playing darts, while another group lustily rehearsed freedom songs. I found Professor Z. K. Matthews queuing for a hot meal served by Indian women. We had met in 1952 at the United Nations, when he had been Visiting Professor of Theology in a New York seminary. With him was a dignified, immensely impressive man with greying hair, Chief Albert Lutuli, who studied me attentively before giving me a warm welcome which dissipated my nervousness. Walter Sisulu reinforced the welcome, as did the quietly spoken, reflective lawyer Oliver Tambo and his partner, Nelson Mandela, whom I had met four years earlier: a young giant with a striking air of authority, debonair in a three-piece suit. Close friends, the three men were a unique political partnership which had vitally influenced the ANC since the early forties.

I met Ruth First and her husband, Joe Slovo, a lawyer; their friendliness did not dispel my unease at being with Communists, unease which *was* dispelled as I came to know them. Soon I had personal experience of the generosity with which they and other Communists supported the fund, getting no credit and asking for none, and learned of their courage and readiness for self-sacrifice over long years of struggle. Ruth had shown exceptional daring as an investigative reporter.

During the trial the judge, referring to the ANC's objective of "one man, one vote," questioned the value of "people who know nothing" participating in the government. Mandela, usually restrained in court, reacted angrily: people were perfectly capable of deciding who would advance their interests, he declared, citing his own father, who had not been formally educated but who would have had the ability and the sense to vote responsibly.

Through the trial the government succeeded in hamstringing many leaders and organizers of the liberation movement for an indefinite period. Mandela spoke to me one day about what it meant to be confined to Johannesburg and its townships. He was giving me a lift to a meeting at the Bishop's House and suddenly his voice, which usually expressed a powerful energy, grew wistful as he told me how he missed the spacious countryside of his youth, how he used to dream of having a small house there. But for years, like so many others, he had been restricted to Johannesburg, first by bans and now by the trial.

But the circumstances of the trial also meant, as Lutuli remarked, that "what bannings, distance, other occupations and lack of funds had made difficult—frequent meetings—the government had now insisted on. We could at last confer *sine die*, at any level we liked." Innumerable visitors turned up at the Drill Hall. Some were messengers or domestic servants wanting to show support for their leaders, others were distinguished foreigners—lawyers, academics, politicians, journalists. And significant figures in continuing protests urgently consulted leaders during lunch-breaks: they included organizers of Alexandra township's successful bus boycott and of a stay-at-home strike on 26 June initiated by Lutuli in support of a demand for £1 a day basic wage.

Meanwhile, outside the City Hall and, later, in "Freedom Square" in Fordsburg—a mainly Indian section of Johannesburg—

Bishop Reeves, Alan Paton and women of the Black Sash movement, as well as speakers from the Congress Alliance, addressed crowds of all races protesting against the Group Areas Act and the Pass Laws.

A last chore for the Treason Trial Fund took me to Johannesburg station to buy scores of train tickets for excited defendants about to return home for Christmas. Then I had to resign and Freda Levson, with whom I had been staying, became secretary of the Fund. Now it was my turn to be a patient in "our" hospital in Pretoria, where doctors gave an ultimatum: only a form of cortisone—a drug which might have harmful side-effects—could reverse the dangerous deterioration in my condition. Soon I was convalescing, and within weeks I had set out to visit friends in the Cape and in Natal.

Nearly two years later, on the way to Bechuanaland, I attended the trial proper, transferred to a disused synagogue which had been converted into a "Supreme Court" in Pretoria. A further sixty men and women had been discharged. Among the remaining defendants were Sisulu and Mandela, Kathrada and Helen Joseph, a British-born social worker who felt honoured to sit alongside such leaders in the dock and who would soon have the added distinction of being the first individual of any race to be placed under house arrest.

In between sessions I lunched with defendants in a vicarage garden opposite the court and dined with members of the defence team, which now included two Queen's Counsel; Isie Maisels, brilliant and imposing, who had not previously appeared in a political trial, and the distinguished Afrikaner and Communist, Bram Fischer, as well as a young advocate, Sydney Kentridge.

Towards the end of January 1960 I flew from Johannesburg to South-West Africa. A letter had come from Chief Hosea Kutako. "I hope that you shall be able to meet me before I return to my last resting place," he wrote, reminding me that he was now eighty-nine years old. And he referred to the death of sixteen men and women: "As an old man the brutality of the shootings in that night of December caused great despair in me." They were among people who had gathered in Windhoek location to protest against forced removals. Police had fired into the crowd. Apart from those killed, a further thirty had been wounded.

Arriving in Windhoek, as before I took the hotel car to the Continental, wondering how to contact the Chief. It was difficult now to visit the location; a journalist from the *New York Times* had recently been arrested for going there without a permit.

As I registered in the hotel I noticed a young Herero hovering near the entrance. I strolled toward him and, when he whispered my name, followed him outside, where he began polishing a shop window while giving me a message from the Chief. Next morning at seven a car would pick me up at the corner opposite the Methodist Church.

It was a Sunday morning, the streets deserted; distant church bells were ringing but there was no sign of life at the Methodist Church. My shadow was immensely long, the sun still low and mild. Each passing minute seemed like ten—was it simply "African time"? At 7:20 a black sedan with two Hereros in front drew up. Greeting me cheerfully, they ushered me into the back, where the blinds had been pulled down, and told me to remain on the floor until we were out of town.

Soon we'd left the smooth roads and were bumping along. "You can come up now!" one said. Winding through anonymous bush they joked about how difficult the Security Police made hospitality. We stopped under a large thorn tree. Before long a truck rumbled towards us. Beside the driver sat Hosea Kutako. I hurried to him as he climbed stiffly down and stood, upright and alert. There was no need for words. It was wonderful to see him again. I felt as if he were the grandfather I'd never known.

Tall young men jumped from the back, bringing chairs. He introduced his new councillors and we sat in a circle, the Chief beside me holding my hand. We all made light of meeting surreptitiously but, he explained through his interpreter, police activity had been intense. Trouble had been brewing for more than a year, ever since whites had begun building houses near the location and the 17,000 black inhabitants had been ordered to move some miles away to a fenced-in ghetto of concrete block houses. New rents would be £2 out of an average wage of £10 a month, whereas in the location they paid 3/6. And there would be ethnic grouping, a system which had already proved destructive of community relations in South African townships. The Chief had petitioned the UN in April 1959, warning that the people were not prepared to accept any scheme based on apartheid, "as they have suffered terribly under this inhuman policy."

By November people were almost unanimous in refusing to move from the location. "This is our home, rebuild here!" they demanded. For the first time nationalist movements had been formed, the SWA National Union and Ovambo People's Organisation, and their leaders, who included Sam Nujoma, like the traditional chiefs, insisted on non-violence. Nujoma had joined Hosea Kutako and Frederick Witbooi of the Namas in warning that the situation was critical. Herero women marched to the administration offices and people boycotted buses, the municipal beer hall and cinema. Then, on the evening of Human Rights Day in December, an angry crowd gathered in the location.

"Hy wat nie wil hoer nie, moet voel!" (He who won't listen, must feel!), the Mayor of Windhoek threatened, before sending armed police to order the crowd to disperse within five minutes. No loudspeaker was used. Only those in front heard and when they tried to retreat, others from behind, curious, pushed forward. Five minutes up, the police fired. Not tear gas, but bullets, the Chief explained.

An official inquiry found that the main cause of the violence was "African provocation." No action was taken against the police.

"For fourteen years now, we have been appealing to the United Nations," the Chief pointed out despondently, "and our position is worse than before. Should we go on trusting that justice will be done? Is there any point in petitioning them again?"

Before replying, I thought about those annual resolutions at the UN, how misleading they were, promising action that came to nothing. When the UN had at last sent a Good Offices Committee to Windhoek, it did not bother to meet Chief Hosea and the other leaders. What if they appealed to the Principal Allied Powers, who had originally consigned them to South Africa's rule, I asked, in the form of an Open Letter? The British Prime Minister, Harold Macmillan, had just delivered his speech to the South African Parliament, declaring, "A wind of change is sweeping through Africa!" And, under Britain, Tanganyika, a Mandate like South-West Africa, was moving towards independence. De Gaulle was getting tough with white extremists in Algeria and the Belgians were planning to grant self-government to the Congo.

The Chief was enthusiastic: the letter should, of course, describe the shootings. A councillor urged that it must also expose the lie that their protests had been inspired by outside agitators: "As if we need to be told of our sufferings! We must speak of the pass laws, of starvation wages and loss of our lands!" All agreed that Macmillan's tolling bell should be included.

The roar of an engine startled us. A small plane, flying low, approached over the treetops. We hid our faces and remained silent as it hovered. When it moved off, we resumed the discussion. But soon it returned, circled and withdrew. The Chief sighed. "You should get back to your hotel. We do not want to cause you any trouble." In Herero he blessed me and we said goodbye. He climbed into the truck, I into the car. We were driven off in opposite directions.

They deputed me to convey their disillusion and anger to the British and American ambassadors. Flying off to Cape Town I looked down on Windhoek's showplace, the cemetery. Nearby were the small houses and shanties of the location. "Why don't they move?" a Christian minister had asked, not attempting to hide irritation. "The new township is really no further away." But there it was, shoved way out on barren land: Katutura, the regimented mass of block houses was called; Katutura, which means "we have no permanent dwelling place."

The British Ambassador spared me ten minutes, the American, forty-five. They listened with apparent sympathy. The former gave me a copy of the Wind of Change speech. Macmillan had referred to the rest of Africa, to Asia, the Commonwealth, the United States and Europe. He did not mention South-West Africa. He spoke of Durban and Johannesburg, Pretoria and Bloemfontein. He did not mention Windhoek. He quoted John Donne's "any man's death diminishes me." What of the dead in Windhoek location?

When the Open Letters reached London and Paris and Brussels, would they be read? Filed? Or tossed into waste-paper baskets? Would no government ever act on such appeals, however often and passionately reiterated? Must it always be violence that brought about change?

As the plane flew south above the Transvaal's cultivated pattern of farmlands and occasional dorps, I wondered what hazards lay ahead.

"A history of the ANC must be written," Anthony Sampson had said, "and you're the one to do it!" Time was running out, he'd explained; the organization had been established in 1912, most of its founders had already died and the survivors, now very old, must be interviewed soon. My protests that I had no academic qualifications and anyway thought an African writer would be more appropriate were overridden. Why not you yourself? I'd asked. Anthony had been a brilliant editor of *Drum* magazine, but, backed by Philip Mason, Director of the Institute of Race Relations in London, he argued that my work with the Treason Trial Fund had given me invaluable connections.

Eventually I agreed and, with a princely advance of £200 from my publisher, set off, excited but also apprehensive. A year earlier, after Sharpeville, the ANC had been outlawed and under the Suppression of Communism Act merely talking about it could be legally construed as "furthering the aims of a banned organization." Quite apart from myself, I was anxious not to endanger the people I interviewed, and I began devising a code for my notes.

At Jan Smuts Airport I went smoothly through Immigration. No sign of the Special Branch. Relieved, I joined [my sister] Poppy and her family, who welcomed me at the barrier.

"So Miss Benson flew in this morning!" a member of the Special Branch remarked to Ruth First, when he happened to encounter her in the city that day. So much for my powers of observation.

Ruth, as always chic and vital, quickly put me in the picture: police searching the country for Mandela had arrested thousands—most of them black—and several leaders had been charged with "furthering the aims" of the ANC. Her husband, Joe Slovo, was to defend them.

As Mandela continued to elude the police and regularly issued statements calling on workers to "Stay at Home!" on Monday the 29th, the press dubbed him the Black Pimpernel.

Next morning came news that Mandela had called off the strike. Feeling excitingly conspiratorial, Patrick and I, with Robert Oakeshott of the *Financial Times,* were driven by Ruth First to a block of flats in Yeoville—one of the less prosperous white suburbs. In a sparsely furnished room dimmed by drawn yellow curtains, with a single electric bulb hanging from the ceiling, we were welcomed by Nelson Mandela. He was far from conspiratorial, relaxed in striped sports shirt and grey trousers, slanting eyes closed to slits as laughter reverberated through his huge frame.

I was content to listen as the "pros" questioned him. The disappointing response to the strike and his decision to call it off, did he concede it had been a failure? asked Robert.

"In the light of the steps taken by government to suppress the Stay-at-Home, it was a tremendous success," he retorted. The mobilizing of army as well as police was "striking testimony of African strength and a measure of the government's weakness."

Three weeks later a friend dropped me at a bungalow in a white suburb, again the drawn curtains but this time, as well as a bearhug of welcome from Nelson, a friendly Alsatian loped in, nuzzling for attention. A tray of tea stood ready. All the police in the country were on the alert and here was their quarry, sociably recollecting the past.

He told of his upbringing as the son of a chief in the royal kraal of the Tembu people, of how at night by the fire he'd listened fascinated to tales told by the tribal elders about the days when the land was theirs, when they'd governed themselves, before the wars against invading Europeans. I mentioned my great-grandfather, who had led a commando against the Xhosa—it made us smile to think how once our ancestors had been at war but now he and I were on the same side. We were also almost the same age; I had thought he was the younger, but in fact he was a year older than I.

At twenty-two, he had run away from the Transkei to escape an arranged marriage. In Johannesburg the only job he could get, this young aristocrat and university student, was as a mine policeman. "I sat at the compound gate, watching people come and go. I wore a uniform and carried a knobkerrie and whistle!" He laughed heartily at what must have been a humiliating experience.

I did not realize how important every detail of Mandela's personal as well as his political life would become and concentrated on the theme of his association with the ANC; nor did I use a tape recorder. During the twenty-six years of his imprisonment, the outside world had heard his voice in only one brief interview, secretly made by a British television journalist during that May of 1961. Pictured in a bleak room and wearing a winter jacket, with a side-parting clipped in his hair (a momentary fashion), he speaks—as he had to us—of the crushing violence of the state which, finally and inevitably, had put an end to the liberation movement's policy of non-violence.

Mandela had eluded the police for more than nine months. One night in mid-November, I waited expectantly in the living-room of that same modest bungalow. As he came in, looking very fit, thinner and bearded, he cast off the chauffeur's white coat and peaked cap he'd been wearing. He was in ebullient mood, just back from touring Natal and the Cape. "A wonderful experience, visiting the rural areas!" he said. "You can't comprehend unless you stay right there *with* the people."

It was eight years since he had been confined by bans to Johannesburg. I recalled our first encounter at that time. In the Indian Congress office I'd come upon him in the thick of a loud and furious quarrel with Yusuf Cachalia. Quite unembarrassed they broke off to respond to my questions about the Defiance Campaign. Neither he, nor Yusuf later, remembered the incident and he had long ago learned to control his hot temper.

Now he could spare only an hour, he said apologetically. Pressure was mounting. But he seemed amazingly relaxed as he described the narrow escape he'd had a few days earlier: "I was waiting on a corner in town, wearing that chauffeur's outfit, when the car due to pick me up failed to arrive. It's vital," he broke off to explain, "to be absolutely punctual when you're functioning underground. And I saw, coming towards me, one of the Special Branch—an African member I knew by sight. He looked straight at me. I thought, it's all up! But he went on by. And as he did so, he winked and gave the ANC salute!"

The incident made Nelson roar with laughter, but he also regarded it as an example of the hidden support the ANC had, even among the police.

When the hour was up he offered me a lift and, after putting on the coat and peaked cap, led me out to a car that was very much the worse for wear. We drove off, with me, as madam, in the back and he, as chauffeur, in front. But the engine kept spluttering to a stop. Each time it seemed an eternity before he managed to rev it back to life. At any moment a police car could have driven by and stopped to see what was wrong. He joked about it, but this was the only transport available to him. At last the car coughed its way to within walking distance of my sister's flat and we said goodbye.

A few weeks later, on 16 December, sabotage broke out in Johannesburg, Port Elizabeth and Durban, launching *Umkhonto we Sizwe*, Spear of the Nation. I realized then how precious even that hour must have been to him, an hour spared from planning the action which had been implied by his remark ". . . we are closing a chapter" on the policy of non-violence.

Six days earlier in Oslo, as if—unwittingly—stamping a seal on that chapter, the King of Norway awarded the Nobel Prize for Peace to Chief Albert Lutuli in recognition, so Lutuli insisted, of the ANC's long record of non-violence and its stand for a non-racial democracy.

The award had been announced on 23 October and Walter Sisulu and Duma Nokwe had asked me to assist "Chief," who was virtually besieged by journalists and swamped with communications from all over the world. After flying to Durban, I was driven northward through lush green sugar plantations and teeming, brightly coloured Indian villages with silvered temples, white planters' mansions and golf-courses in the distance, until we reached Stanger, a small town sited near a sugar mill. There, E. V. Mahomed, an accountant and friend of Chief's, escorted me to the Bantu Affairs Commissioner to apply for the permit required to visit Lutuli, who was confined by bans to the neighbourhood of Stanger.

When we arrived at the humble red-roofed house marked by two tall cypresses, we were welcomed by Mrs. Lutuli, Nokukhanya, a spare, motherly woman. Chief was in the dining-room, seated at a table covered by telegrams and letters. Our first task, he said, was to reply to *the* cable. I promptly did so, sending the historic message from the EUROPEANS ONLY section of Stanger's post office:

GUNNAR JAHN, NOBEL COMMITTEE OSLO. FILLED WITH SENSE OF GRATITUDE AND APPRECIATION. SHALL BE APPLYING FOR TRAVEL PERMIT. LUTULI.

Lutuli was refused permission to attend the celebration. The authorities also blocked the use of buses to transport people from Durban. But nothing could daunt the crowds; convoys of cars packed with Africans and Indians drove into Stanger, disgorging their occupants, who formed umbrellaed queues outside the hall we'd hired. Lutuli, with his wife—ignoring the bans under which it was illegal for him to be with more than one person at a time—joined Alan and Dorrie Paton for an informal lunch given by Indian friends. To Chief's delight, Alan recited a "praise song" he was to give at the meeting:

> You there, Lutuli, they thought your world was small
> They thought you lived in Groutville
> Now they discover
> It is the world you live in . . .

Then, to the freedom song *"Somlandela Lutuli"*—we will follow Lutuli—we all formed a line behind his imposing figure to perform a dance, at once thoughtful and jubilant.

Still elated, Chief settled in a corner of a friend's garage, adjacent to the hall. From there he could just hear sounds coming from the packed meeting and imagine what was happening: the sibilant, long-drawn-out "Shame!" of disgust which greeted the reading of the magistrate's telegram refusing him permission to attend the meeting; the women's ululations as his wife was presented with a scroll of honour on his behalf; the applause greeting Fatima Meer when she spoke of his vision of a free South Africa, the vision which taught people to demand freedom with love and tranquillity, which had led to the martyrdom of many, the vision the world was heralding. Loud and clear he heard the wild excitement following each verse as his close friend M. B. Yengwa declaimed a Zulu praise song:

> . . . The great bull that enemies tried to fence in a kraal
> Has broken the strong fence and wandered far,
> As far as Oslo!
> *Nkosi yase* Groutville! *Nkosi yase Afrika! Nkosi yase* world!

Meanwhile, in the front row, grim-faced members of the Special Branch laboriously made notes.

On my last day I took a stack of correspondence to the Lutulis' house for his signature. He was very tired. Leaving him to tackle the work at leisure, I played with his grandson in the garden. A photographer from an Afrikaner newspaper drove up—the picture he took of Msomi seated on my lap featured in a caustic article about a white woman assisting the prizewinner.

Alan Paton said Lutuli was "the shadow of a great rock in a weary land." In his day he was unique in uniting people of all races. The government, therefore, having failed to crush his rapidly growing influence by a one-year, then a two-year ban, or even a charge of high treason, finally confined him to his home district for five years, a restriction that was reimposed until, in 1967, he was run down by a train and killed.

In my research into the ANC's history, I came to know my country as never before. I travelled by rail, road and air to cities and towns, to remote villages such as Inanda in Natal and Thaba'Nchu in the Orange Free State, as well as townships and Bloemfontein location, where I visited the hall in which the ANC had held its inaugural conference in 1912—a bioscope now, standing among red and yellow brick houses under dusty trees. And I came to know our history, so rich and complex compared with the arid distortions learned in school. This history flowed partly from recollection of individual lives, from people's opinions of each other and, of course, from what it meant to be black.

I was pleased to find [Walter Sisulu's office] was more prosperous than the one I'd visited nearly ten years earlier. Since Walter's movements were dogged by Sergeant Dirker of the Special Branch, a thoroughly lugubrious man, it was difficult to relax and get on with our interview. Late one afternoon, therefore, a friend gave me a lift to Orlando, where mile upon mile of bald little houses covered sloping ground, hardly a tree to be seen, all regimented brick and concrete against brown earth, the only softening element the pall of smoke from a multitude of stoves cooking the evening meal. It made a grim contrast to Sophiatown's anarchic vitality. One day this conglomeration would be officially named South-Western Townships, with the acronym Soweto.

The night was bitterly cold. There were no street lights. Along dirt roads bumpy with potholes people cycled or trudged home. The Sisulus lived near a railway line. Albertina, a nursing sister, generous of spirit as of build, was expecting me. The small front room was lit by lamps and candles. Walter arrived, in overcoat and woollen scarf, and over tea we continued our interview, with Albertina joining in, since she had been the solitary young woman member at the inception of the Youth League in 1944. Their wedding picture hung on the wall, he slender and rather wistful, she modestly smiling—now she was the mother of five and the youngest girl was called Nonkululekhe, Freedom. What struck me when I came to write about Sisulu was that he, more than any other African leader, knew just what it meant to be a "native." He had been a kitchen "boy," studying English grammar in his spare time, a miner and then, working in a bakery for £2 a week, he'd led a strike for better conditions and been sacked. That, the first of countless experiences of jail, had resulted from protesting against a white man's ill-treatment of a black child. Aged forty-one, he had visited Russia and China in 1953, passing through Israel and London, and for the first time had been treated—as he put it—"like a dignified human being.". . .

Afterwards, he led me down the road past a barren area, a danger-ground, he explained, where *tsotsis* preyed on returning wage-earners, on to the Mandelas' house, facing a hill. Inside, it was colourful and full of Nelson's books. I had met Winnie several times at dinner with Nelson in the past. She was putting their baby daughters, Zeni and Zindzi, to bed. A social worker with Child Welfare, her married life had been continually disrupted, first by the Treason Trial and the months of Nelson's imprisonment during the 1960 State of Emergency, then by his disappearance underground.

I could no longer feel unalloyed affection for relatives or for friends from the past who, through prejudice or through apathy, condoned apartheid. To my delight, Poppy had become warmly supportive, but I seemed unable to convey to our cousins how life had been excitingly transformed by coming to know these fellow–South Africans of all races. "You mean you were alone with Natives!" one exclaimed, after seeing me drive up with an Eastern Cape leader.

Even self-styled liberals said: "Don't be so impatient, things are moving. Just give it time." Couldn't they see how every moment mattered when black youths were being driven to become *tsotsis,* their mothers frantic? In this, their only life, in this world of ours? *Time*. What did that matter to the Ciskei babies dying of starvation, babies whose vast eyes had gazed coldly at me from their Belsen-faces? Men claiming to be Christian had committed the subtlest cruelty: depriving fathers and mothers of the humblest and greatest need, to dream dreams for their children.

I wondered how I dared to be stimulated in spite of the persecution and suffering I had witnessed, but there was no doubt that tension sparked adrenalin. Everyone in the "movement" seemed almost casual about the intrusions of the Security Police, as the Special Branch were renamed. Professor Z. K. Matthews met me in Alice, the small town where he had been an eminent figure at Fort Hare University until he'd resigned in protest against Bantu Education. As he led me from my hotel to his car, he indicated a Volkswagen waiting nearby: "The Security Police in these dorps have nothing better to do than harass us," he remarked. "Well, we'll give them a little thrill!" And he proceeded to drive round and round the square, peering into the rearview mirror and chuckling at the sight of the police stolidly following our gyrations. He might chuckle but I, not so accustomed, flushed my notes down the toilet on returning to the hotel.

The Security Police turned out in force, senior officers included,

for a celebratory meeting on Afrika Day, 15 April 1962. In a field at
Kliptown, where the Congress of the People had been held seven
years before, they loitered around the fringes of the crowd. Posters
of Lutuli and Lumumba were held high. Albertina Sisulu and Winnie Mandela wore Xhosa dress, while men in Zulu warrior garb vo-
ciferously approved speeches made from an improvised platform
on a lorry. Interspersed with the rhetoric were sober references to
the huge sums spent on arms, money desperately needed for better
housing and food for the malnourished. "It's true, it's true!" a
young man beside me wearing a silver miner's helmet passionately
affirmed.

Next day I had lunch with a visitor from Britain, Robert Birley,
the headmaster of Eton. It was not all that startling a social leap because this huge, immensely erudite man would soon be teaching in
the most deprived areas of South Africa. Over lunch with Robert
Loder, one of his former pupils, now with the Anglo-American Cor-
poration, Birley spoke of his intention to resign from Eton in order
to become Visiting Professor of Education at Wits University. He
thought his work in Germany after the Second World War should
be relevant—he had been in charge of de-Nazifying education. He
evinced a lively interest in my ANC researches and expressed a determination to meet people of all races, of all political persuasions
and all ages. Each time I had returned to South Africa I had been
struck by how cliquish the various dissidents were, out of touch
with each other, even mutually suspicious in what, after all, was a
lonely situation. Birley's unusual lack of any such caution was very
endearing.

One afternoon in May I went to Orlando with Nat Nakasa and
Peter Magubane, *Drum*'s star reporter and photographer. We had
tea with Zeph Mothopeng, who earlier that day had been released
from prison. A tall, jovial, middle-aged man in a loose-fitting suit,
he was one of the Pan Africanist Congress leaders jailed for organizing anti-pass demonstrations just before the Sharpeville shootings occurred. During the two years in a cell it was, he said, "the
isolation and cramping-in feeling" that he'd felt most sharply. "I
never liked to see a bird in a cage," he explained, "but it never
struck me it was something of an inconvenience for the bird—now
I know what it is like. For an open-air man . . ." He broke off to accept a joyful welcome home from old friends. He was to return to
jail again and again for his militant role in Africanist resistance.

Exhilarated by his spirit, I returned to my sister's flat to learn that in my absence the Security Police had called. They left a message ordering me to take my South African passport to the local passport office. There it was confiscated. Shock was dulled by the urgent necessity of getting a British passport since I had assignments for the *Observer* in Nyasaland and Tanganyika. Fortunately, the British Embassy quickly granted a passport, on the grounds that Dublin, at the time of my father's birth, had been part of the Empire.

In London I lived in the flat in St. John's Wood which once I had borrowed for the dinner with Alan Paton. A terse note in my diary for Thursday, 14 June 1962, states: "Cooked. 7 P.M. Tambo." Oliver Tambo, Chief Lutuli's deputy, had for two years been organizing the ANC-in-exile. A knock at the door and, when I opened it, standing beside him was Nelson Mandela. "And N. Gorgeous!" The note continues, compensating for the brevity. "Talked till 1.30."

Nelson, immaculately suited and looking superb, gave a thrilling account of slipping across the border to tour Africa. Pacing the small room until the floor squeaked, he described the reception he'd been given in country after country, the experience for the first time in his life of being "free." Now, marvellously, he could spend a few days in London. On the Saturday, through David Astor, he met Hugh Gaitskell and Jo Grimond, leaders of the Labour and Liberal parties. On the Sunday, Freda Levson and her husband, Leon, and I, took him sightseeing, to Parliament and Westminster Abbey, then along the Thames to lunch at their house in Chelsea.

Early in August came the news that he had been captured, a few days after his secret return to South Africa. Betrayed by an informer? Horrified and dreadfully sad, I tried to keep busy and helped draft a profile of him which Cyril Dunn wrote for the *Observer*.

He was sentenced to five years for "inciting" the Stay-at-Home in 1961 and for leaving the country without a permit. He was imprisoned in Pretoria jail.

I have always felt at home in America. There was my long love-affair with the movies. I was naturally delighted when the publication in New York of *The African Patriots,* my history of the ANC, led to invitations to speak and give seminars at a number of universities across the continent.

Early in May a member of the UN Secretariat asked if I would

testify before the newly formed Committee on Apartheid. In the
over-heated, gloomy Great Northern Hotel on 57th Street I tussled
with the question. However much I had written and spoken out,
this was the ultimate in verbal attack on the government. But in
South Africa, under the Ninety Day Law, detainees were being tortured, and the country was toppling into ever greater violence. It
would be inadequate simply to recount facts; if I spoke, I must also
recommend action. I felt contempt for those living in safety overseas who glibly called for "armed struggle." The "ordinary" people
were always the ones to suffer. Chief Lutuli had called for economic
sanctions as the international community's only effective alternative to outright violence. Why should trade always be regarded as
sacrosanct?

I would be the first South African to testify. Surely this would
make it difficult, perhaps impossible, to return home? I valued gathering material there for books which could then be written in the
freedom of England; as writer and lobbyist I could only function
confidently on the basis of first-hand experience. Above all, I had
developed a profound love for my country.

There was one final question: would my testimony be useful?
So many fervently worded statements had already sunk without
trace in the morass of international bureaucracy. Besides, I felt cynical about the human rights record of some of the governments to
whom I would be appealing.

I telephoned David Astor in London, who consulted Michael
Scott, Bishop Reeves and Colin Legum, a South African journalist
on the *Observer,* before calling back to say they all urged me to go
ahead.

Tense at the thought of the responsibility, I worked hard on
writing the statement. After four days it was done and a subcom-
mittee of the UN approved my credentials.

The next morning—a Friday—in a committee room of the UN,
I was shown to the lonely seat, with its microphone and a glass of
water, facing the Committee, which consisted of four Africans,
three Asians, a Haitian, a Costa Rican and a Hungarian. To one
side sat the Secretariat staff; beyond, in glassed-off boxes, interpreters mouthed like fishes in bowls. Friends sat in the public
gallery, where there was constant movement as spectators came and
went.

"I am honoured to be the first South African given a hearing by your Committee," I began, and went on to explain that to speak out seemed the least I could do, so desperate were the times in my country. Since the facts of apartheid were already known, my testimony would concentrate on the effects on living human beings, within my experience.

Successive governments, I then pointed out, had used the weapon of fear, yet if we considered history, it was the blacks who, ever since the time of the slave trade, had suffered far more at the hands of whites; it was the blacks, therefore, who had more to fear. I spoke of the special culpability of English-speaking whites and of Afrikaners, who had cut themselves off from the world in "deliberate, deluded self-isolation," whose government understood only one language, that of force. "And the only non-violent way of applying force is the one the United Nations has already chosen, that of economic pressures." My great fear was that the UN would fail, "due to the refusals of the British and American Governments to support its efforts; in other words, to their virtual abandonment of South Africa to a violent solution.

"But," I concluded, "how marvellous if you succeed! If in this age of nuclear dangers you can find the way to use non-violent economic pressures *firmly* towards achieving justice for that tragic country, a country that is the crux of the greatest issue in the world today, whether we, and you"—and I paused to glance at the Africans and Asians facing me—"can live together in mutual confidence and understanding."

The statement had taken forty-five minutes. Drained, I went on to give radio and television interviews. But what mattered most to me was that my testimony should be reported in the *Observer,* so on Sunday I hurried to Times Square to buy the airmail edition. It was not mentioned.

The following evening Josh, a black journalist I had met recently, took me uptown to Harlem. It was drizzling as he guided me down steps to the rosily lit Red Rooster bar, crowded with men and a few stunning girls, drinking and talking against the juke-box jazz. I liked being there as his friend and not a sightseer, although I could not help being conscious that I was the only white in the bar. While he chatted to an acquaintance, I studied the slanting planes of his face, the thick, curling lashes, the up-turning mouth which could be mocking or amiable.

In the street the drizzle had cleared. He tucked my hand under his arm. "What about some real jazz?" and he indicated a club on the corner. A glance at my face and, impulsively, he hailed a cab. In silence we rode downtown to the hotel where he was staying.

We were not in love. But, as he put it, we wanted each other and we were both adult. I found reassurance, even bliss, in the relationship with Josh. Everything about me amused him, amazed him: when he discovered I was assisting lawyers working on the South-West African case, he asked how much they were paying me. "Nothing? You mean you do it all for free!" He laughed until the tears came.

During the days that followed, whereas in Harlem we walked arm in arm, downtown—in "white" surroundings—we were circumspect, relaxing only when we reached the privacy of his room. Our times together were intense. Soon I would have to return to London.

After my return to London, in July 1963 news came of the arrest of Walter Sisulu, Govan Mbeki, Ahmed Kathrada and several others, in Rivonia, a suburb of Johannesburg. When they were brought to trial in Pretoria's Palace of Justice, Nelson Mandela was named Number One Accused. Charged with membership of the National High Command of the *Umkhonto we Sizwe* sabotage movement, they faced a possible death sentence. A worldwide campaign was mounted to put pressure on the South African Government and prevent the men being hanged. At the UN the anger of the international community was expressed in a vote of 106–1 condemning the South African Government for its policies and calling for the release of the Rivonia defendants. Protesting crowds demonstrated outside the UN and at the White House, among them black actors such as Ossie Davis and Ruby Dee, and the novelist John Oliver Killens.

Oliver Tambo, Vice-President of the ANC, testified before the UN Committee on Apartheid, followed by Miriam Makeba, the singer, and representatives of American anti-apartheid organizations. I was asked to speak specifically about the men on trial, since I knew or was acquainted with several of them, and in March 1964 I flew from London to New York. "The press here," wrote Govan Mbeki from Pretoria prison, "have carried the news of your intended visit across the Atlantic." Having spoken of the Rivonia defendants, I went on to describe the lives of African families under apartheid and the role of foreign investment in sustaining the South African Government, and then, in desperation, concluded: "To tell the truth, my heart is so sick at the endless churning out of the horrible facts, which we all know too well, and have known for years, when all the time the iniquities we tell each other about, ceaselessly and so unnecessarily are hurting human beings—and this is their only life. Therefore, I beg that we stop cataloguing facts, and plan action and then *act*. Economic sanctions are surely the obvious civilized form of action when diplomatic and moral pressures long ago failed to make any impact on the South African Government."

On 11 June Nelson Mandela, Walter Sisulu, Govan Mbeki and all but one of the others in the Rivonia trial were found guilty on all counts. What would the sentence be? In St. Paul's Cathedral we kept vigil through the night. Next day came the news: they had all been sentenced to life imprisonment with hard labour. Nelson and the other black defendants were flown to Robben Island, a small rocky outcrop in the south Atlantic, some seven miles from Cape Town. Dennis Goldberg, the only white, remained in Pretoria prison.

I received a message that their spirits were tremendously high. They felt they would not become forgotten men. "To most of the world," said the *New York Times,* "those men are heroes and freedom fighters, the George Washingtons and Ben Franklins of South Africa."

A Negro Leadership Conference on Africa was to be held in Washington in October. Giving only a day's notice, a representative of the ANC asked me to fly there to speak on the organization's behalf—at that time they had hardly any members lobbying in exile. Civil Rights leaders were backing the event and the Secretary of State, Dean Rusk, was guest of honour, Martin Luther King the chairman. Chief Adebo, Nigeria's impressive ambassador to the UN, was the main speaker, and I followed.

After comparing the leadership and methods of the American freedom movement with that in South Africa, I spoke of recent events: leaders such as Nelson Mandela and Robert Sobukwe imprisoned on Robben Island, further arrests, interrogation under torture, innumerable political trials. What lay ahead, I asked, if non-violent resistance was met by massive crushing by the State, by killings, as at Sharpeville, and the outlawing of African political organizations? If underground action and sabotage led to death sentences and prolonged terms in prison? If Britain and America continued, in deed if not in word, to support the status quo of racial tyranny because of trade and investment?

In South Africa, as in the United States, I pointed out, the great majority of black leaders had steadfastly refused to be driven by white racialism into black racialism, and in both countries courageous whites had played a significant role in the struggle. I paid tribute to Martin Luther King, James Farmer, Roy Wilkins and other leaders in the United States for exerting moral authority—the American nation had cause to be profoundly grateful to them. They had already supported UN calls for economic sanctions against South Africa and I was confident that their determination would be strengthened by recent events in South Africa. Surely now they would exert renewed pressure on their government, and also on American investors who helped to bolster apartheid. Emphasizing the increasing significance of the Negro vote, I urged that they set about transforming government policy.

During the summer of 1964 Ruth First had settled in London with her three daughters. It was wonderful to see her again. She had endured 117 days in solitary confinement and long periods of gruelling interrogation. For the time being she would devote her brilliant intellectual powers to political and academic activity in Britain. (After returning to Africa, to academic work in Mozambique, in August 1982, Ruth was assassinated by a letter bomb.)

Bram Fischer also turned up in the autumn. Unexpectedly he had been granted a passport—unexpected because he had just been arrested in Johannesburg and, with twelve others, had been charged with membership of the illegal Communist Party. In London he was leading an appeal before the Privy Council on behalf of a commercial company. He had given an assurance to the South African authorities that he would return to stand trial.

I had first met him during the Treason Trial. What struck me was his courtesy: it never faltered, even when some remark by the prosecutor, some action by the police, angered him, hardening the expression of his blue eyes. Not physically impressive—short, ruddy-faced, with silver hair—he was an immensely captivating man.

His visit was both arduous and celebratory, seeing old friends and new, fitting in theatres between serious discussions. He seldom spoke of himself, was concerned rather to convey precisely what was happening under the Ninety Day detention law. To Hugh Foot (now Lord Caradon), who was on leave from the UN, Bram described the effects of police torture. Suliman Saloojee, a young Indian held in solitary, had somehow managed to smuggle a message to his wife. "Pray for me," he'd appealed. Bram could hardly contain wrath and grief as he explained that Saloojee was not a religious man and that, a day or two later, while being interrogated in Security Police headquarters, he had fallen seven storeys to his death.

In London influential politicians were profoundly impressed by Bram's dignified courage. They tried to persuade him to remain in Britain rather than go back to almost certain imprisonment. "But I gave my word," he told them. And from the bar of the Privy Council, Abram Fischer, QC, prepared to return to the dock in a Johannesburg Magistrate's Court.

I discussed with him my longing to go home. Apart from nostalgia for friends and family, as well as country, I felt it would be a small token of commitment when so many liberal or left-wing whites were leaving South Africa. And there was the continuing dislike of "agitating" abroad without returning to experience developments in the country. London seemed increasingly a neutral zone, an area of withdrawal from Johannesburg or from Jackson. But a lawyer in Cape Town advised me that, since I had advocated sanctions against the South African Government, I could be charged under a law which carried a minimum sentence of five years. Other friends in Johannesburg and in Port Elizabeth thought I would probably be followed by the Security Police and could harm the very people I wanted to assist. Bram, however, was convinced that all would be well and hoped I would decide to go. And I recalled James Baldwin's grave insistence that I would find I would "have to" return to South Africa. . . .

Before leaving London I asked my doctor for something to calm me should I encounter the Security Police. He prescribed a seasickness pill. As the plane flew over the Transvaal on Christmas Eve, I swallowed one and by the time we landed at Jan Smuts Airport I was feeling euphoric. The friend who had sat beside me throughout the flight, a South African academic living in America, made himself scarce. Entering the terminal I glanced around: there, the big man in flannels and blazer, eyes narrowed, hair cropped, surely he was one? A voice over the loudspeaker called: "Will Miss

Benson go to the BOAC counter?" Oh God, I thought, this is it! But at the counter a young woman wanted simply to confirm my return booking. In line for Immigration Control I wondered if they were checking names against a list. It seemed not. When my turn came the official studied my passport: "Hm, so you're a writer!" He smiled. "Well, have a good time in South Africa."

Home again. Even the weeds looked beautiful. And the night sky, when you gazed up at the Milky Way and the constellations—Sirius, Canopus and the Southern Cross—surely nowhere in the world were the stars so opulent and yet so intimate. While crickets shrilled, unceasing.

"It's like the coming of a whole battalion," Bram welcomed me extravagantly, that New Year's Eve of 1964. A few days later I attended his trial, in the "whites only" gallery, sitting nervously among families and friends of the thirteen who had been accused of membership of the outlawed Communist Party. Bram entered the court by a side-door and stood for a moment, looking directly at me. No greeting, only the acknowledgement of my presence. I was glad I had come.

The chief State witnesses were Gerald Ludi, a police spy who had been a member of a Party cell, and Piet Beyleveld, who had been a friend of Bram's—an Afrikaner, long a leading member of the Party. Both witnesses agreed that the activities of the Party centred largely on propaganda about injustices. The very issues about which the English-language press and the Liberal and Progressive parties legally protested, became illegal when taken up by Communists. But Ludi also declared that the Communists aimed to overthrow the government by violent revolution. Beyleveld contradicted this: revolution, he contended, did not mean violence but change; the Party had condemned acts of terrorism and insisted there must be no bloodshed.

"For years, Piet and I were comrades," Bram had told me. "I do not believe that when he comes into court, when he looks me in the eyes, he will be able to give evidence against us." But Beyleveld came into court, he stood in the witness box and he evaded Bram's gaze. When asked by the defence why he was giving evidence, he said he had agreed after persistent questioning by the Security Police; there had been no ill-treatment. Questioned further, he gave a startlingly accurate account of Bram's nature and influence: Fischer,

he said, was well known as a champion of the oppressed, with political views that had never been concealed; a man widely respected
in all parts of the community. He himself, he added, still revered
Fischer.

I could imagine the distress this admission must cause Bram,
who seemed to feel no bitterness towards his old friend, only anger
at the system which manipulated such an easy betrayal. The defence
counsel must have been astounded. "I was interested to hear you
say that," he remarked to Beyleveld, and then asked, "I don't like to
put this in my client's presence, but he is a man who carries something of an aura of a saint-like quality, does he not?"

"I agree," Beyleveld replied.

On a Friday afternoon I met Bram in a coffee-bar. His gaze was
unusually intense, but I put this down to our activity over the previous days. I had encouraged him to write an article expressing his
views about the crisis in the country which would be suitable for
the London *Observer*. Coming from him it was a seditious, illegal
document and he was worried lest I be incriminated as a fellow-
conspirator. Security Police made no attempt to hide the fact that
they were following him, but he was sure that on this occasion he
had given them the slip. He handed me the final copy of the article.
Then, gripping my hands, he asked me to be sure and come to court
on Monday. Of course, I said. With a light kiss and a *"Totsiens"*—
till I see you—he left.

All weekend I brooded miserably on what lay ahead. Perhaps
Bram intended to make a deliberate challenge to the State from the
dock, an action that would precipitate his imprisonment? How little I knew him.

On Monday, 25 January a friend who was staying with the
Fischers stopped me as I approached the court, drew me into an
empty waiting-room and handed me a letter. "Bram has gone underground," she confided.

"I feel incredibly dishonest and have ever since our talk on Friday," Bram wrote.

> This is not because I am about to "jump" my bail. The other side has
> never played according to the rules and has changed the rules when-
> ever it has suited them. That is the least of my "moral" worries. But
> throughout our talk I had to act to you and pretend I would see you
> on Monday and that was a singularly unpleasant experience.

In some ways I suppose this would seem to be a crazy decision. Yet I feel it is up to someone among the whites to demonstrate a spirit of protest. It must be demonstrated that people can fight apartheid from within the country even though it may be dangerous. That is why I returned here from London. I have left the trial because I also want to demonstrate that no one should meekly submit to our barbaric laws. I'm sure we shall meet again.

In the court everything seemed normal. Police and officials, defence and prosecution teams were present, and the other twelve defendants filed into the dock. Except that there was no sign of Bram. As soon as the magistrate had taken his seat, leading counsel for the defence rose to announce that he had a letter from Number One Accused, Abram Fischer, who had decided to absent himself from the trial. There was commotion in the court. The twelve defendants appeared flabbergasted and their families strained to hear as counsel read the letter. Bram stated that he had not been prompted by fear of punishment; indeed, he realized that his eventual punishment might be increased. He believed that white complacency in the face of the monstrous policy of apartheid made bloodshed inevitable. "To try to avoid this becomes a supreme duty, particularly for an Afrikaner," he declared. "If by my fight I can encourage even some people to think about, to understand and to abandon the policies they now so blindly follow, I shall not regret any punishment I may incur. I can no longer serve justice in the way I have attempted to do during the past thirty years."

Under the byline "From a Special Correspondent in Johannesburg," Bram's article, which I had mailed to the *Observer,* was headlined WORD FROM MISSING QC:

> The State thinks it has crushed the liberation movement, but it has not. . . . If the struggle for freedom is smothered in one place or for the time being, it flares up again before long . . .

He concluded with a vision of a free South Africa: at last the country would fulfil its great potential internally and in African and world affairs.

Weeks passed. The English-language press enjoyed taunting the police. BRAM FISCHER STILL FREE. The authorities said he might be disguised as a black-haired priest with dark glasses, or as an elderly

invalid woman swathed in shawls. FISCHER COULD BE ANYWHERE
FROM MALMESBURY TO MOSCOW.

Curtains drawn against the night, two women sat beside me on
a sofa. They had asked to see me urgently. One signalled a warning
that the room might be bugged. Gaps in their soft, quickly uttered
sentences were filled by words they wrote on paper. They had seen
Bram. He was known as Max. I watched the hand as it wrote,
"Max is depressed and isolated, will you visit him?"

"Of course," I said, and wrote, "When?"

"Tomorrow."

One of the women drew a map, showing the street, the house,
a shopping centre some blocks away where I could be dropped, and
a discreet route to ensure no police would follow. "Try to look as
unlike yourself as you can," was the final warning.

Writing now of those events, in the detail made possible by my
coded notes, I can feel again the apprehension—and exhilaration—
of being caught up in such a drama.

On a bright autumn day, wearing heavy suntan make-up and a
headscarf to obscure my face, I took a taxi to the shopping centre.
From there I walked until I arrived at an ugly yellow-brick house
with ornamental iron railings. Head held high but with shaky
knees, I went up a long drive past an unkempt garden and tennis
court. No one was visible in the neighbouring house. Pressing the
doorbell, I heard its chime but no movement. I rang again and this
time the door was opened by an African woman. There had been no
mention of a maid. "Is the master in?"

She motioned me through a bare hall to a large room furnished
only with cane garden chairs and a table. I noticed an ashtray with
pipe and matches. But Bram did not smoke. A sound made me
swing round. A man was standing there, staring at me. Auburn-
bearded, balding with receding auburn hair, his eyes blank behind
rimless spectacles. Jesus, I'd come to the wrong house! How could
I explain and get out?

"Good God!" he said. It was the familiar voice, warm, slightly
accented. "What are you doing here? How wonderful!"

It felt weird to embrace this strange-looking man, but the voice,
the smile, were Bram's. He was delighted and reassured by my failure to recognize him. "You look like Lenin," I teased. He had not
lost a mannerism of clearing his throat, nor a certain gesture of the
hand.

In the days that followed I marvelled that he was living in the heart of Johannesburg, within a mile or so of his old home, while the police were scouring the country. A substantial reward had been offered for his capture. I thought of him, alone but for the maid, in that dreary house. It was sickening that a man of his integrity should be forced to resort to subterfuge and lies.

"Get yourself a hat," he had said. In the OK Bazaars I bought one, emerald green, to match a borrowed green-and-white suit. The object was to look normal when leaving my sister's flat, where I was staying, and to arrive at Bram's house looking, I hoped, like a district nurse. Barney Simon, a close friend, drove me. He was ignorant of my ultimate destination, knowing only that I had to be dropped at the shopping centre—in a time of such tension and complexity friends were careful not to ask dangerous questions. When I nonchalantly put on the green hat, the sight reduced him to uncontrollable laughter, setting me off until we rocked with mirth. Sobering up, absurdly hatted, I strode into a fruit shop while he drove off. By the time I had reached Bram's front door, the hat was in my hands.

I was glad that he chose to have tea in the front garden rather than in the house, which was sparsely furnished, he explained, because he did not want to use his limited funds on unnecessary comforts. He was enjoying the informality of his new life, wearing sports shirts and flannels, and each week he grew more confident.

I did not want to know what he was doing or who he was seeing. The Ninety Day detention law had been suspended but could be brought back at any moment; the less I knew, the better. Clearly, he was having to start from scratch.

Usually we met once a week. He loved to hear about friends. Alan Paton was in town and Bram wished he could see him. "I'd give anything . . ." During the Rivonia trial he had visited Alan in Natal to ask if he would speak in mitigation of sentence. He had hardly made the request when Alan agreed. "But you've not heard all the facts," Bram protested. To which Alan replied, "You told me that it's a matter of life and death."

On judgement day in the trial of Bram's comrades, I waited in the main street of Benoni, a mining town where my brother-in-law had his office. Bram's Volkswagen approached, on time, and we headed for the southern border of the Transvaal. I was happy to be with him and relieved to avoid the tension of the court.

When he spoke of his people, perplexity, anger and love clashed. Their historic Great Trek from the Cape had been precipitated by the desire for freedom from British control, but they also wanted the freedom to own slaves, so were they freedom-fighters or oppressors?

Bram reverted to his family, what made them rebels was the Boer War.

Listening to Bram talk of the war, I was struck by how real it seemed for him although he was born six years after it ended. His family had town and country houses in the Free State and, like many Afrikaners, they were left with little but a few ornaments. British soldiers tore pages from the family's set of Dickens to stuff pillows.

"Today in all South Africa Afrikaners are only about 8 per cent of the population, and who in the outside world backs them?" Perhaps, he mused, oppressed people are always progressive until they get power. So, once Afrikaners attained power, their Nationalism escalated into domination over the blacks, a domination to which it seemed there was no limit.

It struck me that Bram's sacrifice of family, career and freedom had essentially been inspired by his Afrikaner heritage. He had implied as much in his letter to the magistrate: as an Afrikaner, he sought to make some reparation for the misdeeds of his people.

Bram announced that we'd reached our destination, Volksrust.

He turned off the main road to drive down a track to a *kloof*. He was a perfect host—the fire deftly made, the chops well grilled, the drinks iced. Each picnic became a festive occasion. He identified birds and trees and shared a letter from [his son] Paul, proud of the boy's literary style and amusing comments on life in London.

The sun, lighting the shaved area of his head, exposed white roots where the auburn hair began. "Your hair," I said. "It's beginning to show." Later, when we arrived in the suburbs, he stopped at a chemist, where I bought the dye that he used.

Bram had been underground for more than six months.

Back in Johannesburg, I found that he had moved. To my relief he was much more security-conscious and when one evening he drove up in his Volkswagen to where I awaited him on a corner, he asked me to close my eyes until we had driven in the gate to the new house. It was semi-detached but he hardly saw his neighbours, a young couple. He no longer employed a maid. Inside was the same garden furniture. Two garish paintings remained unhung in the nondescript sitting-room.

Warmed by an electric fire, we drank sherry to celebrate our reunion. . . .

I had grown quite accustomed to the strange double-life. Dining with friends, spending Sundays in and out of their pools, it was odd to hear their speculations about Bram. But when such speculations embraced me, I grew anxious. A diplomat remarked on how curious it was that the police hadn't taken any action against me and surmised this might be because, knowing I was a friend of Bram's, they hoped I would lead them to him. However, my only encounter with the Security Police in Johannesburg was when I attended a political trial and Sergeant Dirker, the policeman who had made life a misery for Walter Sisulu, asked for my press card. I watched as he showed it to Ludi, the former spy, who was assisting the prosecution and who gave him some instruction, whereupon he left the court. Meanwhile, I had swallowed the seasickness pill prescribed by my doctor and slipped away to visit academic friends, who were amused when I suddenly dropped off to sleep.

On a day bathed in winter sunshine, Bram and I drove along a road straight across the vast, breathtaking spaces of the Transvaal, the bare veld which previously I had seen as monotonous. The glorious day suited our mood. During the past weeks the *Rand Daily Mail* had published a series of articles by Benjamin Pogrund on prison conditions and the *Sunday Times* had followed with revelations from a white prison warder. Police raided the newspaper offices several times, interrogating the writers of the articles.

"Do you think it's the flaring up of a new flame, or old ashes dying?" Bram asked, his broad smile revealing what he thought, and before I could reply, he exclaimed, "I believe it is a new flame! If, now, people could be brought together, a whole new opposition working together . . ."

We picnicked under a cluster of thorn trees. Suddenly, African women materialized from the bush—there was no sign of a village—and sat beside us, displaying their handiwork. Bram bought grass mats and seed necklaces. After the women had withdrawn we had a last cup of coffee. There was always a slight melancholy when the time came for packing up.

One evening I brought him a gift, German poetry with translations, to mark his seven months of "freedom." It was a kind of milestone for me too. I had found that when you do something risky without being caught, each day is an extension of life that you truly value. Bram and I had separately seen a local production of *The Caucasian Chalk Circle*. Now I wanted to share with him Brecht's poem "*An die Nachgeborenen*"—to those who come after—which I felt expressed the question Camus put, the most important of our age: How cease to be victims without becoming executioners?

On a Sunday morning towards the end of August we drove to the north-west, through veld barren and strange under a sickly yellow sky.

On the wind that swept away the clouds came a host of yellow and white butterflies. Green shoots sprang in the veld. In a *kloof* below a high rocky *krans* Bram and I spread our rugs and cushions under blossoming trees. Kingfishers plunged towards the nearby stream. We gathered wood for our *braaivleis* fire.

Lunch over, I read to Bram from the final chapter of the history of the ANC, which I had been bringing up to date for a paperback: "Laski once wrote, 'The political criminals under a tyrant are the heroes of all free men.'" I broke off to ask, "That's a good quote, hey?" He smiled agreement. As I read on, shouts broke out from the woods on the opposite bank and from downstream.

"Your scarf!" he urged. The shouts sounded nearer and nearer. I quickly tied the headscarf under my chin and, as helmeted heads appeared among bushes across the stream, Bram calmly offered me a banana. Voices now came from behind us. We turned to see soldiers in full battledress running towards us. This is it, I thought.

"*Gooie dag!*" called one brightly.

"*Dag!*" said Bram.

"*Dag!*" I said as they trotted on by. We watched their booted feet climb the almost vertical cliff. More shouts sounded and more men ran past. We were in the middle of army training manoeuvres.

With studied casualness we packed the picnic basket and rugs and drove up the track to the main road. There a jeep was parked. Three senior officers stared out at us and smilingly saluted. We waved back and speeded away.

A few days later came the inevitable but horrifying announcement that Vorster had brought back and doubled the Ninety Day detention law. One hundred and eighty days of solitary confinement. You had no access to lawyers or courts while the Security Police interrogated you.

A man named Isaac Heymann was the first to be so detained. In prison he attempted suicide. I did not know him but was sure he was one of Bram's contacts. Bram's face was grim when next we met. Yes, he confirmed, Heymann was a close friend. "Do you know anyone who would put up a fugitive?" he then asked. I thought about it. I was renting a room in a friend's house; Athol Fugard and his family were also staying there while he rehearsed a new play. "No," I said apologetically, ashamed that I did not want to expose myself or test my friends.

The net was closing in. He confided that he was having sleepless nights. He had assumed a new name, Peter West.

We drove to a suburban hotel. "Let's have a gin and tonic to cheer ourselves up!" he said. We sat on the verandah under a rapidly darkening sky. There was only one other customer, a man at a nearby table. Was he observing us, the tall woman and the short, bearded man? Sensing my unease, Bram said, "If anyone you know comes up, don't forget to introduce me as Peter West, from out of town."

"Open your eyes!" We had arrived back at his house. A jacaranda tree was in bloom, glowing phosphorescently in the light from the street. For the rest of the evening, we hardly talked, just listened to music.

A few days later the woman who had been my contact with Bram was taken into detention: 180 days. When I had last seen her she said that on some days she felt well and was confident she could cope, but on days when she was feeling ill, she was not so sure. Women detainees were usually made to stand while interrogators questioned and threatened them, made to stand all through the day. . . .

Bram and I met, as arranged. In his house he took me through to a small room where a bed was ready. So this had been for the "fugitive." "It was too late," he said. And shut the door on the room. He was distracted from his grave anxiety for what his friend might be going through only by the desperate need to get away from this house. He had found a suitable place, but the owner could not see him to conclude negotiations until the following Sunday.

He wanted to post an important airmail letter. We drove to the main post office in the city. I watched him cross the road in front of a line of cars drawn up at the traffic lights.

Standing, standing, night and day . . .

Next morning, the morning of Thursday, 11 November, I telephoned Bram. He had asked me to arrange an appointment with a visitor from London and, although I had tried to dissuade him from so risky a venture, he had insisted. "Your appointment on Saturday," I told him, "it's all right." He was delighted.

That evening was the first performance of Fugard's *Hello and Goodbye*. On the way to the theatre came news of Rhodesia's Unilateral Declaration of Independence. Surely, I thought, Britain would not stand for Ian Smith's rebellion. This crazy act must help our struggle. I felt suddenly exhilarated, but also sad that the Rhodesian whites could be so deliberately self-destructive. Bram must have seen the evening paper; we would discuss it when we met in a few days' time.

Early next morning an acquaintance called by to collect some photographs. She said: "Bram Fischer's been caught!"

I did not believe it. There had been many false alarms; how he and I had laughed at them. I began to feel nauseated. She handed me a newspaper:

JO'BURG DRAMA: FISCHER IS ARRESTED.

Die Transvaler had a picture of him beside the gross and malevolent Swanepoel, the most notorious of all the Security Police; his fist clutched Bram's arm, while Bram's other hand adjusted his rimless spectacles as he stared into the photographer's flash.

A day of mourning. Athol sat with me on the balcony looking out on the wild garden where we lived. We did not talk. A day interminable, somehow to be survived. "You've saved my sanity, bless you," Bram had said when we parted on that last evening.

The courtroom bristled with Security Police. A handful of spectators, white on our side, black on theirs, sat in the public galleries. While we waited I counted the police milling around the dock. I had reached forty-nine when up the steps from the cells and into the dock came Bram.

He turned once, deliberately, calmly, to look at us, and once to look at the black gallery. He had shaved the beard and reverted to his old, half-rimmed spectacles. He was no longer Max, but not quite Bram—I felt doubly bereaved.

It took only a few moments for the magistrate to announce a remand. A glance from Bram at [his children] Ruth and Paul and he was gone, a prisoner, to be held behind bars and locked doors in a cell in Pretoria prison. I was never to see him again.

———

At his trial early in 1966, . . . he made a statement from the dock.

"All the conduct with which I have been charged has been directed towards maintaining contact and understanding between the races of this country. If one day it may help to establish a bridge across which white leaders and the real leaders of the 'non-whites' can meet, to settle the destinies of all of us by negotiation and not by force of arms, I shall be able to bear with fortitude any sentence which this court may impose on me."

He was sentenced to imprisonment for life.

In 1968, when I was allowed back briefly to South Africa, I applied to visit Bram. The Commissioner of Prisons was a man of few words: "Your request to visit A. Fischer cannot be acceded to."

We were able to exchange occasional letters, 500 words the limit, and no mention of politics or world affairs. For the most part he referred to his studies: he had passed Economics I and was reading "Native Administration." And he described the plants he was growing in the courtyard of their special section: gazanias and roses, Iceland poppies and freesias. He was experimenting with grafting guava and grenadilla and if it bore fruit he would name it guavadilla. He fed crumbs to sparrows, doves and rock-pigeons. "Then we have a thrush coming after worms occasionally and can sometimes hear a Cape robin before dawn."

And he wrote of a thunderstorm, the lightning glimpsed through the barred window of the cell, and in an instant I was back in the little house next door to the jail, with the pain of exile and missing him added to the violence of that never-to-be-forgotten storm.

That Christmas he was in hospital—the hospital I remembered so well—guarded by two warders. After a fall in prison, cancer had been diagnosed. Throughout his dreadful, slow dying he was said to be calm and cheerful, but exhausted. Despite the increasingly urgent appeals of family, friends and innumerable people from many countries, the Minister of Prisons and Justice refused to release him to the care of his family until he was incapable of appreciating their companionship.

Bram Fischer died on 8 May 1975. After the funeral, the authorities demanded that his ashes be returned to Pretoria prison.

———

Each day that passed after Bram's arrest, bereavement and fear of being taken into 180 days were strangely mixed with happiness, the happiness of feeling at home. I loved the dilapidated colonial mansion where I was living, with its large, dark rooms, its long corridors and balcony overlooking the garden of tangled grass, pines and jacarandas. I wanted to stay. I did not want to run away.

The police put out a story that Bram had been followed for several months before his capture. If it were true, they would have known about me, they would have known his phone number and would have overheard our last conversation. Obviously they were watching the airport, hoping his contacts would scatter and run. As I waited and waited I imagined that one of the taxi drivers who had dropped me near Bram's car might recognize him from pictures in the press and report a tall woman with a British accent to the police. If I were to be detained in solitary confinement and interrogated, what would become of my courage, my loyalty? I had glibly condemned those who had given evidence against their friends. Now I wondered: who could be sure of resisting? Many had succumbed, some after brief interrogation, others only after months of solitary confinement and torture. During the Inquisition, men and women sustained by their faith had withstood appalling forms of physical torture. But in our age, did honour really matter more than survival?

It was not that I knew any secrets, but what if I were broken to the point of telling lies which could incriminate the innocent?

Very early on a summer morning in February, arriving in Johannesburg by slow night train, I headed straight for a mailbox to post the preface of the ANC history to Penguin Books. Back in the old house I telephoned friends and as they welcomed me and we chatted, idly I watched the sunlight playing on leaves outside the hall window. A large sedan appeared, circling the drive; from the front seat two men stared directly at me. "A car's just come, two men . . ." I told Barney, the friend I had just called. "Jesus!" he said. As the doorbell rang I put down the receiver.

When I opened the door one of them thrust a sheaf of documents at me, asking, "Dorothy Mary Benson?" while the other announced, "We are from the Security Police. We have to serve these orders."

It was very strange. I had been expecting them to arrest me and instead they were asking me to read a document: "WHEREAS I, BAL-THAZAR JOHANNES VORSTER, Minister of Justice, am satisfied that you

engage in activities which are furthering or may further the achievement of the objects of communism . . ." My eyes jumped a few lines:
"Prohibit you . . . from absenting yourself from the residential
premises"—yes, that was my address—"at any time except between
the hours of six in the forenoon and seven in the afternoon . . ."

"I don't understand," I said.

"We're only serving the orders. We want you to sign here to say
you received them. You must ask the magistrate, or a lawyer."

Dazed, I signed, and they went down the steps. The telephone
rang. It was Barney. They turned to watch me through the window
as I told him, "It seems to be house arrest. I can't understand the detail."

"Shit, man, that's bad," he sympathized.

Nine pages of restrictions: house arrest every night, through
weekends and public holidays; restriction to the city, weekly reporting to the police; and clause after clause of bans. Banned from
schools, courts—I would not be able to attend Bram's trial—factories, newspaper offices and any area for "Bantu, Coloured or Asiatic persons"—I could not visit Dugmore Boetie, a Coloured writer
ill with cancer in hospital. Banned from "gatherings," which, I
knew, was legally interpreted as being with more than one person at
a time. Clause 5 banned any writing, even poetry, with sub-clauses
(a), (b), (c), (d), then (e) (i) and (ii), and (aa), (bb), (cc) and (dd),
which included a ban on "preparing, compiling, printing, publishing, disseminating and transmitting." "Transmitting"—that obviously related to those letters from Washington which had blatantly
been opened.

Clause 6 said no visitors to the house apart from a medical
practitioner. No sooner had I read it than a friend, a journalist,
drove up to the front steps. I hurried out to explain. He was as
stunned as I. I quickly handed him notes about the Eastern Cape,
which, until half an hour ago, had been a perfectly legal act on my
part.

It was a tremendous relief to realize that the police were ignorant of my meetings with Bram. The least suspicion on their part
would have led to immediate interrogation. Yet the shock of the
lesser punishment was intense. No reasons were ever given for such
banning, but in my case I was convinced the restrictions were aimed
at silencing me after the reporting of the Eastern Cape trials.

The first Saturday of house arrest was brilliantly hot. Kurt and
the other "lodger," even the servants, were out. The telephone was

silent and I could not repress the question: did friends want to protect me or themselves? . . .

The pattern of life had changed. Instead of writing by day and visiting friends in the evening and at weekends, I went obsessively to town in the hope of bumping into one of them for coffee or lunch. I say "bumping into" because lawyers advised that any prearranged meeting could be construed as a "gathering." Unexpected people contrived to send messages of where they were likely to be and when. And friends joined me in the Outpatients queue at the hospital, where I went regularly for treatment. . . .

Increasingly, family and friends urged me to leave the country, but Guy Clutton-Brock, who had once been imprisoned in Rhodesia and whom I greatly admired, wrote: "Try to stay and endure to the end. No other weapon than creative suffering can cope with the enormities of the world in which we live."

If I could not write, at least I had one worthwhile if small job: to compile a survey of the Eastern Cape trials. Until lawyers advised that this too was illegal.

Could I leave the country that finally had become "home"? I felt just being there had a certain value. When I thought of London, the Sunday papers' gossip columns filled me with gloom—Forster's, "He could pardon vice, but not triviality"—and our anti-apartheid protests seemed stridently negative rather than supportive of those who tried to create in the face of repression; but of course, much that was creative could not be told about without risking its survival. Yet to stay meant giving up almost all human contact, it meant renunciation, silence. On the other hand, to go could mean "for ever." I would not be allowed to return without permission from the Minister of the Interior. As weeks passed and I toiled with these questions, I wondered at what point self-mockery began.

Agonizing though it was, my father had no doubt that I should go. And somehow Bram managed to get a message to me: "You can do more overseas."

It was midnight. Down the corridor from Kurt's room came the wail of his favourite Fada songs. I put on a record of *"Das Lied von der Erde"* and listened to the reverberating beauty of Kathleen Ferrier singing "Der Abschied," the farewell, for ever, *"Ewig . . . ewig . . ."*

Weary, but with a curious sense of lightness, I decided to leave.

In the end what made it easier was the knowledge that I was going directly to Washington to testify before a Congressional

Committee on Foreign Affairs, recently formed to consider United
States–South African relations. I was already planning my statement.
I would start by saying that the time to confront the South African
Government was now: in five to ten years it would be more powerful, more tyrannical. I would remind the Committee that the Minister of Justice, Vorster, had been detained in the Second World War
for pro-Nazi activities. It was important to try to convey what life
was like for Mrs. Ntlonti and her family and for the 800 men,
women and teenagers recently arrested by police raiding servants'
quarters in Johannesburg's suburbs. While giving some idea of the
psychological effects of bans and house arrest, I wanted to make it
clear that most of the 520 people who had been banned were
Africans, and that the cruellest restrictions were those imposed on
men and women immediately after their release from prison. And
of course I would testify about the trials in the Eastern Cape.[1]

The Chief Magistrate granted a permit enabling me to leave the
city of Johannesburg, "at 10:45 on Saturday, 16 April 1966 for the
sole purpose of proceeding to Jan Smuts Airport in order to leave
South Africa."

At the airport Pa was photographed by the *Sunday Times* mopping up his tears. A large gathering of friends saw me off—watched
by the Security Police.

It was not until the plane was high over the stark hills of As-
mara that I thought: leaving is betrayal. Even *one* counts. I felt it
might be the greatest mistake of my life.

[Two years later Benson returned.] "I think my father is dying!"
I appealed to Helen Suzman, the Progressive Member of Parliament. Since he was alone in South Africa—my sister no longer lived
there—I had applied to the Minister of the Interior for permission
to be with him, but this had been rejected. After a brief convalescence, Pa had returned to his room in a boarding house, where he
again fell ill and it was when his letters abruptly deteriorated into a
scrawl of gibberish zigzagging across the pages that I telephoned
Mrs. Suzman in Johannesburg. Her urgent approach to the Minister succeeded. At last the necessary permit was granted and I flew
out in July 1968.

An ambulance drove us to "our" hospital, now imposingly

1. *African Politics and Society*, ed. I. L. Markovitz, Macmillan Free Press, New
York, 1970.

signposted H. F. VERWOERD HOSPITAL. I had to abandon Pa to a ward where everyone, nurses and patients, seemed to speak only Afrikaans.

I caught a bus to town, haunted by images of the crumpled old man groaning at each jolt as he was wheeled through what had once been his domain.

I went to police headquarters and reported to the officer on duty. He informed me that I would be restricted to Pretoria but I would not be under house arrest. However, the other bans remained in force: I could not meet more than one person at a time and I could not communicate with other banned people. And finally, he added that I would be permitted to stay for only one month.

Pretoria was ugly with symbols of Afrikaner Nationalism's rise to power and prosperity. The massive new Security Police headquarters, the glass-and-concrete banks and office blocks dwarfed the old Boer and Imperial buildings—the Raadsaal and, facing it, the Palace of Justice, where Mandela and Sisulu and the other Rivonia men had been on trial. I crossed Church Square between those relics. Ahead of me strolled a young black couple, the boy in jeans and sneakers, the girl wearing a floral cotton dress. Their laughter, the springing energy of their movements, their appearance of happy confidence at the very heart of Afrikanerdom, signalled, I thought, the future.

On Sunday morning the Salvation Army's tuba and trombone accompanied singing in the ward. Pa stirred. I held his hand and assured him it was all a nightmare, it would come to an end. "I know," he said. In the evening he slipped into unconsciousness. After four hours a doctor came. One of Pa's lungs had collapsed, he said, but pulse and blood pressure were fine. The nurses advised me to go home for dinner.

Pa died an hour later. They said he had not regained consciousness but I wished desperately that I had been with him. *Miseris Succurrere*. I forgot to ask for his ring.

The next day a friend drove me along Potgieter Street, past Defence Headquarters, to the corner next door to the prison. No longer an oasis: our first house still stood, but baldly stripped of jacarandas and flower beds. Where once an orchard of peaches and figs, nectarines and plums had flourished, the ground had been cemented over and a prison warder was washing his car.

My pilgrimage took me on to the jail next door. Locked away

behind those red-brick turreted walls in a new wing built specifically for white political prisoners was Bram Fischer. My application to visit him had been bluntly rejected; this was the closest I could come.

We drove on past the old façade and, turning to the right, from the hillside we looked down on a huge conglomeration of maximum security buildings and defence establishments which had swallowed up the neighbourhood and soon, no doubt, would devour the red-brick prison and our house. Back in Potgieter Street, I gave a last glance at the small barred windows.

At COMPOL, a cream-painted colonial building, a sign on the outside stated COMMISSIONER OF POLICE. Nothing to indicate what was perpetrated inside but, down the passage, a warning, NO ADMITTANCE EXCEPT . . . Except if you are the interrogator, the torturer or the victim. In the foyer a Captain of the Security Police added his signature to the permit given by the magistrate, enabling me to leave Pretoria provided I took a single ticket for the train to Botswana, travelled via the shortest available route and did not leave the train at Johannesburg station.

A last view of the railway yards. Then nothing but brown veld. Inside the compartment, firmly stuffed green leather seats and a display of glassed-in vintage photos of rhinos in the game reserve, Zulu warriors and Benoni town hall. Soothing rhythm of wheels over sleepers, and I thought of the people I was leaving behind—Athol without a passport, Bram in prison for life. And Nelson and Walter, after they'd been sentenced, a lawyer had spoken in amazement tinged with dismay of their euphoria, for did it not reveal the besetting defect of the "liberation movement," evasion of reality? But I recalled Camus's advice that we should say "in the very midst of the sound and fury of our history: Let us rejoice!"

In Johannesburg station we were shunted from one concrete tunnel to another. Suddenly a young woman friend appeared at the door of the compartment with books and messages from the others who could not come. The whistle blew and, "Oh Mary," she said, "it's so awful here now." As the train crawled through the entrails of the city I caught a last glimpse of the skyscrapers and yellow mine dumps, and finally wept.

Mafeking. The last stop before the border with Botswana. Into the compartment came two men. "Security Police. We want to search your luggage. Please open everything." They fumbled through my carefully folded dresses, intently studied gramophone

records, then came to an airways bag crammed with books, press
cuttings, my father's papers and photos and my coded notebooks.
They pulled out a few papers randomly, peered suspiciously at pictures of a robin and a swallow cut from Pa's bird calendar, then
gave up.

"Your person must be searched," said one and, as they left, a
girl appeared and apologetically asked me to strip. Amused rather
than cross, I undid the zip and began to lower my dress. "That's all
right," she said. And departed.

The train lurched into action, leaving Mafeking, leaving my
country. My country . . .

> And the end of all our exploring
> Will be to arrive where we started
> And know the place for the first time.[2]

---

2. From T. S. Eliot, *Four Quartets*. Faber and Faber, 1944.

Ruth First

(1925–1982)

Ruth First (Slovo), the daughter of South African academics and committed leftist reformers, was born in Johannesburg, where she attended university. A gifted journalist, she was already active in the cause of black workers at the age of twenty-one, when she published stories of brutality and repression during a 1946 miners' strike and a series of exposés of near slave conditions among farm laborers in the Transvaal.

Married to Joe Slovo, the leader of the South African Communist party and friend and confidant of the leaders of the African National Congress, First edited a hard-hitting reform journal, *Fighting Talk,* and served as the Johannesburg editor for the *Guardian,* where her dispatches were a constant thorn in the side of the South African government.

Present at the famous African National Congress meeting at Rivonia, which was raided by the South African Security Forces, First escaped without detection but was arrested shortly afterward and detained in solitary confinement for four months, a period of psychological terror and constant interrogation. Secure in the knowledge that her husband had left the country, First was still vulnerable to threats against her aging parents and her three young children. But she held firm and revealed none of her knowledge of ANC activities.

After her release First moved to the United Kingdom, where she taught at the University of Durham until she became one of the founders of the Center for African Studies at the Universidade Eduardo Mondlane in Mozambique in 1979. There she led a team of researchers investigating the conditions of migrant labor in South Africa. In 1982, while completing her report indicting migrant labor conditions in South African mines, First was killed by a letter bomb, the favorite method of the South African Security Forces for disposing of intransigent political exiles.

Her account of her solitary confinement is one of the most gripping and chilling of prison narratives. While many names of male opponents of South African racism are household symbols of courage, none of the great women resisters are as well known. First's account is a classic because of her psychological insight into herself and her interrogators, and her total absence of self-pity. As we read we know such defiance can only be silenced by death, and we feel the shadows of tragedy closing in upon our existential heroine, even as she walks undaunted away from prison.

117 DAYS

For the first fifty-six days of my detention in solitary I changed from a mainly vertical to a mainly horizontal creature. A black iron bedstead became my world. It was too cold to sit, so I lay extended on the bed, trying to measure the hours, the days and the weeks, yet pretending to myself that I was not. The mattress was lumpy; the grey prison blankets were heavy as tarpaulins and smelt of mouldy potatoes. I learned to ignore the smell and to wriggle round the bumps in the mattress. Seen from the door the cell had been catacomb-like, claustrophobic. Concrete-cold. Without the naked electric bulb burning, a single yellow eye, in the centre of the ceiling, the cell would have been totally black; the bulb illuminated the grey dirt on the walls which were painted black two-thirds of the way up. The remaining third of the cell wall had been white once; the dust was a dirty film over the original surface. The window, high in the wall above the head of the bedstead, triple thick— barred, barred again and meshed—with sticky black soot on top of all three protective layers, was a closing, not an opening. Three paces from the door and I was already at the bed.

Left in that cell long enough, I feared to become one of those colourless insects that slither under a world of flat, grey stones, away from the sky and the sunlight, the grass and people. On the iron bedstead it was like being closed inside a matchbox. A tight fit, lying on my bed, I felt I should keep my arms straight at my sides in cramped, stretched-straight orderliness. Yet the bed was my privacy, my retreat, and could be my secret life. On the bed I felt in control of the cell. I did not need to survey it; I could ignore it, and concentrate on making myself comfortable. I would sleep, as long as I liked, without fear of interruption. I would think, without diversion. I would wait to see what happened, from the comfort of my bed.

Yet, not an hour after I was lodged in the cell, I found myself forced to do what storybook prisoners do: pace the length and

breadth of the cell. Or tried, for there was not room enough to
pace. The bed took up almost the entire length of the cell, and in
the space remaining between it and the wall was a small protrud-
ing shelf. I could not walk round the cell, I could not even cross it.
To measure its eight feet by six, I had to walk the length alongside
the bed and the shelf, and then, holding my shoe in my hand, crawl
under the bed to measure out the breadth. It seemed important to
be accurate. Someone might ask me one day—when?—the size of
my cell. The measuring done, I retreated to the bed. There were
four main positions to take up: back, stomach, either side, and
then variations, with legs stretched out or curled up. In a long
night a shift in position had to be as adventurous as a walk. . . .
even when I closed my eyes and sank deeper into the warmth of the
bed, there were other reminders of the cell. The doors throughout
the police station were heavy steel. They clanged as they were
dragged to, and the reverberation hammered through my neck and
shoulders, so that in my neck fibres I felt the echo down the passage, up the stairs, round the rest of the double-storey police station. The doors had no inside handles and these clanging doors
without handles became, more than the barred window, more than
the concrete cell walls, the humiliating reminder of incarceration,
like the strait-jacket must be in his lucid moments to the violent in-
mate of an asylum.

Six hours before my first view of the cell, I had come out of the
main reading-room of the University library. The project that week
was how to choose atlases in stocking a library, and in my hand was
a sheaf of newly scribbled notes. . . .

The librarianship course was an attempt to train for a new profession. My newest set of bans prohibited me from writing, from
compiling any material for publication, from entering newspaper
premises. Fifteen years of journalism had come to an end. I had
worked for five publications and each had, in turn, been banned or
driven out of existence by the Nationalist Government. There was
no paper left in South Africa that would employ me, or could, without itself being an accomplice in the contravention of ministerial orders. So I had turned from interviewing ejected farm squatters,
probing labour conditions and wages on gold mines, reporting
strikes and political campaigns, to learning reference methods, cataloguing and classification of books. . . .

Somehow, in the library as I packed up the reference books on
my table, I managed to slip out of my handbag and under a pile of

lecture notes the note delivered to me from D. that morning. It had suggested a new meeting-place where we could talk. The place was "clean" and unknown, D. had written. He would be there for a few days.

The two detectives ranged themselves on either side of me and we walked out of the University grounds. An Indian student looked at the escort and shouted: "Is it all right?" I shook my head vigorously and he made a dash in the direction of a public telephone booth: there might be time to catch the late afternoon edition of the newspaper, and Ninety-Day detentions were "news."

The raid on our house lasted some hours. It was worse than the others, of previous years. . . . I tried to put firmly out of my mind the faces of the children as I was driven away. Shawn had fled into the garden so that I would not see her cry. Squashed on the front seat beside two burly detectives, with three others of rugby build on the back seat, I determined to show nothing of my apprehension at the prospect of solitary confinement, and yet I lashed myself for my carelessness. Under a pile of the *New Statesman* had been a single, forgotten copy of *Fighting Talk*, overlooked in the last clean-up in our house of banned publications. Possession of *Fighting Talk*, which I had edited for nine years, was punishable by imprisonment for a minimum of one year. Immediately, indefinite confinement for interrogation was what I had to grapple with. I was going into isolation to face a police probe, knowing that even if I held out and they could pin no charge on me, I had convicted myself by carelessness in not clearing my house of illegal literature. . . .

. . . The cell door banged shut, and two more after it. There was only the bed to move towards.

What did They know? Had someone talked? Would their questions give me any clue? How could I parry the interrogation sessions to find out what *I* wanted to know, without giving them the impression that I was resolutely determined to tell them nothing? If I was truculent and delivered a flat refusal to talk to them at the very first session, they would try no questions at all, and I would glean nothing of the nature of their inquiry. I had to find a way not to answer questions, but without saying explicitly to my interrogators, "I won't tell you anything."

Calm but sleepless, I lay for hours on the bed, moving my spine and legs round the bumps on the mattress, and trying to plan for my first interrogation session. Would I be able to tell from the first questions whether they knew I had been at Rivonia?[1] Had I been taken in on general suspicion of having been too long in the Congress movement, on freedom newspapers, mixing with Mandela and Sisulu, Kathrada and Govan Mbeki, who had been arrested at Rivonia, not to know something? Was it that the Security Branch was beside itself with rage that Joe had left the country—by coincidence one month before the fateful raid on Rivonia? Was I expected to throw light on why Joe had gone, on where he had gone? Had I been tailed to an illegal meeting? . . .

Or was I being held by the Security Branch not for interrogation at all, but because police investigations had led to me and I was being held in preparation for prosecution and to prevent me from getting away before the police were ready to swoop with a charge? At the first interrogation session, I decided, I would insist on saying nothing until I knew whether a charge was to be preferred against me. If I were asked whether I was willing to answer questions, I would say that I could not possibly know until I was given a warning about any impending prosecution. The Ninety-Day Law could be all things to all police. It could be used to extort confessions from a prisoner, and even if the confession could not—at the state of the law then—be used in court, it would be reassurance to the Security Branch that its suspicions were confirmed, and a signal to proceed with a charge. . . .

As I dropped off to sleep the remembrance of that neatly folded but illegal copy of *Fighting Talk* rose again. If the best happened I would be released because there was no evidence against me . . . and I would have withstood the pressure to answer questions . . . but I would be brought to court and taken into prison for having one copy of a magazine behind the bottom shelf of a bookcase. How untidy! It would not make impressive reading in a news report.

I slept only to wake again. My ears knocked with the noise of a

---

1. One month before my arrest, in July 1963, Security Police arrested Nelson Mandela and other political leaders in a raid on a house in the Johannesburg suburb of Rivonia. That house was used as the underground headquarters of the freedom struggle headed by the African National Congress. In what subsequently became known as the Rivonia Trial, Mandela and his associates were sentenced to terms of life imprisonment for directing sabotage and planning the armed overthrow of the South African Government.

police station in operation. The cell was abandoned in isolation, yet suspended in a cacophony of noise. . . .

Twice again I was jerked awake by the rattle of doors to find the wardress standing in my doorway. She was on inspection, doing a routine count of the prisoners. "Don't you ever sleep?" she asked.

Suddenly the door rattled open and a new wardress stared in. A tin dish appeared, on it a hard-boiled egg, two doorsteps of bread, and coffee in a jam-tin mug. Minutes later the crow was retreating down the passage. The wardress led me out of my cell, past a second solitary one, into the large dormitory cell which was divided by a half-wall from a cold-water basin and a lavatory without a seat. I washed in cold water and half a bucket of hot, put on my pyjamas and dressing-gown, was led out again into my little cell, and climbed back into bed. My first day in the police station had begun.

I felt ill-equipped, tearful. I had no clothes. No daily dose of gland tablets (for a thyroid deficiency). My confiscated red suitcase, carefully packed from the accumulated experience of so many of us who had been arrested before, was the only thing, apart from me, that belonged at home, and in the suitcase were the comforts that could help me dismiss police station uniformity and squalor. I sat cross-legged on the bed, huddled against the cold, hang-dog sorry for myself.

The door clanged open and a lopsided gnome-like man said he was the Station Commandant. "Any complaints?" he asked. This was the formula of the daily inspection rounds. I took the invitation. I objected to being locked up without charge, without trial, in solitary. The Commandant made it clear by his wooden silence that I was talking to the wrong man. The catalogue of complaints was for the record, I had decided. I would allow no prison or police official to get the impression that I accepted my detention. But the end of the recital that first morning tailed off on a plaintive note . . . "and I've got none of my things . . . I want my suitcase, my clothes, my medicine. . . ."

"Where's her suitcase?" the Commandant demanded of the wardress, who passed the query on to the cell warder.

"Bring it. All of it. Every single thing."

The cell warder went off at the double. Red suitcase appeared in the doorway, tied up with pink tape. The Station Commandant started to finger through it, then recoiled when he touched the underwear.

"She can have the lot!" he said.

The wardress, peering over his sloped left shoulder at the cosmetics, said shrilly: "She can't have bottles. . . . The bottles . . . we can't have bottles in the cells."

The Commandant rounded on her. One person would make the decisions, he told her. He had decided.

The cell warder retrieved the pink tape and the suitcase stayed behind in the cell. Nestling in it were an eyebrow tweezer, a hand mirror, a needle and cotton, my wrist-watch, all prohibited articles. And glass bottles, whose presence made the wardresses more nervous than any other imagined contravention of the regulations, for it was a strict rule that nothing of glass should be allowed in the cells. I was later to find out why.

The next day was Sunday, but pandemonium. The cell door was flung open and the wardress, the cell warder, and a third policeman stared in, disbelievingly, I thought. There was prolonged shouting from the guts of the station, repeated banging of doors overhead. The Station Commandant had the door flung open a half-hour before the usual inspection. He said the usual "Any complaints?" formula but was out of the cell before he could reply to my "What about exercise?" The wardresses were tight-lipped, on edge. A fever seemed to rage in the working part of the police station, and the raised temperature flowed out to the prisoners lying in their cells.

There were four instead of two inspections that night. Trying to reconstruct the noises of the night hours I realized that there must have been an admission into the women's cells, and someone was in the cell opposite me, for there were two mugs of coffee in the hands of the morning-shift wardress.

Unexpectedly a high fastidious voice said, "I am due to menstruate, wardress, how do I get some cotton-wool?"

"Anne-Marie!" I shouted. "Anne-Marie . . . you here! Wardress, I've got cotton-wool."

The cell doors opened long enough for me to pass out the cotton-wool and to catch a glimpse of Anne-Marie Wolpe—wife of our good friend Harold—haggard and drawn, perched on her high bed.

If Anne-Marie had been taken, Harold must have got safely away. The escape had come off, I decided. Thirty-six hours before I had gone into Marshall Square a break-out of the cells was being planned. . . .

"Four 90-day Men Escape," said the newspaper headlines. "Wives Held for Questioning." A massive police search for the fugitives followed. "Goldreich, described as the Security Branch's major detainee, is still on the run. Police Patrols are at work throughout the land." "The police are being swamped with calls about the escapers."

"The Net Closes In." "A price of R1,000 is on the head of each escaper. . . .

On the fourth day I asked the little Station Commandant about exercise.

"Exercise! That'll have to wait. Can't you see this place is in a *dinges*?"[2]

"*A dinges*?" I pretended not to understand.

"Oh, all right, a turmoil then," and he added, ominously, "After this things are going to be tough, very tough. You've seen nothing yet." He was half out of the door, ". . . and you'd better get rid of those bottles!"

"Slovo!" There was the rattle of keys and the door clanged open.

"Goldreich!" Suddenly there was gentle Hazel, Arthur's wife, and we blinked delightedly at one another in the sun. The wardress set off in the direction of the men's exercise yard, and Hazel and I pranced behind her, mouthing enthusiastic welcomes to one another. Too soon we reached the exercise yard where a Security Branch photographer had his camera and flash gun poised, and a list of detainees. While I had my picture taken, my back against the brick wall, Hazel peered at the list. "Anne-Marie's been released," she hissed, spotting on the list next to A. Wolpe the word "*ontslaan*" (released).

"Ai . . . aai . . . they're together . . . they're together!" The Station Commandant had come into the yard and leapt into the air in a series of panicky jerks at the sight of Hazel and me together. The wardress was flummoxed. She had been told to bring Slovo and Goldreich to the photographer. Those had been Security Branch instructions, after all, and no one had explicitly said, "But not the two of them together." Back we were hustled, individually, into our cells. But the encounter had taken place and though precautions

2. Afrikaans slang for "what-d'ye-call-it."

against our seeing one another were stricter than ever, we knew we had company beyond the courtyard wall, and the presence of someone else in the same predicament was selfishly reassuring.

For my part, I found myself slipping with disconcerting ease into a dreary, squalid routine of locked-up life in an airless, grimy concrete space. . . . I was trying to turn isolation into an advantage. But the clang of the steel, the doors without handles, the never-ending inspections were constant physical reminders of the humiliation of being locked away.

Isolation and privacy. Not the same thing by any means. I was isolated, but utterly dependent on outsiders—my jailers, my enemies. I had to shout or bang on the door when I wanted to use the lavatory. The wardress stood by while I washed. The daily programme, whatever I pretended, was not mine but theirs.

Prison routine imposed itself during the first days of bewildered existence in blackness. The electric light burned endlessly but showed nothing but the end of my bedstead, and beyond that, my red suitcase enthroned on the wall shelf. I could dispense with my eyes. Ears were more useful in isolation. There would be the jingle of keys and the clang of doors to announce the approach of an intruder, or a new episode in the regulated monotony of life in a cell.

Marshall Square is the most important police station in South Africa's largest city. . . . The politicals were in separate cells, segregated from the other prisoners, but sounds filtered through the thick walls, especially at night when the roar of the traffic died down. Several times a day I was ushered to the washroom of the large communal cell next door . . . if there were other prisoners there, the wardress stood on duty to make sure I did not try to communicate with them. . . .

Once the prisoners had been shunted off to court and the new shift had taken over the cells, the station could get down to the serious business of the day: cleaning up. . . . I am sure that if the wardresses had any attitude to Ninety-Day detention it was that our uninterrupted occupation of the cells, without a decent exit in the crocodile of the prisoners being taken to Court, obstructed a really good polish. For cleaning meant the floors. . . . Except rarely the basin and the lavatory were not properly cleaned: the budget of the station did not run to the right equipment and cleaners. But the floors, ah the floors . . .

Every morning as the cha-cha cleaners were on their way out, the wardress on duty would thrust a large aluminium bucket at one and order him to bring hot water for the "missus." That was me. Washing in a bucket was the highlight of my day. The hot water would rub away the mouldy blanket smell that pervaded the cell, and when the bucket was brought I would accept with alacrity the invitation to be locked in the large communal cell that sported the wash-basin. The bucket of hot water was a concession to the Ninety-Dayers' permanent residence in the cells; the ordinary occupants had to manage under the cold-water tap. For the first few days I grappled with the water in the bucket unsuccessfully. To pour it over me would have been a wonderful splurge but of few seconds' duration. If I stood in the bucket it would be like an uncomfortable stork, more out of the water than in it. In time I improvised a bath by acrobatics. I poured the water into the basin and perched on it in an inelegant squat, face and stomach towards the wall, legs dangling. Then I poured water over myself with cupped hands. It made a great splash that sounded like fun if anyone cared to listen, and I knew that the prisoners would hold the pools of water on the floor against, not me, but the wardress if they were called in to do a second mopping.

Bath over, it was the start of a new day, another day of torpid inactivity. Lying in bed at night could be excused as a retreat from inactivity. Lying in bed by day had to be an activity in itself, and each hour spent lying flat on my back or leaning against the propped pillow was an exercise in trying to cajole a state of resigned semi-consciousness out of myself.

The cell was too small to move in; it was cold and futile to stand on the floor; I lived on the bed. From the bed I made scratches with a hairpin on the wall next to my head. Each scratch took me at most 120 seconds to make, but I had to await the passage of 1,440 minutes, or 86,400 seconds, before I could make the next. How many marks would I have to make before I got out of this cell?

. . . The excitement of the escape still simmered through the station but routine reasserted itself, and one day when the cell door opened it was not to admit yet another arm of the law but to let me out. One hour's exercise daily. Alone. I was to spend the hour in the bricked-in quadrangle of the women's section of the brick and bar monster that is Marshall Square. . . . The few steps out of the cell were like a hurtle through space on a fun-fair figure of eight, and my stomach leapt as my legs moved across the concrete threshold. But the exercise yard was too like a cell. The sky was trapped by brick walls extending upwards and, like the warders regulating my stay in the courtyard, the brick walls officiously limited the shine of the sun. There was nothing for it but to walk round and round the courtyard.

On chill days I loped but tried to put out of my mind the thought of generations of prisoners doing the same. On sunny days I basked in the patch of sun, moving with it, if I could stay long enough, as it inched westwards across the courtyard and then out of reach.

There was another exercise yard for the women but it was used for men detainees until the women wardresses reasserted their, or our, claim. This was a sandy yard, four times the size of the women's quadrangle, deep in the bowels of the station and closed in by fourteen-feet-high brick walls, with mesh on top. To see what lay beyond the walls I stood in the pit of the quadrangle with my head thrown back. Then like a victim in the gladiators' den I could see and be seen by the elevated spectators, in this case the skyscrapers of Johannesburg's mining and finance houses. . . . I judged feeling on the Ninety-Day detention clause by whether the clerk sorting papers in the office which had a ringside seat on my arena raised his head or hand in answer to my cheery, seemingly unconcerned wave, or stared down in haughty disdain. If it was a lunch-hour, groups of girls would pass along the windowed corridor and one might catch sight of me and call the others to stare and stare. Did they know what they were looking at? Did they care?

One morning in the second week I had barely had time to get used to being outside the cell when the wardress appeared to usher in a neat little man with white hair, shiny starched white shirt, white hands holding a sheet of white paper. The magistrate was paying his weekly call. Any complaints? he asked. I had been complaining endlessly. I intended to permit no one the illusion that I accepted my imprisonment with resignation. I was in a state of buoyant aggression, disarmed of weapons except for the last, my tongue. I complained to the Big Wigs who came on nocturnal inspections. They said nothing or "humpff" and brushed off my rush of words as coming from an intransigent trouble-maker and no wonder the Security Branch locked *her* up, look at the way she never stops complaining. I complained to the wardresses who said, "You'll get more out of them if you don't complain so much." I complained to the nicer policemen who said they were only doing their jobs, and *they* hadn't locked me up. Some said, "We don't make the laws, you know." One said, admiringly, "She's a fighter. . . ."

The magistrate stood before me, pencil poised. Did he know, I demanded, what it was like to be locked up with nothing to do, nothing to read, no one to see? Did he know what it was like to be detained without knowing why, or for how long? Did he not agree that the Ninety-Day detention law was callous, cruel, inhuman? I don't know what he wrote of my rhetorical questions, but the pencil moved conscientiously across the paper. The magistrate said almost nothing. He would convey what I said to the Minister. He said this each time and each time that he returned it was without any reply. . . . So the magistrate listened and wrote, and his notes, when typed out, turned up on the desk of the Security Branch interrogator about whose arbitrary control I was complaining, for the direction of the work both of the magistrates and the Security Branch falls under the Department of Justice. . . .

The little magistrate did the best he could, which was to listen carefully and write painstakingly. When the flow of complaints ceased—and their tenor was always more or less the same—"I demand to be released"—he would say a quiet "thank you. Is that all?" and scurry off to his next detainee, like the anxious White Rabbit always late, late for his appointments in Alice's Wonderland. . . .

At one interview I uttered my usual diatribe against Ninety-Day detention and told the magistrate to tell the Minister it was a sadistic scheme. He wrote with his customary civil-service politeness. He was on his way out when I called over my shoulder, "And tell the Minister I need a bath!" He came back. Was there really no bath? he asked. Only a cold-water tap, I said, and the daily bucket of hot water.

A few days later the Public Works Department arrived. They had instructions to build a shower in the women's section. Builders and planners, paid and amateur, flocked to examine the slope of the floor in the washroom of the large cell, the thickness of the pipes, the outlet to the drain. With great deliberation they argued the best site for the shower and how to cope with its overflow that, if not dammed or run off, would flood the floor of the large cell. Wardresses going off shift reported to their replacements coming on duty the state of the women's shower. In time the cheapest scheme was agreed to by the P.W.D. supervisors. Bricklayer and plasterer moved in with two African labourers and by the end of the day the shower had been screwed in and a small concrete wall, four inches high, had been built to divide the wash-up section from the cell. . . .

. . . A noisy energetic drunk was booked in late that evening. She raged blindly round the cell for some hours, then there was a brief silence: perhaps she was eyeing the bed. I lay in mine waiting for her to settle down. There was the noise of feet shuffling across the floor, then a resounding slap-bump on concrete, then heavy silence. No wardress came until the change of shift the next morning. The drunk woman was found stretched across the low shower wall. Like an obstacle laid across her path it had tripped her at the ankle and caused her to fall headlong into the shower. A doctor was called but he diagnosed nothing more serious than a large head bump. The wall had to go nevertheless; at that rate it would knock out all the drunks as they lurched towards the toilet. The construction of the shower dragged on, the P.W.D. coming back repeatedly to improve the slope of the floor towards the outlet pipe and to put heads together with the wardresses on the perfection of the shower. When finally it ran it gave only cold water, but I used it religiously out of deference to the achievement of the magistrate in reaching the ear of the Minister.

The morning-shift wardress broke her silence.

"Did you hear a shot last evening?" she asked.

I had not.

Dennis Brutus, live-wire initiator of the campaign against apartheid in sport, himself sportsman, teacher, impassioned poet, had been shot in the side only two blocks from Marshall Square. He had been taken to Coronation Hospital for an emergency operation. Two policemen in surgical masks stood watch in the operating theatre, police patrolled the hospital grounds and stood guard outside Dennis's ward on the first floor. His doctor, a woman, tried to see him after the operation. The policeman outside the door stopped her. One of them said to the other, "Shall we arrest her or should I shoot?"

Brutus recovered, despite the complication of pneumonia, and then refused to let the doctors change the dressing on his wound; he demanded to see a representative from the then Federation of Rhodesia and Nyasaland.

Gradually the account was unravelled. Brutus had been in Swaziland at the time that Harold and Arthur had sought temporary refuge there. They had travelled west, by air, to Bechuanaland;

Brutus had turned eastwards, had shown his southern Rhodesian passport at the Swaziland border, and had presented himself to the Portuguese authorities of Mozambique, at Mhlumeni near Goba. The passport was valid, the visa freshly issued. The officials were preparing to stamp his passport for a stay of twenty days when the telephone at the border post rang. An inspector was being sent from Lourenço Marques, the capital, to check Brutus's papers, he was told. Four inspectors arrived. . . . He was taken under escort to Lourenço Marques. A spokesman for the Mozambique Policia Internacional e Defesa Estado (P.I.D.E.) said that the South African Security Branch had been notified of Brutus's arrest.

The Grays dispatched Sergeant Kleingeld and Warrant Officer Halberg to fetch Brutus, who was handed over to them at Komatipoort. The party arrived at Marshall Square as dusk was falling on Tuesday 17 September. As Kleingeld bent to take a suitcase from the boot of the car, Brutus made a dash for it. He sprinted westward, through the peak-hour traffic, chased by Halberg. Kleingeld had fallen and hurt his knee and was out of the chase. Halberg fired and Brutus fell to the pavement outside the Anglo-American building.

An officer of The Grays described Halberg as a "deadly accurate shot."

"FOUR NATIONS INVOLVED IN ROW OVER BRUTUS," said a newspaper headline. . . .

If, it was argued by Brutus's friends, he had been regarded as an undesirable immigrant, normal Portuguese procedure should have been to return him to the country from which he had come (Swaziland), or to the country under whose passport he was travelling (the Federation).

A Federation diplomat called on Brutus in hospital to tell him he could not claim Rhodesian protection or intervention though he had been born in Salisbury and held a Federal passport recently renewed at the Federal diplomatic mission in Pretoria; he had made use of South African nationality, he was told. . . .

The argument went on for a short while, and then withered beside the fact that Brutus was in the hands of the Security Branch (he had been removed to The Fort in an ambulance). . . . The Security Branch patted itself on its back for one of several coups to come involving the capture of political fugitives with the connivance of neighbouring Governments. . . .

Brutus was taken to court and charged on four counts with contravention of his banning orders, among them attending a meeting, leaving Johannesburg, and leaving the country. . . .

Brutus was sentenced to two years' imprisonment with hard labour, which he is serving on Robben Island.

I was called out of my cell one morning and I was sure it was for interrogation by the Security Branch. It was a visit by the children, brought by my mother, and arranged at the sympathetic instigation of a non-political neighbour who had tugged at Colonel Klindt's heart-strings by telephone. It did them good to see that I looked the same and talked not of being locked up but of school and the cat, library books, and holidays. Shawn, a vulnerable thirteen-year-old, seemed closest to tears; serious wide-eyed considerate Gillian exerted her usual tight control; and jolly Robyn was diverted throughout the short visit by a conspiracy of her own. They had handed me a fistful of bubblegum on arrival and when the time came to say good-bye, Robyn whispered in between her hugs: "It's Ch——pp——'s Bubblegum. There are things written on the inside of the paper, something for you to read!"

I chewed the gum and read the wrappings:

"Did you know the skin of an elephant is an inch thick?" "Did you know the giraffe has seven bones in his neck?" "Did you know the stars are hundreds of miles apart from each other?" "Did you know zip fasteners were first used in the nineteenth century?"

"They'll leave you to sweat a while," a knowledgeable policeman volunteered. They did. For nine days. One morning I heard the approach of the keys to my cell. The wardress appeared. "They want you," she said.

Two men were waiting in the small interview room. The taller was Warrant Officer Nel. Lanky, in a drab grey suit, with sandy stringy hair, blue eyes as cold as a fish in an icy bowl, a toneless voice that I never heard utter a spontaneous sound. Sergeant Smit was ginger, an irritable and jerky man. Liverish, it turned out. There was a high deal table and two chairs. The stuffing floated out of the seat of the one so I was offered the second. Nel perched on the edge of the torn seat, and Smit leaned against the wall. This first encounter was hedged in by formal politenesses.

Did I know why I was being detained? Nel asked.

No, I said.

Patiently he read me the lesson of the day. Clause 17 of the General Law Amendment Act of 1963. . . .

Was I prepared to answer questions?

I could not possibly know, I said, until I knew what the questions were. But I was being detained to answer questions, Nel repeatedly insisted. Preliminary to prosecution? I asked. Were they preparing a prosecution? How could I answer questions if evidence was being gathered against me? I needed to know what the questions were before I could say if I would answer them.

Like a pet white mouse in a toy ferris wheel, round and round I went. I was bored, I found to my surprise. I had been through this encounter so often, in my imagination, lying in my cell, that I was surprised not to hear them say: "But you've tried this on us so often before!"

Unexpectedly, Nel took a decision. "You were a member of the central committee of the Black Hand Secret Society," he darted at me.

I answered that question—with an incredulous giggle. I was banned from some thirty organizations, over twenty-four of which I had never belonged to anyway. I had heard of a few dozen organizations other than those listed in the usual banning orders. But the whole country knew that the Black Hand Secret Society was an invention of the Security Branch. A reaction question, surely, I made a mental note. I just had time to register the technique when they moved in with a body blow.

"What were you doing at Rivonia?" I filled in my stunned pause with nervous repetitive chatter that I could give no undertaking to answer questions till I knew the full extent of the investigation.

"Why did Joe leave the country?"

"Why did you hold mixed parties?"—"To mix," I said.

"What were you doing in South-West Africa?"

The questions and the few flippant non-committal fencing replies had become awkward. I felt the producers were noticing that I was missing my cues and not hearing the prompt.

The sergeant had been leaning against the wall. Impatiently he pulled himself erect and said crossly to Nel, "She thinks she's clever. She's just trying to probe."

He was right, of course. I knew enough for one interview. The Security Branch knew I had been at Rivonia.

Five days later the two came again. And six days after that. They asked no new questions. Was I prepared to answer questions? Was I prepared to make a statement? A statement on what? Answers to their questions, they said. What questions? I asked. Everything, they said. They wanted to know everything. Secrets. Nel improved on that. "Top secrets," he said.

Behind the parrying and the fencing we were baring our teeth at one another.

One week there were two different interrogators.

Swanepoel was squat, bullfrog-like. His face glowed a fiery red that seemed to point to the bottle, but he swore that he had never drunk so it must have been his temper burning through, for Swanepoel's stock-in-trade was his bullying. Higher in rank yet deferring to Swanepoel's belligerence was Van Zyl, a lumbering, large man who tried persuasion in a sing-song oily voice. Van Zyl carried "Granpa" headache powders in his top pocket; he sometimes offered them to his victims. On Sundays he was a lay preacher, on weekdays he was Swanepoel's interrogation partner. The two of them peddled a mixture of noisy vulgar abuse and suspect avuncular wheedling.

I had sat around for long enough without telling them anything, they said. I had been detained to answer questions. The replies had to be to the satisfaction of the Minister.

Swanepoel tried another tack, then another. He turned to Van Zyl. "She's too comfortable here. She's having a holiday. We must have her moved to Pretoria. She won't like that."

Once again he asked why Joe had left the country. "Joe is no fool," I said. "Has it ever struck you that he might have provided for this day? How can you know that I know anything at all? Couldn't he have said to me the day he left, 'My dear, when I have gone the chances are that the Security Branch will hold you for ninety days to question you about me . . . so I'm going, but I shan't tell you the reason why. . . . It will be useless for the Security Branch to question you, won't it?' "

Swanepoel's stock-in-trade was to bully and taunt but like most bullies he could not himself stand being teased. His colour rose higher.

"You're an obstinate woman, Mrs. Slovo. But remember this. Everyone cracks sooner or later. It's our job to find the cracking point. We'll find yours too."

During my first weeks in the cell I had been impudently buoyant. I was determined to find the stamina to survive this war of attrition. But now I began to feel encumbered by diversionary actions. My parents, and through them the children, were being pulled into the line of fire. What was the Security Branch planning? Who else was on the list to be detained? Who else had turned informer? I lay and worried, before full awakening in the morning, all day, even in my sleep. I was no longer sleeping well.

I embarked upon a campaign to accommodate myself to the prospect not of ninety days in a cell, but years. The sooner I got used to the idea, I decided, the more easily I would bear it. Once convicted I would be able to read, study, perhaps even write; at worst I could store experiences and impressions for the day I could write. I would struggle to erase self-pity. Hardest of all, I would struggle not to think about the children. They would be elsewhere, where they could grow up without the continuous reminder of me in a prison, and they would have Joe. I had always needed him so; he would give the children his confidence, his optimism, his humour. It could have been so much worse: Joe might have been sitting in a cell upstairs, and by sheer lucky timing he had got away from the Rivonia raid and the aftermath. I had to stop thinking about the children. I needed all my concentration to handle my own situation . . . but of course I couldn't stop thinking about them.

My mother was granted a visit. Colonel Klindt came to the prisons rarely, I gathered. For the most part he sat in his office in The Grays supervising his squads of detective-interrogators, going in person on very important raids, . . . and making himself available, when he was so inclined, to the anxious relatives of detainees. He dispensed visits entirely at his discretion. My mother danced attendance at The Grays with powers of attorney, letters from the bank, forms needing my signature. She was granted one request out of ten.

This time she said, "Do you want to hear all the news, or just the good news?"

"All the news, bad news too."

"Ronnie's been detained," she said. "I'd rather they had taken me."

Ronnie is my brother.

Pained [First's nickname for a warder] fetched me out for exercise. Twice while I walked up and down the yard she had the heavy door opened and put her head through to peer at me. The second time she called in the cell warder and said in my hearing, "She's got a suitcase to pack. We'd better tell her now."

"Tell me what?" I demanded.

"Mr. Nel said we had to get you ready. He's coming to fetch you."

An hour later Nel came, with a new detective, Van Rensburg, who, I discovered, had detained my brother and was in charge of his case, and a woman clerk from the C.I.D. offices who was released from her typewriter for the morning to act as escort.

The car was driven in the direction of Pretoria. Why, I asked Nel, why was I being taken to Pretoria?

"A more permanent home for you, Mrs. Slovo," he said.

The detectives didn't seem to know their way. Perhaps, like me, they were visiting the Women's Central Prison for the first time.

In the Matron's office a bird chirped in a cage on a pedestal and an irritable-looking Pekingese with tiny teeth bared in blackish gums lay on the carpet. . . .

"I've got a lovely room waiting for her," the Matron said.

She looked to the doorway where a row of wardresses in khaki skirts, starched pink shirts and khaki forage caps perched on stiff lacquered hair had formed. They stiffened to attention and the entire row rushed forward and ranged itself about me when the Matron indicated that I should be escorted upstairs. "Not all of you!" the Matron ordered, and three of the wardresses disentangled themselves from the body of eight and ushered me to the stairs. I minced in my high heels and thrust my bosom out firmly in my charcoal suit, free to impress them, I thought, while I was still outside a cell. I was so preoccupied with making a dignified exit that I dropped the biscuit tin I was carrying and had to get down on hands and knees to scoop up the biscuit pieces.

The "nice room" was at the head of the stairs. It was two-and-a-half times the size of my Marshall Square cell, as bright as the previous cell had been gloomy. The bed had sheets. One barred window high in the wall overlooked the front of the prison; a second was an excellent vantage-point from which to view the staircase. The cell had double doors: one was solid steel with a peephole in the centre; the inner one was of mesh and bars at two-inch intervals. The wardresses carried in an enamel water jug, a china cup and saucer and plate, a fork and a spoon, and a gleaming white table-cloth. My housekeeper instincts surged and I arranged these acquisitions in tidy rows, hung my jacket from the bars of the stair window, and placed my shoes under the bed.

I encountered, close-up, only two members of the senior prison staff: the Prison Commandant, Colonel Au'camp, and his second-in-command, Major Bowen.

On the second day of my stay in Pretoria my door was flung open to reveal the colonel. I did not know that prison regulations demand that every prisoner must stand to ramrod attention every time a wardress, let alone the chief, appeared. I had been lying on the bed and the Matron was aghast. Even she stood up for her colonel, she reproved me later. I reminded her that she had voluntarily enlisted in the force; I had not. After that reproof, though my stance would not have passed muster on any parade, I did rise to my feet whenever the Matron or one of her superiors came to the cell. Colonel Au'camp seemed wary of coming in. He stood in the doorway and looked hard at me with small, pig-like eyes in a fleshy face, the faintest suggestion of a smirk on his mouth. On the second day his smirk was a little wider and I decided that he was warming to the idea of having a woman Ninety-Dayer in the clutches of his jail. . . .

I read the Book, from the first page to the last, first the Old Testament, then the New. When I reached the last page I started again with the first. I memorized psalms and proverbs:

> A fool's mouth is his destruction
> And his lips are the snare of his soul

and

> Confidence in an unfaithful man in time of trouble
> Is like a broken tooth, and a foot out of joint

memorizing and storing up references to my predicament at the hands of informers and the Security Branch.

I had been reading the Bible steadily for two months in Marshall Square and there were days—for all the lurid visions and attractive prophecies of disaster—when I could not bring myself to open the covers. Given commentaries I might have advanced to a more profound examination of the Gospels and Paul's sermons and letters but the Security Branch conceded us the Bible not to deepen our faith and understanding and improve our religious erudition, but out of deference to the Calvinist religion of the Cabinet and the Nationalist Party which, mysteriously, justifies apartheid policy by its interpretation of divine teaching, and could therefore deny the ballast of this theology to no prisoner, not even an atheist political. Giving us the Bible, they seemed to think, fulfilled the State's Christian duty to us as prisoners. We had the Book and our consciences in solitude; the interrogation methods of the Security Branch would, it was hoped, do the rest.

I stayed in the cell for all but ninety-five minutes each day. But I stuck to my resolve never to use the po. I hung on till the day shift took over from the night shift at about seven o'clock in the mornings and freed me from my cell to lock me in the bathroom block for thirty minutes. At midday I was fetched once again and locked in the exercise yard for an hour. Lock-up time was at half past four, and about twenty minutes before the day shift left the prison I was let out for a few minutes. This was the usual routine but it was disrupted on Sundays and on prison holidays. In the second week after my transfer to Pretoria lock-up time was inexplicably brought forward to two o'clock and I remained locked in for a stretch of seventeen hours, still without using the po. My bladder passed the jail endurance test as well if not better than any other part of me.

. . . in my cell I would eat my breakfast as slowly as I could, trying to prolong the operation, but somehow I could never get it to last longer than twenty-five minutes. Then I had to pass the time of four and a half hours till my exercise period.

I was in Pretoria Central Prison for twenty-eight days. It was like being sealed in a sterile tank of glass in a defunct aquarium. People came to look at me every now and then and left a ration of food. I could see out of my glass case and the view was sharp and clear, but I could establish no identity with what I could see outside, no reciprocal relationship with anyone who hove in view. In Marshall Square my sooty surroundings and the general air of gloom about the old police station would have justified melancholy, but I had been buoyant and refractory. Pretoria shone of bright polished steel and I grew increasingly subdued. My imprisonment was an abandonment in protracted time. I reflected on the new-found skill of the Security Branch in subjecting people to an enforced separation, a dissociation from humanity. I felt alien and excluded from the little activity I saw about me; I was bereft of human contact and exchange. What was going on in the outside world? No echoes reached me. I was suspended in limbo, unknowing, unreached.

I read the Bible, day-dreamed, tried to shake myself into disciplined thinking. I devised a plot for a novel. . . . When my imagination faltered I turned again to the Bible. I was ravenous for reading matter. One day during the early part of my stay in Pretoria I was in the yard during exercise hour and saw a scrap of paper in the dust-bin for cinders from the kitchen high combustion stoves. I fished it out and held it between my thumb and forefinger to devour the words. It was a prison card and recorded prisoner's name, number, crime, and sentence. Perhaps a dozen words in all but to me they were like an archaeological find, proof that some people in this society recognized the value of written language and were able to use it. . . .

The routine activities I could organize for myself were few, and, however I struggled to stretch them out, they were over disappointingly soon and I had to sink back again into inertia. I made the bed carefully several times a day, I folded and refolded my clothes, repacked my suitcase, dusted and polished everything in sight, cleaned the walls with a tissue. I filed my nails painstakingly. I plucked my eyebrows, then the hair from my legs, one hair at a time, with my small set of tweezers. (When I got into the sun I pulled out the strands of grey hair growing at my temples.) I unpicked seams in the pillow-slip, the towel, the hem of my dressing-gown, and then, using my smuggled needle and thread, sewed them up again, only to unpick once more, and sew again. The repetition of these meaningless tasks and the long loneliness made me a prisoner of routines and I found myself becoming obsessional, on the constant lookout for omens. . . .

Ninety days. I calculated the date repeatedly, did not trust my calculation, and did it all again. Every day I repeated that little rhyme, "Thirty days hath September" and I counted days from 9 August, the date of my arrest. My wall calendar had been left behind at Marshall Square; in Pretoria my calendar was behind the lapel of my dressing-gown. Here, with my needle and thread, I stitched one stroke for each day passed. I sewed seven upright strokes, then a horizontal stitch through them to mark a week. Every now and then I would examine the stitching and decide that the sewing was not neat enough and the strokes could be more deadly exact in size; I'd pull the thread out and re-make the calendar from the beginning. This gave me a feeling that I was pushing time on, creating days, weeks, and even months. . . .

It was not only the pain of existing in a vacuum. It was the indefiniteness of it all. As the Security Branch detectives said at every possible opening: "This is the first period of ninety days; there can be another after that, and yet another." I was convinced that everyone, myself included, could make an adjustment to a known situation. Unknown numbers, many of them in South Africa my closest friends, are living through prolonged prison terms, splendidly adaptable. But the greater part of this matter of adjustment is knowing to what to adjust. Deadly boredom can be withstood if there is an end in sight. A prisoner, even one facing a life term, has some security in the cessation of fear of the unknown.

The Security Branch had devised a situation in which its victim was plagued with uncertainty, apprehension, and aloneness; every day that passed in a state of active anxiety about the outcome of the incarceration and the purpose of the interrogation sessions stripped the prisoner of the calm, the judgement, and the balance which were required equipment to cope with continued isolation and the increased strain of interrogation sessions.

. . . I was determined to endure the first spell of ninety days, and then make a further adjustment to whatever came after that. It would be ignominious to be defeated by enforced solitude and those inept boorish inquisitors of the Nationalists. . . .

. . . I was shaken, though, when on Monday, 7 October, a smart navy-blue frock and matching coat with a red silk lining were sent in to Pretoria Prison with my laundered slacks and shirts, and soup in a thermos flask. This, I realized, was my mother's warning that I should expect to be taken to trial any day, and her equipment for me to mingle in the world again. But nothing happened. The next days went by in yawning emptiness.

From the time I was moved to Pretoria the visits by Nel, the Security Branch officer, had been perfunctory. On the average he came once a week; sometimes eight or nine days went by without a visit. Nel's air was one of bored indifference whether I talked to him or not. Sometimes his visits degenerated into brief sterile sessions of a formal inquiry and answer. "Are you prepared to answer questions or make a statement?" "No I am not."

Some days went by after the arrival of my blue dress and coat, and then one morning Nel had me brought down from the cell into the Matron's office and he opened the interview saying, "Well, Mrs. Slovo, you have not been charged after all. Now you can talk." I feigned ignorance. "Charged with what?" I asked. "Ah, come now," he said, "you know you were worried you would be charged in the Rivonia trial."

This *had* been the worst of the worries. For the rest of the day and the night I breathed in great gasps of relief. I still did not know what was in store for me, but this was one hurdle taken.

. . . I told Nel how my ulcer was playing up and that erratic food deliveries from outside—my overtaxed mother had to travel thirty-six miles there and back to deliver a basket—were not making the situation any easier. I asked Nel to convey my request to Colonel Klindt. He said he would but I did not trust him to, so I asked for paper and pen, which he gave me, to my surprise, and I addressed a letter to the colonel asking for a "transfer" back to Johannesburg.

Colonel Au'camp heard of this request and found it funny. Fancy a prisoner trying to arrange her own transfer; once you were in jail you stayed there until "we" moved you, he said. . . .

Nel enjoyed his role as interrogator in his own cold, calculating way. . . .

They would not permit me to see the children in Pretoria. One morning Nel arrived and opened the interview with, "I see in the Sunday papers that your children are being taken over seas." As he had hoped, I was immediately in a state of agitation. When, I asked, when were they leaving? He knew nothing except that the news of their impending departure had been carried in newspaper columns. "I must see them before they go," I said. "Will you let me see them?" "Why do you want to see them?" he asked. "You have seen them already." I took a deep breath. "You," I said, "are a cold-blooded callous fish of a man." "Why do you say I'm a fish?" he muttered.

I had not been aware that solitude was giving me a craving for conversation, any conversation, even with a detective, and one day, to my consternation, I found that his question, "What were you doing in South-West Africa?" set me off on a round of inconsequential anecdotes and jokes. I chattered and he listened intently and suddenly took me up on my remark, "But surely you know all this . . . ? You know exactly where I went and what I did . . . you had me followed all the time." How did I know I was being followed, he wanted to know. I had seen the Security Branch men, I told him. "Couldn't you have been mistaken? If you saw me in the street would you know I was Security Branch?" "Yes," I said emphatically and he looked disconcerted.

I was taken from my cell one morning to meet not Nel, but my mother. The Grays had granted permission for an interview to discuss business and family affairs only. The detective sitting in on the interview was from Pretoria's Security Branch staff, he knew nothing of me, and was not very interested. I asked my mother if she was taking the children out of the country. She had made no such plans yet, she said, and she knew nothing of a report to that effect in any newspaper. She had news of a different kind. Colonel Klindt was away on leave but his deputy, Colonel Venter, had told her that I was to face a charge at the end of the ninety days. I could barely ask but I did. "What charge?" Possession of illegal literature, it seemed, and once more I was enormously relieved. But if this was their intention, why hold me until the end of the ninety days? My mother said that she had put the same question to Colonel Venter but he had ignored her. We had a jolly interview, my mother telling me that my brother had been released, and that my father was safely out of the country.

I had seven days to go before the end of ninety days. That week I found I was talking to myself, repeating over and over again, "Now, then, get a hold on yourself. These last days will drag worse than any other. Take it easy. Try to coast through the time, not long now . . . and whatever happens you've made the first ninety days. Don't built your hopes too high; be ready for a let-down. The chances are they will not let you go."

Six days before the end of ninety days I was walking among the washing lines during exercise time when the Assistant-Matron unlocked the yard door, beckoned to me, and said I should pack my things, I was being taken away. There was no sense in my asking questions; she did not know the answers and if she had known she would not have told me.

I packed my suitcase to the accompaniment of a thumping heart. . . . I was breezy and cheerful. "Where are we going?" I asked them. "To Johannesburg," they said. "But where in Johannesburg?" I insisted. "There are so many places in Johannesburg, among them my home." The fairer of the two men answered. "I'm afraid you're not going to your home this trip," he said.

. . . By now I realized I was going back to Marshall Square and

the thought of a jail I knew was infinitely more comforting, however unpleasant those cells really were, than one I did not. When I
was led to the counter of the charge office where I was booked in as
a prisoner and I saw the face of the sergeant I had known from my
last stay there, I forgot myself and cried.

The detective who had me taken out of my cell on the first
morning after my return to Marshall Square brought not a torture
instrument, but a piece of bait. . . .

He didn't think I was really at home in a police station. Why
didn't I get myself out of this mess? I need only answer questions,
and I would be free. How did he know I knew anything? I asked.
"You know. You know *plenty*. I know that you know," he said.

I let fly at Ninety-Day detention. The Security Branch followed
me, opened my letters, tapped my telephone, compiled a dossier on
me. Then they had me arrested. They were my jailers. They were
my prosecutors and my persecutors. And he tried to persuade me
that if I talked to him the Security Branch would sit in calm judgement in my case, act not only as prosecutor but as jury and judge,
and come to a free and unprejudiced decision on my future. I
trusted no undertakings of any kind by the Security Branch, I said.
I simply did not trust them. And as for information, I knew nothing
of any interest to them.

The next morning was Monday and to my astonishment I was
called out for a visit from the children and my mother. I was taken
aback, but as I sped along the corridor to the little interview room
I said to myself, "This is a bad sign, not a good one. If they're planning to release you at the end of ninety days, which is tomorrow,
they would not grant a visit from the children today." I had no time
to consider what they were planning. The three bright faces rushed
at me as I entered and we had a fevered session of hugging, with the
three taking turns to sit on my lap with their arms round my neck.
I don't know why I permitted myself to say out loud what we were
all thinking but I said to the detective, Sergeant K——, who sat in
on the interview, "Tomorrow my ninety days is up. Are you going
to prosecute me?" The sergeant's reply was circumspect: he had not
had any papers relating to a charge placed on his desk, he said.
Robyn's eyes had sparkled at the words "ninety days . . . up . . . tomorrow." I would be out in time for her birthday after all. I could
not spoil the visit by uttering the caution which I above all needed,

though I did not seem to realize it at the time: it's unlikely they'll let me out, hold tight for another spell of detention. Sergeant K——'s attention was diverted by someone who asked him to enter the visit in the official book. My mother sidled up to me. "B——'s talking," she whispered. "Something has gone terribly wrong."

When the visit was over a few seconds later I was taken back to the women's section and was about to go into my cell when the wardress said that as I had not yet had my exercise time I might as well take it right then. I sat on the ground, my back against the wall, and tried to stop myself shaking. If B. was talking, that put an end to my prospects of release. He knew so much about me: what I had gone to Rivonia for, who I had met there, some of the meetings—one in particular—that I had attended there, the people I was in touch with in the underground, the work they and I did together. Why had he broken down? How had he broken down? He had always struck me as controlled and confidently self-contained, unimaginative even, but that was all to the good in detention situations. Could he be reached at all? How could I possibly find out if among his revelations to the Security Branch he had included me? My pulse was beating fast and I found it difficult to think in sequence. I felt as though I had been poised on a high diving-board above a stretch of water, timing my take-off, when someone had suddenly pushed me. And in the hurtle downwards the water below had dried up.

I was trying to control my panic at such unexpected betrayal when the wardress appeared to call me out again. Above all else I needed to be left alone to think and regain calm. That morning there was a plot against my privacy, connived at by the wardress who kept calling me away from my thoughts, and, unwittingly, by my own friends, on our side.

When I got to the waiting-room Nel was waiting to see me. He had not come for over a week, since Viktor's appearance.

"I've come to tell you to pack your things, Mrs. Slovo, I'm releasing you!"

The seconds ticked by.

"I don't believe you," I burst out. "You're going to re-arrest me."

"I mean what I say," Nel said. "I've come to release you this morning."

"Don't bluff me," I shouted. "Don't tell me one thing and do another. Don't make a farce of this thing. Don't talk of release if you mean something else."

"I've come to release you, Mrs. Slovo," he said insistently.

The wardress had been hovering in the background. "Don't be like that, Mrs. Slovo," she butted in and took me by the elbow. "Here is your chance to go home. Come, I'll help you pack."

Doubtfully I followed her into the cell but then I was consumed with the excitement of pushing my possessions into the suitcase and getting the lid to close, gathering the basket of dishes and thermos flask, changing out of slacks into my navy frock and coat, giving the wardress the box of dried fruit that had recently been sent in to me. Laden with suitcase, basket, and flask I staggered through the heavy door leading into the lock-up section, which opened smoothly at the twist of the key by the cell warder, and then into the charge office. The sergeant at the desk had been alerted; he had the book open and was already writing out the liberation warrant. He looked pleased; I had decided that the better warders on the Marshall Square staff didn't really like this Ninety-Day detention. They were used to locking people up, but according to the old rules of the game, and to some of these men forty-eight hours without a charge was long enough, never mind what kind of prisoner you were. The sergeant did not ask for any details; he didn't need many for filling in the form. He looked to see that the carbon was working, then stamped the top sheet and the one underneath, ripped out the copy, and handed it to me.

In my hand was a certificate of release.

Nel was still there. "You might have told me twenty minutes earlier," I reproved him. "I could have gone home with my family, and now where do I find a car? I don't think I even have a tickey[3] to telephone."

I asked if I could use the charge office telephone and the sergeant said no, but there was a public telephone box outside on the pavement. I fumbled in my purse (which had been handed to me together with other possessions kept in a prisoner's property bag). A man standing next to Nel who must have been Security Branch but whom I did not remember having seen before, came up and peered over my shoulder. "Look," he said, pointing to the corner of the purse, "There's a tickey." He seemed as pleased as I was to find it.

---

3. A threepenny-piece.

I fished out the coin and made a beeline for the telephone box outside. I was only half-way there when two men, whom I did know as Security Branch detectives, walked up to me.

"Just a minute, Mrs. Slovo," the spokesman said.

"What do you want now?" I demanded, and my mind and hearing were alerted to hear . . . "a charge under the Suppression of Communism Act for possession of illegal literature . . ." or something which would hint at that, but he said:

". . . another period of ninety days."

The second detective grinned hugely from ear to ear.

In the charge office I was sickly silent and tight-lipped. Not till later in the month did I confront Nel with, "I thought you said you were releasing me?" to hear his Jesuitical prevarication. "I did release you. *I* didn't re-arrest you."

I left the suitcase, the basket, and the thermos flask standing in the middle of the charge office floor, and stood at the door leading into the cells, waiting for it to be opened. The two detectives who had done the re-arrest were right behind me. They did not leave me when we reached the women's cells, not even when I stood in the courtyard and waiting for the wardress to take over. They motioned to her to open the cell door and said, "Come inside, Mrs. Slovo," then themselves clanged the door closed, more loudly than I had ever heard it, and snapped the padlock into place.

Left to face my second round of ninety days I was filled with loathing and bitterness against the Security Branch detectives who had stage-managed my humiliating phony release and then re-arrest; but I was also overcome, for perhaps the first time since my initial arrest, by a wave of self-pity. I had said barely a word throughout the cruel pantomime, because I didn't want to give the detectives the satisfaction of an outburst that would reveal my feelings; my instinct told me to keep a tight hold on my emotions and to let no sound of them escape me, but it was more than I could manage. I sat on the edge of the bed, still in my navy outfit, and shook with sobs. My "release" had been some time in mid-morning; by late afternoon I was still sitting in the same position. The heaving of my shoulders had stopped, but a tight pincer-feeling was growing in my stomach.

That reminded me. I had made an arrangement with my mother, furtively, when the back of the Security Branch detective had been turned away from us during a visit, that if at any time I rejected a basket of food, it would be a sign that I had embarked on a hunger strike, and glucose tablets should be sent in to me. I could not endure another period of ninety days as though I were taking the experience calmly, within my stride, as my due deserts at the hands of the Security Branch; I had to draw attention to my plight, and even if I were carried out of the cell on a stretcher, some fussing by jailers and doctors would be preferable to an isolation that was treated as my normal existence. When the basket of food came round at nightfall I called the cell warder back and told him to return the food, I did not want it, or any the following evening either.

If only I could have stood outside myself; if only I had not believed that I would always have the strength to do whatever I wanted and that emotional shock was something separate from and subordinate to my reason. This was no time, at the end of ninety days spent in solitary, to embark upon a hunger strike, certainly not with my ulcer already recording, with a steady dilating pain in my inside, the state of my nervous anxiety. I did not offer myself alarmingly overt symptoms to recognize the effect solitary had had on me. I suffered no claustrophobia, no ringing in the ears, no voices coming from the walls, no nightmares, no double vision, no hallucinations. Disorientation was calmness itself, without my knowing the full extent of it. I was lonely, I was anxious, I longed for human company; I had not yet thought that these were short cuts to a loss of discrimination which could be the stepping-stone to far more alarming reactions.

I lay awake the whole night. I worried without stop about the news that B. was talking. This, I thought, introduced a critical change into my own position. I could not stand the suspense any longer; I felt an irresistible urge to act, to lose no more time, to make some move to force a counter-move from the Security Branch. I felt that I would crumble if I stayed still any longer. . . . How could I get events round me to move? For ninety-one days I had been stubbornly impenitent, obdurate in making no attempt to draw them on in their questioning of me. I was still stubbornly uncontrite but now my impatience was stretched to the point of snap. I could no longer bear to sit and wait while events moved around me; I had to provoke them. I would begin to show some interest in questioning. To find out what they knew, I told myself. To offer them the smallest crumb of useless information as a catalyst. Perhaps I would wait a week before the routine visit and question, "Are you prepared to answer questions?" and I would then make a

tentative move. I didn't have to. Nel arrived the following morning.
I felt withered inside.

"You see, Mrs. Slovo," he said, "we are persistent."

There was silence for a while and then he asked if I would go to
The Grays to answer questions. I said I would.

. . . I got a further shock. There would be no questions. I was
expected to make a statement, starting at the beginning, they said,
and ending at the end, omitting nothing. I was asked to sit on a
chair mid-way between Viktor, who sat with pen poised over paper,
and Swanepoel, who produced a thick file with my name on the
outside "*Heloise Ruth Slovo née First*" and began to go slowly and
methodically through the great piles of paper in it, making notes as
he went along on a stack of paper beside his right hand. Van der
Merwe sat next to him, glancing from the notes that Swanepoel was
making to my face. Van Zyl and Nel lurked in the background behind my chair.

I made a slow, comforting start. And what I told them about
my awakening interest and steady involvement in politics seemed to
be normal behaviour, the only thing to do in South Africa! We
whites who embarked on protest politics side by side with the
Africans, Indians, and Coloureds, led a vigorously provocative life.
Our consciences were healthy in a society riddled with guilts. . . .

I was born in Kensington, Johannesburg, and went up the road
to Jeppe Girls' High School. My university years were cluttered
with student societies, debates, mock trials, general meetings, and
the hundred and one issues of war-time and post-war Johannesburg
that returning ex-service students made so alive. On a South
African campus, the student issues that matter are national issues.

Who had influenced me? they wanted to know. No one in particular. I had been able to read for myself. I didn't have any one
teacher of politics; we students learnt from one another, and from
what was happening around us. Manchuria, Abyssinia, Spain, Austria, Sudetenland, were not events of my own student generation,
but they were close enough to influence us. There were Africans going to war carrying assegais and stretchers; there was bitterness that
war-time costs of living were obliterating the buying-power of
wages, that African trade unions were not recognized, that African
strikes were illegal and the strikers prosecuted in mass trials.

I had graduated with a Social Science degree, but I turned my
back firmly on the social worker's round of poor white families in

Fordsburg, questioning them about what they did with their money to justify an application for State-aided butter or margarine. . . .

Up to six months before my detention I had still been in our newspaper office. Over the years I had been served with banning orders that prohibited me from leaving Johannesburg, so that I could take part in no further exposés of forced labour like my work on Bethal; from entering African townships, so that I could no longer personally establish the contacts of African men and women who alerted our office first of all when some new vicious scheme of the police and the administration came to light; from attending meetings, so that others had to take the notes and the photographs; from writing anything for publication, so that I had to sit at my desk with a legal opinion that sub-editing someone else's copy might just slip past the ban. Working in the midst of these ministerial bans and under the continuous raids and scrutiny of the Security Branch was like going to work each day in a mine field, but we survived, and our editions continued to come out each week. Then finally the bans stopped every literate or available Congressman from writing, and the printer, the last one we could find in the country to publish our notoriously outspoken copy, gave us notice that he could no longer take the risk. We sold the paper to a new proprietor whom we hoped would assemble a fresh team of writers. We were not to know until almost a year later but "Babla" Saloojee, the new owner, was himself detained under the Ninety-Day law, and, driven to despair by the interrogation methods of the Security Branch, he hurled himself to his death from the window of the very room where I was being questioned.

I told the detectives sitting like birds of prey over me the bare outlines of this story, stringing it out for as long as they showed patience to listen, for I did not know what I would say when we came to the end of all legal political activity for the African people and their allies in South Africa. The detectives were clearly not interested in most of what I told them, though Viktor took it all down without comment and at one point ordered a detective to leave the room and check somewhere in the records department of The Grays the dates on which the various papers had been banned.

Why had I fled to Swaziland during the 1960 State of Emergency after Sharpeville? one of the detectives demanded to know. "Because you would have arrested me without preferring a charge or bringing me to trial, like you did to 1,800 others," I said. The

Security Branch knew very well that I had spent emergency months in Swaziland; they did not know that I had come back to live underground in Johannesburg during the second half of the emergency, and I did not tell them.

Towards the end they began to dart questions.

Who wrote articles in *Fighting Talk* under the pseudonym XXX, they wanted to know. I did, I said. (Though I had not.)

What about the Turok conviction for sabotage, after he had planted a bomb in the post office? "I couldn't tell you," I said. "All I know about that was what I read in the newspapers. You might have asked my husband, he was one of the defence counsel, but now it's too late, isn't it, he's no longer here."

"What did your husband do when he went out every night?" "I couldn't say, I made a point of not asking him about his movements."

"What about sabotage?" I was not involved in sabotage and I could tell them nothing about it, nothing at all; this had been something in which I had not got involved.

Who had I met most frequently at meetings? A. and E. and L., I said. (All out of reach of the Security Branch.)

Where had I been to meetings? In my house, in my motor-car parked in some quiet place, in the home of D. (long settled abroad).

"It's a funny thing, isn't it?" said Viktor. "But every name you've given us is the name of someone who has left the country!"

"Perhaps they had good reason to go," I murmured.

My statement had stopped with, to them, alarming unexpectedness. I don't know why my reactions were so appallingly slow but though I had decided at the outset that I would play out a small measure of the rope, it took the slow progress of the interview for me to realize fully that I was winding it fast around me. There was no time to wriggle, to fabricate, to gauge reaction, to probe, to find out anything for myself. I was breaking down my own resistance. It was madness for me to think I could protect myself in a session like this, in any session with them. I had no idea what they knew, what contradictory information they had wrenched from someone else. They were giving nothing away; they had already become too experienced for that.

It was now mid-afternoon. Viktor said that was enough for the day; he left the room.

Swanepoel sorted his notes, pinned them together, and tilted back his chair.

"You don't think that's a statement, do you?" he roared.
"You've told us nothing, absolutely nothing. You've not begun to
talk. Those sheets are absolutely worthless. We know all about that
meeting at Rivonia. It was a meeting of picked people from all over
the country. Mandela was there, and Sisulu. The pick of the bunch.
You're the only woman there . . . and you try to pretend that you
know nothing of what happened, that you can't remember, that
nothing happened worth knowing. We know all about you. You'd
be surprised to know what we know. You're deep in it. You can
count your lucky stars that we still have respect for women in our
country. You could have been charged in the Rivonia case. But we
didn't want a woman in that case. We still have some feeling for
women. We picked our accused. . . . We picked our witnesses. . . ."

Swanepoel's face grew purple as he raged. The other detectives
were now standing and watching me.

"You were in on that Rivonia thing from the very beginning,"
he continued. "What's more, we have a sworn statement that you
paid Jelliman."'

"I paid Jelliman?" I echoed in disbelief.

"Yes, you paid Jelliman. It's in a sworn affidavit."

Jelliman was an old man who had acted as a caretaker on the
Rivonia property when Mandela had lived there in hiding at the start
of his "Black Pimpernel" existence. I knew Jelliman from the old
days of legality; we had seen one another at Rivonia; I had never
given him any money.

That was the end of any statement from me, I told him and the
others still in the room. They said I had paid Jelliman, that there
was even a sworn statement to that effect. That showed the quality
of the evidence they had gathered against me. People under pressure
of continued detention and threats would say anything to buy an
indemnity, and I was in no doubt that the files of statements made
by their victims were full of false information. I had again to protect myself from their persecution in the only way I knew: by remaining silent. "Tomorrow," they said. "Tomorrow."

I was taken back to Marshall Square. I was drained, prostrate
with tiredness. But I could not sleep. I knew so clearly that I should
make no statement, I could not understand—and I was too desolate
to try—how I had allowed myself to think otherwise, even in a wild
gamble for information and relief from solitariness. That was all I
thought the entire night: literally two words "NO STATEMENT
NO STATEMENT NO STATEMENT" over and over again in my

mind. I realized I had to eat again; perhaps my precipitate hunger-strike had helped to unhinge my judgement.

The next morning Viktor had me brought out again. As I walked towards him in the corridor I said, "I'm not going back to The Grays. I am not making any statement." "You're not coming to The Grays?" he said. "Pity. Your mother is there, waiting to see you. Colonel Klindt granted her request for a visit."

I could not refuse to see her. Van der Merwe was with Viktor, driving the car, and on the way through the city he said, "Why no l——," and stopped himself. I knew what he was asking. Why had I put on no lipstick, no make-up that morning? This was the first time even in my detention, apart from the first day when I had no make-up because my suitcase was locked away, that I had permitted anyone to see me without make-up. I had simply forgotten that morning.

. . . My mother was upset; though to me it seemed a lifetime ago, it was only two days since I had been re-detained for a second spell, but her control was as superb as ever. We talked about the children, about the state of my father's health and how he was now safely in England, about her house which she was putting up for sale since it seemed she would continue to live in mine for some time to come. Viktor called the interview to a close after about twenty minutes, but allowed us to embrace. "Are you cracking up?" she whispered, and I nodded. "We're depending on you," she said, and then she had to go. Viktor asked afterwards what she had whispered, and I said, ". . . something like 'Keep your courage up.'"

The following morning Viktor came again to fetch me to The Grays. I refused to go. "Your sister-in-law is waiting to see you," he said.

This was the first time that Clarice had managed a visit; again I agreed to go with him. Nel sat in on this interview and seemed surprised when I said: "Oh Clarice, they'll never let me go, you watch . . . they just won't let me go."

I was appalled at the events of the last three days. They had beaten me. I had allowed myself to be beaten. I had pulled back from the brink just in time, but had it been in time? I was wide open to emotional blackmail, and the blackmailer was myself. They had tried for three months to find cracks in my armour and had found some. The search was still on. Some, many perhaps, of my weaknesses had been revealed to the Security Branch; if they had any inkling of others, I would have no reserves left. I could no longer hold to an intransigent stand because I had already moved from it. It was too late to say stoically that I would say nothing, not one word, to them. . . . I had too little emotional resilience left to resist a savage new onslaught on my vulnerable centre: that above all I was fighting to salvage my respect in myself, in the hope that my associates in the political movement could still preserve confidence in me. Viktor suspected this; but perhaps he was not absolutely sure that this was the point at which to attack me. If he had any hint of what was in my mind, I knew the Security Branch would spread reports that I had made a statement telling "all," that I was broken and useless, had given in under pressure. I was in a state of collapse not for fear of what would happen to me physically, of numberless pealing days in detention, but for the gnawing ugly fear that they could destroy me among the people whose understanding and succour I most needed, and that once they had done that I would have nothing left to live for. I had not signed that useless statement, but it was nestling in Viktor's drawer, had probably been cyclostyled by now and placed in other dossiers, and might be brandished in front of some other detainees remaining silent. "What's the good of holding out? Here's another one who has cracked and told us all."

. . . Sleep had been a refuge in the cell; now it had fled. On top of sleeplessness I had nausea and diarrhoea. It all spelled anxiety, I suppose, but an anxiety that had got out of hand and that I could no longer control with my own resources. I asked for a visit from my own doctor. . . . My doctor came and was marvellously calm and normal, but I feared to embarrass him politically by too close an account of why I was in such an overwrought state. He gave me a mixture to control ulcer pangs and a phial of sleeping-pills.

. . . I accepted that I now had no option but to adjust to indefinite detention, detention for eternity. I had never been afflicted by a fatalism quite so deep.

The days were grey and melancholy. I barely noticed the exercise periods. I had reeled back from a precipice of collapse but I felt worse than ever. I was persecuted by the dishonour of having made a statement, even the start of a statement. Give nothing, I had always believed; the more you give the more they think you know, and the more demanding they become. I had never planned to give anything, but how could I be the judge? It would be impossible to explain such an act, to live it down. Joe had always told me that my weakness was my extreme susceptibility to acceptance and fear of rejection and criticism: were these the qualities that had propelled me to make a statement? Or was it again my arrogance, my conceit that pooled experiences and rules of conduct (under interrogation) were for other people, and that I was different and could try my own way? . . .

. . . I felt unimaginably tired and dispirited. I could not cope any longer. I could not weigh up factors properly. No one could get near me to help me and the help I needed could not be supplied by anyone else. I spent all Sunday making a dilatory attempt at a cross-word puzzle, but filling in the clues was surface activity: a decision was forming in my mind. The Security Branch was beyond doubt planning an act of character assassination against me: I would not give them information out of loyalty to my friends, but they would break me finally with some carefully introduced indication that my friends had abandoned me because I had betrayed them, or so the Security Branch would arrange for the version to be told. This abandonment I would not be able to face; and even until it happened I did not have the strength to survive. There was only one way out, before I drove myself mad, and as the truest indication to anyone who was interested that I had not let the Security Branch have it all their own way. I was anguished when I thought of the children, but what good would I be to them in mental pieces? On the flyleaf of the crossword puzzle book, with the pencil that was the property of the South African Government, I wrote a note that apologized for my cowardice, loved the children once more, tried to say words that would have a special meaning for Joe, and indicated that I had not given in, that those still free should not panic and should proceed in the knowledge that I had kept their secrets. After the last inspection of the night I reached for the phial of pills (which the wardress had left in the cell quite inadvertently . . .), and swallowed the lot.

In the daze of coming out of what seemed like a coma I remembered to rip the message from the front of the crossword puzzle book and flush it down the lavatory.

Somehow the act of taking the pills shocked away any further intention of doing so. I had completely lost track of time and even interest in keeping a wall calendar or sewing stitches behind my dressing-gown lapel; but inch by inch I made a slow adjustment to balance, though I was not sure at the time that I was doing so. I managed to have another visit from my own doctor and I told him I had taken all the pills. He was the only person I told all the while I was in prison, and I told hardly anyone when I got out. He did not seem surprised, or impressed by my surprise that the pills had not worked. "You don't think I'd be so foolish as to leave you with that size dose?" he asked, and I could laugh about my ignorance. "I'm heading for a crack-up, aren't I?" I asked, and he said, "You've had one already.". . .

There was nothing for it but to swallow the tranquillizers which the doctor prescribed (and which I was pleased to note the wardress conscientiously kept in her office) and to try to coast back to normality. I would be on guard against a further relapse of body, of spirit, of confidence. I had sealed myself to solitary, and the longer I stayed "inside" the more certain my friends would be that I had not capitulated. There would be security in detention!

I had always been contemptuous of the State security apparatus. The detectives were distinguishable by the tall hats and Government-issue suits they wore, by their physical appearance, I thought. Their bumbling methods brought them ridicule. But these amateurs in political sleuthing who seized books because they had "black" or "red" in the title had developed into sophisticated sadistic mind-breakers in the matter of a few years. The failure of the treason trial and the few frame-ups tried there had been a painful public and world humiliation. Those held in prison pending political trials or during the 1960 State of Emergency and the days of the 1961 Mandela strike, had emerged from a spell of community jail life with morale marvellously unimpaired. Every new stretch of prison for a group of political prisoners gave birth to a new batch of freedom songs. Jail spells had not broken us; they had helped to make us. The Security Branch had also been painfully aware of its failure to infiltrate informers into the movement, or get politicals themselves to change sides. Our security was good when it had not been severely tested. When solitary confinement and the torture of prolonged interrogations was introduced in the 1963 amendment to the General Laws Amendment Act, we were in for some disastrous collapses. At first I had thought the Security Branch far too unaware of human susceptibility and sensitivity to know what effect the solitary spells would have on people. Not a bit of it. We underestimated them sadly. The Security Branch had launched a deliberate plan of attack, and had studied its texts carefully. Where one detective or the other proved inept as an interrogator, the total impact of all the methods of a group of interrogators, with prolonged solitary confinement, often had its effect.

At first torture was reserved for Africans alone. But Ninety-Day detention had not been in force for fourteen months when torture was turned against whites, even though one of the most sacred laws of apartheid had been, up to then, that whites, all whites, any whites, are different from Africans, and must be handled apart, even in the jails. With the use of torture this, too, changed. Anything was permissible to the Security Branch. The skill of the inquisitor was to know what methods to use against each prisoner. Sometimes the machine was in a hurry and there was no time to wait for the erosion that solitary confinement for a long enough period of time was almost always bound to bring about. Torture, electric shocks, beatings, were then ordered early on in the imprisonment. In other instances they were not in such a hurry or so desperate for results. The interrogators warmed to their task of studying their victims, or leaving time in solitary to make inroads on their resistance while they dealt with other cases.

I could now see unravelled the campaign of attack against me. Solitary confinement for an undetermined period was the basic requirement. . . . From neglect by [Nel] I would then be introduced to the more concentrated attention of Viktor, when three months was almost up and I must be feeling the accumulated effects of so many weeks in isolation. But before he appeared with his apparent concern to spare me the worst of eventualities, I had to be subjected to carefully planted hints about a prosecution for possession of a copy of a banned magazine, which would be an enormous relief compared with the ordeal of the Rivonia trial or another spell of detention. The hints about the prosecution were carefully timed to raise my expectations of easy relief. All Viktor's talk centred round how smoothly that prosecution could be avoided. He had come to make a deal but withdrew, disappointed, when I turned the proposition down, disappointed at my stubborn refusal to save myself. Enter the villains to make the phony release and the re-arrest, but not before a visit from the children, eager and expectant for my release, had given me another emotional jar. The release and the re-arrest had come a day before the actual expiry of my ninety days, and I had lost a day and a night I might have had to adjust to their tactics of springing a surprise (the children's visit) on me before a rude shock of re-arrest. The invitation to an interrogation session had come hot-foot on the release, again before I had had time to find my balance, and on top of one shock they had not planned: the information that B. had probably given me away. . . . I thought I had adapted to boredom and aloneness unlimited, but inside me the effects had accumulated to obscure insight and judgement when I most needed them.

At last I permitted myself my first scent of victory. I determined to shake off the all-devouring sense of guilt at my lapse. I had been reeling towards a precipice and I had stopped myself at the edge. It had *not* been too late to beat them back. I had undermined my own resistance, yet I had not after all succumbed. In the depth of my agony I *had* won.

I braced myself for continued existence in jail; if not this one, then some other. Somehow I would summon powers of survival, kill the part of me that yearned for other lives, and resign myself to continued imprisonment as the price of the life I had chosen myself. I would get used to the idea and the life in prison, and I would manage.

One morning Viktor came to ask me what I would like to read. "What's come over you people now?" I asked. He was behaving like a smug Father Christmas. No, he said, it's just that the colonel said I could have books, one at a time, and all the titles had to be approved by Pretoria. I asked for *The Charterhouse of Parma* which I had been longing to get my hands on for over three months, and I had to give him a potted summary of the plot. He telephoned my mother who brought him a copy of the book, and the next day he brought it to me.

I longed to withdraw to read, but he continued to come practically every day. Once he came twice in a day. I had finished Stendhal and asked for *War and Peace*. He wanted a plot summary. As in Stendhal, I said, Napoleon figures; as an ideal in *The Charterhouse*, very much to the fore in *War and Peace*. "What's this thing you've got about Napoleon?" he wanted to know.

He was getting to know me all the same. He sat in on a second interview with my sister-in-law; he watched a wretched tearful session with the children when the eldest sat on the ground in the exercise yard and howled her heart out with loneliness and pity for her state, and the other two were on the verge of following suit. Pretoria was still reserving judgement on *War and Peace*, but a thriller,

The Night Has a Thousand Eyes came, and for the first time in my life I was afraid of a book, because the thousand eyes were the force of telepathy and I felt the eery presence of Viktor's scrutiny continually at the back of my neck.

He might have been getting impatient but he did not show it except to say his annual leave was due shortly and I should get myself out of Marshall Square before then. "If you go on holiday leaving me here, you'll have me on your conscience, I suppose?" I said. His job as a policeman was very important to him. He was filled with ambition for promotion, anxious to study law in his spare time to qualify sooner and better. . . . He sometimes saw his victims in jail and he prided himself that none of them nursed a grievance against him; he treated them fairly and played the game, and they realized the game was up when he had caught them. That was his version of himself as detective.

It seemed that this would go on for ever. I had read only three books in a fortnight and still Viktor came to the little interview room and we conducted verbal activity, screened and filtered by him and by me, but human contact nevertheless. I was no longer so affected by the gloom of the cell; my own state was not of despair as much as resignation. I had had worse days than these.

I spent a wretched week-end. I entertained no notion of calling Viktor to buy a release, but I had an attack of gloom at being locked up and especially during the birthday week-end. The Sunday dragged interminably.

The following morning I was still washing in the bucket of hot water when the wardress came to tell me that Viktor was waiting.

I was so polite. "I kept you waiting?" I asked.

"I've come to take you home," he said. "I've got an order for your release."

"Look here," I said. "Don't try *that* again. You've done it to me once already, and it's cruel. I won't have it done again."

"Honestly, I have an order for your release. Van der Merwe is in the charge office fixing it up. You can get ready to leave."

I burst into tears. I continued to sit in that interview room for several hours. I did not believe the release was genuine. "You're going to re-arrest me?" "No." "Prosecute me?" "No."

After all that I was not even prosecuted for possession of the illegal magazine.

I don't know why I was released. Perhaps they just didn't have enough evidence. Perhaps they had made up their minds that I would not talk after all. Perhaps I was approaching another cracking-point, a cracking not wide open to them, but of myself, and they might have seen it coming. Viktor said he knew me by then better than I knew myself.

My release had to be part of a wider tactic for dealing with political whites, the errants who would not go into the *laager* of whites against Africans. How deal with us? Some were permitted to leave the country: this was one way of physically removing opposition. If among those locked up there were men who broke under the strain of detention and interrogation, they would be used for information by the Security Branch. Those who were unbreakable were given long spells of imprisonment—eight years, twelve years, twenty years, life. In my case the first spell of detention had not given them the information they wanted from me, nor the evidence in all its strength that they needed to convict me. They could have been releasing me to watch me again and catch me in the act. Viktor delivered a warning against my trying to evade my bans or make a dash over the border by the escape route. "If you try that," he said, "I'll be there to catch you."

We left Marshall Square eventually and by the time I got home it was lunch-time, though Viktor had brought his release order early that morning. When they left me in my own house at last I was convinced that it was not the end, that they would come again.

Emma Mashinini

(1929–   )

Emma Mashinini was born in Johannesburg, the third child of ten born to a black family in which the mother worked as a domestic and the father traveled long distances to a job as a dairy worker. The family's life was constantly disrupted by the extension of white areas and the forced removal of blacks to more distant shanty-towns, so that Mashinini's hardworking parents could never settle and secure the education for their children which was their goal.

Eventually the forced absence of Mashinini's father at his distant job broke up the family when she was fifteen, forcing her into the routine of work as a domestic. Married at seventeen, Mashinini bore six children, of whom only three daughters survived. At age twenty-six Mashinini left her husband to escape physical battering and inadequate economic support and began to support her children as a clothing worker. In a clothing factory in Henochsberg she began her career as a labor organizer and leader of labor protest through the 1960s and '70s, a period of unrelenting suppression of union activity. In 1975 she left her clothing job to become a paid organizer of a union of black shopworkers, the Commercial, Catering and Allied Workers' Union of South Africa. A tireless and innovative organizer, Mashinini showed great physical courage in her work, in which there was always a chance that she would be silenced by beatings or imprisonment.

By 1981 Mashinini's union organizing had become so effective that the CCAWU was a national force, provoking arrests of Mashinini and her white fellow union leaders, and their detention under the notorious law which allowed detainment of persons defined as threats to the state for indefinite periods in solitary confinement.

Held in Pretoria Central Prison for more than six months, Mashinini never cracked, never supplied details of her work or implicated fellow workers. Subject to constant interrogation, intimidation, and threats of harm to her family and second husband, Tom Mashinini, whom she had married in 1967, she experienced severe depression, and, when finally released, needed psychiatric help at a Danish center for victims of torture before she could escape the terrors and panics of her long ordeal. These were constantly being revived by frequent visits from the Security Police, whose cars outside her house and nighttime searches kept her aware of her danger. Always unshakable in her commitment to the cause, Mashinini comments that she was lucky to escape without total psychological impairment, since those imprisoned after her often came out vegetables, unable to function at all.

Despite the loss of a beloved son-in-law to the violence of Soweto, Mashinini's later years have brought her widespread international recognition. Awards from Oxford University and Howard University and from unions in the United Kingdom and Holland have celebrated her courage and leadership, and given this quietly modest woman some awareness of her achievement.

STRIKES HAVE FOLLOWED ME ALL MY LIFE:
A South African Autobiography

I was born on 21 August 1929 at 18 Diagonal Street, Rosettenville, a white suburb in southern Johannesburg. My mother, Joana, although to my knowledge she had never been a domestic worker, did some housework in order to pay for our accommodation. We lived in the backyard.

When I was six years old we moved to Prospect Township, in City Deep, south-east of Johannesburg. My mother became a dressmaker of repute, sewing clothes for people in the community, and since both my parents were working very hard and doing quite well for themselves we children started school early—that is, at what would be the normal age for white children.

So I attended the City Deep Methodist school in Heidelberg Road, Johannesburg, until 1936, when we suffered our first forced removal to make way for a white suburb. We could have moved to Orlando, which is now part of Soweto, but my parents chose instead to go to Sophiatown, which in those days was a racially mixed area, apart from whites, with many African, Indian and Chinese families all living harmoniously together.

That vibrant community of Sophiatown also disappeared, a few years later, when Sophiatown was declared a white area. The whole population passively resisted and was forcibly and mercilessly crushed by 2,500 police and soldiers.

From Sophiatown I was now sent to a Salvation Army school

in the municipal Western Native Township nearby, where I discovered how few of my classmates had started school at the correct age. My family was fortunate in other ways, too. I don't remember any of us running around without shoes, and I had a raincoat, unlike many of the children, although since I was sickly in those days I knew that whenever it rained I'd get tonsillitis anyway, and be unable to go to school.

The memory of our little house in Toby Street always fills me with happiness, and with gratitude to my mother for creating such a home for us.

There was one room and a kitchen. That was all. This one room served as a dining room and a bedroom, and in order for my parents to have some privacy they erected a curtain separating their bed from the rest of the room. Six of us slept on the other side of this curtain, on the floor, with thick blankets as mattresses. The kitchen had room for a table and two long wooden benches which were scrubbed daily, and we had a black coal stove which stood shining in its corner. On our kitchen dresser hung blue Delft china cups, and on the dresser were crystal glasses and shining brass vases. From my childhood and because of my mother I grew to love beautiful things.

I am the only child of my mother to have inherited her dark skin colour, and I have her identical features. I love to dress well, also, and when I think of my mother I always remember how when she went to town she would wear gloves and high-heeled shoes, and how she would always return holding a bunch of flowers and a cake.

There was music in that home. In the bedroom/dining room we had an organ, and on this my younger sister would play hymns. There was a wind-up HMV gramophone on which my mother would play her Columbia records of African choral music. But what I remember with utmost joy was the front *stoep*. This was of red polished cement, glittering around the straw mat in the centre, with two half-cut paraffin tins painted a bright green and filled with the plants my mother always called "elephant's ears" but which today I know as rubber plants, one on either side, while on each side of the front door stood a large half-drum, also painted bright green, and filled with "Xmas" plants (hydrangeas) which flowered pink and blue, in December, in the height of our summer. And in the middle of our *stoep*, in a hanging cage, was a singing yellow canary.

The happiness of this home was shattered for me when my parents separated. This came as a terrible shock to me, even though we weren't seeing much of my father at the time, since he was still working for the same dairy as before, seven days a week, and since he was provided with living quarters he would return home only once a week. Even then he would return home late at night and leave around three in the morning to cycle back to work.

But when my father disappeared now, completely, my family broke up. I, at the age of about fifteen, was the only one who decided to stay near Johannesburg, and try to find my father.

Due to the break-up of my parents' marriage our funds deteriorated and I was forced to leave school before completing my Junior certificate. I had tried very hard to remain in school, and would baby-sit for white children in the suburbs after school was over, earning three rand per month, but finally I had no alternative but to leave. Even then I would not give up my search for my father. I think that was my first fight for human rights, my own right to have a father.

When eventually he came to live in Alexandra I was already starting to work on my own, cleaning, and I visited him regularly. But my education was over, and perhaps that was one of the reasons I married so young, at the age of seventeen. . . .

Although he hadn't been the perfect parent, I loved my father dearly. For one thing, as an old man he was very good-natured, and a good grandfather. Despite his age, he continued to build new rooms on to his house for my family to stay in, in case they should ever need to. . . .

I married in 1947, and then I stayed at home. I was a housewife. My first child was born in 1949, and thereafter I had another baby in 1951, and another in 1952, and another in 1954, so it was just babies, babies, all the time. My last baby was born in 1956. I bore six in all, but three died within days of their birth. I didn't know at the time what had caused their deaths, although I can see now it must have been yellow jaundice. Then, in my ignorance, I didn't see that anything was wrong with them. At that time black people wanted their skin to be lighter. Those children seemed to me beautiful, with their lovely light yellow complexions. And the jaundice was never diagnosed.

It might surprise some people that I could lose three babies, each time soon after birth, and not know the cause. But it is typical of white doctors working in our black hospitals to treat patients, and cram them with pills and mixtures, without ever telling them the cause of their illness. . . .

This thinking that anything that is light-skinned is beautiful has caused so much harm. I don't think anyone escaped it. I myself used skin lighteners when I was working, but I'm one of the lucky people who didn't get cancer from them.[1] . . . When you're working side by side with someone with a lighter skin in a factory and you find they're given preference, it's hard not to believe a lighter skin is better for you. Now black consciousness has saved us from hating the colour of our skin. We used to wear wigs, too, to help give the appearance of being fair, and we used to have terrible struggles with our own hair, to make it straighter. . . .

When I met my first husband, Roger, I thought he was very nice because he was handsome and he used to dress well. And when he chose me to be his wife I was proud, because he had chosen me from all the women he could have had.

It was the tradition then that a newly married woman should spend much of her time staying with her in-laws, on her own. It was a point of pride to be able to say, "I am well accepted. My in-laws love me."

Then I went back to my husband and brought up our children in our one-roomed house in Kliptown. I was fortunate that in the yard where I was living there was a well. The others had come to

---

1. In the late 1960s black women in South Africa, especially the ill-educated, started using skin lighteners, mainly to compete with the fair-skinned, so-called "coloured," women who have better status socially and at work. Little did they know that hydroquinin, the chemical present in these creams, has been held responsible for untold harm when used on the face. Thousands of black women have been treated by skin specialists, and some who have developed skin cancer cannot be cured. For many years, professional organisations like the Dermatological Association of South Africa have been fighting for a total ban on hydroquinin in skin-lightening creams. This matter was further taken up by the National Black Consumers' Union and other concerned women's organisations in the country. But the authorities are not prepared to ban hydroquinin, and the draft Bill which was gazetted on 20 May 1988 to ban this harmful ingredient has now been shelved. The Minister of National Health and Population Development, Dr. Dawie van Niekerk, decided to give the manufacturers of these creams another three years' grace to stop marketing these products.

this same well, and some people had to travel a long way for water. Then came a time when we were told we shouldn't drink the water, as it was polluted, but should use it only for household and laundry work. So I would put my glittering bucket on my head and travel a long way to another well to draw water, but we could never be sure that that well was clean, and whether the person doing the inspection was reliable. Looking back, I realise how often my children were ill, and wonder about that water.

Within five years I had to admit that my marriage was no longer what it had been. There were just too many quarrels. Always it would be one problem that would lead to the quarrels, and that was money. He was working in the clothing industry, in the cutting room, and so was earning slightly more than some of his colleagues, but still we could not manage on his pay.

In 1955 we moved into our own four-roomed house in Orlando West, which is in Soweto. The arrangement was that you would pay rent, and if you could afford to pay for thirty years then you would be granted the lease of the house, but never the freehold, because the law forbids black people to own freeholds. That is the privilege of whites only.

Well, it was our pride to have such a big house. Such luxury! We even had our own yard, for a garden or vegetable plot. But the financial problems came with us.

In our tradition, when a girl married she was married, body and soul, into the family of her husband. And after the wedding, before she went to live with her husband, all the elderly women—grannies, aunties, mothers—would convene a meeting where she was told what to do when she got to her new home. All the taboos were spelt out—how to behave to her husband, her parents-in-law. And especially she was told never to expose the dirty linen in public. This is why it was always to my mother-in-law that I would go when things got really bad between Roger and me, because wife-battering was regarded as dirty linen, and a woman would suffer that in silence and never admit to a doctor what was the real cause of her injuries.

But one day we started arguing and I said to my husband, "I'm going to leave you. I'm going home."

And this man knew I cared about my family, my family unit, and he thought I'd never leave him. So he just said, "If you want to go, why don't you?"

I took my bag—no clothes or suitcases—and I left. I walked to the bus stop and took a bus all the way to my father's place, and that's the last time I walked away from my husband.

My children came afterwards. My people had to go and fetch them. It was not possible to do it any other way.

I left my husband in 1959. In 1956, when I was twenty-six, I had started work in Johannesburg, at a clothing factory called Henochsberg's which provided uniforms for the government forces. It was my first job, apart from working as a nanny to white children when I left school, and I had not begun to develop any political awareness. But I was already angry. The hours my father had been forced to work had contributed to the break-up of my family, and my own need to earn money had put paid to my schooling. And now, when my three children were still young and I could have done with being at home to look after them, I was having to go out to work to earn a tiny wage, which we needed in order to survive.

I remember my first day very clearly. It was November, and when I walked into that building it seemed to me that there were hundreds of people rushing this way and that, and a terrible volume of noise, with a lot of shouting—"Come on, do your job!"—that kind of thing. It was completely bewildering. Immediately I got there on my first day as a worker, I was started on the machines, working very close to people who had already worked as machinists at other factories, so I was a struggler from the start. I was in a department headed first by an Afrikaner called Mrs. Smit and then by a German-speaking man, Mr. Becker. He used to shout and scream at us, sometimes for no reason at all, and it wasn't unusual for ten people to be dismissed a day. They were always saying you had to push. They would say, *"Roer jou gat,"* which means, "Push your arse"—"Come on, push your arse and be productive." You would be on the machine sweating, but they would tell you, *"Roer jou, roer jou"*—"Push, push, push," and you would push and push.

I'd start factory work at seven-thirty in the morning, after travelling about thirty kilometres to get there.

I would leave my children sleeping, and the night before I would have made my preparations for the coming day, because I had to leave everything—bread, uniforms, everything—lined up for my neighbour, who would come and wake my children for school.

I would get home about seven—and in winter, you know, that was pretty dark. When I got home I'd start making a fire on my coal stove. I used to try to prepare for that the night before, but if not I would have to start chopping wood, getting the coal, getting the ashes out and all that. And there was no one to follow my children when they were getting up, and the basin would be full of dirty water, and I would start emptying that as well, picking up the dirty clothes, and the school clothes they took off when they got home from school.

Then they would go to sleep, and there was the tidying up to do, and the dishes, because that was the only time I had to clean my house, at night, after everyone had gone to bed. I would do the washing as well, at night, and in the morning I would get up and before I left I would hang my washing on the line. We none of us had so many clothes that we could last the week, and so I couldn't do all the washing at the weekend. Then, on alternate days, I would do the ironing, with those heavy irons you put on the stove, and my table would be my ironing board.

There was no time to sit and laugh and talk. No time and no energy. Even going to church, trying to cope with catching them, getting them to wash, finding their socks, always shouting. Only on the way there, walking out of that house and holding their hands— I think that was the only loving time I had with my children. Just holding their hands and walking with them to church.

I struggled from the first day I got into the factory. After I had learned the machine better I thought that perhaps the most important thing was to do whatever I had to do perfectly, but because I wanted to do this I couldn't produce the number of garments I was supposed to. It was not possible to chase perfection along with production. They made the choice for you, and they wanted production.

As a result of my attempt to work in this way I was screamed at more than anyone else, but still I couldn't get myself to work as fast as all those other people. Every morning when I walked into that factory I really thought, "Today it will be my turn to be dismissed." But then I was elected a shop steward, and soon after, to my surprise (though looking back it does not seem so unexpected), I was promoted. It was after about three or four years, and I was promoted first to be a set leader and then a supervisor, which was unheard of—a black supervisor in that factory. Instead of dismiss-ing me, they were trying to make me one of them.

We were members of the Garment Workers' Union Number 3. Union Number 1 was for whites, and Number 2 was for Coloureds and Indians. Number 3 was for blacks, headed by Lucy Mvubelo, who had sent me to Henochsberg's in the first place. The union for Africans wasn't registered, of course, but the employers accepted it was there.

I was very glad to have been elected a shop steward and that it was part of my duty to go about and influence people. It's strange, really, that I didn't expect to be elected, but when it came I was more than ready to accept the job. I'd say that has been true of my entire career—that I have never sought to be elected to positions of such responsibility, but when they have been offered to me I have found great fulfillment in the work they entail. You have to work hard, and learn and learn, and work even harder, because you don't have the experience, but despite this, and despite the strain, at the end of the day I can say I have enjoyed my work.

I had a dual role in the factory, but I was very clear where my first loyalty lay. I was appointed a supervisor, but I was *elected* to be a shop steward by my fellow workers.

As a supervisor I had some access to Mr. Becker, who was held in very high esteem by senior management. He was very much feared by the workers, since he had a way of goading, pushing and bullying them to produce more garments than any of his white col-leagues who headed other departments. He was a slave-driver. . . .

I remember that when I first confronted Mr. Becker he was quite taken aback, because he did not expect me to speak out. But with time I saw that he came to respect my views.

Evilly entwined in all the work at our factory was apartheid and all the disabilities which were imposed on us, the black work-ers. Job Reservation was one of those punitive decrees. Many jobs—in the cutting room, and stitching around men's jacket sleeves, for example—were reserved by statute for whites only. As supervisor I was only permitted to supervise blacks and forbidden by law to supervise our "superior" whites, even though some of the jobs reserved for whites were so simple that we laughed to ourselves to see how superior they felt in performing them.

In such a society as this, whites developed into very lazy people, because all the menial and hard tasks were landed on the backs of black people. . . .

I don't know exactly when I became politicised. In 1955, for example, I was in Kliptown when the Freedom Charter was drawn up there, and the square that became known as Freedom Charter Square was like a stone's throw from where I was living. . . .

Friends of mine who knew I was living in Kliptown wanted a place to sleep while they were there. This was before the African National Congress (ANC) was banned. All my friends were members, and I think the reason why I was not was because I had just got back from the rural area, and nothing meant anything to me apart from my children. . . .

The ANC had a uniform then, and these women were wearing black skirts and green blouses. The gold colour was not anywhere in them then, just green and black. So my friends were all in their colours, and I didn't have that, but every other thing which affected them and made that occasion so wonderful for them affected me as well. . . .

It was so good to be there, just to hear them speaking. Every race was there, everybody, intermingling. I would sit under the shade of a tree and listen to everything, and it was as though everything I heard was going to happen, in the next few days. . . .

There were speeches against the pass laws, and cheering, and clapping, and we sang, "*Mayibuye Afrika!*"—"Africa Come Back!"—and "*Nkosi Sikelel' i Afrika*"—"God Bless Africa." . . .

That congress was really an eye-opener for me. That, maybe, is when I started to be politicised. . . . I resent being dominated by a man, and I resent being dominated by white people, be they man or woman. . . .

Soon after this, we went on strike in our factory over our wages, which were still so terribly low.

At that [union] meeting was Tom Mashinini. He was there as an organiser. I must have grown to appreciate Tom more over the next few years, since we eventually married, in 1967. He has always respected my independence, and this, I am sorry to say, is unusual in South Africa. It's also unusual to be married out of community of property, but I was. I wanted to protect Tom, because I already had my own children and he had his, and I didn't want him to be financially responsible for mine.

Always, when I addressed those whites, I would have to stand. We wore uniform for our work, and so I would stand there, dressed in my blue overalls, with my hands behind my back. In all the nineteen and a half years I worked at Henochsberg's I was never once asked to sit down.

A strange thing happened with Mr. Herman, though—a good thing for me, but it could have turned out badly. One day several years later, around 1970, when we were not allowed to remain in the factory during lunch-breaks, I was there filling in an application form for my daughter, Molly, who was now at the University of Turfloop. At that time I was earning around fifteen rand a week, and that was after fifteen years. I used to take five rand home with me, and the other ten rand was kept by the factory, so that I would get it all at once at the end of the year in January and be able to meet all my school fees for my children and so forth. . . .

As I was busy filling in this form, alone in the factory, the big man, Mr. Herman, walked in. I was so absorbed, putting down how I was going to pay the fees myself and so forth, and that I was separated from my husband and all the responsibility was on me, that I didn't see him. Because I am so short he could stand there and look over my shoulder to see what I was writing. I heard him say, "What are you doing in here?" I wanted to take my papers and just run, but he said, "No, I want to know what you are doing here."

I apologised and told him I was filling in this form, and he said, "You have a child at university?" I said, "Yes." He said, "How do you manage to make your payment to the university?" I told him I paid it myself, out of my salary. He was so amazed, he took the form and read it, and then he said, "Do you want me to assist you?"

Now I would say back to a question like that, "It is the salary you give us that makes life impossible." But then it never occurred to me. As workers, when we had our report-back from the union after negotiating, we would boo and say what we were being offered was too little, but it ended there. So when this man said it must be hard to manage with school fees and so forth, all I replied was we had to pay them.

I think he went home and spoke to his wife. Next day he said she wanted to meet with me, and she directed me to a group of wealthy Jewish women, the Jewish Women's Community at Temple Emmanuel. The following year an application was made for a bursary for my daughter, and I must say that then I was very grateful.

After that a man called Loet Douwes Dekker, a trade unionist working for the Urban Training Project (UTP),[2] approached me and said, "Emma, I think you would be the right person to go and start a union for the textile workers." Now all this was a foreign language to me then, and I thought he must be joking. I said no, it wasn't for me, I was okay where I was. But that wasn't the end of it. Next I was approached about a glassworkers' union, and again I didn't accept. But then I was approached by the senior people of the National Union of Distributive Workers (NUDW), the union for white shop-workers, and this time I accepted. I still don't know why, but I did. I discussed it with Lucy Mvubelo and handed in my notice.

Morris Kagan and Ray Altman were my first real experience of friendship between whites and blacks. I had met them before, along with other white trade unionists, at TUCSA meetings, since the NUDW was an affiliate, and I had admired the brilliant speakers there.

My starting salary was 200 rand a month, which was a big jump, and to cover our first few months Kagan's union gave our union a 1000 rand loan, interest free. We were to be called CCAWUSA: the Commercial, Catering and Allied Workers' Union of South Africa.

The union offices were in Princess House, in the centre of Johannesburg. My office was on the second floor. Because of the Group Areas Act we could not, as blacks, rent offices in town, so Morris Kagan rented my office in the name of NUDW. I had an office, a desk and a chair.

My first day was a terrible experience. I had come out of a factory of over a thousand workers, with the machines roaring for the whole day, everybody busy, people shouting and so forth, and here I found myself all alone. The silence was deafening. It was spring, and I was very cold in that office. I was afraid. There were no formalities to be gone through, I just had to get myself ready to go out

---

2. The Urban Training Project (UTP) was formed in 1970 as "an educational or service organisation" for labour organisations, and in 1978 contributed to the formation of the Black Consultative Committee of Trade Unions (BCC), which permitted dual membership of Cheif [sic] and TUCSA. The UTP also contributed towards the formation of the Council of Unions of South Africa (CUSA) in September 1980, which adopted a black exclusivist approach but retained links with the UTP and its white advisers.

and find some members. I didn't know where to start or what to do. When I went home that afternoon I thought I'd made the worst mistake of my life.

I had never been a shopworker and I knew nothing of the ordinances and regulations. I was an ordinary factory worker. I would listen to Morris Kagan speaking and quoting and quoting, and I just thought, "My God, will I ever catch up?"

In a way, this was my university education, at last, my chance to study. And I was lucky to have a man like Morris Kagan to talk to me and say, "Here are the books. Read."

There were other black trade unions that were being set up at that time. Every union was busy getting on its feet, and although their focus wasn't on the particular industry we were representing, at least it was on other problems that we shared, like legislation or recognition.

I needed all the support I could get, because it was clear from the start, in 1975, that the employers weren't going to make it easy for me. Like other black trade union officials, I had the problem of access to the canteens at tea-breaks and lunch-breaks, to meet with the workers at their different workplaces.

This was my first great battle. In December we managed to achieve 200 members, and by 1977 we had reached 1000! The obstacles they put in our way! They were so determined not to let us near the workers. Not only did I have no access to the stores, but even distributing leaflets out in the different shopping centres brought me to my first brush with the police.

The best way of getting the leaflets distributed, to get information across to the workers about the fact that there was a union called CCAWUSA, and where the headquarters were, and what it could do for them, was to go to their workplace and wait for them to come in to work. They had their meals in the canteen, and it was difficult to catch them going home because most of the stores had several different doors, and you wouldn't know where to wait. So I would try to catch them in the morning, as they came streaming in to work.

Management was very upset by this. They used to blame me for making the workers late, even though all I did was hand them the leaflets as they went in. Then they challenged me with trespassing on private property, which was quite interesting, since if I wasn't trespassing as a shopper then I wasn't trespassing by being there with my leaflets. But then the management would phone the police, and the police would come with their dogs, often very many of them, and bundle me into their van, leaflets and all. Oh, it was disheartening to see all those leaflets disappear into their hands, with all the printing that had gone into them. And they would mishandle me, but there was nothing they could charge me with, and that was more important to me than any fear of being injured. I remember the first time they came roaring up to me with their vans and packed me off to the police station, I was horrified, thinking I was now a criminal. I had broken no law, but that was my main fear.

I was married to Tom by this time, and he would help me out, either standing with me to hand out leaflets or driving me around to the various points before dropping me at work and then going on to his own work. He would sometimes be taken to the police station along with me, but we kept on popping up the next day, at a different place, and a different set of police would come and take us away again.

What the police were not aware of was that by intimidating me in full view of the workers they were in a way assisting me, because the workers became interested in this woman who was being arrested, as it seemed, and wished to know who I was and what was going on. So I didn't give up, and when I managed to save up and buy a very old second-hand Fiat car and to learn to drive it properly I could visit many more people. It wasn't easy learning to drive at the age of forty-six, but I was glad I did!

One morning in 1977 workers at the Checkers store in Benoni, about thirty kilometres east of Johannesburg, decided to go out on strike for an unfair dismissal that took place within their store. When they went out they didn't stay in the store but took a train from Benoni and travelled all the way to come to the union office—to me!

This was a great moment, very exciting, but I was nervous. These workers were going to lose their jobs. I had to seek advice, and I was advised to telephone their employers and tell them that the workers were out on strike and were here. I did that. I telephoned, and the employer, who was one of those who didn't want to meet with me before, said, "Well, Mrs. Mashinini, could you send the workers back to us because we have been looking all over for them."

Well, the whole store was outside my office in the centre of Jo-hannesburg—about fifty or sixty people—and this time I felt that the ball was in my court and I was not going to make life very simple for these employers. I said to him, "No, I am not sending the workers to you at your headquarters. The workers chose to come to our union offices, therefore you must come down and meet with me and the workers in our offices."

Oh, they pleaded with me—"Please don't let the newspapers know about it"—and I said, "Okay, if I don't let the newspapers know about it, you too equally don't let the people from the liaison committee know about it, because if they do they will come, and they will come with the police, and there will be police interference in the matter." They promised not to, and they didn't. And when they did come into our union office they discussed the grievances of the workers in the presence of the workers, and for the first time the workers were so outspoken I didn't have much to do. . . .

The employer simply said, "You all go back to work. No one is going to be dismissed. You are going to be paid for the time you have been away from work." In fact they did not go back to work that day, as it was too late. They went back the next day.

When I did get proper recognition for CCAWUSA from an employer, it was less of a step forward than I had expected. It happened in March 1977, and the company involved was Pick 'n' Pay.

The *Financial Mail* had been carrying articles that Pick 'n' Pay were not engaging black cashiers but were engaging black people to do other jobs. To be a cashier there you had to be a foreign worker, a white refugee, coming from Angola or Zimbabwe, or wherever. Ray Ackerman, the managing director, was challenged about this, but he just said there were no black workers available. There were and everyone knew it. All they needed was training.

Now Ray Ackerman was beginning to feel he was being seen in an unfavourable light, and because many companies at this time were becoming concerned with their image, as a result of international pressure, he invited me to a meeting, along with Morris Ka-gan, and made sure everyone knew about it.

After that [first] meeting we were given access to the canteens at tea-breaks and lunch-times, and we had a kind of recognition with Pick 'n' Pay, though no formal agreement. The policy on black cashiers changed only very slowly, but on the whole we felt we had been successful.

. . . We remained a blacks only union until 1984, when the CCAWUSA constitution was amended to admit Coloureds and Indians, and in 1985, a few months before COSATU was formed, we removed all reference to race from our constitution.

It is hard for black workers in South Africa to identify with other workers' problems. Other workers are seen as human beings, and the black workers are seen as underdogs. . . . And as a black worker, if I speak about a transport problem I am speaking about a different transport problem from anything the white worker will have to suffer. We have these very long distances to travel, and we have the poorest possible transport facilities, and our problems concern the pass laws and schooling, and hospitals, exhaustion, and poor diet.

No. Our problems are not the same. We had to fight for our identity as a black union. And we had to fight the dependency we had on the white workers and their unions. It was vital that we should be recognised for who we were, and that we should fight for our identity and respect as human beings. . . .

By 1979 it had become clear to us that the demand for the union was far greater than we could cope with, and that, as our list of postal members showed, we could no longer concentrate just on the Johannesburg city centre. We decided there was a need for a second full-time official in the union.

Then we began to make plans to establish an office in Durban.

This was, all in all, a very exciting time for black workers, because as well as the success of CCAWUSA in building its membership, the other black trade unions were also growing in size and influence. . . . We had international trade links and were affiliated to international trade secretariats, so we had a very strong profile in world trade affairs. There was a lot of travelling involved, and as well as receiving support from organisations abroad we were able to provide information about South African multinationals which had companies in other parts of southern Africa. . . .

In 1977, when the Wiehahn Commission was set up to look into the situation with regard to democratic trade unions, it was especially concerned to plan a strategy for dealing with black trade unions.

When the Commission began asking people to go and make

representations to them, I was elected to represent the workers of the group of unions with which CCAWUSA was working. Of course, the black trade union movement was not represented. I was questioned about political involvement in the trade unions, and I didn't pretend there wasn't any. I insisted that the trade unions have got to be very much involved in politics, and that even if trade unions anywhere else in the world are not involved politically, in South Africa they must be, because this is a country where everything around us is politics. . . .

Well, we had our hopes of the Commission, and when the law was changed and we were informed that we could apply for registration we went ahead and did so. But I must tell you, this was not by any means an easy decision. The issue was sensitive for all the black trade unions, and there were many who felt that to register was to sign up as a willing partner in the whole unjust system of apartheid. We had a sore debate about this in CCAWUSA, and for a long time we could not decide one way or the other whether this would be the right or the wrong thing to do. . . .

We applied for registration that year, in 1979, but we had to wait until 25 November 1981 for it to be granted. By that time I was in detention, safely out of the way. The sequence of events was this: after the law was passed, those trade unions with "difficult" leaders were told their registration was under consideration, and then there was a swoop and those leaders were arrested. The unions were given the right to exist. But the union leaders, who had negotiated this right, were betrayed.

And in the end, registration was not as important to us as being formally recognised as the workers' representatives. We came to realise that while you can be a registered union with no members, you can force the employers to negotiate with you if you are recognised as being the union representing the workers, registered or not.

All our offices were leased under NUDW, because under the Group Areas Act blacks were prohibited from leasing offices in white areas and establishments. In 1981, in order to be rid of us, the owners of the York House building in Johannesburg informed NUDW that when their lease expired it would not be renewed. The office was very modest, with a small room and an anteroom, but they clearly wanted us out.

This brought a very big change in our lives, because as head of CCAWUSA, I had to go and approach Desmond Tutu, the General

Secretary of the South African Council of Churches (SACC), to grant us accommodation, since no one else was prepared to have us. So we became the first union to be granted accommodation in Khotso House (House of Peace), and I found it quite amusing that NUDW, who came in also, did so under our auspices.

In Khotso House we now had access to infinitely superior accommodation. Apart from our office we had a large hall, which could hold most of the strikers from CCAWUSA, and later from other trade unions, and which was used continuously until Khotso House was destroyed by a bomb in 1988.

With the tremendous growth of union workers, education was top of our list in organising members into the unions.

In the end we established a committee of representatives of the progressive unions, including the African Food and Canning Workers' Union, whose regional secretary, Neil Aggett, took a very active interest in the project to build a centre. I chaired the meetings, and the secretary was Alan Fine, who was engaged by NUDW as an organiser, and who also took a very active interest in our plans. He was arrested in September 1981, under Section 22, and Neil took his place as secretary. It was a meeting of all these trade unions that year which saw the birth of an ideal which finally germinated with COSATU, and later COSATU House, which was bombed in May 1987.[3]

We thought and hoped that Alan would be released after fourteen days, and I can remember keeping some chocolate for him in a drawer as a surprise for when he came back, because I knew he loved chocolate, and I was even planning to tease him a little, by marking the calendar and telling him how much time he had wasted while we were working so hard, and that there was much work to be done and he had better get on and do it, after sitting idle for two weeks.

But then the fourteen days were up, and he wasn't released. I

---

3. The Congress of South African Trade Unions (COSATU) was formed in 1985 as a federation of trade unions working with the following principles in mind: (1) control for the workers; (2) non-racialism; (3) one non-racial union per industry; (4) representation based on paid-up membership; (5) national cooperation between unions. In 1988, under Order 335 of the regulations made under the Public Safety Act (1953), the Congress was effectively banned from any activities taking place outside the workplace and not directly affecting the workers as workers.

became very concerned for him, and it was at this time that I grew close to Neil, who would come in every day and talk with me about what was happening.

Alan was now being held under Section 6, which allowed for people to be held indefinitely. I think he was one of the first to be held under that section. There was another white trade unionist arrested at that time, Barbara Hogan, who was also a friend of mine and who is still serving a ten–year sentence, charged in 1982 with "furthering the aims of a banned organisation," the ANC. And shortly afterwards, Neil himself, another white person involved with black trade unions, was arrested, on the same day as I was.

Neil was a medical doctor who was particularly concerned with occupational therapy, and he used to come and speak to us at health and safety meetings. That was his concern with the Food and Canning Workers' Union as well. His girlfriend, Liz Floyd, was another doctor, and she had a friend called Liz Thompson, who also took a keen interest in the workers and their health. We called them Liz and Liz, and all of us used to discuss together what was happening to Alan and Barbara, but I must say we didn't connect what had happened to them with our ideas for a trade union centre.

So I was completely unprepared when, on the morning of 27 November 1981, I woke, very early, to hear loud bangs and knocks at the door of our house. My husband opened the curtains to look out, and saw a string of cars of police and soldiers. He opened up to let them in and they swarmed into our bedroom to find me still in my night clothes. My husband and children were all ordered out of the house, just in their nighties and pyjamas, and locked out there for more than an hour.

They said to me, "Emma Mashinini, we are detaining you under Section 22," and that I still take exception to, because they should have made that statement in the presence of my family and not to me alone.

They searched the house, the dustbin, outside in the yard. They took complete charge of everything while I stayed in my nightie. With the shock and everything I wanted to go to the toilet, and whenever I went there was one policewoman who came with me, accompanied me literally into the toilet—as though something would come out of that place to attack them and she had to be there all the time. And they went on searching. They searched through the piles of letters from my children, and from the friends I had made all over the world, and from the shopworkers' unions in different countries.

The letters were very interesting to them, and the books, especially all the books that had something to do with trade union work. They took piles of them, piles and piles of things, and put them on the table, and just at the time when they were about to leave the house my family was called in and they said to my husband that he should attach his signature to a form saying they were taking these books and materials that had been found in the house.

Tom refused to sign. "I am not going to attach my signature to this when I don't know whether you brought these things along with you or what." They were very rude to him and said he was not making life easier for me, but he said he would not do it. They did not want us to speak to one another. I said "Tom" and was going to say that no, they did take the books from the house, but they would not let me say anything further, so it was to my advantage that they did not let us speak. At one stage they brought a black policeman who thought maybe my husband did not understand what they were saying, and he said, "I hear each and every word that you are saying. I am just not prepared to do it."

They took me out to their cars. Now I was in the street, and my neighbours were standing on the corners to see what was happening. It was as though they had come to arrest a murderer, a criminal. It was only about six-thirty in the morning, and I was busy working over in my mind why it was they had come to arrest me, what offence I had committed. And after some time it came to me—oh no, maybe it is like the other trade unionists who were arrested in September. And then I thought, Section 22 is fourteen days. I was counting—oh my God, fourteen days, two weeks' time, in two weeks' time it'll be . . . I'll be back, I'll be out, just before Christmas, I'll be back home . . . But why, why?

They drove me to town, to Khotso House, where we now had our offices.[4] They didn't even ask me where our union offices were. They went straight to that place to search it. And it was dead silent, dead silent in the back of the car, with me in the centre and two policemen escorting me.

4. Khotso House is well known for housing anti-apartheid organisations. As well as the United Democratic Front, the Detainees' Parents Support Committee and the Black Sash, many church groups have offices there. Police raids like this one are a regular occurrence.

Several cars had gone, but still there were about three or four that came with us to Khotso House. When we got there it was too early in the morning for the door to be open, and we were not able to open it ourselves. The policeman who was standing there said the key was not there. And the man inside would not open. He knew it was too early for there to be anybody in the offices, so anything could have happened. He was very brave and very sensible not to open, and we had to wait until someone from inside came out.

When eventually we did go in, they searched our offices, through all the files—and there was a lot of paper then, not like when I first started the union, when I didn't have one letter. Again they were interested in all of it, and again they took piles of the files and books.

It was now after eight, and the people coming to work were having to wait outside. I was still just standing around, wondering what would happen next. I did at least have a dress on over my nightie.

Finally we went out to the car again, and when the lift stopped at the ground floor we met a group of inmates of Khotso House who were coming from the chapel, because in Khotso House every morning they have prayer meetings held at eight-thirty before people start work. It had been announced that I had been seen accompanied by police and that my offices were being ransacked. Several young men came to say, "What are you doing to Emma?" And even though the police said, "Get away, get away," they still came, just to show that they were with me. And when I walked out of the lift with the police carrying all the books and was taken to the cars, the people did not go into the lift, but instead they followed us. They were singing and chanting, "*Siphe Amandla Nkosi Okunge Sabi*"—"God Give Us Courage"—about fifty of them, black and white, singing "Give her strength, Lord, not to be scared. Give her strength, Lord, for her to stand up and face whatever they are going to expose her to."

I was strengthened by these people, and all the goodbyes, the waving at me, and the good things they were saying, that there will come a day when all this will be over, one day. Right in front of the car they were standing, and they sang the national anthem and chanted, "*Amandla Ngawethu*"—The power is ours—and I was raising my clenched fist back.

We went to John Vorster Square,[5] where I was put into a room, and there I was interrogated and harassed and given a number. And after some time I was called in by other policemen, who were looking through all the books and things which had been collected from my home.

"You're fat, Kaffir maid," one said to me. "You're a nuisance and a troublemaker." And afterwards he said to me, in Afrikaans, "Are you a commie?"

Well, my understanding of that was, "Are you a communicant?" because I saw some Bibles and I thought he meant was I communicant of the Church. So I said yes.

And he said, "Well, I'm not going to give you the damned Bible, because you are a Communist and you admit it."

I was shocked, and all by myself, and it seemed everyone had an insult for me, that everyone who walked past had a word of insult to say to me. I was just in the centre of a mess. Who was I to argue over anything and say I misunderstood and that the last thing I was was a commie? That is how they work. They put you in a room, and confine you there so that you must just think you are the only person who is arrested and detained. They don't want you to be exposed to the knowledge that there are other people who are detained as well.

As fate would have it, with all the shock, I kept needing to go to the toilet, and time and time again I had to say to this lady, "Now I want to go to the toilet."

But this time when I went, just before we turned into the toilet, we passed the lift, and it stopped, and someone walked out and said, "Hello, Emma." It was Neil Aggett. I wanted to respond, to say hello back to him, but the relief of finding I was not the only one who was arrested took it away from me, and I could not bring out even that one word. I always regretted that, that I did not say hello to Neil, because I was not to see him again. But he was being pushed one way, and I that way, and he did manage to say, "Hello, Emma."

---

5. The building called John Vorster Square is used as a form of clearing house. It is the last place a detained person is known to have been taken. Thereafter, every attempt is made to keep the whereabouts of detainees completely secret, in order to prevent demonstrations and any proper investigation of their conditions.

From the toilet I went back to the office where they were writing down my details. They took photographs and fingerprinted me, and later on I was taken downstairs to the car, with just the little bit of clothing I had brought with me. They told me, in Afrikaans, that they were going to drive me to the Wilds, which is a place where all the muggers and criminals hang out. One understands Afrikaans, but only as much as one has to. There is not the willingness to learn to communicate very well.

As they were driving me I was busy looking at their clock, because the radio was on and it was just about one o'clock, and I was anxious to hear the news in case there was an announcement about what was happening to me. But these people are not great fools. Just when the radio said "pip pip pip" for the news they switched off the radio, which was my lifeline. Yes, these were young bully boys.

I don't know where we went. They took me many different ways, just to cause me more confusion, and they were insulting me all the time.

But then we stopped, and I saw we were in Pretoria.

I think it was then I realised I was really in trouble. I was taken to the offices and put into a cell. And I thought then, Now I am arrested. Now I am detained.

Because, to me, Pretoria Central Prison was a place for people who have been sentenced to death.

It was a prison where there seemed to be whites only. A prison of black people would not have been so clean. They would not have bothered. It was November, mid-summer in Pretoria, but I was very, very cold.

I was able to count the days by my meals and by dark and light, by how many nights, how many getting ups. I was able to count that day onwards to day fourteen.

And it was still Emma. I was still sane. I was myself.

I started becoming hypertensive and I told them, "I'm not going to take food with salt," and they said, "Well, you will have to." And I ate. I was looking forward to going home—I said to myself, I need to eat, to keep strong to go home.

On my fourteenth day, when the policewoman came to open the door for me and brought my food in, she said would I like to go and have a bath. I thought that this meant I was going home. After my bath, when she was locking me in, I said to her, "Am

I not going home?" She said to me, "Didn't you see the newspapers—that you are charged with another section?"—as though I could get a newspaper. Yet I think she was not doing this to spite me but was unaware of the system, of her own system.

Now I think that was the most heartbreak I had. The heartache was even greater than when I was actually removed from home, because I was now being held under Section 6. I kept telling myself, Section 6 is one of the worst sections. You can remain in prison for an indefinite time. It depends on the government.

When I went to bed that day—well, from that day onward—I never even thought it was necessary to eat and keep strong to go home because I knew—my God, I knew—that now I'd had my chips.

All my trade union experience of demanding to see and not being refused just fell aside. Even going to bed was an effort. I was just a lump. And this was now heading for Christmas, the time I'd always thought I'd be home. I thought about my children. My children who were not here. . . .

With the cold still, and the horrible food, and the headaches and dizziness from the hypertension, and now this heartbreak and disappointment, this was a bad time. A very bad time.

It was a very frightful thing, that window. Whilst I was sitting on my only sitting place—there was no chair, I had to use the bed to sit, to sleep, to do everything—I was always sitting opposite that window, which was sealed. But then when I was on the bed, trying to sleep, not expecting anybody, I would just see two eyes piercing at me. All I could see was their eyes. It was very, very frightful. I couldn't get used to it. I thought, It's like an animal, to see those two eyes, and I'm in a cage. It was frightening.

One day, two policemen came, together with a policewoman, and they said, "Come on, come, come out of the cell." Nothing like, "Get yourself ready to go" or whatever. It was just "Out" and out I went.

There was this very long corridor that I had to walk through.

I'm a short person. I could not walk as fast as they did, and I had no business to. I did not know where I was going. Eventually, when we reached a doorway, they pushed a door, and there were policemen waiting, with their guns. I did not know whether I was going to be shot or what. Nobody ever says anything. These people have fine ways of torturing you. They let you torture yourself.

We went through and out into a car. Still they didn't tell me where I was going to. I didn't ask. I had no saliva. I was so thirsty— very, very thirsty. I think that was the shock. This is how thirsty I was. I saw one of those police people, it was a woman, a white policewoman, chewing gum. They were busy eating. I put out my hand to say, "Please, I'm dying," you know, of thirst, and she made a joke out of this. "She wants to chew because we are chewing." . . .

This was my first time of being handcuffed. I wasn't handcuffed the time when I left home. And I just asked, "Has any woman been handcuffed before?" I had never seen a woman walking in the streets with handcuffs on.

They deliberately had parked the car very far from where they were taking me. I still did not know where that was. But what a funny, strange feeling. Walking in the street, escorted by them, with the handcuffs.

I did not slump my hands, or whatever. I really held them up. I thought, I must be seen, that I'm handcuffed. I was looking round. This was Pretoria. We had union members in Pretoria, and I thought, I'd like them to see that I'm arrested and I'm in Pretoria. I thought my people thought I was in John Vorster Square and nobody knew where I was.

We got into this building, a huge building. You could see that it was a government building. It must have been yet another police station within Pretoria. I was taken into another room and the handcuffs were taken off my hands. There was a chair where I sat, and after a few minutes my husband and my sister-in-law came into that room.

This was 23 December. It was about four weeks since I'd seen them. Instead of excitement I felt very dampened. All the hell I had walked through, of those people in that long corridor falling on their knees. All that, and it was for a visit from my husband. And still what I wanted was water, water, water.

Well, then it came, at last, the joy, the excitement. But we were not allowed to speak in our own language. There was a white policeman there who wanted to hear everything we were talking about, and conditions were laid down. You don't ask her about the conditions of her arrest. You don't ask her what she does. You discuss family matters and nothing else.

He hugged me and kissed me, and I don't remember them stopping him, to say "Don't do that." And my dear husband had brought a pillow for me. He knew that I needed pillows. I don't know how he thought about it. There was dried fruit, too. There was everything.

And then he said, "Have you been getting all the things we've been sending you?"

I said, "No, I haven't received anything." This was the first time that I'd received something from home, this dried fruit.

He said, "Well, I'm going to make enquiries."

Amongst other things that he brought me were Christmas cards, from Bishop Tutu, whom I knew personally, and Leah, his wife, who is a friend of mine, and some from people working with me. And my children had sent Christmas cards from overseas to Tom. He brought these as well, and I said, "Am I going to be allowed to take these to the cell?" And he told me I was allowed six cards.

And I wondered, did my father know that I had not committed any crime, and insisted, "Tom, please sit my father down and make him understand that I have not committed my crime. I don't know why I am here."

My next concern was, "What's going on in the union? Is the union okay, Tom? Is everything okay?" And he made all the assurances that people were working very hard and all was well in the union. He brought greetings from Morris Kagan to say he was very concerned and was doing everything he could to see that the union continued.

It was about fifteen minutes, and this visit was like a lifetime to me.

When they were asked to leave the room I wasn't able to cry. I wasn't even able to cry, and I felt I wasn't going to cry because it would break his heart. . . .

Back into my handcuffs again, and with the handcuffs I had to cuddle the things he'd brought for me, and a black policeman, another one, had to carry some of the parcels all that long walk back to the car and now back to my cell.

That long corridor I walked now. There were no people. Just that long walk back. But sitting in my cell, looking at those things, having seen my husband for the first time for all those weeks, having heard about how my family was, looking at those cards—I can't explain how I felt. I think it was the greatest day I've ever had.

———————

During this period I had, with my headaches and dizziness, a terrible backache. I complained to the nurse to say, "Your tablets are not giving me any relief from the pain," and they took me to a doctor. When they X-rayed me I had to go on quite a high machine, and it was an effort. I was so weak I couldn't easily get up there. They said the result showed there was nothing wrong with my back, but it was so painful. . . .

I had been in my cell for two months now. And the days went by. The days went by.

In January I was moved from Pretoria to Johannesburg.

A huge cell, after my very small, clean cell. From my very clean cell with a bed to this dirty place. The walls were dirty. The floor was dirty. There was a bundle of black blankets in the corner, and a bit of carpet, and I was shoved into that place. No bed, no chair, nothing. A lavatory, again filthy. I said, "Now this is the end of the road. I can't take this."

I'd lost a lot of weight, during my imprisonment in Pretoria, and now I had to visit the dentist on several occasions. I was losing my teeth, I think from the loss of weight and the kind of food I was eating. I was also taken to the doctor, because of my back, and the warder would give me medicine every evening, because I was not allowed to keep the medicine myself.

There was a black policewoman who came to check on me— "Is everything okay?" and so forth.

The first day I just said, "Yes, yes," but as the days went by I complained to say, "Can I have an extra blanket or an extra mat?" meaning just something to make this floor softer. She gave me that. And when I asked her about the food she said everybody ate this kind of food. She said it was the same food, cooked from the same pot as for every other arrested person, black and white. Because I was saying, "Is it food just for detainees?" And she told me detainees and white persons eat the same food. So I got encouraged and started eating again.

But I was so glad—oh my God, I was so glad to see a black person, even a black police person. I was so sick of seeing those white people. To see always white people, white people pushing you and telling you "Come" or "Go" and what to do—it was making me ill.

It was for me an outing, to visit the doctor, or the dentist, even if the reason was pain with my back, or my teeth falling out. And this was how I felt about my interrogation when it began. An outing to get out of my cell.

There could be about four people, at times six people. At times I would stand, at times I would sit, and these people would take turns. This could go on for the whole day. Questioning you about this, questioning you about that. Sometimes they would ask me if I wanted coffee, but I would always ask for water instead. I didn't want to be seen sitting drinking coffee with these people. They would be at one end of the room, with a table. I would be at the far end of the room. They worked in shifts. One shift would go to lunch and leave me with another shift. Then, at the end of the questioning, they would just leave me. They wouldn't say goodbye or anything. They would just go, and the next thing would be another policeman coming to say, "Follow me." Not to say where to. Just, "Follow me."

I was thoroughly questioned about my trade union work. They weren't interested in the GWU, just in CCAWUSA. And they seemed very interested in the Allied Publishing strike of newspaper workers, which I suppose was really a turning point for us, and showed how strong we had grown. They were also very interested in my relationship with the other leaders who had been arrested before me. At times they would tell me directly that I had been very obstinate and very difficult to the employers. They would remind me of instances, saying, "Do you remember that this is what you were saying to a certain employer?" . . . So it seems that in our industrial relations in South Africa you not only deal with the employers when you negotiate but you deal with the police as well.

And they were questioning me about our meetings and our trade union centre and where this idea had come from, that somebody must have put this or that idea into my head. They wanted to know if I had ever read certain books—I can't remember the names, because in fact I hadn't read them, but they were Marxist books, because Marxists were the sort of people who have that type of thought, of bringing people together. I was interested in a trade union centre for worker education. Not necessarily with any ulterior motives behind it. But I was interrogated for hours to come up with the truth about the idea and where I got it from.

Always they wanted the truth, when I had no more truth to tell. I don't think they ever really understood that in fact there was nothing to give away. But they always tried to find it, this nothing. . . .

Worst of all was one particular day when I was being driven to
John Vorster Square and we were going down Commissioner
Street. Out of anxiety I would always look round to see if I could
see people I knew. I would see them, but I couldn't wave to them because I was with two policemen, sitting next to me. That day I saw
on the posters, "DETAINEE DIES IN CELL."

"Detainee dies in cell, detainee dies in cell . . ." And I can't ask
these people what has happened or what is going on.

I wanted to know from the policeman, "I understand there is a
detainee who has died in the cell. Who is this detainee?" And one
policeman said, "Okay, I will call you somebody senior who will
come in and talk to you." I think it was a Section 6 inspector who
came. And he said, "I believe you have got a question." I said, "Yes,
I want to know who is this detainee who has died in the cells." He
said, "Who told you that? Who told you that?" I said, "Nobody
told me." He said, "Where did you get it from?" He was becoming
aggressive. I told him I had read the posters at the corner of the
street. And he said, "Can you guess who it is?"

He never told me who that person was. And this was a torture
and a hell to me. My husband was now bringing me fruit juice in
five-litre boxes. One time it was peach, orange, apple and so forth.
I had these boxes in my cell. When they were empty I kept them.
The colour meant much to me—the green, the orange—it was my
closeness to nature. It kept me going. It was fun. But then my husband also brought me a transistor radio.

Now I had company. There was music. But also I could listen
to the news. And one day when I was listening to the news I just
heard the radio say that Australian trade unions refused to offload
goods from South Africa because of Neil Aggett's death in detention.[6]

---

6. Neil Aggett's death in detention on 5 February 1982 provoked a public out-
cry, both in South Africa and throughout the world. In the week after he died,
over 85,000 workers in hundreds of South African factories downed tools or
left the shop floor in a half-hour tribute to him, the first time industrial action
of a political nature had been taken on the shop floor rather than in the form
of a stay-away. An official police statement claimed he had been found hanging in his cell and that indications were he had committed suicide, a claim Dr.
Aggett's friends and family, and those who knew about conditions for detainees, found highly improbable. The inquest into his death was delayed by
legal arguments about the admissibility of a statement made by Dr. Aggett
fourteen hours before his death, alleging that he had been assaulted with kicks
and punches on 4 January and given electric shock treatment on 29 January.

I asked at this time for things to clean the place. I was given disinfectant for the toilet, and I cleaned the walls and the floor. It was interesting cleaning the walls, because in places I could read, "I WAS HERE FOR RAPE," and a signature, or "I WAS HERE FOR STEALING CARS." Everybody who had been in that cell wrote on the wall what they were there for, and it kept me busy, reading all this. But then it began to torture me, because I thought I was not a criminal. . . .

But under all this was Neil Aggett. His death affected me very deeply. We were very close friends with this man.

The police hated that white people should work for justice for black people. When they interrogated me they didn't know I had found out that Neil Aggett was dead. They would time and time again tell me, "We're going to question him about this."

Strangely, I was not made more frightened when I went in for my interrogation. Instead I was furious about the whole thing. I was sort of arguing back.

I was still getting the newspapers, and one thing really gave me a lot of pride when I saw it. There was a cutting with a photograph of my husband standing as a lone demonstrator in front of the Supreme Court, demanding my release. Tom standing there, alone, with a placard, demanding. And I read about him even coming to Cape Town and demanding my release, and demanding the release of all the other detainees.

Tom was a very strong and conscientious person. But he was not one to speak out. My being detained, him demonstrating in front of the Supreme Court, the police station, demanding my release there—this Tom was a person who spoke out, which he hadn't been before. So sometimes when the police think they're doing you down, they're building you up. They built me up by harassing me in front of the shopworkers, and helped make the union what it is. And they made my husband speak out. . . .

When it came to Easter, because I am such a staunch member of the Anglican Church, I made my demands during the interrogation to say that I wanted to receive Holy Communion.

Tom had brought me a Bible to read in my cell, and also other reading material, little novels with love stories. I also saw someone from my Be United group, who brought me a dress and warm underwear, because it was winter, and said that all the underwear was from money collected by the Be United group.[7] And any particular day when I had visitors I told them that I wanted to have Bishop Tutu come and give me Holy Communion. I said this openly in front of the police, and the police said that, much as they would look into my demand to receive Holy Communion, I was not to think they would have Bishop Tutu coming into their offices.

When Good Friday came I was fetched from the cell and taken to John Vorster Square. And instead of going to the tenth floor, where I was usually taken, I was taken to the ninth floor.

As I was going to the ninth floor, where I saw several men with handcuffs, and was saying to myself, "Am I going to be tortured together with these men?" a young man came walking down the steps as we were coming up. He noticed me, and he just said, "Don't be so morose." And he kissed me. He had his escorts, but he braved them to speak to me and then to kiss me. His name was Sisa Njikelana,[8] and I carried his kiss with me for a very long time. When people speak about the kiss of life, I tell them that kiss of Sisa Njikelana was a kiss of life to me.

When we reached the ninth floor we went into a room and I found my priest there, Father Telejani, from the Holy Cross in Soweto. When I was demanding Bishop Tutu and Holy Communion they had suggested other Anglican priests, whom I had totally refused. So I don't know what happened or how they ended up with Father Telejani—maybe they found out he was my priest in Soweto and so brought him. He is a very intelligent man, but he never used to preach about politics, about the real things. Human rights.

So in that room were Father Telejani, the two police and myself. And the table. He had prepared the table exactly as he would in church. He had everything necessary. He had the wines, he had the little jars, and he was in full cassock, in full attire.

I was excited to see him, and I kissed him, and that was allowed, and he sang a hymn, "Praise to the Holiest." And after that he made his prayers. As we were singing you could hear the police join in with humming, because they would not leave me alone with

---

7. Be United is an all-women group made up of friends and colleagues who act as a *stokvel* but also meet to discuss politics and other matters of interest and concern.

8. Sisa Njikelana was the Vice-President of the SAAWU. He was detained on 8 December 1981, and on several other occasions, charged, under the Terrorism Act. Two years ago he was paralysed in a motor accident.

my priest. And when it was time to say "Amen" you could hear
them say "Amen," and I thought how, with all the horrible things
that happen in South Africa, this was still meant to be a Christian
country.

So then the priest brought me greetings from the Church, and I
gave him greetings to the Church, and we hugged and we kissed,
and it was wonderful.

Outings—to the doctor, to the interrogation, to my visitors—
served a very good purpose, because it was going out to meet people, to see other things and most of all to see people. Even
interrogation I looked forward to. And if they didn't call me for interrogation, I really wanted to remind them, because interrogation
was better than to be isolated and all by myself for all those
months. I even thanked myself for being so ill, because of the outings to the doctor and the dentist.

I had the Bible to read, and the stories my husband had brought
me, and the radio, newspapers which I would have to destroy when
I'd read them; so much more than at first when it was just me. But
somehow the thing that should have brought me the most happiness instead brought me the most pain.

I had a picture of my grandchildren. I was excited to see this the
first time. It came out of the books my husband brought me. But afterwards when I looked at the picture it seemed as though those
children were talking to me and saying, "Granny, what are you doing here?"

One day, thinking about my own children—Molly, who was in
Germany, my grandchildren, and Dudu, who was in New York—
thinking about their faces, and putting names to them, I could see
my youngest daughter's face and I wanted to call her by her name.
I struggled to call out the name, the name I always called her, and I
just could not recall what the name was. I struggled and struggled.
I would fall down and actually weep with the effort of remembering the name of my daughter. I'd try and sleep on it, wake up. I'd go
without eating, because this pain of not being able to remember the
name of my daughter was the greatest I've ever had. And then, on
the day when I actually did come across the name—this simple
name Dudu, or "Love"—I immediately fell asleep, because it was
such a great relief. But that was after days of killing myself to remember my own child's name.

I thought I was going mad. Really going mad. And I was fighting very much against it because now I could read in the newspapers that people were going into psychiatric hospitals and I didn't understand that you could go mad from being arrested.

It's only now, after years, that I feel I want to speak about this effect of being in detention. Not to talk about it is to deprive a number of people who will come up against it for the first time without knowing what their expectations should be.

So in prison you are anxious and concerned about everything. You are killing yourself about being there and what's going to happen tomorrow, and all that, and you look forward to your outings—to the doctor, to visitors and to the interrogations.

And then, one day, the interrogations just stopped. That was it—bang. No word. Nothing about why. And I missed them. I thought once again I was going to be sitting in that room all by myself. I didn't think I knew myself any longer. There was no mirror. It's odd what happens when you don't see yourself in a mirror for such a long time. You don't recognise yourself. You think, who am I? All I had to recognise was a jersey which was sent to me by a friend. It was her jersey and I could recognise it. But I didn't know any longer how to recognise myself.

One morning in May a chair was brought to my cell, so the doctor's orders were at last complied with. I had a chair. But I had not sat on that chair for too long when there was a knock on the door to say, "Pack your things. Come with us."

This wasn't anything new for me, to bring my things for interrogation. But I had not had any interrogation for so long, I just thought it was a change from one prison to another again. Leaving that chair behind, that chair which I'd waited so long for, I thought, "Oh, my God, I'm going to start life all over again without a chair." The cruelty of people. The cruelty of that chair. I ached. My back ached. I needed that chair.

I was taken to John Vorster Square with all my things, into that office, and in that office I was made to sign papers to say that I would appear in court on a certain day. It was only after signing all those papers and after being made to make oaths about not talking about being in prison that I realised, "Oh, I'm being released."

Then they said, "How are you going home?"

I asked if I could please phone my husband, to tell him that I was being released. They knew the number. Of course. They knew everything about my husband, and myself. During the interrogation they used to tell me about my husband and myself. They rang him and told him that I was released from prison.

So now it was time for me to go home. It was so exciting. My child Nomsa was there, and my neighbours. My neighbours came in very great numbers, and there was one visit especially which was very important to me. Morris Kagan, who until that time had never been to Soweto, came to my house. He said—it was before the permits were abolished—"Permit or no permit, I'm going to Soweto. I'm going to see Emma." All this was very wonderful, but also too much, because in the evening, when I went to bed, I was very exhausted from being alone for so long and then all of a sudden having so many people coming.

I now had a period when I was very concerned and worried and wanted to run away from my home. My home was no longer suitable for accommodating me safely, because they knew where it was and I thought they were coming back to get me.

We called the doctor, and he gave me something to put me to rest, to sleep. But still that feeling went on, for days and days. And all the time people were coming to see me. They were coming in their tens, in their hundreds. We actually had to have arrangements to say which people were going to visit on a certain day. People from trade unions, people from the Church, from prayer meetings. It was just traffic, one after another. And international friends. I was one of those lucky people who had a telephone in the home, and all the time there were telephone calls from all angles.

I'm sure people could tell from my speech that I wasn't normal. And in the end my FIET colleagues in Geneva said, "We want you to come to Geneva, and we are prepared for you to travel with your husband. We are not going to take the risk of you travelling alone."

In May I was out of prison, and now in June I was to travel to Geneva. And from Geneva I was whisked away to go to Denmark, to a clinic for detainees and people who had been tortured.

The doctor who started the clinic was Inge Genefke, a woman about ten or twelve years younger than myself, and a very brave, intelligent person.

Inge Genefke used to want me to speak out.

But for me I was speaking to a white doctor, and I had spent so much time with white police, surrounded by white people. It was a white woman who had refused me chewing gum, and a white woman who had put those bracelets on me. And it was hard, very hard, to trust her, this new white woman. As well as that, I had been told when I was released never, *never* to speak about my detention. So whenever I spoke I was leaving something out. I was fearful, terribly fearful, that this would leak out and get to them, and I would be rearrested and charged for having spoken about things.

So it was thanks to all this—my friends and family, psychotherapy and my beautiful car—that I kept going for those last five years in CCAWUSA. And I needed them, because now that I was beginning to be on the mend there was work for me to do. The union had been going well, but there were many problems—workers in many of the stores were involved in big strikes. CCAWUSA was in a good position to win recognition from many of the companies we dealt with, and I wanted to be there, leading the struggle for workers' rights. I was still at the head of my union.

The doctors told me I should work half-days, or at the most a four-day week, but it was simply not possible. 1982, of all years, was an important one for CCAWUSA. That was the year we made the retailing employers accept that we were here to stay. It wasn't easy. It took strikes at four of the big employers. . . .

But for myself, what with the tension and the exhaustion, I must say that I was beginning to feel the strain, and to realise that I was not so quickly to recover from my experience as a detainee.

Because through all this I just could not forget the prison. This came to a head when Alan Fine, who was still detained, wanted me to go and visit him. I wanted to, but I hated the thought of going to that place. To go back to prison after you've come out is really horrible.

But I did go to visit him. I walked through those gates, and I could hear every gate being locked behind me, and as I listened to all those closing doors I wasn't thinking about Alan. I was just thinking, "Will this door open for me to go out again?"

There was no contact allowed between Alan and me. I could touch Tom when he came to see me, and speak to him and so forth, but with Alan there was glass dividing us. Still, he was very pleased to see me, and I was pleased to see him, even with all that glass dividing us.

But there, in that prison room, we were only able to have general conversation. He wanted to know what things were like, and so forth, and how was the union. . . .

The other thing I had to do was visit Neil Aggett's grave. I called Liz Floyd, Neil's girlfriend, to ask her to take me there. She had come out of prison in February, but she said to me, "Emma, I don't know it. I've never been there."

I said, "It's my tradition. He was dear and close to me. I must go to his grave." And I made this arrangement with Liz. We went to a friend, who gave us some plants, and we took hand forks and so forth, and we went to the cemetery. A woman friend who had attended the funeral accompanied us, and we looked for Neil's grave. When we found it we saw a wreath on top, on which was written that a Communist was buried in this grave.

Well, we told ourselves it didn't come from the people. We just left it there. We had heard that already there was a lot of vandalism with the grave. Many people knew where it was, because Neil had a big cathedral service, with many speakers, and his funeral was indeed a funeral of the people.

By the grave I said a prayer. I said a prayer and told Neil how much I cared for him, how much I loved him. Here we were two women together: myself, a black woman, and Liz Floyd, a white woman I've always respected and honoured. But with this friend we shared, this dead friend, we became as one.

Those six months brought about a great change in me. I tried to get it all out at the time, all the bad feelings and memories, but I could not, and even now there are things that come up, and I remember. These are long-term effects. I have had long-term physical effects, and long-term mental effects.

The first time I caught sight of myself in a mirror after all that time I had been shocked. I was a different person altogether. I am a very big person by stature, a fat person, though not tall. But now I was so thin and small, and my complexion had gone so fair from being in the shade for all that time, that I couldn't believe my eyes that this was me. It shook me a lot. I thought it was my sister in that bathroom with me, my sister who is very fair.

I was to suffer memory lapses. They came at a certain time of year, particularly in December. The first thing that I would experience was a feeling of tiredness, exhaustion, and then I would go into a deep sleep. And thereafter I never knew what happened.

I had nightmares, too. When I first came out every car move shattered me. And the thought of going back—well, when they say one gets cold feet I really know what that means. It's not just a saying. Sometimes, even in great heat, when I am perspiring and so forth, my feet are so frozen I have to cover them up.

I did manage to break my memory lapses, at least. In December 1985 my husband and family suggested I leave South Africa to see if I still suffered a lapse. So I went to Dudu, and indeed it never did come. I try always to travel at this time of year now.

For a long time I didn't talk to my family about my prison experiences. Neither Dudu nor Molly knew about many of the things I had been through until they saw me in *Mama, I'm Crying*, telling of the terrible time I could not remember Dudu's name. They kept saying, "Mom, you never told us about this." They didn't even know about my forgetting Dudu's name. This book will serve as a living memory of the evil of the apartheid regime. It is an opportunity for me to speak to my children.

Indian Nationalism

"Prison was a challenge"

Shudha Mazumdar

(1899–   )

Shudha Mazumdar was born in Calcutta, the fifth child and youngest daughter of Tara Pada Ghose and Giri Bala Ghose. Tara Pada Ghose was a *zamindar*, a landowner living off the rents of the family's forested lands in the delta of the Ganges. The Ghose family was involved in the intellectual life of Calcutta, especially through Jogendro Chandra Ghose (1842–1902), follower of Auguste Comte and leader of the Indian Positivist Society. Mazumdar's father saw to it that she received a Western-style education at a Catholic convent where she learned English, and that she was not married until later than usual in her family's circle.

Even so Mazumdar was married at age twelve to Satish Chandra Mazumdar, son of an educated Indian family, who had entered the Indian Civil Service. Mazumdar's life in her father-in-law's house until the birth of her son two years later was taken up with further education and getting acquainted with her husband, almost twelve years her senior.

After she became a mother, Mazumdar moved with her husband to his various postings and began to adjust her traditional Bengali ways to the mores of the raj. Her husband's career required that she break purdah and mix with the British, and his success as a magistrate rested upon demonstration of total loyalty to the British. Thus, although rebellious and critical of the British, Mazumdar could not join in the Congress movement or show any signs of her support for Mahatma Gandhi and the nationalist cause.

In her early twenties Mazumdar became involved in organizing educated women in efforts to improve the health and welfare of women in whatever district her husband was posted. Her women's groups, known as *mahila samiti*, became nuclei for more professional efforts at welfare work and for Mazumdar's continuing involvement in social work and the Red Cross after her husband's death. During the couple's postings in remote parts of Bengal, Mazumdar also took up writing about typical scenes and themes in rural India, and she began to develop her lifelong interest in sacred Indian texts, most particularly the *Ramayana*, which she translated into English.

In 1934 the couple were transferred to Calcutta, where Mazumdar began her involvement in national women's organizations—the All India Women's Conference, the National Indian Association of Women, and the National Council of Women. Through these groups she expanded her interest in women's welfare, working on the provision of homes for prostitutes and on the needs of women prisoners.

In 1951, following her husband's death, Mazumdar did not take on the role of the traditional Indian widow but instead intensified her welfare work, traveling to Geneva to represent India at the International Labor Organization's Conference on Women's Work. Her comparative study of prison conditions for women in Europe and India, *Women in Prison at Home and Abroad,* was published in 1957. Much of her widowhood then became devoted to helping released women prisoners begin new lives, caring for the children of prisoners, and securing religious counsel and observance for prison inmates.

Freed by her husband's death to participate actively in the Congress movement, Mazumdar met and worked with Gandhi and Jawaharlal Nehru in the struggle for independence, but, although she toyed with the idea of running for elective office following independence, her interests increasingly focused on her faith and on understanding India's religious heritage. The structure of her memoir, in which external events are assigned significance for the religious insight they prompted, makes this last stage of her life readily understandable.

MEMOIRS OF AN INDIAN WOMAN

"Wife brought to bed of a daughter. . . ." The entry was dated 22 March, the year 1899. I was only ten years of age when I found this item, written in English, in an old diary. My advent had been important enough to be noted down by my father!

Mohan Chand House in the Kidderpore area of Calcutta was our home. . . .

The house was enormous. The front wing was Father's. It had an English dining room, a vast Victorian drawing room, a book-lined library, shady verandas and corridors, and a marble staircase that led up to the immense roof-terrace overlooking the Kidderpore Docks. . . .

Mother's room was situated in another wing. Father also had a suite here and so did each of my brothers after marriage. And here too was a cheerful little room, the accouchement chamber, where all the family had been born and were to be born.

Of a family of five, I was the youngest and seemed to be always in the background. My elder sister, thirteen years my senior, had been married a few months before my birth. People always appeared to be occupied with her and her husband in some way or other, for though they lived in Howrah, they often visited us. There was one brother before and two others after her.

The youngest, then six years old, was much disgusted at my arrival. . . .

As time went on I grew more attached to him than to my other brothers and many were the games we had together. . . .

Ours was a very quiet household and we saw little of the world outside the great walls surrounding the garden. . . .

My father, Tara Pada Ghose, was a landowner—a *zamindar,* as they were then called in Bengal. Most of the ancestral property which my father inherited was in the area of the Sunderbans—the sundari forests in the delta of the Ganges. . . .

Apart from his estate, Father had two great hobbies: his health and his horses. He had four horses in his stables, and I remember so well the manner in which he fussed over their food and had them groomed in his presence. . . .

In a specially built gymnasium, he exercised regularly and kept magnificent health in old age. I never saw him eat our food. He dieted according to every book on dieting, experimenting to discover what was best for him. His diet was composed, according to an English recipe book, of meat and fish—boiled, baked, or steamed—and vegetables. . . .

He was also extremely fond of *sandesh* [a milk sweet] which was served in tiny terra-cotta bowls sprinkled with rose petals as a special delicacy at his dinner parties. Mother was never present at these parties for we were all in *purdah* [seclusion] in those days in spite of Father's advanced Western ideas. . . .

My mother was the sweetest soul, but poles apart from my father. While he remained unorthodox to a degree, wholeheartedly adopting Western ideas, she clung to the Eastern ones. He had his ways of living and thinking, but she held firmly to her own.

My mother's people came from nobler lineage than my father's because they had the blood of Maharaja Protapaditya in their veins. Protapaditya of Jessore was the pride of Bengal—the rebel lord famed for his valour and stubborn resistance to Mughal sovereignty. . . .

Mother faithfully maintained the various rituals, functions, and social customs that had been handed down to her by Grandmother. . . .

. . . She kept her [Hindu] faith and lived up to her beliefs, and rigidly adhered to the family traditions she felt it her duty to uphold. . . .

Generous to a fault, endowed with a priceless sense of humour, always self-restrained and fearless, she bravely stood up for what she considered to be true.

She had her own personal establishment including her kitchen, presided over by a Brahmin cook, and a retinue of servants for the daily work. . . .

We had our food from the hands of her Brahmin cook, but were occasionally allowed to taste the Western dishes from Father's table. However, the pleasure was brief. . . . Unorthodox food was considered unclean, and therefore I was unclean until I had been thoroughly washed. . . .

Father was always well dressed, having an extensive wardrobe of European clothes tailored by the best English firms of Calcutta. . . .

Sometimes I was asked to accompany him on one of those afternoon outings that were considered to be so good for one's health. To sit primly dressed in my best frock and straw hat trimmed with pink roses, in silence, was something of an ordeal, but of course I could not dream of refusing to comply with his request. . . .

Mother . . . pressed her points by adding that it was necessary for a daughter of Bengal to do this, or not to do that, concluding most times with, "Remember, you will have to go to your father-in-law's home and if you do not know these things you will be held in disgrace." "The father-in-law's home" assumed awesome proportions for young girls in Bengal; forever it was dinned into their heads what would be approved of there and what would not. To gain the approval of the revered elders of one's husband's family was an important item in the code of good conduct. . . .

One day after my father had returned from his travels, I learned that I would be going to school. . . . Bursting with importance, I brushed my close-cropped hair, put on a clean frock and pinafore, and took my place opposite my father. Soon we arrived at St. Teresa's Convent School, and here I was admitted as a day scholar.

At that time, I was the only Indian girl amongst the English and Anglo-Indian girls at the school. Being quite ignorant of English, I had to speak in broken Hindi to make myself understood. The good nuns, who mostly came from Germany and France, knew some Hindi but not a word of Bengali. I made friends quickly and became very fond of school.

"It won't do to teach her English only," said Mother, so I was placed under the tutelage of one of her relatives and from him I received my first lesson in Bengali. I used to rise early in the morning and trot downstairs to the *amla* quarters for this instruction. In a section of this detached building, separate from the clerks, lived distant relatives whose slender salaries forbade the luxury of bringing their families to Calcutta. . . . Amongst these kinsmen were an uncle of Father's and another on Mother's side, the former lean and lanky, a teacher at the David Hare School, and the latter, not unlike Falstaff, a clerk at the Meteorological Office which Mother always insisted on referring to as the "stormy office."

These two were a jolly couple and had a room to themselves. I was the pupil of the Falstaffian uncle and well remember one of his favourite modes of punishment. When I failed to answer a question in a satisfactory manner, I was lifted up to the top of a wall that partitioned their room from the next and left there with legs dangling miserably until my sin was sufficiently expiated. . . .

Time passed and I was growing. I was now almost nine years old.

"She is not learning any housework. . . . Whatever will she do in her father-in-law's home?" lamented many a well-wisher to my mother. Those dark words were often repeated, but they failed to register with my mother and I went about as usual, giving little thought to the problems of domestic life. My time was divided between school and the carefree hours at home, and except for asking me to fetch and carry during the *puja* days and occasionally hand out plates of sweets to her guests, Mother made no effort to educate me. It was Dada, my eldest brother, who at last made her realize that it was high time to take me in hand.

"She is growing up to be a wild good-for-nothing," he complained, "let her learn something useful." He turned to me. "From tomorrow," he told me firmly, "you are to wash your clothes." . . .

Wasting soap and using much more water than necessary, I washed and rinsed clothes in a most unsatisfactory manner and my arms ached as I hung them up to dry. . . .

One Sunday, he caught me romping around in the garden and promptly led me into the house. "Come and help Mother, her cook is ill," he said. In Mother's kitchen, Bamun Pishi greeted me warmly with her toothless smile. "You have done well," she told Dada. "A girl has to learn all things; no one knows what destiny has in store for her. Yes, she must be able to do everything," she wheezed, nodding her hairless head at me. . . .

. . . School-going was a pleasure except for one or two things, and one was the problem of my hair. The trouble began when it had grown to my shoulders. Mother's notion of hairdressing and that of the good nuns differed so widely that I was left wondering which course to follow. A bath was of course a daily function in the family, and according to Mother, a bath was only a bath if it included some water on the hair. Also, the top of one's head was thought to be peculiarly susceptible to heat and as such needed half an ounce of oil rubbed into the crown. Either Mother or the maid rubbed this well into my head. Now this meant that the hair was wet and had to be left loose to dry. But according to convent rules this was "untidy," so often I was reprimanded and made to tie my loose hair at school.

"Why do you bathe every morning?" my schoolmates asked me. "We don't. We only have a bath on Saturday and Sunday." I told my mother this and begged her to allow me to do the same. She shuddered and said I was to do nothing of the sort and on no account was I to dream of adopting any of their ideas of personal cleanliness. The sanitary habits of all *firingis* [Europeans] were utterly deplorable. She considered them to be so unhygienic that she made me change into fresh clothes after a good wash when I returned home from school each day. "But why, Mother?" I had protested. "They all look quite clean." "Yes, that's just it," she replied grimly, "they look clean but they are not.". . .

. . . My first experience of an English theatre . . . left an indelible impression on me. Charles Vane, a Shakespearean actor, had come all the way from London with his company, and Calcutta was agog with excitement—at least my brothers were. My father, who was an ardent admirer of Shakespeare, had purchased tickets many days in advance for a matinee performance of *The Merchant of Venice*. I was thrilled to the core and utterly loathed Shylock and loved the gallant Bassanio. I had been told the story in a very sketchy fashion by my younger brother and found it hard to follow the entire play, but the court scenes with Portia stirred me to the depths.

"Did you like the play?" Father asked me later, "and did you understand it all?" To further my knowledge of English he spoke to us in that language and insisted on our doing the same. When I replied rapturously in the affirmative he opened his volume of Shakespeare at Portia's immortal lines of—"The quality of mercy is not strained . . ." and read it out with much feeling. Then raising his eyes with a quizzical look he said, "Do you think you could learn this by heart? If you can, this will be yours," and he held up a silver coin.

I took the book and went up to the terrace and pacing up and down repeated the passage till I became word perfect. In the evening I went to him to claim my prize. . . . Father was so delighted with my performance that not only did he give me the coin but, to my great distress, he made me recite the lines before all my brothers, while he commented in glowing terms on my delivery and diction, praising the good nuns for my feat. . . .

. . . I had made many friends at school and one of them, then a boarder at St. Vincent's Home, had encouraged me to live at the school. . . . I was then about nine years old, and one day I crept to Father and from behind his chair expressed my wish to become a boarder. Time passed and I had nearly forgotten all about my desire when one day, at tiffin time, I was told to come to the Home for my food.

I went with alacrity, but my heart sank when I saw the coarse rice and heavily-spiced egg curry served to me. . . . Realizing that I had become a boarder at last, I felt a lump in my throat. The afternoon lengthened; I lost interest in my lessons and began to feel homesick and forlorn. Suddenly one of the Sisters called me from the class and led me to the parlour. Here, to my surprise, was Mother, who had never before come to the school. . . .

"Is this your mother?" Sister Superior asked me with a worried look. I nodded vehemently. "She wants to take you home, do you wish to go with her?" "Yes," was my joyful reply. All I remember after that is that Mother took me by the hand and saying some words in Hindi to the Sisters, led me to the waiting carriage. . . . Mother proceeded to dress me in a sari, and without any explanation for her conduct went on to say that it was necessary to wear this as we were going to the wedding of Susama Didi, the daughter of the widowed Pishima. Pishima was my father's only sister, and if anyone had the last word with Father, it was she. . . .

Feeling very guilty, I effaced myself from her presence. Presently, Mother dressed me properly and I found my own level with some small girls who had come with their parents. The house was gaily decorated and overflowing with people, and I was happily playing about with my little companions. I was suddenly petrified to see Father coming towards me with a face like a thundercloud. He was in Jodhpur breeches, and from the whip in his hand I knew he had driven over in his own "tum tum," the name for gigs in those days. "Well," he said, "so your mother took you away?" I did not know what to say but to my great relief Pishima appeared.

"Ah, here you are, Boku," she began quite casually. "You must have gone out of your mind to put the girl in a *firingi* boarding school. It's a good thing that Bou had enough sense to bring her away." . . .

[Mother] was ever a realist and Father was not. He could not calculate or think so far into the future, nor could he visualize his restless daughter, now in pigtails and frock, as a staid old maid in economic distress. So, when all her arguments failed, Mother did what she thought would save me from disaster. It went against the grain for her to disobey her husband and court her own unhappiness, but it was just like Mother to adhere to her ideas of right and wrong, irrespective of the cost.

There was a rift between my parents, and I could sense the discord between them for many days. The money that had been deposited at the school for my boarding was converted into clothes. It provided work for the needy Anglo-Indian women who lived in the Home, and I wore the many frocks and petticoats they made for me till the time I was married, and then they had to be discarded altogether. I remember my eldest brother's wife using the last of my petticoats under her sari when she came to our home at the age of nine.

I was eleven at that time and my marriage took place the following year, 1911, when, to commemorate the visit of King George V, the capital of India was changed from Calcutta to Delhi and the partition of Bengal was annulled.

In the years following my marriage, I came to learn many new things about politics and religion, although I still enjoyed the games of my childhood. My introduction to politics was in 1905 when I was seven years old and Mother served us with a *phal-ahar* [fruit meal] when it was neither a fast day nor a *puja* day. It was not a holiday nor did I hear of any holy purpose, so I was somewhat puzzled to notice the unusual silence in the kitchen and find that no fires were burning at all. On enquiry I learnt it was associated with the *Swadeshi* movement.

When the Viceroy, Lord Curzon, decided to partition Bengal in 1905, a great wave of national consciousness swept over the country. It had started first in Bengal where, as a sign of mourning, kitchen fires were not lit on the 16th of October, 1905. People at this time took an oath to boycott foreign goods and pledged themselves to wear only *swadeshi* [of our own land] items of clothing. . . .

I became aware of other aspects of the movement three years later, but this time it was through a young cousin of mine. He was a tall and lanky youth who usually teased me, but that evening when he visited us he was unusually quiet. Mother had entertained him with freshly fried *loochis*—*loochis* seemed to be always ready to be served with a curry of seasonable vegetables, together with a sweetmeat, to anyone who happened to visit us in those days.

After partaking of these snacks he came to the veranda to wash his hands and rinse out his mouth. Drying his hands on the towel that I held out for him he looked at me gravely and said, "Do you know what I have got with me?" patting his pocket. I shook my head. He held up a little paper pellet. "The ashes of Khudiram!" he said.

I started. "Yes," he added with a smile, "his body was cremated last evening." "Who was he?" I ventured. "What! You do not know Khudiram? You seem to know nothing!" was his contemptuous reply. "He worked for the *Swadeshi* movement and he gave his life for our country. He was hanged by the British at dawn." . . .

As I look back, I find my father was a man much ahead of his time and also full of contradictions. He felt the English way of life admirable and worthy of adoption, but he never failed to don a *dhoti* during the Durga *puja* to pay his annual visit to Mother Kali in her temple at Kalighat. . . .

One evening, when we were at dinner and Mother was serving us with appetizing *loochis*, I asked [my eldest brother], "Dada, how many gods are there and which is the true one?" Reading the Christian scriptures had raised doubts within my mind. "Why, I thought you knew there was but one God," was the reply. "Yes, but at school . . ." "Oh, is that what is troubling you?" laughed Dada. "Look, it's just like this," he said, and here he raised his tumbler. "We call this *jal,* Muslims call it *pani,* the French *l'eau,* and the English *water.* All these many names mean just one thing. It is the same with God. He has many names, but He is but one."

The convent teaching raised a fresh conflict in my young mind and I came to him again one day with another problem. "Which is the true religion?" I asked. "All religions are true," he replied. "They are but so many roads that lead to God. Some roads are broad and some narrow, some are long and some are shorter ways to the same destination, that is the only difference," was his reply. "Then it does not matter much, does it, which road we take?" I asked, surprised at my own boldness. "But it does matter," he retorted. "It all depends on how you look at it. You may reach your destination through a flower-filled garden, or through an unclean latrine, it is for you to choose which path you prefer."

Dada was pious, but his language was not always polite nor was he inclined to be patient. He was rather blunt in speech and prided himself upon his ability to call a spade a spade. I am indebted to this brother of mine for a good bit of my education. I am also indebted to him for arranging my marriage. . . .

"When are you giving your daughter in marriage?" people frequently asked my mother after Dada's wedding had taken place. One day, in my presence, Young Grandmother raised her scanty eyebrows and asked the same question, adding a few more words in her own inimitable manner. "Surely you are not going to wait for her to become an old woman before giving her in marriage? She is already ten years old. The honour of the Ghose family will certainly be tarnished if you delay much longer." . . .

One afternoon I was told not to go to school. That day my elder sister took an unusual interest in my appearance. She rubbed a few drops of scented oil in my unruly hair, and then plaited, coiled, and pinned it back in a becoming manner and dressed me in a silk sari. I soon learned that some people had come to see me and was unwillingly led to meet them in Father's study. Here I found Father proudly handing round my school reports to two elderly gentlemen. I was given a chair beside them and heard one say to another in an undertone, "Gracious, the girl knows French!" This apparently unnerved them for we never heard from them again! . . .

In the meantime I began to hear about horoscopes. In Hindu

families the parents carefully consider every ingredient that contributes towards a happy union. Not only are birth and breeding, appearance, health, and education taken into account, but the horoscopes of the boy and girl must tally as well. My mother had much faith in horoscopes, and they were consulted on important occasions. When the talk of my marriage was in progress she called our family priest one day and gave him mine. He spread out the saffron-coloured roll, written in Sanskrit, and poring over it for a considerable time, found certain unsavoury facts which greatly perturbed my mother. Didi had been taken into confidence and she became even more disturbed. I found her one day wiping her eyes and sniffing; when I asked what was the matter she shook her head and said it was not for my ears and told me to go and play. I was rather intrigued. What was it that made Mother look at me so sadly and Didi, always my arch critic, treat me so gently?

Gradually I learned the truth: an early widowhood had been foretold for me. This so disturbed my sister that she felt I would better remain unmarried all my life. I doubt if my father was made aware of all this, but his old Pandit, Nakuleswar Bhattacharya, was consulted. "You must not eat anything tomorrow until Pandit has read your palm," I was told one day. He came early next morning. Mother spread a carpet for him on the veranda in front of the *puja* room and gave him my horoscope. He nodded his head many times and, following a long consultation between them, I was called. He took my hand in his and peered at my palms through his steel-rimmed spectacles. "Hmm . . . Hm . . . It can be . . . ," he muttered with puckered brows. Then he lifted my left hand and smoothing out the skin of the palm, bent over it gravely. "A good hand," he murmured. And turning to Mother he added, "but—," and left his sentence unfinished. With great compassion he looked at me and said that I could go. . . .

Sometime later, there was a simple ceremony one morning and I again had to miss school. After worship and prayers, Pandit Nakuleswar Bhattacharya unwrapped a shining heart-shaped locket with my name engraved on it, slipped it onto a thin gold chain, and put it over my neck. The locket was made of five metals—gold, silver, copper, iron, and lead—and held within it a sacred formula written on a piece of *bhurya patra* [bark of a tree]. . . .

When I received the locket I only thought it a pretty trinket. I did not know it was meant to shield my future husband from all harm, and had I known, I doubt if I would have worried over a husband I had never set eyes upon. My concerns at the time were the food restrictions placed on me by the Pandit. His parting injunction was, "You must not eat crab, food that has been partaken by another, or *akhadya* food. And, remember, you must wear this locket always and never part with it." . . . Ever alert, my youngest brother at once accepted the former definition. "Aha!" he cried, wagging an admonitory finger at me, "from now on chicken will be forbidden for you. You can have nothing from Father's table!" . . .

So, when on the following day I refused the chicken and told Father why I was unable to comply with his wishes, he flew into a temper and said that I was not to listen to all that "tommy rot"—a favourite expression of his when roused. Calling Mother, he took her to task for it. Referring to the Pandit, he was most irreverent and said he did not believe that such injunctions could be laid down in our holy books, since the Vedic Rishis [sages] performed rituals wherein it was compulsory to sacrifice animals. . . .

This perturbed Mother and the commotion took away my appetite altogether. That night as I lay beside Mother, she told me quietly that it was a sin to displease one's father and that in future I was not to refuse anything from his table. She also told me that I must conform to the Sanskrit *mantra: Pitah svargah, pitah dharma, pitahi paramantapah, pitari preetimapanne, priyante sarvah devata.* The Sanskrit words, roughly translated, mean something like this: "Father is heaven, Father is religion, the gods are pleased by pleasing Father." I was to learn these words and repeat them before partaking of the forbidden food. Thus peace was established, but it was not permanent!

Some time after my marriage, my husband was puzzled at my refusing a chicken curry that had been specially prepared for us. I told him about the amulet (but he never knew what it was for) and its restrictions. He was much amused. "Well, don't you think your mother's method of overcoming the displeasure of your father may be applied to my case as well? If it is sinful to disobey a father, surely it is not a good thing to disappoint a husband. . . . So, since I would like you to share this with me, you had better insert 'husband' in place of father in that Sanskrit *mantra* and come and finish this curry before it gets cold." And so, except for observing the restrictions against leftover food and crab, which I was never addicted to, it was impossible for me to follow all the Pandit's orders in connection with my amulet.

Although Mother came from a family of landowners and was

married to one, she disliked the class and was determined that her daughter should not marry a landowner. She had democratic ideas and set her heart upon a man who was capable of earning his living by some gainful occupation. . . .

One night as I lay beside her listening to one of my favourite legends, she interrupted the story and quite casually asked my opinion about the matter weighing on her mind.

"Which would you prefer? The boy of one proposal is very good-looking but not at all well educated. He is just a matriculate without a university degree; but he comes from a wealthy *zamindari* [landowning] family of east Bengal. Their home is in Barisal where they have vast estates . . . but I do not approve of *zamindars*. . . .

"The other boy is not so good-looking but has a splendid physique and he has had a good education. His home is in Murshidabad where he has just been appointed a Deputy Magistrate. The family is an old one and known to your Dada's father-in-law who has brought this proposal. The boy's father is the private secretary to the Nawab Bahadur of Murshidabad. But I hear that a Deputy Magistrate does not stay in one station, he gets transferred and works in many places."

The word "Nawab" had romantic connotations, and a roving magistrate sounded more interesting than a dull landowner planted in a remote part of east Bengal. And as for looks, why, only a few days ago I had learned from my Bengali primer about the flamboyant *palash* flower that no one loves because it has no scent. It had been explained to me that men were prized for their merits, and that good looks without good qualities had no value, for the flamered *palash,* because it has no perfume, can never be used for any *puja.* All this was fresh in my memory, while the idea of travelling to new places, being always on the move, and living without any fixed abode, seemed absolutely fascinating. But how was I to voice my thoughts? . . .

One fine day in November of 1910 I was preparing for my annual examination when I was told that I would not have to go to school any more for my marriage had been arranged. It was with the Murshidabad boy, but now I found little pleasure at the prospect of my nomadic life with him. No school! Never to see my schoolmates and the good nuns any more! A gloom descended on my spirits and I moped about the house not at all happy about the idea of marriage.

Soon after I received the news of my impending marriage Mother took me to bathe in the river Ganges. The river on which Calcutta stands is known as the Hooghly, but since it is a branch of the Ganges it is often referred to as the Ganges. I always enjoyed the crowd, the atmosphere, the dip in the water, and the adventure of changing my wet clothes inside the closed carriage. Finally the priest from Orissa would stamp my forehead with cool sandalwood paste in a design I myself had chosen from his collection. . . .

We were particularly early that morning, as the bath was a cer-emonial one in connection with the eclipse of the sun or moon. I drew my sari modestly over my shoulders and dipped in the cool waters. Closing my eyes, I held my nostrils with both forefingers, plugged my ears with both my thumbs, dipped under, and came up panting for breath. Opening my eyes I saw my school bus filled with my schoolmates going over the bridge. My heart sank. I felt left out and forlorn and my eyes smarted with tears.

As we were returning home, Mother noticed the look on my face and asked me what was the matter. I burst into tears and begged her to allow me to go to school. I did not want to get mar-ried, I told her between sobs, I only wanted to go to school. But my opinion did not count and matters proceeded.

One day Dada pointed out a serious looking young man in a group photograph of students and said this was my bridegroom-to-be. Shortly after this I was once again dressed by Didi and sent to Father's study. Here Dada was in Father's chair and with him was a grey-haired man with kindly eyes. He looked at me and smiled. "Where is your father?" he asked me. "He has gone to the settle-ment," I replied, and that was all. He was my future father-in-law.

Afterwards I learnt that he had taken a fancy to me and said he found "something" in my face that was lacking in all the other faces he had seen. Goodness knows what he saw in me then; I had not completed my twelfth year and was gawky and graceless and had little to commend me.

In March 1911 I began my thirteenth year. A few weeks later there took place what is known as my *ashirbad,* literally "blessing," but the ceremony is actually betrothal. In this betrothal it is the par-ents and elders, who, by a little ceremony of "blessings" held sepa-rately in their respective homes, formally announce that the marriage has been arranged. The next step is "blessing the bride" and "blessing the bridegroom," although this too is done in the respective homes.

On an auspicious day, the boy's friends and relations assemble at the home of the girl. The future father-in-law or elder who is arranging the marriage and standing in his place blesses the bride-to-be and makes a gift to her in token of his approval and good wishes. After the ceremony there is an elaborate feast to celebrate the occasion. Later, a similar ceremony is held in the home of the bridegroom. At this time the date of the wedding is decided and the exact auspicious moment announced.

Thus it was that one evening late in April I was "blessed" by my future father-in-law and presented with a heavy silver box of an ornate pattern in which to keep vermilion. It contained a small packet of vermilion and two gold coins from the time of the Emperor Akbar. My father-in-law came with a few friends and relatives, and in token of the happy event had sent to our home many dishes of sweetmeats, bowls of curds, baskets of *pan,* and many kinds of spices. Our family priest and Pandit Nakuleswar Bhattacharya began the ceremony by blessing me with Sanskrit *mantras* as they sprinkled over my head a few grains of golden paddy and blades of *durva* grass betokening wealth and prosperity. Then my father and a few elderly relatives did the same.

Some days later, Dada and a few elderly relatives went to Murshidabad to perform the same ceremony for the bridegroom. Dada was accompanied by servants carrying similar courtesy gifts to the people of the bridegroom-to-be, who was also "blessed" with gold coins. On their return the next day, Mother questioned them at length about her daughter's future home, the son-in-law, and relatives. Dada and our relatives had been feasted and feted, and all were unanimous about the desirability of the match. They felt that the relationship with this Murshidabad family would be a happy one.

The wedding had been fixed for the 7th of July. As the days passed, many interesting things began to happen, and I found myself becoming interested in my marriage. Measurements were taken for my ornaments and clothes. The weaver women came with their merchandise, and Mother chose saris while I hovered around, fascinated by the colours and patterns. The local goldsmith brought glittering gold ornaments, and Dada brought more modish ones from fashionable shops. I was thrilled with the gold wristwatch on a Milanese bracelet, but Mother did not approve of the bracelet as it was not made of guinea gold but merely 18ct English gold. . . .

. . . Khokar-jhi . . . nursed my youngest brother, and when I made my appearance, her services were transferred to me. . . . Having been entrusted with the care of three children of the family she had held a position of her own, and it had been decided that she should accompany me as my personal maid to my father-in-law's home. As Khokar-jhi had become old, Mother felt that she might not be able to care for me in a proper manner, so she decided that Parvati, a younger maid, would go too, much to the disgust of power-loving Khokar-jhi.

I was pleased with the prospect of having Parvati for she held me in respect, whereas Khokar-jhi was forever finding fault with whatever I did. I realize now how dearly she loved me, but in those days I fiercely resented her, and much wordy warfare was waged between us. . . . All this rather clouded the golden days preceding my marriage, for whenever I thought of leaving the old familiar house of my father, my heart became heavy and the glamorous wedding gifts lost their allure.

One morning I awoke to the sweet moving strains of the *shehnai* [an Indian oboe]. The haunting music made my heart ache. Tears pricked my eyes and I was filled with a sense of sorrow at the prospect of leaving the known and a vague fear of meeting the unknown. I turned over and buried my face in my pillow. "Wake up! Wake up!" called Khokar-jhi. "It is your wedding day!" . . .

When the bride reaches her new house she is greeted much in the same manner as the bridegroom was received by the women of her family. Wedding *shehnais* and conch shells blown loud and long signal her arrival as a young girl hastens to lay down the long length of a new red-bordered sari for her to step upon as she enters the threshold. Usually a young sister-in-law takes her hand and lovingly leads her to the *alpana*-painted place, where she stands beside her bridegroom to receive the ceremonial welcome. The bride is thought to be Lakshmi, the goddess of fortune, and she is honoured accordingly. Milk, tinted pale rose with *alta*, is made available to wash her feet, and in token of acceptance she dips her toes into the basin. Gaily dressed maidens and wives gather round to greet her with gifts, but it is her mother-in-law, bearing the lucky symbols on the winnowing fan, who comes forward first. She is very precious, her son's wife, for she is his "other half."

The mother-in-law's gift is generally a pair of gold bracelets and a smooth reed-thin iron bangle that is worn on the left wrist. Like the vermilion, this bangle is the symbol of her wifehood and is only taken off when she has the misfortune to become a widow. The newly married couple is then led to the "worship room" where both pay their homage and receive the benedictions of the men of the family and gifts from other relations and friends. . . .

I well remember my first arrival at my father-in-law's house for I almost died within the gilded palanquin which carried me to my husband's ancestral home. We were very much in *purdah* in those days, and nice women were neither seen nor heard, especially new brides. I had all this explained to me by Jushi-di and others who were anxious that I do the right things among my new relations. Feeling rather sick and forlorn, I looked at Mother. She seemed to have a cold; she cleared her throat several times and then nodded and said in a low voice that I should always listen to Khokar-jhi. When my eyes fell on Father, I noticed he was blinking with a frown on his face. "They will miss the train if there is any more delay . . . ," said someone, and I was led to the landau. In the midst of all these strangers I derived comfort from the thought that Khokar-jhi, formidable though she was, followed in a hired carriage. "Your Dada will come and see you soon and your Sripur uncle will come to fetch you when the 'ten days' are over," were Mother's parting words, and that was also another comfort.

My father-in-law had reserved the entire compartment for myself and my husband and my maids. The train started from Sealdah sometime after 2 p.m., and ambled along in a leisurely fashion till five hours later it reached the small town of Murshidabad. . . .

The family I had now become a part of could trace their history for many generations. Their caste was Kayastha . . . Traditionally, the Kayasthas have been civil servants and administrators, and the Mazumdars conformed to this pattern. . . .

When the ten days were over I rejoiced to see my Sripur uncle come to fetch me at last. The acquaintance with my husband had been forged into good friendship, and we promised to write each other till we met again. I told him that both my Bengali spelling and handwriting were appalling, but he only laughed and said, "Never mind, write in English."

In that year of 1911, the months that followed found me deeply engrossed in our correspondence. I was initiated in the art of letter writing. . . . I cannot but think that my father-in-law was somewhat unusual for at that time I knew of no one amongst us who corresponded with a new daughter-in-law in English. I still cherish those letters written in his neat precise hand giving me news of my new relations at Murshidabad and of his son. He always addressed me as his "Dear Daughter" and ended giving his affection and full signature.

As for his son, he affixed "My dear" before my name, chatted about nothing in particular, and ended decorously with his full name. . . .

The coming of King George V is linked in my mind with the anguish of losing a most loving father-in-law. He had been overworked in Delhi; shortly afterwards he caught a cold in Calcutta that developed into pneumonia and he died, alas, early in January 1912. I remember praying fervently for his recovery and wept bitter tears to hear he was no more. Mother made me follow the austere rules of mourning, but I did not mind having the one dish of boiled rice and vegetables for my midday meal. It had to be done in a new earthen pot every day, and should the vessel crack during cooking there would be no cooked meal that day for the mourner. So Mother would first tap and test the clay pot and cook carefully over a slow fire fed with jute sticks. With a lump of butter and sprinkling of rock salt, I thought this was a delicious meal. Served on a fresh green banana leaf, the meal was concluded with a small marble bowl of thick creamy milk and a banana. In the evening there was a cup of hot milk, fruit, and a small lump of *chana* [curdled milk] sprinkled with brown sugar.

This was my food for the mourning month; my mourning clothes consisted of two cotton saris and a warm jacket, for it was very cold at that time of the year. It was even colder at Murshidabad, where I went before the month was over to be present for the *shraddha*, the ceremonial rites for the peace of the departed one's soul. . . .

My husband was still at Mymensingh but my mother-in-law wanted me at Murshidabad. My presence would help to comfort them, she said, so I was sent there along with Khokar-jhi. The old house had a dreary air which was enlivened only by my brother-in-law and his many small friends. Thakurpo, my younger brother-in-law, became my good friend and companion. He was eight, four years younger than I, but inordinately solemn. I would eagerly wait for him to return from school and give me news of the great world beyond the four walls.

———

Sometime late in 1913 my husband was posted to Faridpore. My heart leapt with joy when I learnt that I should be going with him. Accompanied by Khokar-jhi, an old Brahmin cook called Pandey, and a considerable amount of luggage, we left for the distant station in East Bengal.

In those days brick and mortar buildings were rather rare in that part of the world, so we were considered fortunate to have found one consisting of three small rooms with a veranda and kitchen. In the open courtyard there was a well and an enclosed square to serve as a bathroom. Beyond this was the main road, and by it was a room I rarely entered, for it was here my husband entertained his visitors. We slept on two divan beds made with wooden planks. I arranged my beloved books on a small bookshelf on the wall and thought myself very clever to have contrived a dressing table out of a window sill beside which I hung a length of mirror. The only other furniture we possessed were two folding tables and four chairs with hard wooden seats, but we were supremely happy.

At first we ate our meals separately, as we had in Murshidabad, but as time passed we grew bolder. One day my husband ordered the cook to serve our food in the same room and then leave, for we were too shy to eat together before the servants. "Do you think he will tell the Murshidabad people about this?" I asked my husband in an excited whisper as he closed the door.

I had no fear of Khokar-jhi, but it took some time before I was at ease before Pandey, who had been provided "from the home of my father-in-law." I feared he might carry tales of our improper doings. Khokar-jhi ruled both him and me with an iron hand, constantly reminding me of what I should and should not do. As soon as my husband returned from office I would regale him with some of her injunctions. . . .

Time hung heavy on my hands when he was away, and reading palled after a time, so I was delighted when my husband suggested I write an essay. "What is that?" I asked, for I had not reached the essay stage in my school. "You write on any subject you choose," he answered. At this moment, a cow mooed in the field. "Why," he smiled, "you could write an essay on a cow." "But what do I write?" I said miserably, feeling quite lost. "Oh, all you know about it, what it looks like, what it does," and with this he hurried away to court. I remember writing with great pains about the cow possessing four legs, two horns, and a tail, and nobly giving her milk to nourish mankind. My husband praised this, and I went on to write another essay on the river Ganges.

At first we meekly submitted to whatever Pandey and Khokar-jhi thought best for us, but with the passing of time we began to have our own ideas. Even though I had no knowledge of house-keeping, I did not think that Pandey should use the silver milk jug to hold chilies. "Can't we have our tea in the silver service?" I asked my husband. Since that was the only wedding present we had brought with us we decided to enjoy it. . . .

One day I was surprised to see that a very large parcel had ar-rived from a reputable English firm that sold musical instruments in Calcutta. I could not believe my eyes when I opened the case and found a beautiful folding organ! As I raised the lid, I caught my breath to find on an engraved plate an inscription from my husband saying "with love." "Ooh," I gasped, "whatever will people say when they see this inscription? Don't you think it's a bit too shame-less?" "Not at all," he laughed, pinching my arm, "I hope you like it. And now you can practice your songs by yourself at home." Didi came later to test the volume and tone and teased me about the in-scription. The neighbourhood was now constantly regaled with notes of the organ, and my husband and I spent many happy evenings with it.

Then followed a period of life that was cloudless and carefree, yet marred from time to time when a dark shadow seemed to fall and blot out the brightness of the day. The memory of our Pandit's prophecy was never completely absent from my mind. I had heard that my misfortune would be averted with the advent of a baby, and I found myself desperately longing for one.

"You don't look too well these days," said Didi, looking at me with searching eyes. "It's just because I always feel sick in the morn-ing, something I eat must be disagreeing with me," I answered. Didi was concerned and asked questions. My replies confirmed what she had suspected, and taking me under her wing, she gave much sage advice about diet and mode of life for the future. I was acutely em-barrassed when I came to know about my condition, but gradually this passed and gave place to a sense of relief and shy wonder. Khokar-jhi became jubilant as she now had more responsibility than ever. She urged Didi to write to Mother immediately. "Don't you see, the Murshidabad people must be told through Mother," she said. "Oh, no," I implored, "not just yet . . . ," for I feared I would be snatched away from this new home and separated from my husband.

Sometime in early 1914 Mother wrote to say that Father was planning to go to Europe and if he did, I should come to Calcutta before he left. As I could not delay my departure much longer, one day Khokar-jhi became frantic and the fateful letter was dispatched. Soon after, my mother-in-law arrived from Murshidabad with the family priest to perform the Panchamrita ceremony. For the necessary rites I was to wear an auspicious sari—a handwoven red-bordered one given to me by my mother-in-law which was presented with its two ends still intact, just as it was when taken from the loom. I was terribly embarrassed to have my condition made public by the ritual for the welfare of the unborn child and emphatically told my husband I had absolutely no faith in such ceremonies. Although he was of the same opinion, we had to give in where family custom was concerned. At the conclusion of the ceremony I had to uncover one of the two covered receptacles so that the sex of the child could be predicted. The symbol foretold a boy. "What nonsense!" I told my husband later, "I don't believe it at all." Both of us were of the opinion that it would be very nice to have a little girl.

My mother-in-law left soon after, but not without many injunctions to Khokar-jhi to look after me in a proper manner. Mother wrote reams of sage advice, and one of Father's clerks arrived carrying gifts of food and clothing. One basket contained some carefully packed venison which Mother had taken great pains to procure. It was accompanied by detailed instructions as to how it should be cooked since it was this meat, she wrote, that would make my child "have the large lustrous eyes of a deer."

Sometime later, one of my father's old clerks was sent to escort me to Calcutta. My heart sank when I saw him and I grew sick at the thought of leaving my husband. But the auspicious day for traveling dawned, and accompanied by Khokar-jhi, I left Faridpore with bitter tears in my eyes. For a long time after I came to Kidderpore I would cry in secret, and many were the letters we wrote each other during the time I was there. . . .

I had been entrusted to the care of a midwife called Khirodai who was reputed to be good. She had a kindly pockmarked face, wore a spotless white sari, spoke very little, and seemed to know her work. She had come the day before, and when she found her services would not be required immediately, she promptly started to sew small garments out of my old saris.

Layettes were not looked upon with favor in those days as it was thought they might help foster expectations that might never be realized. So many untoward events might occur to shatter one's hopes, how could one dare to set store on what the future might bring? Whether one's lot would be laughter or tears, only time could reveal. "Let the child come by God's grace," it was said, "and there will be plenty of time for coddling it with new clothes." The main concern was the safe arrival of the infant.

I had two maidservants to look after me and my baby, but the precautions that were taken for our well-being were traditional rather than scientific. I remember being tormented by thirst as it was thought water might be injurious for my health. Nor was fresh air considered beneficial, so the windows were closed to prevent my baby and myself from catching cold. A great fetish was made of "touch." I was not permitted to emerge from the room, nor were visitors allowed to pick up the baby or touch me. Except for the midwife and the maids, no one was allowed entry into the ac-couchement chamber. I did not know then that these were the hy-gienic measures of olden days meant to protect mother and child from infectious germs to which they were susceptible at that critical time. Unaware of the cause of all these precautions, I was full of re-sentment and labeled them silly superstitions. . . .

One day I learnt with dismay that my husband had been trans-ferred to Madaripore. He wrote to say no accommodation was available there, and he did not know when he would be able to se-cure a place for myself and the child. . . .

My husband . . . succeeded in finding an obliging landlord who had built a place for us to live. The walls and roof were composed of corrugated iron. The house was partitioned into two rooms and a veranda. The floors were cemented, but to my dismay the corru-gated iron walls stopped several inches above the floor. Conse-quently, when it rained the rooms were flooded and all manner of crawling life sought shelter through this opening. I remember how I shrieked with horror and loathing one evening when I squashed a frog with my bare foot while reaching for the pedal of the organ. There was a pond on either side, and the torrential rains caused the water to rise so that the house was almost surrounded by water.

When I arrived by country boat, I had to walk on stepping stones till I reached the veranda.

My husband became very popular with the young men of the town and was elected president of their club. A junior doctor who was our neighbour became the secretary, and between them they organized many games and theatrical performances for the benefit of the members. But one day there came a letter from the District Magistrate warning my husband to be careful and to refrain from mixing too freely with these young men, who were known to be involved in the *Swadeshi* movement. This was a great blow to my husband, who had enjoyed the company of these young people, but he had to resign.

Gradually I became aware of how the career of a government officer could be adversely affected by any connection with people who held patriotic views. The government took many precautions and posted spies nearly everywhere. I had become friendly with the wife of a leading pleader and later learnt with dismay that her husband was a paid informer of the government. It was an open secret and people looked on his activities with scorn and loathing. . . . My husband told me not to unbosom myself too freely with my neighbourly "Didis" . . . as I was only seventeen and absolutely ignorant of the art of holding my tongue or concealing my thoughts. My carefree days seemed to be at an end; unconsciously I found I had begun to watch my speech and behaviour and observe that of others. Mercifully, we were not in Madaripore for very long.

After a few months we were moved to a small station close to the Garo Hills in Aymensingh named Netrakona. . . .

At first, we were the guests of my husband's superior officer. Every effort was made to secure some accommodation for us, but when absolutely nothing was available, my husband decided in despair that I should return to Calcutta while he would move to the ramshackle traveler's bungalow meant for touring officers. This did not appeal to me at all, and when our hostess, an old friend from Faridpore days, insisted that we share a portion of their roomy bungalow, we thankfully accepted her kind offer.

The extreme cold told on the baby and he suffered from many ailments. It was here I experienced the sorrow of parting forever with my faithful Khokar-jhi when it was discovered that the scar on her finger was due to leprosy. We sent her to Calcutta with an escort and I gazed after her retreating figure as long as my eyes could follow. When the dear familiar figure could be seen no more I groped my way to my bed and sobbed out my heart. . . .

It was with much relief we learnt that we were being transferred to a West Bengal station nearer home and our people.

Sometime at the end of 1916 we came to Suri, in the district of Birbhum, only a night's journey from Calcutta. We were at Suri for three years and I learnt much while I was there. It was at this place I became interested in what is now called "social work," but I do not remember hearing this phrase in those days. Saroj Nalini Dutt, the wife of the District Magistrate, called on me and a few other officials' wives and proposed that we form a *mahila samiti* [women's society]. She explained that this would be a social organization to provide an opportunity for the townswomen to come out of their homes and meet and get to know each other. This would help foster a better understanding between them and break the monotony of their secluded lives. As women in those days rarely visited each other except on formal occasions such as births, deaths, marriages, or when invited to religious ceremonies, social life was confined to these events mainly amongst one's own relations. Women of gentle birth rarely stirred out of their homes for any other purpose and, no matter how near their destination, they traveled in closed vehicles.

To propagate the idea of the *mahila samiti,* I would accompany her to call on the wives of the leading men of the town. I remember how we waited for the best part of an hour in the home of a well-known pleader, a worthy man of wealth and influence, before we could see his wife. . . . She was all smiles, kind and hospitable, and gave us a patient hearing, but said she could not commit herself in any manner without consulting her husband.

Later Mrs. Dutt met the gentleman, and although he was obviously overwhelmed by her visit—for the District Magistrate and his consort were held in awe by all the people—he flatly refused to allow his wife to be associated with this new movement. "But why?" she asked. "What objection can you have?" and hastened to add that the token subscription would be only one rupee a year. But he only shook his head and said that the addition of his wife's name to the membership list would be sufficient to damage their reputation. Mrs. Dutt was pained, but his resolution remained unshaken.

Most of the local gentlemen held the same view. They felt this new movement would be the death-knell of family life, and that it foretold nothing but discord and disruption in their homes. . . . However, the government officers and their wives, junior pleaders, and such people were flattered by the visits of the District Magistrate's wife, and they promised to cooperate in the venture. Eventually the much discussed *mahila samiti* was formed and Mrs. Dutt became its president.

The inauguration meeting was a grand affair. No men were allowed as almost all the women there were in *purdah*. The carriages hired for the occasion began to arrive in the early afternoon and the elite of the town alighted wearing their best saris and jewelled ornaments.

Mrs. Dutt gave her full attention to the guests and we, the junior officers' wives, helped her in entertaining them. The orthodox ladies, whose menfolk had stoutly opposed this newfangled movement, had nevertheless come in response to Mrs. Dutt's personal invitation to come to the function as her honoured guests. The senior orthodox ladies smilingly declined refreshments, but Mrs. Dutt had been prepared for this and had planned accordingly. She gently led them to a tent in a corner of the spacious ground. Here her husband's head clerk, an orthodox Brahmin, had arranged sliced fruits and sweets and cool sherbet all served in terra-cotta dishes. When they were convinced that the food had not been touched and thus contaminated either by Mrs. Dutt or her Muslim servants, and that the Brahmin clerk had observed all orthodox rules of cleanliness, they accepted the hospitality provided and loudly extolled the merits of their hostess in so thoughtfully providing for them. Those who were not so orthodox enjoyed other delicacies in the form of savoury snacks and sweetmeats. The function was a great success, and Mrs. Dutt rejoiced in the victory scored over the orthodox section of the town. . . .

Subsequent meetings took place in different homes with more or less the same items on the agenda. These became occasions for the display and discussion of saris and ornaments, and indulgence in feminine gossip, but gradually the membership dwindled. The cause was mostly financial. For some reason or other, the meetings happened to fall towards the end of the month when all housewives had to struggle to make both ends meet. At this crucial time the cost of hiring hackney carriages became a luxury most could ill-afford. Yet this was a necessity since the gentlewomen of Suri, like their sisters in other urban areas, never moved through the streets on foot. Then, there was the added problem of providing a very high tea when one's turn came to be hostess. Concerned because attendance was declining, the president raised funds for the *samiti,* and transport was provided for the members. But once again, personal visits had to be made to plead the cause, and only then would members consent to use the vehicle that would call for them at the appointed time.

When the *samiti* had been firmly established, Mrs. Dutt proposed that we help in the war effort by working for the Red Cross. There was no opposition, and soon large boxes of cutout garments arrived from Calcutta. These were to be sewn for the Indian troops who were engaged in the war on the Western front. We met regularly and the garments were distributed by Mrs. Dutt. If we were unable to sew ourselves we could have them made by the local *durzi* [tailor], but for this of course we would have to bear the cost. Although it was an expense many could ill-afford, this was what most did as very few possessed sewing machines. By this time the novelty of freely mixing with the District Magistrate's wife had worn off and, in spite of the free transport, membership had again dwindled. But a small faithful group continued to attend and make a contribution to the war effort. We also made countless little bundles of *nim* twigs to be used as tooth brushes by our troops. Each night a fresh twig is soaked in water and in the morning one end is chewed to a soft pulp. This makes an excellent brush for cleaning the teeth since the *nim* tree has special properties which have beneficial effects on dental hygiene. For the recreation of our men we made multicolored patchwork squares on which to play their game of *pachisi.* . . .

The Birbhum *mahila samiti* continued its good work on behalf of the Indian troops in conjunction with the Red Cross. When the King's Birthday Honours list came out in 1918, it was found that the President, Mrs. Saroj Nalini Dutt, had been made a "Member of the British Empire." A reception was held at our house, and despite the wet afternoon the members all attended. It was I who had to read the painstakingly prepared paper of congratulation even though my knees trembled terribly. . . .

Miss . . . Lees, the sister of the Divisional Commissioner, had been invited to a *samiti* meeting and in spite of the difference in our years, we had become good friends. She was sympathetic, warmhearted, and gifted with that inestimable quality of putting people at their ease. There was a party in her honour and Mrs. Dutt pressed me to make an impromptu speech. "But, what do I say?" I moaned, not far from tears. "Just a few words of welcome. . . ." And I found myself stuttering: "We—we—are all so happy to have you with us today, and—" here I looked around wildly, gulped hard, and added with a piteous look at Miss Lees, "I—I—am sure you understand all I would like to say, but—but—cannot—" and with my face on fire and heart going like a sledge hammer I sat down on my chair. Although I was quite crushed by my own performance, Miss Lees told me afterwards she understood how difficult it was to speak in public, and I loved her for her understanding heart.

I was greatly indebted to her in the following year for helping me maintain my courage during the awful ordeal of coming out of *purdah*. When women do not emerge from the seclusion of their homes they are said to be in *purdah*, which means "screened." We hardly ever appeared at public functions, and on those rare occasions when we did, there would be a special place provided where we sat behind a net curtain or split bamboo screen, able to see but not be seen.

In February 1919, there was an important function organized by the government for the education and entertainment of the people of the district. . . . On this occasion, Mr. Cumming, a high government official, came from Calcutta, and Mr. and Mrs. Guru Saday Dutt gave a garden party in his honour. The elite of the town, including government officials, were invited, but as the women were all in *purdah* Mrs. Dutt found it difficult to find any of them willing to be her guest.

She came to visit me one evening and insisted that I come to her party. "Oh no!" I gasped. "But why?" she queried. "Because there will be so many men present and I shall feel terribly shy." She reminded me of my convent education and brought forth many arguments why I should not be so bashful about appearing before men, but I remained unconvinced. . . .

But alas for my resolutions! Persuaded by my husband, I yielded, and the fateful day found me accompanying him to the garden party. To my horror I found that except for our hostess and the headmistress of the local girls' school, neither of whom had ever been in *purdah*, I was the only Bengali woman in that vast gathering. But my heart leapt with joy when I saw Miss Lees; she greeted me with a kind smile and straightaway took me under her wing. Both my host and hostess did all they could to put me at ease and, except for Mr. Cumming and two or three other European officials,

I was spared the ordeal of further introductions and shaking of hands. . . .

In April 1919, the shooting of unarmed citizens of Amritsar at Jallianwalla Bagh created a great stir. Strict censorship had at first prevented news of those outrageous events in the Punjab from leaking to other parts of India. But nevertheless, news of the atrocities spread, and a mighty wave of horror and indignation swept the country.

One morning in June I opened the *Statesman* and was thrilled to find the historic letter addressed to the Viceroy Lord Chelmsford in which Sir Rabindranath Tagore renounced his knighthood. With breathless interest I read through it again and, like countless others, saluted his valiant spirit with reverence and love.

My heart beat rapidly as I read, ". . . the least that I can do for my country is to take all consequences upon myself by giving voice to the protests of millions of my countrymen surprised into a dumb anguish of terror. The time has come when badges of honour make our shame glaring in the incongruous context of humiliation, and I for my part wish to stand shorn of all special distinctions by the side of those of my countrymen who for their so-called insignificance are liable to suffer degradation not fit for human beings."

"Robi Babu," as we call Tagore in Bengal, was dear to me before, but now this glimpse of his flaming spirit and the beauty of his noble gesture completely captivated me and I longed to set my eyes on him. The opportunity came sometime in September that year when Santosh Babu, the Rector of the Santiniketan School, invited us for the *Sharodotsab* [autumn festival].

Santiniketan was but a few hours journey by train from Suri. The song festival would commence at sundown, so dinner was served at an early hour. My husband dined with our host in a separate apartment, but as I never appeared before Santosh Babu, my food was sent to me in my room. Afterwards, when it was dark, I was escorted to the enclosure reserved for women and, from here, avidly enjoyed the feast of Tagore's melodious songs, so exquisitely rendered by the students of Santiniketan. Later I had the joy of seeing the poet himself on the stage. . . .

My husband's term at Suri was nearing its end, and we discussed at length the possibilities of being transferred to this or that station. He was due to receive charge of a subdivision, and we fervently hoped this would materialize, not only in recognition of meritorious work but also for financial reasons.

The pay and prospects of his service were not too good, and yet the Indian Civil Service was considered one of the honourable occupations open to the young men of the times. A junior officer generally had a hard time trying to make both ends meet after the usual deductions had been made by the government. From the slender remains, a monthly contribution was first sent to Murshidabad for my husband's mother and younger brother. The periodic family rituals were also faithfully maintained in the ancestral home, and after meeting all these obligations there was little left to tide us through the month.

My personal needs, however, were supplied by Mother. This seemed to her the right and proper thing to do as I came from a landowning family of some prestige. When I went on my regular visits to our Kidderpore home she would replenish my wardrobe sufficiently to see me through the year; whenever I was ill I would go there, and my medical expenses would be met. I also received a small allowance each month from Father. This eased our financial situation to a certain extent, but nevertheless we always seemed to live on the edge of our income.

My husband had a little patrimony to fall back upon, and this too helped to balance our budget somewhat. We were not particularly downhearted over monetary difficulties, nor did they tend to make us morbid, for we never forgot we were better off than many. Nor did being perennially short of funds prevent us from building castles in the air. . . .

By the end of September 1919 our financial position became rather precarious. Three months house rent was overdue, the bills for the gifts of *puja* clothing remained unpaid, and we were beginning to take a gloomy view of things. . . .

Before coming to Tamluk my husband had been congratulated on his posting, but friends had also commiserated over his having Mr. Cook as his superior officer. I had heard he was rude and ruthless and had dreaded meeting this ogre. But both he and his wife were so friendly and courteous that I was soon put at ease. I enjoyed that tea party and lost my heart to the beautiful blonde English girl who accompanied the Cooks. I was thrilled to learn she had driven ambulances full of wounded soldiers during the war. I still cherish the memory of that brief encounter in my impressionable years, when she appeared to represent all that was beautiful and best in an English girl during the First World War and the early postwar period.

My husband's predecessor was a senior officer whose wife had been elderly and worldly-wise. When the local ladies extended the usual courtesy of calling on newcomers to me, they made no attempt to conceal their surprise at what a callow creature had been installed in her place. One of them even made tactful enquiries to ascertain whether my husband was an aged widower and I his second wife. I was only twenty-two, and in those days prone to be moved to quick laughter at the slightest provocation. But I had been warned to beware of exhibiting any signs of levity and instructed to act more serious and dignified. I began to realize my husband's onerous administrative duties and tried hard not to jeopardize his position by injudicious behavior. All this weighed heavily on me.

My visitors were nearly all elderly ladies, and their conversation centered on the vagaries of the weather, shocking bazaar prices, knaveries of serving-men and maids, and the illness of children. They arrived at sundown and remained late. As I found it difficult to be always palpitating over the price of potatoes, the visits left me rather exhausted. One day when I was sighing over the dullness of my life, my husband smiled and said, "Why don't you attempt to organize a *mahila samiti* here? I am sure that will make things more lively for you."

I turned the subject over in my mind, was a trifle scared at first, and then became excited at the prospect. I had soon mustered up enough courage to talk to my visitors about this idea. To my delight, it was favourably received, particularly among the wives of the young officers.

None of us knew how to proceed or had any concrete idea of the programme of work to be undertaken, but all were unanimous in their decision that the rate of subscription should remain the same as that in Suri—one rupee. After lengthy discussions we decided to arrange social gatherings with music and subscribe to a couple of popular periodicals for circulation amongst members. With these modest aims in view and the firm intention of expanding our activities later, the Tamluk *mahila samiti* was launched on an auspicious day in April 1920; forty ladies attended the inauguration meeting at our bungalow and the function was considered a great success.

When I found myself the "President," I realized with a sinking heart how much was expected of me and how ill-equipped I was for my task. "The first thing you have to do now is to prepare a set of rules for the *samiti,*" was my husband's cheerful comment. I was rather taken aback at his words. . . . But he laid stress on a "democratic" manner of work. The word was new to me. The implications were explained, and gradually an equitable set of rules was drafted in chaste Bengali. I was also taught how to jot down proceedings of meetings and keep a minute-book. . . .

The draft rules were presented, explained, and formally passed at a subsequent meeting. With our slender resources paper was provided, and as the *samiti* had been established "to work for the welfare of the women of Tamluk," the local press generously printed the little *Book of Rules* free of cost. By this time the members had begun to feel important and realized it was incumbent on them to widen their sphere of activity—but how?

Not far from our bungalow was the small local hospital. The outdoor dispensary was always crowded, but the two little rooms attached to it were rarely occupied, for the people felt admittance to a hospital meant certain death. The last patient was a young English engineer. He had been struck down by cholera while visiting some remote village and brought here the next morning in a palanquin. He never recovered. He had come to Tamluk on tour with his newly wedded wife whom he left with the ladies at the Mission House. . . . The tragic tale haunted me, and I always averted my eyes when I passed the hospital. When my husband suggested we take an interest in it I shuddered, but was nevertheless persuaded to pay a visit.

The room meant for men patients boasted an iron cot with a hard coil mattress under a black striped cover, but the adjoining one had neither of these luxuries. It was quite bare, with only a frayed mat rolled upright in a corner. This was spread on the rare occasions when a woman patient was admitted. This I reported to the members of our *samiti,* and with much righteous indignation it was resolved to rectify the matter. But we were short of funds, so it was necessary to raise some money for a bed. . . .

I was still more or less in *purdah* and would only venture forth to nearby homes after sundown. I was accompanied by the secretary, and our *chaprasi* [office peon] followed with a hurricane lantern to light the dark and narrow streets.

While distributing my booklets and pleading my cause I had some interesting experiences. Many of the houses had either thatched or corrugated iron roofs with walls and floors of beaten earth. Each home had a veranda where guests were entertained during the hot weather. When visitors arrived in the evening, a reed mat would be spread, and a palm leaf fan offered to keep oneself cool while the joys and sorrows of life were discussed. . . .

. . . We were unable to raise the requisite amount for a new hospital bed. They were far too expensive in those days following the First World War, so we had to be content with a secondhand one advertised in the *Statesman*. This was given a coat of paint to make it look more respectable, and was duly presented in the name of the *mahila samiti*.

This gave our members a new impetus, and there were lively discussions as to how else we might further the interests of the women of Tamluk. Opinions were invited and an old lady asked, "Can we not have a 'lady doctor' for our town?" Then she went on to say how awful one felt to be compelled to call a man doctor to deliver babies during difficult cases and attend to other ailments that a woman's flesh is heir to. "Why," she quavered, "he was even called the other day to give douche—." Other members now came forward to support her, and all unanimously agreed that a medical woman was essential.

When my husband heard this he felt the local Municipality ought to help, and advised us to draw up a memorandum stating our grievances and demanding the services of a suitably qualified midwife. "Give it to me," he added, "I shall see that it is placed before the next District Board meeting." Before long Tamluk had its first "lady doctor," a worthy woman whose services were much appreciated by the public, and our *samiti* began to be looked upon with due respect. . . .

. . . At this time . . . my other son chose to come into the world, and to the consternation of all concerned, a doctor had to be called to assist in the delivery. Since this was the first time such a thing had happened in the annals of the family, there was much talk over the matter.

The services of Khirodai had been dispensed with and a hatchet-faced woman by the name of Sumoti installed. "She is a real midwife," said sister-in-law Ava, "and always in demand by the best families." Mother did not care for her much, nor did I—she was too full of gossip about the "best families."

When my time came and I was plunged into the deep waters of

pain, she sat and watched me struggle through the long drawn hours of agony. Day passed into night, and the dark night into another bright day which came to an end before she realized all was not as it should be, and then frankly confessed her skill was of no avail in a case like mine. It was decidedly "difficult," and could only be dealt with by a good doctor.

Poor Mother was at her wit's end. Never had she seen medical aid being administered by a man in these circumstances, and would it be right and proper to bring in one without the permission of my husband and his people? The subject was discussed all through the night while I lay precariously balanced between life and death and Sumoti dropped dark hints that no one should be allowed to blame her if anything happened, for she had given sufficient notice. At daybreak Mejda was allowed to fetch Dr. Biman Das Mukherjee only after Mother decided that there was no harm in him coming to advise Sumoti.

When Mejda arrived he was told that he would have to wait as the doctor was busy with his morning devotions. When he eventually came and had heard Sumoti's version of her "case," he was of the opinion that there was no time to be lost. But, so great is the power of past tradition that even then, with her love for me and her anguish at my suffering, Mother hesitated to take the decision. This annoyed Dr. Mukherjee so much that he was on the verge of departing when Father appeared on the scene. Hearing everything, he requested the doctor to do what he thought best without further delay. And Dr. Mukherjee just managed to save me.

I was unconscious when he came, and in those days perhaps doctors did not follow up their cases with postnatal care, so I never had the opportunity of seeing him. But every time my eyes fell upon my sturdy little son I felt this doctor must have been God Himself. The fame of my saviour spread and no one appeared to think of him as anything else but a doctor whose amazing skill had saved our lives. . . .

My close proximity to death stirred me to the depths. True, death is inseparable from life, yet as far as I was concerned it had been but a word connected with the far-off nebulous future. My lengthy convalescence gave me a legitimate opportunity to muse over my experience, and I came to the conclusion I had learnt all there was to know of life. . . .

We were nearing the end of our three years in Tamluk and expected to be transferred at any time. In the meantime the heavy monsoons had made another breach in the embankment and there was a minor flood that kept my husband busy. There was considerable excitement in the country about the boycott of foreign goods and particularly foreign clothes. We heard of bonfires made of bales of Manchester cloth at public meetings. Some applauded these acts and others criticized them, saying it was a sinful waste when so many in our poverty-stricken country went unclad. Congress volunteers toured the villages and urged the people to eschew foreign goods and buy only those that were produced in their own country. The demand of *swaraj* was explained and the people were encouraged to revive the cult of the spinning wheel.

When Gandhiji first launched his *charka* [spinning wheel] campaign, a large section of the people lamented his attempt to turn back the wheels of progress. But it became the rage nevertheless. "Have you a *charka*?" was what everyone asked each other. Nearly all tried their hand at it and the majority grew bored. "The threads break, I cannot manage the thing!" some confessed, "but my little son can"—"my daughter can." Most of the elders abandoned it, but the younger generation took it up in earnest.

The coarse material woven from the hand-spun yarn was called *khadi*, which became the symbol for the national cause. When Gandhiji first preached the virtues of *khadi*, it became the popular craze. For a dress reform movement it was remarkable. Even effeminate fops flung aside their loose flowered organza shirts and proudly disported their *khadi*. With these clothes also went their fine *dhotis* and pointed *lapaita* [slippers]. For a rough homespun shirt demands a nether garment of like texture, and as exquisite footwear failed to fit in with such an outfit, simple sandals became the fashion. . . .

At about this time, Romu returned from school one afternoon greatly excited. In those times he was always bringing home something new for my benefit. That day he burst in with, "Ma, what does 'Bande Mataram' mean? Everyone seems to be shouting this now. And who is 'Gandhi'? And is it true that he is a saint? I was told the government had ordered him to be hanged and the rope had split. The police tried to pierce him through with a sharp spear, Ma, and it broke! And oh, I am ever so hungry—what is there to eat?"

He had delivered all this in one breath and nearly knocked me over with his usual boisterous embrace. I remember the incident well. The influence of Mahatma Gandhi was filtering into remote villages and wild rumours were current. Many were the tales afloat about the man whose name would later become a household word in India.

I heard of many political meetings and processions, and my husband's official work increased considerably. He found it difficult to keep his confidential reports from being circulated around the town by his gossip-loving clerk. A small Corona typewriter was purchased on the installment system like my Singer sewing machine, and I taught myself to type with two fingers. Before long I was helping him with his correspondence and came to know much about the nature of his work and the trend of the times.

My days passed placidly enough till the end of the rains brought a slow fever to my small son. It persisted in spite of treatment, so we took him to Ranchi hoping he might benefit by the change of climate. . . .

. . . I was detained at Kidderpore for a long time. First, it was Romu who needed expert medical treatment to recover from the after-effects of typhoid; then I was ill for several weeks. . . .

Romu recovered. Returning to Tamluk in June 1923, I gratefully offered my thanksgiving prayers and alms at the ancient shrine of Bhima Devi by the river. It was a halcyon month. Hoping to remain another year at Tamluk, all our savings were invested in a motorcycle to facilitate my husband's tours. This caused great excitement in the countryside, and the youngest generation would run after it with shrill cries while their elders would rush out to watch it ploughing through the dusty streets.

But soon after its arrival we were plunged into gloom at the news of my husband's transfer to Chittagong. Not only did this mean moving to a remote town in East Bengal, but also the lack of a rent-free bungalow such as we were then enjoying. The government accepted no responsibility for officers posted to headquarters, so we would have to find our own accommodations. It was difficult to find a suitable house within one's purse range, and in the meantime the officer had to live in one of the dingy rooms of the dismal Inspection Bungalow. . . .

. . . Our immediate problems were happily solved by a cousin of mine who happened to be posted in Chittagong. He had a spacious bungalow and a generous heart and invited us to stay with him till we could find a home of our own.

The people of Tamluk tried hard to detain my husband. He had endeared himself to them by his service during the devastating floods. But their efforts were of no avail as his allotted term had already been extended by many months. The members of the *mahila samiti* gave me a tearful farewell, and I found it hard to part with these kind friends whose warm affection had enriched my life.

In September we reached our new station after a wearisome journey by train and steamer in most inclement weather. I was entranced by the scenery of wooded hills and undulating roads. My cousin's beautiful bungalow with its well-kept garden sprawled over a low hill. We lived here for three weeks in comfort, and came to know the niceties that had to be observed by him and a few others of our country who belonged to the select group of "covenanted officers."

Their movement, speech, habits, and mode of living were under surveillance, and the slightest deviation from approved standards spelt disaster. From what I gathered, the unwritten law was: never be seen except in European clothes, always speak English, and adopt the British mode of living and thinking. This of course meant that wives could never observe *purdah*.

Despite the handsome emoluments, I could see my cousin chafe under the conditions of his service and harbour bitter hatred for his superior officers, all recruited from the ruling race. Having lived for long years in their country, he was of the opinion that the Britisher at home was of a different breed altogether. He was a dour person, my cousin, endowed with a scathing tongue and a pungent sense of humour. Many were the arguments he had with my husband while I sat astounded to hear his view of things.

He regaled us with brief sketches of officers and their families. . . .

. . . He began to deride them mercilessly and went on to say that most of them were artificial and insincere. "They are divided into three groups," he continued, exhaling a column of smoke from one of his endless cigarettes. "The *bagha,* the *chaga,* and the *chuno.* " I gasped. Gravely he explained that he had made a scientific study of the species and the first were the "tigers." "Blessed with the knowledge of all that is British and best, by virtue of their trip to *Bilat* [England]," they were foremost in bank balance and brains. The next were the "goats," who were not so affluent or influential, but bleating acquiescence, they meekly tried to follow their leaders. Lastly came the "small fry." Numerically they were stronger, but of humble means and station; they valiantly determined to swim in the wake of their superiors. . . .

My husband too was worried, but on a different account. Every day after office he would set out to search for a suitable house and return late, enveloped in gloom. As time passed, it became evident that the kind of accommodation we had in mind might not be available. . . .

But I was to learn later that in Chittagong there were men and women who were thinking along different lines. To liberate the Motherland from foreign rule, drastic measures were being decided upon. Their aim was to further the national cause, not as Congress planned, but according to daring plans of their own. Oblivious of self, they had dedicated their lives to this ideal and joined secret societies to plot revolution.

One evening after I had been teaching our cook a new recipe, we sat down late to the evening meal. The children were fast asleep. The stillness of the night was broken by the clamorous cries of countless cicadas and the wail of a jackal from beyond the hills. The kerosene lamp burnt low. I raised the wick and was proudly serving the dish so painstakingly prepared when heavy footsteps on the veranda made our spaniel "Gypsy" bark in excitement.

The servant came to say a police officer wanted to see my husband. He was often called out at odd hours, and fearing he would be late I implored, "Oh let him wait, you must finish your dinner—" but he shook his head and left murmuring, "It might be something very urgent." When he came back he said he must go out to attend to important work and might be late in returning. The look on his face froze the questions that rose to my lips, and he immediately set out on his mission.

The untouched food was put away and the servants left. Alone in the solitary bungalow I counted the slowly passing hours. . . . It was long past midnight when he returned. I wanted to warm his dinner but he said he had no inclination for food, and hearing the nature of the work he had been summoned for, I did not wonder.

He had gone to record the declaration of a dying police officer. This officer had received a note from a friend who asked to meet him that evening in a secluded part of the Parade Ground. The friend insisted he had something important to communicate. After they had chatted for a few minutes, the friend pulled out a revolver and shot him in the chest because the officer had recently discovered his friend's connection with the revolutionary party of Chittagong. The officer was young and newly married; he died that night.

I had been aware of political activities—*swadeshi* disturbances as they were called at that time—of people being arrested and jailed because they had gone against the British government, but this was the first time I had been brought close to violence and bloodshed in the cause of our country's freedom. I began to ask questions, and from the replies and books and papers that came my way, I realised the tremendous implications of the times we lived in. Long before I had learned of the death of Khudiram, forces had been at work to awaken India to the fact that she must win her freedom from foreign rule. Many influences had helped to form public opinion to this end and to mold the minds of our young men and women revolutionaries.

Sarat Chandra Chatterjee, the Bengali novelist, vividly portrayed the privations, great sufferings, determination, and self-sacrifice of these bold revolutionaries in his novel *Pather Dabi* [The Path's Demand]. Regardless of the price, these young people could justify any means where the liberation of the Motherland was concerned. It was a most human document, written with great courage and understanding, which gained instant popularity and was promptly banned.

When the case came up, every effort was made by the defence to prove that the dying declaration was a concocted document. When my husband was called to give evidence, he maintained that he had recorded exactly what the dying man had said. The counsel for the defence was a brilliant barrister who could terrify occupants of the witness box by lashing out with unexpected questions, and twisting and turning the answers until he confused them and they blurted out things afterwards to be regretted. This barrister was J. M. Sen Gupta, the nationalist leader of Chittagong, who was later called *desha-priya* [dear to the country].

It was at this time that a postcard arrived with the warning, "Mazumdar, be careful, don't overdo things," scrawled in Bengali. Immediately, two plainclothes policemen were posted at our bungalow, but somehow I did not feel we were in any danger. From what was known of these terrorists, barring the British victims, they attacked only under grave provocation. My husband had only carried out the routine work of the administration without fear or favour and was well known for his integrity. I knew their bullets were reserved for other types of men and he would remain unharmed.

The rest of our Chittagong days passed smoothly enough. My leisure was enlivened by writing a short story, and when it appeared in print, I ambitiously began a novel. I had tried to be clever in this story, sketching the follies of a corpulent superintendent of police who had risen from the ranks. Possessing goodwill but no knowledge of Bengali or of the Indian Penal Code, this middle-aged Englishman floundered in situations that were thought to be amusing. . . .

I never succeeded in being at my ease with the people amongst whom we had to move in Chittagong. One of the things that struck me as queer was the habit of talking always in English. It appeared to be the hallmark of excellence to be able to do so and when Bengali was spoken, it was spoken with a foreign accent! Parents spoke to their little children either in English or Hindi.

"I can understand the reason for English," I told my cousin, who never failed to be amused at my reactions, "but why Hindi?" He shrugged his shoulders. "I warned you about the oddities," was the reply, then as afterthought he added, "Perhaps they do it to show that their children are looked after by *ayahs*." "But," I stammered, "what has that to do with it?" "Everything. Have you an *ayah*?" he asked abruptly. I recalled our simple Mokkada from her little village in the backwaters of Bengal. Always bashful, Mokkada kept her veil lowered before "menfolk." I shook my head. "No, we have Mokkada and you know full well we don't call the Bengali maid servant an *ayah* but refer to her as *jhi* [a daughter]." "There you are!" he cried in triumph. "The majority of us employ the humble *jhi* in Bengal, but the *ayah* comes mostly from the distant north or south, and the southern ones generally speak English, for even the street beggars there beg in that language. . . ."

In the autumn of 1926 we moved to Manikgunge, in the district of Dacca. My husband's feeble objection to another East Bengal posting had been overruled by the young Under Secretary who had just arrived from England. "Why," he had said with an amiable smile, "Manikgunge is not far from Calcutta. Let me see (consulting a map), it is only . . . miles as the crow flies. . . ." He quoted a reasonable number of miles, and was convinced that he was quite fair in posting my husband there after distant Chittagong.

The mileage quoted might have been correct "as the crow flies," but by train, steamer, country boat, and palanquin, it took us two days to arrive at our destination. This being an outlying subdivision, the officer in charge had a bungalow to live in, and, unfurnished though it was, we were thankful for this amenity provided by the government. . . .

We were warmly welcomed upon landing. My husband remained with the men while I followed some small girls up a narrow flight of stairs to a spacious hall lighted for the occasion with rented gas lights. There was a large gathering of women and children of all ages sitting on the gaily woven cotton carpet, and I was made to sit on a high backed chair draped with gold-embroidered crimson velvet and garlanded with fragrant flowers. A welcome song was sung by a group of pretty young girls, and then the widowed mother of our host stood up to read her address. It was remarkably well written and delivered with dignity and ease. Speaking on behalf of those assembled, the speaker emphasized the importance of women's education in this part of the world. They had learnt with pride and joy of the attainments of their foreign and Indian sisters and regretted their own educational inadequacies. They wanted education to make themselves real helpmates of their husbands, to help them rear strong and healthy children, and to give widows and other poor women a way of earning their own livelihood. She concluded with the oft-quoted lines, "Until the women of Bharata [India] awaken, Bharata will never awake!"

Then a very old lady rose, adjusted her sari, peered through her steel framed spectacles, and in a quavering voice welcomed me to their village. This once prosperous town was now sadly stricken by poverty and disease. Notable men had been born here, she said, naming a few well-known public figures, but alas, they had forgotten their humble birthplace. If these men would take a little interest in their village, it would flourish. "Our needs are many," she continued. "But the first thing we want is education. We must have knowledge, for only this can give us the power to break our fetters of ignorance and superstition, and then the women of India will be able to regain the honoured position that was theirs in the golden days of the Vedic age." . . .

As I had not been well for some time I returned to Kidderpore in August 1928 and soon after underwent a major operation at the Cavel Nursing Home. I remained with my parents to recuperate while Romu, who had to continue his studies in Manikgunge, returned with his father. His small brother, fighting to keep back his tears, wailed, "To whom will I now tell things?" His elder brother was a merciless tease, but life lost its flavour when "Dada" was not available. He fretted, and so did I. My convalescence was long, and as the tedious days dragged by I began to write to pass the time. My effort, entitled "Choosing a Bride in Bengal," and written from my own experience, was later published in *Asia*, a New York magazine.

December found me still in Calcutta. I went to a *purdah* party given by the National Indian Association for Lady Irwin, the Viceroy's wife, and here I met an English woman with whom an enduring friendship developed. During the same month I also attended a function whose purpose was directly opposite to this one. Seeing my interest in the political life of the country, Dada had allowed me to accompany him to one of the Congress sessions, for in that year the All-India Congress Committee was meeting in Calcutta. At the entrance, Bengali youths on horseback kept the crowd in order. They were in smart uniforms and had gold braid on their shoulders. "Subhas Bose's volunteers," Dada said with an approving smile. Inside the tent, I noticed a slim restless young man with serious eyes and asked who he was. "Motilal Nehru's son Jawaharlal Nehru," Dada replied.

People talked much about the important event of the year: the Bardoli rent affair. As the crops had been unsatisfactory, the impoverished peasants were not in a position to pay the enhanced revenue. They had pleaded with the government to appoint an impartial committee to investigate their condition. When these efforts had been exhausted they accepted Gandhiji's advice and began a nonviolent "No Tax" campaign to obtain redress. The government's attempt to crush the movement failed, and eventually the peasants won their point. It was decided that there should be practically no enhancement of land revenue, and the confiscated lands were restored to the people.

In January 1929 I returned to Manikgunge. . . .

In this isolated place where very little of consequence occurred, I was given ample leisure for reading and reflection. What was happening in the brave new world since the thrilling campaign of Noncooperation launched by Gandhiji interested me enormously. Since I was present when the fateful resolution was passed, the fortunes of those who participated in the fight seemed to become a personal concern. What Gandhiji said and did was endlessly discussed. Some said he was a saint, and others shook their head solemnly and thought him to be insane.

When our allotted term at Manikgunge had ended, but before settling down in our new station, we applied for leave and hopefully planned a trip to North India. . . .

As the day for leaving Manikgunge drew near we realized how fond we had grown of the people and the place. Since gentlewomen did not appear here in public, my husband attended his farewell parties alone and a special one was given for me by the members of the *mahila samiti*. . . .

We started very early next morning, first using a country boat so that we could catch the steamer across the mighty Padma river and then the train for Calcutta. On our way the boat got bogged down in mud, for this was October and the waters were receding. We got out and walked slowly through knee-deep slush, using long staffs to prod each place before we took the next step. The hardy boatmen managed somehow to get our luggage across, and when we finally put our feet on firm ground, it was only to be told we must run for the steamer station. Panting, we reached the steamer just as she started. But alas, for some reason or other she failed to keep to schedule, for we found the Calcutta train had left without us.

With the monument of luggage that always manages to accumulate during transfers, and the uncertainty of obtaining accommodation on the next train, tempers were frayed. When the next train had arrived and we were about to enter a compartment at the extreme end of the ill-lighted platform, a blind beggar appeared calling for alms. My husband harshly told him to move aside and pushed in the last piece of luggage as we scrambled into the moving train. My mind, already depressed, became more so as I watched the sightless man left standing on the platform with outstretched palm.

I shall always remember that ghastly journey. The next morning our younger son, then eight years old, had his eyeball gashed open in the running train. It was drizzling and the window by which he was sitting to watch the fleeting landscape had its glass pane partially lowered. Thoughtlessly our young servant had flung a broken china plate through this and it was thus that the grievous injury was inflicted.

No medical aid could be given. The train rushed along; we were still a long way from Calcutta. Unashamedly, I wept and prayed aloud as I sat with his head on my lap. "Never mind, Ma," he consoled me, "Lord Nelson had only one eye." Then, after a while, he added, "Do you know why this happened, Ma? I think it's because we never gave the blind beggar any alms." When we at last reached the noisy, grimy Sealdah station there was no one to meet us; the car and clerk from Kidderpore had left when we had not arrived on the previous train.

We took Donny to Dr. S. K. Mukherjee on Kydd Street, the only optician I knew, and we never regretted it. For long weeks before the bandage was removed, it was uncertain whether the wound had responded to treatment. When at last it was found that sight had been restored, I tried to stammer my thanks. But the doctor said, "Your gratitude should go to God, it is He who has cured your son. I was not very hopeful when he first came to me. But, he must always be very careful. Out of two horses, one is lame and must be considered accordingly."

Pandit Nehru, presiding over the 44th session of the Congress, declared in an address that the time had come for India to march forward to win independence. Those who would come forward to free the country from foreign rule would be recompensed with suffering, imprisonment, and death, he warned. Following this the decision was taken that the 26th of January would be observed as Independence Day. On this day the Congress flag would be flown each year and the pledge of independence taken.

I do not recollect any great enthusiasm about this amongst the people I happened to meet. Those with vested interests flouted the idea and said the Congress was crazy. Grey heads were shaken in disapproval; it was felt to be a fantastic idea. Only the youthful hearts danced at this daring aim, and those who lacked the courage to openly espouse the cause did so in secret.

I was in Kidderpore in January of that year of 1930. We were gathered round the tea table that morning when loud voices in the street drew us to the veranda. It overlooked the large expanse of the "lotus pond" where at one time, so the legend runs, the flowers really blossomed. A long pole had been planted beside its placid waters, and many people were assembled to witness the raising of the flag at the appointed hour.

A young man in white homespun seemed to be in charge of the function. Two motor lorries containing red turbaned constables appeared on the scene. We could not hear what the European sergeant said, but the young man was seen to shake his head firmly in the negative. The police force waited, and so did the silent crowd. The clock struck eight. The *khadi*-clad youth moved to hoist the Congress flag and the sergeant quietly intervened. Conforming to nonviolence, the youth did not resist, and we saw him calmly follow the sergeant to the lorry.

"Bande Mataram!" cried the crowd in one voice, and this was repeated again and again till he was out of sight. Another sergeant came to the pole, pulled it up, flung it into the "lotus pond," and carried away the flag. The people watched in silence. We were about to leave when a sudden ripple of amusement made us turn to see a tiny paper flag fluttering gaily in the morning breeze. The sergeant walked back in silence, plucked the flag, and thrust it into his pocket. The crowd tittered and began to disperse; a little urchin came capering along the road and shrieked to another who had just arrived: "Hah! You did not see the fun, they took away Gandhi!"

Anyone who came in conflict with the police over the Congress ideals was labelled "Gandhi" by the common people; in fact, the Civil Disobedience Movement itself was given this name. Sometime later at Basirhat, hearing distant cries of "Bande Mataram," defiant yells, and voices raised in anger, I asked our little sweeper girl what was happening down the road. All she said was, "Only Gandhi," as she calmly continued to eat her guava with relish.

When the Viceroy made it clear that independence for India was out of the question, the Congress Working Committee authorized Mahatma Gandhi to start Civil Disobedience. But, before this was done, a moving letter was sent to Lord Irwin in which Gandhi explained how he desired to convert the British people by nonviolence. "It is my purpose to set in motion the force of nonviolence against the organized force of British Rule. This will be expressed through civil disobedience. . . ." The Viceroy's answer was unsatisfactory and Gandhiji wrote, "On bended knees I asked for bread and received a stone instead. The English nation responds only to force, and I am not surprised by the Viceregal reply. India is a vast prison house, and I regard it as my sacred duty to break the monotony of peace that is choking the heart of the nation for want of free vent. . . ."

Amongst the points that had been presented to the Viceroy were total prohibition, protective tariff on foreign cloth, and the abolition of the salt tax. It was felt that salt, like air and water, was the property of the people. On the 12th of March, accompanied by his seventy-nine followers—and my heart pounded to find Sarojini Naidu was in this movement—Gandhiji began his historic march to take the salt depot at Darsana. He reached his destination on the 5th of April.

People pored over the daily papers and discussed the outcome of all this with mounting excitement; it was now realized that non-violence was not a form of negation but a definite scheme of resistance. Civil disobedience came to be termed *satyagraha* [truth crusade]: to be prepared to endure imprisonment, sufferings, and penalties for the cause, to never ask for any monetary help, and to implicitly obey the leaders of the campaign. A large number of people became aware of the spirit of Gandhi's teachings, and were stirred to the depths. They cast aside worldly considerations and joined his crusade with faith and fervour.

"He has been arrested and taken to Yervada Jail," Chorda announced mournfully one morning. Then we came to know of the message he had left—that neither the people nor his colleagues should be daunted. He was not the conductor of the fight; that was God who dwelt in the hearts of all. Only faith was necessary; then God would lead them. Entire villages were to picket or manufacture salt, women were to picket liquor, opium, and foreign cloth shops, and young and old of every home were to daily ply the spinning wheel, twirl the *takli* [spindle] to produce plenty of yarn, and create bonfires made of foreign cloth.

We were at Basirhat when the country was passing through this important phase. . . .

In April of that year I was in Kidderpore for a few days. . . . It was some weeks later that we came to know of the Chittagong affair. While Gandhiji and his followers were engaged in a nonviolent struggle to free the country from foreign rule, a group of young people had pledged to use violence to win independence.

In the town of Chittagong a band of young revolutionaries had organized an armed insurrection. Led by Surya Sen, they had sworn death to the enemy or to die in this effort. They planned to seize the armoury, attack the British Auxiliary Force and Police Lines, raid the European club, destroy the telephone and telegram communications, remove railway lines, and cut Chittagong off from the outer world altogether. Long preparation had been made for this bold scheme, and they did succeed in an amazing manner. But the victory was brief; many were killed, some were captured, and the rest went underground.

They had known full well when they undertook this perilous adventure that they might be defeated, but it had been hoped that their daring attempt would embolden revolutionaries in other parts of the country. They were but sixty-four who figured in this saga, some of them barely in their teens, including a dauntless girl who swiftly swallowed poison, preferring death to captivity. Their self-sacrifice, flaming spirit, and indomitable courage left a lasting impression on the people.

Amongst them was a lad who often came to play with Romu at our hilltop bungalow in Chittagong. I remembered Ananda Gupta well. High-spirited and handsome, he was very lovable, and I nearly wept aloud when I learnt he had been sentenced to "life imprisonment"—that is, twenty years. His younger brother was killed in the undertaking.

At that time, the true account of the "Chittagong Raid," as it was called, was not known. News being censored, no one had any idea as to what was happening in that remote town after the revolutionaries had been vanquished. Very little news was allowed to filter out, and it was not until a student, returning to his college from his home town, told of the reign of terror and the reprisals dealt by the ruthless military police force. Hearing the grim tale, one of his professors, an Englishman of integrity, was so moved that he wrote an open letter to a leading newspaper. The harrowing details were given, but the professor soon lost his job and was shipped back home. It was not known whether he ceased to be a missionary, but he became the idol of the students. . . .

. . . It is only in Bengal that with Durga, the symbol of invincible power, is seen lovely Lakshmi, the power of wealth, protected by the power of arms in the form of the elegant Kartick, the god of war. On her left stands the shimmering form of Saraswati, the power of culture, guided by Ganesha, the spirit of wisdom, and Demos, the lord of the common people. At the feet of this scintillating group full of beauty and grace lies brute force, ugly and evil, vanquished by the glorious goddess. Thousands stand before her with folded hands to cry "Bande Mataram!"—"I bow to Thee, Mother!"

She was the patriot's vision of an India victorious and free, with her wealth and culture restored; she was the pride of her people, released from the bondage at last. To others, she symbolized the yearnings of the spirit towards values that crowned life with fulfillment and bliss—the ultimate aim of human existence.

Durga *puja* in Bengal is celebrated with elaborate ceremony when the heavy rains and gusty winds have subsided and autumn has come. The days of mud and slush are gone, the earth is clothed in tender and bright flowers. The wild tawny rivers are tamed and flow calmly in their course now, reflecting the azure heavens. The sun shines from cloudless skies when the monsoons have passed; the days are golden, the bright moon and starlit nights stir the spirit, and people are heard to say with a reminiscent smile, "Why, already there is a scent of *puja* in the air!"

The wealthy, the needy, the worldly, the spiritually inclined, the happy-hearted, and the miserable, all look forward to this national festival. Though moved by different sentiments, the same shining thread will be found to enrich the texture of their lives and thoughts. It is a joyous occasion that helps to spread goodwill and maintain social obligations. It is a time of blissful reunions—children who had left home to seek their fortunes in distant places join their families during the *puja* vacation. It is a season for exchange of gifts, and the weavers who had stored best *dhotis* and saris raise their prices to make a little extra profit, since the traditional presents are clothing. The poor hope to obtain a new garment and perhaps a proper meal, for almsgiving is a special feature of the festival and the rich are reminded of their obligations. The elders make gifts of garments as a token of their blessing and, attired in these, the younger generations make their obeisance before the Mother and pray for her benediction. It is only here in Bengal that the spirit of the primordial energy is invoked in sculptured clay. Special craftsmen mold, tint, and adorn the image, accurately following the word pictures given by the *rishis* [sages] in our scriptures.

The Durga *puja* would be at its best in the village where the festival is celebrated with pomp and circumstance by the local *zamindar*. His tenants, both Hindu and Moslem, receive new clothes when they come to their landlord's mansion to join the many activities connected with the ritual worship of the Mother. They feast here for the four festive days, and special attention is given to the poor, for it is said that Daridra Narayana, the Lord Himself in the form of the poor, has come to partake of gifts and hospitality from the home that is blessed with the Mother's presence.

As we reached Saidpore [the home of Mazumdar's maternal family], the tinkle of bells and sound of conch shells proclaimed that the ritual worship of Mother Durga had already commenced. The old house wore a festive look, the courtyard was teeming with people, and noisy children were romping about. A group had gathered round the drummers, demanding that drums should be beaten right now rather than later at *arati,* when the drum and gong usually go together.

There seemed to be a current of joy in the air when my uncles and aunts and cousins came forward to greet us. We went together to the temple, for it was nearly time for the *pushpanjali,* the flower offering ceremony, in which everyone participated.

We stood silently with hands folded before the great sculptured group including Mother Durga and her divine children. The snarling lion at her feet had his teeth on the bleeding monster, Mahisasura, around whose neck was coiled a serpent with outspread hood. This was of particular interest to the younger people, but we only had eyes for the serene face of the Mother. A mysterious smile played on her lips and her eyes were tender. Lights and incense and rich offerings of many kinds, including masses of flowers, were placed before her. There were bunches of bananas, large and luscious fruits, and rough clay plates piled high with sugar cakes and other sweets from village folk who had placed their humble gifts before the Mother in thanksgiving.

Vijaya Lakshmi Pandit

(1900–   )

Vijaya Lakshmi Pandit is the elder daughter of Motilal and Sarup Nehru, heirs of a Kashmiri Brahman family destined to shape the fortunes of India in the twentieth century. Sister to the architect of independence, Jawaharlal Nehru, and aunt to one of India's most commanding political leaders, Indira Gandhi, Vijaya Lakshmi Pandit often assumed leadership of the Nehru clan when her brother and her husband were serving jail sentences for opposition to British rule.

Widowed early in life by the death of her husband, Ranjit Pandit, from inadequate medical care during detention, Vijaya Pandit became her brother's close political ally and confidante. Jailed three times for her own political activities, Pandit willingly gave up the family's princely style of life for the cause of independence, watching the confiscation and auction of treasured possessions with aristocratic detachment.

Pandit served as a member of the Allahabad Municipal Board in 1934 and, during one period of cooperation with the British authorities, as a member of the Uttar Pradesh Legislature and as a minister. In this role she showed deep concern for village communities, often visiting plague-infested areas to see conditions firsthand. For two crucial years in the independence struggle, she was president of the All India Women's Congress, playing a key role in mobilizing women for the national struggle.

After independence, Nehru appointed Pandit ambassador to the two countries most critical to India's future as a neutral state, the Soviet Union from 1946 to 1947 and the United States from 1949 to 1952, and leader of the Indian delegation to the newly formed United Nations from 1946 to 1951. Pandit was successful in her roles in the United States and at the United Nations, where she capped her career by service as president of the General Assembly from 1964 to 1968. She was less effective in the Soviet Union, where her Western ways and British manners aroused suspicion. Pandit concluded her diplomatic career as Indian high commissioner to the United Kingdom, a role in which she excelled and won great popularity.

Shortly after her retirement from diplomacy, Pandit reentered

Indian politics as a staunch opponent of her niece, Indira Gandhi, during the latter's suspension of the national legislative body and introduction of semimilitary rule. Pandit was a rallying point for the opponents of the emergency and keeper of her brother's tradition of belief in democratic institutions, a role which earned her the popular name Lamp of India.

Her narrative spans the transformation of India from her traditional childhood in a Brahman household—where the husband and father dined separately from the rest of the family in a room patterned on English models and served by a British-trained chef, while the wife and children ate Indian food and followed traditional Hindu religious observances—to the independent democratic state of the 1960s and '70s. Central to every page is the writer's concern with politics, and her ingrained acceptance of power exercised without ambiguity.

THE SCOPE OF HAPPINESS:
A Personal Memoir

The Nehrus are Saraswat Brahmans[1] and came originally from the Kashmir valley. . . .

My father's father, Pandit Gangadhar Nehru, had settled in Delhi and occupied the position of chief of police at the court of Bahadur Shah, the last Moghul Emperor of Delhi. He died at a young age.

My grandmother, Indrani, known as "Jiyomaji," was a remarkable woman. At a time when life for a Hindu widow was full of every conceivable hardship, she reared a family according to the traditional pattern and was respected and admired in the Kashmiri community. . . .

Of Father's two brothers the eldest, Pandit Nandlal Nehru, was an advocate. My father, Motilal Nehru, was brought up by him, showered with affection and spoiled badly.

Father's education was haphazard and his academic career was

---

1. Brahmans are the first of the four castes that form the social groupings of Hindu society, a system evolved more than two thousand years ago. The divisions of Hindu society are Brahman (priest or learned man), Kshatriya (ruler or warrior), Vaishya (peasant), and Shudra (laborer or serf). Saraswat is one of the classifications of Brahmans.

undistinguished. Beginning at a *madarsa* [Indian language school], in the manner of the times, he went on to a mission school and later Allahabad University, which he left without taking his bachelor's degree. . . . His mother tongue was Urdu, and Persian was his second language. He was proficient in both. It was only after he started practicing law that he began to take life seriously, partly because he became the head of a large joint family at an early age and also because he loved his profession, worked hard, and achieved success rapidly. His law practice was the source of the Nehru family wealth. . . .

We were all one family living together in the manner of those days. The joint family has ceased to exist, but it had its uses since it was a form of social security and insurance and no one was abandoned. . . .

The family house belonged to everybody, and relatives could come at any time and stay as long as they wished. It was their unquestioned right to do so. A *tonga* [horse-drawn vehicle], piled high with luggage, would drive up to the porch and a number of relatives would settle down in whichever room happened to be vacant. . . .

My father's pride in his family was tremendous, a feeling he passed on to each of us. The Nehrus, he seemed to convey without actually saying so, were better than other people, they did certain things but others were just not done. . . .

Father's great satisfaction lay in the fact that he kept the family united. It was not easy because there were powerful forces that could have separated us. During the freedom movement, for instance, there were Nehrus with Gandhi and Nehrus in the government that Gandhi opposed. In spite of this the family tie remained strong and Anand Bhawan's[2] welcoming doors remained open to every Nehru. . . .

A characteristic of the Nehrus was their quick but short-lived temper. In my own case I like to think this may be partly due to the code word "Tempest" by which my arrival in the world was cabled to my father. . . .

Father was a rebel and an iconoclast from his earliest years. His great delight was to attack blindly accepted patterns. At a time when social life was circumscribed and lived according to a confining set of rules, our family, because of Father's courage, was able to

---

2. The name of our family home.

break many artificial barriers erected by caste and community. . . . He put into his fight against reaction and prejudice all the drive he later put into the freedom struggle. There were no half measures with him. . . .

. . . When he sent his only son to Harrow there was a great deal of hostile comment, but when I was allowed the same freedom as if I were a boy, many heads were shaken in sorrow and in anger. I remember one incident when I had just returned from a ride and went into Father's study to greet him. . . . Father had just won a lawsuit for [a client] that was a *cause célèbre* in the province, and the old gentleman looked upon Father as a personal friend as well as a legal adviser. He was very old-fashioned and did not believe in freedom for women. I was the subject of the conversation and he was asking what Father envisioned my future to be. "Is it necessary," he asked, "to let an Indian girl behave in the uncouth manner of the English? Why is she being educated according to foreign standards and being given so much freedom? Do you intend to make her into a lawyer like yourself?" . . .

Twenty-seven years later, when I was a Minister in the Congress government of Uttar Pradesh, I often wished I had studied law. The old gentleman's son sat facing me on the Opposition benches of the State Legislature. He seemed no more reconciled to my position than his father had been to my upbringing, but India was moving forward. . . .

My mother came from a conservative Kashmiri Brahman family settled in the Punjab. She was fourteen when she was married and there had been no Western influence in her upbringing. She was like a little ivory figurine, with big almond-shaped hazel eyes and bright chestnut hair falling in thick waves below her waist. Her actions and behavior were quiet and restrained in the manner of the well-bred Indian woman, and, in spite of many limiting factors, she was never out of place in any society. . . .

. . . In a carnivorous Kashmiri household she was a strict vegetarian, in surroundings where religion was scoffed at she continued, with quiet dignity, her prayers and her religious fasts and all the paraphernalia of Hindu worship. She fed Brahmans and bathed in the Ganga on appropriate occasions, and sometimes she went on pilgrimage to the holy places, Varanasi or Dwarka or Rameshwaram. . . .

No two people could have been more unlike each other than my parents. The only things they shared in common were their children and even in this my mother did not get her fair share, for I was my father's child in all respects. He was the dominating influence in my life. I loved him deeply and he was my ideal of all that was great and good and honorable. . . .

Our home, Anand Bhawan, was situated in the Western section of the town. . . . Anand Bhawan stood in the midst of a spacious garden, which was Father's special joy. It had tennis courts, a riding ring for the children, an orchard, and an indoor swimming pool. . . .

Our home too was divided into Indian and Western sections. The reception and dining rooms and Father's offices were in the front of the house overlooking the garden. It was here that Western-style parties were held. Indian social life went on in another part of the house, which was run in the traditional manner with a Brahman cook and Hindu servants. Although this was Mother's domain it was her elder sister who really attended to all the details. She had been widowed in her teens and, as remarriage was forbidden, such women could only fulfill themselves through service to others. . . .

The Western side of our house was looked after by Miss Smith, the Anglo-Indian housekeeper, and the Christian, Muslim, or "untouchable" servants. . . .

When I think of the way we lived I am amazed at our utter disregard to time and consideration for others. There seemed to be no coordination about meals or anything else and ours was merely a reflection of the well-to-do Indian home. Except for Father, whose meals were regular, adjusted to his working hours, and eaten in the Western dining room, the other members of the large family ate wherever and whenever it suited them. . . .

I have been writing as if I were an only child and in a sense this was true, because the difference in age between my brother, my sister, and myself was so great that we were all brought up separately. My brother was eleven years older and my sister, Krishna, seven years younger than I. He was fourteen when he left for Harrow and at the time of his one brief visit home I was still a very small girl— there could be no question of companionship between us. To my baby sister I was a little mother from the beginning and more and more so as we grew up, for her adolescence came at a time when the foundations of our well-ordered life were being shaken. . . .

In India anyone older than oneself is never called by name but is referred to by the relationship, and, as we have different names for maternal and paternal relatives, it is easy to know who is being spoken of. As our brother was older than my sister and I we called him Bhai. . . .

A brother occupies a very special position in India. He is the guardian and protector of his sister, whose attitude to him borders on adoration. Brother's day—*Bhaiya Duj*—which follows the festival of Diwali, is an important occasion all over the country. The sister and brother renew the pledge of affection to each other and the brother gives his sister a gift. In all religious ceremonies the brother's part is symbolic of this relationship. In a period where women had no rights, personal, civil, or political, where there was no divorce for Hindu women and they were recognized through their relationship to a father, husband, brother, or son, the role of the brother was one of the greatest importance in the life of the sister, and his home practically the only protection she had in case of marital or other troubles. . . .

The years passed and Bhai was home for good. Some cousins had also returned from their studies abroad, and Anand Bhawan was full of young people and their laughter. . . . For me it was, in a very real sense, an awakening, a dream come true. The adored brother was home. He had time to ride with me, read with me, and encourage me to discuss things with him. . . . Bhai made me write essays and brought into my life topics that had not until then had much meaning for me. He also opened a door for me to Buddhism, in which he was at that time much engrossed. . . .

The major event in our life in 1916 was Bhai's wedding. There was not a family in the community who would not have been happy if their daughter had been chosen as the bride of Jawaharlal Nehru. The wedding was lavish to the point of ostentation—again one of those contradictions in Father's personality difficult to reconcile with the kind of man he really was. . . .

Kamala, my sister-in-law, was a beautiful girl. She came from a conservative family of Delhi and was sent to Allahabad to live with an aunt for a year before she was married so that she might get to know the man and family into which she was marrying. But it was hard for her to adapt herself to surroundings totally different from those in which she had grown up. . . .

. . . Kamala's baby was born on November 19, 1917. Eagerly awaited by the expectant grandparents, it was presumed that it would be a boy. The baby was born in one of the rooms across the courtyard from Father's room, and several of us were standing in the veranda awaiting the announcement. Presently Mother came out of the room and said, *"Hua . . ."* Before the others realized the implication Father laughed and said, *"Baccha hua?"* Mother had not said a son is born but "it" has been born. In the traditional way she could not bring herself to announce the birth of a daughter!

Father wanted the baby to be called after his mother, Indrani, but it was considered old-fashioned by some, and finally the name Indira, then much in vogue, was chosen. . . .

A paradox about my father was his championship of women's rights but his disregard for his daughters' education. He provided opportunities but there was no supervision and no plan. . . . As often happens in such cases, I knew more than the average school-going child of my age, but there were subjects with which I had only the slightest acquaintance. . . .

. . . I developed a complex about my lack of a formal education, and a university degree symbolized for me a passport to opportunity. After I was married this attitude annoyed my husband very much. "Stop pitying yourself," he would say if I ever harped on the subject. "Unless you get your values straight, you will never succeed in anything." My values were ultimately set straight by Gandhiji, but it took a national revolution to start a revolution in my mind.

For a girl, all roads led to marriage, and this is still mainly true in India. Suitably, I had been betrothed at thirteen and the custom was so usual that it made no impression on me nor did it change my life in any way. A few years later, the engagement was ended by mutual consent because of the widening political gap between our families.

I was now seriously involved in my Hindi studies, which were opening a door of real enjoyment for me. . . .

. . . Tulsi Das's Hindi version of the *Ramayana* is not only good poetry, it is a book of philosophical concepts and moral values. I was now writing on literary subjects for Hindi magazines. This too I enjoyed, and Sanskrit became a part of my studies. My English reading covered a wide area—Dickens, Shakespeare, Scott, poetry, and biographies. . . .

As the war ended there was discontent on many levels—among the peasantry, from whom soldiers had been recruited and who had helped to win the war; among the Muslims, resentment over Allied treatment of Turkey; and everywhere among the educated middle class, expectations of widespread constitutional reform leading to greater political opportunity. Change came, indeed, but in the form of the Rowlett Bills, which contained drastic provision for arrests and deportations without trial or any check of the law. Expectations were rudely shattered, and every shade of political opinion openly opposed what came to be known as the Black Bills.

Mahatma Gandhi, since his return from South Africa, had been involved with agrarian movements in Bihar and Gujarat. The Rowlett Bills, and the manner in which they were passed by the Imperial Legislative Council despite strong public opposition, shocked him. The constitutional method had failed and he began to think of *satyagraha*. He started an organization called the Satyagraha Sabha and published a pledge. Those who joined the Sabha had to solemnly affirm "to civilly disobey" the new laws and "follow truth faithfully and refrain from violence . . ." Among the first to join the Sabha was Bhai. Father, as deeply stunned as any, would never allow himself to be guided by emotions alone. . . .

I first met Mahatma Gandhi in November 1920, when he came at my father's invitation to discuss his policy of satyagraha with our family. . . .

When he came to our home for the first time there was great excitement in the family. Our house was still geared to the old pattern. There were large numbers of servants in their wine and gold liveries, rooms decorated with glittering chandeliers and beautiful carpets, masses of flowers everywhere. This, obviously, was not the proper setting for a Mahatma, and yet what was one to do about it? It was impossible to dismantle a whole house for a visit that would last only a few days. Finally, Mother's sitting room, which was furnished with *takhts* in the Indian style, was prepared for him, and arrangements were made for sitting on the floor. About Gandhiji's entourage one did not have to bother as they were happy to live comfortably for a day or so and needed no special arrangements.

The world knows now what Gandhiji looked like, what he ate, and what he thought of many issues apart from politics. Various authors, from their imaginations, have added to his known fads, thereby losing sight of the humanity of the man and portraying him as some kind of a freak. To me, with his naked body and his big ears, by no means handsome, Gandhiji was, at that time, a strange new sight. He had by now shed his turban and his Gujarati clothes and begun wearing a loin cloth to identify himself with the poorest Indian. His food was served in tin dishes—a plate, a bowl, and a mug—and these he carried everywhere with him. . . .

It was during his stay in Anand Bhawan that Gandhiji suggested that I should be sent to the Sabarmati Ashram near Ahmadabad, where he lived, for some weeks, to be subjected to a simpler way of life. As far as I recollect nobody asked me specifically whether I wanted to go, but the idea of the simple life was about to begin in India. Bhai had already adopted it and it was obvious that there would be many changes in our life-style before long. I was the pampered daughter of the house and needed discipline.

My heart sank when I first saw the place. Everything was so utterly drab and so unpleasing to the eye. I wondered how long I could survive there. As a concession I was to share Gandhiji's hut. He was known as *Bapu,* which means father in Gujarati, and that is the name I used for him ever after. Life in the ashram was austere beyond belief. Rising at 4 A.M. for prayers, we went on to the chores of the day, which consisted of sweeping and cleaning our living quarters, washing our clothes in the river, cleaning the latrines— which is a task impossible to describe. In order to let me down gently I was not required to clean the latrines, for which I offered thanks to the Almighty! . . .

. . . By the time I had left the ashram I had lost my fear of [Gandhiji] and had, to some extent, come to terms with ashram life, not accepting it but beginning to appreciate the underlying philosophy on which it was based.

Certain things I could not grasp, and it took a long time for me to understand some of Gandhiji's views. . . .

From Allahabad Gandhiji had sent a telegraphic appeal to the Viceroy "respectfully" requesting him to refrain from passing the Rowlett Bills. This appeal was ignored and Satyagraha Day was launched with fasting, prayer, and a nationwide *hartal* on April 6, 1919. A fast is an ordinary event among Hindus, Muslims, and Christians alike, but this fast was different because it was for a political purpose and not for personal salvation. Many of those who did not fully understand the political significance knew that any big task is only undertaken after a process of self-purification. Gandhiji always based his appeals to the people on what was traditionally known to them. This was why he easily carried the common man with him while the more sophisticated and politically complex mind of the educated held him aloof.

The demonstrations were nationwide. Bazaars were closed, public vehicles ceased plying for trade, huge processions marched through cities, and business was at a standstill. For the first time peasants from the villages participated in a political demonstration along with townspeople. There was firing by police in many parts of the country and arrests of numbers of people. The government declared martial law in Punjab, and strict censorship cut off all news of what was happening there. On April 13 a peaceful meeting of several thousand men, women, and children was held in the walled garden of Jallianwala Bagh in Amritsar, and, under orders of General Dyer, troops fired on the people, who could not get out of the garden because it had only one small exit. Over a thousand were killed and wounded in this infamous massacre, and while General Dyer was applauded in the House of Lords, the poet Rabindranath Tagore returned the knighthood he had earlier accepted from the British. . . .

It was in this tense national atmosphere, and strained domestic one, that I met Ranjit Pandit, whom I was to marry shortly afterward. An article published in 1920 in the *Modern Review* of Calcutta entitled "At the Feet of the Guru" had created considerable interest, especially among younger people. The guru of the article was Jawaharlal Nehru, the writer, Ranjit Pandit. At a time when all eyes were focused on Gandhi, the man with a new technique for freedom and about whom there was controversy in all circles, this article asserted that a new star was rising on the political firmament—a guru the young could understand and to whom they would give their loyalty—Jawaharlal Nehru. . . .

. . . We were engaged during Ranjit's visit to Allahabad. No formal announcement was made immediately because my parents wanted us to get better acquainted and also because of my father's growing uneasiness over coming events.

When he was leaving, Ranjit gave me a tiny silk-bound volume almost in tatters. He told me it was a copy of the *Gita* that his father had always read and carried with him. "It is the most precious thing I possess," he said. When I showed it to my mother she was horrified. It seemed quite mad to her that a young man, just engaged to be married, should give his fiancée the *Gita* with its message of renunciation. Where was the diamond ring he should have given me? However, the ring and other gifts of jewelry followed later and somewhat appeased her! The *Gita* has in a way been symbolic in my life. Years afterward Bhai gave me a small beautifully tooled *Gita* as his present on Bhaiya Duj, the brother's day. This gift is always with me. . . .

. . . Gandhiji had been a close friend of Ranjit's father, and this wedding had his consent and approval. Suddenly one day he wrote to inquire what I would wear for the ceremony. . . .

. . . Gandhiji's wife, Ba . . . sent me a piece of cloth spun and woven by her. It was the correct width and also fine enough to be dyed the traditional pink. It certainly was not a wedding sari in any sense but was reluctantly accepted. Instead of the jewelry I should have worn, flowers were woven into various attractive ornaments for my ears, neck, and wrists.

Judged by the standards of the day, the wedding was a simple affair. The list of guests read like a political convention. All the leaders of India were present. The auspicious hour for the religious ceremony was after midnight, so Gandhiji had been persuaded to retire at his usual time. Ranjit and I went up to his room later to receive his blessing. Bapu, as we all called him, was curled up on his bed in the veranda, a ray of moonlight shining on him. He woke immediately he heard our footsteps, gave us his blessings, and spoke of love and responsibility. Then he looked very grave and began to talk of our duty to the country at this time—the strength required could only come from purity of the highest order. Chastity in married life was difficult, he knew, but so was the great struggle for freedom upon which we had entered and which demanded every sacrifice. . . . Suddenly the Nehru spirit asserted itself. I looked at Bapu and said haltingly, "Why did you give your permission to our marriage if you thought it was wrong for us to live together as husband and wife? I love Ranjit and I want a normal married life." I stopped because I was breathless, expecting a sharp rebuke, but none came. Instead, a gentle sigh, then a slap on my burning cheek, "So you love Ranjit? See to it then that you do not distract him from his duty!" And we were dismissed with a loving smile!

Among Brahmans, it is customary to change the name of the bride after the wedding ceremony, when the girl has been accepted into her new family. . . . The name given to me was Vijaya Lakshmi—the conquering goddess Lakshmi. . . .

Two days after the wedding we left for Calcutta. Bhai had an appointment in some village that day but had promised to be back in time to say good-bye. He had not, however, reached home when we were leaving for the railway station. I was unhappy. Friends and relations were waiting to see us off and our good friend, Mr. Clark, the Anglo-Indian station master, came up to shake hands. The time for departure was due.

"Oh, please, can't we wait five minutes?" I begged Mr. Clark. "I know my brother will come."

As we reached our flower-decorated reserved carriage I saw Bhai sauntering up the platform. He was aware that he was late but it was his studied custom not to hurry or show any anxiety on any occasion. I was standing in the door of the carriage and he swung himself up.

"Oh, you came," I said. He took my face in his hands and, kissing me between the eyes, he said, "Be happy, little sister."

The whistle sounded and we were off—a new life, a new beginning, and an uncertain future.

We began our married life in Calcutta. . . .

. . . Time passed quickly and the court vacations drew near. We had not really had a honeymoon, and it seemed right to go to Rajkot where we could have the quiet needed to look at ourselves and the developing political situation objectively, to come to some decision about the future. Gandhiji had now made an appeal to students to boycott colleges and to lawyers to boycott courts. My marriage had not entirely pleased Ranjit's family because they were afraid the association with the Nehrus would come in the way of his success at the Bar. . . . His own political convictions, his deep admiration for my father and brother, and his love for me pulled him toward the national movement. My own feelings were mixed. Coming from a home that had been suddenly uprooted and where new ways of living and thinking were being established, I was acutely aware that unless Ranjit conformed to this pattern he would not have a close place in the hearts of Father and Bhai. . . .

Ranjit had a complex and versatile personality. His early studies had taken place in Bombay, but after graduating with distinction from the university he went abroad where the Sorbonne, the University of Heidelberg, and the Middle Temple claimed him. He was a good sportsman and crack shot and also a fine musician. He had studied both European and Indian music, played the violin with considerable talent, and had a well-trained singing voice. He was also a linguist of ability and had studied many European and Indian languages, which he spoke fluently. He was a barrister by profession but a historian and classicist by choice. His two great loves were music and Sanskrit. . . .

The Pandits were a sporting family, and riding, hunting, fishing, and games of every kind were part of the pattern of their lives in Rajkot. The stables had been drastically reduced after my father-in-law's death because both sons had settled away from Kathiawar, but there were still some riding ponies, and my own beloved "Bijli," my favorite Arab mare, had been sent from Allahabad. Ranjit and I spent the mornings in long cross-country rides and the afternoons in reading—the Sanskrit classics, and poetry, drama, and history. I went through all the winding paths of India's evolution, and, as Ranjit unveiled and interpreted the richness of our cultural heritage, for the first time I became aware of myself as an Indian. It was an exciting discovery. Now I understood better what Gandhiji was saying to us. The national movement, which had seemed remote up till that time, became a compelling force. . . .

. . . I think we both knew what the final decision would be. Our talks about material things were superficial; what really prevented Ranjit from making an immediate break was Gandhiji's insistence on nonviolence as a creed and its observance in thought and action. . . . Ranjit was a son of Maharashtra and the fiery blood of many ancestors intolerant of the foreigner flowed in his veins. He was a man of action and could only fulfill himself through action. In theory, he accepted Gandhiji's reasoning, but could he live up to it? . . . .

The Congress had decided to boycott the Prince of Wales's approaching visit, which was due in November 1921. As the time approached satyagraha gathered force, and it was known that those who were protesting would be arrested. By this time Father had joined Gandhiji, but with some reservations regarding nonviolence. Earlier he had suggested that since he could not give his complete loyalty to Gandhiji's program, would it not be better to continue his legal practice, still a princely one, and donate the money to the cause? Gandhiji's reply, as one might have expected, was almost in the words of Christ. "But it is *you* I want," he said, and in a very short time afterward Father threw in his lot with Gandhiji and never looked back or regretted his decision.

Of the leaders who were arrested for boycotting the Prince of Wales's visit in Allahabad, Father and Bhai were among the first. . . .

. . . It had been understood between Father and Ranjit before we went to Rajkot that whatever political step Ranjit might decide to take, he would stay with Mother during this first political crisis in her life, for which her mind was wholly unprepared. So this was our immediate plan. . . .

Big changes were taking place at home. Our staff had been drastically reduced, a part of the house closed, and our style of living altered to fit in with the new conditions we had accepted. The political situation was deteriorating and there was suffering in many homes where the breadwinner was now in jail. One's personal discomforts ceased to have any meaning. Anand Bhawan was always full, for those who had joined Gandhiji were now one family and were gladly given shelter and help by Mother.

Besides the six-month sentences for Father and Bhai, fines were also imposed. The rules of the national movement forbade us to pay these, and we expected the police to come and take away whatever they wished in lieu of the money. Gandhiji's instructions on this point were clear. The police must not be obstructed in the performance of their duty and should be allowed to take whatever they wished. Mother could not reconcile herself to this invasion of her home and, by the time the police arrived a few days later, she was seething with anger. Kamala, on the contrary, was quite serene and kept trying to persuade Mother that we must let the men who were present in the house deal with the situation. . . .

In lieu of a small fine of Rs.1000, van loads of valuables were removed. Carpets, pieces of furniture, and ornaments were taken and later sold by public auction. This was intended to destroy the prestige of the family and to humiliate us. . . .

The world we now lived in was unfamiliar and also much smaller. It required a continuous effort to adapt oneself to new situations. Many old friends and acquaintances disappeared from our lives and new ones came into them. There was a difference, however, for those who became comrades in the struggle were simple people—men and women who did not share our background or our earlier interests, to whom we seemed as strange as they seemed to us. The bond between us was simply that of association in a common cause. We all dressed in the coarse hand-spun, handwoven material called khadi. . . .

The "boycott" movement was reaching its height—foreign cloth and liquor shops were being picketed. For this purpose Gandhiji enrolled women, considering them better able than men to persuade people. Kamala and Betty [her sister, Krishna] had joined the Congress volunteers and were engaged in active work of various kinds, including picketing. . . .

. . . Ranjit had left the Bar but so far was not occupied in any way. For a man who had worked hard and been active in many fields, the present life was not only boring, it seriously threatened our domestic peace. Ranjit had joined the Congress and did some work at the Congress office, but there were hours of enforced leisure. . . .

In Rajkot we not only organized spinning and weaving centers but, by working in the villages, we came to know our people and problems we had previously not spent much thought on. We also started schools for the illiterate and developed programs of all kinds to arouse social conscience and open up opportunities for Harijans [the untouchables] and other underprivileged persons in the area. It was very good discipline though often dull work. . . .

It was customary for a first child to be born in the maternal grandparents' home, and my first confinement took place in Anand Bhawan. . . . The baby girl born on January 23, 1923, was a healthy and beautiful one. My parents were disappointed, but "Nan's baby" was special and the usual celebrations took place. Ranjit and I were happy, and, as his mother had died only a few weeks earlier, Ranjit decided to give the baby a Maharashtrian name his mother had liked. We called her Vatsala, "Beloved."

To our lasting sorrow little Vatsala did not live. She died in October of the same year—hardly nine months old. . . .

By the end of 1921 the national movement was expanding and Congress volunteers were coming forward in large numbers to offer civil disobedience. Arrests were the order of the day. . . .

Ranjit and I had now settled down in Allahabad. His mother had died and the home in Rajkot had been closed up. My second daughter [Pandit's daughter Lekha was born shortly after the loss of Vatsala], Nayantara, Star of the Eyes, had been born, and the two babies, though three years apart, kept me busy part of the time. I associated myself with the constructive program in the town, and Ranjit completely involved himself in this and worked in a group of nearby villages for rural uplift. Our personal life was slightly more peaceful and orderly than it had been for some time. . . .

[The year 1929] was a landmark in the national movement . . . the Congress voiced the yearnings of the Indian people in the demand for complete independence. A new spirit was abroad, and the solemn pledge taken by the delegates at midnight of December 31, 1929, on the bank of the Ravi River was an unforgettable experience, almost spiritual in its content. Now there was no turning back; we were pledged to the forward march whatever it might cost us. For our family this was the beginning of a deeper involvement in terms of work and prison. . . .

January 26 was declared Independence Day, and on that morning every year after the historic Lahore Congress, we foregathered on the upstairs terrace of Anand Bhawan to read the pledge, hoist the Congress flag, and sing the national anthem. . . .

[The Nehru family's political activities were reinforced by Motilal Nehru's death following serious illness in prison.] [Father] knew he was dying; he also believed that freedom was round the corner. Gandhiji had been released and he had come to Allahabad immediately, as had many other Congress colleagues and old friends, who were with Father up to the time he left us. . . .

. . . For myself, Father's death left a void that I have never been able to fill. . . .

On January 26, 1932, I was the "dictator" of the Allahabad City Congress Committee and was to preside at the meeting where the Independence pledge was to be taken. The Purshottamdas Park, where the meeting was held, was crowded to capacity with men and boys even sitting on the branches of trees. We knew there would be arrests immediately afterward and, indeed, the police were present in full force. The pledge was taken solemnly and the meeting dispersed. That night, Betty, a colleague, Purnima Banerji, and I, among others, were arrested and taken to the district jail.

The Allahabad District Jail was a collection of mud houses in a large yard enclosed by a dilapidated wall. . . . We were taken to the "female" section and told to settle ourselves in a long room known as a barrack, with gratings in the wall at intervals of four feet. Through these gratings we looked onto a dreary yard with one gigantic banyan tree in the center. . . . Our day ended with lockup at six o'clock, and the long night stretched interminably ahead. . . . It was a continuing nightmare.

After three days of such confinement, there was a comic opera trial and we were each sentenced to one year's rigorous imprisonment. In addition, I was fined fifteen hundred rupees or six months' imprisonment in lieu of the fine. Congress policy forbade the payment of fines, so my sentence amounted to eighteen months' imprisonment. . . .

Our transfer to Lucknow, where our prison term was to be served, took place one bitterly cold midnight. No previous intimation was given and we had already gone to bed when the matron, accompanied by several wardresses, came hurrying into the barrack and told us we were to leave immediately for an unknown destination. In a few minutes we had changed and followed her into the main office. The superintendent of police was waiting to drive us to a wayside station from which we were to entrain for Lucknow. This was done to avoid a demonstration of sympathy at the central railway station. . . . We raced at amazing speed through the deserted streets, reaching ahead of time the wayside station where we were to entrain. Political prisoners accepted the discipline imposed on them, so were not strictly guarded. It was cold and I walked up and down the footpath alongside the railroad track. Suddenly I saw a dim shape creeping up the embankment; the first figure was joined by a second and a third. By the time I reached the spot, the place was crowded and our guards were vainly trying to form a barrier between us and the townspeople who, having heard that we were being spirited away, had come to say good-bye. When the train arrived, the place was crowded and cries of Jai! [Victory!] rent the air. Garlands of flowers were piled into our hands or thrown at us over the heads of the guards and policemen who formed a ring round us. The passengers on the train put out their heads to see who the political prisoners were, and some joined in the shouts of greeting as we were recognized. It was a triumphant send-off. . . .

In spite of the advice I had had from Bhai and Ranjit I found that it takes a long time to get over the pinpricks of prison life and benefit from the doubtful advantages it offers. We lived according to a set of rules and regulations that bore no relation to our actual needs. The endless do's and don'ts caused friction with the authorities and often led to open defiance on our part. . . .

The day took care of itself and we learned to use our time to some purpose cooking our meals, reading, writing, and walking in the prison yard or trying to grow a few flowers in the stony soil. . . .

A year is a long period of time, and the inner resources that came to our rescue in later imprisonments were still undeveloped. In my own case the personal problem outweighed those created by jail life. During the excitement of public meetings and arrests there had been no time for quiet thinking. I had not allowed myself a moment to consider whether my decision to take a more active part in the struggle would be harmful to my children's interest. . . .

. . . Prison was a challenge. The British were not going to crush our spirit, let them try their hardest. It would be fun to test oneself and come out of the ordeal strengthened. With this approach came the desire for a planned life with exercise for the body and mind alike. I had regularly practiced yogic exercises and I now resumed them. I also found reading a few pages from the *Bhagavad-Gita* a mental discipline, helping to keep things in perspective. . . .

I was released two months before my sentence ended because I had earned marks for "good conduct," and one fine morning matron came to the barrack to tell me I must be ready to leave immediately as a car was waiting outside for me. . . .

In Allahabad I learned that Mother was in Poona. My three girls were there too in a small private school started by a young and dedicated nationalist couple, the Vakils. It was a school run mainly for children of national workers, and we had come to know of it when Indira had been sent there. So I proceeded to Poona.

It was good to see the children again. Rita, the youngest, had completely forgotten me in the sixteen months of our separation. Lekha, being older and having had more experience of the national movement, had adapted to life away from home. But Tara was a child who needed a home and parents, and she had been most unhappy and had fretted constantly for me. I was shocked to see how she must have suffered, and now I suffered because of what I had done to the children. To this day I cannot forgive myself. . . .

Congressmen and women were allowed to seek election to municipal and district boards and try to improve civil life. . . . We secured a handsome majority. . . .

I was elected chairman of the Education Committee, a position held much earlier with great success by my cousin, Uma Nehru. This committee was controlled by the conservative elements who had a vested interest in it. I came to my first meeting full of enthusiasm and bright ideas, but soon discovered that wherever else my ideas might have been needed, it was not in the Education Committee. A more narrow-minded, backward group of men I had never met before. Hindu and Muslim alike, all belonged to a feudal age. . . .

The period during which Congress functioned in the Municipal Board was marked by a number of changes in the municipal law and in civic life. Unfortunately, the time was short. . . . The British Parliament passed the Government of India Act, 1935, introducing provincial autonomy. This act envisaged responsible government in provincial legislatures but reserved the right of the Center, the federal government, in New Delhi, to have charge of defense, foreign affairs, tribal areas, and some other subjects. It also retained representation on a communal basis, which had been introduced earlier by the Minto-Morley Reform of 1909.

While Congress condemned the Act, which was forced on the people, it decided, after some debate, to contest the elections that were due to be held.

Once the decision to contest the elections was arrived at, the election manifesto was prepared. This manifesto rejected the Government of India Act but resolved to continue the national struggle and resist imperialism by entering the legislatures. . . . A committee in each province selected the Congress candidates who would contest. Ranjit and I were both offered tickets and accepted them. Ranjit's constituency was in Allahabad district—Jamunapar—and mine in Kanpur, known as Kanpur Bilhaur. . . . Ranjit's opponent was the Raja of Manda, a *zamindar* (landowner) of the district. Mine was more formidable for she was Lady Srivastava, the wife of the Education Member in the Viceroy's Council—a powerful and wealthy industrialist, Sir J. P. Srivastava.

. . . My constituency was a rural one and very spread out. Campaigning meant being on the move for several days at a time in village areas, only going to the town of Kanpur for a few hours' rest or for a meeting scheduled there. . . . We had for our use a Ford car which had seen better days. The plan was to stop each night in a village, and I had no clear idea of what was involved. The idea of the election itself was new and exciting and sufficient for the time being. We started off in high spirits, the five young men and I. Canvassing was easy because the issue was clear-cut. . . .

. . . All went well and at dusk we reached the village where we were to spend the night. The villagers, always hospitable, insisted on supplementing the evening meal we had brought with us. Later, when it was time to retire, I found that the little village schoolhouse had been swept and cleaned and all our bedding rolls laid out side by side. For some reason I had expected a place of my own to sleep in. Seeing consternation on my face, which I could not hide, one of my colleagues explained gently that this was how it was going to be throughout the campaign, but I must not mind, they would all take care of me. I thought of the pajama suit packed in my case, but obviously I could not undress. I had never been to bed in a heavy khadi sari, but there was no alternative. . . .

Ranjit and I had agreed that we should phone each other whenever possible and give news of how our respective campaigns were progressing. I phoned the second evening. "Everything is going very well," I told him. "Last night there was no separate place for me so I slept with the boys." A roar of laughter met my statement and Ranjit replied, "Good for you!" I heard him repeat this to Bhai, more laughter. . . .

Polling Day, I speak especially of my own province, Uttar Pradesh, was a day not to be easily forgotten. One wanted to shout with joy and cry at the same time—one was so proud of one's people, so glad to be one of them, so convinced of victory—not the election victory, but that larger one toward which we were moving and of which this was but a small part. The villagers came out in thousands on foot, on cycles, and in bullock carts, with the odd group even in a tractor. All were dressed in their holiday best, the bullocks wearing bright garlands of marigolds, the festive flower, around their necks. Carts, jeeps, and bicycles were festooned with the Congress flag bravely fluttering in the breeze. . . .

. . . I went around the polling areas like other candidates, and many times I thought to myself, "These are the people of India. They and they alone will give the final answer. I will never forget this day. How right Bapu is—we must never forget them. . . ."

Congress won a striking victory in eight out of the eleven British provinces, and the leaders of Congress parties were invited by the governors to form ministries. India was then divided into British provinces and Princely states. The provinces were under the direct rule of the Viceroy, whereas a vast territory, about two-fifths of the whole of India, was under the rule of Princes who had accepted paramountcy of the British Crown. These rulers were autocratic monarchs with little actual authority as their support came from British power, and the administration of the Indian states was carried on under the "advice" of British-appointed Residents. The 1935 Government of India Act, under which elections were held,

applied only to the provinces. According to the new Government of
India Act, executive powers and functions of the Governors were of
three kinds: those to be exercised at the Governor's sole discretion,
those in which he exercised his individual judgment after first consulting his Ministers, and those in which he acted upon the advice
of his Ministers.

The Congress permitted acceptance of office in the provinces
where they had a majority in the legislatures, but subject to the condition that the Governor would not use his special powers of interference or set aside the advice of Ministers in regard to their
constitutional activities. As the necessary assurances were not given
by the Viceroy, Congress leaders expressed their inability to undertake the formation of ministries. . . .

. . . Congress parties in six provinces[3] were invited to form cabinets. In Uttar Pradesh, Pandit Govind Ballabh Pant, or Pantji, was
leader of the Congress party and became the Chief Minister. He invited Dr. Katju, Rafi Ahmed Kidwai, and myself to join his Cabinet. . . .

The portfolios of Local Self-Government and Medical and Public Health were allotted to me. The former I was glad to have, but
with the latter subjects I was less well acquainted. However, I made
up my mind I would study hard. Since my acceptance of Pantji's offer I had frequently cried myself to sleep, wondering if I would be
able to do credit to the family and the country. . . .

The salary of the new Ministers was 500 rupees a month with
a free house and car. This was the Congress ruling. We were not to
use a private railway saloon when traveling, as had been the case
formerly, but were to travel third class whenever possible. . . .

A notice was sent from the secretariat asking the Ministers to
choose their houses, and a list of houses was attached. I decided I
would go after work to look at them, but at lunchtime Pantji sent
for me and said he wanted me to stay with him. "It will be more
proper," he told me. "You can live as you please without interference from me or my family." I was surprised and tried to explain to
him that, as Minister of the Government, I was a responsible person
and must live on my own. Besides, during the session of the Legislature Ranjit would be in Lucknow, and during their holidays my

3. Madras, Uttar Pradesh, Bombay, Central Provinces, Orissa, and Bihar; later,
North-West Frontier Province and Assam.

children would be with me. I wanted to make a home for them. After much discussion I had to agree, most reluctantly, to stay with Pantji for a month. Pantji was the kindest person imaginable. He was, in every sense of the word, my "political guru," but in certain matters we were worlds apart. . . .

When the new Legislative Assemblies opened, the first resolution moved by the new ministries was a demand for a Constituent Assembly to draft a Constitution for India. This resolution should have been moved by the Chief Minister, but Pantji was indisposed and the privilege of acting in his place fell on me. It was the key resolution of the session. I felt honored to move it. . . .

This was the first time a woman had been given the position of Minister and had to work with men as her subordinates and colleagues. It is natural, I suppose, for a relationship tinged with chivalry to have developed. I can remember so many instances when Kher [her parliamentary secretary for Local Self-Government] would work far into the night doing some research for a speech I had to make, or explaining matters he felt I must be acquainted with before facing some knotty problem with the Governor the next day. . . . On this subject I had spoken to Ranjit and Rafi, whom I always consulted when in difficulty. Both were emphatic that what I did not know I must learn, and in any case I and not officials must be in charge of my departments. I have seldom worked so hard as I did in those days. There were many things I had to learn to understand, and this stood me in good stead later on. I had a husband who was always at my side when needed—critical and understanding. I had good colleagues whose sincere interest and help made most things possible for me. . . .

I was fortunate, also, in another matter, and that was the support and admiration of women all over India. Many were my friends and comrades. Many more I did not know, but from all directions waves of affection and encouragement came to me. There was no jealousy at all, just shared pride, which I like to think was special to India and to my Indian sisters. . . .

. . . During the time I was Minister of Health, Hardwar, one of the cities of pilgrimage for Hindus, was to have its Kumbh Mela. This festival falls every twelve years, and it is considered especially auspicious to bathe in the Ganga in Hardwar. Millions of pilgrims come, and nearly always some form of epidemic occurs. . . .Hardwar is a city of *pandas*—hereditary priests of the Hindu families

who go for worship and the performance of various religious rituals on the banks of the Ganga. The pandas are mostly enormously
wealthy, and some are heads of big religious foundations. They are
also, by and large, ignorant and bigoted but very influential with
the pilgrims and worshippers. . . . On my return to . . . the rest
house where I was staying, a deputation of pandas came with a
written petition requesting the government to prevent cow slaughter in Hardwar. This was a perfectly legitimate request as Hardwar
is a city holy to Hindus. In the ordinary course I would have accepted the petition and given an assurance that I would convey it to
the Chief Minister. As it happened, I read the petition carefully and
to my amazement found that the request was for cow slaughter to
be banned in Jwalapur, one of the three areas that made up the municipality of Hardwar. It was also the area where Muslim butchers
and vegetable sellers lived in large numbers. It was obvious that the
pandas did not dare ask for the ban to be applied to the whole city
because a number of English officials lived there and beef was a part
of their diet. The Muslims, on the other hand, could do nothing to
retaliate and were easy victims.

I was furious. I asked the deputation why the ban should not be
applied to Hardwar as a whole, and the reply was that it would be
easier to begin in one area at a time. I then asked them if it was not
true that they were afraid to offend the foreign rulers but did not mind
destroying the livelihood of a Muslim group. At this they lost their
temper and started to shout abuse at me and at the Nehrus for being traitors to the Hindu creed. . . . After their departure the superintendent of police suggested placing a police guard around the rest
house and my parliamentary secretary wanted me to agree to this,
as he felt that the temper of these ignorant men could lead to an
ugly situation. But I refused to have a guard. I told the superintendent of police that my husband would not approve of such an action. Also, I was a popularly elected Minister and if those who had
voted for me wished to demonstrate against me it was their privilege to do so. Within an hour the shouting of slogans gave us warning that a large crowd was approaching. I gave orders that all the
doors and windows should be closed, and the crowd soon surrounded the house screaming vile abuse and threatening to break
down the doors. They did shatter nearly all the window panes. After half an hour of this I suddenly decided to face the mob. In spite
of the entreaties of my companions I flung open the door and surprised the shouting crowd. For a moment they were silent, shocked

at seeing me, and I climbed onto a chair. Taking the watch off my wrist I held it out to them. I told them that if they could behave in a civilized manner I would speak to them and I gave them exactly ten minutes to calm down. If they wanted to harm me, I told them, it was their privilege to do so, but such an act would only hurt them. Here, on the banks of the holy Ganga, an assault on a Brahman woman would hardly be to their credit. For a moment it was doubtful whether or not the violence would continue, but as I remained standing on the chair holding my watch for all to see, the temper of the crowd suddenly changed and they became quiet. . . .

When I returned to Delhi the next day Pantji told me he had passed an anxious night on hearing the police report from Hardwar, and that in future I must have adequate protection. I pointed out with some pride that I was competent to look after myself. Some weeks later an apology was received from the leading pandas of Hardwar for this incident. . . .

Gandhiji was now wholly preoccupied in thinking what form the next movement could take. Japan was almost at our door for Malaya, Singapore, and Burma had fallen. Indian refugees from these countries were pouring in, and the threat to us was a very real one. In July 1942 a meeting of the Working Committee, the Congress executive body, met at Wardha, Gandhiji's home and ashram. It was a long session lasting a week, and the whole war situation as it affected India was thoroughly discussed. The resolution passed was in the nature of an appeal for the British to leave India. It said, in part, "If such withdrawal takes place with good-will, it would result in establishing a stable provisional Government in India and cooperation between this Government and the United Nations in resisting aggression and helping China." Should the appeal fail, however, Congress felt it would be compelled to use all its nonviolent strength for the vindication of its political rights. Any forthcoming struggle would, of course, be under Gandhiji's leadership. No response was really expected from Britain, and none came.

An A.I.C.C. [All India Congress Committee] meeting was called in Bombay to consider the resolution of the Working Committee. It was fully attended, and the atmosphere all over India was very tense. It needed but a spark to set it in flames. . . . This Quit India resolution, as it came to be known, took the decision of starting a mass struggle and called on the people to face the future with courage and endurance. The resolution was passed late on the night of August 8. In the early hours of the next morning, Gandhiji and all the members of the Working Committee were arrested and taken in secret to an unknown destination. . . .

[Shortly after the August decision Pandit took on family leadership.] The university campus is a few minutes' walk from Anand Bhawan and I went there and met some of the student leaders, including Bahuguna, who is now a Minister in the Central Government. I begged them to be absolutely controlled, warning them that they would injure the larger cause if there was any violent action on their part. They promised to march peacefully but told me there would be processions every day. . . .

. . . There was no news at all of where Gandhiji and the Working Committee members had been taken after their arrest. Meanwhile, the messengers I had been expecting arrived under cover of the night. They turned out to be Lal Bahadur Shastri and a colleague. I hid them in our guest room upstairs, locked the door from the outside, and put the key into my pocket. A warrant of arrest was out for Lal Bahadur, and I arranged to take up food to them only at night so that not even the servants would know they were in the house. They immediately started typing and cyclostyling instructions to be sent to the villages. Everything had to be done swiftly and quietly.

On the third day after the Bombay arrests the Vice-Chancellor rang me up saying that he had heard there would be lathi charges and possibly shooting, and could I have the next scheduled procession called off? In any case, could I persuade Lekha not to participate? I replied that I was powerless to do either. I had said everything possible to the students and now it was up to them to show their wisdom. The procession was expected to be very large, divided into two sections, each going by a different route and converging to hold a meeting. When I heard of the possibility of firing I asked the Kamala Nehru Hospital, which is next to Anand Bhawan, to be ready for any eventuality. Some beds had to be kept vacant and a doctor and nurse available on duty in the out-patient's department. I asked Bhai's secretary, Upadhayaji, to pay frequent visits to the university and report what police arrangements were being made. I was under great strain. Lekha had gone off to join the procession and Tara, then only fourteen, had accompanied her. Nothing was normal anymore.

By noon there was no news of where the processions had reached. I sat at home in the veranda straining my ears to hear shouting or any noise indicating the approach of the procession. The two men locked in their room upstairs were equally tense, but no action was possible and we could only wait. About two o'clock in the afternoon I heard the tut-tut-tut of machine-gun firing. The servants rushed into the street to find out what was happening, but the shouts of "Quit India" and other slogans had begun to reach us and I knew the confrontation had taken place. I was just running out of the gate when three lawyer friends stopped their car out on the street and said the procession that had taken another route had also been fired on and that Lekha was gravely injured. They had come to take me to her. My heart almost stopped beating. I felt giddy and sick, and at this moment Upadhayaji rushed up to say that the boy leading the procession in front of the university had been shot dead. I pulled myself together. Like a flash of lightning, Gandhiji's voice passed through my mind—do your duty, it said. I turned to my lawyer friends who were waiting and asked if they would take Upadhayaji to check what had happened to Lekha and the others. I ran like a wild thing to see what was going on on our side. I do not mention this incident in any spirit of self-righteousness— that is far from my nature. But it is important for those who did not know Gandhiji to realize how deep his influence was on the people who loved and trusted him.

In front of the university the spectacle was a frightening one. A barricade had been erected, and before it were police and military facing a vast crowd opposite. The air was full of slogans: "Quit India," "Release our Leaders," "Murderers," and so on. After the shooting of the student who was leading the procession, all discipline had gone to the winds. Lathi charges provoked hand-to-hand encounters between police and students and this, in its turn, led to firing. Many were wounded. I asked the police to let me get to the other side, but they refused. Seeing me, the crowd doubled their shouts and demanded that I be allowed to join them. At last I was permitted to do so. I climbed onto the hood of a car standing nearby and addressed the students, begging them to disperse and let us all attend to the dead and injured. I gave the police superintendent my personal word that I would calm the crowd if he would withdraw his men. The dead boy turned out to be the son of a zamindar of our district. Many injured boys were taken to the Kamala Nehru Hospital. I remember one boy whose testicles had been shot and he screamed in agony; there were others too with serious injuries. It had not been a case of firing on legs and shooting to disperse the crowd. The baton assaults too had led to grave injuries. Meanwhile, news came that the other procession had managed to reach a city park and hold a meeting. Lekha and others were safe and there had been no firing. Knowing this was a tremendous relief, and I devoted myself to giving what help I could to those in need.

I also had another anxiety during these days. There was no news of Ranjit. He had attended the A.I.C.C. in Bombay and so far had not returned. Because of complete censorship names of those arrested were not published in the press, and I could only wait for news to come from some trusted friend. . . .

[Eventually Pandit herself was arrested.] "Why is it necessary," I asked the Magistrate, "for so many armed men to come to arrest one unarmed woman at this amazing hour?" He told me a search was to take place.

I went in and woke the younger girls. They immediately grasped the situation and no useless questions were asked as they helped me to pack a bag. Even the youngest was familiar with police methods by now. She looked at me with her big eyes full of sleep and said, "How wonderful to live in these days, Mummie; I wish I could go to jail too." Tara told me, "Let's say good-bye to you outside. I want the police to see how we take these partings." After I had left, the girls went back to bed and lay on the hidden leaflets while the police search went on. I was very proud of my children that night. . . .

As I got to Naini the jail authorities said that they had received no information about my arrival! After half an hour's wait, the gate of the Female Prison was opened by the matron, who came rushing up, panting and puffing and very annoyed at the disturbance of her night's rest. I was taken to the old familiar barrack. It was four-thirty in the morning. I spread my bedding on the ground, was locked up, and a new prison term began. My head ached and I could not sleep thinking of the events of the past few days. I was especially worried about Lekha, fearing that she would land in jail. The previous evening I had had a brief talk with her, wanting to know her reactions to what she had been through. She spoke with great bitterness. "It will take a long time for me to forget what I have seen, Mummie, and it will be longer before I can root out the hatred that is growing in my heart. We can't think in terms of normal life anymore—there's no going back for us. We have to go on to the end, whatever the end may be." Of course she was right. But

Tara and Rita were still so young to be alone, and the future was uncertain. . . .

I had not been well for some time past and was in need of surgery, but this was no time to think of one's health. I did not sleep well, could not cope with the necessary daily chores, and was in very low spirits. On August 30, I was feeling particularly tired and remained lying down. Suddenly my friend and recent barrack-mate, Purnima Banerji, rushed to the yard, and I heard excited chatter. Looking up I saw Lekha, laden with garlands and a broad grin on her face, striding into the barrack, a prisoner. For a dazed moment I thought she was visiting us but immediately remembered we were no longer entitled to visits. In any case, jail interviews were conducted in the superintendent's office. I heard Lekha telling Purnima how her arrest had taken place but I was so stunned I could not speak to her. . . .

. . . On September 11 a bruised and battered Indu [Indira], with some of her clothes torn, arrived in the barrack. She had been at a meeting and there was a scuffle with the police. She brought us news that Feroze [her husband] had also been arrested and was probably in the men's section next door to us. There was still no news of Bhai, which was disturbing. Ranjit had been ill in Bombay and was leaving to spend ten days in Khali in order to recoup before his inevitable arrest. I worried about him because, in the past few years, even at the best of times, he had not been robust. . . .

After more than seven months in prison my physical condition was still unsatisfactory and I was let out on parole. I did not like the idea of leaving Indu and Lekha but felt that I should go home to see to my health, which must not be allowed to break down at this time. I also was eager to look into domestic affairs. I left Naini in a tonga, not wishing to ask the jail authorities to inform my home of my arrival. I did not want Khaliq, our chauffeur, to bring the car to fetch me.

The first sight that met my eyes as I entered the gates of Anand Bhawan was dozens of policemen and the District Magistrate. A search was in progress, and what a search! Cupboards had been forcibly opened, clothes thrown anyhow on the veranda and in the garden, books taken out of shelves, and furniture and carpets piled on the lawn. It was as if a tornado had hit the house. I asked the District Magistrate severely what he thought he was doing. He answered that he was looking for a letter that Pandit Jawaharlal

Nehru had written to President Roosevelt just before his arrest! I told him I did not think much of his intelligence—are important political documents hidden among clothes or put for safety between the leaves of a book? "Please take my assurance that I know where that letter is," I informed him curtly. "I also know you will not find it, because it is not in Anand Bhawan." . . .

[After her daughters' arrests for political offenses Pandit persuaded them to leave India for further education to prepare them for leadership in the Indian cause.]

I was back in jail at the expiration of my thirty-day parole. . . . A few days later Indu and I were informed that we were to be released next morning but an order would be served on us requiring us to leave Allahabad and go straight to Khali, our estate near Almora. We were to live there at our own expense but under the surveillance of the Deputy Commissioner of Almora. Naturally we refused to do so. Later we discovered that jail rules were being further tightened, and, as neither of us was in normal health—Indu had been running a temperature for some time—it had been decided to remove us. Two days later, on May 13, we were released, but I was back in Naini within a week under Section 127 of the Defense of India Rule. Indu was ill with high fever, and, fortunately, no warrant was served on her. Purnima was still in our old barrack and it was good to have her there. Within a few weeks I was ill again, and by July I had been released on grounds of health. . . .

The emergence of Indian women as an important flank of the national movement had been yet another example of the magic of Gandhiji. His call to women had been answered by thousands, crossing all traditional barriers of creed and caste and encompassing all social and economic levels. The patriotic fervor that had us in its grip was something more than political, and by leaving the age-old shelter of the home and taking part in the noncooperation movement side by side with men, Indian women had achieved a sense of equality denied by immemorial custom. . . .

I had gone to Allahabad from Bengal for a brief rest. There had been no news from Ranjit and no reply to my official letters requesting news of him. I now telephoned my friend, the civil surgeon of Lucknow, Colonel Clyde, and begged him to find out how Ranjit was. Colonel Clyde had been a friend of ours while we lived in Lucknow, and our family physician as well. He was aware of Ranjit's health problem. A few days later a telegram from the superintendent of Bareilly Central Jail reached me saying, "Your husband suffered mild heart attack." The date given was a week earlier. I phoned the District Magistrate and asked permission for an immediate interview, but he expressed his inability to help me because of the new rules for political prisoners. I then wrote to the Governor, enclosing the telegram I had received, and the permission was granted.

I went to Bareilly. It was a tremendous shock to see Ranjit brought in to the superintendent's office on a stretcher. His head had been shaved and he was emaciated and almost unrecognizable. It cost me a tremendous effort to restrain my tears. He had been seriously ill for more than a month and was not receiving proper medical care, yet I had not been informed. I was shocked by his appearance, did not know what to talk about, and did not dare mention that I had asked the Governor's special permission for this interview, for even in extreme illness he would have reacted angrily to this. . . . Knowing how Ranjit hated any show of emotion I just sat by the stretcher holding his hand and trying to give him news of Khali, the garden in Anand Bhawan, and the latest letter received from the girls. Interviews are short, but evidently on orders from above I was allowed to stay an hour. I asked for information regarding his treatment, but the prescriptions I wanted were not given to me. As I was leaving Ranjit said, "I have been hearing rumors that I may be released on some ground. I have reason to believe it is so-called friends who are making this effort with the authorities. Nan, darling, remember that I am in the camp of lions—Gandhi and Nehru. I refuse to howl with the jackals." I promised him I would not encourage any move against his wishes. I did not know how I got to the car and reached the place where I was spending the night. I was frightened by his condition, and I was seething with anger. How dared they treat Ranjit in this barbarous manner! . . .

After a very great effort Bidhan did manage to examine Ranjit on grounds of being our family physician. Knowing how Ranjit felt about the question of release on special grounds, and not wanting to disturb him in his serious condition, Bidhan wrote an official letter to the Governor asking permission to take him to his own clinic in Calcutta as a parole prisoner for the urgently needed treatment. This request was refused, but a week later Ranjit was transferred to the Civil Hospital in Lucknow, as a prisoner, to be treated by Colonel Clyde. He was allowed a brief interview with me every day. There was a guard inside his room and armed police on duty outside his door. Fortunately, the hospital room was clean and comfortable, and Colonel Clyde was not only a good doctor but a close friend and he kept in touch with Dr. Roy in Calcutta.

At first, Ranjit responded to treatment and began to look very much better, but in a month he began to slip again. He had now developed wet pleurisy. At that time we did not have the wonder drugs that later saved so many lives, and by the time he was finally released "on grounds of health" the doctors knew he had not long to live. Even I could see that he was sinking. He was too weak to undertake the train journey home, and a friend in Lucknow kindly offered us the hospitality of his home. For three weeks, with night and day nurses and the best medical attention possible during that period, his condition continued to worsen. He had been neglected too long and his release had come too late.

Ranjit died at 5:10 A.M. on January 14, 1944. Death is always unexpected, and the shock of seeing him die, struggling for breath and not being able to breathe, was torture for me. The nurse and I were the only people with him at the end, and even after death for some minutes his hand continued to grip mine. After the agony of the previous days, he was suddenly still and his face was calm and young—he looked beautiful and might have been sleeping after a disturbed night.

I was absolutely alone and very bewildered. Bhai was incommunicado—in Ahmadnagar Fort, as we later learned; the two older girls were in the U.S.A. The few relatives in Lucknow were in government service and could not be expected to help. But I phoned my cousin Captain Anand Nehru, who was cantonment officer. He came over immediately, and we decided to take Ranjit to Allahabad. Anand took charge of everything and, risking Government displeasure, he got in touch with a few people who might be helpful. He also telephoned to Feroze and Indira in Allahabad and informed Budhilal, my cook, to expect us later that afternoon.

The first thing to be done was to tell Rita, who was still asleep, but I did not wake her. When the news was broken to her, she was naturally hysterical, for the shock had been severe. . . .

The days that followed were not easy. The servants had completely broken down and were, for the moment, useless. But for

Anna, who took charge of Rita, and Indira and Feroze, who made me their special concern, I would not have been able to get through the various necessary formalities. . . .

. . . Ranjit had spoken innumerable times about writing [a will] but it had not been done. Ladlibhai [her cousin] was very grave. "This might have very serious consequences for you," he told me. He was proved right. . . . As the widow of a man who died intestate and was a member of a joint Hindu family, and because I had no "offspring," meaning son, I was not entitled to any part of the joint immovable property. . . . The first thing was to cut down all expenses. . . .

. . . I gave notice to my landlord and told Anna it would be impossible to retain her. With the exception of Budhi, my cook, I gave the other servants permission to look for other work. It was one of the moving moments of my life when one after another, each responded in his or her own way. Anna, gruff and practical, said, "You want looking after now, I can't see any reason to be asked to leave." The reason, I argued, was a very practical one, but she firmly refused to move and said she wanted no salary. The other servants, Lala and Sundar, were in tears. I was their *malik* [master], they had eaten my salt all these years, and now they were being insulted and treated as if their purpose in serving me was money. They would *not* go, and whatever little I had they would share. They would take no salary—only a few rupees for incidental expenses until better times. Budhi, who had been devoted to Ranjit, also gave up his salary and left his own home to move into the servants' quarters on Mukerjee Road. Presently the landlord came. I had insulted him, I had doubted his loyalty to the Nehrus. Did I think his relationship with us was based on the rent paid for the house? He would not permit me to leave, nor was there any question of rent for the time being. . . .

Meanwhile, Bhai had heard of Ranjit's death, but no news of further developments had reached him. As he had not known of Ranjit's long illness in jail, the news of his death hit him especially hard. In his letter to me (to write which he had to seek special permission) he mentioned that he was sure I was financially secure as he knew the amount of movable and immovable property involved. Sitting in far away Ahmadnagar, he had forgotten about Hindu law. It was Pantji, who was interned with Bhai, who raised the doubt that unless something specific had been arranged between Ranjit and Pratap [Ranjit's brother], and Ranjit had left a will, I might be in grave difficulties. This disturbed Bhai greatly, and one day when I had reached a moment of near despair, with an exceedingly small bank balance, I received a visit from the collector who handed me a letter from Bhai enclosing a check for Rs.2,000. In his letter Bhai said he was sure I was not in need, but a doubt had been put into his mind and he had asked for permission to send me this "small check." Soon after this, as freer permission to write and receive letters was granted to the prisoners in Ahmadnagar Fort, Bhai soon learned about the case and other matters. His immediate reaction was that I should not ask Pratap for anything. Later, when he heard of an agreement being possible, he took the same line as Gandhiji' had and said I should accept whatever was offered. The unhappy episode had to be ended and forgotten; we had more important things to do. Finally, against Sir Tej's[4] advice, I signed a document giving up my personal claims and that of any unborn grandsons I might have, and the chapter was brought to a close. I went to Juhu to spend a fortnight with Gandhiji, whose tender care of me was like balm to my wounded heart. With Gandhiji's guidance I was able to still my inner turmoil and to make peace with my brother-in-law. The deep love that Ranjit had had for his family helped me to do this, and, because of the reconciliation, our children did not suffer from a break in the affectionate relationship they had always enjoyed. From Juhu I went back to Bengal to continue my work in the famine area. . . .

Back in Calcutta after Ranjit's death, I joined forces with Dr. Shyama Prasad Mukerji, who was working in famine areas, and our workers cooperated with one another in the district where, by now, severe cholera epidemics were sweeping the countryside in the wake of the famine. . . . It was at this point that I thought of starting a Save the Children Fund on a national basis. My committee was enthusiastic, and Sir Richard Casey, the Governor of Bengal, was helpful. . . .

Money for the Save the Children Fund was coming in, but it was nowhere near the amount needed. The famine and allied epidemics continued, but our children's homes multiplied and, even

---

4. [Sir Tej Bahadur Sapru,] leading constitutional lawyer and family friend.

with the simplest arrangements, and mostly honorary doctors and workers, our expenses increased. I launched an appeal to the women of the world to help us. The response was swift and dramatic—the first check came from Madame Chiang Kai-shek for $10,000, another for $5,000 from Mrs. Roosevelt, yet another from the India League of America, of which Pearl Buck was chairman, for $10,000. . . .

During this period I paid brief visits to Allahabad and learned . . . that Gandhiji was anxious for me to go to the U.S.A. to tell the American public what was happening in India. . . .

. . . The hurdle was that my passport had been confiscated and there was no likelihood of its being reissued to me at this time.

Among those who had befriended me in Calcutta were the Chinese Consul General and his American wife. Dr. Pao was a scholar and had been a friend of my husband's. He was a mandarin, very wealthy, and a member of the diplomatic service. His wife, Edith, was from Boston, equally wealthy and well born, and a charming hostess. . . . One day I received a letter from Edith while I was in some remote corner of the famine area. She said she wanted me to come to Calcutta on a certain day to meet some interesting people at an informal buffet dinner. I sent word regretting and said I was not in a party mood. However, she wrote again, and in the end I went to Calcutta. I could not understand why I had been asked as the party was obviously for the American Air Force then functioning in the Burma theatre of war. I did not know anyone. At dinner we sat at small round tables and I found myself next to a very interesting man in Air Force uniform. As I was not familiar with the various insignia, I did not know the rank of my dinner partner. He asked me if I knew anything about America, and I told him I had two daughters at Wellesley College but had never been to the U.S.A. myself. "I would very much like to go," I added, "but this is a difficult time to go abroad." He agreed, and it was only after I got home that I realized I did not know his name!

Some weeks passed, and I received a telegram passed through the censor but delivered nevertheless, which was unusual. The telegram read as follows: "IF YOU STILL WISH TO GO TO THE U.S., MEET ME IN CALCUTTA ON . . ." signed "STRATEMEYER." This was General Stratemeyer, Chief of the Allied Air Command in the Eastern theatre of war. Ten days later I had a message from the American Consul General in Calcutta informing me that a signal from

Washington, from Mr. Sumner Welles, Undersecretary of State, gave clearance for my visit to be expedited and all help to be extended. . . .

I arrived in New York in the early hours of the morning. There were no problems at the airport. I was met by a smart young WAC who said she had everything under control, expressed surprise at my lack of luggage, and took me to a waiting military car. We drove to a hotel which I later discovered was the Waldorf-Astoria. It was a bitterly cold December day and I was miserable for want of proper clothing, but once inside the hotel I began to feel more cheerful. The young WAC suggested I should go to bed and have a good rest before getting in touch with my friends. In any case it was too early in the morning to do anything else. She also told me that all my expenses in the hotel had been taken care of for a week and that I had nothing to worry about. She left a State Department phone number with me in case of need. I went to my room and got between soft sheets. I was asleep in a few minutes—two days in a military plane with bucket seats had been an exhausting experience.

I awoke a few hours later refreshed and very hungry. Realizing that I had few clothes, none suitable to the climate, and only a twenty-dollar bill that a friend in Calcutta had slipped into my handbag, the first thing to do was to establish contact with people I knew—first of all, Lekha and Tara. It was a joy to hear their voices and to know we were so near to one another and would meet soon. The next call was to Pearl Buck. I told her that my immediate need was clothes, shoes, and a warm coat. She promised to come soon to take me shopping. She also informed me that there had been a message from Bhai to her husband, Richard Walsh, of John Day and Company, who were Bhai's publishers, asking him to advance five hundred dollars to me from his royalties for my immediate expenses. . . .

. . . I did not know exactly what my mental picture of New York was, but I was wholly unprepared for and overwhelmed by what I saw. Great tall buildings, glittering shop windows, cars, well-dressed men and women and signs of affluence everywhere. We went—I now wonder why—to Saks Fifth Avenue, and I was dazzled and bewildered. The stores were all decked for Christmas and I had never before seen such decorations nor been subject to such temptation. It was all an unreal world into which I strayed by accident.

The past, with its jail-going, was more real, and so were the filth and stench of the famine-stricken area from where I had so recently come. Those little abandoned diseased babies were real enough. . . . What was I doing here? Surely I could serve no useful purpose. . . .

. . . I had to decide how to go about my work in informing the American public about India and the conditions then prevailing in my country. Among my friends were many Americans who had sympathy for our freedom struggle and admiration for Gandhi and Nehru. . . . I was assured that I could best reach the public through a lecture tour, and Pearl Buck introduced me to the Clark Getts Lecture Bureau. . . .

. . . A rough tour schedule was prepared for me. On paper it appeared easy and interesting. It was to cover a whole year and extend from coast to coast. After a very few weeks at the job I began to wonder why I had hated being in jail. On an extended lecture program one is literally a prisoner—a prisoner of the lecture bureau and a prisoner of the audiences, few of whom had much information about India. . . . Soon I began to reach people, and demands for my lectures doubled and trebled. . . .

. . . In a remarkably short time the press was with me and India was the focus of attention in various small towns across the country. . . .

As the time approached for the meeting in San Francisco, where the Charter of the United Nations was to be framed, it was the desire of . . . Indian residents in the United States that something should be done to show Americans and the world that the Indian delegation, hand-picked by the British Government to attend the meeting, was in no sense representative of our country; that India's voice was stifled, and her leaders, who alone among Indians were competent to sit at the conference table to take part in reshaping the world, were in prison without trial. . . .

The two Indian freedom organizations got together and decided that a small group of Indians must be present in San Francisco to talk outside the conference hall, and that I must spearhead the attack against the British-chosen Indian delegation. . . .

But in spite of generous financial aid it was a problem to find a place to live in San Francisco at that time. Every hotel, boarding house, and room to let had already been booked far in advance for members of official delegations and those accompanying them, and the accommodation problem, already acute due to the war, was greatly aggravated. We had no credentials and little possibility of being able to stay in the kind of hotels where we would be likely to meet and speak with delegates of other countries. I spent one night in the lobby of the St. Francis Hotel. It looked as if that would be my fate the next night also, but just as I was looking for a comfortable chair a lady in uniform, whom I had noticed the previous evening at a desk, came up and asked if I needed help. I told her I was from India and explained the purpose of my being in San Francisco. She introduced herself and told me that she knew about Gandhi and Nehru and had seen some publicity about me in the press. Very cordially and simply she said, "My name is Mrs. Ogden Mills. I am living alone in a large apartment, and I shall be happy if you will come and stay with me."

I was very touched by her kindness but reminded her that she did not know me. "I'm willing to take the risk," she said, smiling, "if you are willing to look after yourself. I have no servants." So I found myself in a beautiful apartment with every sort of comfort. . . .

Having a base made a great difference to me, and I was able to concentrate on my work. The technique of our group was to issue short statements and have articles printed in the newspapers, to buy time on radio, and to hold public meetings whenever possible. In all these activities we tried to explain that the real India was not represented in the conference chamber. . . .

My lecture tour and my speeches at San Francisco were widely reported in India and appreciated. It was inevitable, in a nongovernmental mission of the kind in which I was engaged, that there could be no brief or prearranged plan. In San Francisco my companions and I were a rebel group, and I had the double disability of not having a passport and of being in the States by the courtesy of the President and the generosity of my fellow countrymen settled there. An effort of this kind is, as it were, played by ear, seizing opportunities as and when they come. There is no doubt that on my return to India I was received as something of a heroine. It is also correct to say that my American experience paved the way for the later role I played on the international stage as leader of the Indian delegation to the United Nations and as an Ambassador of India abroad. . . .

When the Second World War ended, members of the Congress Working Committee were released, as were many others who had spent time in jails, but hundreds were still kept in detention. . . .

In August 1945 the Government of India announced there would be a general election the following year. Bhai had been in correspondence with me in New York since his release from prison, and now wrote that I should come home immediately to take part in the elections, which would be held in January 1946. . . . I flew back directly. It was a great joy to be with Bhai again. So much had happened since we had last seen each other—to us, to the country. I had been through great sorrow, but exhilarating experiences in a new country had enabled me to look ahead with confidence. The most heartwarming of feelings was to know Bhai was proud of me. . . .

During this period I was once again a Minister of the Uttar Pradesh Government and living in Lucknow, and as far as I remember August 16 that year coincided with *Janamashtmi,* the Hindu festival of the birth of Krishna—which is also my birthday according to the Hindu calendar. However, no thought of birthday celebration was in my mind as the day progressed and I sat listening to the radio broadcasts giving news of horrors perpetrated, mainly in Bengal. Thousands of lives were lost and blood flowed in the streets of Calcutta as well as in rural areas, as atrocities were committed and Hindus slaughtered by followers of the [Muslim League]. . . .

It was six o'clock on a hot steamy September morning. I had had a bad night and was still dozing when the telephone rang outside my room. I let it ring. Presently there was a knock on the door and Rajab, my peon [office messenger], said there was a long distance call and that there was some very important person on the other end. Rajab was one of the three peons I was entitled to as a Minister. From the moment he came to the house he appointed himself a sort of majordomo, though he was the youngest of the three. . . .

"I have been trying to reach you for nearly half an hour." I knew that voice very well. It was Sir Girja Shankar Bajpai from the Ministry of External Affairs. In a minute I was wide awake. [Sir Girja was] appointed Secretary General of the External Affairs Ministry.

"What can I do for you?" I asked.

"Haven't you received the Viceroy's telegram?" At that moment I noticed a closed telegram on the telephone table. I opened it hurriedly and told him, "It has just arrived but I don't understand. . . ."

"You must come to Delhi immediately. A plane is being sent to fetch you. The Prime Minister wishes to see you as soon as you arrive. Mahatma Gandhi will see you at 5:00 P.M., and you are having dinner with the Viceroy at 8:30 P.M."

I explained to Sir Girja that I could not possibly come to Delhi for several days as my Gaon Panchayat Bill was before the Legislature and I was having difficulties with the Opposition. The bill was a major reform initiated by Congress to bring self-government to every village in Utter Pradesh. Uttar Pradesh was the largest province in the country and had at that time a population of more than sixty million people. The Gaon Panchayat Bill was founded on the traditional Indian system of village democracy, which went back many hundreds of years, and the experiment we proposed to bring before the Legislature was of the greatest importance in a country composed mainly of villages. As Minister of Local Self-Government I had worked hard on the bill. . . .

I called up Pantji to explain the situation. As I had anticipated, he was very annoyed and seemed to think the whole thing had been my idea. I suggested he phone Bhai for a clarification, and I began to get ready for my departure.

In a beautiful official limousine Sir Girja met me at the airport and told me the reason for my being summoned. Lord Wavell and Gandhiji had decided to send a delegation to the first General Assembly of the United Nations, due to meet later in the month, and I was to be appointed the leader. I was horrified.

"I can't possibly go," I told him. "Apart from my bill, what qualifications have I got to lead a delegation to an international conference?"

Very quietly and in his most cynical manner he said, "You managed pretty well on your unofficial tour—I personally witnessed that!" . . .

. . . Bhai's greeting was loving as always. "Hello, darling. Forgive me for dragging you away from your work, but this is important. I expect Girja has explained everything." I told him that Sir Girja had explained nothing but had bullied me all the way from the airport and frightened me by saying I had to dine with Lord Wavell. Bhai had a good laugh, and while I was having breakfast on a tray in his office he explained that the Government had decided to send a strong delegation to the U.N. as this would be the first from an "about-to-be-independent India." Gandhiji particularly wanted me to lead the delegation. He would explain when I met him, and actually it was he and the Viceroy who had come to this decision.

That afternoon I went to the Bhangi Colony, where Gandhiji usually lived when in Delhi, to see him. We always touched his feet, and to people he loved he generally gave a slap on the cheek or tweaked an ear. But with it was his smile—a smile not easy to describe. It was radiant, loving, comforting, all at the same time. For me it was the most wonderful smile in the world. It had kept me alive in my darkest hour, it had given me hope and courage when I needed them most. I loved it and him more than I would ever have been able to say. Because he pampered me and forgave me many things I burst out, "Bapu, I can't go to the United Nations—I don't have the qualifications."

"*I* am doing the talking," he said, "and *you* are going to sit very still and listen." . . .

"Remember," he told me, "I want the delegation of my country to set an example. I shall be happy if we get votes, but I shall be most unhappy if these are gained in any manner that is divorced from our guidelines." . . .

Because of the delays en route we reached New York only a few hours before the General Assembly was due to open. The announcement of the Indian delegation's departure for the U.N. was welcomed by the whole country. We left with the good wishes of all sections, and our work was widely publicized by the press. . . .

In those early days when colonialism was dying there were high expectations, in what is now known as the Third World, of better days to come. The U.N. was referred to as the "conscience of humanity," and men and women everywhere believed this. . . .

Our main concern was of course the item India had inscribed on the agenda. It was also the most important item of that session. The immediate cause for bringing this question to the General Assembly in 1946 was the passing of the Asiatic Land Tenure and Indian Representation Act, otherwise known as the Ghetto Act, by the South African Parliament.* My formidable adversary in the debate was the late Field Marshal Smuts, who raised the plea of domestic jurisdiction under Article 2(7) of the Charter. In reply to this

---

*This act was a major step towards apartheid. It was of concern to India because of its impact on Indians resident in South Africa. [Ed.]

I said, in part, "For us this is not the mere assertion of certain rights and privileges. We look upon it primarily as a challenge to our dignity and self-respect. India has resisted every attempt to divert the debate to a consideration of the legal aspects of the issue. . . . What the world needs is not more charters, not more committees to define and courts of justice to interpret, but a more willing implementation of the principles of the Charter by all governments." The debate lasted in the First Committee for several days, and Field Marshal Smuts took part in the earlier stages. . . .

Treatment of our Harijans (untouchables)[5] was of course emphasized, but he went on to tell the Committee that "South Africa was upholding a Christian civilization in a dark continent inhabited by polygamous races." This called for an intervention, and I said that I was not aware that polygamy, whether sanctioned by law or otherwise, was confined to the East. As for a Christian civilization, I continued, were Jesus Christ himself to visit South Africa, he would be treated as a "prohibited immigrant."

The last phase of the debate was exciting for the General Assembly as a whole. Our delegation was tense with expectation. Time was passing, and though it was already midnight the final intervention was yet to be made. India had the last approach to the delegates. It was to be an approach to conscience—neither aggressive nor humble, but an appeal to those who held the political fate of Asia, and indeed the world, in their grasp. I said,

> I ask no favors for India . . . no concession for the Indian population of South Africa. I ask for the verdict of this Assembly on a proven violation of the Charter on an issue which has led to acute dispute between two member states; on an issue which is not confined to India or South Africa, and finally on an issue the decision of which must make or mar the loyalty and confidence which the common people of the world have placed on us. Mine is an appeal to a conscience, the conscience of the world, which this Assembly is.

The voting took place at 2 A.M. in a tense atmosphere. We had asked for a roll-call vote, and as each "yes" came we could hardly

---

5. The Congress party stand on the question of untouchables was that all social and religious prejudices must be removed. The word Harijan was applied to them by Gandhiji. The most important item of the Congress Constructive Program was the removal of untouchability.

restrain ourselves. The resolution was passed by a two-thirds majority, and as the President announced this, pandemonium broke out. Those who had voted for us rushed from their seats to shake our hands and congratulate us and themselves. It was an Asian victory and we were jubilant. It was some minutes before order was restored. I went into the lobby and the press surrounded me. "What do you feel?" and similar questions were hurled at me. I was happy, excited, a little proud. Restraining myself I said to the press, "We are grateful to our Asian and African friends through whose help this victory has been possible—it is shared by us all." The next thing I did was to send a message to Gandhiji, glad that I had been able to fulfill his mission. . . .

For the whole of that session my presence in the U.N. continued to surprise people who could not equate me and the position I held with their firmly established view of an Indian woman—a clinging vine subservient to all manner of caste restrictions. I would be untruthful if I did not admit that I enjoyed all this. . . .

[After Pandit's return from the U.N.] Bhai as Prime Minister of the interim government also held the portfolio of Foreign Affairs and he had spoken to me several times about an ambassadorship. . . .

A few days afterward Bhai had another talk with me and said he had decided on Moscow for me, and in a day or two the Government would ask the Soviet Government for an *agrément*. I expressed my doubts about a diplomatic career. *Ad hoc* visits to conferences and the United Nations were one thing, but to take on a task that needed special training, and at a time when the eyes of the world were on newly independent India, might be a mistake. I knew nothing of embassies or of Moscow. He suggested I should speak to Sir Girja, and later we could discuss the matter again.

Accordingly I spent an hour with Sir Girja Shankar Bajpai, who was Secretary General of the External Affairs Ministry. He explained that the Government wanted to select public figures for their first ambassadors. He himself felt it would be good for me to be sent to Moscow because I had already met several of the top Soviet representatives at the U.N. and established contact with them. Secondly, the Soviet Union would be pleased to have a woman ambassador, and there would be no prejudice against me. The third and most important reason, he told me, was that I was neither a pro-communist nor an anti-communist. . . . As regards lack of training, he said I would have experienced officials on my staff and would grow into my job. . . .

I was told by Bhai that I must take my briefing from Sardar Patel, and so I accompanied him on his 5 A.M. walks for three days. What I had wanted was instruction and information regarding government thinking on India's overall approach to world problems as well as her specific approach to Moscow, in terms of politics. As in the earlier case when Bhai "briefed" us to the U.N., Sardar Patel spoke of truth, adherence to values, friendship with all nations, avoidance of war.

"But," I said, "these are expressions of hope, Sardar, you are not outlining a policy. Surely we must have a *positive* and *realistic* policy." With some trepidation I reminded him that in the *Artha Shastra,* an ancient Indian thesis on the art of politics, one of the things Kautilya, the author, lays down as rules for the conduct of diplomacy is that diplomacy is not concerned with ideals but only with achieving practical results for the State. . . .

"There is no point in quoting Kautilya," Sardar answered. "He was a learned man, but quite definitely an opportunist! One unchangeable aspect of *our* foreign policy will always be ideals, from this base it will evolve gradually and honorably." I was in a highly unsatisfied mood when I left him, and more unsure of myself than ever. . . .

I was not in India when the day of freedom came. Despite all my protests I had been obliged to leave for Moscow early in August 1947. On the midnight of August 14 power was transferred from the British Parliament to the Constituent Assembly of India. It was a moment of jubilation all over the country and of mammoth crowds in Delhi cheering our national leaders as well as the Mountbattens. At that historic midnight session of the Constituent Assembly, where Bhai made a most moving speech, all members present took the following pledge:

> At this solemn moment when the people of India, through suffering and sacrifice, have secured freedom, I, ———, a member of the Constituent Assembly of India, do dedicate myself in all humility to the service of India and her people to the end that this ancient land attain her rightful place in the world and make her full and willing contribution to the promotion of world peace and the welfare of mankind. . . .

We left Delhi on August 3, 1947. An Air India plane had been chartered for us, and it stood on the field like a great silver bird flying the Indian flag. We were full of excitement and a sense of pride, for India's first mission abroad was to be opened. Our relationship with the world was about to begin. . . .

We had been in Moscow barely five months when the news of Gandhiji's death was broken to me by Dr. Fu, the Chinese Ambassador. Knowing what a terrible shock it would be to me, he had come over personally to say that he had just heard the news on a B.B.C. broadcast. We immediately turned on the radio, and the chant of *Raghupati Raghava Raja Ram*, Gandhiji's favorite hymn, made us realize that this incredible news was correct. Every little while the chanting was stopped and the senseless manner of his killing was announced. We were stunned and incredulous. How could such a thing have happened, and why? At the moment of Independence I had felt myself discriminated against by having to be abroad, but now, in the time of this national tragedy, I was overwhelmed by bitterness at not being at home. . . . Later we heard on the radio Bhai's now well-known speech, "The light has gone out of our lives," in which he broke the news of Gandhiji's death to the nation. . . .

Moscow and Washington were planets apart, and though this may sound odd, the fact was that I had adapted myself to conditions of life in Moscow far more easily than I settled down in Washington. . . .

In Moscow my simple clothes (I usually wore subdued colors or black) and restrained style of living and entertaining had been appreciated and remarked upon. In Washington the newspapers were constantly commenting on my sari and my hair style. The general expectation was for me to "live up to my position." This was explained to me by one of my early callers, Perle Mesta (of *Call Me Madam* fame!), who was a most friendly person. But the world in which she lived was so different from mine, and her only knowledge of India had come from a Maharaja she had once known. . . . But public life in India immediately after Independence imposed many restrictions on one's way of living, and those who had been through long periods of jail and the rigors of the freedom struggle itself had molded themselves on another and simpler pattern. . . . I did not want to be a target for members of Parliament. I was still the only woman ambassador, and it was difficult enough to persuade Parliament that I did my work as efficiently as a man without having debates about my clothes or my parties. . . .

I had met President Truman briefly during my lecture tour and my relationship with him remained a good one. There were no diplomatic frills about him. Both he and Mrs. Truman were what I call real people, with no pretentions, and I liked and admired them very much.

Dean Acheson, the Secretary of State . . . found it difficult to accept me as my country's official representative.

"Why do pretty women want to be like men?" he once asked me.

"They don't," I replied, "they only want equal rights and privileges, Mr. Secretary of State, and I insist on having mine!" Some of these "privileges" related to protocol. The Chief of Protocol, Mr. Stanley Woodward, was harassed and worried by problems such as whether I was to be treated like a man or a woman at formal dinners. Meaning, thereby, would I join the men for cognac and cigars and political talk after the dinner or go with the women for coffee and gossip? As firmly as I could, I said that I would go with the men, and I stuck to this. A few ambassadors felt uncomfortable in the beginning but they soon got used to my presence, and, I might say, liked it! . . .

During my term in Washington a grave crisis that faced the world was the outbreak of the Korean War. The incursion of North Korea into the South was termed an aggression by the Security Council. India's stand was that this aggression must be condemned, and we supported the Security Council's resolution. From the beginning of the crisis India was greatly disturbed, and, because our Government was among the few represented at that time in China, we felt that we were in some sort of position to offer help to nations that had no contact with Peking. . . .

One of the great disappointments of our time has been that the United States, a beacon of hope during the freedom struggles of the Asian peoples, succumbed to the views and greater colonial experience of nations grown to power in an earlier period. In Asia, it has seemed to us that the United States has always backed "the wrong horse," ignoring the legitimate aspirations of the peoples of the countries concerned and their desire to be rid of political and economic domination. Where India was concerned, the United States accepted the thesis that our refusal to join the so-called "free world"—[John Foster] Dulles termed nonalignment "immoral"— could be balanced only by a closer relationship of the United States with Pakistan. The results of this policy have been all too obvious. Starting with the first "tilt" in the matter of taking sides over Kashmir in 1948 onward, to Nixon's famous "tilt" at the time of the Bangladesh war, the United States stepped into imperial shoes and played one side against the other as in former "divide and rule" days. . . .

Home again, I was kept busy with work in my constituency, Parliament, and family life. After many years I had a home in India, and Rita . . . was with me. I was pleased that she had decided to work with the Red Cross, and when I learned she was doing a really good job, I was very happy. . . .

Bhai had told me that India would seek election to the presidentship of the eighth session of the General Assembly, and, if elected, I would assume that office. Lester Pearson of Canada, Nobel Peace Prize winner for his efforts in Korea, was then President of the General Assembly, and I succeeded him. It was a memorable moment for me because I was the first woman to hold the office of President. At a press conference in the U.N. Building following the election, some of the questions asked by reporters seemed almost unintelligent and it was not easy to reply politely. . . .

"How would you describe the sari you are wearing?"

"Did you ask my predecessor to describe his suit?" I was very put out that in this age of women's emancipation, and after all the years I had been in public life, such inane queries should be put to me simply because I was a woman. No man would have been asked these meaningless questions by the world press. . . .

Actually the role of President was less demanding than that of leader of an important delegation, but it had its responsibilities and opportunities. . . . As President of the General Assembly I had to preside over the Steering Committee to consider the agenda and to decide on the items to be discussed by the various committees. In 1953 the items on the provisional agenda numbered more than seventy. Some of these involved much discussion and, indeed, a basic conflict in the views of member states, and I tried whenever possible to appeal for an objective view in the debates.

[Pandit's next assignment was as Indian High Commissioner[6] in London.] I had known from the beginning that London would present me with many difficulties. Our first High Commissioner there had been Krishna Menon, whose appointment was supported by the Mountbattens but had caused discontent among a part of the large Indian community. There were a number of Indian nationalists settled in Britain who had risen to eminence as doctors and barristers, and among them were some who felt they were entitled to this prize. Though things settled down on the surface after a while, the feeling of having been bypassed remained with them, and a rift was created. . . .

India House was a huge establishment, and everything there was on a grand scale including a fleet of staff cars—and a custom-built Rolls-Royce for the High Commissioner that had been ordered by Krishna. But nothing had been properly maintained. A woman, I think, is quicker to notice such things than is the average man. I made it known to the staff that this would not be tolerated, and for some time we had the kind of spring cleaning that had never been done before. At the end India House had had a face-lift and looked much younger.

Our Embassy Residence in Kensington Palace Gardens had been purchased by Sir Girja Shankar Bajpai from a rich American divorcée. It was a beautiful house. The main salon was paneled with boiserie from one of the famous French chateaux on the Loire. It was completely French, and there was no room to place Indian *objets d'art* or pictures, nor would they have fitted in with the French décor. . . .

The Embassy Residence had deteriorated a great deal by the time I went to London. The chandeliers alone were unaffected by time and neglect. Everything else required attention, especially the beautiful paneling, which was dirty, and the parquet flooring, which needed expert polishing. London demanded a high standard of entertainment, and we were not equipped for this. . . . I began using my own things, which were more suitable than anything our

---

6. Ambassadors of the Commonwealth accredited to other Commonwealth countries are known as High Commissioners.

Government had provided and which gave me pleasure to use. In India this gave rise to much talk of my luxurious living and extravagance. . . .

For an envoy to a foreign country an Embassy is not only a home but a show window of the country he represents. To me India is a land of beauty and generosity, of traditional hospitality and the acceptance of many cultures. And therefore I tried to make 9 Kensington Palace Gardens a congenial setting where people of all backgrounds could meet and know one another, exchange serious talk, or relax. . . .

In the fall of 1956 I had permission from my Government to go home on leave. It had been some time since I had had a holiday, and I was looking forward to being with the family for Diwali.[7] During the summer I had acquired two new granddaughters, and Lekha and Tara were taking the babies and their older children to the family home in Anand Bhawan. Rita was coming from Tokyo with her son, who had been born there and spoke only Japanese, and the whole family was going to be reunited after several years. No sooner had I arrived in Allahabad, however, than I was summoned to Delhi and left by special plane. From Delhi I flew back to London. Suez had been attacked. . . .

The start of the Suez crisis may be dated to President Nasser's need for assistance to build the Aswan Dam. He had asked for aid and expected to be financed by the United States, Britain, and the World Bank. Nasser was at this time at the peak of his popularity, with his dream of Arab unity and his great desire to see the Arab world restored to some of its former glory. . . .

During the months preceding the Suez crisis Nasser was available at all times to the Indian Ambassador, who kept his Prime Minister informed and in touch with Nasser's thinking. The fiery speeches made by Nasser at this time were aimed at the Arab world as much as toward his own people, and on Nehru's advice he modified many of his statements. . . .

We now know that Britain was determined to force the issue from the time the nationalization of the canal was announced and also that secret meetings were held by Britain, France, and Israel. At

---

7. Hindu festival of lights, usually held late in October.

one such meeting at Sèvres David Ben-Gurion, Guy Mollet, and Selwyn Lloyd came to an agreement to stop Nasser's "expansionist ideas" and bring about his downfall. . . .

It was interesting for me as High Commissioner in London to note that the British Government had been in consultation with some of the Commonwealth countries before the Suez crisis broke out in the press, but that they had not informed the Asians in the Commonwealth of their intentions. The trend was obvious to us, and it was felt that Britain had not come to terms with her present position. India was then a member of the Security Council and strongly condemned the action. . . .

At the end of my seven years in England I was restless. . . .

I knew that fifteen years' absence is a long time, especially when those years have been full of change at home and a whole new generation has been growing up. I was also aware of the immense problems facing the country, and because of this I thought every man and woman who could work would be welcomed and permitted to make some contribution to the patterns of new India.

When I said good-bye to London I was sad. After so long I felt almost as if I were leaving home, not going home, and yet I had a sense of purpose—a desire to identify myself once again with that India which Bhai, in one of his speeches, had described as "a myth and an idea, a dream and a vision and yet very real and present and pervasive. . . ." And now she beckoned to me, and I had to go and fulfill myself in her and through her.

While I was still in Parliament in 1967 my daughters had persuaded me to build a house in Dehra Dun. There were several reasons for choosing this location. It is in my home state of Uttar Pradesh. I have had close associations with the town since I was a girl, and we spent summers in the neighboring mountain resort of Mussoorie, twenty miles away. My daughters went to school in Mussoorie, my grandchildren's schools were in Dehra Dun, my husband and my brother spent years in a Dehra Dun prison. . . .

My home is actually in Rajpur, a village nine miles from the town, in sylvan surroundings. . . .

The Rajpur road is lined with jacaranda and laburnum trees. When the jacaranda are in flower the road seems to be covered in a delicate purple mist. Other seasons bring other flowers. I have a garden that some day will fulfill my dreams, and a little pool of wa-terlilies, pink and white, which add charm to the scene. To the northwest of my house is a hill, well wooded and nearly always green. Below it flows a stream that fills up in the monsoon rains, and the sound of running water is pleasant to hear. On this hillside live two friends who treat my garden as their personal property, coming and going at will. These are a pair of panthers whose main interest is the chicken farm across the road, which provides them with chicken dinners. My complaint is that these nocturnal meals are frequently eaten under the cassia tree on my lawn, and the heaps of white feathers left behind make extra work for my gar-dener, who already considers himself an overworked and underpaid man! Sometimes there are invasions of monkeys who destroy my vegetables and eat my fruit. My gardener will not try to scare them away or attack them because they are considered reincarnations of the monkey god, Hannuman. They may do what damage they please and know they are secure.

I like to observe festivals of all faiths in my home whenever pos-sible. There is Diwali, with its lights and joys of the companionship of friends and family who can join me at this time; and *Id*, the Mus-lim festival of brotherhood and rejoicing; and the birthday of the Buddha with its message of compassion for mankind; and Christ-mas with the hope of peace. . . .

During the summer I watch the sunrise while I drink my morn-ing tea on the veranda, and in the evening the sunsets over the Si-walik hills in the west are breathtakingly beautiful, sometimes flaming red and gold, and at other times a mixture of soft shades of rose and pink and purple, all merging into one another. But what I love most are the serenity and silence. On nights when the garden is flooded with moonlight, the mountains look as if they have moved up to the edge of the lawn—good neighbors who know when *not* to speak. . . .

Governments change, men and women come and go, but India will remain and move from strength to strength for there will al-ways be those who will truly serve her and will strive to keep her great. And no matter how many may desire the calm of despotism there will be thousands of others brave enough to launch out on "liberty's boisterous sea."

As I look at the mountains I give thanks for the abundance of God's blessings, above all for His having given me the strength to keep faith with my ideals. I am at peace with myself. I have lived most of my life in the sunlight and enjoyed it. Now that the twilight has come, I welcome it, for I know that the darkness that follows will be the beginning of another day.

Meena Alexander

(1951–   )

Meena Alexander was born in Allahabad, the daughter of George and Mary Alexander, heads of an Indian service family, who were dispatched early in her childhood to the Indian diplomatic mission in Khartoum. Thereafter Alexander struggled to reconcile the inheritance of her paternal family and maternal clan with the Islamic world she encountered when she entered the University of Khartoum at the age of thirteen.

These conflicting influences were complicated when Alexander traveled to England at age eighteen to undertake doctoral studies in English, receiving her Ph.D. in 1973 from the University of Nottingham. A student of the English Romantics and their relationship to nature, Alexander had to square this literary tradition with the Arabic she had learned at Khartoum and her childhood Malayalam. This effort, she says, made her inner life like a mapmakers' grid, in which every word in a stream of consciousness had to be anchored in at least three linguistic and literary traditions.

An example of the cosmopolitan nature of the modern educated classes in India, Alexander added further complexity to her creative life by marriage to an American literary scholar, David Lelyveld, with whom she now lives in Manhattan, along with their two children. A poet, novelist, playwright, and critic, Alexander is understandably deeply interested in postmodern theories about language and the impossibility of translating experience into written expression with any degree of accuracy.

A professional scholar who has taught at Fordham University, Hunter College, and Columbia University, Alexander is intent on exploring the dimensions of modernity in India in poetry and fiction. She has published a novel, *Nampally Road,* concerned with communal violence in India and with brutality to women. Her 1988 volume *House of a Thousand Doors* established her reputation as a poet of unusual technical brilliance. Her memoir focuses on the visual imagery and linguistic forms of each of the traditions in which she is rooted, tracing the moments in her development when each became critical to her interpretation of existence. Postmodern in her insistence on the deceptive nature of linear narrative,

Alexander moves the reader through many periods in her life, treating them as geological strata rather than connected history.

FAULT LINES:
A Memoir

W hat would it mean for one such as I to pick up a mirror and try to see her face in it?

Night after night, I asked myself the question. What might it mean to look at myself straight, see myself? How many different gazes would that need? And what to do with the crookedness of flesh, thrown back at the eyes? The more I thought about it, the less sense any of it seemed to make. My voice splintered in my ears into a cacophony: whispering cadences, shouts, moans, the quick delight of bodily pleasure, all rising up as if the condition of being fractured had freed the selves jammed into my skin, multiple beings locked into the journeys of one body.

And what of all the cities and small towns and villages I have lived in since birth: Allahabad, Tiruvella, Kozencheri, Pune, Delhi, Hyderabad, all within the boundaries of India; Khartoum in the Sudan; Nottingham in Britain; and now this island of Manhattan? How should I spell out these fragments of a broken geography?

And what of all the languages compacted in my brain: Malayalam, my mother tongue, the language of first speech; Hindi which I learnt as a child; Arabic from my years in the Sudan—odd shards survive; French; English? How would I map all this in a book of days? After all, my life did not fall into the narratives I had been taught to honor, tales that closed back on themselves, as a snake might, swallowing its own ending: birth, an appropriate education—not too much, not too little—an arranged marriage to a man of suitable birth and background, somewhere within the boundaries of India.

Sometimes in my fantasies, the kind that hit you in broad daylight, riding the subway, I have imagined being a dutiful wife, my life perfect as a bud opening in the cool monsoon winds, then blossoming on its stalk on the gulmohar tree, petals dark red, falling onto the rich soil outside my mother's house in Tiruvella. In the inner life coiled within me, I have sometimes longed to be a bud on a tree, blooming in due season, the tree trunk well rooted in a sweet, perpetual place. But everything I think of is filled with ghosts, even this longing. This imagined past—what never was—is a choke hold.

I sit here writing, for I know that time does not come fluid and whole into my trembling hands. All that is here comes piecemeal, though sometimes the joints have fallen into place miraculously, as if the heavens had opened and mango trees fruited in the rough asphalt of upper Broadway.

But questions persist: Where did I come from? How did I become what I am? How shall I start to write myself, configure my "I" as Other, image this life I lead, here, now, in America? What could I ever be but a mass of faults, a fault mass?

I looked it up in the *Oxford English Dictionary*. It went like this:

> Fault: Deficiency, lack, want of something . . . Default, failing, neglect. A defect, imperfection, blameable quality or feature: a. in moral character, b. in physical or intellectual constitution, appearance, structure or workmanship. From geology or mining: a dislocation or break in the strata or vein. Examples: "Every coal field is . . . split asunder, and broken into tiny fragments by faults." (Anstead, *Ancient World,* 1847) "There are several kinds of fault e.g., faults of Dislocation; of Denudation; of Upheaval; etc." (Greasley, *Glossary of Terms in Coal Mining,* 1883) "Fragments of the adjoining rocks mashed and jumbled together, in some cases bound into a solid mass called fault-stuff or fault-rock." (Green, *Physical Geography,* 1877)

That's it, I thought. That's all I am, a woman cracked by multiple migrations. Uprooted so many times she can connect nothing with nothing. Her words are all askew. And so I tormented myself on summer nights, and in the chill wind of autumn, tossing back and forth, worrying myself sick. Till my mind slipped back to my mother—amma—she who gave birth to me, and to amma's amma, my veliammechi, grandmother Kunju, drawing me back into the darkness of the Tiruvella house with its cool bedrooms and coiled verandas: the shelter of memory.

But the house of memory is fragile; made up in the mind's space. Even what I remember best, I am forced to admit is what has flashed up for me in the face of present danger, at the tail end of the century, where everything is to be elaborated, spelt out, precariously reconstructed. And there is little sanctity, even in remembrance.

What I have forgotten is what I have written: a rag of words wrapped around the shard of recollection. A book with the torn ends visible. Writing in search of a homeland. . . .

Appa was born in 1921 in the ancestral home of Kozencheri. He was baptized George Alexander. In deference to the tug to Anglicize, his family name, Kannadical, was not officially used. Appa was the third child in a family of four children and the only son. Amma was born in 1927 in Tiruvella. She was the only child of her parents. A similar naming pattern held for her. She was baptized Mary and was first was known as Mary Kuruvilla and then after her marriage as Mary Alexander.

The first child of my parents, the eldest of three sisters, I was born in 1951 in Allahabad, in the north where my father was working, in a newly independent India. My sister Anna was born in 1956 and my sister Elsa in 1961. Amma returned to her home in Tiruvella each time to give birth.

In 1956 my father, who worked for the Indian government, had been "seconded" abroad to work in the newly independent Republic of the Sudan. My mother and I followed him in February of that year. I turned five on the Arabian Sea, my first ocean crossing. For the next thirteen years my childhood crisscrossed the continents. Amma would return to her home in Tiruvella, sometimes for six months of the year. The other six months were spent in Khartoum. In 1969, when I was eighteen, I graduated from Khartoum University and went to Britain as a student. I lived there for four years while I was completing my studies. In 1973 I returned to India to Delhi and Hyderabad. In 1979, just married, I left for the United States and have lived in New York City ever since.

My grandfather Kuruvilla was two months short of seventy when I was born. . . .

Ever since I can remember, amma and I have been raveled together in net after net of time. What was pulled apart at my birth has tensed and knotted up. Without her, I would not be, not even in someone else's memory. I would be a stitch with no time, capless, gloveless, sans eyes sans nose sans the lot. Lacking her I cannot picture what I might be. It mists over, a mirror with no back where everything streams in: gooseberry bushes filled with sunlight, glossy branches of the mango tree, sharp blades of the green bamboo where serpents roost.

To enter that mist, I put out both hands as far as they will reach. My right hand reaches through the mirror with no back, into a ghostly past, a ceaseless atmosphere that shimmers in me even as I live and move. Within it I feel the warmth of the sun in Tiruvella. I smell the fragrance of new mango leaves.

. . . In . . . the present . . . I touch rough bricks where the pigeon perched just an instant ago, on the wall at the corner of 113th Street and Broadway in Manhattan—Turtle Island as it once was in a sacred geography.

Moving west, both arms outstretched, I stand against the park wall, at Riverside Drive. The wind from the Hudson River whistles through my body. . . .

Tiruvella, where amma's house stands, is a small town in Kerala on the west coast of India. There one finds the old religious centers, seminary, graveyards, and churches of the Mar Thoma Syrian Church. Syrian Christian families have house names and Kuruchiethu is the house name amma was born into, my grandfather K. K. Kuruvilla's family name. The old lands are in Niranum where the Kuruchiethu clan, once so powerful, had established its own private church. My grandfather, who was born in 1881, settled, as a grown man, a little distance away in Tiruvella. Buying lands near his wife's paternal home, he built a house with a gracious courtyard and tiled roofs, whitewashed walls and ceilings set with beams of rosewood. The doors and windows of the house were cut in teak, quartered in the fashion of the Dutch who first came to the coast in the mid-century in search of pepper and other precious spices.

When I was a child, the scent of pepper filled my nostrils. When the green flesh around the seed turned crimson, I bit into the sweetness of thin flesh. My teeth grated on the fierce seed within. Yet I found it strange that centuries ago Europeans had killed our people for this bitter prize. . . .

From the veranda of the Tiruvella house I had seen men pick the ripe peppers and toss them into baskets and then pour the harvest onto the sandy courtyard till it made a crimson carpet. In my dreams, it was as if that carpet had come alive, filled with people, raising their arms aloft, singing. And high above them was the clear blue of the Kerala sky.

I think of the Tiruvella house, the courtyard, the clear blue of the premonsoon sky, as filled with the spirit of my grandfather. It is where I trace my beginning. Even now, in New York City, I dream of the sparrow and the coil crying together in the guava tree, the blunt knocks of the woodpecker's beak on the day of my grandfather's death. I see the dry holes under the frangipani tree where the cobras crawled, seeking refuge from the terrible heat of noonday. . . .

. . . When she turned seven, amma was sent off from the Kottayam house next to the old seminary . . . She entered a boarding school run by two Scottish Presbyterian ladies who bore the surname Nicholson. . . .

The school, designed for Syrian Christian girls, stands on a hill with flowering trees and well-tended playing fields, two miles from where the Tiruvella house was built. I imagined my eleven-year-old mother snooping around for pools of water in which to find her face, scouting out bits of polished metal in which she could fix her plaits. What would it be like to be in a boarding school where you could never see your face? I could not imagine. Even boarding school seemed hard to think about, but with grandmother Kunju so preoccupied with political work, it had seemed the only way.

. . . After graduating from Nicholson High School, she left for Madras, for Women's Christian College. There she lived in the shelter of the high walls of the college, enjoying a strict regimen of studies and meals, sedate games of badminton and netball. College was seen as a completion of school, and amma's life in its dark fluid movement of girlhood growth found shelter in Christian institutions for young women.

School and college nurtured her but also cut her away from the daily routines of a parental home and its tight bonds of love. In her later years, in fierce reparation, as if the past might be done over again in the rearing of a daughter, amma brought me and my sisters up in the strict belief that women should stay at home.

"If you ever marry," she told me as I was growing up, "and if you have children, always remember that your role is to be there at their side, at home. It would be wrong for you to take a job. Remember that, Meena, a woman's place is at home, by her family." As she repeated the words over in her soft voice, almost as if she were teaching herself a difficult truth, I pondered the load of pain she had gathered into herself in her quest to live as a woman. And watching her stitch a torn hem, or stir a pot filled with dal, or outside, in the garden stooped in the shade of a neem tree, setting the fragile roots of a marigold into the flower bed, I learnt to love her, to love the slow persistence with which she had learnt how to live her life.

In my rebellion against my mother's advice, in those Khartoum years filled with teenage parties, the writing of explosive poetry, the harsh, addictive throb of desire, in odd moments when my rage against her strictures ebbed away, I tried to understand what it was that made her so stern about a woman's place in the world. Was it because grandmother Kunju's public life had offered her so little time with her only daughter?

Surely, it was amma's bitter longing for her own mother that made her this way. Grandmother Kunju had died an untimely death. She could never return from the grave, draw her lonely daughter to her side, sing to her, smooth her hair, set water to her dry lips as the first grandchild tore through the delicate skin of her daughter's vagina. Did the domestic world give my mother a feeling of safety that she craved? But whenever I have asked her about her own choice of a life, about her feelings for her dead mother, amma has brushed me aside. It was as if a second skin had grown over her mouth, barring her from speech. . . .

When I arrived in America in 1979, five months pregnant, newly married to David, whom I had met in Hyderabad, I felt torn from the India I had learnt to love. In those days I was struck by all the differences between Hyderabad and New York. I could not get over how little dust there seemed to be in Manhattan. Then why pack up the vegetables, celery, broccoli, cabbage, in plastic? My own soul seemed to me, then, a cabbagelike thing, closed tight in a plastic cover. My two worlds, present and past, were torn apart, and I was the fault line, the crack that marked the dislocation. . . .

My mind moves to stones—broken and whole—pebbles, slabs of granite, pink boulders. Lines from the Egyptian Book of the Dead I first read in Khartoum repeat in my head. I had sought the book out after my visit to the Great Pyramid in Giza, a sullen, grotesque thing of sandstone, massive icon of gravity, crouched over its own inner darkness. I was frightened of the spirits of the dead who inhabited it, and had to be coaxed by appa to enter. Amma, who has always suffered from claustrophobia, waited outside with my little sister Anna. So I entered the pyramid with my father and the Egyptian guide, and let the darkness and the dank underground smell wash into my flesh. For weeks later that pyramid cut into my dreams. The huge stones seemed forged from human flesh, broiled by the desert sun into the melancholy gold of

Egyptian sandstone. And out of the stones came voices crying out in Arabic, Syriac, Persian, the words babbling in my head. . . .

. . . My earliest years flow back: skin, cotton, wall, mattress, and quilt. The old mattress mender with the blind blue of a cataract in his left eye, hand raised with the metal hook he threaded into the old cotton, puffing up the crushed stuff inside. It needed air, needed to tumble a little before being shut up in the striped ticking. I remember the clean scented mattresses of Allahabad; air so hot and dry it flayed my cheek; dirt, tons of it; the blue, blue glaze of heaven; moisture, sudden moisture.

How misty it all is, water vapor dashing against mirror and bed and bowl. We needed the water ritual to survive the Allahabad summers. Usually the maid did what was necessary, twice a day, as the heat rose from the Gangetic plains. But one night it was appa's job. He got up and fetched a metal bucket filled high with tap water, crossed into the middle of the room, tipped the water out. It hissed on the hot floor, spreading its wet film over the tiles. Bucket followed on bucket till the iridescent sheet of water petaled the stone floor, making lamplight gleam and flower, an unfinished paradise shifting till the whitewashed walls closed where they touched ground, making a pale bud, a vessel in water, rocking a little, a delicious safety, for I knew the light would subside and with it the motion of the water from the bucket. In its wake a heavenly coolness infiltrated the room, pouring through silks and pottery, metals and glass, and our human skin felt less like a hot tight helmet or body shield made out of copper as in those ancient etchings, and more like ordinary flesh should, smooth, vulnerable, the source of feeling. . . .

Though I was born there, Allahabad is not my home. It is far from Tiruvella, about a thousand miles due north. *Nadu* is the Malayalam word for home, for homeland. Tiruvella, where my mother's home, Kuruchiethu House, stands, and Kozencheri, where appa's home, Kannadical House, stands, together compose my nadu, the dark soil of self. I was taught that what I am is bound up always with a particular ancestral site. Perhaps I will return there to be buried, my cells poured back into the soil from which they sprang. How tight the bonds are, how narrow the passage from birth to death.

But for a woman, marriage makes a gash. It tears you from your original home. Though you may return to give birth, once married you are part and parcel of the husband's household. You enter those doors wearing the rich mathrakodi sari his mother draped over your head at the marriage ceremony. When you finally leave in a simple rosewood casket, the same sari becomes your shroud. . . .

Amma was married into the Kannadical family. She followed appa north to Allahabad and gave birth to me in Kamala Nehru Hospital sometime around nine o'clock on a winter's morning, on the seventeenth of February 1951. No one will tell me the exact time of my birth, perhaps no one knows.

Kozencheri veliappechan, my paternal grandfather, had a horoscope made for me, based, he claimed, on the precise instant of my birth. He would never show it to me. It was locked away with his files and ayurvedic potions, somewhere in a teak cabinet in the large white house he built for himself, high on a hill on ancestral property in Kozencheri. Kozencheri is only twelve miles away from Tiruvella, but in my mind's eye it is a lifetime away; more archaic, more backward, bent to the darkness of blood feuds and feudal torments. The white house, fitted with electricity, was built after veliappechan tore down the house of teak and mahogany that had stood for four hundred years in the lower garden at the edge of the sugarcane fields. . . .

I do not know who cut my umbilical cord. Or how it was cut. Did he or she use scissors? Perhaps it was a harassed doctor. Perhaps a nurse held me, all slippery and mussed, my head a purplish cone with the pressure of entry. Perhaps by this time amma was too worn out with tears to care. But she put me to her breasts as soon as they let her and set the sweet milk flowing.

I know she loved me. I also know that she was broken up, not quite ready for the difficulties of the world, when I popped out. The normal custom was to return to one's mother's home to give birth. While marriage is a parting, an exile from the maternal home, giving birth is a time to return, to celebrate, to feast on rich nutty sweets, to imbibe life-giving proteins, to have your body, numb after childbirth, rubbed over with hot oils and unguents steeped in herbs.

But with grandmother dead, amma had nowhere to return. The closest was her mother's sister, my great-aunt Sara. She lived in Burhanpur where her husband had retired from Simla. Their house was filled with crystal and cigar smoke. Appa went by train to fetch her and brought her back to the little house on the empty field filled with wild flowers that was our first home. She spent her time in Allahabad, preparing muslins and baby woolens, waiting for me to arrive. After my arrival she stayed for a few weeks, then left. Great-aunt Sara was the closest amma could get to home. I know she wept bitterly, missing her own mother at the season of my birth. She felt very far from home. In five years she was to travel even further, again following appa, but this time across the boundaries of a new India, across the Indian Ocean and the Red Sea, further, much further than Allahabad.

Sometimes I think that the journey across the ocean was like a death to her. Or perhaps I should say that it made for an entirely different life for her. As for me, just turned five, my days changed utterly and I became a child of a different sort. My life shattered into little bits and pieces. In my dreams, I am haunted by thoughts of a homeland I will never find. So I have tuned my lines to a different aesthetic, one that I build up out of all the stuff around me, improvising as I go along. I am surrounded by jetsam. It is what I am, the marks of my being: old, overboiled baby bottles, half-used tubes of A and D ointment, applications for visas to here and there, an American green card with my face printed on so dark you can scarcely make out the flesh from the black hair floating around, a diaphragm I no longer use, a wedding ring I cannot wear for my finger has grown plumper, scraps of scribbled paper, a fragment of silk from my grandmother Kunju's wedding sari that I have preserved in a silver box with intricate patterns of mango leaf and the wings of dancing herons that belonged to my mother's mother's mother's mother and is set now on a bookshelf in my bedroom in the Manhattan apartment where I live. . . .

Sometimes I am torn apart by two sorts of memories, two opposing ways of being towards the past. The first makes whorls of skin and flesh, coruscating shells, glittering in moonlight. A life embedded in a life, and that in another life, another and another. Rooms within rooms, each filled with its own scent: rosehips, neem leaves, dried hibiscus leaves that hold a cure, cow dung, human excrement, dried gobs of blood.

I come from there. That conch shell, that seashore, those bellies, that dung, those dried leaves holding a cure for the aching mind, all know me. The rooms, enfolded each within the other, the distant houses all have held me.

I see amma, her hands bent into brown shell shapes for the wind to whistle through. She holds up her hands in sunlight, in moonlight. She stoops to pick me up. I am two, perhaps two and a half. She lifts me high into the wind. I see appa's hands, the veins rising on them. He is almost seventy now, his hair combed back on his head, streaked with silver, that handsome face whittled from within by a blood disease, time and sickness consuming the flesh that just about sustains him. He stretches out his hands to me. I want to dissolve, become a ghost myself so I can race to my father, into his outstretched hands.

Behind him, my mother stands in the doorway. She too has grown older, the laugh lines deepen on her face, the curly hair blown loose from her bun is gray, shot through with black. Now I see her in the half-darkness, the sari drawn over her head. They are utterly quiet, for there is nothing that needs to be said. They wait for me in the Tiruvella house with a sandy courtyard where the ancient mulberry tree blossoms in sunlight.

But the rooms of the house are filled with darkness. I am in that house, somewhere in between my parents, hovering as a ghost might. I cannot escape. This is the house of my blood, the whorl of flesh I am. It is all already written, already made.

Another memory invades me: flat, filled with the burning present, cut by existential choices. Composed of bits and pieces of the present, it renders the past suspect, cowardly, baseless. Place names litter it: Allahabad, Tiruvella, Kozencheri, Pune, Khartoum, Cairo, Beirut, Jerusalem, Dubai, London, New York, Minneapolis, Saint Paul, New Delhi, Trivandrum. Sometimes I think I could lift these scraps of space and much as an indigent dressmaker, cut them into shape. Stitch my days into a patchwork garment fit to wear.

But when she approaches me, this Other who I am, dressed in her bits-and-pieces clothing, the scraps cobbled together to cover her nakedness, I see quite clearly what I had only guessed at earlier: she has no home, no fixed address, no shelter. Sure, everything else looks fine. She has two hands, two feet, a head of long black hair, a belly, breasts. But it is clear she is a nowhere creature.

She babbles in a multitude of tongues: Malayalam, Hindi, Tamil, Arabic, English, French. Desert sands fill her eyes. Bombers spit fire down on her. She crouches right where she is, at the edge of the subway platform that runs under Broadway: uptown local, at 110th Street. She listens to the youth cry out through his harmonica, lisp out of the side of his mouth for a few dimes, the odd quarter: "She is a material girl, and she knows what she is, she is a material baby, she is an American girl, huh, huh," he cries, pitching his voice as high as he can. Now the metal body of the train grinds in, people press bellies, thighs, elbows, fists shoving in the haste to enter. Thrust against a white ceramic pillar she crouches low, witnessing it all. As the train doors smash shut, she sucks in her breath. I am here she thinks. No elsewhere. Here, now, in New York City.

What does it mean to be born, to live in houses, to be held by the hands of mothers? What answer is there except to say, this is what shapes the fluid stuff of desire, warms it, till the very bedposts cry out for us to return and the past rises, fragrant, spiked with the bitterness of a nostalgia that can never be eased. Pothos, a home-sickness that is never sated. When I think of homesickness, the Tiru-vella house . . . rises up for me. Those corridors wind through my blood. But in dreams that house becomes one with the other great house of my childhood, the Kozencheri house that belongs to my father and his father before him. But neither was my first home lit-erally, for I was born in Allahabad. . . .

. . . Sitting here in New York City, at my writing table in a room filled with dust, I recall my childhood fears about what it might mean to be born into a female body. Quite early I was taught how the sexual body enticed men and then was crossed out in the interests of a higher truth. Women had to bear the burden of all that sin, all that forgetfulness. . . .

The Kozencheri family, appa's side, was most particular about appearances. They were also very strict about crossing lines. Playing with a woodcutter's child, or a milkman's child as I did in Tiruvella, would never be permitted in the Kozencheri house. My Kozencheri veliappechan had large holdings of land that he inherited from his paternal side, sugarcane, paddy, rubber, and coconut groves. He had middlemen and overseers working for him, supervising the la-bor of large groups of peasants who plowed the rice fields, trans-planted paddy, and worked with the rubber sap as, still warm, it poured out of the cut bark into the little coconut cups and then, af-ter being bound into round, stringy balls, was transported to the rubber factory where they turned it into the ridged mats that smelt like vomit a day old, laid out in the sun to dry.

After the day's work the laborers would come up to the house and squat outside on the sand as the middlemen stood by watching.

With his legs outstretched veliappechan sat on the rosewood and rattan chair with the immense arms that he had bought from the British Resident well before the British were forced to leave India. In one hand he held the wad of chewing tobacco that he had pulled out of his leather pouch. In the other he held the wad of money that was to be distributed to the laborers for the day's work. . . . Already I was starting to glimpse the curse of property, the lines of power that held us all in.

Later at night as we gathered for prayers around his bedside kneeling, singing out the portions of the Syriac liturgy veliappechan had chosen, I watched the same man weep out loud as he recited the prayers for the salvation of the soul. Then in the impromptu prayers added on, he called upon the Lord to save all of us, entire and whole for the kingdom to come, called upon the Father in Heaven to rescue us from the Communists whose powers were growing. Surely the Almighty knew they had murdered a tax collector in the mountains to the north and three landowners in the east. And now they were threatening him too. We would all breathe loudly, in chorus, after the "Amen" that followed, while behind my shut eyes, my gaze doubly shielded by my clasped palms, I imagined young men and women with their hair tied up in red bandanas sweeping down at night into the Kozencheri property. I always shivered after these thoughts and moved a little closer to my grandmother Mariamma, and she, quite gently, would pull her silken cloak over me for protection. I knew she scarcely spoke to veliappechan and maintained a staunch silence in his presence. Surely the Communists would spare her.

It is in me still, her voice, her bearing: Kozencheri veliammechi, grandmother Mariamma, my appa's mother who loved to scold me for running around in the sun as I did in Tiruvella.

"Only boys do that." She raised herself magisterially on her carved stool. "Only male children; and the other thing," she stopped, sniffing a little into her muslin handkerchief. She had a large, rather dashing wart at the tip of her strong boned nose, a bumpy grayish thing. She refused to have it removed surgically and gave a reason that made perfect sense to me, the logic of instant recognition. . . .

Veliammechi . . . needed to remind me of who I was and then prepare me for my future.

"Child, come here now." She made me stand up close to her, looking straight at the wart on her nose.

"First, never forget the pure blood that flows in your veins, from the Kaitheyil kudumam and the Sankaramangalam kudumam."

She deliberately omitted her husband's family from the accounting of pure bloods. I did not let on I had noticed her lapse.

"Never forget that pure blood. Come here, child, don't shuffle off." She gripped me by the elbow, kinder now, having to break the sore thing to me, a child without beauty, a plump dark-skinned thing.

"The point is you are so dark. You take after your mother's side in that."

Veliammechi had no compunction in saying this. She would have said it even if amma were listening. How straight she sat with her immaculate form, her starched garments drawn upright as if a pin descended her spine, much as they taught me in elocution class years later. "Walk as if a pin were dropped through your spine and an invisible wire held you up to the ceiling." Those words that came out of the Australian mistress's mouth in Unity High School, Khartoum, might have been inspired by veliammechi's gleaming posture.

My grandmother Mariamma was so fair skinned, I imagined all her blood coming from the Syrian side of the family. Her great-grandfather, sent to Antioch for spiritual training in the Orthodox doctrines, had married a Syrian woman and brought her back to Kerala, and many of his descendants had the pale skin and light eyes of the Syrians, or so it was rumored. But indeed there were many servants and others of lower status who were as fair as veliammechi.

She drew me close to her so that I could tell, young as I was, that by her side I seemed a different race altogether, and the whole of beauty lay with her. She drew me so close I could smell the fragrance of the herbs she boiled into her bathwater and the rosewater that was sprinkled over her silken cloak before she pinned it into place.

"Look child, you are dark enough as it is. How will you ever find a husband if you race around in the sun? Now it's time to stop and do a little embroidery and let one of the maids plait your hair properly. See how terribly dry it is? Let her braid those velvet ribbons into it." She placed two dark velvet ribbons in my hand. I trembled with pleasure, in sheer surprise.

Her words never left me. She spoke so little that those sentences constituted a grand speech and I could not forget them. Nor could I ever forget the confusion her words created in me. Already by virtue of what I was, dark like my mother, I was a cut below her and beauty was impossible. And I knew it was only because of the fine ancestral lines and the landholdings that she had permitted her son to marry such a woman. Then, because appa had gone to work in Africa, there was always the danger that I would become a jungli of sorts, ill-kempt, barbarous, impossible to tame. Furthermore, it was clear that amma, having been used to ayahs and maids all her life, had absolutely no idea of how to raise a girl-child properly.

Still . . . I was left with the sense that, if I tried hard enough, behaved well enough, I might overcome these faults, so grievous in me. In time I might even marry a handsome man with large properties. But decorous behavior, embroidery, and some musical skills were essential and what was I doing in that direction? What was I doing to overcome my deficiencies? In my grandmother's eyes, I had to try very hard. I had to learn how to grow up as a woman. I had to learn my feminine skills, labor hard to grab hold of what beauty I could.

I comforted myself with the knowledge that in two hours the black car would have left for Kozencheri with my grandparents inside and I could return to my barefoot pleasures, tree climbing, hiding out in the ash pit or rabbit hutch, mango picking, tapioca tasting. On rainy days, in Tiruvella, with no one telling me what to do, I could amuse myself in Ilya's study, pulling down heavy volumes of the Bible and its various concordances and translations, the lighter volumes of Marx and Engels and Gandhi and Niebuhr and Tillich. I could make them into an unwieldy pyramid of words and dance around them, pretending I was a rakshasi come down from the Vindhya Mountains or an apsara who had suddenly lost her wings and was forced to seek shelter in a human home. . . .

Ilya believed in the social gospel and the uplift of the poor. He had many friends who were Communists, including the great leader E. M. S. Nambudiripad who used to come when I was a child and take tea on the front veranda with Ilya. But Ilya was a staunch member of the Congress Party, which seemed to him, as the party Gandhi had founded, the best means to any truly Indian version of social justice. In any case he never questioned his own class basis. He came from an old feudal family with extensive lands in Niranum, and while land could be given away, as he and grandmother

Kunju did during the years of the Nationalist struggle so that some landless peasants could be resettled, he never questioned the condition of his birth. . . .

Almost seventy by the time I was born, he was well established as an intellectual and community leader, a spokesman for the Mar Thoma Syrian Christians of Kerala. From all those who came to call on him and from the numerous public speeches he gave, I learnt to accept his place in the world around him, his public power. I loved him more than I have ever loved anyone in my life—in that intensity that childhood brings, severing us from ordinary light, the daily bread of routine and orderliness. Still, I sensed that the very things he taught me about—love and equality and the sameness of all human beings in God's sight—were what our lives in Tiruvella did not have and could not brook.

When I think back through earliest childhood, the houses I lived in, the real, solid places I knew shine out of me, various, multiple, bound together by the landmass of India, an accustomed geography. The constancies of my life, the hands I held onto, the rooms or gardens I played in, ripple in memory, and sometimes it is as if the forgotten earth returns. I remember little things, a window ledge with white paint, the fragrance of wildflowers, appa's bicycle.

In Allahabad appa had a black bicycle he rode to work each day. It suited him well. Sometimes the path that led to our house was so bumpy and he rode so fast that the tires jerked up a halo of dust. Appa was full of verve and loved to travel. We lived in Bambrali, near the Civil Aviation Training Centre where appa taught pilots the basics of meteorology, how to tell an oncoming storm, how to navigate their planes through rough weather. The buzz of aircraft filled my infancy.

When we moved to Khartoum, again we lived near an airport and the whine and splutter of low-flying craft, the low drone of the larger flying machines made a constant brown sound against which I lived and moved. My first lines when I made poems as a child were etched in my own head against the metallic sibilance of aircraft. How frail the words seemed when set against the constant reminder of flight, the skies crisscrossed by thundering silver birds. . . .

I lived with my parents in Allahabad till just before I turned four. Each year before the hot season started, amma, with an appropriate female traveling companion, a servant who could help with my things, set off with a four-day supply of food and fresh water. We entered the first-class compartment of the train, with its plush padded seats and shiny electric fans. The train could take us home, all the way to Kottayam. On the first journey, when I was four months old, appa helped amma and the ayah into the train and the porter lowered his red turban, unloading a huge slab of ice. The ice was covered in sawdust and rough sacking. It had the odor of crushed jasmine, a rich, slightly overripe scent. With the fans turned on and the ice secure underfoot, we were kept reasonably cool for the long overland journey. The temperatures outside, as the train sped though the northern dry lands, could rise as high as 114 degrees. . . .

In 1955 appa was transferred to the Meteorological Office in Pune, in the foothills of the Deccan. In Pune, I started a few mornings of school at Saint Mary's, a convent school run by Protestant nuns. Each morning, a van with a driver picked me up. I was helped in and sat by the window, next to another little girl. I was stiff, uncomfortable at first in the dark navy uniform with white blouse that hurt my shoulders with the heaviness of starched cotton. I was proud, though, of my leather belt and little bag. The nuns were kind. They checked our fingernails before class and, in deference to four-year-old needs, laid out mats at noon each day for our naps. . . .

In summer there was the ritual return to Kerala, to Ilya's home in Tiruvella. Amma traveled south when the heat grew too heady, when the green painted screens could not be flung any lower, nor mango juices cool the senses. However hot the season, the Kerala seacoast prevented terrible excesses of temperature. After a few months we returned to Pune. And so my life, though filled with motion, was stable. My childhood had a clear form: parents and then displacing them for part of each year my Ilya, the grandfather I loved so dearly. . . .

In 1956, just before I turned five, I left India in amma's company. In 1956 when the Sudan gained independence, Azhari, the president, turned to Nehru for help. Rather than have the British send technical aid, he wanted assistance from other Third World countries. Appa was thirty-five at the time; amma was twenty-eight, my age when I made the journey to America. A position for a meteorologist had been advertised in the *Government Gazette*, and full-time members of the Indian Service could apply. He applied for the position and was chosen to work "under secondment" from the Indian government. When I was four and a half, he left Pune for his new job. It was five years since his return from London after his studies at Imperial College.

I have often felt that my father was a Royalist at heart. Something in the pomp and circumstance of British rule appealed to him. He was devoted to the secular ideals of the new Indian government, but the British sense of order, of stilling the "native" chaos in the colonies struck a chord with my father. Perhaps that had to do with the tumult of the feudal family he came from and his constant efforts to keep his own emotions under firm dominion. Years later he told me he believed in Newton's conceptions of the universe, the order and clarity presumed in the universe. The instabilities of the winds and waters, of the monsoon and the haboob (the dark desert wind he had to forecast in the Sudanese summers) coexisted in his mind with the geometric precisions of a physics that could refigure all things in a divinity without division.

The photographs of the time show a handsome young man, slender, with strong shoulders, even-featured, with dark wavy hair. His eyes are tender with happiness. Amma by his side is slight, her hair pulled back in a low, tight bun. Her face is delicately molded, the cheekbones high, the forehead wide and handsome. There is something quiet, even reticent about my mother in the photograph. She looks down, away from the photographer to the little child in a smock dress, whose curly hair is pinned to one side. I am there, at four, skipping between my parents, one hand in each of theirs. I am wearing shiny shoes that catch the light and deflect the image. We are standing in the back courtyard of the Tiruvella house where the roof points down in two triangles for the rain water to fall onto granite slabs. We are close to the mulberry tree, a bit of a blur in the photo. Like my Kozencheri grandfather before him, my father has strong shoulders. . . .

. . . That first ocean crossing obsesses me. I think of it as a figuration of death. Losing sense, being blotted out, thrown irretrievably across a border. But it also provokes the imaginary. I am forced to fabricate, trust to the maquillage of words, weave tales. A five-year-old child, I stood still by amma's side on deck watching the dark coil of waves. . . . I felt I hated my mother for taking me away. I let go of her hand. I stared at the thick dark waves. Even now, in memory, they unfold like cut tongues. . . .

In a white painted steamer of the Mogul Lines, the SS *Jehangir,* amma and I sailed from Bombay to Port Sudan. On deck with the shining glass beads that our neighbor from Tiruvella had wrapped up in tissue paper for my birthday, I sat mute, wordless. In spite of amma, sitting in her Kashmir silk sari in a deck chair in the shade, I felt I had no name, no nature. The water was flat and blue and endless. That night, out of the porthole, I saw an oil tanker sailing towards Iraq.

We sat at the captain's table. Amma had tried to school me in how to use my spoon correctly, how to adjust the white napkin on my lap. I felt uncomfortable. A Parsi lady sat next to me. She kept picking at her fishbones with a silver toothpick. . . . Once, after a glass of too much of something, she leant over and kissed me several times on the cheek. Instinctively I lifted my right hand and did what I did with my great-aunts who were given to the same mischief. With great deliberation I wiped her wetness off my cheek, first with the outside of my hand, then with the palm. Then I glared at her with my rakshasi gaze. I imagined my eyes smoking red as Shiva's did in his rage. . . .

Out of the corner of my eye I saw amma gulp down her glass of water. She shifted uncomfortably in her chair. As if from a great distance I saw her trying to placate Mrs. Bootliwalla. I kept my eyes on the lady's large bosom where a red rose, cut and crimped from stiff Bazaar lace, bobbed uncomfortably. . . .

Arriving at Port Sudan in March 1956, I laughed and wept all together, freed onto dry earth, freed from those ocean tongues. I rushed into appa's arms, forgetting about amma who walked with her head modestly covered, her cheeks with the chicken pox scars shaded by her silk sari.

Over and over again in the days that followed, as we ate supper in the cool shade of the Red Sea Hotel, or as we crossed the desert in a railway train to Khartoum and I saw the rough glittering sands on either side, I made appa repeat the tale of recognition. I think it gave him real pleasure to tell the story to me, though sometimes he had to be prodded a little till he fell into the rhythm of it.

The narrative repeated made an entry for me into a new life, affixing a running stitch of child and father, appa and I. Without his words, those inklings of the actual, where would I be? Stuck somewhere on the docks at Port Sudan, in between the huge bales of cotton tamped down with metal. I watched fifteen, twenty men with huge heads of hair sticking up high over their shoulders, their muscles working in sweat and sea heat, straining to lift the bales up to the cranes that waited with metal hooks dangling in place. Cotton, grown in the fields of Gezira and Atbara, was packed into bales and loaded onto ships bound for Lisbon, Manchester, Newcastle.

Lacking my father's recognition as I raced up the pier, shorn of the tale he repeated over and over again for me, I might still be held in the darkened cabin of the SS *Jehangir,* still haunted by an oil tanker bound for Iraq, its hull fit to burst into flames.

On the train journey through the desert, from Port Sudan to Khartoum, I recall the polished wood of the table in the Sudan Railways dining car where we had our meals. There were lamps with hooked brass necks built into the side of the carriage, whose green shades cast double images in the bright wood, and thick glass windows and beige curtains to shield the travelers from desert glare. I saw date palms, clumps of them out of the window. Then a wave of speckled sand blew forward, covering them up.

In Kerala the sunlight was always filtered through the green of a vigorous tropical growth, leaves, coconut palms, new paddy fields, acres of intricately bordered fruit trees, while here in the sub-Saharan desert it glinted off the sameness of one earthly substance—sand in all its forms, sliding, shifting over the surfaces of perception. Sometimes I saw a single lorry in the distance, jousting with its own reflection. Sometimes a camel and its hooded rider and then four or five others in a caravan appeared in the moving window, up-ended, reflected in imaginary water. It took me years to reflect on mirages, consider what is involved in sighting water where there is none, bitter, mimic doublings that dazzle, deflecting gravity, shattering all coordinates.

Reflecting back on that train ride, I am struck by a dry pleasure, a sensation almost aesthetic in the lack of comfort. The desert remains for me a place of austerity, a site where skins are stripped away, where words dance with their illusory doubles.

I enjoyed that train ride immensely. Appa was handsome and well trimmed and I loved to sit next to him, lapping up all his attention. After the efforts of her journey and her recent sickness, amma looked pale, even nauseous. She spoke little. Perhaps she felt that my father, in his pin-striped shirt, was well able to take charge in this strange land to which he had brought us. Over the glass of fresh lemon juice and the cakes the bearer brought in, appa began the story for the third time.

"What did I do? I went up to the top of the Red Sea Hotel. The very top, mind you. And from there I looked out to sea. There it came, slowly up the waterway, the white steamer. And who should I see on the deck?"

Shifting on my seat, I hugged myself in delight, in anticipation.

"I saw Meenamol. Meenamol herself, with two plaits and this very same dress."

I almost knocked over the glass of lemon juice. Now even amma was smiling. By this time all three of us had forgotten the patently fictive nature of this detail.

"Did you see me, appa, did you see me on the ship? Really?"

"Of course, my dear. What do you think? Of course I saw you, right on deck." So on he went with the tale.

"Then I knew it was the right ship. So I rushed down the stairs and jumped into the taxi. The taxi raced the ship to the dock. We were racing neck to neck, my taxi and the SS *Jehangir*!"

I sighed. I was happy now, at peace. I almost didn't need his last words.

"And then you ran down the gangplank, ran and ran into my arms and I lifted you up, up, so high in the air!"

He raised his strong arms above me as he spoke and I felt the air whirl and the mirage outside the window seemed to enter with all its glittering force, till we were lifted, appa and I, in a warm gush of air and we levitated without moving, while amma, so long my guardian, was left behind, a frail, pensive figure seated by the window in a silk sari marked with patterns of mango leaf and bird wing, the very same figures that were etched into the silver box that belonged to her great-great-grandmother, which she was carrying with her in the trunk safely stowed away in our sleeper. . . .

First catching sight of a mirage in the Sudanese desert, a child of five, I found myself clutching the window ledge of the train in sheer excitement. In my mind's eye, the waters of the Tiruvella well, the cool depths of the Pamba River that turns past my Kozencheri grandfather's paddy fields, even the gray welter of the Arabian Sea, all began flowing into this sheer kingdom of doubling, murderous site of vision.

Twelve years later, at the age of seventeen, that season of excess, I gladly accepted the hyperbole of passion when a man whispered, "No mirage, you are my oasis." I tried hard to contain the ache in my soul when he left to return to Prague. That was in the spring of 1968, and our meetings in a small flat left empty by an acquaintance of his, in a white room by the Nile, were filled with tales of excitement in Wenceslaus Square, of how the Vltava was lit at night by the songs of young people, newly liberated, pouring out

poems, plays, stout ideas for reform. He read out the poems of
Pushkin to me in the original and the shining lyrics of Pasternak. In
between sips of mint tea he described a train ride he had made from
Moscow to Vladivostok passing by Siberia. I could only imagine
such a cold landscape and I curled into his arms. From down below
the cries of the seller of melons and the seller of fresh-caught pigeons rose up from the avenue that wound past the Blue Nile.

In his halting English my friend said, "You must understand,
Meena, if you want to be a poet, there is no stopping place. We poets go on and on. Stations. Small stops. Sometimes an oasis. That's
it, on and on and on." In speaking to each other we made do with
fragments of English and French. For I knew neither Czech nor
German, and he had no Malayalam, no Hindi, no Arabic, languages that had served me well. When he left, I longed to follow
him, across multiple borders, leaving all my skins behind me. . . .

. . . Had I been a male child, brought up between two lands,
surely I would have been able to read maps, figure out the crossroads of the world.

But I was a Kerala girl-child brought up abroad and one of my
feet was bound to the raised wooden threshold of my ancestral
home. I often tripped trying to walk out. At times I have sighted
water where there was none. Occasionally I have been overpowered
by maps that covered whole territories so completely that the earth
beneath vanished and I spent all my energies shutting out buried
cries from rubble.

But the rubble is what I am.

Sometimes I think of the English language as a pale skin that
has covered up my flesh, the broken parts of my world. In order to
free my face, in order to appear, I have had to use my teeth and
nails, I have had to tear that fine skin, to speak out my discrepant
otherness. . . .

. . . Sometimes I think I write to evade the names they have
given me. "Mary Elizabeth" I was baptized, the names of my two
grandmothers strung together, anglicized from Mariamma and Eli
as befit our existence in the aftermath of a colonial era when English was all powerful. Fifteen years old in Khartoum, I changed my
name to Meena, what everyone knew me as, but just as important
to me, the name under which I had started to write poems. On all
my papers at the university, I put Meena, crossing out Mary Eliza-

beth. Appa was dismayed: you will get irretrievably confused in the public records, no one will know who you are, he insisted.

And as long as I lived under his protection, I was Mary Elizabeth in my passport. Then I added an alias: Meena. I felt I had changed my name to what I already was, some truer self, stripped free of the colonial burden. The name means fish in Sanskrit, enamel work or jeweling in Urdu, port in Arabic. It is also the home name my parents had chosen for me at birth. It is the name under which I wished to appear. . . .

When I was in Unity High School, arithmetic with its rhythms of crude additions and subtractions and lumpish carryings over offended some internal logic in me. I could never manage it. Algebra with its finer music of compounds and metamorphic elements drew me, however, and once I was introduced to the figure x, I was fascinated by its possibilities. I would sit by the back wall of the Hai el Matar house, while amma or my sisters roamed around crying out for me to come and take tea and samosas, or come and get dressed for we were expected for dinner at the Kanagasundarams or Kannans or Gopalakrishnans and were already late. I sat in utter silence as they whirled about in the distance calling my name, secure in my hiding place by the white stucco wall, under the shade of a neem tree.

I fastened on the way the sunlight moved over the tips of the neem leaves, or the golden surface of the fruits; the way the pebbles were stacked near my bare feet, with streaks of cobalt under them scarcely visible as if a skin colored like my own, only a tinge lighter, had masked the essential properties stone held to itself. I bent over, laid my cheek against that warm surface, felt the sunlight ripple from tree leaf and bark over my body, or sitting straight felt the rough wall behind me. Each surface in turn echoed my own, made for a shining thing that rendered my own consciousness, held in a growing child's body, less arbitrary, less senseless.

Though I had not started writing poetry, it was in a mood akin to this that poetry began in me, words welling from a voice freed for an instant or two from the prison house of necessity—the calls to duty, the round of taking tea, sitting pretending to read a book at the edge of a circle of idle chatter about where the newest chiffons might be found, or how Mrs. So and So had received a pile of old kanjeevarams from her mother-in-law's tumbledown house in Madras. . . . Yet without those duties, those social rounds where I was held in a net of women's voices, what would have become of me? What if the *x,* the shining symbol I now gave to all that moved me—the gleaming intricate surfaces of the world, the feelings that welled up from too deep for words to reach—were to become all that I was, a spirit on the brink of dissolution, nothing, literally nothing. Such moods used to fling me into a wordless condition and amma would run out of the house worried at finding her eldest daughter crouched in utter silence at the side of the house, gazing at nothing in particular.

"What is this, child? Why do you behave as if the cares of the world were on your shoulders? What are you thinking of?"

There was little I could say in my defense for I had no language for what was passing through me. It might have pleased amma that the clear perception of beauty, in leaf and stone and sky, allowed me to join again with the gardens of my Tiruvella childhood. For by now Ilya was dead and amma was my thickest bond, the blood bond with that life. She turned to me not unkindly and said:

"Come put on that new striped dress, there'll be ice cream, I'm sure, at the party. The Vijaykrishnans have cousins who are coming from Canada to visit. . . .

"Come, come. Manorama's brother, you know, is married to a Canadian, Chloe. This is her first visit abroad. She is said to be rather nervous. Perhaps you can speak to her."

At that dinner party there were tall lamps set out on the lawn at the edge of the house in Khartoum North, cries of mongoose and jackal from the area of darkness that surrounded the lamplight, and Chloe, beautiful, pallid in a low-cut printed dress, seated very still, her freckles and reddish hair in all that lamplight making her seem like a creature out of one of the books of poems I had found in the library. I was fascinated by her looks and wondered what it would be like to live in such a body and have a tall dark man like the Tamilian Tiru drawn to her. I do not think she opened her mouth except to him, and he hovered over her the whole time as chicken was borne out to the table in the garden, and golden brown puris and the chapatis, and dal and paneer saag, and as the expatriates from South India and Sri Lanka, Malayalees and Tamilians, hung together over glasses of whiskey and cold lemonade, laughing into the night. Over the hedges of acacia and tamarind, across the rough dirt road, wild creatures gathered: asses and hounds and jackals came in from the desert places, and scorpions summoned by the dim moonlight out of the cracks in the earth. . . .

When I open the journals I kept as a teenager in Khartoum, the thin cardboard of the covers slips through my hands. I see lines of bold, upright script scrawled in between the pages of poetry and quotes from Marcel Proust, Albert Camus, Wallace Stevens. These lines tell of the misery I went through:

"If you want me to live as a woman, why educate me?"

"Why not kill me if you want to dictate my life?"

"God, why teach me to write?"

The invocation to God in the last was not to any idea of God, but rather a desperate cry aimed at my mother. The fault lay in the tension I felt between the claims of my intelligence—what my father had taught me to honor, what allowed me to live my life—and the requirements of a femininity my mother had been born and bred to.

Essential to the latter was an arranged marriage. It was the narrow gate through which all women had to enter, and entering it, or so I understood, they had to let fall all their accomplishments, other than those that suited a life of gentility: some cooking, a little musical training, a little embroidery, enough skills of computation to run a household. In essential details and with a few cultural variants, the list would not have differed from Rousseau's outline for Emile's intended, the young Sophie. Indeed, I was to be a Malayalee version of Sophie, or so it sometimes seemed to me. There was a snag though. Amma was living quite far from the decorum of her Syrian Christian peers, and the expatriate life of Khartoum set up singular difficulties in her path. How was she to cope with the parties to which I went in the company of Sarra or Samira, where I met boys, even danced with boys? And what of the University where she knew I read out poems I had written in secret, hiding out in the bathroom at home? What was I learning there? How would I live?

I poured my pain into my journals. I sensed that my sexual desires—which were budding at the time, though they had hardly been satisfied in the flesh—were essential to my poetry. But how did they fit within the rational powers that enabled me to think, pass exams, maintain some independence of thought? I had no answer here. . . .

One night, filled with longing for a young man, a Gujarati whose parents lived in Omdurman, on the other side of the river, filled too with despair at the memory of a dead body, tortured, swollen, lifted out from the Nile River, I walked out into the garden at night. The brilliant desert stars came close, swooping down towards me. I lay down on the grass. I put my cheek to the ground, took the blades of grass into my mouth. I put out both my hands and ran them across the ground till I reached a slight crack in the soil. I was convinced by the evidence of my touch and of my beating heart, that there was a crack in the earth nothing could heal, a fault in the very nature of things, treachery in creation.

What I could not admit, as my parents wished me to, was that sexuality made for that fault, had caused the Fall of Man appa reverted to, time and again, in his discourses to me. Appa was pleased that I was being educated, that my rationality, as he liked to think of it, was developing, but he was clearly anxious about my desire to study philosophy, a discipline that he believed could only confound the religious sentiments he sought to inculcate in me.

"First acknowledge God," he said, "then all things, including human intelligence, can be perfected."

When I was fifteen, he insisted I go with him and amma to the sandstone cathedral the British had built in the center of Khartoum. Worn out with fighting, I went, but shut my heart and soul to the vicar of the Church of England who had confirmed me in the Christian faith, had checked my knowledge of its teachings over Sunday breakfasts of scrambled eggs and toast that I shared with him and his wife and their three boisterous children.

My struggles over received religion have caused me some anguish. Even now I am sometimes pierced with a longing to believe but I know that were I to try to enter the steps of the American cathedral two blocks from where I now live, I would be swept out, as if by a hot dry wind, flung onto the stone steps. . . .

They sit around the long dining table that almost fills the room, appa and amma, side by side. Behind them, the long windows of the Khartoum house edged with white shutters. Through the windows the sky and the acacia hedge are visible. The sky is white hot. There they are, appa and amma, male and female, the beginning of me, discussing their daughters' clothing.

"They can't travel to Kozencheri like this."

Amma was worried. The lines on her forehead were just beginning to form. She was approaching forty. I sensed in her a heaviness of flesh, a settling in, a being there. A mother with freckles and small lines on the face, never picture perfect. So close at hand that she shut the light out. The fine bones in her face were growing coarser, as she put on a little weight, as mothering troubles rose up.

Appa sat there, arms crossed, looking grim.

"Of course they can't." The words seemed to be torn out of him.

"Why not?" I was being daring now, foolhardy even.

I leant across the polished tabletop. The sunlight from the window was in my eyes. I was squinting, trying hard to see. There didn't seem to be anything terribly wrong in what I was asking.

"Why on earth not?" I persisted, hearing my voice in my ears, as if it were going nowhere, as if it could not be heard.

He straightened up. He was an honest, decent man, but one who held in his passions with great effort.

"Know what they do with women? If you go sleeveless in the marketplace, they stone you."

Amma was appalled in spite of herself.

"Shh, Mol." She was trying to calm me down. "You're too headstrong. . . . Of course you won't wear sleeveless blouses. You'll cover your arms up. You'll dress well." . . .

How exaggerated it all grew in my fifteen-year-old mind, all hot and feverish and blurred. The thick-skinned grapefruit from the garden, the taut lemons, the slippery dates, shone with an internal heat. The blue painted ceramic bowl in which they sat grew heavy, bearing the naked fruit. I pulled myself round.

"So what am I going to wear? Are you going to make a new set of clothes for us, all over again?" . . .

That morning, at the dining table in Khartoum, I felt amma's nervousness and gave in. In my mind's eye I saw my arms, bare all the way from Khartoum to Tiruvella, covered up in cotton sleeves for Kozencheri consumption; my skirts suddenly two inches longer; the necks of the blouses cut so high I could hardly breathe.

It was only in Kozencheri, appa's ancestral place, that we had to be careful. Elsewhere women from the family dressed in diaphanous saris and revealed all the plumpness of their tender forearms. And who cared? Some even wore backless blouses at dinner parties on Pedder Road. But Malabar Hill in Bombay was one thing, the ancestral home in Kerala was another. . . .

It is summer in Manhattan and a hot wind blows. The wind blows in through the window. I feel it against my cheek almost as if I were in Khartoum or Tiruvella. I lay out my old journals on the white desk and gaze at them. Time contracts into the scrawl of my teenage years. The journals composed when I was a teenager in

Khartoum contain within them a desperate awareness of my femaleness, a sense of shame, of power drawn back that in its very intensity was a threat to the order that governed my young life.

For not only did I bear the shame from the Kerala world within
me, but I set by its side the burning horror of clitoridectomy that
many of my friends had described. . . . In my years growing up,
from time to time I was filled with the image of what women might
suffer—whether through mutilation or through shame—sufferings
caused purely by being female. And I felt in a dim, unspoken way
that there was a connection between how I came to language and
what it meant to be cast out, unhoused.

As a small child in India, I had learnt to speak English along
with Malayalam and Hindi. Syllables, phrases, sentences of English
flowed along as part of the river of my experience. In Khartoum,
however, as a young child of five, cut from the fluidities of my Indian world, I had to learn English all over again. Now it was not
just one language spoken among many: it was the most important
one and I was an outsider confronting it. No doubt my English tutor, Mrs. McDermott, had a lot to do with my feelings of utter in-
eptitude when faced with the complexities of her mother tongue.
Over and over she made me repeat the words she felt I should learn
till their sharpness overwhelmed me, made my mouth hurt.

I see myself, a small child of six, sitting at a polished wooden
table with a sheen so bright it reflected all that was cast onto it, an
ivory vase with roses, a place mat, a knife, a fork pushed to the side,
two faces, one small and dark, the other older and pale. The book I
was trying to read was flush against the wood and so didn't make a
double image: an old old book with pictures of Tom and Bess, little
English children who wore knickerbockers and pinafores, carried
caps in their hands and drank milk. They were forever loitering by
ponds filled with ducks, racing down lanes towards windmills with
red wooden slats. Mrs. McDermott leant forward. Over and over
she made me say: "duck," "duck," "pluck," "pluck," "milk,"
"milk," "silk," "silk." It was hard for her. I pouted, I fidgeted under the table, knocking my knuckles against the wood, then tried
over and over. It was a ruinous waste of time but she persisted. I
was all wrong, I knew it. And I felt quite ashamed. The trouble was,
I knew the words already but in a different way. And she tried her
level best to polish out my Indian English and replace it with the
right model. From her point of view she did a good job. Traces, perhaps even more than traces, of that speech linger on my tongue.

How could she know that more than two decades later, that very diction would work against me, make me an oddity in the eyes of the white Midwestern feminists at a university in the colder reaches of this country who wanted nothing to do with me, who turned and said: "Of course they'll hire you. They'll trot you out because you speak such good English."

In Khartoum, after the year with the Scottish tutor, I enrolled in the Clergy House School, the first non-white child. At first they wouldn't let me into the school: it was officially known as the Diocesan School for British Children. But faced with the wrenching prospect of sending me away to Saint Joseph's in the hills of India, amma spoke to her uncle, C. P. Maathen, who had just come to the Sudan as the first ambassador from India. My great-uncle put in a word with the Anglican bishop and I was let in, by the side door as it were. . . . I was miserable in that school for the first two years. My blackness stuck out like a stiff halo all around me. I was imprisoned there, I could not move beyond it. I felt myself grow ugly under their gaze. . . .

. . . For almost a whole year in class I was dumb, I refused to open my mouth. It was my way of resisting. "You were considered very slow, you wouldn't read in class when you were asked to," amma reminded me. "I came to school," she explained, "and told that English woman: 'My child is not slow, just shy.' She let you be. Then it got a little better." I remember amma walking me to the gate to wait for the school bus, helping me over and over with English words so I wouldn't be puzzled or get lost. But when I began to write poetry at ten and eleven, she grew anxious, perhaps justifiably so, about the disclosures that a writing life commits one to, quite contrary to the reticence that femininity requires.

As a child in Khartoum I used to hide out to write, either behind the house where there was a patch of bare wall and the shade of a neem tree, or better still, in the half-darkness of the toilet. I gradually found that the toilet was safer. There I could mind my own business and compose. I also learnt to write in snatches, a skill that has served me well. If someone knocked at the door, I stopped abruptly. I hid my papers under my skirts, tucked my pen into the elastic band of my knickers, and got up anxiously. Gradually, this enforced privacy—for I absorbed, perhaps even in part identified with, amma's disapproval of my poetic efforts—added an aura of something illicit, shameful, to my early sense of scribblings. Schoolwork was seen in a totally different light. Essays, exercises, notetaking, reading and writing about the literary works on the school syllabus, were always encouraged. It was good to excel there, interpreting works that were part of a great literary past. The other writing, in one's own present, was to be tucked away, hidden. I had to be secretive about the writing that came out of my own body, but still a fierce pride clung to it.

Little did I know that years later the hot unease I had first felt as a small child learning to repeat English words, and trying to get them right, that dense tissue of feeling (unease, embarrassment, a fear of being exposed, a shame, finally, of being improper, not quite right, never quite right) would return sharply, enveloping me. Once again I felt that hot scent: forcing me back onto myself, onto a border existence. But this time it was my intellectual work that was called into question, not because of itself, but because of what my body made me: female, Indian, Other.

I was once called into the office of the chairman of my department at the Jesuit university where I worked. He leant forward in his black garb, stiff, quite clear about his own position. "It has been pointed out to me that you do not publish in the area in which you were hired, British Romanticism."

I perked up. "What about that?" I pointed to a book lying on his table. He picked it up, a little puzzled. "Look at the table of contents," I pointed at it with my finger. He glanced at me. I was sitting there, quite proper in my Kashmir silk sari, erect at the edge of the chair. His eyes shifted to the titles of chapters listed in the table of contents. There was a gap there, a split second. I shivered, not because I was cold—it was early fall and quite warm still—but because I suddenly saw something. There was no way the man who sat in front of me could put together my body with any sense of the life of the mind. I had fallen under the Cartesian blade. "Yes, yes," he muttered, looking at the chapters with names like Wordsworth and Coleridge littering them. "Yes, yes."

I stood up. The trouble was what I was, quite literally: female, Indian. Not that I had not published in my designated area, but that I had also published outside that docket. A paper on Jayanta Mahapatra had just come out in London. Some senior colleagues had seen it. Was this stuff really literature? Also, I was active in the reading series, Art Against Apartheid, and my poems were coming out in journals. It was all quite improper. Later, when I was denied tenure in the spring of 1986, when my body was swelling with a second child, going into work I sometimes smelled that old shame.

The sharpness of the recollection excited me, but by then I was too tired to sort it out. I left it hanging there in memory. . . .

The language I used, English, was part of my reaching out for this new world. It was braided in for me with the Arabic that was all around me, the language that my first poems were translated into, the language in which I first heard words of love and anger. English was woven too with the French I had learnt in school and chattered with my friends, the language of Verlaine and Mallarmé, of the most exquisite lyricism imaginable, of tears, of storms of tears, of betrayal.

> Le ciel est, pardessus le toit
> Si bleu, si calme!
> Un arbre pardessus le toit
> Berce sa palme.

I loved those lines, for quite early I understood the necessity of beauty, of an atmosphere of silence, of a void even in which the imagination might blossom. And without the space made for beauty, of what use was the political struggle? The heart would grow hard, numb, turn into a desert stone.

. . . In my teenage studies I was deeply attracted to the poetry and prose of the English Romantics, whose intense, even tormented probings into the nature of image and language were underwritten by the call for a revolutionary knowledge. I will never forget the first time I read Coleridge. It was in Khartoum, and I carried with me the magical thought of what he, borrowing from Schlegel, developed as the notion of organic form, the idea that any living existence, a cloud, a plant, a poem, a person, might have its own unique inner teleology, apparent only in the flowering of the fullest form, a logic, a *svadharma,* that could not be questioned. Given this, no one could say: you're all wrong, you don't do things right, you don't get the final syllable in the stanza right. The inner form had a logic so powerful it was best spoken of in the language reserved for passion and it tore through the mesh of decorum, of the principled order the disparate social worlds had established.

Yet even as these liberating thoughts came to me in English, I was well aware that the language itself had to be pierced and punctured lest the thickness of the white skin cover over my atmosphere, my very self. The language I used had to be supple enough to reveal the intricate mesh of otherness in which I lived and moved. My very first poems were composed in French when I was twelve and thirteen: I felt this was the way to attain the heights of lyricism Verlaine had opened up. Slowly I revised my thoughts and turned to English.

In the late sixties, I was part of a small group of poets at Khartoum University. My friends all wrote in Arabic and were strong supporters of the use of contemporary language. They felt that the decorum of the classical meters could only violate the quick of the spoken form, the pressing needs of the poet. These friends easily translated my poems into Arabic. My first publications were these poems printed in the Arabic newspapers in Khartoum. While this gave me a great deal of pleasure, I was also surprisingly compliant about accepting my illiteracy in Arabic. . . .

It seemed to me . . . that one script was enough, the one that I had been forced to learn. And I truly believed that I could translate myself in and out of it, together with all the languages that welled up inside me. Perhaps there was also something else at stake, a greater fragility than I could acknowledge, a need to protect the quick of the self.

Through an inability to read and write the script in Arabic, and even in Malayalam, my mother tongue, I maintained an immediacy of sound and sense in those two great languages of my childhood years that enabled me to dissolve and dissipate, if only in a partial, paradoxical fashion, the canonical burden of British English. And so a curious species of linguistic decolonization took place for me, in which my own, often unspoken sense of femaleness played a great part. I set the hierarchies, the scripts aside, and let the treasured orality flow over me. After all, that was how Malayalam had first come to me: in chants, in spoken voices that held a community together. Perhaps deep within me was a fear that learning the script would force me to face up to the hierarchies of a traditional society, the exclusionary nature of its canonical language. . . .

I did not know any women who were writers, at least not firsthand, though indeed, I was aware that such beings existed in the libraries of the world. And it was only dimly, if at all, that I was aware that the illiteracies I clung to helped me steer clear of the elaborate hierarchical machine that set women apart, lower, different from men. . . .

I was fascinated by the corrosive magic of the first person singular: its exuberant flights, its sheer falls into despair. Still there was always a desire to tell the stories of my life, to write of Ilya's garden. My experiences as a young child, as a guardian of the cashew nut grove, were sufficiently troublesome to lead me to want to set down those feelings in words. I needed a fictional form that would allow me more than the intensities of the lyric voice: I needed others, many voices, a plot however simple, a form from which history could not be torn out any more than a heart could be torn from a living animal. At thirteen I thought I would write a short story. But in my first attempts the supple skin of language turned into a barbed wire that trapped me. . . .

. . . Two things became clear: one was that I could never write fiction, for that would mean translating the words of the people I knew best, the life and the practices I was closest to; and the other was a sudden bitter realization of the sheer force of English and how I had been made to learn it. I had had no choice in the matter. It was presented to me quite literally as the only way to go. Living in Khartoum as an expatriate Indian child, I had to learn English. How could I possibly have received an Arabic education? What would that have equipped me for? And in any case the Sanskrit and Malayalam tutors were far away, across the burning waters I had traveled with amma.

Bit by bit I realized that the form of the poem offered something I needed, a translation out of the boundaries of the actual, a dance of words that might free me from my own body. And I took to reading poems day and night so that history might not consume me, render me dumb. But that realization came slowly when, years later in North America, I had to strip my partial knowledge away so that I could learn to write the truth of the body, pitted, flawed, unfinished. . . .

Was English in India a no man's land? No woman's either? I could not be sure in those tumultuous years of the early seventies when I lived and worked there. At the Central Institute of English in Hyderabad where I started work in 1975, there was much discussion of precise speech, correct pronunciation, appropriate usage, the status of English in India, the function of the language, how knowledge imparted in English, including technical knowledge that had to do with modernizing the country, must surely have a trickle-down effect as it was called, from the elite—who unabashedly saw themselves as such—to the rest of country. English then had this superior status in the eyes of some who taught there, superior that is to any Indian language. But there were others who realized that the future of English in India lay in its ability to blend itself with the life all around, the world of the streets, of the marketplaces.

Often I would spend long evenings with my dear friend Susie Tharu, thinking through what it meant to write in India, what sort of art could come out of the streets, the marketplaces. In her company, I learnt to think afresh of aesthetic forms and consider how they are bounded by the public spaces of our lives. Susie too had spent her childhood in Africa—in Uganda, rather than the Sudan— and then, after her studies in Britain, had returned to India. In those days I learnt from her about femaleness, about resistance, and the possibility of political action. In 1979, just before I left Hyderabad, she took me to the first meetings of the women's group, Shree Shakti Sanghatana. Even after I left Hyderabad for New York our friendship, stretched taut by absence, survived, deepened.

In India, my quest to make sense of poetry written in English— what role would it have in terms of Indian literature, who would read it?—took me to Cuttack, to meet the poet Jayanta Mahapatra. First, I wrote to Jayanta, whose work I admired, and asked if I might call on him. It was 1976: I was twenty-five years old. I took the train to Cuttack and then set out in one of those high-backed rickshaws in search of Tinkonia Bagicha. The rickshaw driver took me to the gate. I peered in through the bamboo that grew by the house and saw a bay window filled with books and then Jayanta's slight figure dashing out, calling me. I spent several days there, immersed in the life of poetry, feeling the soil under my feet. Jayanta and his wife Runu grew to be dear friends. Through Jayanta, who had lived his whole life in Cuttack, I learnt to understand the poet's bond with place; learnt to understand how the elegiac voice could gather sustenance from the landscape around; learnt, too, how to accept the ravages of time.

The years when I taught at the Central Institute in Hyderabad, 1975 to 1977, were the years of the Emergency in India, when Prime Minister Indira Gandhi withdrew civil liberties and people could be jailed on mere suspicion of an oppositional stance. Behind my office window was a police station and sometimes I could hear the cries and the hoarse whispers of those who were taken there. I wrote a poem about a police station called "Within the Walls," which appeared in the *Democratic World* in Delhi, but the next poem I sent in and they accepted, "Prison Bars," about prisoners being beaten, was never published. Instead, in the spot where it should have been, the magazine maintained a blank white space, the exact size of the poem, a signal of censorship.

In 1977 I moved a few miles away to Hyderabad University, a very new institution, and there, in an atmosphere of academic excitement, I debated the question of poetry all over again, particularly poetry written in English. My special friend there was the poet Arvind Krishna Mehrotra, who was reading *After Babel* in those days and thinking hard about multilingualism and the composition of poetry in English. For my part I could not forget my Khartoum experiences and how English, the language in which I made poems, had come to me.

Colonialism seemed intrinsic to the burden of English in India, and I felt robbed of literacy in my own mother tongue. The English department of Hyderabad University was housed in "The Golden Threshold," home of the poet Sarojini Naidu. Reading Naidu's poetry and her political speeches—she used English for both purposes—I noted how the discourse of her poetry stood at odds with the powerful language of her speeches. The former was pained, contrived, modeled on the poetry of the English Decadents, filled with images of the female body wasting away. Her speeches, in contrast, were impassioned, concerned with the British abuse of power, with the possibility of a new Indian beginning: they were forcefully directed to her audience, a people struggling for national independence.

I was fascinated by how English worked for her, and how in her political speeches the language could be turned to the purposes of decolonization. What would it be like if Naidu as a poet had been able to break free of the restrictive ideology that bound her in? What would she have needed in order to make poems of resistance, poems that voiced the body?

The questions have not left me. They reverberate in my head. Sometimes a voice rises in my dreams, as floodwaters rise, subsiding suddenly. And the parched landscape of Hyderabad, in the season before the rains fall, starts to crackle with flames and the flames become the blue gas flames in the stove in my New York City kitchen and in my dream I have to hold myself back with both hands, tie the end of my sari to the refrigerator handle to prevent me from tumbling over the slopes into the fault lines that split my imagined earth. . . .

. . . At the age of eighteen, I went to England, to Nottingham University to study for my Ph.D. Initially, amma had had other thoughts in mind. She was keen that I join Madras University where she had studied and where grandmother Kunju had studied and taught. Her fond hope was that I could be drawn back into the web of traditional life as if the fabric which had been stretched, even battered, by our life abroad, might be woven afresh and I wrapped up in it again, a fresh generation entering adulthood. An M.A. from Madras University was not wholly inappropriate for an intelligent young woman. It should certainly be possible to find a good husband after that. And then would follow a life in a comfortable home, with servants and children, somewhere in India. But to amma's shock, for she had started all the investigations herself, through her many cousins who lived in or near Tambaram and Chinglepet, Madras University refused to accept a degree from Khartoum University, which must have seemed in its eyes a poor, postcolonial cousin. London University would accept the Khartoum degree, but not Madras. So I was left with the old colonial route seemingly the one credible possibility: go to England, young woman, they all said. Then you can return to India.

The external examiner at Khartoum University had come from Nottingham University. Jim Boulton, a handsome man, shortish with a shock of white hair and piercing blue eyes. He had been a fighter pilot during World War II and, landing his plane in Madras, had been billeted in Pune. He met us at the cathedral where appa and amma in a renewed spirit of Anglicanism took us each Sunday. "I will meet you after the service and then come home for dinner," he said. After dinner, sitting on the lawn, under the desert stars, he spoke to appa privately. "You have a very talented daughter. I have just marked her papers, and she would have got a first anywhere. I would like her to study further, to do her Ph.D. in England. She can certainly come to Nottingham, but perhaps she would like to try for Cambridge, where I am sure she would get in." This is the conversation that appa, in fulsome manner, relayed to me a few days later.

I did not go to Cambridge. When one of my professors who had studied there wrote to Girton College, Miss Bradbrook, on learning that I was just eighteen, wanted me to fulfill the second half of the Tripos exam. I was dead set against it. The thought of ever doing exams again filled me with irritation: I did not see how reading a set text had any connection with the learning requisite to the composition of poetry, which was what my heart was set on.

My poetry professor, Alasdair Macrae, also counseled against it. "Don't go there, Meena. People who go to Oxford or Cambridge always think of themselves as superior, as set apart for the rest of their lives." Alasdair, who had read us the words of Hugh MacDiarmid and sung ballads in Gaelic to illustrate the music of poetry, had grown up as a proud Scotsman and had studied at Edinburgh. He was a great influence on me. . . .

At night I used to lie awake and wonder what the high tower of Trent Building was like—I had seen a photo in the brochure that the university sent me. I used to wonder if the whole city was filled with Raleigh factories and what was left of Lawrence's coal mining town, and the poverty he had written of in *Sons and Lovers,* a book that had moved me greatly.

Khartoum airport, August 1969: the travelers waited by the concrete wall with their relatives, just by the runway. Amma was fighting back tears, then let them spill. She turned her face all puffy with weeping. Anna and Elsa stood arms linked, a little to her side. Appa, stepping forward to hug me, seemed tired, his eyes slightly red with the glare off the metal airplanes lined up on the concrete. My suitcase, the blue one with the expanding frame that we had taken on all our trips to India, had gone already into the metal hold of the plane. I think I was calm, ready to move on. I had already cut my bonds, I would fly loose.

"Meena, don't forget our people, go to church too," amma had begged me. Now her arms were wide open and empty as I stepped away.

I will never forget that plane ride: the temperature dropping precipitously at each stop—Khartoum, 110; Cairo, 90; Rome, 70; London, 60 with frozen fog—so that in the little semidetached outside Heathrow the body trembled in its thin covers, then trembled all through the next day, entering another life. . . .

At Nottingham, Jim and Margaret Boulton took the place of a second set of parents, and I grew to depend on them greatly. I appreciated their rose garden and the delicate herbs Margaret placed on her roast beef, the Yorkshire pudding they cooked up. Jim gardened for hours and often, spending Sunday at their house in Beeston, I would talk to him of the difficulties I was facing. . . . I also shared with him troubles caused by various young men who kept asking me out, one even going so far as to say he would kill himself if I did not marry him. I felt quite helpless in the matter. I did not know what to do. Shovel in hand, or trimming a rosebush, Jim would listen patiently, and his acute intelligence when he responded always clarified my confusions.

In all these narratives, without consciously intending to do so I kept my sexuality carefully out of the picture. I painted myself as the passive recipient of male desire. I was not touched deep inside; they wanted me, I told myself, and told others: such percipience seemed the feminine part. It was with a shock, a year later, still in England, when I realized that the world I had so carefully constructed, of intensive study, of a few late night parties that I attended more out of a sense of duty than anything else, beers, cigarettes, heady intellectual talk of the sixties, all the accoutrements of a young student's life, could all blow apart. I wanted a man, and I had not wanted anyone so much since the friend I had met in Khartoum when I was seventeen. The intensity of sexual passion forced me back into my bodily self, made me turn against the "reason" of the world. Though all the Romantic texts I was studying seemed to work against the sorts of Cartesianism that split mind from body, I could not move from those intense visualizations of personal space into my own ravaged history.

I felt I had nothing to hold onto and was falling and falling through empty air. I felt I had transgressed in some unspeakable way and the arms of the father could not hold me. That is how I couched it in my journals: "father" or alternately "Father," as if I had fallen through the arms of God or as if my own father, in lifting me high in the glittering air as I ran off the ship at Port Sudan, had suddenly vanished and I had dropped through hot air. I struggled for familiar sensory attachments that might hold me, but there was little my eye or ear could attach to, little to revive a web of memory that might connect me to my past. The whole world had caved into the apocalypse of the mind.

Even when I could not read, I held tight to my well-thumbed copy of *Fear and Trembling,* often tucking it in under the bedcovers, where it would get lost in the pale pink blankets the University Health Centre favored. For that was where I found myself, heavily sedated, so I would sleep. Indeed I was grateful for sleep when it came and willing to give up my nervous pain for the pacification the sleeping tablets provided. Awake, I was acutely conscious, my mind trembling with knowledge it could not piece together. My research into the structures of Romantic self-consciousness, into the refined articulations of internal time-consciousness, had led me here. I did not know who I was. I felt as if I were paying with my life.

. . . My study of Romantic identity was predicated on the erasure of my own. . . .

Returning to India after my studies in Britain, as a grown adult in 1973, I had to unlearn my tortuous academic knowledge, remake myself, learn how to read and write again as if for the first time. Thinking this out, I take courage from Rassundara Devi, who in 1876 published the first autobiography in Bengali, *Amar Jiban* (My Life). As a married woman, held within the confines of domesticity, she taught herself to read and write in secret, hiding a page from the *Chaitanya Bhagavatha* in the kitchen and scratching out the letters on the sooty wall. It took me many years to get where she got, many years to find my own sooty wall on which to scratch these alphabets.

To help me recover my strength I went away from Nottingham for three months, into the countryside outside Basingstoke, to Pamber to live with an old bricklayer and his wife. I had never seen such poverty, such plainness of living close at hand: a small cottage, no books, just the beds and chairs and table and a small pile of vegetables, a few cheap cuts of meat. . . .

. . . I did return [to Nottingham]. I did finish my thesis on Romanticism and the structures of self-identity, pondering how memory was opened up by the complications of lived space, how the "now" of recollection permitted internal time to unfold, a moment, constantly shifting, constantly returned to, much as the opening note of a piece of music is held always at the brink of consciousness, guaranteed by the fragile, living body. . . .

In 1973 I returned to Pune where appa and amma were living. The city was recovering from a bad flood that, coming after a season of drought, had devastated life. I saw women picking up shards of glass, bits of broken bottle, wire, paper, anything but stones, to recycle them for a few paise, and this with the right hand while the left scrounged around for scraps of food that might have been thrown out of the houses nearby: rice, dal, chapatis, half-cooked vegetables. Seeing all this, I could not eat and grew very thin.

I needed a job, so I could live my own life, but it was several months before I finally found one, in Miranda House in Delhi, in

1974. I had just turned twenty-three. Delhi made me. I cannot conceive of myself without those years, 1974 and 1975, when I threw myself into the life of the city. I was young enough to be taken for a student and enjoyed the life of the hostel and cafes. I used to attend the meetings of the Philosophy Society at Saint Stephen's College, at the home of Dr. and Mrs. Gupta. Old Bose Saab, the elegant philosopher, used to attend regularly and we would sit in silence and hear him speak of Spinoza and the intellectual love of God, this very old man whose bones seemed to be shining through his frail skin.

It was at these gatherings in 1974 that I met Ramu Gandhi. . . . Through him I learnt to see India for myself, started to glimpse the deep troubling truths about the land of my origins. Through our conversations, I sensed afresh something of the pain and pity of what it meant to feel one's self spiritually cast out. He taught philosophy in those days in Delhi University and we would sit and talk under the trees in the campus gardens or in the coffeehouse. He came from a distinguished family, his father's father was Gandhiji, his mother's father was Rajagopalachari and he might have considered himself part of the most privileged in a new India. But Ramu, with his intensity of soul, had a true empathy in those days for those who were truly cast out, considered polluted. And knowing how new I was in Delhi, indeed in India, at least where adult life was concerned, he pointed out all sorts of people to me: the poor children picking rags by the truck stops, the beggar squatting by the pile of garbage outside Saint Stephen's College, the mother with three naked infants clinging to her back. His brilliance broke loose from the language of the Oxford philosophers—he had studied with Strawson—and turned to the concrete, vivid landscape around him. . . .

With [my friend] Svati [Joshi] I went on the great march that J. P. Narayan led in 1974, in Delhi, and we watched in wonder as very old ladies clad in khadi came out of their seclusion and climbed onto jeeps that moved them in slow motion, through the hot air, towards India Gate. When my little daughter was born in the summer of 1986, Svati and Bapuji were visiting the United States and they came and stayed with us and Svati held out her lovely arms and picked up her little namesake and sang songs to her, and walked with me, the week after the baby was born, in the summer heat of Broadway.

Why did I leave India? Why did I feel as if there still were a part of my story that had to be forged through departure? I am tormented by the question. All I knew was that something had broken loose from inside me, was all molten. And what was molten and broken loose had to do with India as I saw the land, and to write I had to flee into a colder climate. Else I would burn up and all my words with me.

"I am falling," I said to David when we first met. "I keep dreaming I am falling." It was a long time ago, 1979. We were sitting at Manju's, the new bar on Abid Road in Hyderabad. It had a dull orange light and excitable men who had left their wives behind to come and drink. It had a bar lady with a cleavage and fish that swam sullenly in a neon-lit aquarium with water two feet deep and enough artificial pearls to smother even a fictive Nizam of Hyderabad.

"I am falling. I keep seeing that, falling off the edge of a cliff. I am holding on with two fingers, wrapped around a bit of rough grass." He was very tender. "I'll hold you," he said. "I'll be a safety net for you." And he told me about the extreme cold of Minneapolis where he worked, where breath froze, and the car froze, where just for the heck of it bearded men went out on the ice when the temperature was minus forty, punched holes in the ice with metal picks, and sat and fished for pike, all red with cold, never trembling, never falling.

I was fascinated by those tales and by his own gift of narrative. David loved telling stories, and wrapped me in his voice and held me there. We had met at the home of a mutual friend in Hyderabad and very quickly, in three weeks, had fallen in love and decided to marry. We used to meet in his high room with a balcony in the Taj Mahal Hotel. He was retracing all the steps that he had traveled ten years earlier and had gone from Athens to Jerusalem and now was in India. On his old Hermes typewriter he set up pages of the Jerusalem journal he was writing. I was fascinated by the sense that through narrative he was making up his life, his autobiography.

There was a neem tree outside his balcony and the quiet shadows of a garden of marigolds and roses. I felt a peace, a great pleasure in that room with him and knew I could be there forever. But when we reached Minneapolis a year later, where he had his teaching job at the university, I felt chilled by this strange new world:

baby food in jars and shopping malls and at home books stacked high in piles with no time to read them. When my cigarette dropped into a wastebasket in the attic room of the house David shared with a colleague in the history department, and the basket started smoldering, the thought sprang to mind: I am this basket, this burning thing, how shall I bear my life here? And I tossed the basket out of the high window to put out the flames and to cool off, pushed my little Adam—who was born in New York just two months earlier— around and around the sidewalks of the neat suburban area and watched other wives lay out the washing and roll out their carpets and thought, I am a wife like that, I am, I am. And I saw the mailman come with the mail, and lay it down in a neat pile under the laurel tree and heard my son cry out with delight. But in my mind's eye I kept seeing that basket burning, filled with waste paper from writings that never had time or space to come to anything, torn pages of a Sears catalog, fourth-rate junk mail, bits of soiled tissue paper. Where was the life I had led? Who was I? . . .

In September 1979, ten years after I left Khartoum never to return again, I made another continental crossing: from Hyderabad to New York. By this time I was twenty-eight years old and I was not alone. David Lelyveld and I were married. I remember the evening we first met. It was February 21, dark, clear, so that the rounded moon and stars were visible. A cool breeze was blowing as I entered Syed's house. David was sitting on a mura, talking to Syed. I recall something being said about the fake books in a Nawab's library, walls filled with them, concealing liquor cabinets; the old stables in Rampur converted to a garage for antique cars.

David is a historian of India and he had come to Hyderabad to work on his ideas of nationalism and the formation of Urdu as a public language. In the daytime he would wander about the marketplace, talking to people, scholars, ancient graybeards who gave orations. He was also deep into the Hyderabad archives. After that first meeting, our friendship picked up quickly. We were lonely, each of us, deep inside and our meeting made for a sheltering space. There was a great innocence to our falling in love, a sheer sense of possibility. We felt we had each lived our separate lives and now could come together. I had just turned twenty-eight; David was ten years older. Within three weeks we decided to get married. We traveled north to spend a long summer in Chail at the foothills of the Himalayas. Already in Chail, I was filled with excitement at the thought of coming to America, a country I had read about, but never seen.

Our first stop on the route west was Paris, where we thought we could combine a holiday, part of an extended honeymoon, with some work at the Sorbonne. But after a few weeks in Paris, under the green leaves of the plane trees in late summer, I grew so dizzy I could hardly stand and was forced into the University Hospital on Boulevard Jourdain. I did not get to do any of the work on Walt Whitman that I had wanted to do. "I am fascinated by his notion of the body," I had told Professor Roger Asselineau, "surely it is relevant even now. All that space stuck out flat, the bits and pieces added onto the body, the corpses carried out of the old house. But how?" He had listened carefully over coffee. But my own body, heated by the malarial virus that had developed during the long trip through India, overtook me, stopped my intellectual questioning. The nausea of early pregnancy coupled with the headaches and chills of acute malaria made Paris in the summer a fearful thing. . . .

Svati Mariam was born in New York City, late at night, on May 12, 1986, almost born in the taxi cab. I will never forget the full moon behind the Guggenheim, a pale lemony color as the cab raced down Fifth Avenue. David didn't know I was fully dilated, nor the cab driver, whistling through his teeth. I bit into my lips to stop the pain. One red light, I thought, and that will be that and the child will be born here, now. But we got into the emergency room and I was on the stretcher, and in another half minute she shot out all blue and gray and mottled, my little one, and I trembled and laughed, all at the same time, an experienced mother now. "What is her name, her name," Dr. Wolf asked, when he got there. "Here she is, she must have a name." I took the strength of speech into my own lips and said, "Svati, Svati Mariam is her name."

She was all mottled and discolored then.

"That was before you became a beauty," I tell her, when she asks me what color she was when she was born. "I am varnish now," she replies or sometimes she fixes herself a color change: "peach." And then continues: "You are brown mama, papa is blond papa, Adam is brown Adam, and I am peach Svati."

What shall I be for her, my little one? I push her each day towards Broadway. The days pass. She is still so young, packing in her years, one, two, three, four. Sometimes I worry for her, a little Indian-American girl-child. Whenever I can I hold onto the reality of mechi and mechan, her grandmother and grandfather in Kerala, her aunts, her cousins. Another soil, another earth. But what might she wish to be, that other soil cast into invisibility years down the road, when her small breasts flower and boys line up for her? What will she make of me, her South Indian mother? Will she recall I loved her, loved her brother too, throwing my arms around them, trembling at the sound of trucks roaring past, ambulances that halt to the stench of burning rubber at Saint Luke's emergency room? . . .

I cannot forget Adam just before he turned three. He lay on the airport floor at Trivandrum. Words tumbled out of his mouth, mixed in with the tears. He beat at the cold floor. "No. No. Don't take me away, no, no." He was a well-built child with rosy cheeks. His tears made a mess on the floor. He could not bear to leave Kerala and his grandmother and grandfather and the rough and tumble of all that love, scents of cows and chickens and goats, the safety of so many arms to hold him.

I bent to pick him up, preparing for the passage through the metal detectors and body searches, then over the tarmac into the plane, all ready for the first step, in long return to New York. But as I stooped I felt myself dissolving, a sheer bodily memory I have no words for. I was all tears. I cupped his struggling little form to my breasts and looked at my mother's face. Through her tears, she looked back at me quite steadily.

A few days after Adam returned to New York, he lay on the floor in his American grandmother's house and drew a little picture: his map of the world. On the brown paper there were squiggles running up and down and a square shape somewhat at an angle to the up and down lines.

"Kozencheri, Delhi," he explained, reading his map to us, "India, sixth floor."

"What's the sixth floor?" We peered over his shoulder.

"Grandma's house, right here."

He beamed in delight at his own creation, the hereness, the honey of life included in it. Looking at him, I learnt to forget the little clenched form on the airport floor, the pain, the refusal. How close to danger we so often are, I think to myself, how little the present reveals the complicated amassing discord out of which alone our words can rise to music. In the little kitchen behind us, Toby was warming up a zucchini preparation she had cooked for our homecoming. That tangy, alien fragrance, and the sweetness of bread pudding steaming on the stove top distanced me from those thoughts and I shifted my weight in the new shoes I had bought for our return to this island city by the Hudson. . . .

In America you have to explain yourself, constantly. It's the confessional thing. Who are you? Where are you from? What do you do? I try to reply.

As much as anything else I am a poet writing in America. But American poet? What sort? Surely not of the Robert Frost or Wallace Stevens variety? An Asian-American poet then? Clearly that sounds better. Poet *tout court*? Will that fit? No, not at all. There is very little I can be *tout court* in America except perhaps woman, mother. But even there, I wonder. Everything that comes to me is hyphenated. A woman poet, a woman poet of color, a South Indian woman poet who makes up lines in English, a postcolonial language, as she waits for the red lights to change on Broadway. A Third World woman poet, who takes as her right the inner city of Manhattan, making up poems about the hellhole of the subway line. . . .

Franz Fanon, that great, tormented man whose work I have long loved—I read first in Khartoum, then in India, each time with a shock of recognition—speaks of the dividing lines, the barracks, the barbed wire that exist in a colonized state, of the "zone of occult instability" to which we must come in our art, our culture of decolonization.

In America the barbed wire is taken into the heart, and the art of an Asian American grapples with a disorder in society, a violence. In our writing we need to evoke a chaos, a power co-equal to the injustices that surround us. A new baptism. Else even without knowing that we are buying in, we are bought in, brought in, our images magnified, bartered in the high places of capitalist chic. I think of Bulosan's powerful novel I am reading these days, *America Is in the Heart*.

Wallace Stevens is a poet I treasure. His lines often repeat for me in the mind's privacy. Somewhere he speaks of the imagination as a violence from within that presses against the actual, the violence from without. But Stevens's world is not mine. . . .

. . . It was only after I got here that I read the bitter, fierce words of Frederick Douglass and Harriet Jacobs, Toni Morrison and Audre Lorde, and stitched together that pain with the postcolonial heritage that is mine as an Indian woman, the sense of English I got from Sarojini Naidu in India in her struggle during the Nationalist years, or more recently Ngugi wa Thiong'o in Kenya.

There is a violence in the very language, American English, that we have to face, even as we work to make it ours, decolonize it so that it will express the truth of bodies beaten and banned. After all, for such as we are the territories are not free. The world is not open. That endless space, the emptiness of the American sublime is worse than a lie. It does ceaseless damage to the imagination. But it has taken me ten years in this country even to get to think it.

It was in America that I learnt all over again about the violence of racism and understood that a true poetry must be attentive to this. It must listen and hear. Our lines must be supple enough to figure out violence, vent it, and pass beyond. . . .

If I live here and write mellifluous lines, careful, obscure lines about the landscape by the Hudson, trees and clouds and all that and forget my bodily self, our bodily selves? Or if I write dazzling, brilliant lines filled with conjuring tricks, all the sortilege of postmodernism and forget the body, what would that be like? Didn't Baldwin say somewhere that being a Negro was the gate he had to unlock before he could write about anything else? I think being an Asian American must be like that. Through that bodily gate the alphabets pour in. This is our life in letters. . . .

My ethnicity as an Indian American or, in broader terms, an Asian American, the gateway it seems to me now to a life in letters, depends upon, indeed requires, a resolute fracturing of sense: a splintering of older ways of being, ways of holding that might have made the mind think itself, intact, innocent, without presumption. Now it may well be, indeed it probably is the case that talk of wholeness and innocence and all that really doesn't make sense, or if it does only as a trope for the mind that casts back wherever it is and whenever for a beforeness that is integral in precisely the ways that only a past can be. After all it is in the very nature of a present time to invade, to confront, to seize. It is the present that bodies forth otherness.

But does this mean that faced with the multiple anchorages that ethnicity provides, learning from Japanese Americans, Chinese Americans, Filipino Americans, Mexican Americans, Jewish Americans, African Americans, Native Americans, and, yes, Indian Americans, I can juggle and toss and shift and slide, words, thoughts, actions, symbols, much as a poor conjurer I once saw in the half darkness of the Columbus Circle subway stop? Can I become just what I want? So is this the land of opportunity, the America of dreams?

I can make myself up and this is the enticement, the exhilaration, the compulsive energy of America. But only up to a point. And the point, the sticking point, is my dark female body. I may try the voice-over bit, the words-over bit, the textual pyrotechnic bit, but my body is here, now, and cannot be shed. No more than any other human being can shed her or his body and still live. . . .

Ethnicity for such as I am comes into being as a pressure, a violence from within that resists such fracturing. It is and is not fictive. It rests on the unknown that seizes you from behind, in darkness. In place of the hierarchy and authority and decorum that I learnt as an Indian woman, in place of purity and pollution, right hand for this, left hand for that, we have an ethnicity that breeds in the perpetual present, that will never be wholly spelt out.

So that the deliberate play of poetry, the metamorphosis of images that we prize, throwing things up in the air and changing them, a dove out of an empty cut, cabbage from bootsoles, a comb out of a throat, charged images that discolor against the plainness of our daily lives, is only one small part of the story, a once shining truth all broken up and its bits and pieces turned into sequins on a conjurer's sleeve.

SECTION FOUR

Postcolonial America

"They say the loss of your mother will cause you to sing the old songs"

Vivian Gornick

(1935–   )

Vivian Gornick, journalist and scholar, was born in the Bronx, the only daughter and second child of Louis and Bess Gornick. Educated at City College of City University of New York, she earned her B.A. in 1957 and an M.A. in English from New York University in 1960.

She has divided her working life between teaching English at SUNY–Stony Brook, and Hunter College, and sustaining a career as a working journalist, first as a staff writer for *The Village Voice* and then working as a freelance. An early and important feminist author and speaker, Gornick published *Woman in Sexist Society: Studies in Power and Powerlessness* with Barbara K. Moran in 1971 and *Essays on Feminism* in 1979.

In Search of Ali Mahmoud: An American Woman in Egypt (1973), written to capture Gornick's effort to understand an Arab male friend, shows her mature style and her capacity to describe and evoke powerful human passions with the sparest of language. Never a doctrinaire feminist, Gornick tried in this volume to capture both the life of women constrained by traditional Islam and the reality of the male experience in Islamic society.

In 1978 she published a history of American Communism, a book in part a tribute to her mother, a committed Party member, and in part an effort to trace the links between earlier leftist criticisms of American society and those of her own generation. This work shows the same concern to get to the facts and dispel the myths that her 1983 study of the factors which inhibit women's successful pursuit of scientific careers displays.

The research and analysis present in these historical narratives and careful ethnographic studies undergird the sense of history and the capacity to evoke the past that are so powerful in *Fierce Attachments,* a work in which we feel the anxiety of the Depression years, smell the passageways of the tenement in which the Gornicks lived, and participate intensely and simultaneously with Gornick and with her archetypal Jewish mother.

Her triumph as a writer comes from her ability to make us hunger for her release from bondage to her mother's emotional demands while we see her mother in all her many dimensions and can no more dismiss her than can her angry but loving daughter. Gornick's ability to convey the physical—the touch, smell, and sense of bodies—means that her characters, both male and female, are among the most fully embodied of any we read about in twentieth-century America, just as the narrator herself has a physical three-dimensionality usually left out of women's writing.

FIERCE ATTACHMENTS:
A Memoir

My mother and I are out walking. I ask if she remembers the women in that building in the Bronx. "Of course," she replies. I tell her I've always thought sexual rage was what made them so crazy. "Absolutely," she says without breaking her stride. "Remember Drucker? She used to say if she didn't smoke a cigarette while she was having intercourse with her husband she'd throw herself out the window."

. . . My relationship with my mother is not good, and as our lives accumulate it often seems to worsen. We are locked into a narrow channel of acquaintance, intense and binding. For years at a time there is an exhaustion, a kind of softening, between us. Then the rage comes up again, hot and clear, erotic in its power to compel attention. These days it is bad between us. My mother's way of "dealing" with the bad times is to accuse me loudly and publicly of the truth. Whenever she sees me she says, "You hate me. I know you hate me." I'll be visiting her and she'll say to anyone who happens to be in the room—a neighbor, a friend, my brother, one of my nieces—"She hates me. What she has against me I don't know, but she hates me." She is equally capable of stopping a stranger on the street when we're out walking and saying, "This is my daughter. She hates me." Then she'll turn to me and plead, "What did I do to you, you should hate me so?" I never answer. I know she's burning and I'm glad to let her burn. Why not? I'm burning, too. . . .

Our building was all Jewish except for one Irish family on the first floor, one Russian family on the third floor, and a Polish superintendent.

. . . Here, in this all-Jewish building, she was in her element, had enough room between the skin of social presence and the flesh of an unknowing center in which to move around, express herself freely, be warm and sarcastic, hysterical and generous, ironic and judgmental, and, occasionally, what she thought of as affectionate: that rough, bullying style she assumed when overcome with the tenderness she most feared.

My mother was distinguished in the building by her unaccented English and the certainty of her manner. Although our apartment door was always closed (a distinction was made between those educated enough to value the privacy of a closed door and those so peasantlike the door was always half open), the neighbors felt free to knock at any time: borrow small kitchen necessities, share a piece of building gossip, even ask my mother to act as arbiter in an occasional quarrel. Her manner at such times was that of a superior person embarrassed by the childlike behavior of her inferiors. . . . She seemed never to be troubled by the notion that there might be two sides to a story, or more than one interpretation of an event. She knew that, compared with the women around her, she was "developed"—a person of higher thought and feeling—so what was there to think about? . . . I absorbed the feel of her words, soaked up every accompanying gesture and expression, every complicated bit of impulse and intent. Mama thinking everyone around was undeveloped, and most of what they said was ridiculous, became imprinted on me like dye on the most receptive of materials.

. . . The apartment was a five-room flat, with all the rooms opening onto each other. It was a tenement flat not a railroad flat: not one window looked into an airshaft. The apartment door opened into a tiny foyer that gave directly onto the kitchen. To the right of the kitchen, in the foyer, stood the refrigerator, propped against a wall at right angles to the bathroom: a tiny rectangle with a painted wooden door whose upper half was frosted glass. Beyond the foyer stood two rooms of equal size separated by a pair of curtained glass doors. The second of these rooms faced the street and was flooded with afternoon sunlight. Off this front room, at either end, were two tiny bedrooms, one of which also faced the street, the other the back of the building.

Because the front room and one of the bedrooms faced the street, ours was considered a desirable apartment, an apartment "to the front." A few years ago a man who had also grown up on my block said to me, "I always thought you were richer than us because you lived to the front." Although living to the front usually did mean that the husbands made more money than did the husbands of those living *tief, teier in draird* (deeply, dearly in hell) to the back, we lived to the front because part of my mother's claim to a superior grasp of life's necessities rested on her insistence that, unless we stood nose to nose with welfare, an apartment to the back was not within the range of domestic consideration. Nevertheless, it was "to the back" that we—that is, she and I—actually lived.

. . . The alley caught the morning sun (our kitchen was radiant before noon), and it was a shared ritual among the women that laundry was done early on a washboard in the sink and hung out to dry in the sun. Crisscrossing the alley, from first floor to fifth, were perhaps fifty clotheslines strung out on tall wooden poles planted in the concrete ground. Each apartment had its own line stretching out among ten others on the pole. The wash from each line often interfered with the free flap of the wash on the line above or below, and the sight of a woman yanking hard at a clothesline, trying to shake her wash free from an indiscriminate tangle of sheets and trousers, was common. While she was pulling at the line she might also be calling. . . . Friends were scattered throughout the buildings on the alley, and called to one another all during the day to make various arrangements. . . . So much stir and animation! The clear air, the unshadowed light, the women calling to each other, the sounds of their voices mixed with the smell of clothes drying in the sun, all that texture and color swaying in open space. I leaned out the kitchen window with a sense of expectancy I can still taste in my mouth, and that taste is colored a tender and brilliant green.

. . . Here in the kitchen I did my homework and kept my mother company, watched her prepare and execute her day. Here, also, I learned that she had the skill and vitality to do her work easily and well but that she disliked it, and set no store by it. She taught me nothing. I never learned how to cook, clean, or iron clothes. She herself was a boringly competent cook, a furiously fast housecleaner, a demonic washerwoman.

The kitchen, the window, the alley. It was the atmosphere in which she was rooted, the background against which she stood outlined. Here she was smart, funny, and energetic, could exercise authority and have impact. But she felt contempt for her environment. "Women, yech!" she'd say. "Clotheslines and gossip," she'd say. She knew there was another world—*the* world—and sometimes she thought she wanted that world. . . .

. . . Passive in the morning, rebellious in the afternoon, she was made and unmade daily. She fastened hungrily on the only substance available to her, became affectionate toward her own animation, then felt like a collaborator. How could she not be devoted to a life of such intense division? And how could I not be devoted to her devotion?

. . . I had known since early childhood that my parents were fellow travelers of the Communist Party, and that of the two my mother had been the more politically active. By the time I was born she had stood on soapboxes in the Bronx pleading for economic and social justice. It was, in fact, part of her deprivation litany that if it hadn't been for the children she would have developed into a talented public speaker.

During the Depression the Communist Party sponsored and ran the Tenants' Councils, organizations formed to fight eviction for nonpayment of rent. My mother became the head of Tenants' Council Number 29 in the Bronx. . . . Mama running the council was a childhood classic. "Every Saturday morning," she would tell me, the way other mothers told their children Mary had a little lamb, "I would go down to Communist Party headquarters in Union Square and receive my instructions for the week. Then we would organize, and carry on." How she loved saying, "Then we would organize, and carry on." There was more uncomplicated pleasure in her voice when she repeated those words than in any others I ever heard her speak.

My parents slept, alternately, in either of the two middle rooms, some years in the back, some years in the front, whereupon the unused other room became the living room.

. . . When I was in my twenties I asked my mother why. She looked at me just about thirty seconds too long. Then she said, "We knew that the children each needed a room for themselves." I gave her back the same thirty seconds. She had made such an intolerable romance of her marriage, had impaled us all on the cross of my father's early death, and here she was telling me that the privacy needed for sexual joy was given up for the good of the children?

. . . An ideal of marital happiness suffused the atmosphere my mother and I shared that made simple reality a circumstance not worthy of respect, definitely not what it was all about. What it was all about was Mama's worshipful attitude toward the goodness of her married life, accompanied by a sniffing dismissal of all marriages that did not closely resemble hers, and the single-mindedness of her instruction to me in hundreds of ways, over thousands of days, that love was the most important thing in a woman's life.

Everything from work in the kitchen to sex in the bedroom was transformed by Papa's love, and I think I knew early that sex did have to be transformed. She did not hate sex, but she did seem to put up with it. She never said physical love was unimportant or distasteful to a woman, but sentences like "Your father was a very passionate man. Your father was always ready. Your father could use ten women a night" left me feeling: To take your clothes off and lie down with a man you had to really really love him—otherwise the whole enterprise backfired.

. . . Love, she said, was everything. A woman's life was determined by love. All evidence to the contrary—and such evidence was abundant indeed—was consistently discounted and ignored, blotted out of her discourse, refused admission by her intellect. Once, in my presence (I must have been ten), a friend told her she was dead wrong, that her notions of love were absurd and that she was a slave to her idea of marriage. When I asked my mother what her friend meant she replied, "An undeveloped woman. She doesn't know life."

. . . It's a cloudy afternoon in April, warm and gray, the air sweet with new spring. The kind of weather that induces nameless stirrings in unidentifiable parts. As it happens, it is also the anniversary of the Warsaw Ghetto uprising. My mother wants to attend the annual memorial meeting at Hunter College. She has asked me to come with her. I've refused, but I've agreed to walk her up Lexington Avenue to the school. Now, as we walk, she recounts an adventure she had yesterday on the street.

"I was standing on the avenue," she tells me, "waiting for the light to change, and a little girl, maybe seven years old, was standing next to me. All of a sudden, before the light changed, she stepped out into the street. I pulled her back onto the sidewalk and I said to her, 'Darling, never never cross on the red. Cross only on the green.' The kid looks at me with real pity in her face and she says, 'Lady, you've got it all upside down.'"

"That kid's not gonna make it to eight," I say.

"Just what I was thinking." My mother laughs.

We're on Lexington in the lower Forties. It's a Sunday. The street is deserted, its shops and restaurants closed, very few people out walking.

"I must have a cup of coffee," my mother announces.

My mother's wishes are simple but they are not negotiable. She experiences them as necessities. Right now she must have a cup of coffee. There will be no sidetracking of this desire she calls a need until the cup of steaming liquid is in her hand being raised to her lips.

"Let's walk over to Third Avenue," I say. "There should be something open there." We cross the street and head east.

"I was talking to Bella this morning," my mother says on the other side of the avenue, shaking her head from side to side. "People are so cruel! I don't understand it. She has a son, a doctor, you should pardon me, he is so mean to her. I just don't understand. What would it hurt him, he'd invite his mother out for a Sunday to the country?"

"The country? I thought Bella's son works in Manhattan."

"He lives in Long Island."

"Is that the country?"

"It isn't West End Avenue!"

"Okay, okay, so what did he do now?"

"It isn't what he did now, it's what he does always. She was talking to her grandchild this morning and the kid told her they had a lot of people over yesterday afternoon, what a nice time they all had eating on the porch. You can imagine how Bella felt. She hasn't been invited there in months. Neither the son nor his wife have any feeling for her."

"Ma, how that son managed to survive having Bella for a mother, much less made it through medical school, is something for Ripley, and you know it."

"She's his mother."

"Oh, God."

"Don't 'oh, God' me. That's right. She's his mother. Plain and simple. She went without so that he could have."

"Have what? Her madness? Her anxiety?"

"Have life. Plain and simple. She gave him his life."

"That was all a long time ago, Ma. He can't remember that far back."

"It's uncivilized he shouldn't remember!"

"Be that as it may. It cannot make him want to ask her to sit down with his friends on a lovely Saturday afternoon in early spring."

"He should do it whether he wants to or not. Don't look at me like that. I know what I'm talking about."

We find a coffee shop on Third Avenue, an upwardly mobile greasy spoon, all plastic wood, vinyl leather, tin-plated chandeliers with candle-shaped bulbs burning in the pretentiously darkened afternoon.

"All right?" my mother says brightly to me.

If I said, "Ma, this place is awful," she'd say, "My fancy daughter. I was raised in a cold-water flat with the toilet in the hall but this isn't good enough for you. So okay, you pick the place," and we'd go trudging on up Third Avenue. But I nod yes, sit down with her in a booth by the window, and prepare to drink a cup of dreadful coffee while we go on with our weighty conversation about children and parents.

. . . "Say what you will, children don't love their parents as they did when I was young."

"Ma, do you really believe that?"

"I certainly do! My mother died in my sister's arms, with all her children around her. How will I die, will you please tell me? They probably won't find me for a week. Days pass. I don't hear from you. Your brother I see three times a year. The neighbors? Who? Who's there to check on me? Manhattan is not the Bronx, you know."

"Exactly. That's what this is all about. Manhattan is not the Bronx. Your mother didn't die in her daughter's arms because your sister loved her more than we love you. Your sister hated your mother, and you know it. She was there because it was her duty to be there, and because she lived around the corner all her married life. It had nothing to do with love. It wasn't a better life, it was an immigrant life, a working-class life, a life from another century."

"Call it what you want," she replies angrily, "it was a more human way to live."

We . . . continue on up Lexington Avenue. The air is sweeter than before, warmer, fuller, with a hint of rain now at its bright gray edge. Delicious! A surge of expectation rises without warning in me but, as usual, does not get very far. Instead of coming up straight and clear it twists about, turns inward, and quickly stifles itself to death; a progress with which I am depressingly familiar. I glance sideways at my mother. I must be imagining this, but it seems to me her face reflects the same crazy journey of detoured emotion. There is color in her cheek, but her eye is startled and her mouth pulled downward. What, I wonder, does she see when she looks at me? The mood of the day begins to shift dangerously.

We're in the Fifties. Huge plate-glass windows filled with color and design line the avenue. What a relief it's Sunday, the stores are closed, no decisions to make. We share an appreciation of clothes, my mother and I, of looking nice in clothes, but we cannot bear to shop, either of us. We're always wearing the same few articles of clothing we have each picked hastily from the nearest rack. . . . I know it is precisely because we *are* mother and daughter that our responses are mirror images, yet the word *filial* does not seem appropriate. On the contrary, the idea of family, of our being family, of family *life* seems altogether puzzling: an uncertainty in her as well as in myself. We are so used to thinking of ourselves as a pair of women, ill-starred and incompetent (she widowed, me divorced), endlessly unable to get family life for themselves. . . . The clothes in the window make me feel we have both been confused the whole of our lives about who we are, and how to get there.

Suddenly, I am miserable. Acutely miserable. A surge of defeat passes through me. I feel desolated, without direction or focus, all my daily struggles small and disoriented. I become speechless. Not merely silent, but speechless. My mother sees that my spirits have plunged. She says nothing. We walk on, neither of us speaking.

We arrive at Sixty-ninth Street, turn the corner, and walk toward the entrance to the Hunter auditorium. The doors are open. Inside, two or three hundred Jews sit listening to the testimonials that commemorate their unspeakable history. These testimonials are the glue that binds. They remind and persuade. They heal and connect. Let people make sense of themselves. The speeches drone on. My mother and I stand there on the sidewalk, alone together, against the sound of culture-making that floats out to us. "We are a cursed people," the speaker announces. "Periodically we are destroyed, we struggle up again, we are reborn. That is our destiny."

The words act like adrenaline on my mother. Her cheeks begin to glow. Tears brighten her eyes. Her jawline grows firm. Her skin achieves muscle tone. "Come inside," she says softly to me, thinking to do me a good turn. "Come. You'll feel better."

I shake my head no. "Being Jewish can't help me anymore," I tell her.

She holds tightly to my arm. She neither confirms nor denies my words, only looks directly into my face. "Remember," she says. "You are my daughter. Strong. You must be strong."

"Oh Ma!" I cry, and my frightened greedy freedom-loving life wells up in me and spills down my soft-skinned face, the one she has given me.

. . . The year after my father's death, the year in which I began to sit on the fire escape late at night making up stories in my head. The atmosphere in our house had become morgue-like. My mother's grief was primitive and all-encompassing; it sucked the oxygen out of the air. A heavy drugged sensation filled my head and my body whenever I came back into the apartment. We none of us—not my brother, not I, certainly not my mother—found comfort in one another. We were only exiled together, trapped in a common affliction. Loneliness of the spirit seized conscious hold of me for the first time, and I turned my face to the street, to the dreamy melancholy inner suggestiveness that had become the only relief from what I quickly perceived as a condition of loss, and of defeat.

I began sitting on the fire escape in the spring, and I sat there every night throughout that immeasurably long first summer, with my mother lying on the couch behind me moaning, crying, sometimes screaming late into the night and my brother wandering aimlessly about, reading or pacing, the only conversation among us that of barely polite familiars: "Get me a glass of water," or, "Shut the window, there's a draft," or, "You going down? Bring back milk." I found I could make myself feel better simply by swinging my legs across the windowsill and turning my face fully outward, away from the room behind me.

. . . My father died at four o'clock in the morning on a day in late November. A telegram was delivered at five-thirty from the hospital where he had lain, terrified, for a week under an oxygen tent they said would save his life but I knew better. He had had three heart seizures in five days. The last one killed him. He was fifty-one years old. My mother was forty-six. My brother was nineteen. I was thirteen.

When the doorbell rang my brother was the first one out of bed, Mama right behind him, and me behind her. We all pushed into the tiny foyer. My brother stood in the doorway beneath the light from a sixty-watt bulb staring at a pale-yellow square of paper. My mother dug her nails into his arm. "Papa's dead, isn't he? Isn't he?" My brother slumped to the floor, and the screaming began.

"Oh," my mother screamed.

"Oh, my God," my mother screamed.

"Oh, my God, help me," my mother screamed.

The tears fell and rose and filled the hallway and ran into the kitchen and down across the living room and pushed against the walls of the two bedrooms and washed us all away.

Wailing women and frightened men surrounded my mother all that day and night. . . .

With me they did as they pleased. Passing me among themselves in an ecstasy of ritual pity, they isolated me more thoroughly than actual neglect could have done. They smothered me against their chests, choked me with indigestible food, terrified my ears with a babble of numbing reassurance. My only hope was retreat. I went unresponsive, and I stayed that way.

Periodically, my mother's glazed eye would fasten on me. She would then shriek my name and "An orphan! Oh, God, you're an orphan!" No one had the courage to remind her that according to Jewish custom you were an orphan if your mother died, only half an orphan if your father died. Perhaps it wasn't courage. Perhaps they understood that she didn't really mean me at all. She meant herself. She was consumed by a sense of loss so primeval she had taken all grief into her. Everyone's grief. That of the wife, the mother, and the daughter. Grief had filled her, and emptied her. She had become a vessel, a conduit, a manifestation. A remarkable fluidity, sensual and demanding, was not hers. She'd be lying on the couch a rag doll, her eyes dull, unseeing, tongue edging out of a half-open mouth, arms hanging slack. Two minutes later she was thrashing about, groveling against the couch, falling to the floor, skin chalky, eyes squeezed shut, mouth tightly compressed. It went on for hours. For days, for weeks, and for years.

I saw myself only as a prop in the extraordinary drama of Mama's bereavement. I didn't mind. I didn't know what I was supposed to be feeling and I hadn't the time to find out. Actually I was frightened. I didn't object to being frightened. I supposed it's as good a response as any other. Only, being frightened imposed certain responsibilities. For one, it demanded I not take my eyes off my mother for an instant. I never cried. Not once. I heard a woman murmur, "Unnatural child." I remember thinking, She doesn't understand. Papa's gone, and Mama obviously is going any minute now. If I cry I won't be able to see her. If I don't see her she's going to disappear. And then I'll be alone. Thus began my conscious obsession with keeping Mama in sight.

The funeral. Twenty years later when I was living as a journalist in the Middle East, I witnessed Arab funerals almost weekly—hundreds of men and women rushing through the streets, tearing at their clothes, uttering cries of an animal-like nature at a terrifying pitch of noise, people fainting, being trampled, while the crowd whirled screeching on. Westerners who might be standing beside me in the street would shake their heads in amazement at a sight so foreign it confirmed them in their secret conviction that these people were indeed not like themselves. To me, however, it all seemed perfectly familiar, only a bit louder than I remembered, and the insanity parceled out quite a bit more. The way I remembered it, Mama had center stage at all times.

. . . Mama's suffering elevated Papa's death, made us all participants in an event of consequence, told us something had occurred we were not to support, not to live through, or at the very least be permanently stunted by. Still, it was Mama who occupied the dramatic center of the event while the rest of us shuffled about in the background, moving without tears or speech through a sludge of gray misery. It was as though we had all been absorbed into her spectacular abandonment, become witnesses to her loss rather than mourners ourselves. It was Mama who was on our minds as we roamed the gloomy apartment—who could think of Papa in the midst of such tumult?—Mama who must be watched and attended to, Mama whose mental agony threatened general breakdown. Disaster seemed imminent rather than already accomplished.

. . . At the funeral parlor she tried to climb into the coffin. At the cemetery she tried to fling herself into the open grave. There were other moments at the funeral worthy of permanent record—my brother passed out, I looked so long into the casket I had to be pulled away, a political comrade announced at the grave that my father had been a wage slave in this America—but these moments are without clarity or sharpness of outline. They pall in memory beside the brilliant relentlessness of Mama's derangement.

. . . The kitchen was by far the most interesting place to be. Invariably, two of the women were my aunt Sarah and Mrs. Zimmerman, each of whom had less than a loving attachment to her own husband and certainly considered marriage an affliction. Both, however, had been silenced by my mother's awesome performance. Except every now and then irrepressible Mrs. Zimmerman, stirring her own soup at the stove, would mutter, "She lays there crying like a lunatic. If I would come home and find mine dead, it would be a blessing."

. . . I didn't know that not every woman who had lost a husband would be carrying on like Mama, but I did know that the conversation in the kitchen was immensely interesting. One spoke sharply, another speculatively, a third imperiously. The talk was hard and bright, gave the room charge and intensity. . . . I loved it. Felt nourished and protected, delighted and relieved by it. I remember, especially, the relief.

. . . The difference between the living room and the kitchen was the difference between suffocation and survival. The living room was all monotonous dread, congealed and airless. Here you took a deep breath, held it until you were smothering, then either got out or went under. In the kitchen there was pitch and tone, the atmosphere fell and rose, dwindled away, churned itself up again. There was movement and space, light and air. You could breathe. You could live.

. . . It rained earlier in the day and now, at one in the afternoon, for a minute and a half, New York is washed clean. The streets glitter in the pale spring sunlight. Cars radiate dust-free happiness. Storefront windows sparkle mindlessly. Even people look made anew.

We're walking down Eighth Avenue into the Village.

. . . We cross Abingdon Square and walk into Bleecker Street. The gentrified West Village closes around us, makes us not peaceful but quiet. We walk through block after block of antique stores, gourmet shops, boutiques, not speaking. But for how long can my mother and I not speak?

"So I'm reading the biography you gave me," she says. I look at her, puzzled, and then I remember. "Oh!" I smile in wide delight. "Are you enjoying it?"

"Listen," she begins. The smile drops off my face and my stomach contracts. That "listen" means she is about to trash the book I gave her to read. She is going to say, "What. What's here? What's here that I don't already know? I *lived* through it. I know it all. What can this writer tell me that I don't already know? Nothing. To *you* it's interesting, but to me? How can this be interesting to me?"

On and on she'll go, the way she does when she thinks she doesn't understand something and she's scared, and she's taking refuge in scorn and hypercriticality.

The book I gave her to read is a biography of Josephine Herbst, a thirties writer, a stubborn willful raging woman grabbing at politics and love and writing, in there punching until the last minute.

"Listen," my mother says now in the patronizing tone she thinks conciliatory. "Maybe this is interesting to you, but not to me. I lived through all this. I know it all. What can I learn from this? Nothing. To you it's interesting. Not to me."

Invariably, when she speaks so, my head fills with blood and before the sentences have stopped pouring from her mouth I am lashing out at her. "You're an ignoramus, you know nothing, only a know-nothing talks the way you do. The point of having lived through it, as you say, is only that the background is familiar, so the book is made richer, not that you could have written the book. People a thousand times more educated than you have read and learned from this book, but *you* can't learn from it?" On and on I would go, thoroughly ruining the afternoon for both of us.

However, in the past year an odd circumstance has begun to obtain. On occasion, my head fails to fill with blood. I become irritated but remain calm. Not falling into a rage, I do not make a holocaust of the afternoon. Today, it appears, one of those moments is upon us. I turn to my mother, throw my left arm around her still solid back, place my right hand on her upper arm, and say, "Ma, if this book is not interesting to you, that's fine. You can say that." She looks coyly at me, eyes large, head half-turned; *now* she's interested. "But don't say it has nothing to teach you. That there's nothing here. That's unworthy of you, and of the book, and of me. You demean us all when you say that." Listen to me. Such wisdom. And all of it gained ten minutes ago.

Silence. Long silence. We walk another block. Silence. She's looking off into that middle distance. I take my lead from her, matching my steps to hers. I do not speak, do not press her. Another silent block.

"That Josephine Herbst," my mother says. "She certainly carried on, didn't she?"

Relieved and happy, I hug her. "She didn't know what she was doing either, Ma, but yes, she carried on."

"I'm jealous," my mother blurts at me. "I'm jealous she lived her life, I didn't live mine."

Mama went to work five weeks after my father died. He had left us two thousand dollars. To work or not to work was not a debatable question. But it's hard to imagine what would have happened if economic necessity had not forced her out of the house. As it was, it seemed to me that she lay on a couch in a half-darkened room for twenty-five years with her hand across her forehead murmuring, "I can't." Even though she could, and did.

. . . She got a job clerking in an office for twenty-eight dollars a week. After that, she rose each morning, got dressed and drank coffee, made out a grocery list for me, left it together with money on the kitchen table, walked four blocks to the subway station, bought the *Times,* read it on the train, got off at Forty-second Street, entered her office building, sat down at her desk, put in a day's work, made the trip home at five o'clock, came in the apartment door, slumped onto the kitchen bench for supper, then onto the couch where she instantly sank into a depression she welcomed like a warm bath. It was as though she had worked all day to earn the despair waiting faithfully for her at the end of her unwilling journey into daily life.

Weekends, of course, the depression was unremitting. A black and wordless pall hung over the apartment all of Saturday and all of Sunday. Mama neither cooked, cleaned, nor shopped. She took no part in idle chatter: the exchange of banalities that fills a room with human presence, declares an interest in being alive. She would not laugh, respond, or participate.

. . . Widowhood provided Mama with a higher form of being. In refusing to recover from my father's death she had discovered that her life was endowed with a seriousness her years in the kitchen had denied her. She remained devoted to this seriousness for thirty years. She never tired of it, never grew bored or restless in its company, found new ways to keep alive the interest it deserved and had so undeniably earned.

. . . A woman-who-has-lost-the-love-of-her-life was now her orthodoxy: she paid it Talmudic attention.

Papa had never been so real to me in life as he was in death. Always a somewhat shadowy figure, benign and smiling, standing there behind Mama's dramatics about married love, he became and remained what felt like the necessary instrument of her permanent devastation.

. . . The air I breathed was soaked in her desperation, made thick and heady by it, exciting and dangerous. Her pain became my element, the country in which I lived, the rule beneath which I bowed. It commanded me, made me respond against my will. I longed endlessly to get away from her, but I could not leave the room when she was in it. I dreaded her return from work, but I was never not there when she came home. . . . On Friday I prepared myself for two solid days of weeping and sighing and the mysterious reproof that depression leaks into the air like the steady escape of gas when the pilot light is extinguished. I woke up guilty and went to bed guilty, and on weekends the guilt accumulated into low-grade infection.

She made me sleep with her for a year, and for twenty years afterward I could not bear a woman's hand on me. . . .

A glorious day, today: New York hard-edged in the clear autumn sun, buildings sharply outlined against the open sky, streets crowded with pyramids of fruits and vegetables, flowers in papier-mâché vases cutting circles on the sidewalk, newspaper stands vivid in black and white. On Lexington Avenue, in particular, an outpouring of lovely human bustle at noon, a density of urban appetites and absorptions.

I have agreed to walk with my mother late in the day but I've come uptown early to wander by myself, feel the sun, take in the streets, be in the world without the interceding interpretations of a companion as voluble as she. At Seventy-third Street I turn off Lexington and head for the Whitney, wanting a last look at a visiting collection. As I approach the museum some German Expressionist drawings in a gallery window catch my eye. I walk through the door, turn to the wall nearest me, and come face to face with two large Nolde watercolors, the famous flowers. I've looked often at Nolde's flowers, but now it's as though I am seeing them for the first time: that hot lush diffusion of his outlined, I suddenly realize, in intent. I see the burning quality of Nolde's intention, the serious patience with which the flowers absorb him, the clear, stubborn concentration of the artist on his subject. I *see* it. And I think, It's the concentration that gives the work its power. The space inside me enlarges. That rectangle of light and air inside, where thought clarifies and language grows and response is made intelligent, that famous space surrounded by loneliness, anxiety, self-pity, it opens wide as I look at Nolde's flowers.

In the museum lobby I stop at the permanent exhibit of Alexander Calder's circus. As usual, a crowd is gathered, laughing and gaping at the wonderfulness of Calder's sighing, weeping, triumphing bits of cloth and wire. Beside me stand two women. I look at their faces and I dismiss them: middle-aged Midwestern blondes, blue-eyed and moony. Then one of them says, "It's like second childhood," and the other one replies tartly, "Better than anyone's first." I'm startled, pleasured, embarrassed. I think, What a damn fool you are to cut yourself off with your stupid amazement that *she* could have said *that*. Again, I feel the space inside widen unexpectedly.

That space. It begins in the middle of my forehead and ends in the middle of my groin. It is, variously, as wide as my body, as narrow as a slit in a fortress wall. On days when thought flows freely or better yet clarifies with effort, it expands gloriously. On days when anxiety and self-pity crowd in, it shrinks, how fast it shrinks! When the space is wide and I occupy it fully, I taste the air, feel the light. I breathe evenly and slowly. I am peaceful and excited, beyond influence or threat. Nothing can touch me. I'm safe. I'm free. I'm thinking. When I lose the battle to think, the boundaries narrow, the air is polluted, the light clouds over. All is vapor and fog, and I have trouble breathing.

. . . I go to meet my mother. I'm flying. Flying! I want to give her some of this shiningness bursting in me, siphon into her my immense happiness at being alive. Just because she is my oldest intimate and at this moment I love everybody, even her.

"Oh, Ma! What a day I've had," I say.

"Tell me," she says. "Do you have the rent this month?"

"Ma, listen . . ." I say.

"That review you wrote for the *Times*," she says. "It's for sure they'll pay you?"

"Ma, stop it. Let me tell you what I've been feeling," I say.

"Why aren't you wearing something warmer?" she cries. "It's nearly winter."

The space inside begins to shimmer. The walls collapse inward. I feel breathless. Swallow slowly, I say to myself, slowly. To my mother I say, "You *do* know how to say the right thing at the right time. It's remarkable, this gift of yours. It quite takes my breath away."

But she doesn't get it. She doesn't know I'm being ironic. Nor does she know she's wiping me out. She doesn't know I take her anxiety personally, feel annihilated by her depression. How can she know this? She doesn't even know I'm there. Were I to tell her that it's death to me, her not knowing I'm there, she would stare at me out of her eyes crowding up with puzzled desolation, this young girl

of seventy-seven, and she would cry angrily, "You don't understand! You have never understood!"

. . . I entered City College, . . . [which] seemed . . . concerned
with laying siege, to the ignorant mind if not the intelligent heart.
Benign in intent, only a passport to the promised land, City . . . did
more violence to the emotions than . . . Mama . . . could have
dreamed possible, divided me, . . . provoked and nourished an un-
shared life inside the head that became a piece of treason. I lived
among my people, but I was no longer one of them.

I think this was true for most of us at City College. We still used
the subways, still walked the familiar streets between classes, still
returned to the neighborhood each night, talked to our high-school
friends, and went to sleep in our own beds. But secretly we had begun to live in a world that separated us from our parents, the life of
the house and that of the street.

. . . At City College I sat talking in a basement cafeteria until
ten or eleven at night with a half dozen others who also never
wanted to go home to Brooklyn or the Bronx, and here in the cafeteria my education took root. Here I learned that Faulkner was
America, Dickens was politics, Marx was sex, Jane Austen the idea
of culture, that I came from a ghetto and D. H. Lawrence was a visionary. Here my love of literature named itself, and amazement
over the life of the mind blossomed. I discovered that people were
transformed by ideas, and that intellectual conversation was immensely erotic.

We never stopped talking. Perhaps because we did very little
else, . . . we talked so much because most of us had been reading in
bottled-up silence from the age of six on and City College was our
great release. . . . Our life burned in us. While we pursued ideas we
felt known, to ourselves and to one another. The world made sense,
there was ground beneath our feet, a place in the universe to stand.
City College made conscious in me inner cohesion as a first value.

I think my mother was very quickly of two minds about me and
City.

. . . "Where is it written that a working-class widow's daughter
should go to college?" one of my uncles said to her, drinking coffee
at our kitchen table on a Saturday morning in my senior year in
high school.

"Here it is written," she had replied, tapping the table hard with
her middle finger. "Right here it is written. The girl goes to college."

"Why?" he had pursued.

"Because I say so."

"But why? What do you think will come of it?"

"I don't know. I only know she's clever, she deserves an education, and she's going to get one. This is America. The girls are not cows in the field only waiting for a bull to mate with." I stared at her. Where had *that* come from? My father had been dead only five years, she was in full widowhood swing.

The moment was filled with conflict and bravado. She felt the words she spoke but she did not mean them. She didn't even know what she meant by an education. When she discovered at my graduation that I wasn't a teacher she acted as though she'd been swindled. In her mind a girl child went in one door marked college and came out another marked teacher.

. . . What drove her, and divided us, was me thinking. She hadn't understood that going to school meant I would start thinking: coherently and out loud. She was taken by violent surprise. My sentences got longer within a month of those first classes. Longer, more complicated, formed by words whose meaning she did not always know. I had never before spoken a word she didn't know. Or made a sentence whose logic she couldn't follow. Or attempted an opinion that grew out of an abstraction. It made her crazy. Her face began to take on a look of animal cunning when I started a sentence that could not possibly be concluded before three clauses had hit the air. Cunning sparked anger, anger flamed into rage. "What are you talking about?" she would shout at me. "What *are* you talking about? Speak English, please! We all understand English in this house. Speak it!"

. . . I was seventeen, she was fifty. I had not yet come into my own as a qualifying belligerent but I was a respectable contender and she, naturally, was at the top of her game. The lines were drawn, and we did not fail one another. Each of us rose repeatedly to the bait the other one tossed out. Our storms shook the apartment: paint blistered on the wall, linoleum cracked on the floor, glass shivered in the window frame. We barely kept our hands off one another, and more than once we approached disaster.

. . . Compounding our struggle, stimulating our anguish, swelling our confusion was sex. Me and boys, me and maidenhood, me and getting on with it. Safeguarding my virginity was a major preoccupation. Every boy I brought into the house made my mother anxious. She could not but leap ahead in her thoughts to the inevitable moment when he must threaten her vital interest. But she knew the danger came not so much from them as from me.

. . . Once, when she was positive I'd slept with the boy I'd gone out with, she pinched my arm until my eyes crossed in pain. "You've tasted him, haven't you," she said, her voice flat with accusation and defeat. That was her favorite euphemism for intercourse: "You've tasted him, haven't you." The phrase never failed to shock. I felt it in my nerve endings. The melodrama of repression, the malice of passivity, the rage over an absence of power, all of it packed into those words and I knew it from the first time I heard them. When she spoke them we faced each other across a no-man's-land of undefined but unmistakable dimension.

. . . "Why can't you find a nice man to be happy with?" my mother is saying. "Someone simple and good. Not an intellectual or a philosopher." We are walking down Ninth Avenue after a noon-hour concert at Lincoln Center. She places one hand palm up in the air. "Why do you pick one schlemiel after another? Tell me. Do you do this to make me miserable? What *is* it?"

"For God's sake, Ma," I say weakly. "I don't 'pick' men. I'm out there, I'm just *out* there. Things happen, an attraction begins, you act on it. Sometimes, way in the back of your mind, for a fraction of a second, you think: Could this be serious? Is it possible this man will become my intimate? my partner? But mainly you push the thought away, because this is our *life*, Ma. Affairs. Episodes. Passions that run their course. Even when they include getting married."

She knows I'm speaking now from a losing position, and she moves right in.

"But an alcoholic?" she says.

"An ex-alcoholic, Ma."

"Alcoholic, ex-alcoholic, what's the difference?"

"Ma! He hasn't had a drink in four years."

"He also hasn't called in two weeks."

Marilyn Kerner had said almost the same thing. Marilyn (she never did get married), now forty-six, a lawyer living on the Upper West Side, remains a corrective voice in my life. When I want not the easy reassurance of the therapeutic culture but the unsparing appraisal of the standard-bearer of the Bronx, I call Marilyn. There are no euphemisms in Marilyn's vocabulary. Be prepared for an analysis that will strike like a body blow, or don't call Marilyn. But

I had called Marilyn over this newest rapture of mine and she, too, had said, "An ex-alcoholic? Doesn't sound promising."

"But Marilyn," I'd protested, "it's just the opposite. He's *been* there. He's been as powerless as a woman. He's got wisdom. Believe me. This man is extraordinarily undefended. The friendship between us has been marvelous. With every word, every gesture, every bit of behavior, he has said to me, 'I'm as vulnerable to this as you are, as sensitive to your fears and insecurities as I am to my own.'"

"But he hasn't been sensitive to his own," said Marilyn. "He's been pickled in alcohol for fifteen years."

"He's different now," I said. "Jesus Christ. Nobody gets a second chance in the Bronx, do they?"

"It's not that," Marilyn said. "It's that if you come from the Bronx you don't ignore the evidence. You can't afford to."

Now, of course, the evidence is weighing heavily against me. This man and I had met at a journalists' conference. Desire had flared quickly, and then happiness had taken us both by surprise. We had spent a month together. Now we had separated, I back to New York, he to the Midwest to finish an assignment. Our plan had been to meet in New York in six weeks. Meanwhile, he was to call the day after I got home. Two weeks have now passed: no phone call.

. . . My brother graduated and left the house. . . . We were alone in the apartment, Mama and I, as I had always known we would be. She lay on the couch and stared into space. I hung out the window. Her stare was dull, silent, accusing. She would not be roused. I sat in the room, spoke the thoughts in my head, and nothing happened, absolutely nothing. It was as though I had not spoken. Her refusal was powerful. It hypnotized me, awed me into collaborative submission.

Failing to get what she wanted from life, what she thought she needed, felt was her due, my mother disappeared under a cloud of unhappiness. Beneath this cloud she felt helpless, fragile, and deserving of sympathy. When she was told her relentless melancholy was oppressive to those forced to witness it, she was surprised. Her mouth and eyes flashed angry hurt and she said, "I can't help it. This is how I *feel*. I can only act as I feel." Secretly she considered her depressed state a mark of sensitivity, of stronger feeling, finer spirit. She would not take in the idea that her behavior affected others adversely, and the notion that a certain level of social exchange is required below which no one has the right to fall was foreign to her. She could not see that her insistent unhappiness was an accusation and a judgment. "You?" it said with each resentful sigh. "You're not the right one. You cannot deliver up comfort, pleasure, amelioration. But you are my dearest of dears. Your appointed task is to understand, your destiny to live with the daily knowledge that you are insufficient to cure my life of its deprivation."

. . . When I was a child the feel of things went into me: deep, narrow, intense. The grittiness of the street, the chalk-white air of the drugstore, the grain of the wooden floor in the store-front library, the blocks of cheese in the grocery-store refrigerator. I took it all so seriously, so literally. I was without imagination. I paid a kind of idiot attention to the look and feel of things, leveling an intent inner stare at the prototypic face of the world. These streets were all streets, these buildings all buildings, these women and men all women and men. I could imagine no other than that which stood before me.

That child's literalness of the emotions continued to exert influence, as though a shock had been administered to the nervous system and the flow of imagination had stopped. I could feel strongly, but I could not imagine. The granite gray of the street, the American-cheese yellow of the grocery store, the melancholy brownish tint of the buildings were all still in place, only now it was the woman on the couch, the girl hanging out the window, the confinement that sealed us off, on which I looked with that same inner intentness that had always crowded out possibility as well as uncertainty. It would be years before I learned that extraordinary focus, that excluding insistence, is also called depression.

. . . I began leaving home at nineteen and kept leaving until I was married in the living room at twenty-four in a noisy act of faith that announced the matter accomplished. My husband was small (my size); blond ("insignificant-looking," as Mama put it); foreign (he couldn't defend himself in English). We were drawn to each other by a common love of the arts, but he was a visionary painter and in me literature had aroused the critical faculty. He was wordless, I was all words. In him repression was demonic, in me explosive. . . . The course I had followed to lead me to this man and this marriage was not difficult to trace (any child analysand could have delivered a creditable description of the psychological terrain), but I remained deep in the woods a quarter of a mile from the road.

. . . I remember entering graduate school at Berkeley. . . . The English department . . . was itself a model for human relations in the world. There were those in power: the brilliant, famous, full professors, and those seeking power: the brilliant young men ready to become the disciple, the protégé, the son and intellectual companion. Together, professor and protégé formed the interlocking links in the chain of civilized cronyism that ensured the ongoingness of the enterprise being served: English literature in the university.

Side by side with the young men were the women students. Most of them came from the Midwest, wore Peter Pan collars, were choked silent with intensity, and in the third year at school became engaged to one of the promising young men. Many of these women were also brilliant. . . . It was interesting to observe how people in the department spoke of such a woman once she became one half of the future academic couple. Before she had not really been spoken of at all. Now she was referred to in muted tones, as though the conversants were in a sickroom speaking of an invalid, and inevitably one heard one of them saying, "Poor Joan. Gifted girl, really." . . . The mixture of ritual and relief in the speaker's voice was both peculiar and palpable.

Then there were the other women students. . . . Brash, difficult, "gypsy-dark" (meaning Jewish from New York), the intelligence strong not subtle, the sensibility aggressive not demure, the manner startling in its overdirectness, without grace or modesty, disorienting. These women did not fall in love with Mark, who sat next to them in Medieval Lit 101. They studied with him, argued with him, sometimes slept with him, but they did not marry him. Or he them.

. . . The men were able to retreat from anxiety into a readymade identity. They got their Ph.D.'s, married Joan, and went off to walk the carefully prepared road that had been assigned them. The women had no such luck. Who were they to identify with? Where were they to go? At Berkeley I know where they went. They fell into affairs with married professors, black activists, antisocial mathematicians; or they hung out at the bars on the other side of Shattuck Avenue.

. . . I need hardly say among which group I took my own uneasy place. I had come to Berkeley also trailing a list of "inappropriate" attachments. I already knew I had hopeless trouble with the Marks of this world, trouble I thought originated in their insecurities, their fears, their defenses. Me, I was ready. It was they who didn't want a wife who talked back, they who were afraid of a woman like me.

. . . What I could not register was this: In each of these affairs a necessary element of control devolved on me. If a man was short or stupid or uneducated or foreign, I felt sufficiently superior to risk tenderness. I might be socially uncomfortable but I was freed up. Love was a swamp of overwhelming proportion.

. . . Stefan was neither stupid nor uneducated, but he was short and foreign and an artist. . . . We met one night at a party in North Beach, not far from the art school where he was a student, and immediately began to discuss the significance of Art, the privilege of being allowed to serve, the promise and the glory, the meaning and the transcendence. The conversation mesmerized us. We met repeatedly to hear ourselves speak the magic words again and again. Very quickly I began to image a life together, intense and highminded, devoted to the idea of the Great Work.

. . . I called home and announced I was getting married. At the other end of the phone my mother was speechless. When she found her tongue it was to revile me for bringing her a goy. *But, Ma! We were communists!* She calmed down, asked me when I was coming back to New York and what kind of a wedding I wanted. Homemade, I laughed. *Thanks, Ma.*

I came back and she gripped me in a hard, angry embrace. She *did* try, but repeatedly her head filled with blood, over what, I think she hardly knew . . . oh yes, I was marrying a goy. I was elated. I began to feel embattled. Now I wanted to marry Stefan more, I thought, than I would ever again want anything. I must fight for the integrity of my opposed love, fight her to the death. But each day at noon I was overcome by a wave of nausea, and chaos beat inside *my* head. What was I doing? Why was I getting married? Why was I marrying *him*? Who was *he*? I was going to stand up before a judge and swear, call this man husband, take his name. . . . I felt myself plunging. . . . Don't think about it, it's too late now, all too late. If she wins this one you are lost.

. . . In the late afternoon we suddenly ran out of flour and sugar. Mama pulled off her apron and said she needed air, she would go to the grocery store. I couldn't let her out of my sight. "I'll come with you," I said. She nodded wordlessly, as though she had expected no less.

We left the house and trudged up the block. It was late August.

I was wearing a thin dress that was one summer too old. The hem had come down that very morning and I had pinned it up. Now as we walked a mild breeze rippled the dress, exposing the pins. My mother said sharply, "What *is* that?" I followed her gaze. "The hem came down this morning." I shrugged. "I couldn't find the sewing box." Right then and there, on the street, halfway between the house and the grocery store, she lost her mind.

"You are dis*gust*ing!" she yelled at me. "Disgusting! Look at you. Just look at you. You're a mess! That's what you are. A mess! When will you ever learn? You think you'll learn? You won't learn." People began to turn around. She didn't notice. Suddenly her body trembled. Her skin lost its color. She pushed her face at mine. "He'll never marry you," she hissed.

The pain in my chest cracked open, and an angry frightened excitement ran quickly into the cleared space. She was jealous. It wasn't just that I was getting married, it was that the glamorous goy was taking me out into the world. I could see it in her eyes. We stood there, immobilized. I felt my face going gray like hers. Without another word, we turned away from each other and continued on to the grocery store.

. . . My mother and I are walking past the Plaza Hotel at noon, on our way to eat lunch in the park. Gathered around the fountain in front of the hotel a swarm of people: sitting, standing, strolling out to the sidewalk to buy shish kebab, soda, pretzels, falafel, egg roll, and hot dogs. They are eating out of tinfoil, drinking out of plastic, being entertained by street performers who pass the hat: break dancers, mimes, string quartets. One of the street performers not passing the hat is a fundamentalist preacher pacing back and forth in front of the fountain, thundering at individual people: "You are going straight to hell! Not tomorrow, not tonight, *right now*!" He makes the mistake of stopping my mother. She dismisses him with a brusque "What's *your* problem?" (she can't spare the time for this one), and keeps walking.

I laugh. I'm exhilarated today. Today *I'm* a street performer. I've always admired the guts, the skill, the command of the one who plays successfully to the passing New York crowd. Last night I spoke at a large public meeting in the city: on the barricades for radical feminism, also not passing the hat. I spoke easily and well, and I had the crowd in my hand. Sometimes I don't, but last night I did. Last night all the skill I've acquired at this sort of thing was there at my command, and I knew it. It was the knowing it that made me clear-headed, lucid, expansive and expressive. The crowd was being stirred. I felt it, and then I had confirmed what I felt.

My mother was in the audience. I didn't see her afterward, because I was surrounded and carried off. Today, right now, is our first meeting since I walked onstage last night. She is smiling at me now, laughing with me at the pleasure of the day, the crowd, New York acting out all over the place. I am properly expectant. She is about to tell me how wonderful I was last night. She opens her mouth to speak.

"Guess who I dreamed about last night," she says to me. "Sophie Schwartzman!"

I am startled, taken off balance. This I had not expected. "Sophie Schwartzman?" I say. But beneath my surprise a kernel of dread begins growing in the bright bright day.

Sophie Schwartzman had lived in our building for some years, and she and Mama had been friends. After the Schwartzmans moved to another neighborhood in the Bronx our two families had continued to meet because the women liked each other. The Schwartzmans had three children: Seymour, Miriam, and Frances. Seymour became a famous composer who changed his name to Malcolm Wood. Miriam grew up to become her mother. Frances, a pretty girl with "ambitions," married a rich man. Sophie has been dead a good ten years now. I haven't seen any of her children in more than twenty years.

"I dreamed I was in Sophie's house," my mother says, crossing Fifty-ninth Street. "Frances came in. She had written a book. She asked me to read it. I did, and I wasn't so enthusiastic. She became very angry. She screamed at her mother, 'Never let her come here again.' I felt so bad! I was sick at heart. I said, 'Sophie. What is this? You mean after all these years I can't come here anymore?'" My mother turns to me as we reach the sidewalk and, with a huge smile on her face, says, "But then it was so wonderful! I woke up, and it was only a dream."

My feet seem to have lead weights in them. I struggle to put one in front of the other. My mother doesn't notice that I have slowed up. She is absorbed by her own amazing narrative.

"You dreamed this last night, Ma?"

"Yes."

"After I spoke?"

"Well, yes, of course. Not *right* after. When I got home and went to sleep."

We enter the park, find a bench, sit down, take out our sandwiches. We do not speak. We have each fallen into reverie. After a while my mother says, "Imagine dreaming about Sophie Schwartzman after all these years."

. . . For a long time, a few years in fact, Stefan and I described the tension between us as intensity. (Tension we knew was in the negative, but intensity—ah, intensity!) Our lovemaking was almost invariably tight and explosive, a pent-up release from the gloom that marked so many of our days.

. . . The difficulty was chronic, not occasional. Every other day some little thing would set one of us off. There would be an inconsiderate exchange and we would each feel hurt. . . . At last, when the air was so thick we could hardly breathe, one of us would break through. More often than not it was Stefan. He would sink to his knees before the rocking chair, wrap his arms around my legs, and murmur, "What is it? Tell me." Then I'd burst into tears, cry, "I can't go on like this! I can't work! I can't think!" And we'd go to bed.

. . . Yet those years were a true beginning for me. I did actually try to sit at the desk and think. Mostly, I failed miserably. Mostly, not always. In the second year of my marriage the rectangular space made its first appearance inside me. I was writing an essay, a piece of graduate-student criticism that had flowered without warning into thought, radiant, shapely thought. The sentences began pushing up in me, struggling to get out, each one moving swiftly to add itself to the one that preceded it. I realized suddenly that an image had taken control of me: I saw its shape and its outline clearly. The sentences were trying to fill in the shape. The image was the wholeness of my thought. In that instant I felt myself open wide. My insides cleared out into a rectangle, all clean air and uncluttered space, that began in my forehead and ended in my groin. In the middle of the rectangle only my image, waiting patiently to clarify itself. I experienced a joy then I knew nothing else would ever equal.

. . . We lived together five years. Then one day Stefan left the house and he didn't come back. Our marriage was ended. And indeed why not? We had each wearied of the struggle between us. We each wanted to take a breath in rooms free of that oppressive tension. We wanted that more than we wanted to be together. I dismantled the flat, sold everything in it, left graduate school (always an abstraction to me), and returned to New York. I was thirty years old, and I was relieved to be alone. I moved into the little tenement apartment on First Avenue and got myself a job writing for a weekly newspaper. I fixed up the apartment. In no time at all the place was cozy. The colors all worked this time: no surprises between the can and the wall.

. . . These were years when women like myself were being called New, Liberated, Odd (myself I preferred Odd, I still do), and indeed, I was new, liberated, odd during the day when I sat at the desk, but at night when I lay on the couch staring into space my mother materialized in the air before me, as if to say, "Not so fast, my dear. All is not done between us."

. . . I sat at the desk and I struggled to think. That's how I liked to put it. For years I said, "I'm struggling to think." Just as my mother said she was struggling to live. Mama thought she deserved a medal for swinging her legs over the side of the bed in the morning, and I guess I did, too, just for sitting at the desk.

In the little tenement apartment on First Avenue the fog came rolling in the window. Vapor thickened the air, and mist filled the room. I sat with my eyelids nailed open against the fog, the vapor, the mist, straining to see through to my thoughts, trapped inside the murk. Once every few weeks the air cleared for half a second, and quick! I'd get down two paragraphs of readable prose. Time passed. Much time. Much dead time. Finally, a page. Then two pages. When there were ten pages I rushed to print. I looked at my paragraphs in print: really looked at them. How small, I thought. How small it all is. I've been sitting here so long with these pages, and they're so small. A man said to me, "Good insight. Pity you didn't have time to develop it." A woman said, "What you could do if you didn't have to meet journalistic deadlines. A shame there's no government subsidy." I started to speak. Misery dissolved in my mouth, glued my lips shut. What would I say if I could speak? And to whom would I say it?

I "struggled" on.

It is August: New York under siege. A mountain of airless heat presses down on the streets of the city. Not a bit of summer sensuality in this heat. This heat is only oppressive.

Yesterday I sat with a friend drinking iced tea in Paley Park, recovering for a moment from the exhaustion of the day. The wall of rushing water behind us created a three-sided courtyard of miraculous cool. We gazed out at the street shimmering only fifty feet from where we sat.

My friend and I, usually quite talkative, spoke listlessly of this and that: projected work, work in hand, a movie he had seen, a book I was reading, a mutual friend's new love affair. I thought I had been equally responsive to all of our small talk, but then my friend said to me, "You're remarkably uninterested in men."

"Why do you say that?" I asked.

"Every other woman I know, or man for that matter, if they've been without as long as you have, it's on their minds constantly. First priority. Not you. You seem never to think about it."

As he spoke I saw myself lying on a bed in late afternoon, a man's face buried in my neck, his hand moving slowly up my thigh over my hip, our bodies striped with bars of hot light coming through the window blinds. The image burned through me in seconds. I felt stunned by loss: the fun and sweetness of love, the deliciousness, the shimmer. I swallowed hard on empty air.

"No," I said. "I guess I don't."

Life is difficult: a glory and a punishment. Ideas are excitement, glamorous company. Loneliness eats into me. When the balance between struggle and self-pity is maintained I feel myself one of the Odd Women—that is, I see myself on a continuum of that amazing two-hundred-year effort—and I am fortified, endowed with new spirit, new will. When the balance is lost I feel buried alive in failure and deprivation, without love or connection. Friendships are random, conflicts prevail, work is the sum of its disabilities.

Tonight I am hanging on by my fingernails, barely able to hold it all together. I sit at my mother's kitchen table, drinking coffee. We have just eaten dinner. She stands at the sink washing her dishes. We are both edgy tonight. "It's the heat," she says. The apartment is air-conditioner cool, but we both love real air too much. We have turned off the machine and opened the window. For a minute the crowded noisy avenue down below invades the room, but very quickly its rush subsides into white noise, background buzz. We return almost without a pause to our own restless gloom.

My mother is conversant with all that is on my mind. She is also familiar with the usual order of my litany of complaint: work, friends, money. This evening yesterday's conversation in Paley Park seems to drift in the window on the sexy summer air, and to my own surprise I find myself saying, "It *would* be nice to have a little love right now."

I expect my mother to laugh and say, "What's with you tonight?" Instead, not even looking up from the dishes, she goes on automatic and says to me, "Well, now perhaps you can have a little sympathy for *me*."

I look up slowly at her. "What?" I say. I'm not sure I have heard right. "What was that you said?"

"I said maybe you can understand *now* what my life was like when Papa died. What it's been like all these years. Now that you're suffering from the absence of love yourself, maybe you can understand."

I stare at her. I stare and I stare. Then I'm up from the table, the cup is falling over, I fly against the kitchen wall, a caged animal. The pot she's washing clatters into the sink.

"What the hell are you talking about?" I shout. "What *are* you talking about? Again love? And yet again love? Am I never to hear anything but love from you until I die? Does my life mean nothing to you? Absolutely nothing?"

She stands at the sink rigid with terror, her eyes fixed on me, her lips white, the color draining from her face. I think I'm giving her a heart attack, but I can't stop.

"It is true," I rage on, my voice murderous now with the effort to keep it down. "I've not been successful. Neither at love, nor at work, nor at living a principled life. It is also true I made no choices, took no stands, stumbled into my life because I was angry and jealous of the world beyond my reach. But *still*! Don't I get any credit for spotting a good deal, Ma? That one should *try* to live one's life? Doesn't that count, Ma? That counts for nothing, Ma?"

Her fear dissolves into pity and regret. She's so pliable these days, it's heartbreaking. "No, no," she protests, "it's another world, another time. I didn't mean anything. Of *course* you get credit. All the credit in the world. Don't get so excited. I was trying to sympathize. I said the wrong thing. I don't know how to talk to you anymore."

Abruptly, the rush of words in her is halted. Another thought has attracted her attention. The line of defense swerves. "Don't you see?" she begs softly. "Love was all I had. What did I have? I had nothing. *Nothing*. And what was I *going* to have? What *could* I have? Everything you say about your life is true, I understand how true, but you have had your work, you *have* your work. And you've traveled. My God, you've traveled! You've been halfway around the world. What wouldn't I have given to travel! I had only your father's love. It was the only sweetness in my life. So I loved his love. What could I have done?"

But mutual heartbreak is not our style. "That's not good enough, Ma," I say. "You were forty-six when he died. You could have gone out into life. Other women with a lot less at their disposal did. You *wanted* to stay inside the idea of Papa's love. It's crazy! You've spent thirty years inside the idea of love. You could have had a life."

Here the conversation ends. She is done with pleading. Her face hardens. She draws herself up into remembered inflexibility. "So," she reverts to Yiddish, the language of irony and defiance. "You'll write down here on my tombstone: From the very beginning it was all water under the bridge."

She turns from the dishes in the sink, wipes her hands carefully on a towel, and walks past me into the living room. I stand in the kitchen looking down at the patterned linoleum on the floor, but then after a while I follow. She is lying stretched out on the couch, her arm across her forehead. I sink down into a chair not far from the couch. This couch and this chair are positioned as they were in the living room in the Bronx. It is not difficult to feel that she has been lying on this couch and I have been sitting in this chair almost the whole of our lives.

We are silent. Because we are silent the noise of the street is more compelling. It reminds me that we are not in the Bronx, we are in Manhattan: the journey has been more than a series of subway stops for each of us. Yet tonight this room is so like that other room, and the light, the failing summer light, suddenly it seems a blurred version of that other pale light, the one falling on us in the foyer.

My mother breaks the silence. In a voice remarkably free of emotion—a voice detached, curious, only wanting information—she says to me, "Why don't you go already? Why don't you walk away from my life? I'm not stopping you."

I see the light, I hear the street. I'm half in, half out.

"I know you're not, Ma."

Gloria Wade-Gayles

(1938–)

Gloria Jean Wade-Gayles was born in Memphis, Tennessee, one of two daughters of a striving but stable black family. Her grandmother, mother, aunt, and uncles watched over the two Wade children, while Wade-Gayles's father, working in Chicago, supported his daughters with money, phone calls, and annual visits.

Wade-Gayles earned her B.A. from LeMoyne College in 1959, a master's degree in English from Boston University in 1962, and a doctorate from Emory University in 1981. After 1963 she taught permanently at Spelman College, earning the rank of full professor in 1989. Before that, Wade-Gayles was a visiting professor at Howard University, Morehouse College, Emory University, and Talladega College. In 1967 she married Joseph Nathan Gayles, one of her generation of black students in the Northeast, by whom she had two children. She earned a Danforth Fellowship in 1974 and a National Endowment for the Humanities Fellowship in 1975, awards capped by her appointment as W. E. B. Du Bois Research Fellow at Harvard University in 1990.

A literary scholar and poet, Wade-Gayles has published *No Crystal Stair: Visions of Race and Sex in Black Women's Fiction* (1987) and *Moving in My Heart: African American Women's Spirituality* (1994). Her poetry and critical essays have appeared in a wide range of periodicals. Her memoir traces her journey north to graduate school; her rejection of the spirituality of her mother's and grandmother's Christianity, which she then saw as a cause of their subjection to white society; her rediscovery of her own spiritual life; and her fear that the next generation will be so saturated by the imagery of a slick, media-shaped culture "that they might be desensitized to the spiritual world." The strength to which she is "pushed back" in the title of her memoir is the spirituality of her mother and grandmother, a strength threatened during her years of rebellion and training in critical rationality.

PUSHED BACK TO STRENGTH:
A Black Woman's Journey Home

I remember the city of my birth as a big country town overlooking the muddy Mississippi River and bounded by Arkansas and Mississippi, two of the meanest states in the Union for black people. . . . I will admit, however, that it was a clean city. The "Cleanest in the Nation," billboards advertised. A quiet city. . . .

Black people saw the public relations signs, but did not bother to read them. By law, we were forced to read other signs, the ones that established boundaries and territories on the basis of race, making mockery of the city's claim to progress. "For Whites Only" and "Colored" were more numerous than magnolia trees.

I remember they prevented me from splashing in swimming pools where the water seemed clearer than the finest crystal and from checking out books in the downtown library where overhead lights were as bright as the sun, but softer. They were always there, the signs, locking me out and pushing me back. Even at the zoo where caged animals had no knowledge of race, I saw the signs except on Thursday, which was "colored" day.

I remember walking to Main Street—which we called "downtown"—on hot summer days to avoid the humiliation of sitting in the back of buses or enduring the hateful looks of white people who weren't pleased even when we moved to the back, often past empty seats. . . . They had a way of lynching us with their eyes which said they were capable of lynching us with their hands. Especially on Main Street.

. . . In the bright of day and out in the open, we were often well-behaved and cooperative. "Good colored boys and girls" in the eyes of whites. We were playing it safe, being careful and following our parents' admonitions. "Don't talk back to them. Don't touch them even when you put money into their hands. Don't walk too close to them. Don't look at them hard. Don't do anything to give them a chance to beat you."

As teenagers, many of us were caught between our anger at white people and our respect for our black elders; between a need to vent our rage in the light of day and a desire to remain alive; and between two images of our people: one for downtown and the other for ourselves.

Sometimes my grandmother's stories dulled my anger. . . . Other times, however, they exacerbated my anger. If only for her, I wanted to fight every white person I saw.

"They're pushing us back. Always." I would emphasize, "*Always* pushing us back."

"They don't know it," Grandmama would respond. "They don't know it, but they're pushing you back to us, where you can get strong. Get some strength."

Black people of her generation had no illusion about their lack of power, but they believed in their strength. For them, strength was total immersion in a black community grounded in values that translated into a sense of self. . . . Hardworking ordinary and beautiful people were the mirror in which we saw ourselves whole. We learned at an early age to avert our eyes from the mirror white people held before us, the one they had systematically shattered for distorted reflections. White definitions of blackness.

Today, in part because of integration, many black people try in various ways to be validated and legitimized by white standards. But in the forties, when I was growing up in Memphis, black people validated and legitimized themselves. . . . That was the meaning of my grandmother's words about being pushed back to strength.

. . . We were able, the church told us, to dream beyond the narrow confines of our world and to realize our dreams. The churches prepared us to do precisely that. They improved our reading skills in Sunday school and in tutoring programs. They gave us leadership training by requiring us to plan and execute, even to raise money for, children's day activities.

Back then, the way our parents handled segregated education made such good sense. In the outside world, whites were in charge. Hence our parents' emphasis on what we *should not do*. But inside the world of black schools, we were in charge. Hence the emphasis on what we *had to do*. Achieve and excel. As in church, so also in schools, we were Amened into high self-esteem.

I attribute our arrogance not only to our parents, but also to black teachers who were tough, challenging, and uncompromising in their insistence on excellent academic performance and exemplary character. They kept us in after-school detention for infractions as minor as chewing gum, being tardy, and speaking barely above a whisper during silent time.

Unlike black students in today's inner-city schools, we never

had a reason to chant, "I am somebody! I may be black, but I am
SOMEBODY!" . . .

I grew up believing I was somebody with a special future, in
spite of the fact that I lived in a low-income housing project. In
those days, a housing project was a stopping-off place. A decent,
but temporary, home you lived in until you were able to buy a real
home, and that was often not possible until all of the children were
"through school."

My housing project—called the Foote Homes—was a thirty
minute walk from Main Street and only fifteen minutes from Beale
Street. It was a colorful city within a city composed of attached red-
brick apartment buildings, cheap versions of Philadelphia row
houses. . . .

If care for one's surrounding is a sign of dignity and pride, residents in the projects had both in abundance. They framed their
windows with starched curtains and tailored drapes and planted
begonias, roses, and petunias which grew in profusion in the small
patches of earth they called their "yards." . . .

The project did not shrink in shame from the rest of the city.

Neither did the children who lived there. We, too, were scrubbed
clean. Only by our address could our teachers identify many of us
as residents of the project. We wore starched hand-me-downs or inexpensive clothes bought on time and in basement sales at stores on
Main Street. . . . Children in the project were adorned.

I grew up . . . as one of two girls in a small, closely knit family
of three women and three men. My father, who was a joyous
melody sung at a high pitch, lived in Chicago. . . .

I do not remember a day in my life when my Uncle Jack, my
mother's baby brother, was not present to bring me laughter and give
me advice. . . . My belief in the power of transformation is the result
of changes I saw him make in his life. He put aside dancing and waiting tables at a hotel on Main Street for preaching the word of God. Of
my grandmother's four children, he is the only one who earned a college degree. By sheer determination, in his later adult years, he studied
at what had once been the all-white state university in the city. . . .

The men in my family were buttresses and protectors, but it
was the women who gave meaning to the expression "pushed back
to strength." Each one in her own way provided antidotes to the
city's racism.

Ola Mae, my pretty and petite aunt of grey eyes, had the genius of song. . . . In her early twenties, many years before I was born, she used them in a local nightclub to help the family through hard times. . . .

. . . I remember her preoccupation with correct grammar, enunciation, and etiquette. She turned our small kitchen into a finishing school where we learned what fork to use, when, and how. My sister and I could have eaten an eight course meal at a high state dinner without having to follow someone else's lead. And we could have "talked with kings" (my mother's words) without making mistakes. My aunt taught us to dot all our i's, make our A's broad, and avoid all contractions. . . .

My mother was the brains of the family—an avid reader and a passionate polemicist who had a love affair with ideas. She preceded us at the high school we attended where she earned a reputation as a very bright and gifted student. . . .

. . . I was proud of my mother's mind.

. . . Mama envisioned my sister Faye and me—"my precious girls," she called us—earning graduate degrees, giving speeches, publishing, traveling abroad, winning medals. Any honor that could be conferred on a human being would be ours, my mother told us. And toward that end, she "scrimped and saved," as she put it, and "went without." She sacrificed for one reason—to send us to college. We had one thing to do with our lives—achieve. . . .

My grandmother was the fighter in the family. Prissy. Fiercely proud. Independent. If you pushed her too hard or in the wrong direction, you would never push her again. My peers attributed her toughness to her "Indian blood," visible in the small mountains that rose beneath her cheeks and in black hair so straight it barely held braiding. She was more vocal in her racial anger and less willing to accept humiliation than most people in the units. . . .

At my sister's college graduation, Grandmama carried herself like a grand duchess of whom pomp and circumstance was a routine part of every day. She did not applaud too loudly, did not lean out of her chair too conspicuously to see the colorful procession of graduates, and did not cry out with emotion when my sister turned her tassel. Nobody would know that Grandmama was attending her very first college commencement. No one could have valued dignity and education more than she.

All five of her grandchildren finished high school and continued their education, three earning college degrees and two graduate degrees. All three of her great-grandchildren have earned master's degrees and have plans to continue their education. This is a testimony to my grandmother's belief in the efficacy of education. . . .

Like other southern cities, Memphis has changed significantly since the civil rights movement of the sixties. . . .

The Main Street I once feared and hated is no longer the center of life in the city. It is a ghost town which attracts poor people, 95 percent of them black, who have no way of getting to suburban shopping centers. . . .

I drive past my old housing project and wonder, in disbelief, if I ever lived there and loved living there. . . .

I wonder how and why the old mirror was shattered.

It is a world I do not recognize. Children here are old beyond their years; girls become mothers before they outgrow playing paper dolls and jumping rope. They do not entertain themselves with parades in the courtyard because they live in a world of ready entertainment. There are discos and X-rated movies in the outside world, and in their apartments they sit imprisoned by exciting sex and violence on televisions which come from easy-rental stores.

We live in an "integrated nation" which has forgotten how to love children and how to make them into angels with satin wings and wire halos. The children are lost because adults are lost. . . .

I began college in the early fifties, when all across the South black people were becoming intolerant of Jim Crowism. . . . I was angry and impatient. . . .

. . . I wore my racial anger like a badge. . . . I understood what could happen to any black person who responded to racism with consuming rage. Mama said rage was a corrosive emotion: "If you give in to it, you never win." I wanted to win. . . . For all of them.

Understandably, I was pleased when, in my senior year, I was named a finalist for a Woodrow Wilson Fellowship. Such an honor called for family singing at high octaves; our singing was muted because I had to travel to Birmingham for an interview. Everyone was concerned about my safety. . . .

. . . I came close to losing my life in Birmingham.

When the train arrived in Birmingham, I went immediately to the brightest area in the terminal. Light was no small consideration because I had planned to study for a philosophy exam during my six-hour wait before the interview. The terminal, I remember, was empty, and I did not see—or did not make an effort to see—"Colored" signs. I sat down and opened my book. Within minutes, a tall, big-boned white man was standing in front of me, shaking a fist the size of a grizzly bear's paw. "You better move your nigger ass," he snarled. "Colored supposed to sit over there." He pointed to an area that was too dark for reading. I did not move, but only because I couldn't. I was frozen in fear. He continued shouting, and just as suddenly as he had appeared, he left. I do not know how many minutes passed before a middle-aged black man rushed toward me and pulled me from the bench. "You gotta run, Miss," he said. "You gotta run." As we ran out of the terminal, I looked behind me. The bear-clawed man, now carrying a stick and joined by several other angry-looking white men, was headed in my direction. I followed the courageous black man, running for my life. We ended up in a small "colored" cafe, dimly lighted, but safe. "They would have beaten you half to death," the man said. I spent six hours in the cafe, but I never once opened my book. I wept uncontrollably, out of shame, out of fear, out of rage. There were only a few people in the cafe, but all of them understood my pain and the danger I had faced. The cook, a short and thin black woman, fed me. All of them counseled me, and when it was time for me to go to Birmingham Southern University, the site of the interview, they called the bravest taxi driver in town. He was as kind as my rescuer; not only would he take me to the university, he said, but he would also wait for me because on "that side" of town, there was no telling what would happen to a "colored" girl.

The panel of white men who interviewed me, sitting like judges around a grand oak table, did not know that for every question they asked me about literature and history, I had a hundred to ask them about racism. They could not have known that I was suppressing my rage only because they had something I wanted and needed, something my experience in the terminal had given me the right to receive.

My Birmingham experience . . . prepared me for involvement in the civil rights movement. Everyone in the family understood that and, therefore, no one was surprised when I wrote a year later from Boston, where I was enrolled in graduate school at Boston University as a Woodrow Wilson Fellow, that I had joined an organization that was "picketing places," as my mother put it. They had no fear of tame experiences in the East. The *real* movement, the southern movement, which I joined when I returned South from Boston, was something different. My family *did* fear my involvement with it. They wanted a new South, but they did not want me to sacrifice my life to bring it into existence. In time, however, they substituted pride for fear and began to give accounts to neighbors about what I was doing and, after each release, would report exactly how long I'd been jailed *this* time.

. . . My husband Joe and I went to Memphis three days after Christmas in 1969, following a holiday celebration with his parents and two brothers in Birmingham. Christmas at home was always wonderful. It would be especially so this year because we were bearing special gifts for the family: our son Jonathan, whom they had seen as an infant the previous year, and daughter Monica, an infant of two months. Mama had not yet told me about what had happened to Uncle Prince because I had been in my ninth month with Monica when it occurred. With a composure that did not succeed in concealing her rage and her pain, she now told us the heart-breaking story.

When he did not return home and the family did not receive a call from the downtown precinct, no one was overly concerned. . . . By the third night, though, they knew something was wrong. My mother called every precinct in the city and in outlying areas. There was no record of his arrest. She called John Gaston, the only hospital in the city that admitted poor people, blacks and whites, and hospitals in West Memphis, Arkansas, across the bridge, where he sometimes went with drinking buddies. There was no admissions record for a Prince Albert Reese. . . . They knew something was wrong. Terribly wrong. "It is that way with love," my mother would say when she talked about that night. They feared for his life.

On the fourth night, my family made the calls again, and this time John Gaston had a record of his admission. He had been in the hospital for three days, transferred there from the workhouse where he had been taken after his arrest for drunkenness and vagrancy. The police had not informed us of his arrest. They had concealed his whereabouts. En route to the hospital, my family feared the worst because the authorities—white people—had kept him from us for three days.

He lay unconscious, hooked up to wires, in the black section of the hospital. My mother said she became a mad woman wanting answers. Insisting on them at the risk of being arrested for disorderly conduct. A police sergeant came. He was careful with his words. My uncle was arrested. Taken to the workhouse. He became sick there. Very sick with seizures. So they transferred him to the hospital. No one explained why my uncle was unable to talk coherently.

I heard the tragic story that Christmas with disbelief. Extreme sadness. Grief. Wrenching pain. Rage. Guilt. I wished I had been home when he needed me most. Rationally, I knew I could have done nothing to protect him, but I had never been rational about my uncle.

In spring of the following year, my uncle was admitted once again to John Gaston Hospital and, while there, he suffered third-degree burns. He was smoking in bed when the sheets caught on fire. A nurse was called only when another patient saw the flames. My uncle, unable to speak, could not call for help.

When we went home for Christmas in 1972, he was moving more slowly and with stiffness because of the skin grafting. Genius. Artist. A gentle man who didn't hurt anyone. My uncle deserved more from life. "How are you, Uncle Prince?" I asked. He would answer, "You know."

Through the years, I have preached, literally preached, to my children about the dangers of alcohol. My sermon is not unlike my mother's sermon: "You got it in your family. Don't ever drink." The sermon worked for my sister and me; it also worked for my children. Both of them are very conscious about what they eat (making efforts to be vegetarians), and neither one touches alcohol. Their good habits, I tell them, are gifts from my Uncle Prince. They remember him only vaguely, but they know who he was and what he meant to me. Because of the stories—his and the real ones I share about my life with him.

... My son, at twenty-three, wears my uncle's face. Like my uncle, he has a winning personality. He performs for the family—singing, dancing, delivering speeches, telling jokes, reciting poems. He loves and even writes poetry. He draws and paints. He talks race and change. My uncle was a renegade; my son is a young revolutionary. I think that my Uncle Prince has had his final homecoming in my son. ... The only difference is in the hat. My uncle wears a Stetson; my son, an African kufu.

I remember . . . trains in the Memphis terminal. Explaining the excitement of that terminal to my children, who have known only airports, is almost as difficult as explaining the richness of jazz to someone who has never heard Coltrane or Sarah or Ella or my father's favorites, Dizzy and Louie. It can't be done. . . .

I can see the train belching white smoke. I can hear it exhaling every few seconds. And I can taste the aroma of the heavy oil that greased the rails. The conductor—always white, usually old and often wrinkled—walks up and down the platform in a black uniform which is shiny in places where it should not be. He wears glasses ringed with wire and a silver badge shaped like a star. I remember his eyes. Not the color of them, but the absence of a smile.

He walks authoritatively, giving orders to porters—always black—who shorten their tall structures by bending at the waist, ever so slightly. He takes the large-faced watch from his right pocket, unsnaps its cover, and reads the arrowed hands. He signals to porters. They remove small stepping stools and close the doors to all coaches except one. All is clear now.

The conductor climbs the steps and, leaning half in and half out of the open coach, sings, "All aboard. All aboard." Slowly, the train departs from the station, its metal wheels screeching against metal, its engines breathing a choo-choo sound.

I cannot remember trains and terminals without thinking about my father. Like the trains, he was dependable and strong. Like the trains, he stood still waiting for my sister and me at the same place, capable of taking us safely to a destination he had chosen and we desired. And like the trains, he was physically in and out of our lives. Returning and then departing. He lived in Chicago. We lived in Memphis.

As much as I missed my father and wanted him physically present in my life, I never thought my family was supposed to be structured differently. . . . I have since learned that such a positive attitude toward the separation of one's parents is rare for young children, but no other attitude was possible for my sister and me. We were nurtured on annual trips to Chicago, frequent long-distance calls, occasional letters, generous checks, and most especially by my mother's kind words about our father. Over the years we would love him for what he meant to us, but in the beginning we loved him because Mama did.

. . . He was "Daddy." In the fairy-tale sense of the word. A kind and gentle man who loved us more than he loved anyone else on the face of the earth. Who took us to fun places and bought us almost everything we wanted. Who was never tired. Never impatient. And never angry. Who always smiled love. Every summer, my father lived up to those expectations.

With money Daddy had sent for the trip, Mama would shop wisely for items we *had* to have in Chicago. . . .

Mama would remind us how proud our father was of us—our intelligence, our character, our demeanor.

"Don't disappoint him," she would say, and then add, "but I know you won't. You never disappoint any of us."

I remember there were special words for me. Rightfully so because I was so very different from my sister Faye. . . . She was the lady; I was the tomboy. I had no interest in the order of things on my side of the closet nor in the whiteness of the socks I wore. I was mannerable, especially to adults, but exceedingly and consistently mischievous. . . .

We always arrived on a Saturday, and my father was always there with a broad smile that made the gap between his teeth more noticeable. I remember that he always strutted out of the terminal with my sister holding one hand and me holding the other. I remember, too, that he always asked, "How's Bertha?" calling my mother by name.

In the early years, he would take us to a two-bedroom apartment on Calumet Avenue and in the later years to a nicer two-bedroom on South Cottage Grove. In both places, we knew to expect Daddy's sister and three brothers to gather as soon as we arrived in celebration of our summer homecoming.

Aunt Mae, my father's only sister, would be at the apartment waiting for us. A thin woman with skin as dark and smooth as rich fudge and slanted eyes, which explains her nickname "China Mae," she was my adult twin in mischief.

Every summer, Daddy would open the door and call to her that we were home. She would pretend to be too busy cooking to welcome us.

"Bob," she would say, "can't you see I'm busy."

My father's throat would vibrate with laughter. "Come on, Mae," he would say, participating reluctantly in the game. "Someone is here to see you."

"Who?" my aunt would ask, still not looking at us. "Who is it? Can they speak?"

"Me, Aunt Mae," I would answer, enjoying the game.

"And who is me?"

"Me. Gloria Jean."

"And who else?"

"Faye," my sister would answer.

"Faye and Gloria Jean," I would say. "That's who."

"Well, if that's who it is!" My aunt would take us into her arms and hold us tightly. "Where you been for so long? Where you been?"

She would turn us around, measuring with her eyes the number of inches we had grown since she had last seen us. She had sad eyes, but I remember that, like my father, she punctuated her sentences with laughter. And like my father, she asked, "How's Bertha?"

If my father had lived in the deepest regions of Alaska, reachable only by a sled drawn by a rare breed of dog difficult to find and twice as difficult to train, his three brothers would have located him and moved near by. Like my aunt, they worshipped my father and had never lived for any length of time away from him. They would arrive later in the afternoon with kisses, hugs, and the greeting we knew to expect: "How's Bertha?"

I do not believe it was an accident that I never saw Daddy in his porter's uniform. He chose the image he wanted us to see. Only in terminals and on trains was he a hat-tipping black man. Downtown on State Street, where he took us shopping for school clothes, he gave no hint of his occupation. Salespeople treated him with deference as he counted out the bills with ease, and regarded my sister and me with deference as we tried on outfits, and hats as well. . . .

In addition . . . Daddy, without fail, would take us on a car tour of the University of Chicago. "This is where the smart white boys go to school," he would say, pointing to white men walking to and from buildings that we never entered and carrying the books that Daddy said made them so smart. He could not foresee that many years later his first grandson, Loren, would be a student at the Lab School in one of those buildings. He never talked about the university opening its doors wide to black students. That was beyond the realm of possibility in his thinking, but there was a reason for the centrality of this place to his tours. He wanted us, in spite of racial restrictions, to think education.

. . . Daddy loved *his* Chicago because it was black. I would return home and brag to my friends about having lived for months without answering the door to a white salesman or opening our apartment to white inspectors who, once a year, rated us on cleanliness, checking even our dresser drawers and closets. Daddy's Chicago belonged to us, I would tell my friends. . . . It was a world in which my sister and I lived like princesses because we belonged to Bob Wade.

I believe my sister deserved the answers [to our parents' separation] more than I because, even as a young girl, she understood the difference between a father and a "Daddy." I loved "Daddy." I think she worshipped him as "Daddy," but she wanted him as father. . . .

Why did he leave us? Leave Mama?

The story of their marriage and their divorce unfolded like a large and special quilt kept for years in the top drawer, removed, shaken, and used only when nothing else will end the numbing cold.

Without apology, she shared her memories. They were in their late teens when they married. Mama had graduated from high school and was working at her first job putting together wooden straight-backed kitchen chairs at the Wabash Screen Company in Memphis. Daddy, who went no further than the eighth grade, was working as a delivery boy at a corner drugstore. They met. They fell madly in love. They married. They moved into the two-bedroom house on McLemore when Mama lived with my grandmother, my aunt, and my two uncles.

"Robert Junior," Mama's name for Daddy, "was a good man, but a weak man."

Shortly after their marriage, Daddy's brothers and sister moved in with them. Somehow Grandmama found space for everyone.

"Didn't that bother you?" we ask.

We knew how she would answer. It was common in those days. A way to get ahead. To make ends meet. To be connected as a family. Besides, they were such "loving boys" and "so very talented." Johnny was a leather craftsman, capable not only of repairing shoes, but also of making them. Edmund was a tailor. With his one good eye, he could turn fabric into a good-looking man's suit.

And there was, of course, Daddy, who, in my mother's opinion, was the best barber in the South, or in the nation. Word of his ability spread so quickly throughout Southside Memphis that my grandmother's small house became a thriving barbershop. Daddy was generous with his money, sharing it with Grandmama, his brothers and his sister, and, Mama adds, "friends."

. . . Why didn't the marriage work?

They were simply too young to be married and too young to start a family. Their first child, a son born a little better than a year after they married, died when he was less than two months old while sleeping, peacefully they thought, in his crib. . . .

. . . Though the marriage was weak in Memphis, it might have survived if they had remained in the South.

Daddy was working at an optical store in downtown Memphis. If my research is correct, it was the same store at which Richard Wright worked and about which he writes with bitterness in his autobiography, *Black Boy*. Like Wright, like all black men in the early forties, Daddy was a "boy" in the eyes of white men although he was already twice over a man, caring for not one family, but two. In order to survive, he endured the humiliation, but a charge of theft made continued endurance an act of emotional and spiritual suicide.

Mama remembers the night the police came to their apartment, bursting in without a search warrant and asking contemptuously for "the nigger Robert Wade." They pulled everything out of the closets and dumped the contents of dresser drawers on the bed. One drawer was locked. This, they were certain, contained the stolen goods. They broke the lock with a sharp knife and cussed openly when they found birth certificates and death certificates. Only papers, valuable only to Daddy and Mama. She remembers shaking uncontrollably when they left. Out of fear because they might return, next time to beat her, and out of anger because she was powerless against their rage.

"Why didn't you stay in Chicago?" we ask.

Confession. She missed the South. She missed home. She was lonely. She hated the city that stole Daddy from her. All his life he had known cramped places, confinements and limitations, burdens and responsibilities. He was finally free in Chicago. A good-paying job, a decent place he would call his own, a family, and friends familiar with the fast life in Chicago. Daddy lost all sense of direction. He found the childhood, the freedom, and the open places he had been denied.

There was nothing for her in Chicago except Daddy, whom the city had stolen and would not return. Going back would have brought misery to both of them. Perhaps instead of one slap, there would have been more, and more, and Mama would have found herself a battered wife. The thought crosses my mind, but I reject it. There was only one slap. One too many. But only one. That is what I must remember. There was only one slap.

I am angry with Daddy not for abandoning my sister and me, but rather for breaking my mother's heart.

"He would have lost his mind in Memphis," she explains. "It was a mean city. It would have destroyed him."

Together, they decided what was best for all of us, especially for the girls. A divorce. Financial support. Nurturing from a distance. And their close friendship. *They* decided, she tells us, saying nothing about her consummate grief. Nothing about pain so acute it almost became, like Chicago, a thief taking another parent from us. . . .

. . . There never was a time during his life that Daddy was not in our lives. He continued to call on a regular basis, talking at length to Mama after talking briefly to us; to send clothes, especially the heavy winter clothes available only in a cold place like Chicago; and to write our names on special delivery envelopes containing money just for us. I felt privileged when the mailman knocked on the door and asked us to sign for cash and for money orders. But the amount was never enough. Mama needed more.

We had a difficult time.

Mama worked miracles with what she had. Bacon was strick-o-lean she fried crisp after boiling it long enough to remove the heavy-grained salt. Margarine began as a soft white substance in a cellophane package, in the center of which was a ring of red liquid the size of a penny. We would massage the liquid until it turned the white substance to yellow, becoming our margarine. For special dinners, Mama bought cheap cuts of meat and beat them repeatedly, and hard, with a metal mallet in order to make them tender enough for eating. Only when Mama was pained by not being able to give us something we had requested, but could do without, did I feel deprived, and then only of her smile.

She had a habit in those difficult years of counting on her fingers at the beginning of every month. "Let's see now," she would say, touching the thumb of her right hand. "I owe Goldsmith's twenty dollars and Sears, twenty, and . . ." She would move from her thumb to all the fingers on her right hand and then to the other hand, naming her debts.

I do not ever remembering my mother complaining about debts or whining about problems. She was upbeat, optimistic, stoic, and spiritual. Only once do I remember her being none of these. That was the night she came home, later than usual, in a state of murderous rage.

She had stayed after work, at [her boss's] request, to finish something he said he needed the next morning. By then, she had been promoted from clerk in the insurance company to chief book-keeper, a move up that made only a minor difference in her salary. He buzzed for her to come into his office. When she entered, he rushed to the door and locked it. He unzipped his pants and told her what he wanted her to do. "I got on my knees," Mama told us, "and begged him. 'Please. Please don't do this to me.'" She cried and pleaded. Calmly, he told her that it didn't make sense for her to say no. He could fire her. Without cause if he wanted to and she could do nothing.

She continued to say no. The physical battle began. "I fought him the way a man fights another man," Mama said. Words. Threats. Physical force. She fought him. After an hour, he gave up. His parting words: "Don't tell anybody about this and you'll keep your job."

"Depend on yourself. Always depend on yourself." How often did my sister and I hear those words when we were growing up. If our husbands abandoned us or died, we had to be able to take care of ourselves. Hence her emphasis on education.

Three important events took place between May and June in 1959. I graduated from college with a Woodrow Wilson Fellowship for graduate study at Boston University. I married Jimmy, my college sweetheart; professors and administrators saw us as "twins" in academic achievement and integrity, students "most likely to succeed." *And Daddy said he wanted to return home.* This time, I was praying he would keep his promise. Faye, married a year earlier, was living in Chicago; I was preparing to move to Boston. I was concerned about the imminent void in Mama's life, and I hoped Daddy would fill it. I thought he could do this because, at forty-two, Daddy was a changed man. At a different time and under different circumstances, he and Mama would have remained together and grown old together. Gracefully. There was still a chance. Though their branches did not touch, their roots were intertwined. I believed they had never loved another person as they loved each other.

Which is why, I thought, they should try again. Begin a second life together. Which is why I was delighted when they slept together in the same bed. I asked Mama the next day if they had made love; she smiled and answered no.

I remember that they were like two old friends sharing stories from a long trip they had taken together. They talked endlessly over coffee, touching each other with their laughter. . . . I remember their conversation. Daddy praised her for being a good woman. A good mother. He was brittle with regret. Faye and I had done well because of her. We were the ladies he knew she would raise. He had been such a fool. Nothing out there is more important than family. He wanted to come home. This time, really come home. He wanted to come home, back to her, never to depart again. He would make it up to her. Could he?

They were sitting at the kitchen table, the family gathering place. Mama leaned over and kissed him on the cheek. She touched his hand and said, "Robert Junior, I will never see you again."

"I'm going to surprise you," he said. "This time, it's for real."

The words were familiar, only this time they were spoken in Memphis, not in Chicago. He would go back North, get things in order, and return. He would live with her in our apartment in the project that would be empty with my departure and my sister's.

"I believe you mean it, Robert, but I don't think I'll ever see you again."

I left Memphis headed for graduate school in Boston, praying that Daddy would keep his promise this time.

He left Memphis headed for Chicago with a mental checklist of things to do.

A week later, on a Saturday afternoon, the phone rang. Mama says that she had a strange feeling when she answered. A friend was calling. At a civic club meeting, Daddy had complained of a maddening headache. Two hours later, his blood pressure was dangerously high. Three hours later he died.

. . . Even though most black women worked, and thereby contributed to the family income, men, by and large, decided how money was spent. Men in the community would say, "It's just the way we been taught. A man is supposed to be the head of the family."

Women would advise us: "Always have money put aside which your husband doesn't know about." No matter how good a husband is, a woman must be prepared to take care of herself.

These caveats were central lessons about gender which were as important as lessons about race. Both furrowed our path toward wholeness.

We learned early about biological differences between girls and boys, but the women rarely explained the differences in explicit terms. In fact, their language danced around biology. I remember hearing "kitty cat" for vagina, "worm" for penis, and "number one" and "number two" for bodily functions. . . .

Adults were contradictory in their treatment of sex. On the one hand, they used coded words; on the other, they talked very openly about pregnancy. White women might have told their children about a white stork with long stick legs flying among cumulus clouds with a bundle of joy hanging from his beak. Black women in the project told the graphic truth: "A woman can get a baby when she opens her legs to a man." We were told to open our legs only on our wedding night. "Keep your pocketbook closed" and "Heads Up, Dresses Down" were common sayings in the project.

The onset of menses catapulted girls into a world of old wives' tales ("when you're on your period, wash your hair with coal oil, not with water"), preoccupation with cleanliness ("change your pad frequently, even when you think you don't need to"), and stories about the time when some unsuspecting girl got pregnant "the very first time." We were taught to be "good girls" which meant being virgins.

I would think about my gender upbringing years later when I studied nineteenth-century black women's history and read about women activists championing black women's virtue. "Lifting As We Climb," though not used by all black women's organizations, was an appropriate motto for nineteenth-century efforts to challenge myths about the sexual licentiousness of black women which was in direct contrast to the piety and virtue the Cult of True Womanhood prescribed for white women.

The women in my community were not unlike their ancestors. Their insistence that we remain virgins until we married was in large part a response to myths about our sexuality. . . . These myths motivated white men of means in the South to hire high-class black prostitutes for their sons' first sexual experience because they believed the saying, "A boy can't become a man until he's had tan."

Mama . . . believed a mother had to be her daughter's friend and that she should hold back nothing, especially in matters of sex. Which is why in one breath she advised us against premarital sex and in another she discussed sex in a way that could have easily tempted us to do the very thing she said we should not do. She tried to teach us about sexual exploitation, but not at the expense of our sexuality. Mama actually wanted us to *enjoy* sex. But at the right time.

"It's a wonderful experience," she would tell us. "It feels good. And it's beautiful."

If it's all that, I remember saying to myself, why should we deny ourselves?

Mama's explanation made sense. "It's beautiful but not in the back of a car and not in a motel room. It feels good but not when you have to worry about someone finding out."

You can't experience the "real thing," she would tell us, when you have all those worries interfering with your pleasure. "You have to be able to take your time. Take your own good unworried time."

She was expecting too much of me. What about the hormones? They had centrifugal power pulling me toward a sexual center.

But Mama trusted us.

What should I do about the centrifugal pull?

She had no easy answers.

She trusted us.

"I want you to have it all," she would tell us. "Education. Education. Economic sufficiency. And sexual passion. Pleasure."

Confusion. Struggle. Hormones. Conflict.

But Mama trusted us.

"You'll be glad you waited," she said with certainty that we would wait. "Trust me. You'll be *so* ready. You'll be glad."

Mama was right.

I went because I was required to. Even infidels and atheists (if there were any in the black community) believed children should go to church. Mama would say, "It was the yeasayer in a world of nays." We designed it, controlled it, and made it work for us. It was the only institution in the community in which we never saw white supervisors, white inspectors—white people in charge. It was an empowering institution.

When I make that statement to today's Africentered students, they laugh. Scoff even.

"What about the white Jesus?" they ask. "And white angels?"

I answer, "What about them?"

They also belonged to us. They were in *our* world, saying what we wanted them to say to us, speaking in cadences and metaphors we had taught them. Instead of feeling inferior, we felt special, empowered, chosen. We were as assured of liberation and empowerment on earth as we were of salvation in heaven.

Like secret religious gatherings of slaves, the black church during my growing up years in the South was never exclusively about the salvation of our souls. It was a finishing school, a reading program, a leadership institute, and a counseling center, and in all of these services, the focus was on developing the children into articulate, respectful, well-mannered, responsible, disciplined, and self-affirmed individuals wearing a green light for success.

Salvation required that we keep the commandments Moses brought from the mountain top. . . .

"You must love yourself and your people."

"You must believe that you can do anything you set your mind to."

"You should let no circumstance remove you from the center of your dreams."

"You must never forget from whence you came."

"You must reach back to others."

"You must serve."

These black commandments, and others, made hatred of white people foolish and self-destructive. . . . We were never silent about our injuries and their iniquities. But we stopped a good distance from hating them. Let *them* do the hating, and let them lose. . . . Hatred was a corrosive emotion. It rusted the soul.

. . . Mama was a deeply religious woman who believed in prayer and meditation and in the Bible as a book of eternal truths. Metaphors in the Bible were lessons about life that she passed on to my sister and me, and to her grandchildren. "Read this often, but with comprehension," she wrote on an inspirational poem about the parable of the mustard seed she sent to her grandson Loren during a difficult period in his life. It began with the question she put to all of us in her own words: "Would you like to undertake some mountain moving?" We could be mustard seeds, she taught us, and we could move mountains, she told us. Her texts for parenting came, we knew, from the Bible.

When the church gave me the "right hand of fellowship," I felt better about what I was doing. God said repent of your sins. I had done that. The minister said accept Christ as your personal savior. I did that every day I entered the church. I had a right to stand next to my sister.

When we told Mama that we had joined church, she wept and began wringing her hands, which always meant deep emotion she was having difficulty controlling. Faye cried the Christian's cry. She could feel her hands looking new and her feet, too. She was going to be a different girl, a better human being. That wouldn't take much for her since she obeyed all the rules. I remember going upstairs and getting on my knees at the bed I shared with my sister. I prayed that the Lord would make my joining the church as real for me as it was for Faye.

Baptismal Sunday was the most spirited of days in my church. Increasing the fold brought to the worship a joy, a passion, an intensity that only the most hard-hearted person would not feel. The choir marched down the aisle in bright green robes, swinging from side to side, in step, their voices richer than usual.

> Pass me not O gentle saviour.
> Hear my mournful cry.
> While on others thou art calling.
> Do not pass me by.

One by one, we walked into the cold water to the middle of the pool where [the minister] was waiting to receive us. He placed one arm around our waist and the other on top of our head. "In the name of the Father, the Son, and the Holy Ghost." He dipped us backwards into the water, held us under for a second, and brought us up to the sounds of the congregation's praises to the Lord. I did not choke.

My life *did* change. Perhaps because my baptismal and puberty happened simultaneously, but it changed. I changed. I was less mischievous and more mature. I was not fanatical. I never said, "Praise the Lord." I did not become "saintly." I dressed the same. I continued to go to parties and to dance and to joke. To have fun. . . .

I held on to my religious convictions and to the church through college and graduate school, two experiences black people back home considered a threat to one's faith. Lectures by learned professors, they feared, would challenge sermons on which we had been nurtured. Hence, the text for commencement Sunday: "Goodbye, God. I've Gone to College." I held on until reason and rage convinced me to let go. Christianity, I decided, had crippled my people. Made us too forgiving. Too submissive. Too resigned to suffering on earth as a prerequisite to eternal life. Too incapable of organizing and executing the revolution we needed. I would march with ministers, assemble in churches for rallies, and bow in prayer before demonstrations, but I was not a member of the community of believers.

While I was marching in the sixties . . . I was fighting to hold on to my faith. After four young girls lost their lives in the Birmingham church bombing, I decided never again to believe in my people's religion. And with the advent of Black Power in the seventies, I made what I thought would be a permanent disconnection from the black church. In my new so-called revolutionary thinking, I saw it as the white man's weapon against my people. During the sixties I listened to Martin. During the seventies I meditated politically to the sound of Malcolm's voice on tapes that were selling on every street corner in black neighborhoods. I wished that I had followed him when he was alive. Christianity, he said, is a slave religion. I agreed with him.

They say you can't stay away for long. They say that age and marriage and motherhood pull you back from the other shore. They say that the loss of your mother will cause you to sing the old songs and to bow in prayer again to the God in whom you once believed. They say you do indeed go home again.

I went home for all of those reasons, and for another that is not as easy to explain. I call the reason change. Change in the terrain of black life following integration which, along with other factors, has made us spiritually desolate. In communities that lay like wastelands in America, the black church is the only place where elders feel wanted and needed. There, they can sit erect and, in security and pride, share what they feel and what they know. In a nation where much of the music blasted into the psyche of the young is an introduction to sex and violence, the black church is the only place where the young can hear elders sing the old songs that once sustained us as a people.

"I love the Lord, he heard my cry," a single voice sings. It is a call for response from a chorus. Lining, as it was called, stretched a line from one person's soul into a song that could last for half an hour. Each word in the line, each single word, became a melody. Not only in jazz did black people improvise. No one could write the notes of lining songs on five lines marked by a G clef because, with each singing, the songs were different. Improvised for the Lord.

And where else except in the black church will the young hear "sorrow songs." Created by slaves, spirituals are among the most musically brilliant and moving of songs. To sing them is to be in touch with the spirit of our ancestors. To hear them is to be reminded of the resilience of their spirit and, therefore, to be renewed. "Jordan's River is chilly and cold; it chills my body but not my soul" has relevance for us today for, ultimately, it is our soul that we must save.

The church to which I am returning is not a perfect institution. It cannot be in this, our imperfect, world. Like other institutions in this nation, the black church has high levels of sexist toxicity. Men make policy decisions and women fan fainting worshippers. And cook meals, serve meals, make choir uniforms, type church programs, raise funds. Work. Though dominated by men, the church gets its strength and power from the spirit of the women. Call it nurturing, call it maternal, call it humanistic, call it healing—that spirit is what we so desperately need today.

Boston in 1959 was a strange city. Unattractive, cold, and spiritually desolate. Disappointing. At least for me, a black woman from the South. A daughter of the sun. I was accustomed to people talking with animation on street corners, in grocery stores, and across dusty courtyards. People sitting on front porches watching children, all of whom "belonged" to them. People approaching me with smiles followed by warm hellos. Nothing seemed right about this city. Even its music was wrong. Monotone. Without soul.

I tried to take comfort in the fact that the city had a river, but the name left me unmoved. "Charles" made me think of a young boy bored with life. Privileged and pampered. . . . In contrast, the Mississippi (now that's a name for a river!) was serious. Its wide bosom attracted big boats. . . . Barges big enough to carry cargo to a hundred different cities along the Mississippi. Real destinations.

I was forced to admit that, even without a serious river, this was a significant city. Historic. The birthplace of America as a free nation. On any day of the week tourists of every hue and ethnicity, every political and religious persuasion, boarded double-decker buses near Copley Square and headed for the Old North Church, Bunker Hill, and other historic places bearing the names of patriots—most of them men, all of them white. And some of the buses toured the many prestigious colleges and universities that faced one another across the Charles River. One of those universities had brought me to this northern city.

And I was supposed to be grateful for being there. A black girl from a housing project in the deep South attending graduate school in the East. A Woodrow Wilson Fellow at that. I couldn't remember in what circle Dante placed ingratitude, but I remembered where it belonged in my mother's cosmology of hell. For her, violence against self and violence against others were the only sins closer to the inferno than ingratitude. Being ungrateful in my new home—academic and temporary only—placed me in the hottest region of hell. In 1959 Boston was a venomously racist city.

Boston failed every test on racial sensitivity and racial justice. With its rigidly drawn lines, it failed miserably in employment. I wondered who employed blacks in Boston since even waiters, busboys, and cleaning women were white. For me, it failed most miserably in housing. Black students at universities in Boston and Cambridge had identical stories to tell about realtors who sent us searching for apartments in communities that hid custom-made racial signs behind sugar-sweet politeness that soured quickly when we heard, "If only you had come here yesterday." Many of us succeeded in finding affordable and decent housing close enough for a not-so-long walk or a safe bicycle ride to the universities only with the aid of civil rights organizations. If we suspected discrimination, white volunteers would attempt to rent an apartment we had been denied. Only rarely were they told, "I'm sorry. Someone is moving in tomorrow." Together, we would confront the landlord who would either rent to us or find himself, or herself, in a lawsuit, which we would publicize in a demonstration. Picket signs and all. How humiliating it was to find a decent "home" only through confrontation and entrapment.

Universities . . . were a microcosm of the world outside their gates. Alien places for a student who graduated from a historically black college where professors knew us by name and pushed us, confident of our performance, into rigorous academic challenges. At big universities students are often faces without names, and many professors are scholars without dedication to the faces without names. I had grown up in a learning environment where mentoring outside the classroom was every bit as important as lecturing inside the classroom, and creative teaching was as valued as a significant essay in a scholarly journal. Scholarship was not narrowly defined as publication. It included serious preparation for lectures that would inspire students to pursue excellence and the highest of goals. I was at this university in the city without a serious river because of that definition. Because of scholars who taught with passion, and who inspired by example. They reminded me when I left home why I was leaving in the first place.

"Remember what you're there for."

"Don't get behind in your studies."

"Don't let them make you doubt yourself."

"Remember you're every bit as smart as white students, and smarter."

"You're doing this for black students who will come after you."

"Remember what we've taught you."

"Make us proud."

"Excel!"

I missed them. I missed the small campus in Memphis which was resonant with the history of my people. I missed the lectures and convocations and conversations about mission which meant giving back to the place from whence you have come. . . . The cold whiteness of universities in Boston made me dislike the city even more.

. . . In the beginning I did not believe I would ever adjust to living in Boston. I am sure I would have remained detached and angry if Jimmy had not been with me. He was my friend and my soulmate, holding my hand through each new Boston experience. Having spent a year at M.I.T. as a Danforth Fellow the year before I began my studies at Boston University, he had grown to know well the Boston touted in brochures and in feature stories on culture printed in magazines and award-winning newspapers. He loved the white city. That is not to say, however, he was blind to Boston's racism. Far from it, he was a fighter, bold and unrelenting in his struggles with racist whites. In fact, it was in part his refusal to let them control his life, along with his love of adventure, that made him a connoisseur of every delectable the city had to offer.

I allowed my eyes to see a rainbow of ethnicity that never arched over Memphis. At home, whites were whites. Southern and white. Period. In Boston, whites were divided into distinctively different groups who claimed different sections of the city as home: the Irish in South Boston, the Italians in North Boston, the Jews in Brookline. There was Chinatown and Greektown. Whites expressed their distinctiveness in cuisines, music, ways of worship, and sometimes in dress. . . . And that explains, in part, why blacks could not seek asylum in those ethnic neighborhoods. If anything, we found more outward hostility. I resented the way these groups looked down on and treated blacks, but I went to their neighborhoods as one goes to a fair or to a carnival. With excitement. In anticipation of experiences only they could offer.

. . . With all its faults and in spite of my anger, I began to love Boston and to claim it as my nonsouthern home. Academic and temporary, but "home."

I knew about Roxbury, the black community to the east, but I went there only when it was time to get my hair "fixed." Looking back on those years with very different eyes, I realize that I could have easily been accused of disconnecting from my people. . . .

. . . I was an integrationist of the first order.

That explains why Jimmy and I, along with a few other blacks, joined the Unitarian Church. It's been so long since I worshipped there that I don't remember where it was located. Somewhere near the Common, I think, or in that general neighborhood. I was convinced this church offered what I needed at the time: open dialogue about religion; respect for all denominations and even for non-Western religions; a nonliteral reading of the Bible; and, most important, an integrated congregation that dared be different, that dared challenge the status quo.

In those days the heightened racial turmoil in the South, the struggle for freedom had to be central to all of my experiences, including religious worship. If any church were to make a difference in the Boston area, I was convinced it would be this one.

I confess, however, wishing many Sundays for the sound of a black choir singing gospel or a woman shouting unashamedly as the holy ghost touched her. I wanted to see black mothers hushing crying babies or walking proudly down the aisle in their ushers' uniform. I even wanted at times to see a black preacher strutting across the pulpit, singing and dancing. And although I had long since stopped taking the Bible literally, I sometimes wanted to hear sermons about a real Daniel who fought off real lions and a real Jonah who stayed in the belly of a real whale—until a real God released him.

But I was comfortable, even happy, in my new church home primarily because the people were real, and sincere. . . .

I believe the church directed me to the Boston Committee on Racial Equality (CORE) or perhaps, with Jimmy, I happened by Trailways one day and saw the pickets. I can't remember. I know only that my life changed when I became an activist with CORE in 1961. The South which I had left was changing. In 1960, black students challenged segregation at lunch counters. I saw the beatings on television, and I wept. In 1961, the Freedom Rides began. I saw the beatings, the bloodied faces, and the eyes of hatred. And I wept. I began to remember horror scenes from my past. There were flashbacks of the lynching of Emmett Till and the picture of his bloated body in *Jet Magazine*. Flashbacks of the lynching of Mack Johnson. Flashbacks of white policemen in Memphis beating a black man near my community. Flashbacks of my grandmother's stories and my uncle's stories and my father's stories. My people's stories. My guilt was profound. My people were struggling and dying; I was walking safely into large libraries and reading books about white people which I wrote about in papers only white professors would read. I needed to be involved in the movement. Actively involved.

I could have joined the Boston chapter of the NAACP, but CORE appealed to me more. It attracted a different type of activist. Instead of working in the courts, it worked in the streets. I needed visible and public proof of my commitment, especially since I was living in a white world. . . .

It was called Boston CORE, but many of our meetings took place in Cambridge in a small, three-bedroom apartment not far from Harvard Square—symbolically in a mixed (not to be confused with integrated) community. What I remember most vividly about the long hours Jimmy and I spent in that neighborhood, planning demonstrations, painting picket signs, and preparing leaflets in the small, modestly furnished apartment, was our sense of ourselves as a family, as brothers and sisters fighting a common foe. I don't remember any of the whites in CORE apologizing for what other whites were doing to black people in the South or in Boston. Nor do I remember feeling that I was the "beneficiary" of white paternalism, ingratiating sweetness, or authoritarianism. Perhaps my own racial pride made such postures unthinkable, or perhaps the whites with whom I developed a close friendship were not the kind who later would be called "white liberals" and held under close scrutiny and suspicion in the wake of the Black Power Movement.

. . . What I see now, and could not and did not see then, however, is the extent to which, in spite of genuine bonding between blacks and whites in CORE, the cultural exchange taking place was essentially a one-way street. I was eating their cuisine, studying their literature, listening to their music, admiring their art, worshipping in their church—immersing myself in their culture. I taught them very little about African-American culture. And there was so much I could have taught them. So much they should have learned. Ironically, if they had asked me to educate them about my culture, I would have taken offense and accused them of seeing me only in racial terms.

If I could walk back into history as the person I am now, I would change the Boston chapter in my life.

. . . I would go alone to Roxbury to connect with people who could interrupt my sentences and complete them with words I was prepared to speak. I would look for the children and, after them, for the older people who, even when I was in Boston, knew the art of sitting outside on concrete steps because they understood that only by going outside can you see, know, and bond with your neighbors. I would not give up my life in Boston. I could not and continue with my graduate studies. But I would expand it. Roxbury would be as much a part of my schedule as all-day study sessions for literature classes that ignored the existence of black writers. I would work in both worlds, for both worlds, hoping for one world.

. . . My stay in Boston . . . was an important chapter in my life, the beginning of my metamorphosis into a different woman. A different self. . . . That is what Jimmy and I felt when we decided, with regret but without pain, to separate in 1963 and, a year later, to divorce. We never had an argument or conflict of any kind. We had had the best of times as friends who were close enough to be blood kin. As the best of friends and as co-activists, we moved to Atlanta in 1963. At the end of the year, Jimmy returned to Boston and, some years later, received a cabinet position in the state government. I remained in the South. I was home.

I have not always worn an Afro. My mother reminds me of that fact when she turns the pages of our family scrapbook or my high school and college yearbooks with pride. "You see how you used to look," she says, stopping short of telling me she prefers the way I "used to look." I claim the face in the pictures, and the smile. "You always did smile," she says. But I am reluctant to claim the hair. It is greasy, unnaturally straight, shiny, and, I think, very unbecoming. I try to imagine how I would have looked on Easter Sunday in a white eyelet dress, a pink bonnet, black patent baby dolls, and an Afro. . . .

Twice a month (either on Friday night or late Saturday afternoon) and sometimes more frequently if we had been caught in a hard rain or if we were participating in a special activity, my sister and I prepared for the ritual that would change our hair. We would brush our hair vigorously in order to stimulate the scalp. In order to make the hair grow. Then, black girls did not want short hair. When the brushing was finished, we would place our heads under the faucet in the deep kitchen sink and feel fingers dancing on our scalp. Mama scrubbed our hair with Ivory soap. Rinsed out the suds. Scrubbed again. The ritual had its own rhythm. Water off. Water on. Scrub. Rinse. Off. On. Scrub. Rinse. Off. On. Scrub. Rinse. Only when our hair was squeaky clean, did the rhythm end.

Mama . . . would decide when it was "good and dry." . . .

When it was dry to her satisfaction, Mama would sit in a straight-backed kitchen chair dangerously close to the stove. On a blue flame, she placed a metal fine-toothed comb bought at the five-and-dime. In the middle of the stove, where there were no flames, she placed a wet heavy towel. Sitting on the floor between her legs—one at a time, of course—my sister and I could not see Mama at work, but we knew exactly what she was doing. When the comb was hot, she removed it from the flame, rubbed it several times on the wet towel, and began to straighten our hair.

I welcomed the suffering because I wanted to be "beautiful" and that required straightened hair. I was proud that my hair was not too kinky and even bragged about its shoulder length. Even had the nerve to sling it around and, in the presence of would-be boyfriends, twirl it around my fingers. And yes, I thought I was rather cute in the greasy hair that looked good in pigtails in elementary school, in a ponytail in high school, and in stylish curls in college. . . .

When I look back on the experiences and the people who were responsible for my giving up the metal straightening comb and, later, scalp-burning chemicals, for a pick—a simple, inexpensive, and easy-to-clean pick—I think immediately of the civil rights movement and the women and men, blacks and whites, who risked their lives for change. But they only made possible that which was started long before I met them. I would never have joined the movement and, therefore, never have changed my hair had it not been for my family. . . .

In their own way, my family taught me racial pride that would eventually find expression in an Afro. That explains why no one in my family ever doubted that I would become one of those militants they were reading about in the newspaper. And why I was at home in the movement before it ever began. Having listened to their stories and having seen my family's example of quiet and steady

resistance, I knew how to walk when I hit the pavement for freedom, and though I could not carry a tune (but I had learned from
my Uncle Jack how to dance!), I knew I would sing the freedom
songs passionately. They were resonant with my grandmother's
spirit of defiance.

When I moved from Boston to Atlanta in 1963, I immediately
joined the hundreds of thousands of blacks and whites who called
themselves civil rights workers or activists. My involvement began
when I participated in a demonstration at the largest white Baptist
church in Atlanta located on Peachtree Street next to the historic
Fox Theatre. We were protesting the very "unChristian" behavior
of church ushers. A week prior to the demonstration they had
thrown from the church vestibule an elderly white man, an activist,
and several black students from the Atlanta University Center.
Thrown them. The white Baptists used the "word of God" to justify segregation in the "house of the Lord."

I remember circling the church with other demonstrators,
blacks and whites, as the white worshippers came out of the
church, carrying Bibles bound in leather with special verses high-
lighted in gold. We sang church songs and carried picket signs.
Nonviolently. The worshippers taunted us, their faces demonic with
hatred. I expected only words from them. I did not know at first
what had caused the sharp pain I suddenly felt until I saw a woman
moving from me. She had thrust a long hat pin into my right but-
tock and walked away in her sanctimonious self-righteousness. Resisting the urge to chase her and pound her with my fists (as my
grandmother would have done) was my first test in nonviolence.

. . . My first arrest occurred in 1963 when I was a new instructor at Spelman College and, because of my CORE experiences,
somewhat familiar with movement activism.

Spirit was high, genuine, and infectious in the Atlanta University Center. We held rallies in front of Trevor Arnett, the old library,
and at Rush Congregational Church, a block away from the library.
The Student Nonviolent Coordinating Committee (SNCC) headquarters were located in a small frame house on what was then
Chestnut Street, but is now James T. Brawley. It was approximately
ten blocks from the library and fifteen blocks from Spelman's front
gate. Activists would work there all day, especially on Saturdays,
and late into the night seven days a week. . . .

. . . Rich's was a symbol of all that was racially wrong in white
Atlanta. It was within walking distance of our community and sym-

bolically close to the statue of Atlanta's birth from the ashes. Whites in Atlanta had not forgotten Sherman's march and the pain of defeat in a war that hurt slaves, they believed, more than whites.

We were engaged in a new war, without the devastation of land and people which characterized the Civil War, but our nonviolent troops were, in their own way, as deadly as Sherman's soldiers. . . . I marched with my hair straightened and stylishly curled.

Not until we picketed Leb's, a Jewish delicatessen located a block south of what is now the new Fulton County Library and directly in front of the Rialto Theatre, did the mass arrests begin. The wagons came by the dozens, and the police (all white at that time) twisted our arms, grabbed us by the legs (females knew to wear pants), jabbed us with billy clubs, and threw us into the wagons. Arrests were always dramatic, but this one was even more so because of the presence of Morris Eisenstein, a Jewish professor at the Atlanta University School of Social Work, his wife Fannie, and their two teenage daughters. The Eisenstein family was known to many students in the Atlanta University Center for their genuine support of racial equality. They were the only whites in the center (and there were more than a few on the faculty) whose children were enrolled in public schools in the black community. When they appeared, we knew they were there not as spectators, but as participants. That was the first time, and perhaps the only time, during the Atlanta movement that an entire white family had chosen arrest with demonstrators rather than the protection their color gave them.

At the downtown station, we were separated into groups on the basis of sex and race, fingerprinted, mug shot, and placed behind bars. The women demonstrators were in a cell that was large and long, narrow and cold. The inmates, all women of course, greeted us with cheers, and we literally danced into the cell block, serenading them with our repertoire of freedom songs. . . .

Demonstrations were cruel to my hair. They always made me perspire. Sweat. Because the sun was hot. Because my emotions were high. Because I was moving, expending energy, up and down, back and forth, on picket lines. Incarceration was even crueler because, out of fear, I perspired more. When I was released from jail the next morning, my hair really looked awful. It needed to be "fixed." Once back on Chestnut Street, I went around the corner to a beauty shop.

There were many arrests, but I remember one most vividly because it was so different from any other experience I had in Atlanta.

I was placed in solitary confinement with a tenth-grade girl from Washington High School. Without my grandmother's phenomenal memory, I don't remember why the girl and I were in solitary confinement. . . .

On the second night (I learned later that we had been in solitary for two whole days), we were awakened in the early morning hours and loaded like cattle into police vans protected by a ferocious German shepherd large enough to be a pony on its way fast to becoming a stallion. He barked at us from behind a screen that seemed too fragile to hold him. The ride took forever. The road was rough, the night was dark, and the dog never stopped barking. Worse, we had no idea of our destination.

When we arrived at the workhouse somewhere in the county, we were relieved. Lights and four walls are always safer than dark roads and ferocious dogs. I remember two things about this experience: I was cold most of the time and I worked in a huge kitchen, along with other women, preparing food for inmates. I also remember the obscenity of white jailers. In their eyes we were sexually talented because we were black and should be sexually available because we were black. . . .

Two days later, untouched by the white jailers, I was released along with my fellow demonstrators. The cold I had experienced in the workhouse lingered. I felt chilled. Sick. I wondered if I would ever again be warm. Demonstrations were suspended for a few days while our attorneys worked on legal matters. . . . This arrest had taken its toll on my body. And on my hair. . . . I went to the beauty salon for a touch-up.

. . . Faculty at the black colleges who were tampering with Atlanta's image risked losing their jobs. At the end of the school year, I was fired at Spelman. . . .

When the Confederation of Freedom Organizations (COFO) announced what some called "a nonviolent invasion" of the state of Mississippi, I signed on without hesitation. . . . I drove my little Volkswagen bug (I think it was green in color) from Memphis . . . to the University of Miami, in Ohio, where I joined hundreds of volunteers for a week-long training program in nonviolence. During the day, we were kept busy in workshops that examined everything from the power of redemptive love to the corrosive nature of anger. . . .

. . . By the third day of workshops, we were forced to see the face of danger: CORE activists Chaney and Schwerner and SNCC volunteer Goodman, who were working in Philadelphia, Mississippi, had mysteriously disappeared. Everyone feared the worst. Tears flowed easily, even for men. I have heard that not all of the participants remained true to the words of one of our favorite songs: "Ain't gonna let-a nobody turn me round." Some of them left Ohio for the safety of their own communities.

On the night before our descent into the bowels of Mississippi, I wrote letters to everyone—my family, old friends, new friends, passing acquaintances, my favorite elementary school teachers. . . . I did not want to forget anyone because I was not sure I would return from Mississippi alive.

Our chartered Trailways Bus pulled into Memphis for what we thought was a rest stop. The driver announced that the bus was going no farther. "But you were paid to take us to Mississippi," we screamed. It didn't matter. Trailways had decided not to cross the line from Tennessee into Mississippi. Even white people who were not particularly sympathetic to the cause feared a bloodbath.

There we were. Stranded. Without a plan. . . .

I was never a leader in the movement. Women weren't. But outside the bus depot in Memphis, I wielded some influence. I knew where the train terminal was located, and I knew who could transport us there. My mother and my uncles. I called them, and they organized a carpool. Between the few taxis that dared get involved and my Memphis friends, in one trip after another, we made it to the train terminal.

I was never prouder of my mother than I was that night. She was rich in beauty. The fear in her eyes when she first saw me surrendered without struggle to pride. Mama had stood many times on the very platform on which the volunteers gathered when she waved goodbye to my sister and me as we boarded the Illinois Central bound for Chicago. This time, my sister was not with me. I was not headed north for fun and joy with my father. With a group of people who were total strangers to Mama and new acquaintances to me, I was headed south to the Mississippi of my mother's birth and my grandmother's painful memories.

"I'm not going to tell you what to do and what not to do," Mama said. "You're a woman now. And you are serious about what you are doing." . . .

. . . I was eager to get my assignment. It was in Valley View, a small rural area about thirty miles or more north of Jackson. Canton was the closest town, but it was a "one-hoss town," we were told, with mean white folks.

The trip from Canton to Valley View was singularly unimpressive. The road was narrow and dusty, sometimes straight and sometimes winding, moving past open fields, a trio of lean cows, now and then a mule, clotheslines propped at a slant, and frame houses that looked uninhabited. In our arrogance, we decided the area was sorely in need of change.

When we reached Valley View, I discovered the sky overhead. Clearer than any I had ever seen. Nothing disturbed our view of its expansive beauty because there was nothing in Valley View except trees reaching gracefully upward from dry, flat land.

As our caravan approached the small church, I could see the welcome committee, men and women from the community, many of whom had agreed to let us live with them, in spite of the danger. Some of them shook our hands stiffly, many embraced us as if we were old friends returning home, and a few praised the Lord for our arrival. In the midst of this warm celebration, the police arrived. The guns on their hips looked like small cannons to me. They had orders to take us downtown for fingerprinting.

I remember riding in the back seat of a police car with three other women. I remember my fears. Rape. A beating. Death. I remember my rage. They undressed us with vile language. Remembering the "don'ts" from my early days in Memphis and the sermons on redemptive love from the nonviolent workshop prevented me from responding to them in any way. I confess, however, I failed at pitying them and loving them seemed utterly ridiculous.

. . . They fingerprinted us, made photo IDs, and threatened us with violence. But they released us unharmed.

Activists in overalls, the standard uniform of the civil rights movement, drove volunteers to the families with whom we would be living. Along with Madeline Levine and her husband Steve, who were studying Slavic languages and Asian studies, respectively, at Radcliffe and Harvard, I was driven to the home of the McKinneys. Reverend and Mrs. McKinney. It was a three-bedroom white frame house set back from the road. Alone.

. . . I admired them when they responded with courage to the Ku Klux Klan. I remember the evening clearly. We heard cars speeding past the house and within minutes we could smell burning wood. Only in movies at the Georgia Theatre had I seen a burning cross. I was frozen in fear. Mrs. McKinney was calm, but angry. Rev. McKinney went into action. He went into a closet in their bedroom and emerged with a long rifle. It looked old enough to have been used in the Civil War. He opened the front door and fired two shots into the lighted darkness. Later that night, calmer and more secure, I could not conceal my laughter. Rev. McKinney's rifle made the sound of a cork popping from an under-fizzed bottle of champagne. It was his courage that I heard exploding.

Our schedule was as routine as the McKinneys'. Immediately after breakfast, we went to work, teaching in the freedom schools and registering voters throughout the valley. In the evenings we attended meetings. When we returned home to the McKinneys in the evenings, usually before sunset, we were often physically exhausted, emotionally drained, and frustrated. We could not see our own handiwork, and we began to miss the comforts of our former lives.

Mississippi Summer ended in late August when most of the activists, blacks and whites, left the South, promising to continue the struggle in their own cities. I went home to Memphis to recuperate before leaving for Washington, D.C., to begin teaching at Howard University. Mississippi dust had claimed every strand of my hair, and the Mississippi sun had made every strand brittle. On my second day home, I washed my hair in the deep kitchen sink. I did not need Mama's straightening comb and curling irons, however. Years earlier I had begun using perms that straightened my hair with chemicals rather than with heated metal.

I can see the road stretching out before me and myself with straight hair driving once again my trusty VW bug. I was thirsty. I stopped at a drive-in restaurant in a small town in North Carolina, for a simple hamburger and a vanilla milkshake. Behind a screen, a white woman told me to leave. I told her that I did not have to leave. She was required by law to serve me. This was not the first time I had heard tires screeching, moving fast and angrily to arrest me, but this was the first time I was alone. And I had become impatient. Angry. Less tolerant than I had been earlier in the movement.

Two burly white policemen rushed toward me wearing badges that were grotesquely large and shiny. They twisted my arms behind my back, handcuffed me, and threw me into their car. "If you say one smart thing," one of them said, "I'll slap the black shit out of you."

The coward in me wished I had stayed in my "place." Did I really need the hamburger and milkshake? Why had I forgotten how very alone I was? This was the kind of senseless defiance adults warned us against. Defiance that we think gives us dignity, but claims our lives. . . .

I was placed in a cell with a strange woman whose appearance and penetrating eyes frightened me. She was a dark-skinned black woman. Large. Silent. She stared at me and said nothing. Just stared. I was afraid and physically uncomfortable because my bladder was about to explode. Using the toilet was a problem because it was in full view of the jailer, an old white man, who walked up and down the long hall, up and down, down and up, peering in. What would be worse: to pull up my dress and relieve myself in his presence, or sleep the night in wet clothes?

Concentrating on making my bladder double its size exhausted me. I fell asleep. When I opened my eyes, the woman was staring at me. She began to talk.

"You scared, ain't you?"

"Oh, not of you," I said. "Just the jailer."

"I ain't gone hurt you," she said.

"Oh, I never thought you were," I answered.

She knew I was lying. Her voice was like gravel. Her hands were calloused. Her hair was plaited in small short braids, so thick that Mama's old rubber, large-toothed comb would have been of little help. My hair, permed straight and styled attractively, began to crawl. I had the strange feeling that a hundred small bugs had invaded my hair and begun marching zigzag, in circles, and in straight lines on my scalp. I realized that I was ashamed of my hair. Ashamed that I had altered it. Ashamed because it was too neat and "pretty" for that place and so very different from her hair.

"Why you in here?" she asked. "You kill somebody? Your boyfriend?"

I told her about the movement. She told me about herself. She had murdered her husband because he had beaten her one time too many. In self-defense, she killed him with a large kitchen knife. A "butcher knife," people in the project called it. She was not distraught over her incarceration. She was grateful to be alive.

I came to see her as a gentle woman and an attractive woman with unblemished skin and a perfectly round face. Her laughter was deep and musical, like a bass singing a capella. She seemed to like the sound of her voice and to take pleasure in her humor. She was hungry for an ear, a shoulder, a smile, a warm voice. I gave her all of that, and more. I was her company. She was my protection. I wondered who had ever loved her and had she ever loved herself? I multiplied her by thousands and realized how tragic was the plight of poor black women in this country.

When I was released four days later, I cried. She did not. I told her that I would work on the outside for her release. She only smiled with her sad eyes. "You be good to yourself" was all she said.

I could never be the same again. Nor could my hair. A metal comb placed on an open flame, heated, and then pulled through my hair suddenly seemed utterly ridiculous. A chemical packed into hair and burning my scalp. That, too, seemed utterly ridiculous. Straightened hair became a weight pulling my head down when I wanted to hold it up. High. I remembered that some of the women in Mississippi (one a student at Spelman who joined a group which would later become "Sweet Honey in the Rock") had worn Afros in Valley View. I was ashamed that I had not followed their example. An Afro would have said more to my cellmate in North Carolina than all of my well-chosen words about the movement.

An activist with straightened hair was a contradiction. A lie. A joke, really. The right to tout the movement gospel of self-esteem carried with it the obligation to accept and love one's self naturally. . . .

. . . In August of 1967 I said goodbye to graduate school and the East Coast. Joe and I married and began our life together in San Jose.

My pregnancy was uneventful, but not without worry. My grandmother had been paralyzed for a year following the birth of her second child. Was that hereditary? My mother's first child, though born healthy, had died at the age of two months while sleeping in his crib. Was that hereditary?

And what about labor pains and delivery pains? Would I be able to endure them? Mama said that they are the "worst pain imaginable," but you forget them as soon as you hear the baby's cry. I was lucky, I thought often to myself. My baby would be born in a hospital where attending nurses and physicians would administer injections for pain. My mother was not as lucky. When I think about what poor black women went through to give life years ago—and my God, don't let me think about slave women—I wonder why our communities are not decorated with shrines bearing their likeness.

———————

. . . Intellectually, I supported, and strongly, woman's reproductive rights, but emotionally I was in conflict. The women of my youth held on to me. Between the lines of scholarly position papers on abortion, I would read their nonscholarly, but passionate words: "You never reject what God gives you because you don't know what you killing."

When I am asked now how I, a black woman, can "hook up" with white feminists on the abortion issue, I make my own private soap box and wax eloquently on the compelling relevance of choice to black women, who are disproportionately represented among the poor in this nation and the most victimized by self-righteous positions on choice. I tell those who castigate me for my politics about the day I visited a young mother who had no choice but to live in one of Atlanta's abandoned neighborhoods with her newly born child. I silence them with four words: "The woman was black."

The survival of interracial friendships is not a new problem for race relations in this nation. In the nineteenth century, blacks and whites were allies and often friends working together to abolish slavery. When, because of ideological differences created by race, the political alliance ended, so did most of the friendships.

The problem did not solve itself in the wake of the feminist movement of the sixties. Nor did feminists solve it. It stares at us in the most successful of coalitions across racial lines. It is an unblinking stare that holds the most committed white feminist in its gaze. To paraphrase bell hooks, the racism of white women is a given. Let us move on from there. We should be concerned about the current backlash to the feminist movement which is injected like a drug into the psyche of the nation, dulling our sense of right and wrong and giving us hallucinations of women as monsters set on destroying the world. Many black women feel that we should be equally concerned about racism which was injected long ago into the psyche of white women, dulling their sense of justice and creating hallucinations of themselves as interpreters of black women's reality. Racism is every bit as capable of weakening the movement as organized misogyny.

The break in black-white alliances was sharp and painful, but predictable given the lesson from history and given the many mistakes we made during the movement. One mistake was the decision to send out a nationwide call for white volunteers to work in black communities. The error was not the call, but rather the placement of volunteers. No one worked with white people. We left them alone or, as the old folks used to say, "We let them be." In essence, we planned for a wedding, but told only one party to walk down the aisle.

Some of the white activists should have been assigned to white communities where change was needed most. The problem, after all, was not a black problem, but rather a white problem. In large numbers, white volunteers should have set up camp in the waste-lands of the white South, cuddling white babies, teaching white children, bonding with white women, and educating white farmers and businesses about losses they were incurring as a result of their own racism.

And why didn't we ever consider this strategy? Because it was too dangerous? Yes. Connectedness to the racial struggle was, to white southerners, the worst type of betrayal, deserving punishment. The deaths of Chaney, Goodman, and Schwerner, as well as the beatings of countless white workers, evidenced this fact.

And no. Danger was not the only reason we never considered this strategy. Most of us saw white southerners as lost people, beyond redemption and hopelessly mired in ignorance. Backwoods ignorance that speaks wrong, dresses wrong, worships wrong, eats wrong. But that was not logical given our belief in the power of redemptive love. If we were working to change whites, why didn't we work among them? If redemptive love worked in demonstrations, why couldn't it have worked in their communities?

Another explanation for the placement is the unique experience of being around black people, especially black people of the soil. They are warm, embracing, accepting, spirited and spiritual, musical, and, given their big-bosomed religion, nonthreatening. They made all of us feel like saviors, messiahs, angels bearing gifts. They took us in, gave us their best beds, and prepared their best meals. They remembered us in their prayers and in naming ceremonies for children born after our departure.

Is it possible that black southerners were a fascinating primitive people, racial and cultural artifacts whom we activists, black and white, could talk about in the life of comfort to which most of us returned? I think so.

I think also working among them connected us to a humanity

we could not, for obvious reasons, associate with whites. "Did you see their eyes?" is a refrain in the black community.

"Did you see their eyes?" Mama would ask whenever I complained about moving to the back of the bus.

"Did you see their eyes?" we asked when whites, among them mothers with children, jeered at little black children walking to school carrying books escorted by men carrying guns.

"Did you see their eyes?" we asked when white policemen laughed as they unleashed dogs on demonstrators in Birmingham.

"Did you see their eyes?" we asked when the water lifted children from their feet and pinned adults against poles and cars and other demonstrators.

"Did you see their eyes?" I ask students who open the pictorial documentary *The Black Book* to the horrifying picture of the charred body of a black man lying naked on still smouldering logs. Fathers with sons, dressed in jackets, knickers, and bow ties, smile broadly for the photographer. I see eyes that see nothing except their own power.

If our first mistake was the result of how we saw white southerners, our second mistake was a result of how we saw ourselves: as brothers and sisters in spite of differences in race. We believed—perhaps we had to for the sake of the movement—that race was not an issue for us. After all, we were, by choice, living together and had pledged ourselves to die together, if necessary. Whatever was wrong in black-white relationships in the South had left us alone.

But we were naive to believe that, in one hot summer, we could erase the damage of centuries. Only after the movement, not during, did we admit that, early on, there were mumblings among black workers that whites felt empowered enough (or superior enough) to take over, and mumblings among white workers that blacks were too hypersensitive and hostile.

There is more to black rage than how African-Americans feel about white people. There is more to our rage than the stories which are currently considered to be the only good copy on the subject. In them, black rage is reduced to a hatred of white people, especially of Jews, which translates into murderous designs on their lives. This definition of black rage makes the obsolescence of African-Americans a necessity for national safety. It depicts us as simple-minded people incapable (probably because of genetic inferiority) of understanding the dynamics of a system. Worst of all, it minimizes our phenomenal achievements and ignores the thousands of projects in our communities designed, supported, and sustained by us. In a word, it continues the miseducation of white America.

Although I am "mixed," as all African-Americans are (we *do* have "some Indian blood" and white blood in our veins), I choose to identify genetically and culturally with women and men who were stolen from Africa centuries ago. America is my home. I was born here, I live here, and like so many who have gone before me, I will die here, but Africa is my motherland.

By choice, I have chosen to teach at historically black colleges for over twenty years because I believe in the excellence and mission of these institutions and I am inspired by their history, at the center of which is dedication to our people. I believe they must survive, or we will not survive. Teaching there has been my way of contributing to their struggle for survival which, until the millennium comes, is my people's survival as well.

I study and research, with passion, African-American history, literature, and culture, and regardless of the title of the course, I make our contributions central. I work, when time permits, on service projects in our communities. I am not comfortable with what I am doing. It is so very little for a need so very large. I want to do things that will make a difference, but I think we need a movement for that. No such movement exists. If one came into existence tomorrow, I would again become an activist. And if I thought I could start one, I would.

I make an effort to hear the soul of my Ancestors speaking to all of us. Their voices are in the winds, and in the universe itself is their spirit. I struggle, sometimes in strange ways, to become spiritually connected to them. I believe that, without that connection, we will not reap the harvest of freedom and wholeness we have worked so long to realize.

. . . There is no one way, no more authentic way, no more-African-than-thou way to express that commitment. There are many ways. For me, hating white people is not one of them. I can embrace other races without giving up either my racial birthright, or my racial loyalty. Indeed, I want to be so large in my humanity that I will never feel compelled to shut anyone from my life on the basis of race, or from the struggles of my people. If I am true to my study of African-American history—and out of respect for my people, I must be—I will have reason to call the names of whites who chose to struggle on the side of justice. They are in the diaries and stories and memories of my people. To remove them would be tantamount to changing the script my Ancestors wanted us to read.

Of course . . . I no longer make integration the number one item on my agenda for change. How can it be when the masses of African-Americans are colonized in ghettoes across this nation? I would not make mockery of our suffering by proposing that our song for the nineties should be "black and white together." We tried that and, because of America's misinterpretation of integration, we lost. We lost because we were psychologically enslaved as a people.

White America said, "Let a few enter," and we began the wild rush to their world, abandoning our own. Unintentionally, we weakened black businesses, black colleges, black community schools, black communities, and, indirectly, black families. Tragically, we believed that anything white was better than everything black. This time, we must try a different strategy, at the center of which must be black pride and self-determination. . . .

I believe in racial solidarity and racial separation, not as the end, however, but as the means to the end. I believe racial integration is the only logical goal for all of us. Either we will live together in harmony or this nation will self-destruct, and soon. Africa is our motherland, but it is not in her bosom that millions of us live, suffer, and dream of a different future. And it is not on her soil that we will die.

I believe this is how the masses of black people feel and, consequently, I am not convinced that the wholesale hatred of white people reported by the media is a true rendering of our feelings. Black rage is not to be interpreted as hatred of whites. It simply does not compute when we look at the behavior of African-Americans. Of course there are African-Americans who hate white people! But the masses of my people have never been and are not now preoccupied with hating others. Resisting their control of our lives, yes. But hating them, no.

For me, the most moving expression of our sentiments about white people came from an elderly black woman in a small community in Florida. After sharing her vivid memories of the day whites slaughtered her parents and other members of her family, she was asked: "How do you feel about whites?" She answered: "Some of them is too nice to be white people."

My friends are too nice to be white people.

I remember my friend Naomi, a formidable opponent to anyone who did not believe in racial justice. An irritant who put long briars in your skin if she suspected you of racism. On the canvass of my memories, she is very much in focus, as loved in death as she was in life. She had different eyes.

I think of Dick Eakin, who, in his late seventies, makes time to call and to write. Who values the friendship he has with Joe and me. When I think about him, I do not think white. Rather, I think large heart, unconditional kindness, and authentic friendship. And I see different eyes.

And of course I think of my friend Fannie, who in her seventies leaves her home at six in the morning to work in a community center in Manhattan that has programs for the homeless, the elderly, and high school students who, in spite of their matriculation in poor inner-city public schools, are determined to go to college. Need, not race, is the criterion for being served at the center. Dedication and skills, not race, are the criteria for serving. Fannie understands my rage and meets it with her own.

It was late August in 1987. I was helping my daughter Monica pack for college and thinking to myself that only yesterday I was screaming, "I've changed my mind. Give me something," and Joe was rushing into the delivery room to protect me. There is truth in the cliche that "time flies." Faster than the speed of light or sound, I said to myself, and certainly faster than Monica, who seemed to be taking forever to decide what she would *not* take with her.

She moved slowly, but with excitement. I watched as she placed heirloom items into a trunk I feared we would not be able to close: her first hard-toe ballet shoes; several swim trophies; a handful of swim and track first-place ribbons; music books containing her favorite recital pieces; a small plaque her father and I gave her for reading her first novel (Bette Greene's *Philip Hall Likes Me. I Reckon*); and her favorite stuffed animals. She knew what I was thinking. "Don't even say, Mom," she said. "I know it looks like I'm going a long, long way from home." The drive to Spelman College would take no more than thirty minutes by car, if that long, but I encouraged her to pack whatever she wanted. She would be *in* the city, but *away* from home. Away in her own home. As her brother was during his freshman year in the dorm at Morehouse. Joe and I had promised both children that we wouldn't intrude on their new lives and we wouldn't demand that they come home on weekends. We were letting go.

Monica's departure for college and my leave from Spelman were not the only major changes that took place in my life in 1987. Another, and a very painful one, was my separation from Joe. This change was brought on, I am certain, more than anything by my need for redefinition or perhaps, on a subconscious level, by my response to what therapists call the "empty nest syndrome." Whatever the reason, I found the separation painful, but I reasoned, on one level, that I needed at this time in my life to try my hand, finally, at writing. I was convinced that the separation would be temporary and that it would strengthen our love rather than weaken it. Two weeks after Monica moved into her dorm room, I moved into a small one-bedroom apartment which I called my writer's space.

Words ran from me, sometimes because of the pain of the separation and other times because of my worry over Mama's health. Having suffered from high blood pressure almost all of her life, at seventy-four Mama had heart problems. I was reading in my aunt's conversation coded messages that Mama's health was deteriorating. Stopping short of begging her for fear that too much concern would cause her alarm, I tried to persuade Mama to come to stay with me. Each time she said no because she felt her presence would be a deterrent to a needed reunion with Joe. My insistence, or a feeling she had, finally convinced her to give in to my persuasion.

"I will come for a visit," she told me in October, when I called to celebrate her birthday. She was still beautiful. Still young in spirit. "Just for a visit. But not until the weather is warm."

"What about April?" I asked. "It gets warm here in Atlanta early in April."

"*Sometimes* it gets warm in April," she said. She was right. In the mid-seventies an April ice storm crippled Atlanta for ten days.

We agreed on June, the safest month of all in Mama's opinion. She did not know Faye and I had decided we would not let her return to Memphis, where she lived alone in a very modest two-bedroom frame house in a neighborhood that had changed for the worse over the years. . . . It was time, Faye and I decided, for us to take care of Mama. She would live with me when the weather was cold in Chicago, and during the summer, with Faye.

"Girl, you are something else," my aunt said. "Driving all the way here by yourself. Making it here on time."

Mama held me the way a child holds a doll she has wanted for years and finally gets. "You made it," she said. "All by yourself, you made it."

I went to the phone prepared to answer Faye's questions: Had Mama lost weight? Was she steady on her feet? How did she look? I answered her truthfully: "Mama is beautiful."

Only later that night, after Mama had gone to bed, did I call Faye to tell the larger truth. Mama was thin and unsteady on her feet. She was not well, but she didn't appear to be seriously ill. She was witty, full of fun, feisty, smart as ever. *Herself,* only older and weaker.

Three days later, Mama and I left before dawn for Atlanta. We took her tape recorder with us and a bag of tapes my aunt and I had purchased the day before: selected favorites by B. B. King, Muddy Waters, Billie Holiday, Sarah Vaughan; sermons; and the latest in commercial religious music. We were going to sing our way to Atlanta.

She entered Atlanta in a mood I did not like.

"Gloria, I don't think I'll ever make it back home," she said.

"So you know, huh?" I ignored her reference to death. "Good. That's good. Now Faye and I won't have to pretend that you will be staying with us for more than a visit."

"I don't think I'll ever go home," she said again. She began singing a popular white gospel: "One step at a time, sweet Jesus. That's all I'm asking of you."

With the start of school and the departure of Faye and Aunt Mae, Mama and I returned to our quiet days and intimate nights. I continued to write, but I became preoccupied with plans for her birthday in October. Words began to run from me.

Mama said, "Don't worry. I'll catch them."

I remember returning from the grocery one day to find Mama more excited than she had been since Faye and Aunt Mae had returned home.

"You didn't tell me you had finished the book. You didn't tell me!"

"I haven't," I said.

"You needn't try to surprise me, baby. The agent called. The agent called and said she would be in contact with you in a few weeks. Hot dog! You finished the book! You finished the book!"

The agent had called about a manuscript of poems I had sent her so many months ago that I had ceased expecting to hear from her. That wasn't "the book" I was working on, the one Mama's memories and presence were helping me write.

"Oh that?" I said nonchalantly. "That's the poetry."

"Whatever," she answered, no less excited. "It's something you wrote, isn't it? And it will be published."

"Let's hope, Mama."

A month later, I was back at work and very distraught because the woman I had hired to stay with Mama for three days a week had taken another job. As if she were a fortune teller, Mama had told me in Memphis that my plans for her care would fall through. Negative thinking, I had said. "You'll see," she had responded.

She didn't need anyone. "I'm not an invalid, you know," she told me as I fought my tears and my anger at the woman who had disappointed me. "I can cook, wash, straighten up a bit. You don't need to pamper me."

On Friday, September 17, I did not go home during my break.

I was late reaching my three o'clock class, Images of Women in Literature, in which we were beginning a new unit on "mother as person." I gave the students an idea of what the unit meant by telling them about Mama. Images of her came faster than I could share them with my students, speaking without my voice and bringing moisture to the eyes of everyone. I remember ending the class by saying, "If you could meet my mother, you would love her."

When I returned home, Mama was unusually energetic. She did not ask why I had not come home in the middle of the day. Apparently, she had not missed me. She had cooked a big pot of chicken stew and a pan of cornbread. I learned later from Aunt Mae that Mama had called her and talked for over an hour. She never called long-distance in the middle of the day and even when she called at night, she did not talk that long.

That night we cuddled together in her bed. Her laughter was hearty, and her wit had never been sharper.

"How's your writing coming?" she asked me. Before I could answer, she said, "You're going to hear from that agent."

We talked about Faye, "who must write," and Aunt Mae and the grandchildren and Chiquita—about the family. Nothing maudlin. We seemed to be returning to the joy of her first days with me.

"Just think, Mama," I said, jumping from the bed and doing a silly dance. "Just think, today is Friday and tomorrow is Saturday. No school! No school! I will be here all day. *All* day."

"That will be good," she said, sitting up on the side of the bed. "Hand me my purse."

She opened it and took out several cards wrapped with a rubber band. "These are my insurance cards." She reached in for a five-by-seven blue notebook wire-ringed at the top. "I wrote down all the names of my medicines."

I was speechless.

"Don't let them perform surgery on me for anything. Don't let them put me on life-support systems. Don't—"

"Mama, why are you doing this? Why are you doing this?"

"Hush," she said, "and listen to me. I know what I am doing. Don't let them perform surgery on me. It won't do any good. When it is my time to go, I am supposed to go. Don't let them put me on life-support systems and don't let them perform an autopsy. The cause of death will be that it's my time to go."

"Mama, I . . ."

"Do what I tell you, Gloria," she said with firmness. "Put all of this in your purse. And don't worry about me. Wherever I am, I will be connected to you and Faye. I'll be fine, and you'll have to let go, baby. All of you. Now give me a kiss and turn off the light."

I did not sleep well that night. I kept thinking about Mama's belief in psychic feelings and the "other dimension." Her heavy breathing in the next room reassured me. She was fine. As long as I could hear her, we were in *this* dimension. Together.

That's where we were when I awoke on Saturday morning. Mama was unusually beautiful. Glowing really. Her skin was firm and her eyes were tiny jewels, glittering. The world outside was a perfect skyblue, sunny and decorated with fluffy white clouds close enough to touch.

I was behind with my paper grading, especially the themes I had assigned in freshman composition. When I began grading the papers, I smiled to myself. I must have been teaching Mama in all of my classes. The papers were portraits of mothers.

I had finished the last paper in the set and was writing, "You should show this to your mother. It is a testimony of your love for her," when I heard what sounded like the gasp one makes when surprised. I hesitated for only a second before running to Mama.

Mama never returned to Memphis. We buried her in Atlanta.

For weeks after her death, I went to the cemetery every day, sometimes twice a day. I knew she was not there. I remember her saying, "Only the body dies. The spirit lives. And that is what we are. Spirit." I knew I was disobeying her. She had told me that we had to let her go, but I couldn't.

A month after Mama's death, the phone rang. The voice on the other end said, "I never make business calls from my home, but I'm making this one. I just finished your manuscript and . . ." There was a pause. "Something has been directing me to it for days. I read it before reading others I received before yours." There was another pause. "It's . . . I just can't tell you what a moving experience it was. Reading your poetry. I love it. And I wanted you to know that I have a publisher."

The words I had wanted to hear, had wanted Mama to hear, did not move me. Instead of responding jubilantly, I said, "I lost my mother a month ago and . . ."

The agent interrupted me. "Now I understand everything," she said. "I know what was happening to me." She called my name. "Gloria. Gloria. I am your mother's medium."

Unfortunately, in America, becoming educated means worshipping that which is rational and minimizing that which is spiritual. It means believing that the world of ideas is the only important world, or at least the only world to which upwardly mobile people should be connected. And who more than people of African descent want to make gains in American society, even if doing so means dismissing the importance of a dark woman from the Motherland who has a way of seeing and being we cannot explain.

. . . Many of our students, products of a media-saturated culture, might be desensitized to the spiritual world. From the media, all of us learn the pleasure of the now, the glitter of the material, the power of men with money and position, and the beauty of youth. . . .

What I remember most vividly from my youth is my respect for women, especially my elders. To me, they were powerful beings, forces that belonged, I thought, to another world, but chose to live in this one because we needed them. As blacks, we struggled for personhood and freedom in the physical world, but that was not the only world in which we lived. Women guided us to the other world, the spiritual world, where neither race nor gender was of consequence, and there they nurtured us and made us whole. We called the women wise; they were, in fact, spiritual.

My mother was one of those women. She was, and is, spiritual. . . . I remember her as a woman who made decisions rooted in logic, but also decisions for which there were no logical explanations—only a feeling she had, a dream that woke her in the night, a premonition that came to her during the day, an encounter with a stranger whose eyes held messages, or a sign from nature.

When I was a young girl, and even into my teenage years, I considered my mother an enigma, two different persons in one body. She was both intellectual and spiritual. She sent my sister and me to college, but she made us humble ourselves in the presence of forces unrecognized in academia. She believed in medical science, but told engaging stories about strange illnesses which no one could explain. . . .

I remember Mama telling us, again and again, that everyone has the gift of prophecy; we could become connected to it by claiming it, she would say. That was spiritual.

But I remember most of all her litany about women as special beings who, unlike men, do not fear the unknown. They reach for it. It embraces them; it empowers them. That was spiritual.

I shared these and other experiences with my students, and with choruses of "Amen," they told their own stories. They had known women like Mama all their lives. Their mothers, their grandmothers and great-grandmothers, women in their communities and in their churches read signs, listened to the winds, studied the heavens, related stories about strange incidents, laid on healing hands, and humbled themselves before unseen powers. Their strong sense of self as empowered black women came, the students told me, from the spiritual power of women they had known in their youth.

I had succeeded in concealing my grief from colleagues and friends so well that they marveled at how quickly I had returned to Spelman and become my "bouncy" and "spastic" self, and while the children knew my grief was profound, they thought I was handling it well. I never "broke down" in their presence.

Only with a counselor did I permit myself to cry. Once a week I would ring the front bell at the Catholic Church in which Jim's office was located and feel relief when he answered on the second ring. We would walk together to a room of muted colors and warmth that contained, of course, the proverbial couch. In the first session, he handed me a box of tissues and told me to cry. "Go ahead and cry as much as you need to. As long as you'd like." . . .

The sessions were painful, but liberating . . . as Jim guided me to the inside where I saw fears my conscious mind had not accepted. Once inside, I learned that I was obsessed with my mortality. In fact, paranoid about dying. As a result, I had a sense of terrible urgency about life. I was impatient with everything: a short line at the bank, a slow-moving salesperson, a recording on a phone answering machine, and even a traffic light. To avoid stopping, I would turn right on red, and right again, circling blocks in order to continue moving.

I was also obsessed with a need to have every issue in my life resolved and every question answered. I wanted to step out of myself and in one quick glance see my past, my present, and my future— separate and then together. I now understood what women and men in my community back home meant when they said they were "weary to the bones." I was weary. Very weary.

I learned that I was also suffering from guilt which, like anger, is often one of the stages of grief. We can do everything for our loved ones while they are living, but after their death we remember only what we did not do. I remember being too rushed to prepare a big breakfast for Mama one morning. "But there's more, isn't there, Gloria?" Jim asked. "I want you to go inside. Go deep inside and tell me what you really feel guilt about. Once you name it, you can ask your mother's forgiveness. That's what you want, isn't it? You want her to forgive you for something you have not named." He gave me the box of tissues, and I wept as I had during the first session. "Get in touch with your real feelings," he continued to say in a comforting voice. "Get in touch with your real feelings." I could not deny them any longer. I was experiencing guilt because we had buried Mama in Atlanta. She never went back home to Memphis. . . .

"Now I want you to hear your mother's voice telling you about her core beliefs. About death and dying."

I could hear myself speaking in Mama's voice and saying, as she often had, how foolish it is for the living to spend thousands of dollars on funerals and burials for the dead.

"Why did she feel that way?" he asked.

I spoke again with her voice. "Because we are spirit, not flesh." The sound of the word—"spirit"—was liberating.

"What does that tell you?" Jim asked, knowing that he had made a breakthrough.

I remembered Mama telling me that she did not expect to go home again, telling me not to worry, to let go.

I smiled as I explained that no matter where we had buried Mama, no matter where we lived and where, one day, we ourselves would be buried, Mama was connected to us in spirit.

Edith T. Mirante

(1953–   )

Edith T. Mirante was born in New Jersey, the only daughter and second child of Albert R. and Irma S. Mirante, and educated at Sarah Lawrence College, from which she graduated in 1974. Immediately after graduation Mirante left for California and Marin County to pursue her career as a painter and to enjoy the center of the youth culture of the 1970s.

For Mirante, like so many Americans of her generation, Asia was the region of mystery and romance which promised self-discovery through encounters with other, older cultures. Her travels in Southeast Asia, initially pursued as the typical American youth's *wanderjahr*, opened her eyes to the political oppression of Burma's authoritarian regime and eventually formed her vocation as an activist working for the rights of tribal peoples, the needs of third world women, and the impact of the AIDS epidemic on women forced into the Asian "entertainment" industry. Founder of Project Maje, a nonprofit organization devoted to publicizing offenses against human rights in Burma, Mirante writes and circulates regular reports on conditions in Burma and the situation of its tribal peoples.

Her memoir of her discovery of Burma and its Karen, Mon, and Shan peoples is a fast-paced adventure story, ironic in its commentary on relationships between Europeans, sensitive and sympathetic in its depiction of tribal people. Her writing shimmers with imagery and intertextuality, evoking contemporary equivalents to earlier European adventure stories. She is a smuggler of information from the Golden Triangle, a modern pirate in her voyages with Mon rebels on the Andaman Sea, an utterly fearless female soldier of fortune. Her adventures are told with wry, self-deprecating humor, which makes her laugh at the glitzy outfit presented to her by the opium drug lord Khun Sa but doesn't diminish her empathy and identification with the victims of Burma's autocracy or of its drug trade. A black belt student of karate, Mirante needs no protector, and she settles in with the troops of Shan and Mon women soldiers she visits as though they were her college roommates. Her drive for adventure and love of the region which captures her imagination are reminiscent of Margery Perham, though her style and sensibility are authentically postmodern.

Mirante continues to work at publicizing human rights issues for third world women and, very occasionally, to paint the scenes of Asian life that first led her to Burma.

BURMESE LOOKING GLASS:
A Human Rights Adventure
and a Jungle Revolution

My childhood, in the time of peace just after American troops left Korea, was full of history's wars. My brother and I played all kinds of war games, even ancient Scottish Clan Wars (in kilts, with wooden swords). In the overgrown backyard of our New Jersey house, we stalked through the underbrush with our toy Remingtons and Colts, ready for anything.

. . . Coming from an eccentric family must be one of life's great strokes of luck. My parents indulged their son and daughter in all the exotica of *Just So Stories, National Geographic, Ripley's Believe It or Not,* "Frank Buck's Bring 'Em Back Alive," and ceaseless trips to New York's Museum of Natural History. . . . My father, a Princeton honors graduate, worked hard selling Frigidaires and Speed Queen dryers in his appliance store. He wore Brooks Brothers suits, smoked cheap Italian cigars, and read verse in Latin and Old English. My mother, an Irish-American beauty, read and read until her books were stacked into a book maze, a book city in the attic that we called "the Library." Dinners were always interrupted by someone's running upstairs for a book to settle a dollar bet, prove a point, reveal some tantalizing fact.

. . . I despised school—it interrupted my reading with the horrors of algebra and geometry. I cultivated a "bad attitude," and by my teens I was considered a full-fledged troublemaker.

. . . I managed to get accepted at Sarah Lawrence College, an enclave of independent intellectuality just north of New York City, and I began painting seriously there. I developed my painting style on my own because I was the only student who painted people and landscapes (abstraction still reigned in those days). . . .

. . . I graduated in 1974 and went straight to California, where

I lived among towering madrona pines in the canyons of Marin County, north of San Francisco. Marin had the winter I had always wanted, green and moist as a terrarium, and in those days it was a tough little rock and roll world, burrito stands and biker bars, before every last hill got fitted out with a condo.

. . . When the 1980s began, I began my travels to Asia's timeless lands. . . . I started in Kyoto, then visited Bangkok and Kathmandu. Along with the art, I found the people, and among the people I found friends: punk-rockers, aristocrats, teachers, artists. I returned to California after two months in Asia. . . .

. . . In 1981 I returned to the Himalayas, and then, en route to Thailand, I stopped in Rangoon, the capital of Burma. Rangoon had been nothing more than a steamy implication to me, some vague Joseph Conrad evocation of intrigue and palm trees. As Conrad had, I checked into the Strand Hotel, which had survived Burma's days as a British colony in gently moldy elegance. Tourists were only allowed a week in Burma (a country the size of France), and I spent mine looking at pagodas and talking with people. I hung out in the city tea shops with semi-hoodlums who wheeled and dealed on the black market. I committed my first violation of Burmese law by going to the Diplomatic Store to purchase several cartons of export-only Duya cigarettes, which the hoods bought from me to resell on the street.

Burma's rigidly state-controlled economy had become so strangled since the military dictator, General Ne Win, had taken control in 1962 that few cars had been imported after the tail-finned early sixties. "If you want to buy one of those cars, miss," a hood at The People's Patisserie told me, "the black market can take it apart and people will carry it over the mountains to Thailand, and it will be put back together for you in Bangkok, the old car good as new."

I asked about the smuggling route. "Oh, the border of Thailand is the fighting place, miss. Burma has many kinds of people. In this city we have Burmese people, and India and China people. Outside they are many kinds, who live in forests and mountains, and they are all the time fighting. This government sends the army to fight those ones all the time. To get anything nice you must go through the fighting place, because anything nice comes from the other countries. We don't have any 'Made in Burma' things like watches, calculators, radios, or even our shoes to wear.

". . . Can we do anything? No jobs for us, no real money, only black market. If I speak about it, secret police can take me away.

We speak, we die. The Old Man makes us live like dogs. My country is nothing now. The fighting ones in the mountains, maybe they are right. But we cannot do anything. Must stay here and work for the black market." . . . In my week I had managed to discover that Burma was not simply a romantic third world backwater but one that seethed with the suppressed resentments of its citizens against a virtually omnipotent military regime. From state-run factories incapable of turning out shoes or medicine to a vast network of secret police all too capable of torturing dissenters to death, Ne Win's army had Burma stuffed in its khaki pockets. . . . Rangoon and the up-country places, Mandalay and Pagan, exuded a gripping charm. The people tiptoed between army and police, rice-growing drudgery and starvation, but they did so with such grace, such wild creativity. They were hungry people with attics full of books, artists in ripped sarongs, beggars with degrees. . . . Power failures blacked out heartsick Rangoon and the rats fled the light of a candle given me by some criminal, jobless student. I found my way to the wide staircase of the Strand Hotel. How could I ever be the same again? One week was more than enough to pull me headfirst into all of Burma's pain, Burma's extreme beauty.

After my seven days in the Socialist Republic of the Union of Burma's worker's paradise, I flew on to Thailand.

. . . On the train . . . to Bangkok, I realized my direction was crystal clear. Chiang Mai was the place to paint. . . . I would return to live in Thailand, to the orchid-adorned art colony right next to Burma.

I spent one more year in California. I took Thai lessons, rode in the park, worked out, and learned to shoot guns and sail. I read whatever I could find on Southeast Asian culture and politics. Then, in September 1982, I left for Thailand. . . .

. . . I had enough money saved up from market research and painting sales to retire to Chiang Mai and paint full-time for a while. At twenty-nine, I was free to do as I pleased.

. . . I lived in Chiang Mai, a provincial capital that called itself "The Rose of the North" even though it was mostly a hodgepodge of dreary "shophouses." It was a flat town, surrounded by mountains that gave it a cooler climate than sweat-soaked Bangkok. Hidden amid Chiang Mai's concrete blocks were Buddhist temples of teak lacquered in the northern style, urban islands of serenity. Flame trees flared vermilion over the crumbling ancient wall and stagnant moat that surrounded the older district.

. . . Chiang Mai was home to narcotics agents (both pro and con), militant missionaries, sinister Rhodesian tobacco planters, secretive Japanese investors, alcoholic European artists, and ex–Air America pilots grounded there since the days when they supplied the CIA's covert war in Laos. Added to the mix were operatives of every insurgent group out of neighboring Burma and Laos, some of the world's top-echelon Chinese racketeers, and assorted Thai spouses and counterparts. Plus the ubiquitous agents of Thai Army Intelligence, an agency that all of the above considered an oxymoron.

. . . Jere, a pale shambling Dutchman who had been batik artist to the Laotian court, [said,] ". . . you should know about a place where I go." . . . "We're going there soon, for a festival, the Shan National Day. Can you come along, too?"

. . . Jere produced a map of Thailand, and . . . drew a line snaking from Chiang Mai north, then sharply west. When it reached the border of Burma, Jere's shaky hand printed *Pieng Luang*. "Because it is winter and the roads are dry, we can go by truck."

. . . I had found out enough about Burma to understand that its geography had been its destiny. Over the centuries, several different ethnic groups had migrated into Burma, funneled along three great river valleys. The *Burmese* ethnic group established itself in the central plains. They built cities and monuments of stone and brick, as did the civilizations that arose to rival them: the Mons in the south, the Arakanese in the west, and the Shans in a vast, fertile plateau in the northeast. These four groups warred with each other for hundreds of years, while in the mountainous border regions fiercely independent tribes maintained their own separate cultures.

. . . In 1982, when I went to Pieng Luang, three different Shan armies proclaimed their opposition to Ne Win's regime and their support for Shan independence.

. . . I didn't know the difference between the three, but I knew that Pieng Luang was where the leaders of Sura, who included an aristocrat named Prince George, lived in a fortress compound, a law unto themselves.

. . . In a convoy of pickup trucks and Jeeps, we drove through a cold morning fog to Pieng Luang. The group included Thais, Europeans, and American residents of Chiang Mai. It was evening when our vehicles finally slipped into Pieng Luang, following an unpaved road past tightly shuttered teakwood houses and up a hill to the Sura compound.

. . . Sura had some women soldiers, and Prince George had married one of them. She was said to be politically ambitious, and my friends from Chiang Mai called her "Evita" behind her back (a back they said was covered with magic Shan tattoos of lions).

. . . Prince George lived simply, but what little he had was arranged to provide as much comfort as possible to his guests. We unrolled our bedding and went out to the welcoming bonfire.

We unwound from the long drive with a cocktail hour or two, and then dinner: rice, potatoes, pork, vegetables.

During dinner, Prince George apologized to us.

"I'm afraid that the festival is indefinitely postponed," he said. "It seems that our prognosticating Buddhist monks at the Mai Sung temple have judged the date we'd set for Shan National Day to be inauspicious. We hope you'll indulge us and wait for a few days."

Most of the Chiang Mai contingent decided not to wait. You couldn't tell with the Shans, they grumbled, it could be delayed for days, or for weeks. . . . The Golden Triangle, where Thailand, Laos, and Burma's Shan State converged, was prime growing territory for opium poppies, the raw material of heroin. The Shan State had the largest opium crop in the world. We had passed fields of red and white opium poppies on the way into Pieng Luang, but Sura denied all involvement in narcotics.

Despite Sura's denials, mountain dwellers all over the area were producing opium. In the winter, the poppies blossomed and then dropped their petals, exposing heavy pods. Hill farm women and children patiently cut slits in each pod so the narcotic sap would drip out overnight. In the morning, the opium gum was scraped off, pod by pod. The accumulated opium would be sold to traders, who would pass it on to hidden forest refineries where skilled Chinese chemists processed it into successive stages of purity.

. . . Although most of the guests returned to Chiang Mai when they learned the festival was postponed, I stayed on another day, along with Jere and a couple of the Americans.

. . . That night Prince George, Jere, and I drove across the border into Burma. As far as I could see was Sura territory, but I couldn't see very far in the dark, even from Mai Sung's own hilltop temple. I did not want to look any farther than the Sura headquarters pagoda, its *chedi*, anyway. The night was as cold as Hell frozen over, but it held a celestial sight: the *chedi,* with a round base and a whole cluster of spires glittering with electric fairy lights. It made me certain that there was something truly magical about the Shans. I had seen some humongous gold-plated pagodas in my time in Southeast Asia, but this ice-white one, ethereal on its drum base, enchanted me. It looked more the product of sorcery than masonry.

In the army camp just below the temple we joined a crowd of soldiers watching a movie projected on an outdoor screen.

. . . "This cinema show is called *Khun Sa, Opium Warlord,*" Prince George told me with a drunken laugh. "You know about Khun Sa. Very famous. The King of Opium they call him. The Heroin Godfather. He is public enemy number one."

Khun Sa was indeed infamous throughout Asia for his conspicuous drug trafficking and control of heroin trade routes. He was the warlord of the Shan United Army (SUA), a great rival of my Sura hosts.

. . . My Chiang Mai friends and I left the following morning. Prince George and his fellow officers saw us off at the gate of the Sura compound.

"Miss Edith, we are happy that you were able to visit our place and be introduced to the Shan nation," the Prince said. "We want you to know that you are most welcome here at any time. You needn't wait for a festival or an invitation. Like Jere, you are welcome to bring your art materials and use our land and people for your inspiration. There is much for you to paint here."

. . . I did not know how to get to Pieng Luang by myself, so instead I went to Mai Hong Son, a town farther south on the Burma border. It was simple enough to get there, a twenty-minute flight in a small plane.

. . . I took a room at the Mai Tee, a Shan-owned hotel of 1960s design: blue concrete exterior, linoleumed lobby with a wide staircase to the two floors above. My bed had pink wool blankets. With its mountain ring, Mai Hong Son got frosty at night all year round, but Thailand was, of course, a tropical country, so heating was unheard of. Heavy blankets compensated.

A Chiang Mai friend who did agricultural development work with hill-tribe people had told me about a Shan woman named Nang Lao who sometimes guided foreigners around the border area outside of Mai Hong Son.

. . . She wasn't in the mood to play trekking guide, but she decided I could come along while she went to visit some border villages where she knew people. She didn't want my money but said I could buy a few things in the Mae Hong Son bazaar to take to the villagers. I purchased nylon fishing nets and malaria medicine. I hadn't even thought about malaria when I'd gone to Pieng Luang; it had been so cold there that no mosquitoes were around at all. But the border from Mae Hong Son south was infested with the anopheles mosquitoes that spread the disease.

. . . For a few days I walked with Nang Lao and began to learn my way around the forest and the border. We stayed with the Shans in the valleys and in tribal villages in the hills. Nang Lao brought along a pistol because bandits infested the border area, *dacoits* who robbed and killed and slipped in and out of Burma. The gun was a nickel-plated automatic with no brand name, only a Thai serial number. We took turns carrying it. All along the way we met people with guns (hunters, smugglers, rebel Shan soldiers) as we followed trails from village to village. I liked being armed. The heavy gun was protection, but it was also a kind of totem of belonging in the frontier scene.

. . . As one of Thailand's resident aliens, I had to leave the country every three months to get a new nonimmigrant visa. Penang, a resort island in neighboring Malaysia, was the closest place with a Thai consulate. After I'd lived in Chiang Mai for three months, I made a visa run to Penang, but the next time I decided to go to Burma. A Burmese dissident, whom I'd met through an antique-dealer friend in Bangkok, heard that I was going and asked me to bring a package to his wife in Rangoon.

. . . I agreed to take the package. Able to come and go as a tourist, I carried what I learned were documents into Burma, past Mingaladon Airport's haphazard Customs inspectors, and delivered them to N., the wife of the dissident.

In Rangoon, I found a superb bookshop near the National Museum. It was full of books abandoned by foreigners who had been thrown out of the country when Ne Win took over in 1962.

. . . Rangoon's surviving intellectuals still thirsted for the whole world. The bookshop was bursting with literature from Kipling to Nabokov to Borges, and a long shelf held worm-eaten art books. Browsers in the back room leafed through historical tomes written in Portuguese, Russian, Italian, Urdu. I asked the proprietor, who wore a coffee-stained undershirt and checked sarong, if he had any books about the Shans.

"You want books about the Shans?" he whispered conspiratorily, as if I had told him I wanted rubies or opium or stolen jade Buddha statues. "Wait one minute, please."

He vanished up a back staircase and I heard him rummaging through what I imagined was a city of stacked-up books like my mother's attic library. He returned with *The Shans* by W. W. Cochrane, published in Rangoon in 1915.

. . . I left Burma carrying some documents for the dissident, plus books and newspapers someone I'd met in the Strand Hotel lobby had asked me to bring to a magazine correspondent in Thailand. I had become a smuggler of information. It was one of Burma's most precious commodities. Foreign mail was opened and censored, as if the country was one big prison. The newspapers were Tatmadaw[1] propaganda organs. Radio, and the one television station, existed to sing the praises of army, party, state. The Burmese, Chinese, and Indian people of central Burma were ensnared. Unless they ran—and ran far—they had no reprieve from secret-police control, block wardens, arbitrary search and seizure, detention without charges, and disappearance. The frontier groups like the Shans, Karens, and Mons at least had access to the borders and their own armed camps, and the hope that they could overcome the Tatmadaw by force. The people in the towns and cities, the Burmese ethnic majority as well as the Chinese and Indian minorities, seemed to have lost all hope.

. . . Aside from forays to Burma and Penang, I spent eight months in Chiang Mai painting.

. . . Arriving in the States broke, I took a temporary customer relations job at Tiffany in New York to earn my airfare back to Asia.

. . . Before the winter was out, I made my way to China, where I put my language lessons to work. I took trains and talked my way from one end of the country to the other.

. . . One of eight passengers, I took the once-a-week flight from Kunming, Yunnan's capital, to Rangoon.

---

1. Burmese Army.

. . . I went directly up-country, by plane and "cooperative Jeep taxi" (a genuine World War II American Jeep crammed with passengers), to Maymyo, a mountain town above Mandalay, on the edge of the Shan State. In the days of the British Raj, Maymyo had been a hill station where weary colonists escaped the tropical heat.

. . . I stayed at Candacraig, a hotel that in the old days had been a home for British teak-company employees recuperating from job-related stress and fevers. Everything east of Maymyo was forbidden territory, but I saw Tatmadaw casualties from the frontier war being brought to military hospitals in town. In its present incarnation Maymyo was a Tatmadaw training center with an officer's school. I wondered was it here that they were trained in ways of torture and other forms of human rights abuse?

. . . Back in Rangoon I visited N., the wife of the dissident whose packages I'd carried. A thin, genteel, young woman, she lived in one of the better-off neighborhoods. Her family had enough military connections to pursue various business interests, and to see that N. didn't escape over the border. She served me *khao soi,* chicken curry over yellow noodles, a dish I'd enjoyed in Pieng Luang and Mae Hong Son.

". . . I think you are having your last trip to Rangoon now. If you go around the border on the Thai side, plenty of spies will know your face. You're eating *khao soi* with Shan rebels in Pieng Luang, they know who you are. You can't do that and still get tourist visas for Burma."

. . . I had known there would be a point when the Burmese authorities would get suspicious of me, but I thought I'd have a few more trips before being banned outright. It was depressing, to love Burma and not be able to visit, like some exile.

. . . After I returned to Thailand, I was again brought to the Burma border by an artist, this time to the southern territory of the Karen rebels. The Karens were a huge tribe who had migrated south from the steppes of northern Asia, long before the Burmese and Tai civilizations had appeared on the scene.

. . . The Burmese military considered the Karens a threat to national unity. When some Burmese soldiers massacred Karen churchgoers at a Christmas service in 1948, the Karen rebellion ignited. And it never stopped. The Karens believed the Burmese government

wanted to exterminate them and were convinced that the only way
to survive was to fight back. With their British Army background,
the Karens fought well, but the more they fought, the more vicious
became the counterinsurgency tactics of the Tatmadaw.

. . . The Karens lived far from the opium region and had nothing to hide. To them a visit from a journalist was not "inauspicious." [Brando P.] Bryant [an American artist] began recording
what he called "the Karen people's struggle for self-determination."
Now, six years into his Karen video, Bryant was heading to a Karen
rebel settlement just over the Burma border from the Thai city of
Kanchanaburi, and I accompanied him.

. . . Suddenly with a screech of brakes, we stopped short of a
red-and-white bamboo pole that extended across the trail.

WELCOME TO KAREN NATION KAWTHOOLEI, a wooden sign read.

"They call their rebel nation 'Kawthoolei,'" Bryant told me. "It
means 'Flower Land.'" We were in a place full of jungle blossoms,
quivering with butterflies and shaded by massive vine-draped trees. . . .
In the Shan State, higher elevation and large-scale deforestation had
produced a sparser landscape. Kawthoolei, though, was wet, and it
shone in infinite shades of green. It buzzed with insects and sang
with birds.

Karen rebel soldiers (teenagers and a few who were no more
than children) appeared, lifting the bamboo barrier and waving us
through.

. . . We stayed in the village two more days, and I interviewed
some people for Bryant's videotape. Daniel spoke about Karen history. When I asked him why the Karens were fighting he quoted an
early Karen rebel leader: "Because surrender is out of the question." It seemed to sum up their struggle. The Karens did not appear to be fighting out of a wounded sense of superiority like the
Shans (a conquered civilization) but from gut fear for their survival
as a tribe.

. . . I asked the district's university-educated agricultural director about the crops the rebel village grew. "We want to irrigate the
fields and have rice crops like in the old villages of the delta region,"
he said, "so we can have a bigger rice supply each year. But too
many refugees keep coming to us from the frontline villages taken
by the Tatmadaw. They come here because it is safer and close to
Thailand. They think they can run into Thailand if the Tatmadaw
comes here. Now we have no rice crops to trade, and we have

hardly enough for our daily bread." He smiled sadly. "We have gone back to the Stone Age."

Naomi, Daniel's wife, showed me photographs of some of the "interior refugees" who had fled the fighting and Tatmadaw abuse but hadn't made it to another country. They were still in Burma—Kawthoolei's rebel zone—hiding in the jungle. The Karen educators tried to keep track of them, searching them out, keeping photographic records, boarding their children at the schools near the border. Each photo showed a family in front of its makeshift palm-leaf and bamboo hut. Few of the families were complete—they were missing fathers, mothers, or children, dead from war and its companions, disease and hunger. The children stood up straight and smiled for the camera no matter how malnourished they were, but the parents looked into the lens with anguish.

When we returned to Bangkok, Bryant and I made an effort to get some help for the Karen refugees. But we soon found out that the Karens weren't even considered real refugees, just "displaced persons."

. . . The Burmese government defined its opponents as *dacoits,* bandits. Insignificant bandit activity didn't produce refugees; only big wars did. Or so went official government logic. And this was the logic that denied aid to those families in the palm-leaf huts and thousands camped precariously around Mae Sot.

. . . When I had returned to Thailand from Tiffany and China, I had not gone back to live in Chiang Mai. . . . I rejected Chiang Mai in favor of Bangkok, a city that was so polluted, chaotic, and obnoxious that it defied tourism. . . . I lived with friends at the city's edge. The "jungle suburb," as we called it, was the place where Bangkok terminated abruptly in banana and palm groves and ripe green undevelopment. A road stretched west to Kanchanaburi and the Burma border. Beside that road stood what might have been the last row of "town houses" east of India. I lived there amid the artifacts (Khmer bronzes, Balinese masks, old Burmese tapestries) of the antique dealer who owned the place.

. . . One February night, I went to the Foreign Correspondents' Club for a panel discussion on Afghanistan. I was curious about one of the panelists, a photojournalist, because he had written an article about the Shans for an Asian magazine. His name was Crispin Dunbar, but he was known simply as "Spin." A handsome, gawky New Zealander, he told of his travels with the Afghan *muji-hadeen* to the forbidden city of Kandahar. As he spoke of giving first aid to a wounded Afghan child, my heart began to pound violently. True love hit me like sniper fire.

. . . Over the next month, Spin and I met frequently at his miserable hotel in Bangkok's hippie-tourist neighborhood. And we would run into each other in that city of five million, by chance, like the lovers in Cortazar's *Hopscotch*. Spin began to photograph me. He called me "The Dragon Lady" (out of the *Terry and the Pirates* comic strip), and he called me "Blade," which was short for "Bladerunner," after a William Burroughs story about smugglers of surgical tools. He adored Beat literature and all kinds of aliases or noms de guerre. His favorite sport was illegally crossing international borders, an activity I was no longer unfamiliar with. We talked about the Burma border all the time, night and day, in his sweat-box room and at grubby canal-side food stalls. But Spin stayed in Bangkok, writing stories to go with his Afghanistan photographs, while I penetrated the Burma frontier again.

. . . A show of my paintings was scheduled in Bangkok that spring, and I wanted to paint some Shan pictures for it. Along with Karen scenes I'd painted, they might interest people in the cultures and causes of Burma's rebel zone. Also, I was worried about the Sura people, since I had read some vague newspaper accounts of a massacre in Pieng Luang by the Rangers, a Thai paramilitary force. If I could get there and find out what had happened, I could get the information to journalists and human rights groups. So I took the train to Chiang Mai, which was on my way back to the Burma border.

Up in Chiang Mai, rumors were rife. Ugly, too.

. . . I went to the TRC safe house, a nondescript building in Chiang Mai's worst slum. All the rebel groups had safe houses (in Chiang Mai or Mae Hong Son or Mae Sot) to provide severely wounded or ill soldiers with a place to recuperate after treatment in Thai hospitals, and officers with a place to stay when they came across the border to buy weapons.

. . . A Shan boy in a camouflage T-shirt and torn jeans met me at the front door.

"Greetings," I said in Thai, "I'm a friend of Prince George's.

. . . "I am planning to return to Pieng Luang, just me this time. Is anyone from this house going back there?"

"No, miss, we are all sick and injured. But the *songtaow* [pickup truck converted to bus service with seats in the back] goes to Pieng Luang at eight o'clock tomorrow morning, leaving from the bridge."

"Is it a problem to get there? I understand there's been trouble with the Rangers."

"No, it is no problem at all," the Shan boy said with a smile.

. . . In the morning, at the *songtaow* stop by the bridge, I spoke with a pair of young Buddhist monks who were on their way to meditate at the monastery at Mai Sung, where the TRC headquarters was located. Things were off to a good start, since having monks along was considered auspicious for travel. Sitting in the front seat, they would probably discourage *dacoits* from raiding the *songtaow* (it was bad luck to attack a monk). I sat in the back with a few old Chinese people and their bundles and cardboard cartons.

The *songtaow* stopped several times to pick up Lisu tribespeople, the rice and poppy growers of the mountains. The Lisu women dressed in layers of vibrant blue and magenta cotton. Ribbons festooned their glossy hair and their mouths brimmed with red betelnut juice. A teenage tribesman dressed in blue jeans climbed onto the roof and I noticed a pistol tucked in his waistband.

. . . We arrived at Pieng Luang's new Ranger post. The other checkpoints had been neat little booths with light-weight metal roadblocks, manned by soft-spoken border men in clean, pressed olive drab. The Ranger post was something else entirely. It was a slapped-together shack that reminded me of tree forts I'd built as a child. Crude skulls and crossbones were painted all over it, and a big, cracked wooden heart was nailed up over the door. I decided to call it "Fort Broken Heart."

Some teenage Rangers with utterly menacing expressions surrounded the *songtaow* brandishing M-16 rifles. They looked like a South Bronx street gang. Their basic black fatigues were accessorized with all kinds of nonregulation gear: pirate headscarves, earrings, wristbands, brightly colored basketball socks. The Rangers had spiky punk haircuts, skull tattoos, and Rambo survival knives. They combed through the passengers' belongings—all except mine. And they didn't ask me any questions. . . .

. . . Pieng Luang was a string of small teak buildings surrounded by rice paddies in a narrow valley. It was a very quiet village. "Pieng Luang's like Little Italy in New York," my friend

Ringer had said. "Nobody steals your car because you might be the Mafia don's nephew. In Pieng Luang nobody's going to pick pockets because they just might belong to a KMT general's friend." Old-fashioned Chinese music played on the Taiwan tape decks of Pieng Luang, Burmese Duya cigarettes were sold in the shops, and posters of James Dean—the great rebel without a cause—adorned the fronts of some of the old steep-roofed houses. In its mysterious little way, Pieng Luang seemed a crossroads for the trade and cultures of the Himalayas, China, and Southeast Asia. It drew me in as Asia had enticed me, with an atmosphere as familiar as a remembered dream, but as unpredictable as a hallucination.

The *songtaow* dropped off most of the passengers at the market in the center of the village before continuing uphill. I jumped out at the top of the hill and walked into the TRC compound, where the Shan guard seemed to recognize me. I went to Prince George's house, cutting through his garden of orchids, pineapples, and tomatoes.

... "Pieng Luang was known as Las Vegas!" [said the TRC foreign minister, K. Sam]. "The Chinese hid their gambling casinos behind those closed-up shophouse doors at night, and the Thai soldiers finally came to clean them up."

"It happened very fast," Prince George continued. "Two hundred, maybe three hundred Rangers came in by helicopter with a list of Pieng Luang's undesirable elements."

"A hit list?" I asked.

"Yes. And they went around with that list and gathered up fifty Chinese men and brought them to the forest. Casino men, small drug-trade men, small gun-trade men." Prince George raised his arms and imitated the raking motion of an M-16 firing on full auto. "They use plenty of ammunition, those Rangers. Everyone on the list is finished."

"Frontier justice," I said.

"Like a cowboy movie," Prince George said.

... The next day I woke up before anyone else and walked to the Pieng Luang market, which took place every day between the crack of dawn and seven A.M. I could not understand why markets like Pieng Luang's and Mae Hong Son's began so early. The Shan and tribal vendors were forced to travel in the chilly dark, to sell their wares to Chinese customers who had been up half the night running *fan-tan* games of chance.

The market straddled a short lane on a dusty main street. Under a palm-thatched roof, along two rows of wooden platforms, sellers sat with their goods. Across from the entrance, a Chinese coffee shop had just opened its heavy teak doors for business. So my reward for rising early was a cup of coffee and the chance to watch the market world come and go.

. . . I asked the coffee-shop man about the Ranger invasion.

"Oh, they just took the bad men away and shot them," he said, smiling. "No problem. We can still make good business here. Just have to pay a little to the Thai soldiers for a while. They will go away."

I had the feeling that this attitude probably extended from the humblest shopkeepers all the way up to the highest echelons of the KMT drug syndicates. The unlucky fifty, whose families were mourning over bloody shoes, were just lower-rank gangsters, unessential to the business at hand.

Under the market roof people bargained over cabbages and mushrooms, selected oranges, and weighed pieces of pork on old hand-held scales. They remembered to buy beans or forgot to buy a bottle of fish sauce. A dark-haired teenage girl sat in the doorway of a shop tapping her foot to a Chinese pop tune and stroking a black cat. I realized that there was something radically different from the first time I'd been in Pieng Luang: nobody was shopping with an M-16 slung over a shoulder. In the old Pieng Luang every other person packed ostentatious heat. I supposed they were afraid of having their weapons confiscated by the Rangers. None of the boys in black was showing his face in the market, anyway. Maybe they were still asleep at Fort Broken Heart.

When I returned from the market, I went to visit the neighbor who was baby-sitting Prince George's son. She was a TRC medical officer whose husband was also in Mo Heing's rebel army.

. . . I asked about the TRC's women soldiers. "They are mostly for special security," she told me. "But sometimes they go to the front line. They are brave soldiers, but they make a lot of problems with the boys. The boy soldiers fall in love, want to marry the girl soldiers. Then they both want to run away with each other, thinking of themselves only, not the revolution. But a thing we Shans know: if a woman soldier shoots a man who has a magic tattoo against bullets, the tattoo won't work, the man will die anyway. So a woman soldier is very powerful that way. Nowadays I am teaching the TRC women first aid. If they go to the front line, no hospital there, so if you don't have first aid, maybe you are dead."

"Where is the front line?" I asked. "It seems like the TRC has enemies on all sides."

". . . Now that the SUA's General Khun Sa has agreed to join our TRC, we can all cooperate together in the revolution. Have you had enough tea? I'm going to visit a friend in Mai Sung. Please come along. My son will drive us in our new Toyota truck."

I climbed into the front seat, realizing that a number of new trucks had supplanted the Shan compound's former fleet of aged Jeeps. Sura's sworn enemy, Khun Sa, had consented to join their TRC—the old fox consenting to guard the henhouse, I thought.

. . . I slept a last night in my corner bed before returning to Chiang Mai. In that bed I always felt like I was in the upper left-hand corner of something bewitching. I felt the edge of Thailand, the beginning of Burma, the Himalayan foothills, one angle of the Golden Triangle. Surrounded by intrigue and danger, I slept in a safe place. I had escaped the bad situation the British writer in Chiang Mai had warned me about. My *songtaow* had passed the lair of *dacoits* unscathed. The Rangers were no longer in a murderous mood, so their painted death's heads held no menace. Well-garrisoned Mai Sung seemed far out of reach of the Tatmadaw. The KMT held back, and Khun Sa had been won over. The streets of the mountain capital were as enchanting as ever, and I was sure I would come back again, no matter what roadblocks appeared.

And yet this Arcadia's enchantment, its ceremonies and processions, obscured the true nature of the bad situation: the unspeakable corruption of the Shans. They had always been romantics. Their literature, their architecture, showed the lofty dreams of an aristocratic past, a golden age of Tai civilization. And who was more corruptible than the romantic? I had begun to comprehend that such fine ideals required some filthy deals to keep them alive. I suspected I was capable of it myself, willing to get really dirty for a fine cause. The TRC showed me just how low you could go. They were buying their precious cultural freedom with heroin, the enslavement of countless others. They were so far from conventional morality, so far above the law, so removed from sordid deaths in squalid cities and even from the starving tribal opium farmers in the mountains just beyond us. How could anyone care about such things when there was the shining dream of the Shan nation to fight for? El Cid and all that. The Land of the Tai.

Safe and warm under thick counterpanes, I slept in my corner bed. I was remote from the rest of the world, in the Shans' own land. Their dreams were my dreams, and I dreamt that their war was my war. Deep in the black night, I awoke for a moment to the sound of bells. The sweet jingling of brass was all that betrayed the passage of a pony caravan, moving through Pieng Luang under cover of darkness.

. . . The Thai press was running obscure, garbled reports about fighting between the TRC and Karen forces in a valley called Mae Aw, near Mae Hong Son. This development concerned me, and since I knew both groups I thought I might be able to function as some sort of liaison between them. I wanted to help the Burma rebels communicate with each other, as well as with the outside world.

. . . The main problem with my plan was the season: monsoon rains would deluge my entire route, pounding roads into mud sloughs, making travel hazardous and slow. . . . Spin . . . was now in a Bangkok hospital, raving with cerebral malaria that had infected him at a Karenni rebel camp on the Pai River near Mae Hong Son. I brought him flowers and candied pineapple and told him how nice it was "to see a crazy person get delirious." Much as I loved him, I didn't really mind that he wouldn't be along on my border trip. An unspoken kind of rivalry had developed between us. He was used to competing with other journalists for territory, and I didn't want him elbowing me aside to get his photographs. Deep down, I wanted to go places he hadn't been and see things he hadn't photographed.

. . . I always carried my folding Kershaw lock knife with me; I also had an army surplus poncho, a pair of Wellington-type rubber boots, and malaria pills galore (the chloroquine and Fansidar that had kept the disease at bay without side effects so far). Now all I needed was a map.

. . . I settled for one that at least showed the rivers—the Tenasserim, the Salween, the Moei, the Pai—that crossed the border. Thailand was colored pink, green, and orange, while the surrounding terra incognita, including Burma, was bright purple. It would have to do.

. . . My trip did not get off to a good start. Thinking like a Shan, I would have called it inauspicious. I had written to Daniel, the education official I had met in Kawthoolei, telling him I would be returning, and he had written back, saying he'd meet me when my bus arrived in Kanchanaburi. But when I arrived, a young Karen man handed me a letter from Daniel that informed me he had gone to Bangkok for a few days.

. . . The young man who'd met me and his two brothers had a Jeep. Despite Daniel's recommendation, they charged me for the trip, and at an exorbitant rate. . . .

. . . We drove to a large teak house with a broad porch. Adjacent was a tin-roofed shed where sparks flew from the saw that cut jungle hardwood into planks for Thai purchase. The driver's young wife welcomed me from the porch, saying, "Please come up." I took off my muddy boots, and we sat drinking tea and looking at framed photographs of the boys' father, a Karen politician, meeting with various rebel leaders.

. . . He was a revolutionary diplomat traveling the war zone. Meanwhile, his sons were sawing the jungle into veneer with desperate zeal, trying to make enough money to get out and stay out of the war zone. The revolution had been going on since 1949; I could understand how some third-generation Karens might not be as gung ho about it as the first two.

. . . In the past, war came to a virtual standstill in the rainy season, but in recent years the Tatmadaw kept up attacks all year round. Decades ago, Ne Win had sworn to "exterminate" the Karens (perhaps meaning just the rebels), and their continued existence seemed a personal affront to him. . . .

A gentle teacher in a commando beret said, "We will hold off the Tatmadaw militarily, we always have. The real difficulty is the economic situation. The price of tin is down so low. Karen government did not expect this, so we have no reserve currency, not even reserve rice. Very hard to get ammunition because our black market currency is exhausted. We try to sell our corn in Thailand, and our cashew nuts and honey from jungle bees. But now everything here goes to feed the refugees who keep arriving more and more. The Tatmadaw make press-gang sweeps through villages before launching their offensives. People fear for their lives and run to our revolutionary place. When we had money from tin, we could take care of all. Now our Karen government can only give rice and salt to the refugees." The Karen revolution was running on empty.

Daniel arrived in the evening . . . with . . . great enthusiasm for my river trip.

. . . I unfolded my Thai map. Daniel laughed and said, "That is no bloody map of your mission! It shows the river but nothing else—a big purple nothing! Wait a minute." He ducked into the bedroom and emerged with a silk map that had belonged to some World War II aviator. As I spread it open, I was suddenly transported into a page from *Terry and the Pirates*. The map was foxed with a few brown blotches, but was clearly legible. Daniel pointed out roads built by prisoners of the Japanese imperial forces (now paths that ran beside the river) and showed me villages and places where river rapids disrupted travel.

. . . I showed Daniel my planned route north from Kawthoolei. He gave me the names of Karens to visit near Three Pagodas Pass and in Mae Sot. He told me I would probably have to backtrack through Thailand, perhaps all the way to Bangkok, to get from Three Pagodas Pass to Mae Sot, because no border roads between the two were usable in the rainy season.

"You can borrow this map for the rest of your mission," Daniel told me. Thrilled with it, I folded the soft silk map and put it in my shirt pocket.

. . . After three days, the rain let up enough for the boat trip. We embarked at noon in a narrow craft powered by an Isuzu truck motor. The Tenasserim River writhed past thick jungle fringed with tall plumes of free bamboo. Rising water engulfed trees at the banks. Our boatman, a middle-aged man with a canny smile, was an ace navigator. A teenage soldier perched on the bow to call out warnings of obstacles ahead. His left hand was wrapped with iodine-stained gauze. He sat stiffly, diverting his concentration from the river only to blow his nose through the bandage once in a while.

. . . Cruising the Tenasserim, eased back on a pile of supplies and weapons, I was comfortable except for an M-16 stock that jabbed between my shoulder blades no matter how I shifted. We traveled at a perfect speed: not too slow to lose a sense of urgency, not too fast to observe the jungle shoreline. Black-and-white hornbills took flight from tall dipterocarps as we passed by. The boat's motor buzzed steadily. We rode quietly, alert, waiting for what each turn in the river would bring.

Our first stop was an old Karen village beside the World War II road. We walked up a muddy path from the river and crossed an open square where cows grazed in front of a white wood-frame church.

. . . When we left the village we brought another crew member with us, a young soldier who wore a green plastic necklace with his patched uniform. It rained all day, and the new boy bailed water from the boat. We sheltered ourselves and the supplies with ponchos and sheets of green vinyl. The bow boy, with a cape of plastic around his shoulders, shivered and sneezed as the boatman steered us over a stretch of rapids.

The seesawing river smoothed out after a couple of hours, and we stopped where a big teak house was visible from the boat. The people in the riverside village collected tin from the Karen mines to sell in Thailand.

. . . At noon we got back on the river, which was rising into flood, and the rain felt cold. The boat walloped over the rapids in the downpour. Hours passed by in a green haze.

In the afternoon [of the following day], the river thrust up waves and whirlpools, roaring until it drowned out the noise of our engine. We stared fixedly ahead. Only the boatman was smiling. I realized that if we capsized, swimming would be impossible. Not even the strongest would survive. But at the same time I savored the roller coaster ride and the lush jungle and even the rain in my face. The bow boy shouted and waved his bandaged hand, sighting a rushing vortex like a tunnel in our path. We hastily pulled ashore.

Our stop turned out to be the new refugee settlement. The Tatmadaw occupied their old village, a few miles upriver, on the other side of the vortex. About a dozen families had sought refuge in the small jungle clearing. Rain glistened on the palm-thatched roofs of their bamboo huts. The old, established village they'd abandoned two months before had boasted schools, a church, a Baptist library, and orchards. Now they huddled in a dank glade by the flooding river. They had left their year's stock of rice when the Tatmadaw approached their village. The jungle wasn't going to give them anything easily.

We unloaded bags of rice and salt for them. Rebecca gave out malaria tablets. The refugees—women, children, and old men— were in the jaws of the fever diseases: malaria, dengue, typhoid. The young men were all off fighting near the occupied village. Camouflage clothing hung on bamboo walls, uniforms awaiting husbands who might not return alive. The children were cleaner and healthier than those at the tin-smuggling post, but how long could that last? A couple of weeks before, one of the giant trees had fallen and crushed a little boy to death. As soon as we arrived, Daniel began arranging for some of the children to come to his village as boarding students. They showed him, with charcoal on scraps of rice bags, how well they could read and write. Daniel would send boats back to fetch them. Their mothers looked grateful—the children would be safe.

We stayed in the hut farthest from the shore. It belonged to an emaciated man in his seventies and his family. The old man lit a kerosene lantern and we talked above the sound of heavy rain.

"We Karens have always been afraid of the Burmese," he said, his voice creaking, his hands trembling. "When the Tatmadaw came this last time, we took only the first things we could touch. The lantern, a small ax, this pullover. I had to leave my Bible and hymn book. Disgraceful. We ran to the river and took boats across. The whirlpools were too strong to go downriver by boat, so we walked through the jungle to this place. The Tatmadaw can come at any time, so my daughters are afraid. Still, we are happy that you have come to see us. Perhaps you could photograph us, to show the outside world how we are stranded here."

"Will you be safe from the river here?" I asked.

"Soon we must try to find a better place," the old man said. "If we can send the small children to the safe school, we can go into the jungle again and start a new place, plant orchards, build another church."

We headed back the next day so Daniel could dispatch boats to pick up the refugee children. I spent a few more days in Daniel and Naomi's village, waiting for transportation out.

. . . I wanted to hike through the mountains to Three Pagodas Pass, but as long as it rained there was no way out of the village by foot or even truck. I was coughing badly, trying to deny (to medical missionaries) that I had bronchitis. Three Pagodas Pass obsessed me. The name alone was wonderful and it was the point where World War II's River Kwai "Death Railway" crossed into Burma from Thailand. . . .

Three Pagodas Pass was not in the guidebooks. It was a black market Wild West town, always ready to erupt in violent conflict: Karens and Mons against the Tatmadaw, Karens against Mons, Mons against Mons. In the dry winter season just past, the Tatmadaw had approached within a few kilometers of Three Pagodas' bazaar and shelled it. Although they were driven back, the area still was not considered secure. Tourists didn't often go there, but the border watchers did, and they savored the experience like gourmets discovering a great little restaurant hidden in the French country-side.

. . . After I had been in the village for a week, it stopped raining and a big-wheeled *songtaow* returned me to Sangklaburi. The next day I took a *songtaow* to the Songklia River. The rest of the journey to Three Pagodas Pass had to be made on foot. I crossed the river on a pontoon bridge of lashed-together bamboo. A collection of dirt-floored shacks waited on the other side for anyone who wanted to change Thai currency for Burmese kyat (or vice versa) over a glass of Burmese tea. I kept walking a mud path that led across a logging road into the jungle. Smuggling porters carried loads in both directions. When the path forked I asked one of them which way went to "Chedi," using the Thai word for pagoda.

About twenty minutes from the river, I caught up with a non-porter who was walking to "Chedi." A Thai, he was wearing a counterfeit Dior golf shirt, a golf hat, and a Karen sarong. By way of introduction he produced from his Shan shoulder bag an identi-fication card. He flashed it so quickly I didn't have time to read it.

. . . Snakeman, as I called him, told me he was going up to Three Pagodas Pass to "check on something." . . . I could tell he was a Thai Army Intelligence officer. The golf shirt was the dead giveway, like an FBI man's shiny black shoes.

. . . We slogged through the mud. I was wearing my rubber boots, which helped. Snakeman took off his rubber sandals, which would have been swallowed up, and hitched up his sarong.

. . . In Three Pagodas Pass the path was arched with green bam-boo, and limestone mountains jutted above. Three hours after the Songklia River, Snakeman and I reached the Thai border post. Through an eccentricity of geography, the post stood on a piece of Thailand that extended—a small peninsula—into Burma. We had been walking through Burma since the river. I said good-bye to Snakeman there, and continued on.

Three pagodas were visible next to the Thai Army post. They were no more than seven feet tall, the three of them all lined up in a row looking just like white Parcheesi counters. I had expected something more along the lines of the dramatic Mon *chedi* of Sangklaburi. But unimposing as they were, I was happy to see the three pagodas—I had arrived at last.

. . . Joshua played host to the dozen or so foreign visitors who made it up to Three Pagodas each year. . . .

[He] immediately provided me with a routine. Each morning we went to the bazaar for coffee and rumor collection, then we visited what he called "Chinatown," where most of the shops were owned by demobilized KMT Yunnanese or urban Chinese who'd fled Rangoon's institutionalized discrimination and violence. We stopped in at the district office of one of the Mon factions, where a few soldiers, enervated by malaria, sat beneath a Mon flag: a gold flying duck and a little blue star on a red background.

Joshua warned me that the foliage beside the path covered Karen land mines. They were meant to cripple rather than kill, so the Tatmadaw would have to use two soldiers to carry the wounded man, putting three out of action instead of just one. Reportedly, the idea didn't work all that well, as the Tatmadaw tended to simply abandon their wounded soldiers in the jungle. Joshua and I walked to the sound of bamboo, the stems knocking hollowly in the wind. Long-haired, bleary-eyed soldiers trudged past us, back to Three Pagodas from the front line. Smugglers strode doggedly into the danger zone, goods strapped to their backs.

. . . The big commodity moving from Three Pagodas' bazaar to the interior was Aji-no-moto, a monosodium glutamate powder manufactured by a Japanese company. A huge demand existed for it among the Burmese, who were convinced that it made their food taste better, which may have been true, especially when people were so poor that they often ate rice without any meat or vegetables. Strong men and women smuggled Aji-no-moto in big metal tins lashed together in stacks. When it reached Burma's towns and cities, it was often adulterated with rice flour. The Aji-no-moto trail was a weird parody of the heroin trade in the north; a white powder that's not good for you, but people think they need it to enhance their lives. Foreigners were making the bucks on it—Chinese on the heroin, Japanese on the Aji-no-moto. And both powders were adulterated—to add to the profit motive.

. . . I decided that it might not be so bad to return to Bangkok (south on my way north), get some money from the bank, read my mail, maybe see Spin. I had a lot to tell him, tales of the Tenasserim and Three Pagodas Pass.

Joshua arranged for me to walk down to Sangklaburi with some Mons.

. . . My Mon companions traveled with an ox cart that held their goods—eight rice bags. After hours of plodding through mud in light rain, we got to the Songklia River. The Mons hired porters to carry the bags across to a *songtaow* that waited on the other side. The porters strained to lift the bags and carry them over the sagging pontoon bridge. It became obvious that the contents were heavier than rice. Riding in the *songtaow* with the cargo, I touched one of the bags. It felt like it contained large, smooth rocks. The Mons were going to great trouble and expense to bring eight bags of rocks out of Burma in the height of the rainy season. It seemed the Mons had gotten their hands on raw jade. From Burma's northern mountains, in the Kachin State, the precious rocks were smuggled to border towns where they would be cut and polished. When we reached Sangklaburi, the bags were unloaded at a shop that sold the same prosaic wares as the other shops in town: rope, boots, blankets, thermos bottles, flashlights. It was also the only shop in Sangklaburi where I'd seen jade on display, fine jade, the color of bamboo leaves and mountain mist.

. . . I arrived in Mae Sot the next morning, after an uncomfortable night on a speeding over-air-conditioned bus. I took a taxi to the home of a Karen officer. I showed my laissez-passer to the officer's wife, Gloria, a smooth-skinned matron with an upswept hairdo. She wore traditional Karen dress: a striped sarong and embroidered tunic. She looked at the pass with a distinct lack of enthusiasm. "Well, what is it you want to do while you're here?" she asked distractedly.

"I would like to visit the refugee camps and then go to Karen headquarters at Manerplaw."

"The roads really are bad now. You can't get to Manerplaw. Perhaps one of the refugee camps. Why don't you check into your hotel and I'll send someone over later to let you know if it can be arranged." I was dismissed.

It was obvious that she was busy. Her women's organization was effectively in charge of the refugee camps, where food distribution and health and education programs were Karen-administered and Gloria also had to meet with the foreigners who came to Mae Sot: reporters, missionaries, aid workers. From her large, comfortable house she sold Karen handicrafts and textiles from Burma's frontiers to raise funds for the camp. I noticed the sarongs on display.

"Have you got any Kachin sarongs?" I asked. "The black ones

with the embroidery?" She found a black Kachin sarong for me to buy and the atmosphere warmed up a bit.

"I'm sorry we can't do more for your mission," Gloria said. "But we are so busy with the camps right now. More refugees keep arriving and the weather is so bad. But I think that tomorrow when I go to Wangkha camp for a women's group meeting, you can come along."

The next morning we left for Wangkha camp in a *songtaow* accompanied by other women from Gloria's organization. Their husbands made enough money in the tin, teak, and cattle businesses to afford houses in Thailand, Thai immigration payoffs, and education for their children in Thai schools. The women devoted most of their waking hours to work on behalf of the Mae Sot district's fifteen to eighteen thousand other Karens who were not as lucky.

. . . It took me ten and a half hours and three stupefying bus rides to get from Mae Sot to Mae Sariang.

. . . At the morning market I asked about transport to the Salween River. There wasn't any, not that day in the rainy season. If I couldn't get to the Salween, then I couldn't get to the Moei River, and Manerplaw was near the confluence of the two. I was a month and a half into my three-month visa, and rather than wait around in Mae Sariang for transport to Karen headquarters, I decided to continue north, where other rebel groups awaited on the Pai River.

I took a bus to Mae Hong Son, got a room at the Mae Tee for the night, and went to visit a young woman I had met briefly on my first visit to Mae Hong Son. Emma was the daughter of a British diplomat and a Shan princess, and she had grown up in England.

. . . Emma showed me how to get to the Pai River base, home of the Karenni rebels, by hiring a longboat with an outboard motor, which buzzed along the Pai River between jungle cliffs until it stopped at a settlement of stilted houses. The Karennis were a Karen-related tribe, called red Karens because of their clothing. Those who weren't in red wore olive drab, and I asked one of them to show me the way to the house of Arnold We, the Karenni rebels' foreign minister, whom Spin had visited a few months before.

. . . The Karenni headquarters, like Kawthoolei's utopian communities, was an enclave of university-educated city people marooned in the jungle amongst illiterate but savvy tribal relatives. The rebel leaders tried to make the best of things. Their bamboo houses were beautifully crafted and gardens of corn and tomatoes thrived by the Pai River. Arnold We tuned in to the BBC on his shortwave radio as we ate dinner in the kitchen. We had pumpkin vines and dried fish with our rice.

I noticed a worm-eaten set of the works of Thomas Merton on a kitchen shelf. The Karennis here were Catholics and Baptists. Photos of Pope John Paul II, cut out of *Time*, faded to blue on split-bamboo walls.

. . . After the night's stopover in Pai, I went to Chiang Mai on a bus that had to be pushed out of the mud several times. I slept in Chiang Mai and left for Pieng Luang the next day on the early morning *songtaow*. The road arched into the sky over a ripple of hills. For once the day was sunny, the road was smooth, and we flew. Then the *songtaow* broke down. Whatever the problem was, it could not be repaired easily. While the driver dismantled the engine, his passengers sat on rocks sharing Chiang Mai junk food and chatting in six different languages. A special camaraderie existed since this was, after all, the *songtaow* to Pieng Luang; every passenger probably had something to do with smuggling, drugs, gambling, guns, and/or disreputable politics.

Eventually some trucks came by that picked up the stranded passengers. The truck I boarded was bound for the village just before Pieng Luang. The back was piled high with cargo. I took the best seat possible, on a motorcycle that was strapped to the heap of goods. It was like riding a winged rhinoceros through the air. The truck sailed down the newly surfaced road until the pavement gave out, then took an elaborate detour through a Lisu cornfield, where it got inextricably bogged down. Everyone but the driver abandoned it. Another truck heading for Pieng Luang made it through the cornfield and stopped for us. But on a muddy hill, that truck stalled and nearly overturned. We passengers gave up and began to walk through the darkening forest. We trudged on, and when the trees gave way to a village we boarded yet another truck. It was pitch dark, about ten o'clock, when we finally reached Pieng Luang.

The sleepy soldiers of the Thai Army checkpoint, which had replaced Fort Broken Heart, were not amused by our late arrival. They shined their flashlights in our faces. Here they were, curtailing the smuggling trade, controlling the KMT, keeping Khun Sa's influence out of Thailand. How could they do all that with people in trucks waking them up at all hours? Some small gratuities were offered by the KMT shopkeepers on board to apologize for disturbing the checkpoint staff. One of the Thai soldiers asked me what I was doing there.

"I've come to visit a friend," I said.

"Who's your friend?"

"Prince George at the Sura—TRC—compound." That seemed acceptable. The soldier wrote my passport number in his logbook and waved the truck through.

There were a few changes at the Prince's compound. I was surprised to see electric lights illuminating the Prince's house (a generator had been installed since my last visit). Some new soldiers were staying there, but my old friends . . . were still in residence. Prince George showed me to my usual corner bed that was now draped with a mosquito net. The new lights flickered and went off, and we all went to sleep as rain began to pound the tin roof.

. . . I returned to Mai Sung to attend the graduation ceremony of some five hundred recruits who had finished their training. (The Thai Army had added the day to my border pass, but maintained the ten o'clock curfew.) A painted tiger crouched on a boulder above the training camp's parade ground. The new soldiers stood silently at attention, uniforms brightened with neckerchiefs of orange monks'-robe cloth to symbolize the holy crusade to save Shan Buddhism from Ne Win's Burmese socialism. They carried good expensive weapons, mostly M-16s, and I wondered if they still borrowed them from the KMT for such occasions.

When the graduation ceremony ended, I went with Prince George and Acharn Somkit to the furniture factory. There a stage had been set up with a banner above it proclaiming MORALE BUILDING CELEBRATION FOR THE YOUNG WARRIORS. The new soldiers had preferential seating on the ground in front of the stage, while the other soldiers and civilians crowded behind them inside the big shed. . . .

The show commenced at twilight, a vibrant extravaganza of military songs, Shan and Burmese classical dancing, pop tunes, comedy skits, and romantic duets. The highlight was the Yak Dance. No yaks lived in the Shan State, but long ago these people had known the high yak pastures of the Himalayas. Through all the years as the Tais migrated and settled and fought, the yaks danced alongside. That night at Mai Sung, three yaks appeared, each formed by two men in a brown costume with a white mask. The masks had antlers (instead of proper yak horns) and slanted battery-lit red eyes. The masks sat atop the front men's heads, so the yaks stood tall. They had the bulk of yaks but moved gracefully. The crowd cleared space for them in front of the stage.

Long drums, cymbals, and gongs beat entwined rhythms as the yaks stepped into the light. Two dancing *sayahs* in blue trousers, loose white shirts, and white turbans guided the yaks. The tall beasts shook their antlered heads from side to side, red eyes glowing. They pivoted in unison, pranced lightly one minute, then stomped heavily the next. They approached Mo Heing with offerings of wildflowers in their mouths, which he replaced with envelopes of Thai money. The yaks bowed and swayed, and then they were gone. The music drifted away after them.

The music recommenced, this time more ethereal. Two boys and two little girls moved into the light, dancing the Canary Dance. Circus spangles covered their pink and green costumes and their fanned gauze wings trembled with the vibration of the bronze gongs. The canaries exchanged flowers for money with the warlord then danced into the dark: a Shan fantasy of winged being, pure and noble and free.

The celebration was still going on when I left. I crossed into Thailand at midnight, Cinderella exceeding her border pass, but nobody bothered me.

. . . Pieng Luang's regular *songtaow* to Chiang Mai was out of operation for the rest of the rainy season, but I managed to flag down a white pickup truck whose Chinese occupants were going as far as Chieng Dao, a town just north of Chiang Mai. I rode standing in the back with an old man in threadbare clothes and a chubby young man in expensive Thai sportswear. When we passed through villages, other passengers jumped in: local Shan farmers, a young Thai Army soldier, half a dozen unarmed Rangers going on leave, a Lisu family.

We rode through forests into the mountain zone where valleys lay below us, all around us, green. Smoke and dust were gone, cleansed away by the monsoon. The driver was superb. I had seen some great driving during the previous rainy season, but this man was unquestionably the champion. In the muddy parts where all other vehicles became hopelessly stuck, he put chains on the tires and plowed right through.

. . . Descending from the mountains between cliffs of red earth exposed by recent road improvements, we reached the main road to Chiang Mai. The chubby young Chinese man from Pieng Luang banged on the roof of the cab to let the driver know he wanted to get off. He pawed through his pockets for change with which to pay the driver. "Why doesn't fat boy get it together and pay the guy so we can go?" a Ranger grumbled. We soon had an answer. A yellow Mazda with blacked-out windows roared out of nowhere and screeched to a halt in front of the truck. Four Thai men in jogging suits jumped out. We were looking at three pistols and a shotgun.

"Oh great—cops!" a Ranger snarled. "Dope busters! Just what we need."

. . . "We know you're smuggling heroin," the policeman with the shotgun announced, "and we will take this truck apart piece by piece until we find it." They were going to take the driver into custody in Chieng Dao.

"What about all of us passengers?" a Ranger had to ask.

"Oh, we're taking all of you into custody in Chieng Dao, too. Get back in the truck."

We followed the yellow police car. Two cops sat in the back with their guns trained on us. During the search and seizure, I was thinking what a great story I'd have to tell my friends back at Nit's. I was secure in my very American sense of innocence, sure that since I carried no drugs no harm could come to me. But as the truck bounced toward Chieng Dao, I looked down at my knapsack. It was just like the Rangers' bags. What if one of the Lisus got rid of their dope by dropping it into what they thought was a military pack? The police hadn't searched the outside pockets of my bag— yet. *How will I ever explain what I'm doing on the border? "Liaison with the Shans" might not go over well at the Chieng Dao police station. My Thai Army passes won't cut any ice with Thai narcotics police. . . .*

I remembered that it was my birthday, and I cast out all anxieties by thinking like a Shan. Nothing bad will happen on your birthday, I told myself. Nobody ever gets arrested on their birthday. It's unheard of.

When we reached the turnoff for Chieng Dao, the police said that they only wanted the driver after all. The rest of us were free to go. The driver insisted on collecting his fares from us. "He won't keep the money for long," sneered a Ranger.

With exquisite timing, a bus bound for Chiang Mai appeared and we all ran for it. As the bus pulled away, I thought of the Thai newspaper accounts of traffic accidents that inevitably ended with "The driver fled the scene." In this case, the passengers fled the scene, leaving the driver to his fate.

. . . With a week remaining before I was to depart for China and the U.S., I returned to Three Pagodas Pass. This time, I brought Spin with me. We took a boat to Sangklaburi and marched on in the mud through the waterlogged Pass. At the Mon village we met an English-speaking Mon rebel who invited us to the headquarters of his faction. There, young women recruits in rain-darkened uniforms shouted "Boom, boom, boom" for effect as they charged a bridge with bamboo practice guns. Men, young and old, mostly barefoot, rehearsed ambushes with Chinese rifles. The women soldiers laughed in the rain. The boys wore scarlet ribbons on their guns. We watched them drill, counting their ancient numbers in their Mon language.

The next day the Mons sent us off to walk unescorted through their territory to Three Pagodas Pass. We followed the old Death Railway line. Every so often we noticed signboards at the side of the narrow trail, which bore skull-and-crossbones symbols and lots of writing in the curlicued Mon script.

Spin veered off the trail to take pictures of the signs. He was lucky that day. Later we found out that the signs said: "This area is heavily land mined. Do not under any circumstances leave the trail. Unless you're Tatmadaw."

The Parcheesi *chedis* and the bazaar delighted Spin. . . .

The villagers greeted me as if I was a long-lost daughter. They gave me presents as I gave them their portraits. My favorite Bengali tea shop owner, whom I'd photographed standing at the *roti* pan wearing a purple T-shirt that said "Bowling," gave me a small iron weight shaped like a duck. A Yunnanese grandmother pressed a wad of kyat into my hand when I gave her a photo I'd taken of her in front of her smugglers' shop. Spin started keeping a list in his notebook called "Blade's Tribute." We also listed the different ethnic groups at Three Pagodas' bazaar, and came up with a dozen—a microcosm of Burma living a commercial harmony. . . .

. . . "Miss Edith, there is a Shan man in the bazaar who was human rights abused. You can interview him," Joshua said to me one morning.

"OK," I said. "Spin can tape him for his magazine story."

"I mean you, not your boy," Joshua said with his famous gap-toothed smile. "This is *your* job. Human rights."

"Well, Spin can take his picture, anyway." We went to the house where the Shan was staying. He didn't speak Karen and Joshua didn't speak Shan. Burmese was the shared language and Joshua translated for us.

. . . "I was working at the tin mine, a day north of here. Just a few weeks ago, the Tatmadaw came to the mine. They told us, 'Come here, we won't hurt you.' They caught all of us and tied our hands with rope. They said, 'You work for the Karens in this mine, so you are our enemy.' Five men they took away to be their porters, to carry their things. They left then, but we were still tied up and one Tatmadaw man stayed behind to kill us. Six of us were there with our hands tied. The soldier looked at us and raised his machine gun. . . . This soldier shot us. We all fell to the ground, and then he was gone away. I am dead, I thought. But I was only wounded, and not even badly. The other miners, all five were dead. Now I come here to stay with my relatives. I am a man who comes back from the dead, they say. I was saved by the Lord Buddha, and also by my Shan tattoos, which are of a very powerful *yah* that prevents death by penetration of knives or bullets."

. . . I knew how to interview people and process the information into clear, useful reports. People trusted me and wanted to tell me their stories without even being asked. I had exceptional access to the border and had set up a network of rebel contacts that few others had. Through the rebels, I could reach the civilians and gather information on the war's effects. I would record Pota's story and others like it to send to the United Nations, to human rights groups, and to my government, to try and force them to pay attention to Burma's war zone.

[Mirante returns to the United States to publicize the cause of Burma's ethnic tribes.] . . . In the courtyard [of the Freer Gallery], a young dancer swayed to the taped tones of a bamboo xylophone. Her hips switched the long train of her turquoise brocade sarong. She bent swiftly to the ground, turned her shoulders, and rose slowly. She bent, turned, and rose; bent, turned, and rose, her hands extended in the formal gestures of Burmese classical dance. The jewels on her blue gauze jacket glittered with her movements and flowers quivered in her black hair.

. . . I searched the crowd for familiar faces. Knots of Burmese from the embassy stood chatting with American academics under the Oriental arches of the Freer Gallery in Washington, D.C. The academics' June 1986 Burma Studies conference had just ended, without controversy or political commitment as usual. I had not been included in the conference, but I'd managed to get an invitation to the closing cocktail party.

Wearing a black and red dress from Jim Thompson's Bangkok silk shop, I sipped a glass of Coca-Cola and eavesdropped carefully until an American professor I'd met in Thailand appeared. This no-nonsense, gray-haired man was a Burma expert of impeccable credentials and a rebel sympathizer, so he was someone I could talk to (quietly) in the midst of Burmese government apologists and informers.

. . . He introduced me to the stocky man in the dark suit who'd known that the dancer was Russo-Burmese.

"Edith has just started an information project about Burma," the professor said.

"It's to get the word out about what's going on over there," I added.

"And what is the word these days?" The man in the dark suit smiled.

"Right now I'm particularly concerned about the 2,4-D spraying program that the State Department is sending to Burma," I said.

The man's smile faded. "When did you find out about that?" he asked.

"Only two months ago. I got a letter from the Shan State Army and one from the Tailand Revolutionary Council. I might have discounted the whole thing as a weird rumor, except that it came from two different Shan groups who hate each other."

. . . The letters I had received from the SSA and TRC had claimed that the Tatmadaw was spraying some kind of chemical from aircraft in the Shan State, and that people were getting sick from it, and cattle were dying. The SSA letter was an emotional appeal to call international attention to the abuse of civilians, while the TRC letter included charts showing how many people and animals had died in each sprayed area. I investigated and found that the chemical had been donated by the United States government to Burma for narcotics suppression. It was supposed to kill opium poppies, but I suspected that Ne Win wouldn't mind if it killed more than poppies in the hills of the Shan State.

"You're on to something with this," the man in the dark suit said. "I told them at State that this is Ranch Hand all over again, but they didn't listen."

"Ranch Hand" was the code name for Vietnam War herbicide spraying, and the comparison was appropriate. In Burma, the herbicide being used was 2,4-D (2,4-Dichlorophenoxyacetic acid). The Vietnam War formula called Agent Orange was 50 percent 2,4-D and 50 percent 2,4,5-T. The 2,4,5-T herbicide had been banned in the U.S. when it was discovered to be contaminated with TCDD, the most toxic dioxin substance known.

I had spoken with officials at the U.S. Environmental Protection Agency, who told me 2,4-D was contaminated with "moderately toxic dioxins." Both of Agent Orange's ingredients had been extremely hazardous. 2,4-D was under Environmental Protection Agency review, a process that could take years. Meanwhile, the State Department was giving it to Ne Win's Tatmadaw to rain on the hill tribes.

. . . The legal guidelines for herbicide spraying in the United States were ignored when the chemicals were enlisted in the international war on drugs. The State Department's Burma officer told me that 2,4-D was "only a harmless weed killer." Indeed one could buy 2,4-D anywhere in the U.S. and sprinkle it on the front lawn to kill dandelions. But one certainly could not take it up in a helicopter and spray the whole neighborhood with it, which was what the Burmese government seemed to be doing. . . .

"You'll find that an Environmental Impact Assessment was done before the program started," the man in the dark suit said softly. "It made clear that spraying in Burma would be environmentally risky and of dubious effectiveness. State buried the report and went ahead with the program anyway. Spraying began last winter."

"The program was never tested adequately," I said. "And it's not monitored at all. The Burmese government doesn't let anyone from the U.S. check on the conduct of the spraying or its effects."

. . . I had found congressional staff members sympathetic about the alleged spraying effects but unwilling to attack an anti-narcotics program. An anthropologist, David Feingold, had brought word of the 2,4-D damage to United Nations narcotics meetings, but no one seemed very concerned there, either. I could see that exposing the chemical spraying of the Shan State was going to be difficult.

. . . I prepared a background report called *Burma Frontier Insurgency* (which included a map showing where the war was and where the Wa were) to give to congressional staffers and human rights workers. I mailed a questionnaire to every English-speaking person I knew on the Burma border asking for specific data on human rights abuses that had occurred during the previous three years. I compiled the responses into a report to show the big, international human rights organizations that Burma documentation was available, despite its being a "closed country."

My research revealed a consistent pattern of abuse by the Tatmadaw in the frontiers. The horrors were not the spontaneous acts of soldiers lost in alien jungles, or of isolated warlords—they were counterinsurgency strategies carried to the nth degree by well-disciplined troops. The Tatmadaw was aiming to deprive the rebels of civilian support by terrifying, dehumanizing, and eliminating the civilians themselves.

. . . The same methods were used to extract information: with electricity where available; otherwise with bamboo stakes, molten plastic, boiling oil.

Soon the word was out that I had Burma information. I got calls and letters from academics, journalists, and other researchers. I provided copies of documents and news articles, human rights data, reprints of scientific literature on 2,4-D, and border contacts for researchers who wanted to conduct firsthand investigations. New information arrived daily by mail from my network of insurgents and observers.

. . . It was one thing to study remote tribes—one might get grants for that—but to take up their cause, particularly when the tribes bore arms and raised opium poppies, was more than faintly disreputable. I paid the postage and Xerox bills that kept the information flowing with a series of dismal temp jobs I took while staying in New Jersey at my mother's house. The most memorable job entailed wearing a cardboard sign advertising running shoes while handing out coupons to lunch-hour passersby near Wall Street. I was cold and my feet (shod in the damned running shoes) ached. The only positive part of the job was making friends with the three-card monte dealers, shoeshine men, and African umbrella peddlers who shared the pavement. And it paid for the human rights survey report. Eventually I got an indoor job taking phone orders for college textbooks, which lasted long enough to pay my way back to Bangkok.

I had been stranded in the U.S.—in New Jersey, which I detested—for a year. . . . Needing exercise, I found my way to a karate school. I loved it from the start. Karate was so graceful and deadly. I became one of those tattooed people who hang out at karate studios, getting bruised and strong.

At the beginning of December, just as I was about to go back to Asia, one of the tougher black belts said to me, "You wouldn't catch *me* going to the middle of no war zone!"

"Oh, I'm not going to the middle," I demurred. "Just around the edges."

But this time I knew I had to go further than the border. I had to try to reach the hidden valleys of the Shan State where American chemicals were being sprayed. I had to reveal the lives of the people who lived trapped behind Burma's lacquered screen of isolation.

. . . When I arrived in Chiang Mai at the end of 1986 tourism was already rampant.

. . . My main purpose in Chiang Mai . . . was to get into the sprayed area of the Shan State. If I could go there and obtain evidence of the spraying's effects, then maybe reporters and camera crews would follow. The sprayed areas closest to the Thai border were in southern Keng Tung Province, and Khun Sa's bases lay between that zone and Thailand. A few days before Christmas, I met with Prince George . . . to discuss the possibility of travel in Keng Tung. Christmas in Chiang Mai brought gusts of frosty mountain air and skies that wanted to snow but just couldn't. Patrons of the charming tropical outdoor restaurants shivered while hill-tribe urchins in dirty sweaters pestered them to buy roses and strawberries.

. . . I had managed not to say anything to the National Democratic Front people about the upcoming Tailand Revolutionary Council (TRC) festival, which was to feature Khun Sa. Nobody brought it up, so I figured it was a secret and let it remain one. Only Emma knew, because she knew everything that went on in Mae Hong Son. When I got back from Mae Aw, however, Emma showed me a copy of the previous day's *Bangkok Post*. It announced that Khun Sa would be holding a press conference at his new Shan State headquarters due west of Pai. "A *press conference*!" I groaned. "I told Spin it was his exclusive interview!"

I presented myself with invitation, as instructed . . . at the new TRC safe house. An English-speaking Shan teenager recognized me from Pieng Luang. "You can go up tomorrow, in our truck," he said. "Two other foreigners will go as well, the writer Mr. Kevin Corry and his wife, Mrs. Hannah Corry, who come from England."

. . . When I left in the morning I gave the Shan kids at the Mae Tee desk a note for Spin, informing him that I'd gone on to the festival and he could arrange a ride at the safe house. An hour up the road from Mae Hong Son, Kevin became feverish and thought it might be malaria coming on, so he and Hannah got out of the truck to catch a *songtaow* back to town. The TRC truck drove on, packed with Shans, many of whom had come from Pieng Luang for the festival. We left the Pai road and veered off onto a newly bull-dozed dirt logging track. Thai logging camps were hacking away at the forest in a feeding frenzy on the last stands of precious hard-wood left on the Thai side of the border.

No Thai checkpoints existed to disrupt our trip, and no welcome sign indicated our crossing. I knew we were on the other side when I saw Shan soldiers lurking in a shady bamboo grove, with a field of poppies in heavy bloom just around the bend. We drove down into a valley, entering a Shan village, and the village gave way to Tiger Camp. Khun Sa had conquered the valley and was making it into his own Utopia. Well-irrigated rice paddies spread out from the village and camp, and vegetable terraces were being built up the hills. Ornamental gardens and pristine pathways connected Tiger Camp's neat bamboo huts. All sorts of festival structures were being raised: triumphant bamboo archways with painted Shan slogans, reviewing stands, and snack bars. The truck pulled into a festival parking lot and I climbed out, brushing off dust. A TRC video unit taped my arrival, presumably expecting a grander contingent of foreign guests. K. Sam and Prince George were there, and they introduced me to a Shan education official and Khun Sa's English-speaking aide-de-camp.

A row of *bashas* (temporary huts) had been built for the expected guests.

. . . The parade of newly trained recruits had been rescheduled—pushed back two days—because the parade ground wasn't finished. The TRC had hired three Thai bulldozers, with drivers, from a road crew that was supposed to be working on improving the highway between Mae Hong Son and Pai. They worked around the clock to flatten out Khun Sa's parade ground. Their grinding gears resounded all night and a generator that lit the whole area hummed accompaniment. Cold mountain wind whipped through the loose *basha* walls.

Soldiers, jogging and chanting cadence at dawn, woke us. After breakfast K. Sam announced, "You will now meet our general." On cue, Khun Sa walked up from his *basha*, which was somewhat larger than the others and distinguished by a fence with an arch painted with a Shan phrase, "Brave Blood," which K. Sam helpfully translated as "Old Blood and Guts."

The first thing I noticed was Khun Sa's military bearing. He had superb posture, which made him seem taller than he was. He strode with his head thrown back, hands clasped behind him, in pressed green fatigues (no insignia of any kind) and a bulky olive drab jacket. His straight black hair was combed neatly from a left part. I noticed something familiar about his face, but I wasn't sure what. Everntually one of the guests identified it: "Mao at Yenan. The young Mao Tse-tung before he got bloated. In the old filmstrips." Khun Sa had that same oval Chinese face, the same bearing. "Our general has charisma!" Khun Sa's aide-de-camp beamed, pronouncing the "ch" as in "charm." *Ch*arisma.

Prince George introduced me, and the man known as the opium king of Southeast Asia shook my hand in a strong, two-handed clasp. His skin was remarkably smooth, except for crow's-feet that emerged when he smiled. His eyes had a strange, amused look, like those of a child with a big secret or an old, old man who doesn't give a damn about anything anymore. He was a few weeks away from his fifty-fourth birthday.

"*Ni hao ma?*" I greeted him in reasonably respectful Mandarin.

"*Hen hao, hen hao.*" Very good. Deep crow's-feet. He liked my Mandarin. "Please excuse these very poor accommodations," he continued. "We are only a poor, lousy old army camp. We've lost so much face."

"Please, never mind," I said, Chinese style. "This camp is beautiful, better than I deserve. It is I who have lost face, because my country is giving the Tatmadaw a chemical to spray on the Shan State."

Our conversation continued, nattering old-fashionedly about the weather, as if we were a pair of senile Mandarins in a Suzhou garden.

. . . I spent most of the afternoon seated at a picnic table in the warm sun, using [a borrowed] . . . typewriter. The Shan education official had given me handwritten lists of villages affected by 2,4-D spraying, with statistics on acreage sprayed, ethnic identity of villagers, and persons and animals killed. I retyped them with carbons, to distribute to the journalists who were still supposed to arrive. I had brought along my own press releases about the spraying program and I hoped I could use the press conference to interest reporters in the 2,4-D issue. The statistics claimed that crops were destroyed by spraying in twenty-three Lahu, twenty Akha, three Chinese, and two Shan villages. The hill tribes certainly seemed to be bearing the brunt of it. I was skeptical about the casualty claims. Certainly if planes flew low over a village spewing noxious fumes on the crops subsequent deaths would be blamed on the spraying, no matter what the actual cause was. 2,4-D was a dangerous chemical, but the only way to determine for sure if it was causing fatalities in the Shan State would be to send in pathologists to perform autopsies. And that wasn't going to happen—I would be lucky to get myself in.

The Shan official gave me a few sets of photos taken in sprayed fields. They showed Shan farmers standing among whitened, distorted plants. Thin people in drab clothing, they stared bleakly. These people should be on the cover of American magazines, I thought. Americans should know what we're doing in Southeast Asia in 1987.

I had written a flyer that was translated and distributed by rebel groups called "How to Survive a 2,4-D Attack." It put American safety measures in simple terms, and one of its main directions was to avoid touching anything that had been sprayed. Labels on the 2,4-D weed killer sold in American hardware stores said to wear protected clothing and wash exposed skin with plenty of soap and water because the chemical could seep right through your skin to your nervous system. But the farmers in the photographs didn't own shoes, and if they had water to wash with, it was near the sprayed fields. Were they supposed to wash their 2,4-D exposed feet in 2,4-D contaminated water?

. . . My *basha*-mates and I walked back to Tiger Camp after dinner, and met up with Kulok. He handed me two manila envelopes full of mail and told me he'd driven his truck up with Kevin, Hannah, and Spin. The boys at the Mae Tee had given them my note.

"Where's Spin?" I asked.

"Oh, the big asshole's up at the dining hall. He's *still* eating."

I ran over to the guests' dining hall, and Spin was there—shoveling in the rice—at a table with Kevin (who had turned out to be malaria free) and Hannah. I *wai*'d Spin and said, "Welcome to my island." He swallowed his rice and leaned over and kissed me. I sat down and a soldier brought us border coffee.

"We have got to go to the Salween River from here," I said, taking out my map (a *National Geographic* map showing "The Peoples of Mainland Southeast Asia"). "In the old days this was the SSA trade route, right along the trail that goes behind the village. Prince George let it slip that it's only a couple of days' walk from here to the river."

. . . I was in my *basha* struggling to load my Pentax to take parade pictures when the Shan official appeared at the door with two packages.

"The general wants you to wear this," he said. "Also, you have been granted permission to travel in the TRC territory to the sprayed part of Keng Tung."

He left and I unwrapped a package to find a pink-and-silver lurex sarong and high-collared blouse. Milt Caniff's idea of Shan State evening wear. As I slithered into them, I thought, this is just like a movie: they have to get the female lead into an evening dress instead of her jungle-desert clothes, so the warlord presents her with one. I smiled and brushed my hair out of its ponytail.

It must be my Shan tattoos, I thought. People on the border were always giving me things—flowers, tea, old books—their generosity was endless. I fought for their cause in my own way and was rewarded with infinite kindness every step of the way. Even a "womanizing" drug despot had treated me with respect and had given me shimmering Dragon Lady lurex to replace my worn old camouflage.

The other package contained a black cotton aviator's jacket for when it got cold later on. The sun was still strong, so I carried it and put on my pitch-black Ray-Bans to go outside. Fortunately, I happened to have silver plastic sandals to wear because my hiking boots would have ruined the effect. I walked down to Khun Sa's front garden for a photo session with him and Mo Heing, then I went to watch the parade. Spin caught me in the sunlight and I posed for his camera. "Blade is dazzling," he said. He loped off to the *basha* he shared with Kulok and returned with a little brown paper packet. "Here, Blade, I've been waiting for the right moment," he said. I unwrapped a pair of tiger earrings made of thin lacquered wood. He had bought them for me in Bali, on his way back from New Zealand, and had managed to bring them all the way to the Shan State without breaking them.

. . . Three flags flew over the parade ground: the Shan national flag with its red, green, and yellow stripes; a training camp flag with a fountain pen and an M-16 (the same size) crossed over an open book; and a flag showing three yellow mountains—which Si Paw told me was "the SUA flag, Golden Triangle." The new troops, hundreds of them, marched by in precise formation, goose-stepping.

"They goose-step because they were trained by KMT drill instructors," Kulok explained to me, puffing on a Shan cigar. "And the KMT was trained in the 1930s by Germans." A girls' drum corps, crisply uniformed, beat time. Many of the new soldiers were little boys of nine or ten, and none had guns. At least seven times as many troops paraded at Tiger Camp as I'd seen in the Pai River National Democratic Front Training graduation ceremony, but there was no question in my mind who the real soldiers were: the NDF boys—the ones with the guns, who bumped into each other in close-order drill, who had ragged uniforms, flute music, and a battle with the Tatmadaw staring them in the face—those were the young warriors. Tiger Camp, in contrast, was a Chinese opera or a page from *The Three Kingdoms*: beat the drums, fly the flags, and hope your enemy will run away or, better yet, strike a deal.

. . . While Spin and I were eating breakfast the next morning, Si Paw walked up and said, "They are readying your horses. Will you be able to set off in one hour? I shall accompany you on your trip to the Salween River." Six well-armed young soldiers and their sergeant would also make the trip, on foot.

At the edge of the village, poppy fields were bright with ivory petals. I wondered why Khun Sa hadn't gotten rid of them, since he was trying to present himself as the man with the solution to the Shan State's opium problems.

. . . The Salween trade route was a slim tack that curved into the mountains. Spin, no rider, decided to walk, which put us at eye level, quite a novelty. My Shan pony was Khun Sa's favorite, black and lithe with a bridle trimmed with red tassels.

. . . The route was busy. Men, boys, slender women, all humping black market cargo over the mountains. The smugglers traveled in small groups. When Spin and I passed them, they managed not to look terribly surprised, although we were the first foreigners on the route since Khun Sa's takeover. It was simply Shan courtesy not to make outsiders feel ill at ease by gawking at them. I greeted them with a Shan phrase Lisa had taught me: *"Gwa lul?"* (Where are you off to?) They replied that they were off to Thailand, or Taunggyi, "to sell things," and smiled courteously. This was Burma: refined and noble people reduced to beasts of burden.

We traveled all day, and at dusk we stole quietly through a darkening grove of silvery bamboo and birdcalls. Spin walked at my side and whispered, "This is the enchanted forest." The pale dust of the trail glowed and twisted under vaults of bamboo. When light vanished completely, I dismounted and led my pony, shining a flashlight ahead. Spin and I had met watching an old sepia film of the Shan State, and now we were walking in the film. Smugglers camped around small fires in the clearings, like picture-book gypsies.

We reached a Shan village, where our hostess was an old lady who lived in a big bamboo house with her children and grandchildren.

. . . Sunrise flooded the village with a golden light. The shaggy rooftops glittered with it and the sky above was the most intense blue possible. The villagers, in indigo homespun and sun-bleached calico, warmed themselves at small bonfires. The women and girls wore towel turbans and glass earrings. Some of them had goiter-bloated necks. Far from the sea, the lack of iodine in their diets enlarged thyroid glands, and Si Paw told me that not far away a whole village was populated by victims of goiter-induced cretinism. UNICEF's injectable iodized oil was all it took to prevent the disease, but Burma's war zone was off-limits to such measures.

. . . Early that afternoon we reached a hill overlooking the Salween River at a crossing point where the TRC provided a ferry service to the smugglers (for a fee). After stopping at the ferry master's house for tea, fried peanuts, and chunks of palm sugar, we walked down to the wide, slate-blue river. Mountains rose steeply from the Salween's banks like fins, in graduated shades of blue and gray.

. . . We headed back to the Tiger Camp the next day and stopped again at the Shan village for another smoky night, another golden morning. We traveled on along a different route until poppy fields filled forest clearings and the festival flags, arches, and peaked rooftops of the warlord camp came into view.

. . . I had tried to follow through on Khun Sa's permission . . . but . . . the situation on the northern border was in flux. As the Year of the Rabbit began, Thailand had announced a campaign against Khun Sa, and had moved troops north along the Burma border. Nothing came of it—the war was fought only in the Thai newspapers—but the troop presence blocked my access north to Keng Tung. . . . I . . . left for the U.S. I made lobbying trips to Washington, roaming the corridors of power in my scuffed pumps. Lugging a dented Halliburton attaché case full of reports on human rights abuses, I argued that Burma's narcotics production could only be ended if the war was ended.

The level of apathy I was up against in Washington was exemplified by a State Department report on the use of herbicides for narcotics eradication that blandly stated: "U.S. citizens visiting or residing in foreign countries involved in the eradication program should not be adversely affected. Spraying programs will be employed in remote areas where the public is not likely to be exposed." The fact that people actually lived and worked in those remote areas was of no importance, for they weren't Americans. They were just what a State Department official called "the criminal hill tribes."

I kept . . . cultivating interest in Burma wherever I could find it. When people asked why Burma, why me, I told them it was like a cave-in in a mine. If a miner was trapped underground and you walked on the earth above, not knowing, then you didn't have to do anything. But if you heard his cries for help, you were morally obligated to try and rescue him. Knowledge bred responsibility, and I lived with it. The spraying season, winter, arrived. I got a Thai visa, borrowed money, and headed for northern Thailand.

. . . I received a written message informing me that my laissez-passer from the year before was still valid and that I should proceed to Ban Kong, a KMT village on the northern border, as soon as possible.

. . . When I arrived at my contact's house, hopes high, the scholarly Shan agent was surprised to see me. I told him why I'd come to Ban Kong and he said, "But we have no such information here. I have heard nothing from the general; I would have no idea how you are to proceed across the border. I am so sorry, they haven't set anything up here for you."

I was furious. The Shans must be the most disorganized people on earth, I thought.

. . . "Miss Edith, I will send a message to the general's headquarters about it. I, for one, want your mission to succeed—this chemical war in Keng Tung is a very terrible thing. Stay here tonight, and then spend three days or so in town, and come back at the week's end. I will have got a reply by radiogram by then."

Three days later I returned, sure that Khun Sa's permission would not come through and prepared to settle for interviews with smugglers and refugees in Ban Kong.

"I have good news for you," the agent said. "You'll go into Keng Tung Province tonight. A boy has arrived to bring you over the border to the TRC base." Khun Sa had issued orders to his TRC to get me into the sprayed area and then get me out of Keng Tung before the Burmese, the rebels, or the Thais heard of a foreigner's presence. It was to be a surgical strike, and Khun Sa risked antagonizing his sponsors and trading partners.

. . . I set off in moonlight with a Palaung soldier boy who'd been sent for me, a Yunnanese to act as interpreter (translating everyone else's Shan to Chinese for me), and another man to carry the provisions that my contact and I had selected in Ban Kong. I had walked the road to the refugee village the year before in hot sunlight. Now there was a cool breeze. I tucked my hair up underneath my felt "Gurkha" hat, and pulled the brim low over my face whenever we passed other night travelers. No one came close enough to get a good look at me. It was the smuggling route, so they avoided contact with other moonlight walkers.

My party climbed into the hills. To avoid the refugee village, we scrambled up a field and pushed our way through thick scrub. When we found the path that led high into the hills over the border, we sat beside it to rest. Then, just as we got going again, the Palaung boy whispered that some people were coming. Maybe our crashing about in the thicket had alerted Border Patrol Police from the refugee village. The Yunnanese interpreter stayed back to investigate, and the rest of us quickened our pace. Voices drifted up. Our pursuers were catching up to us. I realized the language spoken was Yunnanese. They were not Thai police, but smugglers. They passed us without a look or a question.

We walked on, single file, along a ridge, in and out of patches of moonlight. A human form emerged suddenly from a shadow, a

Shan sentry with his M-16. The Palaung gave him the password. I was out of range of the BPP. I was back in the Shan State. We had crossed into Keng Tung Province. We continued on, in dense forest, the path rippling with deeply eroded ruts. The TRC camp lay all around us, but the moonlight had ebbed and I saw nothing of it. At a cluster of *bashas* my companions asked for water, and an officer came out and talked to me in Chinese. He told me that we had another two hours to reach the local commander's campsite, where I was expected. Tired, I walked slowly, stumbling from rut to rut. A couple of hours later, we came to a low bamboo building where Shan girls appeared with glasses of cold water for us. A lieutenant, Sai Neng, introduced himself. This must be the place, I thought, but another half hour of plodding over ruts remained.

Everyone was waiting up for us at division headquarters, even though it was two in the morning. The commander was away, but his next in command, a thin major in his fifties, welcomed me in Thai and shook my hand. They showed me to a bamboo *basha* with two rooms, one for me and one for my Yunnanese bodyguard/interpreter. But since this was the Shan State, I couldn't just crawl inside to sleep. Soldiers lit a charcoal fire and cooked up noodle soup and began serving tea. The major told me my expedition to the sprayed area, with a military escort, would get under way in a day or so. I could rest up at the camp while we waited for mules to arrive the next day. . . . I excused myself and retired to the *basha*, where border blankets of soft gray recycled wool had been provided. I put two over my sleeping bag and was perfectly warm. A few hours later, I awoke to hear the Yunnanese next door murmuring in his sleep. I drifted back to sleep, feeling safe, and feeling happy to be back in the forest.

When morning came, the headquarters, a huddle of *bashas*, was a picture of tranquility. Tall trees shaded and camouflaged the hilltop. A soldier climbed a bamboo ladder propped against a tree to send coded radiograms. Soft music came from a cassette player. Breezes wafted through. The day began with Chinese tea, then milky coffee. A late breakfast was served at a table behind the major's flimsy little *basha*. He chided me about my appetite: I only managed one bowl of rice, while the officers kept refilling theirs. After the meal, the major brought out salted watermelon seeds and lemon candies to go with more Chinese tea. Young soldiers asked if I was the lady in the *Freedom's Way* book, and I admitted that I was. The TRC had printed up a colorful Shan propaganda paperback with that title after the Tiger Camp festival. It contained a photo of me, the Dragon Lady in pink lurex, posed between Khun Sa and Mo Heing. I rarely looked that glamorous, but the soldiers seemed impressed. The day passed in peace and quiet.

. . . Lieutenant Sai Neng would head the expedition force and he spoke enough Thai to communicate with me. . . . Sai Neng said, "I don't want you to starve from our poor food." Sai Neng was well briefed on my mission to get evidence of the 2,4-D spraying, and he was totally committed to it. In his thirties, he had deep brown eyes and a devastating white-toothed smile. He wore a pistol slung gunfighter-style on one hip and a walkie-talkie in a knitted case with a Shan emblem on the other.

. . . The major had sent about a dozen soldiers off with Sai Neng and me. They were all rather young and seemed a bit Boy Scoutish, lacking the hard aura worn by seasoned NDF jungle fighters. The TRC cat-and-moused it around the Thai border, avoiding conflict with the Tatmadaw. Its troops were Shan, Palaung, Akha, Kachin, and Wa kids who were taught to read and write Shan and were paid one hundred baht a month (a salary no rebel dared dream of) to fight for the TRC.

. . . When we reached the bottom of the hill, we entered a bamboo forest. The bamboo grew in panpipes and blades and thin feathers. I loved its cool darkness and hollow sounds. . . . I rode through the bamboo forest, my own forest with my own little army, Alice through the glass at last.

. . . We continued along mountain ridges overlooking a vast valley without any sign of human inhabitants. The valley narrowed, and I saw a large building on a high bluff. As we neared it, I realized it was a Palaung Buddhist temple, with a double-cupolaed thatched roof. When we rounded a bend in the trail, the village adjoining the temple became visible. Two boy novices in crimson robes ran across the temple yard. I called the village Shangri-la.

. . . Flavorful red rice was cooked for our lunch, and Sai Neng used Thai money to purchase some more for the soldiers.

. . . In the midday heat we were sequestered for siestas in various longhouses. I was on the longhouse veranda, amusing the children with the Velcro straps on my high-top Reeboks, when a buzzing sound came from the air. Sai Neng told me to get inside, a plane was coming. It was a small black plane, one of the Turbo Thrushes donated by the United States for spraying. Now it was being used for reconnaissance, something forbidden by the terms of the foreign aid agreement. The Tatmadaw had apparently heard of troop movements in the area and sent the Thrush over to check us out.

. . . The afternoon was a long push through elephant grass and tall weeds that overgrew our trail. The grass hit me in the face constantly, the trail was narrow and bumpy, and I had to keep jerking [my mule's] mouth out of the weeds so she'd watch where she was going. Ai Lo looked very tired. I offered him my canteen of tea, but instead of drinking from it, he carried it, a burden added to his rice-roll and AK-47.

It began to get dark. I could see no villages, but opium fields lay alongside the trail. The poppies were mostly a deep, seductive shade of mauve, with some white ones interspersed. Although the harvest had been underway for a month, many were still at the stage where the petals had just fallen and the pods were slit to release the narcotic resin overnight. The smell of the raw opium seeping out awakened a strange craving in me. The fumes from the tribal smokers' pipes had only turned my stomach, but this raw, pure smell made me long for a taste.

I dismounted when Seenuan began stumbling in the dark, and led her. I walked into a Palaung village, dogs barking at us. That night I stayed in a longhouse, at the hearth of a headman who presented me with a chicken and a basket of rice and told his *dokka* (his troubles) to Sai Neng and me.

At dawn, Ai Lo brought me a glass of milky tea and a few crackers, and then we set off. I rode the white mule and Seenuan was given the supply panniers. We moved through an arid zone where new fields were being burnt, and plunged along paths overgrown with fire-toasted weeds. Southern Keng Tung's villages were so hidden from our route that any buildings came as a surprise, and it was particularly startling to ride into a thatch-roofed bridge in an area where most streams were forded, not bridged at all. Inside, it was graffitied with charcoal words of Shan, and the new Akha script's Roman letters. Akha had been unwritten until some Western missionaries in Thailand had devised a script, using the alphabet of their own language.

When the troops and I crossed the bridge, an Akha woman crouched in the tall weeds as if to hide, although her silver-studded headdress reflected the sun. As we filed past, she stood and watched us, silently. We began a long, hot ascent of a hill. One of the Palaung porters pulled himself upward by clutching my mule's tail. An Akha village of many houses spiraled around two adjacent hilltops.

The hilltop village I dubbed "Camelot" was tidy and well laid-out.

. . . When I dismounted, I noticed a mirror hung on a house post. I hadn't seen my reflection since leaving Thailand. I looked incredibly pale. My eyes were an absurd green. My hair was a bizarre color like toasted weeds. The Akha mirror showed me as the Akha must have seen me.

A woman asked me in Shan to wait and meet her mother, who was in her eighties and had never seen an American before. The octogenarian, bent but handsome, was helped out of her low bamboo house into the sunlight. Her gray hair was long and thick under her Akha helmet of silver buttons and coins. Her earrings were Raj relics, George V in imperial profile. Grinning and exclaiming to her daughter, she examined the silver lacquer on my fingernails. She gestured that she wished to touch my hair. I pushed my hat back and bent my head down so she could stroke the strange mane. After a while, we smiled to each other, and I walked on to a house with a sunny elevated porch.

The "sheriff" of Camelot, a thin man in well-mended Thai clothes, beckoned me up to the porch. He pulled out a rough wooden chair for me, placing a folded red blanket on it as a cushion. . . . The sheriff told Sai Neng and me that a field that had been sprayed with 2,4-D a little over a month before was not far. He said it was "about an hour-and-a-half walk away," so we left for it after our lunch of chicken, *pakkard,* and red rice. Spirit gates decorated with carved wooden figures stood sentry at Camelot's exit, and we were careful not to touch them as we passed through.

As we hit the third hour of walking since Camelot, Sai Neng and I realized that the "hour and a half" was an Akha estimate. They sped through the mountains like Inca runners in the Andes, but our footsore soldiers trudged at a slower pace. We halted at a charred hilltop with a view of the next valley. We could see three small Akha villages, one of which had been deserted because of the spraying. It was the Akha custom to abandon a village if evil events had transpired there, leaving it to the ghosts.

"The planes came to the valley from over that hill, and sprayed the whole day long," the sheriff told us. "And at the end of the day, they flew over the ridge and sprayed the field just above those three villages."

"Like dumping the last drops of water out of a canteen before you fill it," Sai Neng commented, looking through a battered pair of field glasses.

"It is not far to this hillside field," the sheriff said.

"We can't go to the next valley," Sai Neng told me. "The Tatmadaw is definitely there, and we had better not run into them. But I think we can reach this field that we see. Is that good for your purpose?"

"Yes, it's good, but we ought to get moving," I replied. "I have to photograph the spraying effect, and I need daylight to do so. We have to get there before the light fades."

An hour later, we were on the hillside but the small, thinly planted fields we passed were unsprayed. The sheriff sent a boy to run ahead and fetch the headman of the nearest village. I steeled myself for failure. Sai Neng, sensing it, said, "Don't worry. We will proceed with your mission to find a sprayed field, no matter what our risks, until we reach one, even if it means going all over the province."

The headman trotted up. . . . He led us off the main path, into an extremely steep field of poppies and vegetables. The sprayed field was just above it, at the ridge top. I suggested that the soldiers take a rest, and Sai Neng and I continued to climb with the Akha guides. I walked, as the steepness might endanger the mules. The dark, dry soil was loose and soft. I found it difficult to hike uphill after riding with my legs locked in one position all day, and I was out of breath. I forced myself to keep going. Near the top, the sheriff reached out his hand for mine and pulled me along, and we crossed into the sprayed field.

The plants were an unnatural bleached-out white, with purplish tinges in the leaves. Poppies and *pakkard* had grown tall and spindly, in baroque deformation. The herbicide worked by attacking growth hormones through the plants' leaves, causing them to grow themselves to death over a week or two, then dry up and decay. The mutants included cilantro, ferns, and long white hanks of dead bean vine. Undersized pods topped elongated poppy plants, and some had been slit in the villagers' desperate attempt to salvage opium from them. The headman said they'd been unsuccessful in getting resin from the pinheaded plants. Since the spraying, a few green weeds had poked through the dry soil among the ruined crops. It was ironic that the State Department's "weed killer" had managed to kill everything *but* the weeds. *Pakkard,* the staple winter vegetable in Keng Tung, which I'd had at every meal, was here collapsed in a rubbery phase of decay.

I walked through the steep, rocky field shooting hundreds of pictures of the destroyed foliage, working fast before the light would fade. Sai Neng reloaded my Pentax for me, to save time. I was at once elated to be at last at the scene of the spraying, getting the evidence; and depressed by the repulsive science-fiction scene of crop eradication. I was overjoyed and broken-hearted. No chemical smell remained, but I felt dizzy there. A strong wind blew down over the hillside as the sun began to set in gold. I thought how spray drift would have been unavoidable on the windy slope, perhaps wafting down to the villages. The next field over lay fallow. The villagers had meant to plant rice there.

I used my knife to gouge a soil sample from underneath one of the poppy plants. We returned to the field below, where the soldiers waited. One of them had been dispatched to gather a water sample from a stream that flowed down from the sprayed field to the village. It was presented to me in a small bottle that had contained Lipovitan, one of the unsweetened vitality tonics popular in Thailand. "When I have this tested, they'll think the Tatmadaw is spraying the field with Lipo," I remarked to Sai Neng. "At least we'll find out what's really in Lipovitan."

. . . As darkness fell completely, Sai Neng made the decision to stop for the night at the Akha village just below the fields rather than march back to Camelot. Both options were risky. By staying, we would be on low ground, which Sai Neng hated, with the Tatmadaw only about five hours away. In the headman's dark, dirt-floored house, I drank a Coke with a bowl of instant noodles prepared with the probably contaminated water, had a small shot of searing rice whiskey, and washed at the bamboo aqueduct that brought water from the hillside. I slept deeply and woke before dawn.

We returned to Camelot, to spend another day in its lofty security.

. . . The stories related that afternoon described repeated 2,4-D spraying of Akhas' fields, and made clear that they felt trapped by the Tatmadaw. They no longer had enough currency or trade goods to follow the well-worn escape route to Thailand. Their food and trade crops had been devastated. "What the government did is not good," a sixty-three-year-old man said, "and the things that I have told you now, I want them to reach the authorities. Will it reach them? Whatever we do, they don't see us as human beings. We are looked down on like dogs and pigs. The government is useless. There is trouble all over the country. I'm very sad, but come rain or sun, we must stay here. We must bear it all."

. . . The tribespeople told of children who, having been exposed to 2,4-D, had hard coughs and bloated faces, lingering illnesses. Villagers had drunk the water from the mountain streams. When vegetables rotted after the spraying, they dug them up and fed them to their pigs, because that's what they always did with rotten vegetables, and the pigs began dying off.

. . . As we neared the TRC camp, I noticed . . . precious debris: Coke cans, plastic bags, old batteries. In the tribal zone, these things would have been scavenged and put to use.

. . . When we ascended the last hill, the major greeted us, and over Chinese tea he asked me if the expedition had been successful.

"Yes, it was a complete success," I told him.

. . ."I am very happy that your mission was accomplished." The major smiled. "Now, perhaps it is best that you proceed back to Thailand tonight. We have had no word that the Thais know about your Keng Tung presence yet, and there is no troop alert on the Thai side of the border. Best to go before that situation changes."

. . . I bathed with heated water in a green bamboo enclosure, and dressed in civilian clothes. I would take a different route back to Ban Kong, in case the BPP was watching the way I'd come. I would go by mule, so Seenuan was saddled up again. Ai Lo would accompany me. So would a young Shan corporal and the Palaung boy who'd guided me up to the base the first night. . . . .

I rode through the base, and in the daylight I could see that it was a well-fortified stronghold. It was the kind of place where Khun Sa's franchised chemists refined the year's opium crop into morphine and heroin. As we left the base, we veered off the main path and began descending a steep trail. . . .

[In Chiang Mai] . . . I found a translator for my Keng Tung tapes, and I made the transcriptions into a report called *The Victim Zone*. . . . I was home free.

When I slept, I kept dreaming of escaping Burma, fleeing it like a Keng Tung refugee. . . . Waking, I tried to picture the remote TRC camp. Soldiers would be coding radiograms, washing uniforms, eating red rice. I tried to imagine that tranquil, isolated place. I wondered about the looking-glass world the camp was gateway to: how fared the Palaungs in their red sarongs, the coin-spangled Akhas, and the forlorn Lahus?

Early in March, I went south [to learn about the Mon people and their battle against Ne Win]. . . . I began my . . . travels with a visit to a . . . renegade Mon group. . . . It was an all-night drive along Thai highways and through coconut plantations, until we reached the Thailand/Burma border and the base commanded by Pakomon.

. . . He was a young warlord—an anomaly in Burma. Pakomon, trained and educated in Taiwan in the 1970s, was in his thirties, and he had an Afro hairstyle and a goatee. Wearing a green beret, he was a hipster in tight camouflage. His army, a mere hundred troops or so, wore expensive camouflage uniforms, and had long, rock-and-roll hairdos.

. . . A Mon doctor brought me on his motorcycle to the camp of Nai Non La. . . . Mild-mannered, white-haired Nai Non La's English was not bad, but he felt more comfortable with a fluent translator, so he called Nai Tin Aung up to his rustic headquarters. Nai Tin Aung had curly, steel gray hair and wore a gun belt strapped around his thick, saronged waist. We discussed the recent press conference.

. . . "Many foreigners attended the press conference," Nai Tin Aung told me, "including a film crew from Germany. We were going to allow them to go on a long trip with our soldiers, but one of the Germans fell ill with stomach trouble, so they all packed up and went back to Bangkok instead."

. . . I . . . asked, "Where had they been planning to go?"

"Oh, we were going to send them from here to the coast of the Andaman Sea."

I had never heard of any foreigner, even Thai Mons, making that trip before.

"I'd go in a minute," I said.

Nai Tin Aung and Nai Non La exchanged surprised glances and said something in Mon. "But you would have to walk too far. Over very high mountains, for many days," Nai Tin Aung said.

. . . I let the subject change, all the while scheming to get myself on this terrible march to the sea. Now that I'd found it was possible, there was nothing I wanted more than to explore the utterly hidden world of Mon seacoast villages.

. . . I said as an inspiration hit me . . . , "I just had an idea. If I decided not to go to Karen Sixth Battalion headquarters in the Tenasserim, where I've been before, then I'd have time to go to the Andaman Sea with your Mon soldiers instead."

A few words were exchanged in rapid Mon.

"We will send some of our women soldiers to accompany you," said Nai Tin Aung, "and you will visit many villages on your way. You can make human rights interviews." It would take at least four days to reach the sea. My Thai visa would expire in about three weeks, so I had just enough time to make the trip and return to Bangkok in order to *properly* exit Thailand.

. . . At Nai Non La's camp, I met Nyundthun, a nineteen-year-old Mon soldier who would be my interpreter on the seacoast expedition. No English speakers were available, but Nyundthun had gone to school in Bangkok for two years and spoke Thai well. "When you reach the coast you will meet a general who speaks English," Nai Tin Aung assured me. "And he will arrange for your interview translation."

"Would you like a small firearm to take with you?" Nai Non La inquired. I declined, much as I was fond of guns and would have liked to swagger past the tourists in the bazaar with one on my belt. I'd have plenty of well-armed soldiers around for protection, and in the event of capture by the Tatmadaw, carrying a gun would only make things worse for me.

. . . I was accompanying an expedition delivering a Chinese rocket-launcher and a dozen or so rockets to troops on the seacoast. We went to the bazaar and waited around while porters' back-baskets were loaded with the heavy, finned rockets. One of the three women soldiers who would be going along brought me iced sugarcane juice, presenting it to me with a wonderful smile.

The officer in charge was a young sergeant ("Sarge") with a light beard. He wore a broad-brimmed hat and had slung a pink Karen shoulder bag beside his M-16. Sarge led us off through the bazaar and down a dusty gulch. I marched in line with nine soldiers and four porters. One of the women soldiers slipped and slid down the gulch, her carbine clattering. She got up, laughing, and brushed the dust off her green fatigues.

We climbed into the hills, sweating. Our pace was slow. The two younger women soldiers paused frequently, gasping for breath. Like the men, who were mostly in their thirties and forties, the women (early twenties) carried rifles, packs, and ammo pouches. In a fire zone where fields were being burnt from jungle, black ash radiated heat and cinders blew in our faces. Eventually the trail leveled off, and we walked through fields at dusk until we arrived at a small village. Sarge, Nyundthun, the women, and I were billeted at a farmhouse. The men would sleep on the veranda, we women on the floor of the front room.

I went with the women soldiers to the river to bathe. We had a new cake of red perfumed soap to share. I learned their names. The serious one, who was a couple of years older than the other two and had no problem with hill climbing, was Pakuson. The youngest—shy, with short hair and muscular legs—was Rad Aung. And the third, a dreamy-eyed soldier with a lovely big smile, was Chu Win.

. . . The women lay down on either side of me, their rifles stacked against the wall within easy reach. Pakuson had an M-16 (the American status symbol), Chu Win had an AK-47 (practical, lightweight), and Rad Aung had an old, worn carbine. They slept under red-and-white Thai cotton sarong material, and they'd brought a sheet of maroon plaid Burmese cotton for me. The night was cold, and we slept fitfully, shivering. I wished I'd brought my sleeping bag, which I'd left in Bangkok. I had not expected to end up sleeping in such cold mountain air.

At five A.M. we woke up, strapped on gear, and moved out—breakfastless, coffeeless. With the dawn's light came the realization that I was not going to get any special treatment. In Keng Tung, I'd been the visiting Chinese princess, with mules to ride and cans of Coca-Cola at every stop. Now I was a foot soldier: no sleeping bag, no blankets, no porter for my gear.

We marched noisily through thick jungle and crossed several streams. I was wearing Reebok high-tops, which were soft inside and had decent traction. But my socks absorbed water when we waded through streams. The wet socks chafed my feet, starting blisters. All the Mon soldiers wore rubber thong sandals, except Nyundthun and Sarge, who had new Chinese canvas jungle boots (with socks). After a few hours, we stopped for rice and curry at a cluster of bamboo shacks, and I took my Reeboks off. I put the soggy shoes in my daypack and buckled on my silver plastic sandals,

but my raw, red toes showed that the damage had already been
done.

We climbed. We hoisted ourselves from root to root, rut to rut,
rock to rock. Midday on the mountain, sweat made mud of the dust
caked on our skin. The women soldiers and I rolled our trouser legs
up; the porters and some of the older, male soldiers who wore
sarongs hitched them up for coolness, revealing thighs tattooed
with magic blue whorls.

We reached a summit and rested in the breeze. Descending the
other side of the mountain strained my knees and ankles, so I went
slowly. The effort made my legs tremble when we stopped on the
trail to rest. Finally we reached a valley and marched through cool
ravines. Refugees were building huts by a river. They had ice buck-
ets full of weak Chinese tea to refresh passing smugglers and soldiers. We stopped and drank glass after glass. We rested in a refugee
woman's open hut.

. . . Our own madness was apparent as we continued on our
way by night, climbing another mountain. My knees were buckling,
but I managed not to fall. The wet shoes sagged in the bag on my
back. The mountain was on fire. Burning bamboo exploded in loud
reports. Sparks dive-bombed us. Smoke billowed across our path as
we trudged upward. We pulled ourselves along, grasping whatever
branches weren't thorny or on fire.

. . . The women soldiers spread out a plastic sheet to sleep on,
at the foot of a huge tree. They said their evening Buddhist prayers,
wai-ing and bowing to the tree. Wrapped in our cotton sheets like
mummies, we lay among rifles, canteens, and ammo clips. We got
thorns in our feet from a bush at the bottom of the plastic. Sarge
and Nyundthun gathered the thorn branches into a bonfire and
hunkered down to talk all night. The crackling of bamboo on the
mountain below us did not abate, but the stars above were brilliant
as the jungle's smoke began to drift away.

. . . Late in the afternoon some new Mon troops arrived from
the west, the direction of the sea, and we jumped up and followed
them back the way they'd come. We marched quickly on rocky
paths to a village. . . . That night we slept in a village house that
provided little shelter from the cold.

. . . We made our usual frantic departure before dawn. Nothing
seemed to be calm or quiet with the Mon Army. Having slept in uniform, all they had to do was take a quick pee in the bushes, strap on
their packs, and sling their rifles over their shoulders. But this was

always done with such commotion that it looked like we were being ambushed.

. . . We stopped just after noon at another village, where we
were given big green coconuts, lopped off at the top so we could
drink the sweet, clear "water" inside. The village was drab and dry,
the people bone thin. But the women and girls were all dressed in
vivid blues and purples—violet, lavender, hyacinth, heliotrope, peri-
winkle—and smiled bravely.

. . . On we marched, up another mountain. We double-timed it
up a slope and along a ridge. Then we went downhill and we all had
to move fast because a bamboo grove was on fire right beside the
trail. We ran downhill through the flames. Chu Win fell, slid,
laughed, and kept running. Then we climbed again, munching red
jungle fruit. We ripped along mountain paths, cooled at last by a
stiff breeze.

When night fell, we descended to a plantation. The fruit forag-
ing did not cease, but now weapons were carried at the ready,
safeties off. We were now very close to the Tatmadaw positions on
the outskirts of Ye City. To reach the sea, we would have to sneak
past the Tatmadaw and cross a paved road that ran south to
Kawthaung.

. . . After hours of pointless wandering in the dark, we finally
managed to hit the "motorcar road." The two-lane thoroughfare
glowed eerily white in the night. We marched quickly along it for a
mile or so. Perhaps Tatmadaw truck convoys owned it by day, but
now, at midnight, the road was ours.

We cut off from the road, on an ox-cart track, into brushland.
The track consisted of two parallel ruts of very uneven depth, with
scraggly bushes growing down the center. I had poor night vision,
and I began to stumble over things—roots? stones? I didn't quite
fall, but I was about to, so Sarge told Pakuson to guide me. She
took my hand in hers, which was reassuringly dry, and led me
along.

. . . We stopped suddenly and everyone sat down on the trail.
Sarge whispered jokes. We ate the last orange candies from a jumbo
bag the soldiers had brought from Three Pagodas' bazaar and spat
in the dust. We sat and whispered and laughed quietly at nothing,
waiting for our guides to figure out where the hell we were.

At last the guides appeared from farther up the trail, with a
Mon Army scout who reported that we were safe. No Tatmadaw
patrols were out hunting that night, so Sarge told me I could use my

flashlight. We all went crashing off cross-country through patches of thorny scrub.

. . . Adjacent to the vegetable field was a palm plantation, our shelter for the rest of the night. It was about two in the morning when the women soldiers and I took over a rickety, derelict stilted hut.

. . . It was daylight when I awoke, and soldiers were just stirring from sleep in nests they'd made of fallen palm fronds. The women soldiers went to work preparing the looted vegetables for breakfast. Some local people appeared and sold the Mon Army a couple of chickens, which the men grilled on a camp fire. That morning it all felt like we were just children having an adventure, playing games in an abandoned house, playing war in a vacant lot. We had survived the night, forgotten the war, slept. We woke up and ate chicken.

We marched away through a stretch of green rice fields. When we reached a village, some people came up to me and said, "Please take a group photo of us, to show the world that we Mon people really exist. Ne Win tells the world that we do not exist anymore." I took their picture—lined-up, barefoot, underfed, proud. The Burmese government liked to claim that the Mons were completely assimilated into Burmese culture. It was accepted by the rest of the world that they were a vanished race. I had half believed it myself before I saw such Mon villages of two hundred houses, three hundred houses, more. Village after village resounding with Mon speech, full of Mon people of all ages wearing their Mon National Day T-shirts smuggled from Three Pagodas' bazaar.

. . . We hiked down an ox-cart track in blazing sun until we reached a town near the sea. The streets were lined with fine two-story teak houses, shops, and covered market stalls. Mon soldiers were everywhere, and I was taken to the home of the coastal area's commander, a thin, older man with a bristly beard. The launcher and rockets were handed over to him, and he was very pleased.

I was given a lemon barley soda and told to sit on the veranda.

. . . When I got up to leave, I realized that blisters had formed under the balls of my feet. The sun was searing. During a rest halt in a scrap of shade, Captain Min Kyaw Soe politely asked me, "Would you like to listen to a Mon song?"

"No, thank you, perhaps later," I said, not in the best mood. He played it anyway, on a small tape deck. It was nice music, soft and strange, and it helped me walk the rest of the way to the beach.

This was, as I had suspected, *a war with a great beach*. The Mon soldiers marched along the sand, ocean shimmering in the background, tropical islands offshore, azure sky above. My mood went swinging up. I had reached the Andaman Sea! I had walked and walked and walked. Now there would be boats.

. . . Soon we were on longboats heading out to a fishing junk moored in the bay. The soldiers made a lot of commotion boarding the junk. It rocked a bit, which turned several of them very green at the gills. Sarge and Chu Win were definitely the worst sailors of the group. Before we'd even hoisted anchor, they were vomiting their guts out over the side. I gave them each a Dramamine tablet. Chu Win promptly puked that out, too. Sarge fell asleep. The more seaworthy, like Pakuson, Radio Boy, and me, loved the cruise; we were out on the open sea, the air was perfect, the light divine.

Our weathered old junk had a Japanese engine with Rambo stickers plastered on it. We cruised past tough Mon fishermen rowing their wooden boats. Then a shot rang out and everyone started yelling and scanning the horizon for Burmese gunboats. It turned out that Nyundthun's M-1, lying on the roof with its safety still off from the night before, had been jarred by the engine vibrations and had fired.

The next crisis was more serious. Black smoke began pouring out of the Rambo engine. This is an interesting way to die, I thought. I figured the boat would explode before we'd have to worry about drowning or shark attacks.

. . . Slowly a rowboat headed our way from the beach and collected the sickest soldiers. Eventually all the troops were transferred ashore.

The sun was setting into the Andaman Sea as we headed down the beach. The troops looked grim. They're not even enjoying this, I thought. . . . It became an *extremely* long walk on the beach. Fatigue set in and my blistered feet were killing me.

. . . The sun bulged and glowed and cast ruby sparkles over the waves. It was beautiful, it was awful, it was endless. Back in the mountains, I had decided that the only way I could deal with the hard march was to keep complaints to myself and just keep going, however slowly. On the flat sand I would not complain and I would keep going. I began to repeat to myself a phrase I'd seen on a Japanese lady wrestler's T-shirt in a newspaper photo. It made a good Zen koan for walking meditation or walking death. I repeated it to myself fifty, one hundred, one hundred and fifty times. It was everything I wanted. It was a cool breeze and a warm blanket. *A Radiant Obstacle in the Path of the Obvious,* I chanted. It was everything I wanted to be, that night and forever.

Pakuson began to sing as she walked beside me, slowing her strong steps to match my faltering pace. I hadn't heard her sing before. It was a strange, pretty song, like the ones on Captain Min Kyaw Soe's tape. The Mons sang ethereally, in contrast to the harsh tones of their spoken language.

At the far end of the beach we found a fishing village and collapsed at a shack on the sand. I examined my feet by oil lamp. The blisters had gone septic. They oozed yellow fluid and were embedded with sand. Nyundthun and Sarge had big, disgusting blisters, too, like mushrooms after a rain. We were all dead tired. Even insomniac Sarge stopped talking and slept that night.

"We will have to walk for a while, to reach a boat," Nyundthun told me in the morning. I wrapped my blisters with gauze and tape, jammed my swollen feet into the plastic sandals, and hobbled down the trail like an old Chinese lady with bound feet. We descended a gray mud bank to a small boat that reeked of rotting shrimp. It brought us to a mangrove swamp. We squished through the mud to a hut whose owner let us use his well water to rinse our feet. The gauze bandages on mine were now gray, salt-soaked tatters. One of the Mon officers hired an ox cart to bring me, Chu Win, and Rad Aung to the next village. The cart jolted along uneven ruts. When we had to go downhill, the oxen would break into a gallop, throwing us into the air.

In a large village we were greeted by dozens of women soldiers resting on shady verandas. I met General Htaw Mon at last, and he did speak English well, in a slow, deliberate voice. He had startlingly light brown eyes and an ironic, feline smile.

"We will arrange for you to visit coastal villages," the general said, "but I don't think you can walk anymore."

"Sure, I can walk, but slowly," I said. "I am starting to think that my country couldn't win in Vietnam because the American soldiers had very good boots, but they wore them in the jungle and got blisters—while the Vietcong had only rubber sandals and didn't get blisters."

The general laughed and said, "Well, you won't have to walk much now. We shall proceed by boat."

. . . The village headman invited me to his house, and we located the village on my map. He told me I was the first Western visitor in twenty years. We drank Dragon American Special Cream Soda and ate bowls of watermelon pulp mixed with sweet, condensed milk. Then I went to the village monastery to meet its abbot. He asked me to take his photograph and arranged his red robes. He sat on a baroque, gilded throne. It seemed very Mon to me that a dirt-poor village would spend whatever money it had making an ornate throne for the head monk, to evoke the ancient Mon civilization.

. . . We left, Mi Kyide Soi Mon and I riding in an ox cart with wooden ox bells jangling. At least forty women soldiers were marching with us—an extraordinary spectacle, a female army. Civilian girls accompanied them out of the village, holding their hands, kissing them, giving them flowers. Mi Chon De, laden with her heavy weaponry, gripped the hand of a local beauty. "Take our picture!" she called to me.

Our evening march ended up at a Buddhist monastery. Most of the soldiers bedded down in the monastery yard, but the general and his staff would sleep in the main temple building. So would Mi Kyide Soi Mon, Pakuson, and I, with rifles stacked at our feet. I was amazed. In Thailand it was utterly taboo for women to sleep in temples. I found the Mon Army as socially subversive as it was politically insurgent.

When I awoke, another ox cart had arrived to give me an hour's ride to a town with a large market place and a Buddhist pagoda. The townspeople poured out of their houses to watch the women soldiers march in and were astounded to see me with them. I was installed at a small house, and people crowded around the porch to gawk at me.

. . . I interviewed ten men who had been captured and tortured by the Tatmadaw. The last time the Burmese forces had come through, they had suspected the men of aiding the Mon rebels and had beat them, hung them down wells, and slashed them with bayonets. One man's daughter had been shot dead by the Tatmadaw in front of his house. The Tatmadaw used the same anticivilian counterinsurgency tactics, and the same torture methods, all over Burma, but for different purposes, depending on the victims. The hill-tribespeople I had talked with in Keng Tung understood very little about politics and insurgency, and the Tatmadaw tormented them to drive them off their land. For the Mons—literate people with a strong nationalistic sentiment—the Tatmadaw used torture to procure information.

When it was time to move out, three young captains joined us. Captain Sai Htaw was the liveliest, with shaggy hair, and mustache, and a big, crooked smile. Captain Rai Chia was a Moulmein University graduate, and Captain Chan Rot had a degree in veterinary science.

. . . At the Ye River we boarded boats, and Captain Sai Htaw stood in the front of mine, George Washington style. "You will see many beautiful views of our Mon land!" he shouted to me. A flotilla of longboats, each flying a brightly colored pennant, carried us down the river. Thick palmettos lined the shore. The boats overtook each other as if it were a race, and the women soldiers cheered. The sun set, reflecting on the river in vibrating lines.

We changed over to bigger, open motorboats, and took to the sea. The troops had their usual yelling crisis, this time over hitching up a boat to be towed. By now I understood that when everyone started shouting, it did not *necessarily* mean the boat was sinking.

. . . I could see fires burning on distant mountainsides when we went ashore. We had walking to do—"About three furlongs," old Nai Aung Shein informed me—but I had no idea how long a furlong was. It turned out to be an hour's painful hike along rice paddy embankments. The reward at the end was a magical little village suffused with the heady scent of frangipani.

Pakuson, Mi Kyide Soi Mon, and I were billeted in the candle-lit front room of a big teak house. Captain Sai Htaw dropped in to work on my blisters.

"I am a front-line doctor," he announced. "I have cured many cases like this." He snipped off the puffed skin with scissors. It didn't hurt, but after a while he got carried away and cut the unblistered skin.

"Stop that!" I snapped.

"Okay, okay, I am only a *barefoot doctor*," he laughed. He then insisted on painting the soles of my feet liberally with iodine, so they looked like the hennaed feet of a Bedouin bride. He gave me an Ampicillin capsule and many assurances that the blisters would be dried up completely the next day.

. . . When I awoke, my blisters did seem much reduced under the coat of crimson iodine. We weren't going anywhere for a while. The women soldiers washed their uniforms and relaxed in sarongs, powdering their faces with *thanaka*. They managed to carry plenty of cosmetics with them in the field: jars of *thanaka*, lipsticks, vials of black "Chum" (labeled "made from the finest chemicals, this eye liner is the best beautifer for modern girls"). The men used *thanaka* too, sometimes, and even tough Sarge packed a glass spray bottle of cologne. Although a respected guerrilla force, the Mon Army was not given to Rambo commando machismo. One of the older men had a decal on his M-16 stock with the tacky Vietnam-era slogan "Kill 'Em All, Let God Sort 'Em Out," but ribbons, flowers, and magic duck emblems were more the norm.

I did a group interview with some of the women soldiers, with Captain Sai Htaw as my English translator.

. . . Mon women in the towns and villages always "congratulated" them for joining the army, they said. Civilian men asked them questions: Were they carrying the same gear as men? (yes), were they marching the same amount as men? (yes), were they sleeping with the male soldiers? (no). Regulations stated that enlistees must stay in the army for five years. After three years, they were allowed to marry. None was married, so I asked if they had boyfriends. "No, no, we don't want boyfriends!" they chorused, possibly for Captain Sai Htaw's benefit.

. . . We left for another pretty village under palm trees. The people there were very thin. Children's bellies were bloated, their ribs stuck out.

. . . I would have liked to at least stay overnight, but we moved out at eight in the evening. Most marched but a few of us went by boat.

The moonlight was bright, and the sea was high. Spray hit us hard as we sped north out of Tavoy Province, back to Ye. We passed a *chedi* gleaming white on a point of land, the Mon equivalent of a lighthouse, and stopped at a small island with a rock-strewn beach. The women found a shelter of sticks and leaves that someone had left and spread plastic sheets beneath it. The men arranged themselves among the boulders on the beach. A bonfire would have dried our spray-soaked clothes, but we didn't want to give any sign of our presence to Burmese government boats that might patrol the night, so we slept in our wet clothes, pretending to be lumps of stone and clumps of leaf.

It might have been a pirate camp. Brigands, often Thai, roamed the seas of Southeast Asia, preying on fishing fleets, cargo ships, and boatloads of Vietnamese refugees. Theirs was a cruel trade of rape and murder as well as plunder. En route to Pieng Luang by *song-taow,* I had realized that I looked like a bandit, sinisterly wrapped up against the road dust. Indeed, I was going to Pieng Luang to meet with outlaws and steal the news of Tatmadaw abuse in the Shan State. When I dodged in and out of Keng Tung Province, I was in the company of smugglers, on their secret nocturnal routes. Then I, too, was a smuggler, of information about tribal villagers and a deadly chemical mist. Now the Mons and I camped like buccaneers on an obscure island in the Andaman Sea. We were pirates, our treasure the interviews, images, information. Established, respected human rights groups could not go to those places. Government agents did not tread there. I had become a pirate, a human rights pirate, raiding the coast for all the information I could thieve from Ne Win's Burma.

. . . I showed my slides of Mon women soldiers on the unknown seacoast to an Asian newsmagazine, which considered the pictures good enough to feature in "Eyewitness," its photo-essay section. Getting one's photographs in "Eyewitness" was an honor, and paid well. Spin, the professional photographer, had never had an "Eyewitness" spread. The photo essay, and Trinka [Spin's new girlfriend], distanced us from each other like coils of barbed wire.

. . . It was evening when I landed in Hong Kong. I caught a swift ferry to Lantau Island, where a college friend welcomed me into her antique-strewn beachfront condo. I slept on the sofa, which was made up with pristine, white sheets. It was so quiet. It was quiet enough to think straight, at last, but I slept instead of thinking.

. . . My love would turn from ruby to copper to ice. Soon after my return to the United States, I would be doing office temp work in the relentlessly monotonous confines of an engineering firm. The day before my thirty-fifth birthday, early in August 1988, I would be sitting in a beige cubicle typing the words *chargeable service* over and over again on forms:

Chargeable service
Chargeable service
Chargeable service

Mesmerized at the Selectric, I would, that day, fall out of love with Spin with the inevitability and decisiveness of gravitational pull. I would suddenly acquire the prescience of the lapis beads. Within the week, Burma would explode: a massive combustion with millions demonstrating in the cities; a shadow play of Ne Win's henchmen; Tatmadaw massacres of Burmese students, monks, and children. Burma would be on the network news every night, and on CNN all day. Burma would achieve the reality of the world's front pages. I would have no time to spend on Spin. The U.S. would cut off all aid to Burma, and Senator Moynihan of New York, with my Keng Tung report in hand, would force a high-level investigation of the 2,4-D program.

I would practice the art of collating, and other menial tasks, at the engineering firm by day and the art of revolution by telephone and typewriter by night. I would urge the rebels to take advantage of the urban uprising, to be real armies of liberation, to take towns, seize territory. But, for the most part, the rebels would sit on their hands. Immobilized by the monsoon season and years of black market inertia, they would fail to act until it was too late and the Tatmadaw would have overpowered the resistance of the cities with a reign of terror.

Additionally, the rebel armies would turn on each other at Three Pagodas Pass. Karen civilians would flee deeper into Kawthoolei, Mons and others would cross the Thai border, and then the Karen and Mon forces would go at each other with their expensive black market weaponry, obliterating the whole Three Pagodas bazaar with their shells until nothing was left and a National Democratic Front team came down from Manerplaw to contrive a truce. Over three hundred people would die in the weeks of fighting. . . .

At the height of the demonstrations in Burma's cities, Khun Sa would prepare to move his operations into corrupt, authoritarian Laos, and refuse outright to fight the Tatmadaw.

. . . Still, hope held on in Burma. Burmese students and other urban dissidents fled to the frontier areas by the thousands. Those who survived waves of malaria stayed on in rebel camps, and hundreds fought side by side with the NDF troops. The young idealists gave the rebellion a much needed infusion of urgency and an infiltration network for the cities. The war went on in the muddy trenches of Kawthoolei, the Mon seacoast, the Kachin mountains, but it was no longer unknown. That fall, the Karennis finally attacked the Loikaw power plant. The commandos' rockets damaged relay transformers enough to shut the lights off all the way down in Rangoon for twenty-four hours.

I belonged in the thick of the revolution, but, blacklisted by Thailand, I could not return to the frontier.[2]

. . . And that September, while calls for democracy could still be heard from Rangoon, I was in a New York library one day, trying to track down a news story quoting a Drug Enforcement Administration spokesman calling the doomed 2,4-D program "a disaster." As I left, I stepped aside to let a Tibetan monk into the elevator ahead of me. Outside, sunlight warmed the air, and I took off my tweed jacket as I walked. I heard a clink of metal on the pavement and a passerby said, "You dropped something." On the sidewalk was the old Tibetan copper coin that was the amulet from [last year's] goldfish dress dream. I'd been sure I'd lost it, but it reappeared, just like that. With copper in my pocket, ice in my heart, and a head full of revolution, I knew now that everything would end up well.

. . . In Hong Kong, that post-deportation June morning, I drank all the orange juice I wanted. . . . I had lost Thailand, but I would never lose Burma. Then thoughts left, and I looked out the glass doors at the path to the beach. The path was shaded by tall casuarina pines that swayed slightly in the sea wind. The breeze stirred two gauze goldfish, remants of a Chinese lantern festival, that hung just beyond the doors. Barefoot on the polished floor I performed *kata,* reaching my best, *Matsukaze,* becoming calligraphy, turning like the pine tree in the wind. I had to be ready.

---

2. Mirante had been deported by Thai immigration authorities.

EDITIONS CITED

Meena Alexander, *Fault Lines: A Memoir* (New York: Feminist Press at the City University of New York, 1993).

Mary Benson, *A Far Cry* (London: Viking Penguin, 1989).

Vera Brittain, *Testament of Youth: An Autobiographical Study of the Years 1900–1925* (New York: Macmillan, 1934).

Isak Dinesen, *Out of Africa* (New York: Random House, 1938).

Ruth First, *117 Days* (New York: Monthly Review Press, 1989).

Angelica Garnett, *Deceived with Kindness: A Bloomsbury Childhood* (San Diego: Harcourt Brace Jovanovich, 1984).

Vivan Gornick, *Fierce Attachments: A Memoir* (New York: Farrar Straus Giroux, 1987).

Elspeth Huxley, *The Flame Trees of Thika: Memories of an African Childhood* (London: Penguin, 1962).

Emma Mashinini, *Strikes Have Followed Me All My Life: A South African Autobiography* (New York: Routledge, 1991).

Shudha Mazumdar, *Memoirs of an Indian Woman* (Armonk, N.Y.: M. E. Sharpe, 1989).

Edith T. Mirante, *Burmese Looking Glass: A Human Rights Adventure and a Jungle Revolution* (New York: Grove Press, 1993).

Vijaya Lakshmi Pandit, *The Scope of Happiness: A Personal Memoir* (New York: Crown, 1979).

Margery Perham, *African Apprenticeship: An Autobiographical Journey in Southern Africa* (London: Faber & Faber, 1974).

Gloria Wade-Gayles, *Pushed Back to Strength: A Black Woman's Journey Home* (Boston: Beacon Press, 1993).